The State of
Working America

The State of
Working America
2000-2001

LAWRENCE MISHEL

JARED BERNSTEIN

JOHN SCHMITT

Economic Policy Institute

ILR Press
an imprint of
Cornell University Press
Ithaca and London

Copyright © 2001 by Cornell University

First published 2001 by Cornell University Press
First printing, Cornell Paperbacks, 2001

Printed in the United States of America

ISBN 0-8014-3823-3 (cloth)
ISBN 0-8014-8680-7 (pbk.)

Recommended citation for this book is as follows: Mishel, Lawrence, Jared Bernstein, and John Schmitt, THE STATE OF WORKING AMERICA, 2000–2001. An Economic Policy Institue Book. Ithaca, NY: ILR Press, an imprint of Cornell University Press, 2001.

Cornell University Press strives to use environmentally responsible suppliers and materials to the fullest extent possible in the publishing of its books. Such materials include vegetable-based, low-VOC inks and acid-free papers that are recycled, totally chlorine-free, or partly composed of nonwood fibers. Books that bear the logo of the FSC (Forest Stewardship Council) use paper taken from forests that have been inspected and certified as meeting the highest standards for environmental and social responsibility. For further information, visit our website at www.cornellpress.cornell.edu.

Cloth printing   10 9 8 7 6 5 4 3 2 1
Paperback printing   10 9 8 7 6 5 4 3 2 1

To Sharon, for love, hope, and renewal
—LARRY MISHEL

To Elizabeth Jin Ying Bernstein
—JARED BERNSTEIN

To Brian, Michelle, and Megan
—JOHN SCHMITT

VISIT WWW.EPINET.ORG

The Economic Policy Institute's web site contains current analysis of issues addressed in this book. The DataZone section presents up-to-date historical data series on incomes, wages, employment, poverty, and other topics. The data can be viewed online or downloaded as spreadsheets.

Table of Contents

Acknowledgments

The preparation of this publication requires the intensive work of many people on EPI's staff. Abe Cambier provided extensive, and enormously valuable, research assistance in all of the areas covered in this book. He also created all of the graphs. David Webster and Danielle Gao provided extensive computer programming and data analysis for this book. Both have been critical assets for all of our labor market work. Monica Hernandez did a nice job of helping to prepare much of the text.

Unfortunately, this will be David Webster's last version as he is moving to another city. David worked on the 1994-95, 1996-97, 1998-99, and the current version, and has made many contributions to our work over the years.

Chauna Brocht and Edie Rasell made helpful contributions to the regions chapter. Christian Weller's concurrent work on the role of technology and investment on recent growth provided needed background. Eileen Appelbaum provided guidance to our work on information-technology labor market trends.

It has been a pleasure to continue the partnership with Kim Weinstein and Patrick Watson in the development and production of this book. Patrick reviewed every word we wrote and effectively edited, checked, made consistent, and substantially improved the text and presentation. Patrick is a behind-the-scenes author, and we owe him a great debt for making us look like better writers and for the equanimity with which he conducts the editing process in a short time period. Kim produced and designed the book. Joe Procopio and Tom Kiley proofread and, with Nan Gibson, offered valuable advice and generous assistance during the production process. Nan Gibson, Brian Lustig, and Tom Kiley work to provide a large audience for the book.

Many experts were helpful in providing data or their research papers for our use. We are particularly grateful to those who provided special tabulations: Ed Wolff and Peter Gottschalk. Others who provided data, advice, or their analysis include Daniel Aaronson, Steve Camarota, Mike Ettlinger, Ann Ferris, Debora Fisher, Howard Hayghe, David Johnson, Kurt Kunze, Allen H. Lerman, Mark Levitan, Virginia Mannering, Robert Manning, Robert McIntyre, Jack McNeil, Tom Nardone, Chuck Nelson, Steven Sabow, Timothy Smeeding, Reid Steadman, John Stinson, and Ed Welniak.

We are grateful to the Ford Foundation, the John D. & Catherine T. MacArthur Foundation, the Joyce Foundation, the Charles Stewart Mott Foundation, and the Rockefeller Foundation for providing support for the research and publication of this volume.

The State of
Working America

Executive summary

A comprehensive review of the vast amount of data that describe the working world at the turn of the new century reveals three important new developments in the state of working America.

The first development is rapid wage growth. After more than 15 years of stagnation and decline, inflation-adjusted wages began to rise in 1995. What's more, these increases have been largest for workers at the bottom.

The second new development is an acceleration in the growth of labor productivity—the value of the goods and services that an average worker produces in an hour of work, probably the best indicator of an economy's capacity to provide for the material needs of its population. Since 1995, labor productivity has grown about 2.5% per year, well above the 1.3% rate that prevailed from the mid-1970s through the mid-1990s.

The final development is a subtle but important change in the shape of wage inequality. In the 1980s, inequality "fanned out"—the top pulled away from the middle, and the middle pulled away from the bottom. In the 1990s, however, wages at the bottom and the middle grew closer, while the top pulled further away from the rest.

One of the major tasks of this book is to document and explain these important new features of the economy. Persistent low unemployment—the unemployment rate has remained below 5.5% since February 1996—plays a key role in the explanation of these recent and dramatic improvements in the labor market. When unemployment is low, workers can more easily press for higher pay, better benefits, and improved working conditions because employers cannot easily replace dissatisfied workers with less demanding ones from the pool of the unemployed. When unemployment remains low for a prolonged period, the work environment changes. Workers feel more and more empowered and employers become more and more sensitive to workplace issues that can affect recruitment and retention of workers.

Sustained low unemployment helps to explain all three of the new features of the economy at the turn of the century. Both unionized and non-unionized workers have translated the increased bargaining power that comes with low unemployment into higher wages, a move that helps to explain the reversal of long-term wage stagnation. The tight labor market also means that the economy is operating closer to its full capacity, where efficiency is often highest, and this capacity utilization can account for at least part of the acceleration in productivity. Sustained low unemployment has also probably contributed to the new shape of inequality. A tight labor market most positively affects the workers who have the fewest skills, the least attachment to work, the most exposure to discrimination, and typically the lowest wages. As a result, the tight labor market of the late 1990s boosted the wages of workers at the bottom even more than it did those of workers at the middle and the top.

Another factor that contributes to understanding these recent developments is the "new economy." Our reading of the available data concludes that investments in information technology (hardware and software)—and the high productivity of sectors producing information technology—are the major reasons for the recent acceleration in productivity growth. Taken together, various aspects of the investment in and deployment of information technology account for about two-thirds of the acceleration in average labor productivity between 1974-90 and 1996-99.

At the same time, though, the information technology (IT) sector has not contributed significantly to job growth or wage improvements in the 1990s. Although information-technology-producing industries generated jobs at a substantially faster rate than did other industries in the 1990s, information technology industries still contributed only a small share to total job growth—about 7.5% of all new jobs. Information technology occupations, such as programmers, systems analysts, and so on, made up just 2.0% of all employment in 1999, up from 1.3% in 1989. IT sectors were not wage leaders: among men, IT wages were stable relative to those of comparable workers since the mid-1980s; among women, IT wages fell relative to those of similar workers. Nor did information technology drive wage growth in the 1990s. Among men, workers in information technology jobs did no better than workers in other kinds of jobs with comparable education and experience; among women, information technology workers actually lost some ground relative to comparable workers in other sectors.

Two other developments help to explain recent improvements in wages, especially wages for women. One is the series of increases in the federal minimum wage implemented in 1990, 1991, 1996, and 1997. These increases represented a sharp reversal of the situation in the 1980s, when the minimum wage's purchasing power eroded continuously. The other development was the decline in the employment share of retail trade, a sector known for its low wages and extensive use of part-time and women workers. Any shift of employment out of retail trade into other sectors would help to raise overall wages; given the high concentration of women in the sector, women's wages benefited most from the shift.

Do these many improvements mean that we are living in the "best economy ever"? Any serious analysis of the condition of today's workers must distinguish between "things getting better" and "things being good." The last five years have seen significant improvements over a broad range of economic indicators important to workers, including unemployment, wages, and incomes. But these improvements follow a long period of stagnation and decline in living standards—wage and income inequality remain high; tens of millions of workers still lack health insurance, pension plans, and vacation and sick pay; families are working more hours and feeling the "time squeeze" more acutely than at any point in the postwar period; and households are burdened with the highest levels of debt in history. Recent improvements are heartening, but much remains to be done.

Incomes rising, with slower growth in income inequality

Despite strong growth in inflation-adjusted incomes in the last half of the 1990s, real income growth over the entire decade was slow and unequally distributed. Between 1989 and 1999, the inflation-adjusted income of the median, or typical, family grew just 0.6% per year—slightly higher than the 0.4% average growth rate of the 1980s and well below the 2.6-2.8% average rate from 1947 to 1973. Even the income gains of the late 1990s—median inflation-adjusted income grew 2.5% a year—fell short of the average rate achieved during the first 30 years of the postwar period.

Income inequality continued to grow in the 1990s, though at a slower rate than in the 1980s. Between 1989 and 1999, the share of total income received by the bottom 20% of households fell 0.3 percentage points, while the share received by the top 5% grew from 17.9% percent in 1989 to 20.3% percent in 1999.

Income inequality continued to grow even during the boom in the second half of the 1990s. From 1995 to 1999, the real incomes of low-income families, or families in the 20th percentile, grew 2.6% each year, the same as for families in the middle (60th percentile) but far slower than the 3.5% rate for families at the top (95th percentile).

Blacks and Hispanics made moderate progress over the 1990s as a whole, but saw historically impressive gains in the 1995-99 period. Over the entire decade, the average income of black families grew 1.6% per year, more than double the rate for whites (0.6% per year). This pattern persisted over both the stagnant growth period of the early 1990s and over the boom period of the latter 1990s, when black median incomes grew 2.9% per year compared to 2.4% for whites. Hispanic family incomes were essentially unchanged during the 1990s, but Hispanic families did much better than whites during the boom years, when average Hispanic family income grew 4.2% per year.

For the first time in the postwar period, the division of total corporate income between income paid to workers and income paid to owners of capital shifted strongly in favor of owners of capital during the 1990s. In 1999, owners of capital received 20.5% of the income paid out by the corporate sector, up from 18.2% in 1989. This 2.3 percentage-point rise in the "profit share" was more than four times larger than the 0.5 percentage-point increase between 1979 and 1989.

The general conclusions about slow income growth and rising inequality stand even after we consider changes in family composition (the increase in numbers of women raising families alone), changes in family size (the long-term decline in average family size), different definitions of income, and changes in tax structures.

The most important factor contributing to the income growth of the last decade was the increase in the number of hours that families worked each year. In 1998, for example, the typical middle-income married-couple family worked a total of 3,885 hours (adding spouses' total annual hours together). This represented an increase of 247 hours—or about six weeks more than a similar family worked in 1989.

African American and Hispanic families worked far more hours than white families in the same income range. White married-couple families in the middle 20% of the overall income range, for example, worked an average of 3,789 hours per year. Black families in that same income range, however, worked an average of 4,278 hours per year, a difference of almost 500 hours per year. Hispanic families in the middle-income range worked an average of 4,050 hours per year, or about 140 hours more than white families with similar incomes.

Wages rise sharply in late 1990s

After more than 15 years of stagnant or declining wages at the middle and bottom of the wage range, the purchasing power of wages at all levels grew rapidly between 1995 and 1999. After adjusting for inflation, the median wage for all workers grew 7.3% during 1995-99. For male workers, the median rose 5.5%; for female workers, it rose 5.8%.

Wage growth during those years was even stronger for workers at the bottom, as the real wage of the 10th percentile worker rose 9.3% (9.8% for men and 9.1% for women). Wages for workers at the top grew even more: at the 95th percentile, real wages jumped 8.5% between 1995 and 1999 (11.7% for men and 7.8% for women). Workers in the middle experienced the smallest gains (median male earnings actually fell 1.2% during the 1990s). Wage inequality in the 1990s, then, involved the bottom and the middle growing closer, and the top pulling farther away from the rest. This pattern of wage growth represents a sharp break with inequality trends of the 1980s, when the top pulled away from the middle and the middle pulled away from the bottom.

Two forces seem to have influenced this new shape of inequality. The first is the series of increases in the federal minimum wage in 1990, 1991, 1996, and 1997, which boosted wages at the bottom but had less impact on wages in the middle. The second is the sustained low unemployment of the late 1990s, which had a beneficially disproportionate impact on the wages of workers at the bottom, where unemployment fell the most.

Other important developments in the wage and compensation distribution include the following:

- The real wage of the median CEO rose 62.7% during 1989-99, helping the average CEO to earn 107 times more than the typical worker. This ratio of CEO to worker pay was almost double the ratio of 56 in 1989 and more than five times greater than the ratio of 20 in 1962. According to the most recent data, U.S. CEOs also earn about 2.5 times more than their foreign counterparts.

- The wage gap between men and women narrowed in the 1990s. In 1999, the median woman earned 76.9% of what the median man earned, up from 73.1% in 1989.

- In 1999, just over one in four (26.8%) U.S. workers earned poverty-level wages—the wage required to lift out of poverty a family of four headed by a full-time, full-year worker (about $8.19 per hour in 1999). Women are much more likely to work in poverty-level jobs than men: about one in five (20.7%) men and one in three (33.4%) women earned poverty-level wages in 1999. Poverty-level work was especially common among racial and ethnic minorities. In 1999, 29.5% of black men, 40.7% of black women, 40.3% of Hispanic men, and 51.8% of Hispanic women were in jobs that paid poverty wages. At the national level, however, the share of workers earning

5

poverty-level wages declined—among both white and black workers—as wages grew in the 1990s.

- In 1998, 62.9% of private sector workers had employer-provided health insurance, about the same rate of coverage as in 1989 (63.1%). Coverage is highly unequal across wage levels. In the same year, 82.3% of workers in the top fifth of the wage distribution had coverage, compared to just 29.6% of workers in the bottom fifth.

- In 1999, fewer than half (49.2%) of private sector workers had employer-provided pension plans. As with health insurance, the rate of pension coverage varies considerably across wage levels. Almost three-fourths of workers in the top fifth of wages had pension coverage in 1999, compared to less than one in five workers (17.9%) in the bottom fifth.

- In 1999, 27.3% of workers had a four-year college degree or more. Of these workers, about one-third (8.6% of the total workforce) had an advanced degree. Just over 10% of the workforce had less than a high school diploma. About one-third (32.3%) had a high school diploma or equivalent, but no further education. About the same number of workers (29.6%) had some college, but had not earned a four-year degree.

- Entry-level wages increased substantially in the second half of the 1990s. Between 1995 and 1999, real wages of young high school graduates increased 6.3% for men and 6.2% for women. Among young college graduates, real wages rose 14.9% for men and 9.4% for women.

- Between 1995 and 1999, real wages grew across almost all race and ethnic groups. Among men, median wages grew 6.2% for whites, 8.1% for blacks, and 11.8% for Asians. The median wage for Hispanic men, however, fell 3.5% over the same period. Among women, median wages grew 6.5% for whites, 5.5% for blacks, 8.2% for Hispanics, and 9.1% for Asians.

- Total compensation for union workers substantially exceeds that of non-union workers. Even after controlling for differences in the characteristics of union and non-union workers, union workers' total compensation is about 27.8% higher than that of non-union workers.

- Even after four increases in the federal minimum wage in the 1990s, its inflation-adjusted value was more than 20% lower in 2000 than in 1979. The erosion of the real value of the minimum wage over the 1980s and 1990s was responsible for a significant share of the increase in women's wage inequality over that period.

Sustained low unemployment key to improvements

One of the keys to recent improvements in hourly wages and family incomes is the sustained low unemployment that began in 1996 and continues through 2000. In mid-2000, the unemployment rate stood at about 4.0%. Since 1996, the unemployment rate has remained below 5.5%, a development that has significantly boosted the bargaining position of workers, especially those at the bottom and middle. The current period of sustained low unemployment is unprecedented in recent economic history: at no other time since 1970 has the unemployment rate remained below 5.5% for more than two consecutive years.

The national unemployment rate was low in 1999, but unemployment rates vary significantly by race and ethnicity. In 1999, unemployment for whites was 3.7%, less than half the rate for blacks (8.0%) and well below the rate for Hispanics (6.4%). Between 1989 and 1999, however, the unemployment situation improved more for blacks (down 3.4 percentage points) and Hispanics (down 1.6 percentage points) than it did for whites (down 0.8 percentage points).

The underemployment rate (which includes unemployed and discouraged workers, workers with only a marginal attachment to the labor force, and involuntary part-time workers) was 7.5% in 1999, about 3.3 percentage points higher than the standard unemployment rate.

All measures of employment—total non-farm payroll, total civilian employment, total hours worked, and full-time equivalent employment—show that employment grew more slowly over the 1990s than it did in earlier postwar business cycles. The share of working-age women with jobs grew significantly in the 1990s, from 54.9% of all working-age women in 1989 to 58.5% in 1999. Corresponding employment rates for men, however, declined slightly, from 74.5% in 1989 to 74.0% in 1999.

One welcome feature of the expansion of the late 1990s is the apparent reversal in the long-term trend toward a greater share of nonstandard jobs, or jobs that aren't regular full-time positions. Between 1995 and 1999, the share of regular full-time employment rose from 73.6% to 75.1% of all jobs. During that same period, the prevalence of various forms of nonstandard work declined: part-time work dropped from 16.5% to 15.5% of all jobs; self-employment from 7.5% to 6.7%; and independent contracting from 6.7% to 6.3%. Other forms of nonstandard work remained flat over the period: temporary help agency employment held steady at 0.9-1.0%; on-call work at 1.5-1.7%; and work with contract firms at 0.5-0.6%.

Nonstandard workers, however, continue to suffer relative to their regular full-time co-workers. While many nonstandard workers prefer the flexibility of their arrangements, they generally receive lower pay than their full-time counterparts. Nonstandard workers are also far less likely than standard workers to have health insurance or pension benefits.

Involuntary part-time work declined substantially over the 1990s, from 4.3% of all employees in 1989 to 2.6% in 1999. The share of workers holding two or more jobs also fell in the 1990s, from 6.2% in 1989 to 5.9% in 1999.

Household wealth mostly untouched by stock boom

Wealth is the total value of a household's assets minus its debts. The stock market boom of the 1990s left the impression that most Americans were experiencing an unprecedented growth in wealth. The truth, however, is that most Americans have no economically meaningful stake in the stock market. The most recent government data show that less than half of households hold stock in any form, including mutual funds and 401(k)-style pension plans. The same data reveal that 64% of households have stock holdings worth $5,000 or less.

The distribution of wealth remains highly unequal. The wealthiest 1% of households control about 38% of national wealth, while the bottom 80% control only 17%. The ownership of stocks is particularly unequal. The top 1% of stock owners hold almost half (47.7%) of all stocks, by value, while the bottom 80% own *just 4.1% of total stock holdings.*

The total wealth of the typical American household rose only marginally during the 1990s. The net worth of the average household in the middle 20% of the wealth distribution rose about $2,200 in the 1990s—from $58,800 in 1989 to $61,000 in 1998. Over that same period, the value of the stock holdings of the typical household grew by $5,500 and the value of non-stock assets grew by $8,500. Meanwhile, typical household debt increased $11,800. The relatively modest gains in stock and non-stock assets, combined with the explosion in household debt, meant that the 1990s were far less generous to typical households than business-page headlines often suggest.

For the typical household, rising debt, not a rising stock market, was the big story of the 1990s. While households in the middle 20% of the wealth distribution captured 2.8% of the total growth in stock market holdings between 1989 and 1998, these same families were saddled with 38.8% of the unprecedented rise in household debt. While low nominal interest rates have made it easier for households to carry this greatly expanded debt, many households appear to be straining. About 14% of middle-income households have debt-service obligations that exceed 40% of their income; 9% have at least one bill that is more than 60 days past due. Meanwhile, despite the robust state of the economy, personal bankruptcy rates reached record highs in the late 1990s.

Poverty remains high despite recovery

Despite the economic boom in the second half of the 1990s, the national poverty rate in 1998 was 12.7%, just one-tenth of a percentage point less than in 1989 and a full percentage point higher than in 1979. Thanks to a larger-than-expected decline in 1999, the poverty rate fell to 11.8% that year, about the same as in 1979. Nevertheless, it took a number of years for the poverty rate to respond to the 1990s recovery.

Child poverty followed a similar path. In 1998, 18.9% of American children—almost one in five—lived in poverty. By 1999, the rate for children had declined to 16.9%, only slightly higher than the 1979 rate of 16.4%

In 1999, about one in four African Americans (23.6%) and Hispanics (22.8%) lived in poverty, a rate about twice that of whites (9.8%). Racial disparities in poverty rates were even worse for children. In 1999, about one in three African American (33.1%) and Hispanic (30.3%) children were growing up in poverty, compared to 13.5% of white children.

During the 1990s, however, overall poverty rates declined much more for blacks (down 7.1 percentage points) and Hispanics (down 3.4 percentage points) than they did for whites (down 0.2 percentage points). The gains for minority children were even more dramatic, as black and Hispanic child poverty fell 10.6 and 5.9 percentage points, respectively, while child poverty among whites fell just 1.3 points.

The official poverty measure almost certainly understates the true level of poverty. One alternative estimation procedure implemented by the Census Bureau suggests that, during the 1990s, the true share of the population living in poverty was an average of 3.6 percentage points higher than suggested by the official estimate.

The poor, like all workers, are working harder than ever. In 1998, for example, poor families with children worked an average of 1,213 hours per year, about 140 hours (almost three full-time weeks) more than in 1989. The increase was greater for poor minority families than for poor white families. Between 1989 and 1998, the average annual hours worked rose by 152 for poor African American families and by 175 for poor Hispanic families; over the same period, poor white families worked an average of only 3 hours longer.

Improvements in the national economy on the one hand and reductions in the generosity of public assistance on the other have combined to increase the share of poor families' income earned through work and to decrease the share received through public assistance. Between 1989 and 1998, for example, among poor working families with children, the share of earned income rose from 58% to 71%, while the share of public assistance income fell from 25% to 11%.

9

South and Midwest make big gains

Trends in wages, incomes, poverty, employment, unemployment, and other economic measures vary widely across the country's four major regions (Northeast, South, Midwest, and West) and the 50 states. In general terms, during the 1990s the South and Midwest were the biggest beneficiaries of new economic developments. By several important measures, economic conditions actually worsened in the Northeast and West.

Between 1989 and the end of the 1990s, for example, median hourly wages and median family income grew fastest in the South and Midwest. Meanwhile, median hourly wages fell in both the Northeast and the West, while median family income declined in the Northeast and remained unchanged in the Midwest. Over the same period, unemployment rates and poverty rates fell most in the South and Midwest, but poverty rates rose substantially in the Northeast.

Between 1989 and 1999, growth in hourly wages also varied greatly across regions. For low-wage workers (those in the 20th percentile of each region's wage distribution), inflation-adjusted hourly wages rose 13.1% in the Midwest and 7.5% in the South. Over the same period, hourly wages fell 2.3% in the Northeast and 0.2% in the West. The pattern of wage growth was similar for workers in the middle of the wage distribution. Median hourly wages rose 4.9% in the Midwest and 4.7% in the South, but fell 2.4% in the Northeast and 2.7% in the West.

Regional differences in wage growth carried over into regional differences in income growth. Over the 1990s, median family income rose 1.0% annually in the Midwest and 0.7% annually in the South. But it did not grow at all in the West and fell at an average rate of 0.3% per year in the Northeast.

In 1998, poverty rates were highest in the West (14.0%) and South (13.7%) and lowest in the Northeast (12.3%) and Midwest (10.3%). But again, during the 1990s the biggest improvements occurred in the South and Midwest. Between 1989 and 1998, the poverty rate fell 1.6 percentage points in the Midwest and 1.7 percentage points in the South, while it rose 1.5 percentage points in the West and 2.3 percentage points in the Northeast.

In 1999, when the national unemployment rate stood at 4.2%, unemployment rates differed significantly from state to state—from 2.5% in Minnesota, Nebraska, and South Dakota to over 6.0% in New Mexico, West Virginia, and the District of Columbia. As with many other trends in the 1990s, the jobless situation improved most in the Midwest, where the unemployment rate fell 1.9 percentage points between 1989 and 1999, and the South, where it fell 1.7 percentage points. Improvements were much smaller in the Northeast (down 0.2 percentage points) and the Midwest (down 0.4 percentage points).

Over the 1990s, employment growth varied from region to region. Between 1989 and 1999, employment grew rapidly in the South (25.7%), West (24.4%), and Midwest (18.3%), but was almost stagnant in the Northeast (4.1%).

For the world, a poor role model

The United States is often offered as an economic model for the rest of the world, but the analysis presented here argues for caution. While the United States has succeeded in lowering unemployment and has been particularly successful in incorporating women into the labor force, it lags behind the rest of the developed world in many other important measures of economic performance. Several other rich countries have managed to achieve low unemployment rates and to incorporate women into the labor market without the high—and rising—level of inequality that has characterized the United States over the last two decades and longer.

In 1998, the United States had one of the highest per capita incomes of all the rich industrialized economies. Using market exchange rates, only Norway, Switzerland, Denmark, Finland, and Sweden had a higher per capita annual income than the United States ($32,051). Using purchasing-power-parity exchange rates, which take into consideration differences in the relative prices in different countries, the United States actually had the highest per capita income in 1998.

Despite strong economic growth in the second half of the 1990s, growth in per capita income in the United States landed in the middle of the range for the rich industrialized economies. Between 1989 and 1998, per capita income in the United States grew at a 1.6% annual rate, above the rates in Germany, Japan, and France but below those in Norway, Denmark, the Netherlands, Australia, and several other advanced economies.

The United States has led the world in productivity (the amount of goods and services produced in an hour of work) for most of the postwar period. During the 1990s, however, several countries (Belgium, western Germany, France, the Netherlands, and Norway) reached and even exceeded U.S. productivity levels.

The United States has the most unequal income distribution and one of the highest poverty rates among all the advanced economies in the world. The U.S. tax and benefit system is also one of the least effective in reducing poverty (though the U.S. Social Security system compares favorably with other countries when it comes to reducing poverty among the elderly).

Contrary to widely held perceptions, the United States offers less economic mobility than other rich countries. In one study, for example, low-wage workers in the United States were more likely to remain in the low-wage labor market five years longer than workers in Germany, France, Italy, the United Kingdom, Denmark, Finland, and Sweden (all the other countries studied in this analysis). In another study, poor households in the United States were less likely to leave poverty from one year to the next than were poor households in Canada, Germany, the Netherlands, Sweden, and the United Kingdom (all the countries studied in this second analysis).

The United States had a low unemployment rate (4.2%) in 1999. But so did Austria (3.7%), Denmark (5.2%), Japan (4.7%), the Netherlands (3.3%), Norway (3.2%), Portugal (4.5%), and Switzerland (3.5%).

The international data also show that workers in the United States put in more hours per year (an average of 1,966 in 1998) than do workers in every other advanced economy except Portugal. The average hours worked in other large industrialized economies—even Japan (at 1,898), the previous world leader in hours worked—are typically well below those of the United States.

The living standards debate

For most workers the early part of the economic expansion that began in 1991 was disappointing: incomes continued to decline and poverty increased during what came to be called the "jobless" recovery. This was also a period of great worker insecurity, downsizing, and low productivity growth. But economic conditions have improved remarkably since 1995. Persistent low unemployment helped to boost wages, brought new workers into the labor market, and allowed workers to move from substandard jobs—temporary, part-time, or without benefits—to better, more regular jobs. The best news is that low-wage workers and low-income families have benefited most, thereby reversing nearly 20 years of declining wages and incomes.

The turnaround from widespread wage decline between 1979 and 1995 to widespread wage growth since is a significant new development for working Americans at the start of the 21st century. But the late 1990s were remarkable for two other stories as well:

- The growth of labor productivity—the value of the goods and services that an average worker produces in an hour of work—has accelerated. Labor productivity is probably the best indicator of an economy's capacity to provide for the material needs of its population, and since 1995 it has grown about 2.5% per year, well above the 1.4% rate that prevailed from the mid-1970s through the mid-1990s.

- The shape of wage inequality changed in a subtle but important way. In the 1980s, inequality "fanned out"—the top pulled away from the middle, and the middle pulled away from the bottom. In the 1990s, however, wages at the bottom and the middle grew closer, while the top pulled further away from the middle. Nevertheless, inequality in the U.S. remains high, and the gap between the best-off and those in the middle continues to grow.

New trends in the 1990s

Broad-based wage growth. From 1995 to 1999, the average hourly wage, adjusted for inflation, grew 2.7% a year, far better than the 0.6% annual growth during the 1989-95 period or in the two prior business cycles of 1973-79 and 1979-89. Because the value of employer-paid health insurance and pensions fell, though, recent overall compensation growth of 1.8% has been less than the 2.7% in wage growth. The real wage growth in the late 1990s was enjoyed across the wage structure, by low-, middle-, and high-wage earners and by both men and women (see **Table A** on the next page). Wage growth has also been greater among lower-wage workers than among high-wage (or middle-wage) workers, marking a dramatic turnaround from the early 1990s and the prior two decades, when low-wage workers not only fared worse than other workers but actually saw their wages continuously decline after inflation. For instance, the wages of low-wage men ($8.02 in 1989) fell 0.9% a year from 1989 to 1995 and then grew 1.7% a year from 1995 to 1999. Moreover, the growth for low-wage men was faster than for middle-wage men (1.3%) and comparable to that of high-wage men (1.8%). Similarly, the wages of low-wage women grew faster (2.0%) than they did for middle-wage (1.4%) or high-wage (1.9%) women.

The quality of jobs has also brightened as unemployment has remained low. The share of workers who are "involuntary" part-timers—working part time but wanting a full-time job—dropped to 2.6% in 1999, down from 3.7% in 1995 and lower than at any time over the last few decades. This is equivalent to shifting 1.4 million involuntary, part-time workers into full-time jobs. At the same time, the number of workers counted as "marginally attached" to the labor force—those wanting work but who had stopped looking several weeks prior to the unemployment survey—dropped by 400,000.

Moreover, the attributes of jobs have improved remarkably since 1995. The share of workers with employer-provided health insurance—a clear dividing line between a "good" and a "bad" job—has grown since 1995, reversing the downward slide in health insurance coverage during the 1980s and early 1990s. The growth of part-time jobs relative to full-time jobs slackened, to the point that there were proportionately fewer voluntary part-time workers in 1999 than in 1995.

Work through temporary help agencies continued to grow throughout the

TABLE A Pay and productivity trends, 1989-99

Labor market indicator	Annual growth		Acceleration 1995-99 vs. 1989-95
	1989-95 (1)	1995-99 (2)	(2)-(1)
Labor productivity	1.4%	2.5%	1.1%
Average hourly:			
Wages	0.6%	2.7%	2.0%
Compensation	0.6	1.8	1.3
Real hourly wages*			
Men			
Low	-0.9%	1.7%	2.6%
Middle	-1.1	1.3	2.4
High	0.1	1.8	1.7
Women			
Low	-0.3%	2.0%	2.3%
Middle	-0.3	1.4	1.7
High	0.7	1.9	1.2

* Measured as 20th, 50th, and 90th percentiles.

Source: Tables 2.1, 2.2, 2.7, and 2.8.

recovery, but the growth slackened considerably after 1995—the share of workers employed by temporary agencies grew 60% from 1991 to 1995 but by just 26% from 1995 to 1999. Had the 1991-95 growth continued, there would have been 826,000 more people employed through temporary agencies in 1999. In addition, during the 1995-99 period the share of the workforce working more than one job—multiple job-holders—fell from 6.2% to 5.8%, reflecting fewer people working two part-time jobs or supplementing their full-time job with a part-time one. In terms of all types of nonstandard work—including regular part-time, temporary help agency, on-call, independent contracting, and contract firm work—the share of workers in these arrangements fell from 26.4% to 24.8% of total employment during 1995-99.

The tight labor markets have not only boosted pay and pushed job quality higher, but they have also allowed greater participation in the labor market, in particular by female heads of household affected by welfare reform. Both the employment rates and the hours worked by low-income single-mother families rose to historically unprecedented rates over the recovery, with much of the growth coming in the latter half of the 1990s. For example, the employment rates of mother-only families with some income from welfare grew from 40.4% in 1995 to 56.0% in 1998. Among poor families with children headed by single mothers, hours of work grew 40% in the 1990s, far more than for any other family type.

The shift to better job quality and the demand for the work of previously unattached or marginally attached persons reflect an improved bargaining position for workers, both individually and through unions. In other words, as a result of low unemployment workers have been able to obtain jobs that better fit their needs.

Productivity growth. The 2.5% annual growth in labor productivity since 1995 compares favorably to the 1.4% productivity growth of the early 1990s as well as the rates of the 1970s and 1980s. Productivity growth has been as fast in other recent decades, but, unlike in this instance, the fast growth tended to occur in the early years of recoveries.

The new shape of inequality. One feature of the economic landscape that has not changed is the unequal distribution of income and wage gains among the different economic classes and the continuing rise in these disparities. However, in the case of wages, the growth of inequality has shifted: the top earners are still pulling away from the middle class and the working class, but now low earners and the poor are closing the gap. The wage gains described above bear this out: low-wage men and women posted gains as high as those posted by 90th percentile earners, while the smallest gains went to workers in the middle. The widening of the wage gap between the top and the middle is even greater than that illustrated in the accompanying table, because the highest wage earners (say, those at the 95th percentile, who earn more than 95% of all workers) have had better wage growth than the merely high-wage earners (90th percentile). Climb even further up the ladder and into the ranks of the corporate chief executive officers and one will find pay growth that is indeed extraordinary—62.7% for CEOs versus 12.9% for the 90th percentile earner over the 1989-99 period.

At the bottom of the wage scale, the share of workers earning poverty-level wages dropped considerably during the 1995-99 period. Among black and Hispanic men, for instance, 5.4% of the workforce left poverty-level jobs for higher wages. Among women, 4.3% shifted to higher-than-poverty-level wages.

Income inequality, unlike wage inequality, continued its historic pattern even through the late 1990s boom, with the top pulling away from the middle and the middle pulling away from the bottom (although somewhat more moderately for the latter than in the past). This continued rise in income inequality is evident no matter how one calculates income—using the conventional Census measure of money income; measuring on an after-tax basis; adjusting for family size; or including government non-cash transfers (e.g., food stamps, Medicaid, and so on). Although estimates of income inequality in a particular year will differ depending on the definition used, all income measures show a significant rise in inequality over the 1990s.

The pattern of this new inequality is somewhat different than that for wages because family income comprises more than wage income. A significant amount of income at the bottom comes from government assistance (Temporary Assistance for Needy Families, or TANF, Social Security, unemployment insurance), and the top derives a huge share from capital income (dividends, capital gains, interest). As with wages, the incomes of those at the top—the upper 1%, 5%, or 20%—have grown significantly faster than those in the middle. For instance, the median family's income grew 6.5% from 1989 to 1999, while that of a high-income family (at the 95th percentile) grew 16.6%. This divergence would be even wider if these numbers included the sizeable capital gains of recent years, gains that primarily accrue to the best-off families. For instance, capital gains made up about 7% of income in 1998-99, about double the share a decade earlier. The most comprehensive income measure available shows the ratio of the incomes of the upper 5% to the middle fifth rising continuously over the 1990s, from 6.7 in 1989 to 7.8 in 1999. By this measure, the growth of inequality at the top in the 1990s is about half as strong as in the 1980s.

Another benefit of low unemployment has been a lessening of the black/white wage and income gaps. For instance, the median family income among African Americans grew 2.9% a year from 1995 to 1999, compared to 2.4% growth among whites. The median hourly wage of black men grew faster than the wage of their white counterparts. The wage growth for black women has been comparable to that of white women since 1995, while in the early1990s the wages for black women grew more slowly. Given these impressive wage and income gains, it is not surprising that poverty fell after 1995, especially among minorities: it was down by 7.5 percentage points among Hispanics and 5.7 points among African Americans, but by just 1.4 points among whites. Even more impressive is that, after 1995, poverty rates fell by over 8 percentage points among minority children and by 3.0 points among white children.

Explanations for the recent trends

One major factor behind faster wage and income growth has been persistent low unemployment, which has helped spur productivity growth and has given workers leverage to obtain better wages and better jobs and to shift away from part-time and irregular, contingent-type work. Low unemployment has also been an important factor in lessening inequality at the bottom. Information technology (IT) is associated with these new trends in some ways, but there are also some trends—such as the new patterns of inequality—that are not associated with IT. For instance, the increased use of information technology has been a major factor propelling faster productivity growth, and yet high-tech-sector employers have not been wage leaders. Nor has technological change been associated with the rise of wage inequalities in the late 1990s or over the last few decades. Rather, globalization, deunionization, and the shift to low-paying industries have kept wage inequality at the top growing, while increases in the minimum wage have helped lessen wage inequality at the bottom in the 1990s.

Persistent low unemployment. The economy has not only achieved a relatively low unemployment rate—just 4.2% in 1999—but unemployment has remained low for several years. In fact, the unemployment rate has stayed at or below 5.6% since 1995, the first time since 1970 that unemployment has remained so low for more than two years in a row. This is what we call "persistent low unemployment," unemployment that remains low enough long enough to require economic actors—businesses, workers, unions, and others—to adjust to the new environment.

Low unemployment is both a consequence and a cause of the higher productivity growth since 1995. The greater productivity growth offset the greater wage growth that accompanied low unemployment, thereby keeping inflation stable and forestalling any Federal Reserve Board action to slow the recovery's growth rate. On the other hand, low unemployment likely led to higher productivity, because employers, unable to find or hire new workers in the tight job market, were forced to produce more with the same workforce, i.e., by increasing investment, upgrading worker skills through training, reorganizing the work process, and introducing new technologies.

Low unemployment has helped fuel faster growth and has lessened inequality at the bottom. But what is responsible for current low unemployment? Part of the answer is that inflation hasn't accelerated, for two reasons. First, continued high levels of worker anxiety and corporate policies have suppressed wage growth, even among white-collar workers. Second, no major "supply shocks," such as those that led to soaring energy and food prices in the 1970s, have beset the U.S. economy. In fact, the rapidly falling prices of computer-related equipment and the import price declines following the "East Asian" financial crisis might be considered positive supply shocks that helped reduce inflation. With inflation low, the Federal Reserve Board did not radically raise interest rates and end the recovery.

Another reason for the low unemployment is that the Federal Reserve Board has not followed the traditional policy of ending a recovery when unemployment fell below some benchmark, such as 5.5%. Instead, its wait-and-see policy has allowed unemployment to fall and, when no inflation ensued, the recovery to continue.

Rapid growth in demand for goods and services, due to faster consumption based on consumer debt and a higher stock market as well as a pickup in the growth of computer-related equipment investment, has also helped to lower unemployment.

Low unemployment has clearly contributed to the greater wage growth among low-wage earners relative to other workers. Low-wage earners benefit more from low unemployment, as reflected in a greater growth of annual earnings: this occurs because they experience both greater gains in employment and hours worked and attain a greater boost to their hourly wages.

As discussed above, this period of persistent low unemployment has allowed workers to obtain the types of jobs that better fit their needs. This shift to better job quality reflects an improved bargaining position for workers, both individually and through unions, and establishes that more leverage for workers, as well as greater productivity, is associated with the recent acceleration in wage growth.

The 'new economy.' This section explores the role of information technology in generating faster productivity, as well as one other dimension of what is referred to as the "new economy": the rapid rise in stock market values and increased ownership of stocks. We also explore the role of the IT sector on labor market trends. We conclude that investments in information technology—hardware and software and the high productivity of sectors producing information technology—are a major reason for the higher productivity growth. But, we note that the IT sector has not contributed significantly to job growth, nor has it demonstrated any wage leadership. In fact, IT wages have failed to rise any more quickly than those of other sectors with similarly skilled workers. We also find that technological change has not been a significant factor in the growth of wage inequality in either the 1980s or the 1990s. As for the stock market, its growth in the late 1990s has been no more than a minor feature of economic life for most families, primarily because most families have little or no stock holdings.

Technological change, and particularly the increased use of information technology equipment and software, has been a major reason for the recent acceleration of productivity growth, accounting for between a third and a half of the faster productivity growth in the late 1990s, relative to that of the 1974-90 period (see Appendix C). Why there was a surge in IT investment starting in 1996 is something our analysis cannot answer and remains to be addressed by other researchers. It is our opinion that the 1995-99 IT surge was driven more by technological developments rather than any proximate economic policy (budget or tax policy, interest rates, deregulation). Other factors that help explain the recent productivity acceleration include: fast demand growth at low unemployment forcing greater efficiency; faster improvements in the organization of work; and, a faster growth of workforce skills. Contrary to the popular perception, the IT sector has not played a leadership role in the labor market. Although IT-producing industries generated jobs at a substantially faster rate than other industries in the 1990s and in the 1992-99 recovery, IT industries contributed a small share of total job growth—about 7.5% of all new jobs. IT occupations, such as programmers, systems analysts, and so on, made up 2.0% of all employment in 1999, up from just 1.3% in 1989. Thus, the IT sector contributed disproportionately to job growth, but was still not a major job generator.

Another common misperception regarding IT workers is that their wages are skyrocketing, reflecting the high demand for their skills (see Chapter 2). Yet a comparison of the wage growth among IT workers relative to comparable workers—those with similar education, experience, and occupation—finds that IT sectors were not wage leaders: among men, IT wages were stable relative to those of comparable workers since the mid-1980s; among women, IT wages fell relative to similar workers. Thus, the IT sector apparently is not experiencing any labor shortage and has not contributed directly (except through the overall productivity effect) to wage acceleration.

There is no evidence to support the notion that the growth of wage inequality reflects primarily a technology-driven increase in demand for "educated" or "skilled" workers. Indeed, technological change has led to a demand for education and skill during the entire 20th century, and probably no more during the 1980s or 1990s than in the 1970s. Without any evidence of "acceleration" of change, there is no reason to believe that technological innovation shifted in a way that led to the post-1979 growth of wage inequality. Second, skill demand and technology have little relationship to the growth of wage inequality within the same groups of workers (i.e., workers with similar levels of experience and education), which was responsible for half of the overall growth of wage inequality in the 1980s and 1990s. Technology has been and continues to be an important force, but there was no "technology shock" in the labor market in the

1980s or 1990s, and no ensuing demand for "skill," that was not satisfied by the continuing expansion of the educational attainment of the workforce.

Moreover, the conventional story about technology leading to the increased demand for skills and the erosion of wages among the "less-skilled" does not readily explain the 1990s pattern of growth of wage inequality: neither the trends in education and experience differentials nor the trends in wage inequality among workers of similar skills. In particular, the 1990s are seen as a period of rapid technological change. Yet, this was the period of the lessening of wage inequality at the bottom. Similarly, education differentials grew slowly among men during most of the 1990s—it was the growth of other dimensions of wage inequality, not easily linked to technology, that kept male wage inequality at the top growing in the 1990s. During the technology-led boom of the late 1990s, there was a growth of education differentials, but other differentials, such as for experience, declined; so there was no growth of "skill differentials" overall during the technology boom.

Another widely heralded feature of the "new economy" is the rising stock market. Indeed, the last decade or so has witnessed a breathtaking run-up in the price of stocks. For instance, the inflation-adjusted value of the Standard & Poor's 500 index of stocks tripled between the beginning and the end of the 1990s. These increases have focused enormous media and public attention on the stock market. Some pundits have even suggested that what happens to a family's stock portfolio is more important than what happens to its paychecks. Yet, while stock ownership has spread and a small number of individuals have ridden the stock market boom to great personal wealth, data on stock ownership establish that the stock market, in practice, is of little or no financial importance to the vast majority of U.S. households.

Even well into the stock market boom of the 1990s, a majority of U.S. households had no stock holdings of any form, either direct or indirect (in 401(k)s, defined-contribution pension plans, or IRAs). In 1998, just under half (48.2%) of households owned stock in any form and only about one-third (36.3%) held stock worth $5,000 or more. In fact, the distribution of stockholdings is more unequal than the distribution of wealth in general. While the wealthiest 1% of all households control about 38% of national wealth, the top 1% of stockowners hold almost half (47.7%) of all stocks. In contrast, the bottom 80% of households (in terms of stockholding, many of whom own no stock) hold just 4.1% of total stock. The value of stockholdings grew across the board in the 1990s, but in dollar terms—and relative to the typical household's retirement needs—the increases were small for 80% of households. For example, the value of the stock held by the middle 20% of households grew only $5,500 between 1989 and 1998 (and this growth includes any shifts they made from non-stock assets into stocks).

The high concentration of stock ownership means that the gains associated with the recent stock boom have been highly concentrated as well. Between 1989 and 1998, almost 35% of the growth went to the wealthiest 1% of households, and almost 38% of the total increase went to the next 9% of households, meaning that 73% of the gains from the stock market accrued to the upper 10%. The middle 20% of households accounted for only 2.8% of the rise in the overall value of stockholdings over the period.

The rising stock market may or may not be a consequence of an information technology "new economy," but in any case its gains bypassed most households.

Rising minimum wage, contracting retail sector. Two developments in the 1990s help explain the better wage and job quality trends for women, especially those in low-wage employment. First, increases in the minimum wage in 1991-92 and again in 1996-97 raised its value in real terms by 14.4% over the 1989-99 period, sharply reversing its continuous erosion during the 1980s. Second, retail trade, the lowest-wage sector and an extensive user of part-time, mostly female workers, expanded in the 1980s but contracted (relative to total employment) in the 1990s. Together, these factors—along with low unemployment—help explain why low-wage women fared far better in the 1990s than in the 1980s and why wage inequality at the bottom among women declined in the 1990s.

The relatively continuous growth of wage inequality at the top, reflected in the wage gap between the 90th or 95th percentile and the median worker, appears to result from trends that have been ongoing since the early 1980s—continued globalization, a shift toward lower-paying industries (except among women), and a weakening of unionism.

Problems remain

Getting better versus being good. In spite of the widespread living standard improvements accompanying the strong recovery of the late 1990s, the fundamental economic situation, given the dramatic, broad-based wage erosion and rising inequalities of the 1979-95 period, can still not be considered "good." For instance, over the 1989-99 period productivity, which might be considered the economy's "ability to pay," or its yardstick to measure good growth, rose 20.5%. However, typical workers received virtually none of this increase—the median hourly wage among men was slightly less in 1999 than in 1989, while for women it was up just 4%.

The divergence between the wage growth of typical workers and productivity growth arises because of two phenomena—rising wage inequality and a shift of income from workers to owners of capital. Of course, the wage gap between those at the top and those in the middle has grown steadily. In addition, a growing share of corporate income is paid to owners of capital, with a corresponding lower share paid out as compensation. Consequently, the returns to capital have soared in the 1990s to historically high levels. Without this ratcheting-up of profitability, average compensation could have been 4.3% higher in 1999.

Also, while a middle-class, married-couple family's income grew 9.2% from 1989 to 1998, a substantial part of this growth reflected a growth in family work hours, up 182 hours to 3,600 total, or about 4.5 extra full-time weeks a year since 1989.

The continued growth of inequality over the 1990s, compounding the dramatic inequality surge of the 1980s, leaves the nation with very high levels of inequality both in historic terms and when compared to other industrial countries. Despite a higher average-income level in the U.S., low-wage workers here earn substantially less than those in other advanced countries. In fact, the typical low-wage worker in an advanced European economy earns 44% more than in the United States, and the percentage of U.S. children who are poor is twice as high as in other advanced countries. In 1999, the U.S. poverty rate was 11.8%, lower than the 12.8% rate of 1989 but equal to the 11.7% rate of 1979 and higher than the 11.1% rate of 1973—despite nearly 30 years of growth. About one in six (16.9%) children were poor in 1999, including roughly a third of African American and Hispanic children.

Other persistent economic problems include a low share of the workforce having employer-provided health insurance coverage—62.9% in 1998 compared to 70.2% coverage in 1979—and the share of the workforce—nearly half—without pension coverage.

So, although the current income boom has generated substantial improvements, by many measures of adequacy, inequality, and income, the current economy still does not match up to reasonable expectations. We now turn to two particular stress points for working families—increased work hours and increased indebtedness.

The time-squeeze on working families. Family earnings growth over the past few decades has come increasingly from greater work effort—a rise in the number of earners per family and in the average weeks and weekly hours worked per earner. Along with the income generated by more work come greater costs for transportation, clothing, and child care. And more paid work comes at the expense of leisure and time for "household production"—laundry, car-pooling, cleaning, and other maintenance activities. Generally, the increase in work hours has made the ability to balance both work and family a major challenge of family life today.

Over the 1980s the increased work effort of families occurred simultaneously with a fall in real hourly wages for men and for some groups of women. While this pattern changed in the 1990s as husbands' wages rebounded, the fact remains that over the 19-year period from 1979 to 1998, increases in annual family earnings were primarily achieved through more work rather than through higher hourly wages.

Much of this increased work effort has, of course, come from wives. The ability of women to enter the labor market and reduce decades of gender discrimination represents a positive social and economic change. At the same time, though, for many families the increased work effort of their female members has been forced upon the family as the only way to keep income growing. ("Work" in this section refers exclusively to labor market work. Of course, women have long been the major contributors to non-market work.) In this regard, families are clearly worse off if their primary means to obtain higher incomes is more hours of work rather than regular pay increases.

The average family, with the combined help of all of its members, now works 83 weeks a year, up from 68 weeks in 1969, or an additional quarter-time worker in every married-couple family with children. The greatest increase in weeks worked has been among middle-class families, whose weeks worked grew by the equivalent of a person working more than one-third of a year (19 weeks). The growth in weeks worked among higher-income households, by contrast, was only half as much. We can track trends in family hours, but only back to 1979. As would be expected, the pattern for hours is similar to that of weeks, with smaller increases in the 1990s relative to the 1980s. While the number of hours worked by married couples in the lowest fifth is consistently lower than those of better-off fifths, their increase in hours over the 1980s—11%—was greater than that of higher income families. Middle-income families experienced the greatest percent growth of hours in both periods: 11.2% over the 1980s and 6.8% in the 1990s. The result: middle income families have added 12.5 weeks (just over three months) and 613 hours since 1979.

Some critics have argued that the increase in inequality has been generated simply by those with higher incomes working longer and harder while other less well-off families did not increase their work effort. But the data on weeks and hours worked belie this claim: the increases in hours and weeks occurred throughout the income distribution, with the greatest increases among middle-income families.

In a similar vein, work hours have increased about as quickly among families headed by someone with more ("at least some college") as with less ("high school degree or less") education. Among middle-income families, hours are far higher among families with less education (4,156 per year, or two full-time workers) than with more education (3,712 hours), and hours growth since 1979 has been greater among the less-educated families. Thus, again we see that problems balancing work and family are not "upper-income" problems and that families that are falling behind (those headed by someone with less education) have done so despite a greatly increased work effort. Hours of work have grown especially quickly among black families, particularly among those in the lowest fifth of the income distribution. In fact, average work effort of African American married-couple families with children grew more than it did for either whites or Hispanics in both the 1980s and the 1990s. Although they started out the period working fewer hours, by 1998 low-income black families worked more hours than either white or Hispanic low-income families. Among middle-income families with children, African American families worked more hours than families in other racial/ethnic groups in 1998. Their 4,278 annual hours were 489 more than for white families and 228 hours more than Hispanics. Therefore, an average middle-income black family with children needed over 12 more weeks of work than the average white family in order to reach the middle-income ranks.

High-income minority families consistently had hours of work above 4,500, suggesting full-time work by both parents, with contributions by other family members as well. Thus, these data suggest that, due to their lower wage levels, for minority families to make it to the top or middle of the overall income distribution they have to put in extremely long hours relative to whites. By 1998, the highest-income minority families were working at least 500 more hours per year than white families with comparable incomes. Across education and racial groups, and across the income scale, hours spent in the labor market have clearly increased for prime-age, married-couple families with children. By 1998, the average middle-income family was spending 87 weeks and 3,600 hours at work, compared to 75 weeks and 3,041 hours in 1979. Clearly, the time crunch is a real phenomenon, and it is one experienced by the majority of working families, not just the elite lawyers, money managers, or "knowledge workers" of the new economy. These data also deny the notion that increased income inequality among families is due to a greater increased work effort among upper-income families.

Greater debt. In 1999, the total value of all forms of outstanding debt was greater than the total disposable income of all households. In contrast, household debt was about 20% of total disposable income after World War II and 60% in the early 1960s.

For typical households, debt levels are high compared to the value of assets.

In 1998, the average outstanding debt (typically, outstanding mortgage debt plus credit card debt) for households in the middle 20% was $45,800, about five times greater than the corresponding $9,200 average for stockholdings and about half the total value of other assets (overwhelmingly the family home). The increase between 1989 and 1998 in the average household debt held by the middle 20% (up $11,800) was much larger than the corresponding increase in both stocks ($5,500) and non-stock assets ($8,500). While middle-class households captured 2.8% of the total growth in stock market holdings between 1989 and 1998, they absorbed 38.8% of the unprecedented rise in household debt over the same period.

In and of itself, debt is not a problem for households. In fact, credit generally represents a tremendous economic opportunity for households, since they can use it to buy houses, cars, and other big-ticket consumer goods that provide services over many years; to cope with short-term economic setbacks such as unemployment or illness; or to make investments in education or small businesses. Debt becomes a burden only when required debt payments begin to crowd out other economic obligations.

Fortunately, the average household's debt burden—the minimum required payments on outstanding debt as a share of disposable income (13.4% in 1999)—has not changed much over the last two decades, primarily because lower nominal interest rates have offset the higher debt. Consequently, though, households are much more vulnerable to high interest rates than in the past.

An increasing portion of households, however, are experiencing financial hardship from their debts. One indicator of "hardship" is service payments equal to more than 40% of household income. By this measure, about 14% of middle-income households and 20% of households in the $10,000-24,999 income range experienced financial hardship. Despite the strong recovery of 1995-99, the share of households with high debt-service payments increased significantly in the 1990s. Between 1989 and 1998, for example, the share of households facing high debt burdens increased 4.7 percentage points among households in the $25,000-49,999 range and 4.9 percentage points among households in the $10,000-24,999 range. The ultimate indicator of debt-related difficulties is personal bankruptcy, and in 1999 about six out of every 1,000 adults declared personal bankruptcy, almost twice as many as in the last business cycle peak in 1989. Despite the strong economic recovery during the second half of the 1990s, personal bankruptcy increased continuously.

The future

The dramatic improvement of trends over the 1995-99 period raises the question of what will happen in the future. Are we now enjoying a temporary reprieve from the wage declines and surging inequalities of the 1980s and early 1990s? Are we in a "new economy" that will generate continued prosperity?

If we are right about the explanations for the recent prosperity, then the future is partly dependent on the policy choices we make and partly dependent on the unfolding logic of today's technologies. A major part of the recent good news regarding wage growth is that it is connected to faster productivity growth, which was brought about, in large part, by the increased use of information technology hardware and software. Precisely what brought about this technology surge is beyond the scope of this work, yet it is safe to say that technological change is partly the result of economic trends and public policies (government research and development, education policy) and partly of the result of a host of factors—invention, or pure accident—that are beyond prediction. But if the technology trend continues, then productivity growth will remain strong, although probably not as strong as in recent years. The result will be continued real wage growth, at least on average.

The persistent low unemployment of recent years has generated much of the gains documented in this book, especially the improved quality of jobs and the stronger-than-average wage and income growth at the bottom. Although some external (to the economy and to policy makers) factors affect unemployment levels, the achievement of low unemployment—below the 6% rate many economists previously recommended—is primarily a policy outcome. At some point the recovery will end and a recession will ensue, and how fast and by what means we reestablish low unemployment will be a major public issue, particularly for low-income families. In the wake of welfare policy changes, low-income families now depend much more on wage income and less on government assistance than before. When unemployment rises in the next downturn, low-wage workers will certainly experience the greatest rise in unemployment, and their families will have a weaker safety net to fall to. Therefore, limiting the next downturn as well as ameliorating its effect need to be on the public agenda.

Another policy, the raising of the minimum wage, has helped promote growth at the bottom. Policy decisions on further increases will determine how low-wage workers, especially women, fare in the future.

Thus, how the future gains from productivity are shared is still an open question. Unbridled globalization, continued deunionization, an eroded minimum wage, and further privatization and deregulation will not only reinforce today's high level of inequality but expand upon it. Keeping unemployment low, providing income supports for the bottom (through the minimum wage, tax credits, housing subsidies, child care, and so on), facilitating collective bargaining by workers, providing national health insurance, and strengthening private pension coverage will lead to a sharing of productivity growth and a lessening of inequality. Whether the inequalities that have emerged are reversed in the near future will greatly affect the future living standards of working families.

Documentation and methodology

Documentation

The comprehensive portrait presented in this book of changes in incomes, taxes, wages, employment, wealth, poverty, and other indicators of economic performance and well-being relies almost exclusively on data in the tables and figures. Consequently, the documentation of our analysis is essentially the documentation of the tables and figures. For each, an abbreviated source notation appears at the bottom, and complete documentation is contained in the Table Notes and Figure Notes found at the back of the book. (In rare circumstances, however, we incorporate data in the discussion that are not in a table or figure.) This system of documentation allows us to omit distracting footnotes and long citations within the text and tables.

The abbreviated source notation at the bottom of each figure and table is intended to inform the reader of the general source of our data and to give due credit to the authors and agencies whose data we are presenting. We have three categories of designations for these abbreviated sources. In instances where we directly reproduce other people's work, we provide an "author-year" reference to the bibliography. Where we present our own computations based on other people's work, the source line reads "Authors' analysis of *author (year).*" In these instances we have made computations that do not appear in the original work and want to hold the original authors (or agencies) blameless for any errors or interpretations. Our third category is simply "Authors' analysis," which indicates that the data presented are from our original analysis of microdata (such as much of the wage analysis) or our computations from published (usually government) data. We use this source notation when presenting descriptive trends from government income, employment, or other data, since we have made judgments about the appropriate time periods or other matters for the analysis that the source agencies have not made.

Time periods

Economic indicators fluctuate considerably with short-term swings in the business cycle. For example, incomes tend to fall in recessions and rise during expansions. Therefore, economists usually compare business cycle peaks with other peaks and compare troughs with other troughs so as not to mix apples and oranges. In this book, we examine changes between business cycle peaks. The initial year for many tables is 1947, with intermediate years of 1967, 1973, 1979, and 1989, all of which were business cycle peaks (at least in terms of having low unemployment). We also present data for the latest full year for which data are available (usually 1998 or 1999) to show the changes over the current business cycle.

We also separately present trends for the 1995-98 or 1995-99 period in order to highlight the differences between those years and those of the early 1990s (or, more precisely, 1989-95) and earlier business cycles. This departs from the convention of presenting only business-cycle comparisons (e.g., comparing 1979-89 to 1989-99 trends) or comparisons of recoveries. We depart from the convention because there was a marked shift in a wide variety of trends after 1995, and it is important to understand and explain these trends.

Growth rates and rounding

Since business cycles differ in length, we usually present the annual growth rates in each period rather than the total growth. We also present compound annual growth rates rather than simple annual rates. Compound annual growth rates are just like compound interest on a bank loan: the rate is compounded continuously rather than yearly. In some circumstances, as noted in the tables, we have used log annual growth rates. This is done to permit decompositions.

While annual growth rates may seem small, over time they can amount to large changes. For example, the median incomes of families headed by persons age 24 and below fell 2.4% per year between 1979 and 1989; over the full period, however, incomes declined a considerable 21.7%.

In presenting the data we round the numbers, usually to one decimal place, but we use unrounded data to compute growth rates, percentage shares, and so on. Therefore, it is not always possible to exactly replicate our calculations by using the data in the table. In some circumstances, this leads to an appearance of errors in the tables. For instance, we frequently present shares of the population (or families) at different points in time and compute changes in these shares. Because our computations are based on the "unrounded" data, the change in shares presented in a table may not match the difference in the actual shares. Such rounding errors are always small, however, and never change the conclusions of the analysis.

Adjusting for inflation

In most popular discussions, the Consumer Price Index for All Urban Consumers (CPI-U), often called simply the consumer price index, is used to adjust dollar values for inflation. However, some analysts hold that the CPI-U overstated inflation in the late 1970s and early 1980s by measuring housing costs inappropriately. The methodology for the CPI-U from 1983 onward was revised to address these objections. Not all agree that it should have been revised. We chose not to use the CPI-U so as to avoid any impression that this report overstates the decline in wages and understates the growth in family incomes over the last few decades.

Instead of the CPI-U, we adjust dollar values for inflation using the CPI-U-X1 index, which uses the new methodology for housing inflation over the entire 1967-93 period. The CPI-U-X1, however, is based on small-sample, experimental indices for the 1970s, and there is some slight variation in methods over the entire period. Nevertheless, use of the CPI-U-X1 has become standard (e.g., it is generally used by the Census Bureau in its presentations of real income data). Because it is not available for years before 1967, we extrapolate the CPI-U-X1 back to earlier years based on inflation as measured by the CPI-U.

Some economists have argued that the CPI (both the CPI-U and the CPI-U-X1) overstates the growth of inflation. We are skeptical that this is the case, and we continue to use the CPI-U-X1. Many adjustments have been introduced to the CPI in the last few years in order to address various concerns.

In our analysis of poverty in Chapter 5, however, we generally use the CPI-U rather than the CPI-U-X1, since Chapter 5 draws heavily from Census Bureau publications that use the CPI-U. Moreover, the net effect of all of the criticisms of the measurement of poverty is that current methods *understate* poverty. Switching to the CPI-U-X1 without incorporating other revisions (i.e., revising the actual poverty standard) would lead to an even greater understatement and would be a very selective intervention to improve the poverty measurement. (A fuller discussion of these issues appears in Chapter 5.)

Household heads

We often categorize families by the age or the race/ethnic group of the "household head," that is, the person in whose name the home is owned or rented. If the home is owned jointly by a married couple, either spouse may be designated the household head. Every family has a single household head.

Hispanics

Unless specified otherwise, data from published sources employ the Census Bureau's designation of Hispanic persons. That is, Hispanics are included in racial counts (e.g., with blacks and whites) as well as in a separate category. For instance, in government analyses a white person of Hispanic origin is included both in counts of whites *and* in counts of Hispanics. In our original analyses, such as the racial/ethnic wage analysis in Chapter 2, we remove Hispanic persons from other racial (white or black) categories; using this technique, the person described above would appear only in counts of Hispanics.

Family income: slower growth, greater inequality, and much more work

We begin our analysis of the economic lives of America's working families by looking at the single most important determinant of living standards: family income. The story we tell is not a simple one—there are many angles through which to view the question of income growth, and this analysis is fairly exhaustive. When all is said and done, however, we find that the incomes of most families grew at a historically slow rate over the entire 1990s, as they did in the 1980s. Furthermore, the growth of inequality has meant that the benefits of growth were not evenly shared.

Yet the second half of the 1990s stands apart. Thanks to the positive conditions that prevailed over this period—most importantly persistent low unemployment, faster productivity growth, and relatively low inflation—income growth over this period was much stronger and more equally distributed than in any comparable period since the mid-1970s. Thus, in order to learn more about this important period, many of the tables below break from the usual "peak-to-peak" analysis employed in this book and separate the 1989-99 period into 1989-95 and 1995-99.

Nevertheless, aside from these last few years, much of what follows stresses the longer-term finding that, over the last two decades, family incomes have grown more slowly and more unequally. Of equal importance is the fact that American families are spending more time than ever before at work. In fact, due to the long-term stagnation of hourly wages (a topic addressed in Chapter 2), the only way for most working families to keep their incomes from falling has been to increase their time spent in the paid labor market.

We examine trends in the annual weeks and hours of work by race and education, and find this result to be pervasive—the "time crunch" that many working families report is strongly supported by the data, and it is experienced by the majority of working families, not just the elite lawyers, money managers, or "knowledge workers" of the new economy. In 1998, an average middle-income, married-couple family with children was working 97 weeks and 3,885 hours per year in the paid labor market, compared to 78 weeks and 3,272 hours in 1979 (these figures sum hours of work across the family). Hours spent at work have grown especially quickly for minority families, who, due to their lower earnings, must work that much more to gain a foothold into the middle class. For example, in 1998, the average middle-income, married-couple African American family with children worked 489 more hours per year than a comparable white family in the same income range. That is, the middle-income black family worked 12 more weeks than the average white family in order to reach the middle-income ranks.

Inequality has also persisted in the 1990s, though it grew more slowly than during the 1980s. Some analysts have mistakenly argued that the trend of rising inequality was stopped in the 1990s. As we point out in some detail, a more accurate assessment is that the trend has been slowed, not stopped. In addition, we emphasize a theme raised in the introduction: compared to the previous decade, the nature of inequality's growth shifted in the 1990s. Over the 1980s, gaps expanded throughout the income scale, as the top pulled away from the middle, while the middle pulled away from the bottom. In the 1990s, middle and low incomes grew at comparable rates, thus leading to some lessening in the gap between these sections of the income distribution. The top, however, continued to pull away from the rest of the pack.

We also explore two sets of counter-arguments that have been raised to discount the growth of inequality over the past two decades. The first set of arguments is essentially about measurement, suggesting that different measures of income yield different conclusions about the course of inequality. While we show that different measures—such as alternative ways of defining income, or measures that account for families' income mobility over time—lead to different levels of inequality at a point in time, each definition shows a rising inequality trend. The second set of arguments that we examine acknowledge the increase in inequality but dismiss it as being "non-economic," meaning that it stems from some other forces such as increased taxes or demographic shifts (e.g., the shift from married-couple to single-parent families). These arguments are also examined and found to be lacking.

The chapter begins by examining the history of inflation-adjusted income growth of the median, or typical, family. We explore this history of income trends by age cohort, showing that, while incomes have grown more slowly for most age groups, younger families have seen the biggest slowdown in growth rates. We also examine trends by family type and race/ethnicity. This latter analysis reveals that the black/white income gap narrowed somewhat in the 1990s, helping to close much of the gap from the 1980s. We then document the increase in inequality using various measures to be certain that the finding of high and increasing inequality is not sensitive to measurement choices.

The growth of inequality over the 1980s and 1990s has also been fueled by large increases in capital incomes, the returns to wealth such as interest and dividends, and realized capital gains. Since, as Chapter 4 documents, most wealth is held by upper-income groups, this growth of capital income generates greater inequality. In the 1990s, these gains stem in large part from the increase in the rate of profit, or the return to capital holdings. The after-tax corporate profit rate prevailing at the end of the 1990s was far higher than at the end of other economic recoveries since World War II. Had these returns to capital been at their historic average, compensation could have been 4.3% higher in 1999.

Unexceptional median income growth, but glimpse of change in late 1990s

Viewed as a whole, income growth in the 1990s has been unexceptional, much like that of the 1980s. But by separating the 1990s into two different time periods, countervailing trends emerge, and the latter part of the decade stands out as a period of strong growth for families throughout the income scale.

The official recovery from the relatively mild downturn began in the middle of 1991, but median family income did not begin to increase until 1994, later than in all previous postwar recoveries. Thus, even with the fast pace of growth over the last few years of the period, median family income grew only slightly faster over the 1990s than it did in the 1980s (0.6% per year vs. 0.4%).

Tables 1.1 and **1.2** show changes in family income, adjusted for inflation, in various cyclical peak (or low-unemployment) years since World War II. As explained in the section on documentation and methodology, examining income changes from business-cycle peak to business-cycle peak eliminates the distortion caused by the fact that incomes fall significantly in a recession and then recover in the subsequent upswing. However, in order to gain more insight into income trends over the recovery of the 1990s, the first few tables of the chapter separate out the first six years and last four years of the cycle so far. This approach shows that, while median family income fell through 1994, it then reversed course (see also **Figure 1A**). Since 1995, income growth has been rapid enough to more than recover the lost ground; by 1999, median family income in the 1990s had surpassed the growth rate of the 1980s by 0.2%. Furthermore,

TABLE 1.1 Median family income,* 1947-99 (1999 dollars)

Year	Median family income*
1947	$20,866
1967	36,409
1973	42,536
1979	44,097
1989	45,967
1995	44,395
1999	48,950
Total increases	
1947-67	$15,542
1967-73	6,127
1973-79	1,561
1979-89	1,870
1989-99	2,983
1989-95	-1,572
1995-99	4,555

* Income includes all wage and salary, self-employment, pension, interest, rent, government cash assistance, and other money income.

Source: Authors' analysis of U.S. Bureau of the Census data.

TABLE 1.2 Annual growth of median family income, 1947-99 (1999 dollars)

Period	Annual median family income growth		Adjusted for family size*
	Percent	Dollars	Percent
1947-67	2.8%	$777	n.a.
1967-73	2.6	1,021	2.8
1973-79	0.6	260	0.5
1979-89	0.4	187	0.5
1989-99	0.6	298	0.7
1989-95	-0.6	-262	-0.5
1995-99	2.5	1,139	2.5

* This is the annualized growth rate of family income of the middle fifth, divided by the poverty line for each family size.

Source: Authors' analysis of U.S. Bureau of the Census data.

FIGURE 1A Median family income, 1947-99

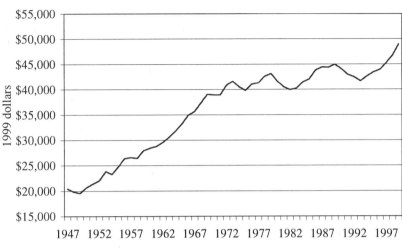

Source: U.S. Bureau of the Census.

since the positive trend of the 1995-99 period has certainly persisted through at least mid-2000, by the time of the next downturn, median income growth in the 1990s will further surpass that of the prior decade.

Family income increased substantially in the two decades immediately following World War II (1947-67). During that time, median family income increased by $15,542 in 1999 dollars, for an annual rate of growth of 2.8% (Table 1.2). Family incomes continued to grow into the early 1970s, but since 1973 have risen at less than one-quarter of that annual rate. In 1989, the median family's income was $1,870 greater than it was in 1979, translating into growth of just 0.4% per year from 1979 to 1989, or two-thirds of the sluggish 0.6% annual growth of the 1973-79 period and only one-seventh the rate of the postwar years prior to 1973 (see **Figure 1B**). In fact, the $1,870 income growth during the 10 years after 1979 equals the amount that incomes rose every 22 months in the 1967-73 period.

Even though the 1990-91 recession was significantly less severe than the downturn of the early 1980s, median family incomes fell about the same amount in both cases: 7.4% in 1979-82 and 7.3% in 1989-93 (note also that it took an extra year for median income to begin growing in the 1990s recovery). One reason for the more sluggish pace of income growth in the early 1990s recovery was that job losses in the 1990s recession were experienced more broadly than usual by occupation (see Chapter 3). Also, partly due to the restrictive growth policy of the Federal Reserve, unemployment was notably slower to fall in the

FIGURE 1B Annual growth of median family income, 1947-99

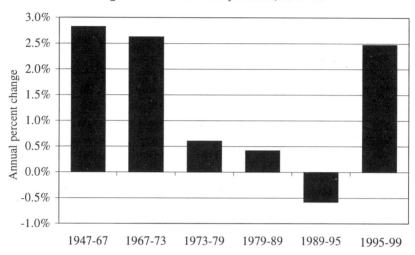

Source: U.S. Bureau of the Census.

1990s recovery, and this dampened wage (and thus income) growth throughout the first half of the decade.

But in the last few years of the 1990s, unemployment fell and the labor market moved toward full employment. Productivity rates also increased, helping to fuel income gains without inflationary pressures. Median family income grew quickly, at 2.5% per year, adding back more than the income lost over the early years of the recovery. Since the growth of median income slowed in the early 1970s, there have been other short growth spurts of this magnitude, but they have typically been the expected rebound from a recessionary trough, as in the early 1980s. The late 1990s median income gains have come uncharacteristically late in the cycle.

It is common practice also to examine measures of family income growth that adjust for changes in family size, since the same total family income shared by fewer family members can be interpreted as improved economic well-being for each family member. However, trends in incomes adjusted for family size can be misleading, since the recent decline in the average family's size is partially due to lower incomes; that is, some families feel they cannot afford as many children as they could have if incomes had continued to rise at early postwar rates. As a result, a family deciding to have fewer children or a person putting off starting a family because incomes are down will appear "better off"

38

FIGURE 1C Average number of persons per family, 1947-98

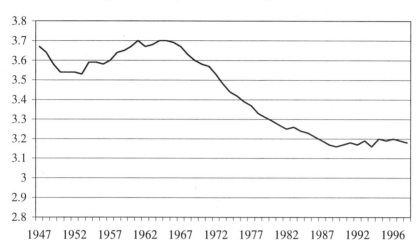

Source: U.S. Bureau of the Census.

in size-adjusted family-income measures. It also seems selective to adjust family incomes for changes in family size and not adjust for other demographic trends such as more hours of work and the resulting loss of leisure.

Nevertheless, even when income growth is adjusted for the shift toward smaller families (Table 1.2, column 3), the income growth of the 1980s and 1990s was about the same by both the adjusted and the unadjusted measures. In fact, the trends in size-adjusted income never differ more than 0.2 percentage points from the unadjusted measure in any period, suggesting that the shrinking size of families has only marginally offset the slow growth of median family income since 1973.

One possible reason for the similarity in the growth of size-adjusted family income and unadjusted income is the leveling off in family size. **Figure 1C** shows the average number of persons per family from 1947 to 1998. At the beginning of the figure, in 1947, families had, on average, about 3.7 members. In the mid-1960s this number began to drop, and by about 1986 had declined to 3.2. Since that time, the trend has been fairly flat, and therefore, we would not expect size adjustments to play a role in income trends. Below, we return to a more detailed investigation of the impact of other aspects of demographic change on family income growth and inequality.

An income 'generation gap'

The income data examined thus far take no account of age differences. As **Figure 1D** shows, up to a point, older families tend to have higher incomes than younger families, primarily because both earning capacity and wealth expand with age. As families retire and spend down their assets, income tends to decline. This section addresses two questions related to income and age. First, how have the median incomes of different age groups moved over time? An examination of this question allows us to compare, for example, how young families are doing today relative to those of earlier periods. Second, how has median family income grown within cohorts? In this examination, we compare the age and income profiles of families starting out in different time periods and track and compare their progress over time. Both of these analyses show that the slower income growth observable in the first set of tables is evident here as well. Recent cohorts have not done as well, in terms of median family income growth, as earlier cohorts.

Table 1.3 shows that income stagnation has been most severe among the youngest families. The average income of families headed by someone under age 25 declined at an annual rate of 2.4% from 1979 to 1989 and 1.8% from 1989 to 1995. Post-1995 growth reversed sharply, especially for younger workers (4.0% annually). But even with this boost, these young families in 1999 had $2,790 less income to spend in real dollars than their 1967 counterparts had when they were starting out. This pattern of income loss has meant that the income gap between the median income of these youngest families and that of older persons has grown since 1979.

The next two columns show that families headed by someone between the ages of 25 and 44 have also fared poorly relative to earlier years. The incomes of families headed by someone 25-34 fell during the 1980s and through the mid-1990s and grew 0.4% from 1989 to 1999. Thus, the median income of these young families was about the same in 1999 as it was two decades earlier in 1979. Many families in this age group are likely to be bringing up young children and trying to buy a home of their own. This latter expenditure has become more costly over time, and these families now have no more resources with which to seek affordable housing.

Families headed by someone age 35-44 experienced a sharp deceleration in their income growth in the 1970s, as their annual growth rate fell from 3.0% in the 1967-73 period to 0.4% and 0.5% during the 1970s and 1980s business cycles. Furthermore, their median income growth continued to decelerate through the mid-1990s, falling 1.0% annually through 1995. Median income for these families rose by 1.9% after 1995, and by 1999 their income was $920 above its 1989 level. The income of the 45-54 age group grew modestly—0.8% per year—

FIGURE 1D Median family income by age of householder, 1999

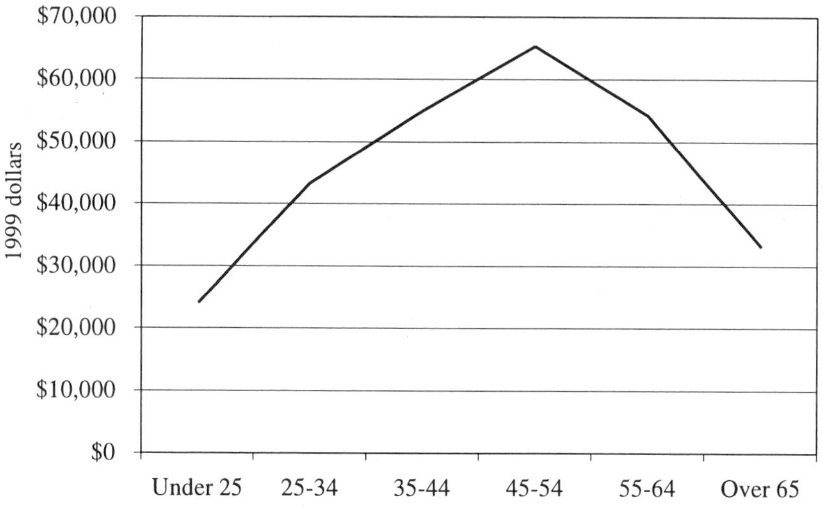

Source: U.S. Bureau of the Census.

TABLE 1.3 Median family income by age of householder, 1947-99 (1999 dollars)

Year	Under 25	25-34	35-44	45-54	55-64	Over 65	45-54 compared to 25-34 relative incomes
1947	$16,144	$20,178	$22,670	$23,682	$22,044	$12,584	1.17
1967	26,821	37,152	42,403	44,408	36,909	18,028	1.20
1973	28,287	43,083	50,499	53,732	45,113	22,682	1.25
1979	29,292	43,469	51,587	56,959	49,338	25,490	1.31
1989	22,926	41,479	54,013	61,939	50,575	31,013	1.49
1995	20,504	39,376	50,862	60,156	49,482	30,938	1.53
1999	24,031	43,309	54,933	65,303	54,249	33,148	1.51
Annual growth rate							
1947-67	2.6%	3.1%	3.2%	3.2%	2.6%	1.8%	0.1%
1967-73	0.9	2.5	3.0	3.2	3.4	3.9	0.7
1973-79	0.6	0.1	0.4	1.0	1.5	2.0	0.8
1979-89	-2.4	-0.5	0.5	0.8	0.2	2.0	1.3
1989-99	0.5	0.4	0.2	0.5	0.7	0.7	-0.3
1989-95	-1.8	-0.9	-1.0	-0.5	-0.4	0.0	0.4
1995-99	4.0	2.4	1.9	2.1	2.3	1.7	-0.3

Source: Authors' analysis of U.S. Bureau of the Census data (1999).

41

between 1979 and 1989, compared to growth of 3.2% per year between 1947 and 1973. Incomes of families headed by someone over 65 also decelerated post-1973, but less so than most other age groups, presumably because they are less dependent on wage income than the other groups.

The last column of Table 1.3 compares the median income of families headed by someone age 45-54 years old to that of families headed by someone 20 years younger. The median income of the older family type was 20% greater than that of the younger family in 1967, but due to their faster income growth over the 1970s and 1980s, their advantage grew to 53% in 1995 (i.e., their 1995 median income was 1.53 times that of the younger family). Note, however, that the pattern of growth in 1995-99 reversed this trend, as the median incomes of 25-34-year-olds grew 0.3% faster than that of 45-54-year-olds. While these few years have ameliorated the economic "generation gap" that has grown since 1967, younger families continue to start out much lower on the income scale relative to older families.

Some income analysts have discounted the importance of the general trend toward slower income growth by noting that families receive higher real incomes as they age, as shown in Figure 1D. But this truism does not solve the problem of the slower growth of income and wages that have persisted since the mid-1970s. The slower growth of median income means that the living standards of today's working families are improving less quickly as they age compared to the experience of families in earlier periods. In the next table, we examine how this dynamic has changed over time by tracking and comparing the progress of various cohorts. We find clear evidence that the economic progress of recent cohorts has lagged behind that of their predecessors.

Table 1.4 tracks various cohorts over time and compares two dimensions of real income growth. First, we can compare how quickly one cohort's income grows relative to a different cohort. The top panel of the table does this by following five different cohorts over time, beginning in 1948. Each column contains the median family income of families headed by persons in three different age groups: 25-34, 35-44, 45-54, which we reference as young, middle, and older, respectively. Note that these data do not track the same families over time (i.e., they are not longitudinal; however, cohort analysis offers a useful proxy to the longitudinal approach).

Cohort 1 starts out in 1948. The real median income of families in this cohort grew by about half as they aged through each period. As they went from young to middle, their income grew by 50.9%; as they grew from middle to older, it grew by 52.3%. Cohort 2 started out in 1958, and their income grew faster than that of Cohort 1 as they started out, 60.6% versus 50.9% (note also that they started from a higher level; this is discussed below). But as Cohort 2

TABLE 1.4 Family median income growth by 10-year cohorts, starting in 1948 (1998 dollars)

Age of family head	Cohorts (median family income in 1998 dollars)					
	Cohort 1: Starts in '48	Cohort 2: Starts in '58	Cohort 3: Starts in '68	Cohort 4: Starts in '78	Cohort 5: Starts in '88	Cohort 6: Starts in '98
25-34 (Young)	$19,622	$27,030	$37,706	$41,955	$40,689	$41,074
35-44 (Middle)	29,610	43,409	49,453	53,516	51,883	n.a.
45-54 (Older)	45,108	54,611	58,134	61,833	n.a.	n.a.
Percent growth:						
Young to middle	50.9%	60.6%	31.2%	27.6%	27.5%	n.a.
Middle to older	52.3	25.8	17.6	15.5%	n.a.	n.a.
Young to older	129.9	102.0	54.2	47.4%	n.a.	n.a.

Addendum:

Growth between cohorts	1948-58 (Cohort 1 compared to Cohort 2)	1958-68 (Cohort 2 compared to Cohort 3)	1968-78 (Cohort 3 compared to Cohort 4)	1978-88 (Cohort 4 compared to Cohort 5)	1988-98 (Cohort 5 compared to Cohort 6)
25-34 (Young)	37.8%	39.5%	11.3%	-3.0%	0.9%
35-44 (Middle)	46.6	13.9	8.2	-3.1	n.a.
45-54 (Older)	21.1	6.5	6.4	n.a.	n.a.

Source: Authors' analysis of U.S. Bureau of the Census data.

passed from middle to older age, its rate of growth decelerated, to 25.8%, as compared to 52.3% for the earlier cohort.

Cohorts 3, 4, and 5 saw considerably slower growth as they aged, relative to earlier cohorts (since Cohort 6 starts out in 1998, we have only one observation for this group). Families starting out in 1978 (Cohort 4) saw their median family income grow by 27.6% as they moved into middle age, and 15.5% as they entered older age. Over the full 30 years, the median income of their cohort grew by 47.4%, about one-third as fast as that of Cohort 1. Since Cohort 5 starts out in 1988, we can observe their income only as they move from young to middle age, and their rate of growth is identical to that of Cohort 4.

Thus, each cohort's real income growth has been successively slower than that of the previous cohort. The bottom panel, however, makes the point that, at least through the late 1970s, the income starting line was higher for each successive cohort. In the 1948-78 period, the broadly shared benefits of the growing economy ensured that each cohort started out ahead of the last. For example, Cohort 2 began its trajectory in 1958 at a level 37.8% above Cohort 1's, and Cohort 3's journey began in 1968 at a level 39.5% above Cohort 2's. But as Cohort 4 began in 1978, its income was only 11.3% above that of Cohort 3, and the next cohort, Cohort 5, was the first to start out with lower income in real terms. Nor did Cohort 5 catch up; its income in middle age was still 3.1% below that of the previous cohort. Note that the most recent cohort, Cohort 6, which started out in 1998, began at about the same level as Cohort 5.

This table clearly shows that, as families age, their incomes tend to rise—a fact that was never in question. It also shows that, at least through the late 1970s, each cohort started out ahead of the last. But the table also reveals that the rate of income growth of later cohorts is considerably slower compared to that of earlier ones.

Among racial/ethnic groups, African Americans make relative gains

Table 1.5 examines some interesting differences in growth rates by race and ethnicity. One notable trend that has emerged over the 1989-99 period is the relative gains made by African American families, who experienced faster income growth than other racial groups. Although black incomes remain well below those of whites, this pattern significantly raised the ratio of black/white incomes. The median Hispanic family, however, experienced no income growth over the 1980s and, despite very strong gains in the latter half of the 1990s, its 1999 median was about the same as it was 1989.

TABLE 1.5 Median family income by race/ethnic group, 1947-99 (1999 dollars)

Year	White	Black*	Hispanic**	Ratio to white family income of:	
				Black	Hispanic
1947	$21,734	$11,111	n.a.	51.1%	n.a.
1967	37,790	22,374	n.a.	59.2	n.a.
1973	45,311	24,837	$30,761	54.8	67.9%
1979	46,015	26,057	31,899	56.6	69.3
1989	48,334	27,152	31,501	56.2	65.2
1995	46,620	28,390	26,859	60.9	57.6
1999	51,244	31,778	31,633	62.0	61.8
Annual growth rate					
1947-67	2.8%	3.6%	n.a.		
1967-73	3.1	1.8	n.a.		
1973-79	0.3	0.8	0.6%		
1979-89	0.5	0.4	-0.1		
1989-99	0.6	1.6	0.1		
1989-95	-0.6	0.7	-2.6		
1995-99	2.4	2.9	4.2		

*   Prior to 1967, data for blacks include all non-whites.
** Persons of Hispanic origin may be of any race.

Source: Authors' analysis of U.S. Bureau of the Census data (2000).

The median income growth of both blacks and Hispanics slowed after 1973. Hispanic income growth was flat during both the 1980s and the 1990s. The final two rows of the table show, however, that these losses were concentrated in the 1989-95 period, when Hispanic median income fell sharply—2.6% per year. In the 1995-99 period, Hispanic income rebounded quickly, growing at 4.2% a year. The benefits of full employment are much in evidence for these families.

Figure 1E plots the ratio of black-to-white and Hispanic-to-white family income. (Hispanic data become available in 1972. Note also that the data for white families includes Hispanics who identify their race as white. Data on non-Hispanic whites are available from 1972 forward; using this series for whites does not change the trends shown in the figure.) Throughout the 1960s, the median income of black families increased relative to that of whites, with the ratio peaking in the mid-1970s. Over the 1980s black families lost ground rela-

FIGURE 1E Ratio to white median family income by race/ethnic background, 1947-99

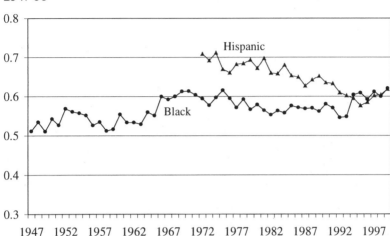

Source: U.S. Bureau of the Census.

tive to whites, but this trend was reversed in the 1990s so that, by 1999, blacks had returned to the relative income levels of the 1960s. (The figure reveals that this gain occurred in one year: 1994. There are no obvious data reasons, such as a coding or weighting change, that would explain this one-year jump. It is, however, unusual for a trend to change this dramatically in one year, and there may be a non-economic explanation. However, blacks made relative gains in other areas over these years, including poverty and hours worked, so, while the change probably occurs more gradually than reflected in the figure, it likely has occurred.)

Though Hispanics also gained relative to whites in the late 1990s, their relative income has trended downward since the Census Bureau began tracking its progress. By 1999, their median income, relative to whites, was the same as that of African American families.

For family types, strong growth in 1990s among dual-earner couples

Along with age and race, it is also revealing to examine trends in family income growth by family type. In fact, some analysts argue that changes in family composition, especially the shift from married-couple families to those headed by a

TABLE 1.6 Median family income by family type, 1947-98 (1999 dollars)

Year	Married couples Total	Wife in paid labor force	Wife not in paid labor force	Single Male-headed	Female-headed	All families
1947	$21,403	n.a.	n.a.	$20,212	$14,953	$20,866
1967	38,740	$45,693	$34,931	31,273	19,707	36,409
1973	45,984	53,781	40,302	37,916	20,461	42,536
1979	48,244	55,971	39,862	37,841	22,243	44,097
1989	51,790	60,817	38,623	37,414	22,091	45,967
1995	51,447	61,024	35,392	33,187	21,526	44,395
1999	56,676	66,529	38,626	37,396	23,732	48,950
Annual growth rate						
1947-67	3.0%	n.a.	n.a.	2.2%	1.4%	2.8%
1967-73	2.9	2.8%	2.4%	3.3	0.6	2.6
1973-79	0.8	0.7	-0.2	0.0	1.4	0.6
1979-89	0.7	0.8	-0.3	-0.1	-0.1	0.4
1989-99	0.9	0.9	0.0	0.0	0.7	0.6
1989-95	-0.1	0.1	-1.4	-2.0	-0.4	-0.6
1995-99	2.4	2.2	2.2	3.0	2.5	2.5
Share of families						
1951*	87.0%	19.9%	67.1%	3.0%	10.0%	100.0%
1967	86.9	31.8	55.1	2.4	10.7	100.0
1973	85.0	35.4	49.7	2.6	12.4	100.0
1979	82.5	40.6	41.9	2.9	14.6	100.0
1989	79.2	45.7	33.5	4.4	16.5	100.0
1999	76.8	47.6	29.2	5.6	17.6	100.0

* Earliest year available.

Source: Authors' analysis of U.S. Bureau of the Census data (2000).

single person, is the primary explanation for many of the trends we discuss in this chapter. In a later section, we show that, while such shifts have had an important impact, the evidence does not support any dominant role for demographics in shaping income trends. We begin this analysis in **Table 1.6**, which focuses both on changes in median family incomes by family type and changes in the shares of different family types in the population.

Since 1973, the fastest median income growth has consistently been among married couples with both spouses in the paid labor force. Incomes among married couples where the wife was not employed declined 0.3% annually over the

1980s and 0.2% over the 1990s (with the declines again concentrated in the 1989-95 period). Single-mother families experienced relatively fast income growth (compared to other family types) during the 1970s (note, however, that the median income levels of this family type are less than half those of married couples). But their income growth decelerated sharply in the 1980s and has recovered only somewhat in the 1990s.

Thus, only families with two adult earners made noteworthy gains in their median income since 1979, suggesting the importance of working wives in explaining these trends. In 1979, the share of married couples without a wife in the labor force was about equal to the share of couples with a wife in the labor force (41.9% versus 40.6%). By 1999, married couples with two earners (assuming the husband worked) made up 47.6% of all families, while one-earner married couples were 29.2% of the total.

While this shift toward two-earner families has been a major factor in recent income growth, the shift appears to be attenuating, since the rate at which wives (and women in general) have been joining the labor force and increasing their hours of work has slowed in recent years. For example, among married-couple families, wives joined the paid labor force at an annual rate of 1.3% in the 1970s, 0.8% in the 1980s, and 0.4% in the 1989-99 period. It is difficult to know the causes of this deceleration. It could be that, at 62% (47.6%/76.8%), the country is approaching the "ceiling" of the share of wives that will work. Second, wives' willingness to work has generally been found to be more sensitive to both their own and their spouses' earnings than it is among most other groups of workers, meaning that they are more likely than other groups of workers to cut back their hours when their earnings or their spouses' earnings rise. However, while this effect has consistently been found to prevail, its estimated magnitude is small, and it can thus only explain a small part of the trend in women's labor force participation.

Married-couple families, although still predominant—representing 76.8% of all families in 1999—make up a smaller share of families than they did in the 1950s and 1960s. There has been a continuing rise in the importance of female-headed families; in 1998 they represented 17.6% of the total. Although this phenomenon has been the focus of increased attention in recent years, the share of female-headed families grew more quickly in the 1967-79 period than in the period since 1979. Note also that the median income of these female-headed families grew over the 1967-79 period, when their share of the population of families was increasing. This pattern suggests that income trends *within* demographic groups were a more important source of income loss than the often-cited shift to female-headed families, an argument we return to shortly. (Chapter 5 examines this issue in the context of poverty.)

Growing inequality of family income

Along with the slower growth rates discussed thus far, the other important trend in the analysis of American family incomes has been increased income inequality. Even while this trend has attenuated lately, there is no question that the last few decades have witnessed a historically large shift of economic resources from those at the bottom and middle of the income (or wage or wealth) scale to those at the top. The result has been an increase in inequality such that the gap between the incomes of the well-off and those of everyone else is larger now than at any point in the postwar period. This section examines the income trends of families at different income levels and growth of income inequality in the 1980s and 1990s. It also critiques a number of arguments that attempt to deny the increase in income inequality.

An arcane but significant methodological issue has an important impact in this analysis. In 1993, the Census Bureau raised the "top-codes," i.e., the highest income levels it records. This led to a marked jump in income inequality that year, much of which is merely a result of the coding change (since those with the highest incomes were suddenly reporting more of it, inequality measures registered a large jump). In the previous edition of this book, we provide extensive analysis of this issue using a specially constructed data set. That analysis suggested that the coding change accounted for about one-third of the increase in income inequality between 1989 and 1996, meaning most of the growth was "real" (i.e., not an artifact of the coding change). Below we present some further evidence of the upward trend in inequality controlling for the top-code change. We also note that any such change becomes less important the further back it is in time. That is, the Census Bureau has lifted its top-codes numerous times in the history of its income surveys (annual earnings in the 1940 Census were top-coded at $5,000). In general, it is only the years right around the top code increase that are significantly biased by the change.

Figure 1F shows the values and the underlying trend in the family "Gini ratio," a standard measure of inequality, bounded by zero and one, wherein higher numbers reveal greater inequality. The coding-induced change in 1993 is clear in the latter part of the figure. The smooth trend line (see figure note for details), however, statistically controls for this shift and plots the underlying trend in family income inequality. Clearly, this trend has been positive since the mid-1970s. It appears to have picked up speed over the 1980s, and, importantly, decelerated in the 1990s. But there is no evidence that the trend in family income inequality was either flat or falling in the 1990s.

Table 1.7 presents information on the share of all family income received by families at different points in the income distribution. Families have been

FIGURE 1F Family income inequality, Gini coefficient, 1947-99

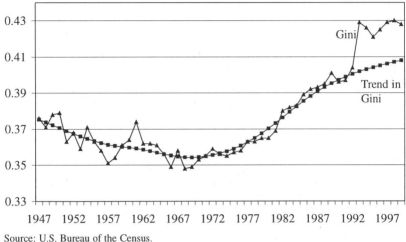

Source: U.S. Bureau of the Census.

TABLE 1.7 Shares of family income going to various income groups and to top 5%, 1947-99

Year	Lowest fifth	Second fifth	Middle fifth	Fourth fifth	Top fifth	Breakdown of top fifth First 15%	Top 5%	Gini ratios
1947	5.0%	11.9%	17.0%	23.1%	43.0%	25.5%	17.5%	0.376
1967	5.4	12.2	17.5	23.5	41.4	25.0	16.4	0.358
1973	5.5	11.9	17.5	24.0	41.1	25.6	15.5	0.356
1979	5.4	11.6	17.5	24.1	41.4	26.1	15.3	0.365
1989	4.6	10.6	16.5	23.7	44.6	26.7	17.9	0.401
1999*	4.3	9.9	15.6	23.0	47.2	26.9	20.3	0.428
Point change								
1947-67	0.4	0.3	0.5	0.4	-1.6	-0.5	-1.1	-0.018
1967-73	0.1	-0.3	0.0	0.5	-0.3	0.6	-0.9	-0.002
1973-79	-0.1	-0.3	0.0	0.1	0.3	0.5	-0.2	0.009
1979-89	-0.8	-1.0	-1.0	-0.4	3.2	0.6	2.6	0.036
1989-99*	-0.3	-0.7	-0.9	-0.7	2.6	0.2	2.4	0.027

* These shares reflect a change in survey methodology leading to greater inequality.

Source: Authors' analysis of unpublished U.S. Bureau of the Census data.

divided into fifths, or "quintiles," of the population, and the highest income group has been further divided into the top 5% and the next 15%. The 20% of families with the lowest incomes are considered the "lowest fifth," the next best-off 20% of families are the "second fifth," and so forth.

The upper 20% of families received 47.2% of all income in 1999. The top 5% received more of total income, 20.3%, than the families in the bottom 40%, who received just 14.2%. In fact, the 1999 share of total income in the three lowest-income fifths—the 29.8% of total income going to the bottom 60% of families—was smaller than the 34.5% share this group received in 1979. As we will see in a later chapter providing international comparisons (Chapter 7), income in the United States is distributed far more unequally than in other industrialized countries.

The 1980s were a period of sharply increasing income inequality, reversing the trend toward less inequality over the postwar period into the 1970s. Between 1979 and 1989, the bottom 80% lost income share and the top 20% gained. Moreover, the 1989 income share of the upper fifth, 44.6%, was far greater than the share it received during the entire postwar period and even higher than the 43% received in 1947. Even among the rich, the growth in income was skewed to the top: between 1979 and 1989, the highest 5% saw their income share rise 2.6 percentage points (from 15.3% to 17.9%), accounting for the bulk of the 3.2 percentage-point total rise in the income share of the upper fifth.

The increase in inequality persisted over the 1989-99 period. (Due to the 1993 top-coding change noted above, we do not show 1995 separately, since we cannot accurately judge the extent of the bias this close to the 1993 coding change. We are, however, confident that by 1999 the effect of the coding change had faded such that comparisons are reliable, although, as noted below, there is still an upward bias.) The income share received by the top 5% grew from 17.9% in 1989 to 20.3% in 1999; about a third of this increase is due to the coding change. Comparing the bottom two rows of the table reveals that the rate of share loss among the bottom 60% was slower than in the 1980s. Aside from the small gain in share by the families in the 81-95 percentile range (0.2), the top 5% continued to gain at the expense of the bottom 95% in the 1990s.

The increase in the income gap between upper- and lower-income groups is illustrated in **Figure 1G**, which shows the ratio of the average incomes of families in the bottom 20% to those of the top 5% from 1947 to 1999. The gap between the top and the bottom incomes fell from 1947 to 1979 but grew to a historic high of 19.1 by 1999, reversing three decades of lessening inequality.

Another way of viewing this recent surge in income inequality is to compare the "income cutoff" of families by income group, as in **Table 1.8**. These values represent the income at the top percentile of each fifth. By focusing on

FIGURE 1G Ratio of family income of top 5% to lowest 20%, 1947-99

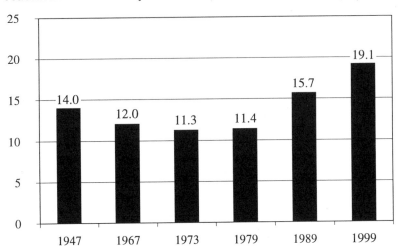

Note: The 1999 ratio reflects a change in survey methodology leading to increased inequality.

Source: Author's analysis of U.S. Bureau of the Census data.

this measure, we are able to discuss income gains and losses for complete group-ings of families (e.g., the bottom 40%). Also, since the cases affected by the top-coding change are typically above the 95th percentile, the 1999 values in this table are not upwardly biased relative to earlier years.

Over the early postwar period, from 1947 to 1973, there was strong and even income growth across the income spectrum. From 1947 to 1967, for in-stance, the growth in the top value in each fifth ranged from the 2.5% annual pace obtained by the top 5% to the 2.9% annual pace obtained by those in the second fifth. Because incomes grew slightly faster for lower- and middle-in-come families than upper-income families (the top 5%) from 1947 to 1967, there was a general decline in income inequality over this period.

The pattern of income growth since 1973 has been far more uneven and far slower than in the earlier period. From 1973 to 1979 the fastest income growth was the 1.3% annual growth at the 95th percentile, which, though modest in historical terms, was twice the 0.6% and 0.5% annual income growth among the first and second fifths. Incomes across the spectrum continued to grow slowly in the 1979-89 period, but the pattern of growth was even more unequal. The fami-lies with the lowest incomes actually lost ground from 1979 to 1989 (incomes fell 0.3% annually), while the top 5% accelerated to a 1.5% annual rate.

TABLE 1.8 Real family income by income group, 1947-99, upper limit of each group (1999 dollars)

Year	Lowest fifth	Second fifth	Middle fifth	Fourth fifth	95th Percentile	Average
1947	$10,905	$17,596	$23,861	$33,857	$55,570	$24,412
1967	18,858	30,956	41,512	56,910	91,442	40,392
1973	21,464	35,417	49,415	67,957	105,943	48,081
1979	22,201	36,506	51,718	71,215	114,247	50,241
1989	21,501	37,619	54,817	80,008	132,962	55,765
1995	20,847	36,058	53,549	78,993	135,178	56,138
1999	22,826	39,600	59,400	88,082	155,040	62,636
Annual growth rate						
1947-67	2.8%	2.9%	2.8%	2.6%	2.5%	2.5%
1967-73	2.2	2.3	2.9	3.0	2.5	2.9
1973-79	0.6	0.5	0.8	0.8	1.3	0.7
1979-89	-0.3	0.3	0.6	1.2	1.5	1.0
1989-99	0.6	0.5	0.8	1.0	1.5	1.2
1989-95	-0.5	-0.7	-0.4	-0.2	0.3	0.1
1995-99	2.3	2.4	2.6	2.8	3.5	2.8

Source: Authors' analysis of U.S. Bureau of the Census data.

In the most recent period, 1989-99, average annual growth picked up slightly, to 1.2%, but some important changes occurred in the distribution. Over the full period, income inequality continued to grow, but income growth at the top of the scale, from the 80th percentile up, decelerated relative to the bottom 80%, and inequality grew more slowly. Note also that the nature of inequality growth shifted in the 1990s relative to the previous decade. Over the 1980s, inequality expanded throughout the distribution as the top pulled away from the middle and the middle pulled away from the bottom. In the 1990s, however, the middle and the bottom grew at comparable rates, while the top continued to diverge from the rest of the distribution. For example, the difference in the growth between the middle-income cutoff and the lowest fifth cutoff was only 0.2% in the 1990s (it was 0.9% in the 1980s), while the gap between the 95th percentile and the middle cutoff was 0.7% (compared to 0.9% in the 1980s).

Once again, two distinct trends can be traced over the 1990s. Through 1995, the bottom 80% of families experienced income losses, and these losses were larger for lower income families. For example, income for the 20th percentile fell by 0.5% annually, while income for the 95th percentile grew 0.3%. Thus, the top income cutoff grew 0.8% faster than the bottom. Between 1995 and 1999 income trends reversed at each income cutoff, though here again the top grew more quickly than the others. In fact, the difference between the 95th percentile's growth rate and the 20th percentile's was 1.2% annually, meaning that, by this measure, income inequality accelerated over the latter part of the 1990s. However, this difference is quite sensitive to the choice of starting year within the 1990s recovery. For example, between 1994 and 1999, income grew 2.5% at the 20th percentile and 2.8% at the 95th, suggesting only a slight increase in inequality by this measure over that time span. We conclude that inequality clearly decelerated in the 1990s, but neither ceased rising nor declined. The pattern of growth did shift, however, as the deceleration was generated primarily by the convergence of middle- and low-income growth rates. The wealthiest families continued to pull away from the rest.

Figure 1H presents a revealing picture of incomes growing together in the first 30 years of the postwar period and then growing apart. The bars in each panel represent the growth rate of average income by income fifth over the periods 1947-79 and 1979-98. The top panel, covering the years 1947-79, shows strong and even growth, with average incomes nearly doubling for each income fifth. Note also that, during this period, growth was slightly faster at the bottom of the income scale than at the top; that is, growth was equalizing. The bottom panel shows a very different pattern. Since 1979, the annual growth of family income has been slightly negative for the bottom fifth; it fell 1.4% through 1999. Income growth was positive for the top four fifths, though significantly more so for the wealthiest families. Between 1947 and 1979 income grew 26% more slowly in the top relative to the bottom fifth; since 1979, income has grown 44% more *quickly* in the top fifth than in the bottom fifth. Thus, the 1947-79 pattern of equalizing growth has sharply reversed since 1979.

Counter-arguments to the evidence on income trends

A number of questions have been raised regarding the evidence presented thus far about the high levels and increasing trend of inequality. We've already noted the lifting of the Census top-codes and shown that controlling for this change does not alter the finding that inequality continued to grow in the 1990s. In this section we evaluate the validity of two sets of counter-arguments.

The first arguments we analyze are essentially about how one defines income: should it be pre-tax or post-tax? Should it include various income components such as capital gains or the cash value of food stamps? Also, some econo-

FIGURE 1H Family income growth by quintile, 1947-99

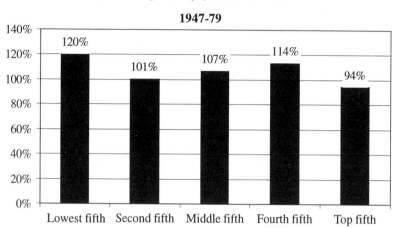

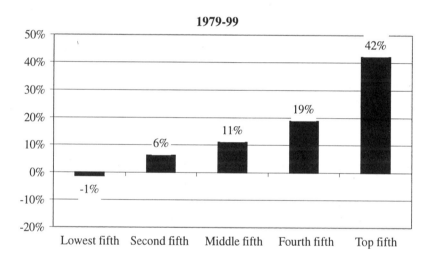

Source: Authors' analysis of U.S. Bureau of the Census data (various years).

mists argue that consumption, a proxy measure for "permanent" income, is a better measure of family well-being than annual income. This raises the question of whether the inequality of consumption has increased along with that of income.

The second set of arguments accepts the increase in inequality that we have demonstrated, but discounts its importance (at least in an economic sense) in two ways. First, critics invoke a demographic explanation, suggesting that non-economic factors (such as the shift to single-parent families over time, for example) are the main reasons for inequality's rise. This is an important distinction, because an incorrect diagnosis of the problem will lead to inappropriate policy responses. Second, critics grant that inequality has increased using the measures we have presented, but argue that, since many families are able to move up the income ladder as they age and gain experience, inequality is not a real problem.

We examine each of these arguments in some detail and find:

- The increase in inequality occurred both pre- and post-tax; thus, tax policies do not explain away the problem;

- Different measures of income lead to different levels of inequality at a given point in time, but, regardless of how income is defined, the *trend* over the 1980s and 1990s is toward more inequality;

- Consumption inequality has grown along with income inequality over the 1980s; its trend flattened, however, though the mid-1990s.

- Controlling for the changing demographics of American families does not reverse the trend in income inequality. In fact, over the period when demographic shifts would have been expected to increase inequality (the 1970s), it grew much more slowly than over the latter periods, when family structure played a smaller role. Thus, most of the growth in inequality has occurred within each family type;

- Income mobility can offset income inequality only if the rate of mobility has increased; there is no evidence of such an increase over the period when income inequality was growing most quickly.

We begin this section by focusing on the role of taxes in the debate over income growth and distribution. The next sub-section examines alternative income definitions.

Are taxes the reason for rising inequality and disappointing growth in family incomes?

Some participants in the national debate over family income inequality blame the stagnant family incomes and widening inequality documented above on rising taxes. All the preceding data on family incomes, however, have referred to *before-tax* incomes. Since the analysis has relied on income data before taxes have been taken out, changes in the tax code cannot be responsible for the observed trends. Slow family income growth and the rise in income inequality, therefore, have nothing to do with changes in the tax system.

Nevertheless, the tax code can act to reduce or to reinforce the income patterns documented above. In this section, we will briefly review the most important changes since the end of the 1970s in federal, state, and local tax rates. In general terms, taxes became more regressive over the 1980s—higher-income families saw their tax payments fall relative to lower-income families—and more progressive during the 1990s—higher-income families saw their tax payments rise relative to lower-income families. Changes in tax policy over the 1980s, then, reinforced the overall trend toward inequality. Changes in tax policy during the 1990s, on the other hand, helped to reduce the growth in inequality.

Table 1.9 summarizes the basic changes in federal tax rates over the last two decades. The first section of the table reports estimates of pre-tax household income from the Congressional Budget Office (CBO). These estimates differ from earlier figures drawn from the Current Population Survey (CPS) in several ways. The data here are for households, which include single people, rather than for families, which are defined as two or more related people living together. Households include single people as well as families. The inclusion of single people lowers household income relative to families, which often include more than one earner. Unlike the CPS data for 1999, which are taken from actual survey results, the CBO data for 1999 are projections of family income based on earlier data from the CPS, the Consumer Expenditure Survey, and the Internal Revenue Service's Statistics of Income. The CBO used data from all three sources together with their best forecasts for economic growth at the end of the 1990s to produce the estimates for 1999 in Table 1.9. The CBO data also incorporate information on a wider range of income sources than is available in the CPS, including income from realized capital gains. A final important feature of the CBO data is that they allow us to conduct an analysis of before- and after-tax income for the top 1% of households, a group whose income growth and tax patterns differ substantially from the rest of the population and even from the rest of the top fifth of households.

Historically, the CBO's estimates have been fairly close to actual outcomes. In any event, the main concern here is about how changes to the tax code, not changes in before-tax income, have affected the distribution of income. The CBO estimates for 1999 reflect federal tax law through 1998, including the last major changes to the federal tax code incorporated in the Taxpayer Relief Act of 1997.

With these caveats in mind, the pre-tax household income figures in the first section show the same basic trends seen for family incomes in the CPS data discussed earlier. Before-tax income inequality grew sharply in the 1980s and continued to grow, albeit at a slower pace, in the 1990s. As the bottom portion of

TABLE 1.9 Pre- and post-tax income and effective tax rates, by income level,* 1977-99

	1977	1989	1999(p)	1977-89	1989-99	1977-99
Pre-tax household income (1999 dollars)						
Bottom four-fifths				*Percent change in income*		
Lowest fifth	$10,494	$9,839	$9,183	-6.3%	-6.7%	-12.5%
Second fifth	25,362	23,394	23,175	-7.8	-0.9	-8.6
Middle fifth	39,573	38,261	38,698	-3.3	1.1	-2.2
Fourth fifth	55,096	55,643	57,938	1.0	4.1	5.2
Highest fifth	$107,459	$128,995	$144,299	20.0%	11.9%	34.3%
Top 10%	142,113	181,467	205,517	27.7	13.3	44.6
Top 5%	195,678	257,990	301,717	31.8	16.9	54.2
Top 1%	425,245	694,167	785,993	63.2	13.2	84.8
Income ratio				*Percent change in ratio*		
Top/bottom	10.2	13.1	15.7	28.0%	19.9%	53.5%
Top/middle	2.0	2.3	2.5	18.9	7.4	27.7
Upper 5%/bottom	18.6	26.2	32.9	40.6	25.3	76.2
Effective federal tax rates (%)						
Bottom four-fifths				*Percentage-point change in rates*		
Lowest fifth	8.4%	8.8%	4.6%	0.4	-4.2	-3.8
Second fifth	14.9	15.3	13.7	0.4	-1.6	-1.2
Middle fifth	19.2	18.9	18.9	-0.3	0.0	-0.3
Fourth fifth	22.1	21.5	22.2	-0.6	0.7	0.1
Highest fifth	28.5%	25.9%	29.1%	-2.6	3.2	0.6
Top 10%	30.5	26.8	30.6	-3.7	3.8	0.1
Top 5%	32.6	27.4	31.8	-5.2	4.4	-0.8
Top 1%	37.3	28.1	34.4	-9.2	6.3	-2.9
Tax ratio				*Percent change in ratio*		
Top/bottom	3.4	2.9	6.3	-13.3%	115.2%	86.6%
Top/middle	1.3	1.2	1.3	-6.6	8.8	1.6
Upper 5%/bottom	3.9	3.1	6.9	-19.8	122.3	78.2
After-tax household income (1999 dollars)						
Bottom four-fifths				*Percent change in income*		
Lowest fifth	$9,613	$8,973	$8,761	-6.7%	-2.4%	-8.9%
Second fifth	21,583	19,815	20,001	-8.2	0.9	-7.3
Middle fifth	31,975	31,030	31,384	-3.0	1.1	-1.8
Fourth fifth	42,920	43,680	45,076	1.8	3.2	5.0
Highest fifth	$76,834	$95,585	$102,308	24.4%	7.0%	33.2%
Top 10%	98,768	132,834	142,629	34.5	7.4	44.4
Top 5%	131,887	187,300	205,771	42.0	9.9	56.0
Top 1%	266,629	499,106	515,612	87.2	3.3	93.4
Income ratio				*Percent change in ratio*		
Top/bottom	8.0	10.7	11.7	33.3%	9.6%	46.1%
Top/middle	1.8	2.2	2.3	22.2	3.7	26.8
Upper 5%/bottom	13.7	20.9	23.5	52.2	12.5	71.2

* Average income level for each group.

Source: Authors' analysis of CBO (1998) and unpublished CBO data.

the first section shows, the gap between household earnings at the top and the bottom and even the middle and the bottom increased across both decades. The ratio of the income of the top fifth to the bottom fifth of households, for example, rose from 10.2 in 1979, to 13.1 in 1989, and to 15.7 in 1999. As inequality rose, household incomes were stagnant or falling at the middle and bottom through most of the period. Between 1977 and 1999, the before-tax incomes of the bottom three fifths declined after adjusting for inflation (down 12.5% for the bottom fifth, 8.6% for the second fifth, and 2.2% for the middle fifth. For the fourth fifth, incomes increased just 5.2% in the 22 years between 1977 and 1999. Meanwhile, real before-tax incomes for the top fifth jumped 34.3%, with the strongest before-tax gains for the top 1% (an almost 85% jump between 1977 and 1999).

The second panel of the table shows the effective federal tax rates paid by each income quintile (including finer gradations of income for the top fifth). The effective federal tax rate is the share of the household's total income that is actually paid out in all federal income taxes, including personal income, payroll, corporate income, and excise taxes. This panel shows the fundamentally progressive nature of the federal tax system (primarily a function, as we shall see later, of the personal income tax). In all three years in the table, the effective tax rate rises with household income. In 1999, for example, the bottom fifth of households paid only 4.6% of their income in all forms of federal taxes. The next fifth paid about 13.7%; the middle fifth, 18.9%; the top fifth, 29.1%. Even within the top fifth of households, effective rates increased with income: the top 10% paid an average of 30.6% of their income in federal taxes; the top 5% paid 31.8%; and the top 1%, 34.4%.

The bottom half of the second panel, however, demonstrates that the progressivity of federal taxes varied substantially over the period. In 1977, the effective federal tax rate for the top fifth of households was 3.4 times higher than the effective rate paid by the bottom fifth. Changes to the tax code implemented in the 1980s made the tax code less progressive, lowering the ratio to 2.9 by 1989. Further changes in the 1990s made the tax code, by this measure at least, dramatically more progressive, with the ratio rising to 6.3 by 1999. The most important reason for the rise in the ratio of effective tax rates was the steep drop—from 8.8% to 4.6%—in the effective tax rate for the bottom fifth, primarily as a result of the expansion in the generosity of the Earned Income Tax Credit (EITC), which boosts the after-tax income of low-wage earners in low-income families.

From the standpoint of progressivity, one of the most important developments over the period was the big swing, back and forth, in the effective tax rates for the high-income households. In 1977, the top 1% of households paid 37.3% of their income in federal taxes. By the end of the 1980s, the effective federal tax rate for this group had fallen to 28.1%. Countervailing changes to the tax code in the 1990s pushed the effective rate for these top-earners back to 34.4%, leaving effective federal tax rates about three percentage points shy of their levels at the end of the 1970s. The effective tax rates for the top 5% and the top 10% of households show similar, though less pronounced, swings.

The last section of Table 1.9 applies the effective tax rates in the second section to the pre-tax incomes in the top section. By comparing growth in before-tax household income with growth in after-tax income, we can judge the impact of changes in the tax code on the pre-tax income trends that we analyzed earlier in this chapter. During the 1980s, changes in the tax code reinforced the rise in pre-tax income inequality. For the bottom three fifths of households, growth in after-tax income was worse than it was for before-tax income. Between 1977 and 1989, for example, incomes for the bottom fifth fell 6.3% before taxes and 6.7% after taxes. Meanwhile, incomes of the top 1% rose 63.2% before taxes and 87.2% after taxes.

In the 1990s, however, changes in federal tax law worked to counteract some of the rise in pre-tax inequality. For the bottom three-fifths, income growth was at least as good after federal taxes as it was before taxes were taken out. Changes in the tax code were particularly beneficial to the bottom fifth: pre-tax income for this group fell 6.7% between 1989 and 1999, but declined only 2.4% after taxes. At the same time, for the top 1% of households, after-tax income grew considerably more slowly (3.3%) than did before-tax income (13.2%).

The data in Table 1.9 established that tax policy was not responsible for disappointing income outcomes in the 1980s and 1990s. **Tables 1.10-1.11** illustrate this same point in a different way. Table 1.10 shows the share of all after-tax income received by households at different points in the after-tax income distribution in 1977, 1989, and 1999. In 1999, for example, the bottom fifth of households received just 4.0% of all after-tax income. In the same year, the top fifth received almost half (49.5%) of all after-tax income. The table also demonstrates that between 1977 and 1989 the after-tax income shares of the bottom 90% of the income distribution fell, while the shares going to the top 10% grew. Over the 1989-99 period, after-tax income equality deteriorated further. The wealthiest fifth of households gained a 0.5 percentage-point share of total after-tax income, while the bottom four-fifths of households saw their income shares fall 0.5 percentage points. Within the bottom four-fifths, losses concentrated at the bottom, with the poorest, the second, and the third fifths losing, while the fourth fifth gained 0.5 percentage points of all after-tax income.

Table 1.11 takes this analysis a step further by decomposing (i.e., breaking down into their component parts) the changes in after-tax income shares be-

TABLE 1.10 Shares of after-federal-tax income for all families, 1977-99

Income group	1977	1989	1999	Percentage-point change 1977-89	1989-99
Bottom four-fifths	56.1%	51.0%	50.5%	-5.1	-0.5
First	5.7	4.4	4.0	-1.3	-0.4
Second	11.5	9.8	9.7	-1.7	-0.1
Third	16.3	15.7	15.2	-0.6	-0.5
Fourth	22.6	21.2	21.7	-1.4	0.5
Top fifth	43.9%	49.0%	49.5%	5.1	0.5
81-90%	15.5	15.1	14.9	-0.4	-0.2
91-95%	9.8	9.8	9.7	0.0	-0.1
96-99%	11.3	12.1	12.6	0.8	0.4
Top 1%	7.3	11.9	12.3	4.6	0.4
All	100.0%	100.0%	100.0%		

Source: Authors' analysis of CBO data.

TABLE 1.11 The effects of federal tax and income changes on after-tax income shares, 1977-99*

Income group	Change in after-tax shares (1) 1977-89	(2) 1989-99*	Change in shares due to: pre-tax income shifts (3) 1977-89	(4) 1989-99*	Change in tax progressivity (5) 1977-89	(6) 1989-99*
Bottom four-fifths	-5.1	-0.5	-4.6	-1.9	-0.6	1.3
First	-1.3	-0.4	-1.1	-0.6	-0.2	0.2
Second	-1.7	-0.1	-1.6	-0.5	-0.2	0.4
Third	-0.6	-0.5	-0.5	-0.9	0.0	0.4
Fourth	-1.4	0.5	-1.3	0.1	-0.1	0.4
Top fifth	5.1	0.5	4.6	1.9	0.6	-1.3
81-90%	-0.4	-0.2	-0.4	-0.3	-0.1	0.1
91-95%	0.0	-0.1	0.1	-0.1	-0.1	0.0
96-99%	0.8	0.4	1.1	0.6	0.0	-0.2
Top 1%	4.6	0.4	3.8	1.7	0.7	-1.2
All	0.0	0.0	0.0	0.0	0.0	0.0

* CBO projections based on 1999 income levels under 1998 tax law.

Source: Authors' analysis of CBO (1998) and unpublished CBO data.

tween 1977-89 and 1989-99 into the portion due to pre-tax income shifts and the portion attributable to federal tax policy changes. The first two columns in Table 1.11 reproduce the last two columns in Table 1.10. The third and fourth columns show the portion of the overall change in after-tax income that was due to pre-tax income shifts in each period. The last two columns show the corresponding portion of the overall shift due to changes in tax progressivity. Of the 5.1 percentage-point decline between 1977 and 1989 in the share of total after-tax income received by the bottom four-fifths of households, 4.6 points were due to a relative loss of pre-tax income and only 0.6 points were due to shifts in the distribution of the tax burden. Thus, shifts in the tax burden, though significant, were clearly not the primary mechanism of the overall redistribution of income from 1977 to 1989. Over the same period, the top 1% of households captured a 4.6 point larger share of after-tax income. But, again, most of this improvement (3.8 points) was due to changes in pre-tax income share and much less (0.7 points) to changes in the tax structure.

Column 2 demonstrates that the after-tax income share for the bottom four-fifths of the population fell 0.5 percentage points over the 1989-99 period. This decline was the result of two countervailing forces. The share of pre-tax income for the bottom four-fifths fell 1.9 percentage points, indicating a further growth of pre-tax income inequality. The greater tax progressivity built into tax changes in the 1990s, however, partially offset these declines, raising the after-tax income share for the group by 1.3 percentage points. At the top of the income distribution, the share of after-tax income going to the top 1% of households rose 0.4 percentage points during the 1990s. The top 1% saw their pre-tax income share rise even more (1.7 percentage points) over the same period, but increased tax progressivity significantly reduced the increase in after-tax shares (by 1.2 percentage points).

The CBO data also demonstrate how little impact the various tax changes in the 1980s and 1990s have had on typical middle-income households. Table 1.9 shows that the effective federal tax rate for the middle fifth of households was 19.2% in 1977 and 18.9% in both 1989 and 1999. Thus, there is no truth to the claim that government taxes, at the federal level at least, are taking a bigger chunk out of middle-class family incomes.

Even if we narrow our analysis to the stereotypical "family of four" (with two children and one earner), changes in federal taxes have had little impact on family living standards, except for low-income families. **Table 1.12** shows separate data from the Department of the Treasury on the effective federal tax rate for families of four with low, medium, and high incomes in 1979, 1989, and 1999 (see also **Figure 1I**). A family of four receiving the median annual income paid 23.1% of its income in federal taxes in 1979. The effective rate rose slightly

TABLE 1.12 Effective federal tax rate for a family of four with one earner, 1977-97

Income level**	Effective federal tax rate*			Percentage-point change		
	1979	1989	1999***	1979-89	1989-99	1979-99
Low	17.4%	20.3%	14.1%	2.9	-6.2	-3.3
Middle	23.1	24.4	22.8	1.3	-1.6	-0.3
High	23.4	24.1	25.0	0.7	0.9	1.6

*   Average rate for combined federal income, employee plus employer Social Security, and Medicare taxes.

** Low income is one-half median income for a family of four; middle is median income; high is twice median income.

*** Projected; taxes rates calculated using laws enacted as of January 1998.

Source: U.S. Department of the Treasury (1998).

to 24.4% in 1989 and then fell to 22.8% in 1999. On net, federal taxes for this typical family fell about 0.3 percentage points over the full 1979-99 period. Effective tax rates rose slightly for a high-income family of four (about 1.6 percentage points between 1979 and 1999). Low-income families of four saw the widest variation in effective tax rates. Their federal taxes rose 2.9 percentage points in the 1980s (mostly reflecting an increase in payroll taxes that fund Social Security) and then fell 6.2 percentage points in the 1990s (mostly as a result of the increased generosity of the EITC).

So far, the analysis of taxes has examined the combined effects of all federal taxes. In fact, federal taxes take a variety of forms, some progressive and some regressive. Changes in the relative importance of different kinds of federal taxes can have an important impact on the progressivity of the federal tax system as a whole. **Table 1.13** shows the effective tax rate for households at different income levels for the four most important types of federal taxes. The data in the table compare effective rates in 1977, before income stagnation and inequality began to rise strongly, to rates in 1999. The first two columns show effective rates for the personal income tax. In both 1977 and 1999, the personal income tax was strongly progressive, with effective rates rising smoothly with income. Refundable tax credits administered through the personal income tax actually increased the income of the poorest fifth of all households in both years. Middle-income households paid about 6.9% of their income in federal income taxes in 1977 and 5.4% in 1999. The top 1% paid, on average, substantially more than the middle fifth did in both years (25.2% in 1977 and 22.2% in 1999).

FIGURE 1I Effective federal tax rate for family of four, 1955-99

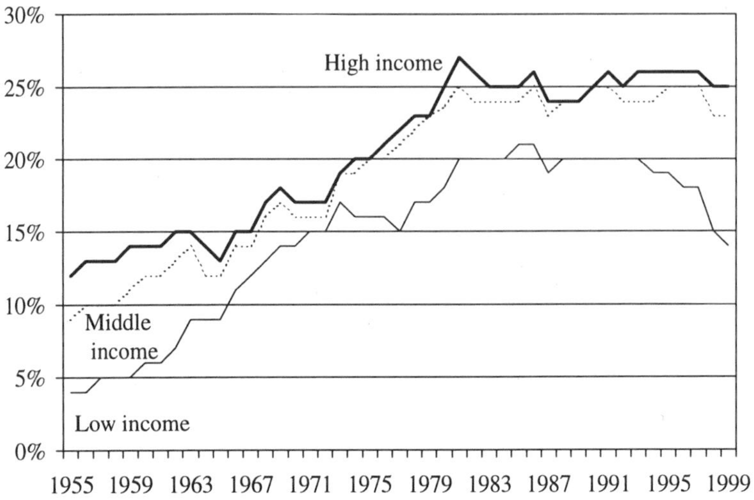

Source: U.S. Department of the Treasury.

TABLE 1.13 Effective tax rates for selected federal taxes, 1977-99(p)*

Income group	Personal income tax		Payroll tax		Corporate income tax		Excise tax	
	1977	1999(p)	1977	1999(p)	1977	1999(p)	1977	1999(p)
Bottom four-fifths								
First	-0.6%	-6.8%	5.1%	7.9%	1.9%	0.5%	2.9%	2.9%
Second	3.4	0.9	7.5	10.0	2.7	1.0	1.8	1.8
Third	6.9	5.4	8.1	10.8	3.0	1.3	1.5	1.3
Fourth	9.6	8.4	7.8	11.4	3.2	1.3	1.3	1.1
Top fifth								
81-90%	12.0%	11.4%	7.4%	11.1%	3.4%	1.8%	1.1%	0.9%
91-95%	13.9	13.7	6.5	10.3	3.9	2.5	1.0	0.8
96-99%	16.6	16.8	4.4	7.4	5.1	4.3	0.8	0.5
Top 1%	25.2	22.2	1.3	2.7	8.8	9.2	0.3	0.3
All	11.1%	11.1%	6.5%	9.2%	3.9%	3.0%	1.3%	1.0%

* CBO projections.

Source: Authors' analysis of unpublished CBO data and CBO (1998).

The third and fourth columns of Table 1.13 show effective rates for the payroll tax, which is used primarily to finance Social Security and Medicare. All workers pay the payroll tax at the same rate (15.3%) from their first dollar of earnings until the point in the year when they reach an income cap ($72,600 in 1999). With the lowest earners paying the full rate from the first dollar earned and high earners paying no payroll tax on earnings over the cap, the payroll tax is regressive, and the effective rates in Table 1.13 bear this out. Effective rates rise through the bottom, second, and middle fifth of households, but fall steeply thereafter. In 1999, for example, households in the middle fifth paid 10.8% of their income in federal payroll taxes, compared to just 2.7% for the top 1%. Comparing rates in 1999 with those in place in 1977 demonstrates that effective rates rose about 2.5 percentage points as a result of increases in the payroll tax made in the 1980s to improve the long-term finances of the Social Security and Medicare systems. While the payroll tax is regressive, the government uses the revenue to fund two programs that are progressive (Social Security and Medicare). This suggests that the most appropriate way to judge the progressivity or regressivity of a particular tax or tax system should involve looking at the effect of the tax or tax system after all the taxes have been taken out and all the associated transfers and services have been provided.

The fifth and sixth columns in Table 1.13 display the effective rates on the corporate income tax, which are portioned out to households according to their estimated income from capital. The corporate income tax is progressive, with effective rates rising sharply with income. In practice, the progressivity of the corporate income tax, however, simply reflects the ownership structure of corporations, with few poor and middle-income households holding any substantial amount of stock. The last two columns of the table report effective rates on federal excise taxes (such as those on alcohol and cigarettes). These taxes are highly regressive, with the bottom fifth of households spending almost 10 times more of their income on excise taxes than do the top 1%. In fact, the poorest fifth of households paid more in federal excise taxes in both years than they did in corporate income taxes.

Of course, in addition to these various federal taxes, households also pay taxes to state and local governments. **Table 1.14** displays the average effective state and local tax rates paid by non-elderly married couples in 1995 (the most recent year for which such an analysis is available). These data differ slightly from those used in the preceding discussion of federal tax rates, but are sufficiently comparable to allow basic conclusions about the incidence of state and local taxes. The first column shows the combined effective tax rates for the four most important types of state and local taxes (personal income, corporate income, property, and sales and excise taxes). Taken together, the data indicate

TABLE 1.14 Effective state and local tax rates in 1995 as percentage shares of income for non-elderly married couples

Income group	Total tax	Personal income tax	Corporate income tax	Property tax	Sales and excise tax	Total after federal deduction for state/local taxes
Bottom four-fifths						
First	12.5%	1.2%	0.1%	4.5%	6.7%	12.4%
Second	10.4	2.2	0.1	2.9	5.2	10.3
Third	9.8	2.8	0.0	2.8	4.2	9.4
Fourth	9.5	3.1	0.1	2.8	3.5	8.6
Top fifth						
81-95%	9.0%	3.5%	0.1%	2.8%	2.6%	7.7%
96-99%	8.4	3.9	0.1	2.6	1.8	6.5
Top 1%	7.9	4.6	0.3	1.9	1.1	5.8

Source: Citizens for Tax Justice (1996).

that state and local taxes are strongly regressive. The bottom fifth of families, for example, paid 12.5% of their income in state and local taxes; the middle fifth paid 9.8%; while the top 1% paid only 7.9%. The next four columns, which break down the overall effective tax rate into its main components, help to explain the regressivity of these non-federal taxes. State and local governments rely on the most regressive types of taxes—sales and excise taxes and property taxes—to raise the bulk of their revenue. These governments raise a much smaller portion of their revenues from progressive taxes such as personal and corporate income taxes.

State and local taxes are even more regressive if one considers the state and local taxes paid after allowing for federal tax deductions (see the last column of Table 1.14). Since taxpayers can deduct part of the state and local taxes they pay from their income for purposes of calculating their federal income tax payments, the state and local taxes families pay can reduce the amount they pay in federal income taxes. Since, as shown in Table 1.13, the best-off households pay the most in federal income tax, these well-off families benefit disproportionately from the ability to deduct state and local taxes. (In fact, since most middle- and low-income families don't itemize their deductions, they take no separate deduction for state and local taxes). The deductibility of state and local taxes lowers the effective tax rate for middle-income families from 9.8% to 9.4%. The

TABLE 1.15 Types of federal vs. state and local taxes, as a percent of revenue at each level, 1999

Type of tax	Federal	State and local
Progressive	59.5%	25.6%
Personal income tax	47.6	21.5
Corporate income tax	11.9	4.0
Regressive	39.2%	70.6%
Excise/customs/sales/other*	4.6	43.7
Contributions for social insurance	34.6	1.2
Property	0.0	25.6
Nontaxes**	1.3%	3.9%
Total	100.0%	100.0%

* Other taxes include vehicle licenses, severance taxes, etc.
** Fines, certain fees, rents, royalties, tuition, hospital fees, etc.

Source: Authors' analysis of NIPA data.

effect, however, is much larger for the top 1%, for whom the effective rate falls from 7.9% to 5.8% after taking deductibility into account.

The preceding discussion of different types of federal, state, and local taxes makes clear that the mix of taxes—including whether government revenues are collected locally or nationally—can have an important impact on how the tax burden is shared. Federal taxes, driven by the progressivity of the federal income tax, are far more progressive than state and local taxes, which rely heavily on regressive sales, excise, and property taxes. **Table 1.15** shows the share of federal and state and local tax revenues collected by progressive and regressive taxes in 1999. Almost 60% of federal tax revenue is raised through progressive taxes, compared to just over 25% for state and local revenues.

Changes over time in the share of taxes collected at the federal versus the state and local level, therefore, can change the progressivity of the overall tax system. **Table 1.16** shows data on tax revenues raised at the federal and the state and local level from 1959 through 1999. Between 1959 and 1979, total tax revenue grew 3.3 percentage points of gross domestic product (GDP), with more regressive state taxes increasing at a faster rate (1.8 percentage points of GDP from a base of 6.9% of GDP, compared to a 1.5 percentage-point rise from a base of 17.1% of GDP). During the 1980s, overall tax revenues rose 0.5 per-

TABLE 1.16 Federal vs. state and local tax burdens, 1959-99, revenue as a percent of GDP

	Federal	State and local	Total
1959	17.1%	6.9%	24.0%
1967	17.4	8.1	25.4
1973	17.9	9.5	27.5
1979	18.6	8.7	27.4
1989	18.4	9.5	27.9
1999	20.2	9.9	30.1
Percentage-point change			
1959-79	1.5	1.8	3.3
1979-89	-0.2	0.7	0.5
1989-99	1.8	0.4	2.2

Source: Authors' analysis of NIPA data.

centage points of GDP—the net result of a 0.2 percentage-point decrease in more progressive federal tax revenues and a 0.7 percentage-point rise in more regressive state and local taxes. In the 1990s, tax revenues rose sharply (2.2 percentage points of GDP), mostly as a result of increases in federal revenue collection (1.8 percentage points).

The data in Tables 1.9 through 1.16 make a strong case that taxes have not played a major role over the last two decades in slowing income growth and widening economic inequality. Rather, these are primarily before-tax phenomena. Taxes exacerbated the rise in inequality in the 1980s, but important changes to the tax code in the 1990s, especially the expansion of the EITC, actually helped to reduce income inequality somewhat in the 1990s.

Is the increase in inequality sensitive to income definitions?

Studies in income distribution, as in all areas of empirical work, have to be careful and complete as to how they defined the items being analyzed. More specifically, it is important to ensure that any conclusions drawn from a data analysis are not sensitive to particular measurement decisions.

Other than the tax data just discussed, the income definition used so far in this chapter is the Census Bureau's primary definition of income: pre-tax, post-cash-transfer money income, which includes earnings (including self-employment), interest, dividend, pensions, and rental income, as well as cash transfers from government programs such as public assistance (welfare benefits) and Social Security. This measure leaves out a variety of income components, some of which, like the cash value of publicly provided near-cash benefits, like food stamps, are equalizing, while others, like capital gains, tend to increase inequality. Fortunately, the Census Bureau provides an alternative series so that we can examine the extent to which any of our conclusions are sensitive to alternative income definitions.

Before we turn to these data, however, we want to emphasize that the central question under investigation here is how the *trend* in inequality is affected by the alternative definitions. These alternative series indeed typically produced different *levels* of inequality at a point in time, but we are primarily interested in whether there is some important income component missing from the above analysis that would change our conclusions about the *trend*.

Census Bureau alternative income definitions: The Census Bureau offers an array of household income measures (most of the tables up to this point have referred to families, i.e., two or more related persons; the data in this section are available only for households, which include persons living alone). We have selected four of the 15 available measures for analysis so that we can identify how results change as incomes become more comprehensively measured and as changes in the tax system are integrated into the analysis (see box). The first measure is the official Census Bureau "money income" definition used thus far. The limitations of this definition are that it excludes any effect of the tax system or employer-provided health benefits, realized capital gains (i.e., gains from selling assets such as stocks), and the value of government non-cash programs (housing subsidies, Medicaid/Medicare, food stamps). The second definition is "pre-tax market income," obtained by subtracting government cash assistance from money income and adding in realized capital gains and employer-provided health insurance. The third definition puts market incomes on an after-tax basis. The last measure, "Comprehensive Income," adds the value of government cash transfers, health programs (Medicare/Medicaid), food stamps, and school lunch programs in order to have the broadest measure of income (see table note for more information on how these values are derived).

Table 1.17 presents several measures of inequality for each definition of income for the years 1979, 1989, and 1998 and the percent growth over time. The top section employs the Gini coefficient (see Figure 1F). There is a persistent and comparable growth of inequality since 1979 for every income definition, with 1990s' income inequality growth about 30% to 40% as much as in the 1980s. For instance, over the 1979-98 period the Gini coefficient grew 10.7% for the first two income definitions and 12.8% for the last two income definitions. Plus, the Gini coefficient grew about 4% in the 1990s. Thus, regardless of definition, income inequality has grown in each of the last two decades.

ALTERNATIVE INCOME DEFINITIONS

Money income: The Census Bureau's official definition of income used to compute income and poverty trends. This definition combines all labor income (wage and salary and self-employment), all government cash transfers (unemployment insurance, Temporary Assistance for Needy Families, Social Security), pensions, alimony, rent, interest, dividends, and other money income. This definition does not take account of non-cash government assistance (e.g., Medicaid), taxation, and capital gains.

Market income, pre-tax: This definition adjusts money income by subtracting government cash assistance and by adding market incomes excluded from the official definition: employer-provided health insurance and realized capital gains (gains from selling assets such as stock). Thus, this definition includes only income generated by the market.

Market income, after-tax: This definition adjusts market income to an "after-tax" basis by subtracting estimates of federal income and payroll taxes, the EITC, and state income taxes. There is no adjustment for other federal (corporate, excise), other state (sales) taxes, or any local taxes.

Comprehensive income: This definition adds the value of government assistance to income. It includes both cash assistance (Social Security, unemployment insurance, etc.) and the value of various subsidies and programs, such as housing subsidies, food stamps, school lunch programs, and health programs (Medicare/Medicaid). This definition is thus the most comprehensive in including both market income and government assistance as well as adjusting for most taxes.

The second two sections of Table 1.17 use a variation of the income ratio approach shown in Figure 1G. Here, we use Census alternative definitions to track the incomes of the highest fifth relative to the lowest fifth of families and the incomes of the highest fifth relative to the middle fifth of families. These panels reveal that income inequality, both between the top and the bottom and between the top and the middle, grew persistently over the 1980s and 1990s, regardless of income definition. In fact, each income inequality ratio grew roughly 25% over the 1979-98 period for nearly every income definition examined in the table. The inequality of market-based incomes grew the fastest in the 1990s for both income ratios. The income gap between the top and the bottom grew as quickly with the official Census measure as with an after-tax income measure, at least in the 1990s (11.7% versus 12.7%). These data thus provide no basis upon which to claim that the use of the Census Bureau money income definition in the first section of this chapter distorts the trend in income inequality.

The reduction of market inequality by progressive tax shifts in the 1990s has meant that the federal government has had to increase its redistributive ef-

TABLE 1.17 Growth of household income inequality using different income definitions and inequality measures

Inequality measure and income definition	Includes: Capital gains & health insurance	Government cash transfers	Subtracts taxes	Value of non-cash government subsidies and programs	Inequality measure 1979	1989	1998	Percent change in inequality 1979-89	1989-98	1979-98
Gini coefficient										
Census money income	No	Yes	No	No	0.403	0.429	0.446	6.5%	4.0%	10.7%
All market income, pre-tax	Yes	No	No	No	0.460	0.492	0.509	7.0	3.5	10.7
All market Income, after-tax	Yes	No	Yes	No	0.429	0.465	0.484	8.4	4.1	12.8
Comprehensive income	Yes	Yes	Yes	Yes	0.359	0.389	0.405	8.4	4.1	12.8
Family income ratios										
Top fifth/bottom fifth										
Census money income	No	Yes	No	No	10.6	12.1	13.5	14.1%	11.7%	27.5%
All market income, pre-tax	Yes	No	No	No	41.7	44.8	51.8	7.4	15.8	24.4
All market income, after-tax	Yes	No	Yes	No	33.9	34.9	39.3	2.9	12.7	15.9
Comprehensive income	Yes	Yes	Yes	Yes	7.7	8.7	9.7	12.6	11.8	25.9
Top fifth/middle fifth										
Census money income	No	Yes	No	No	2.6	2.9	3.3	12.9%	13.8%	28.5%
All market income, pre-tax	Yes	No	No	No	2.8	3.3	3.8	16.2	15.3	34.0
All market income, after-tax	Yes	No	Yes	No	2.6	3.0	3.3	12.8	9.7	23.8
Comprehensive income	Yes	Yes	Yes	Yes	2.4	2.7	2.9	12.9	7.4	21.3

Source: Authors' analysis of U.S. Bureau of the Census data.

forts in order to offset market forces. If one wants to downplay the growing inequality of pre-tax incomes in the 1990s because after-tax income inequality grew less, then one must be supportive of increased tax progressivity. However, many of those who take comfort in after-tax trends actually opposed the increased tax progressivity implemented in the early 1990s. Moreover, if market forces continue to widen pre-tax income inequality, then even further increases in tax progressivity will be required to forestall a growth in after-tax income inequality. Needless to say, such an agenda is not prominent among those who downplay growing inequality.

Table 1.18 presents an additional tabulation of income trends using the same CBO data used in the tax section above, which adjust family income for family size in the same manner as the last column of Table 1.2. This adjustment is made so as to measure income relative to "needs," on the basis that smaller families need less income than larger families, and visa versa. Some analysts have suggested that the trend toward smaller families means that income declines are less onerous. As noted earlier, this family size adjustment is not uncontroversial, since some households may not increase their size (by marrying or having children) precisely because of disappointing income growth.

Nevertheless, it is worth assessing whether adjusting family income trends for changes in family size affects our conclusions regarding trends in incomes and income inequality. In fact, the family size adjustment does not change any of the results. Using this measure, the incomes of the bottom 40% have stayed flat or fallen over the last 20 years, while incomes for the upper 1% have grown 78.9% on a pre-tax and 89.4% on an after-tax basis. Income inequality, when measured with family-size-adjusted data, increases sharply in the 1980s and continues to grow (again, at a slower rate) in the 1990s. The ratio of the size-adjusted incomes of the upper 5% to those of the bottom fifth grew about 70%, both pre-tax and after-tax, over the last two decades.

Whether or not we adjust by family size, look at pre-tax or post-tax income, or add in the value of various other income sources, including capital gains and food stamps, there is nothing in either the CBO or Census data to suggest that alternative measures lead to alternative conclusions regarding the trend toward more inequality. The CBO data, in fact, show a larger growth of inequality and a broader and more severe decline in income at the bottom than that shown by our analysis of the Census Bureau data.

Inequality as measured by consumption: Some economists express doubts about analyses of income because the incomes of families fluctuate from year to year in response to special circumstances—a layoff, a one-time sale of an asset, and so on. As a result, a family's income may partially reflect transient events and not indicate its economic well-being over the long term. For ex-

TABLE 1.18 CBO-adjusted household income growth for various income groups

Income definition/fifth	Percent change		
	1979-89	1989-99	1979-99
Pretax household income			
(adjusted for family size)			
Bottom four-fifths			
Lowest fifth	-6.4%	-3.4%	-9.6%
Second fifth	-1.9	0.0	-1.9
Middle fifth	3.1	2.7	5.9
Fourth fifth	6.5	4.9	11.7
Highest fifth	22.8%	11.4%	36.8%
Top 10%	29.2	12.9	45.9
Top 5%	34.3	15.0	54.5
Top 1%	59.4	12.2	78.9
Income ratio			
Top/bottom	31.2%	15.3%	51.3%
Top/middle	15.3	6.2	22.4
Upper 5%/bottom	43.5	19.1	70.9
After-tax household income			
(adjusted for family size)			
Bottom four-fifths			
Lowest fifth	-7.0%	0.0%	-7.0%
Second fifth	-2.2	1.7	-0.6
Middle fifth	3.4	2.6	6.1
Fourth fifth	7.8	3.6	11.7
Highest fifth	27.7%	7.1%	36.7%
Top 10%	36.5	7.6	46.8
Top 5%	45.2	8.8	58.0
Top 1%	83.6	3.2	89.4
Income ratio			
Top/bottom	37.3%	7.1%	47.0%
Top/middle	18.4	3.3	22.4
Upper 5%/bottom	56.1	8.8	69.8

Source: CBO.

ample, a family experiencing a "bad year" in terms of income may dip into its savings to continue consuming at the same level as during a better year. In this view, consumption levels of families provide a better measure of inequality, since families typically gear their consumption to their expected incomes over the long term.

Figure 1J shows the trend in the Gini coefficient for consumption along with the Gini ratio for income from this same data source: the Bureau of Labor Statistics' Consumer Expenditure (CE) Survey (this analysis is available only through 1995). The income inequality trends from the CPS data—the focus of most of this chapter—are considered more reliable in that they derive from a larger sample and are based on a more detailed set of questions. Nevertheless, we include the CE income trend in the figure for comparative purposes (in fact, the income inequality trends from the two surveys are similar). Both series in the figure are indexed to the starting year, 1981, to allow a comparison of their growth rates. Consumption inequality increased consistently over the 1980s (recall that higher values for the Gini ratio mean more inequality). Although the trend in income inequality from the CE is less consistent, rising steeply over the early 1980s and flattening in the second half of the decade, both income and consumption inequality grew by about 10% over the period.

Income inequality continued to grow over the early 1990s in the CE data, but the trend in consumption inequality was flat from 1989 to 1995. By the last data point available, the consumption coefficient was up 10% above its 1981 level. Thus, by this measure, consumption inequality, unlike that of income, did not increase further over the 1990s. It is possible that the late 1990s run-up in the stock market led to further growth in consumption inequality in the latter part of the 1990s, since, as shown in Chapter 4, this run-up favored the very wealthy who are most likely to consume "big-ticket" items out of the reach of lower-income consumers. But until such evidence is available, the figure clearly shows a flattening in the growth of consumption inequality through 1995.

Alternative explanations: mobility and demographics
Does income mobility counteract the inequality problem? Other critics accept the fact that inequality has grown over time but argue that the data reported so far, which are essentially snapshots of the income distribution at different points in time, miss the extent to which families move up and down that distribution over the course of their lives (an exception is the cohort analysis in Table 1.4). Essentially, this critique agrees that the distance from the basement to the penthouse has grown further over time, but it argues that a family that starts out in the basement has a better chance these days of making it to the top floor than it

FIGURE 1J Income and consumption inequality, CE Survey, 1981-95

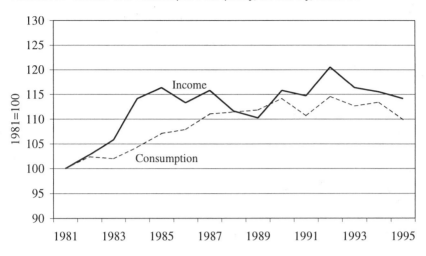

Source: Johnson and Smeeding (1998).

once did. In other words, these critics implicitly argue that an increase in income mobility has served to offset the increase in income inequality.

In fact, those who make the mobility argument fail to either articulate or substantiate this claim. Instead, they simply show evidence of economic mobility and leave it at that, as if mobility in and of itself should lessen our concern over increased inequality. But unless the rate of mobility is increasing relative to that of earlier decades, families are no more likely today to span the now-wider income gap. That is, income inequality trends as measured thus far accurately portray the growth in income inequality over people's lifetimes unless one can demonstrate that mobility is greater now than in the past. As we show below, there has been no such increase.

The economist Joseph Schumpeter derived a useful analogy to explain the concept of mobility, that of a hotel where the quality of rooms improves as you move up to higher floors. If everyone simply ended up in the same room they started out in, society would be totally immobile, with the poor stuck in the basement and the rich ensconced in the penthouse. The reality is that some stay where they start while others move up and down.

How does this analogy help explain the interplay between increased inequality and income mobility? The fact that, as this chapter has demonstrated, the income gap between those at the top, middle, and bottom of the income scale has expanded over time means that the quality of life for a resident of the basement is now worse relative to his neighbor in the penthouse than it was two decades ago. The proponents of the mobility argument acknowledge this, but they say that this family won't always be in the basement. This is true, but unless their chance of making it to the higher floors has increased over time, the increase in inequality means that they are sure to experience more inequality over the course of their lives. The wider income gap means that the higher floors are "further away," and their chance of reaching them has not increased.

These mobility issues are best addressed with longitudinal data, or data that follow the same persons over time. Each person is assigned to an income fifth at the beginning and end of the relevant periods of observation based on his or her family's income. Different income cutoffs are used for each period, meaning that the 20th percentile upper limit in, for example, 1979 will be different than that of 1989. This approach to income mobility examines whether a family becomes better or worse off relative to other families, as opposed to better or worse off in terms of their actual incomes.

In particular, the analysis tracks how families are doing relative to the others they started with at the beginning of the periods in the same age cohort and income class. If each family's income grew by the same amount (in percentage terms), there would be no change in mobility, i.e., no changes in the relative positions of families in the income distribution. If, however, a family that starts out in the bottom fifth experiences faster income growth than other low-income families, it may move into a higher fifth, i.e., this family will experience upward mobility.

Table 1.19 presents a "transition matrix" for the period 1969-94. Going across each row in the table, the numbers reveal the percent of persons who either stayed in the same fifth or "transitioned" to a higher or lower one. For example, the first entry shows that 41.0% of persons in the bottom fifth in 1969 were also in the bottom fifth in 1994. At the other end of the income scale, 38.8% of those who started in the top fifth stayed there. The percent of "stayers" (those who did not transition out of the fifth they started out in) are shown in bold.

Note that large transitions are uncommon. Only 5.8% of those who began the period in the first fifth ended up in the top fifth, while only 9.5% fell from the top fifth to the lowest fifth. Those transitions that do occur are most likely to be a move up or down to the neighboring fifth. For example, among the middle three-fifths, slightly less than two-thirds of the transitions were to neighboring fifths.

Though Table 1.19 does not reveal a great deal of income mobility, the data do show that mobility exists and that families can and do move up and down as their relative fortunes change (as we show in Chapter 7, the U.S. is no more mobile than Europe). How does this fact comport with the historically large increases in inequality that we have focused on throughout this chapter? Refer-

TABLE 1.19 Income mobility, 1969-94

1969 income group	1994 income group					
	First fifth	Second fifth	Middle fifth	Fourth fifth	Top fifth	Total
First fifth	**41.0%**	24.9%	16.2%	12.1%	5.8%	100.0%
Second fifth	22.4	**24.7**	23.9	16.1	13.0	100.0
Middle fifth	16.9	21.0	**23.5**	22.8	15.9	100.0
Fourth fifth	11.3	18.5	19.7	**24.2**	26.3	100.0
Top fifth	9.5	10.6	16.6	24.5	**38.8**	100.0

Source: Unpublished tabulations of the PSID by Peter Gottschalk.

ring back to the above discussion, has there been an increase in the rate of mobility that would serve to offset the rise in income inequality?

Table 1.20 provides the data needed to answer this question. It presents two transition matrices, one for the 1970s and the other for the 1980s. Unfortunately, there are not yet enough years of longitudinal data available from this data source—the Panel Study of Income Dynamics—to measure the rate of income mobility over the 1990s. However, as we have shown, the increase in income inequality was greater over the 1980s than the 1990s. Thus, these transition matrices provide an excellent test of the mobility hypothesis. Also, unlike the previous table, this table uses three years of family income data for each year, e.g., a family's 1969 income is actually the average of its 1968-70 data. This approach is preferred in mobility analysis since it "smoothes out" temporary transitions.

These tables again show relative stability (the largest shares of persons are stayers, located along or close to the diagonal). For example, both 10-year periods reveal that about 85% of persons in families stayed in the first or second fifths. But more important in this context is the fact that mobility has not increased. The shares of both stayers and those who made transitions are very similar in both periods. For example, 61.5% remained in the lowest fifth over the 1970s, and 61.0% remained there in the 1980s. The shares that remained in the middle were also very close (29.6% versus 29.5%), and only a slightly larger share remained in the top fifth in the 1980s. Thus, there is no evidence here of an increase in mobility to offset increased inequality.

In fact, as **Figure 1K** shows, the rate of mobility appears to have declined since the late 1960s. This figure uses the same longitudinal data source as Table 1.20 to plot the percent of persons who stayed in the same fifth from one year to

TABLE 1.20 Income mobility over the 1970s and 1980s*

1969 income group	1979 income group					
	First fifth	Second fifth	Middle fifth	Fourth fifth	Top fifth	Total
First fifth	**61.5%**	24.0%	8.7%	4.4%	1.5%	100.0%
Second fifth	22.7	**31.3**	27.5	12.9	5.6	100.0
Middle fifth	9.6	22.5	**29.6**	26.1	12.2	100.0
Fourth fifth	3.3	17.3	22.4	**31.6**	25.4	100.0
Top fifth	2.9	5.0	11.9	25.1	**55.2**	100.0
	1989 income group					
First fifth	**61.0%**	23.8%	9.5%	4.6%	1.1%	100.0%
Second fifth	22.9	**33.2**	27.7	13.5	2.7	100.0
Middle fifth	8.3	25.2	**29.5**	25.7	11.4	100.0
Fourth fifth	4.6	13.0	23.0	**33.2**	26.2	100.0
Top fifth	2.7	4.9	10.8	22.8	**58.8**	100.0

* Unlike the previous table, this table averages family income over three years to "smooth out" temporary transitions.

Source:Unpublished tabulations of the PSID by Peter Gottschalk.

the next. An upward trend therefore suggests declining mobility rates, as persons are less likely over time to make the transition across income classes. For example, in 1969, 62.7% of persons ended up in the same quintile they started in one year earlier, in 1968. At the end of the period, between 1990 and 1991, 65.9% failed to transition to either a lower or higher income group. The fact that the graph drifts upward over the period under analysis implies that the rate of mobility, as measured by the probability of moving to a different income fifth in an adjacent year, has fallen.

The impact of demographic changes on income: It is often suggested that changes in the demographic composition of American families have been a major cause of the slow growth and rising inequality of income documented so far, implying a lesser role for economic causes such as wage decline. While it is unquestionably the case that the increased share of economically vulnerable families has put both downward pressure on income growth and upward pressure on inequality growth, this process is a dynamic one that has not been constant over time. In addition, some demographic factors, such as the increase in edu-

FIGURE 1K Percent staying in same fifth in each pair of years, 1968-69 through 1990-91

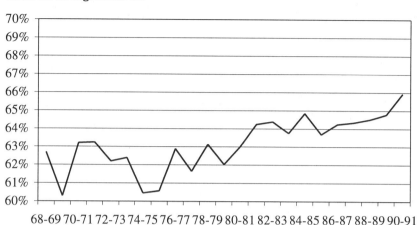

Source: Gottschalk and Danziger (1998).

cational attainment, have led to increased family income. It is important, then, to look at the net effect of the different types of demographic shifts in various time periods.

Table 1.21 shows the impact of age, education, family type, and race on household income (all refer to the head of the household; households, unlike families, include one-person units). The challenge of this analysis is to quantify the impact of changes in these factors on income trends over time. For example, of the list of factors we examine, the two with the largest impact are family type and education level. Over time, as seen earlier in the bottom panel of Table 1.6, there has been a demographic shift toward family types more likely to have low incomes, such as single-parent families or individuals living alone. A countervailing trend, however, has been the higher education levels of heads of households, a demographic trend that would lead to higher income levels over time.

Which of these two factors—educational upgrading or the shift to lower-income family types—has had a larger impact, and how has the impact varied by income level? (Race and age, while important, have played a secondary role in income trends.) Contrary to the conventional wisdom, which has typically assigned the primary role to changes in family type, there is clear evidence that, while the shift to less well-off families has put downward pressure on incomes,

TABLE 1.21 The impact of demographic change on household income, 1969-98

Actual household incomes (1998 dollars)	First fifth	Second fifth	Middle fifth	Fourth fifth	Top fifth	Average
1969	$8,690	$22,141	$34,807	$48,559	$83,391	$39,518
1979	9,309	22,222	36,474	53,413	91,938	42,671
1989	9,524	22,962	38,053	57,598	109,421	47,511
1998	9,906	23,695	39,374	60,855	123,777	51,522
1969-79						
Actual change	7.1%	0.4%	4.8%	10.0%	10.2%	8.0%
Change due to:						
Age	-1.0	-1.6	-1.8	-1.8	-1.8	-1.7
Education	5.5	5.8	5.4	4.5	4.6	4.9
Type of household	-15.3	-11.9	-8.8	-5.9	-3.6	-6.5
Race	-1.3	-1.0	-0.8	-0.5	-0.4	-0.6
Total demographic effect*	-8.8	-7.5	-5.4	-2.6	0.5	-2.6
Income change, holding demographics constant	15.9	7.9	10.2	12.6	9.8	10.6
1979-89						
Actual change	2.3%	3.3%	4.3%	7.8%	19.0%	11.3%
Change due to:						
Age	1.3	0.6	0.6	0.5	-0.1	0.3
Education	5.0	5.4	4.8	4.5	4.8	4.8
Type of household	-5.6	-5.4	-4.1	-3.0	-2.2	-3.2
Race	-1.4	-1.3	-0.9	-0.5	-0.4	-0.7
Total demographic effect*	-1.0	-0.1	0.6	1.4	3.0	1.7
Income change, holding demographics constant	3.3	3.5	3.7	6.5	16.0	9.7
1989-98						
Actual change	4.0%	3.2%	3.5%	5.7%	13.1%	8.4%
Change due to:						
Age	0.4	0.8	0.9	1.0	1.1	1.0
Education	5.0	5.4	4.9	4.2	3.9	4.3
Type of household	-3.5	-3.2	-2.6	-1.9	-1.7	-2.1
Race	-1.2	-0.7	-0.5	-0.5	-0.5	-0.5
Total demographic effect*	0.6	1.7	2.0	2.5	3.3	2.6
Income change, holding demographics constant	3.4	1.5	1.5	3.2	9.8	5.8

* Components do not sum to the aggregate effect due to interactions between the groups (see table note).

Source: Authors' analysis of March CPS data.

educational upgrading has more than compensated for this effect. Most importantly, during the 1979-98 period, on net, when income inequality was increasing most quickly, these demographic factors led to rising, not falling, average household incomes. Thus, explanations that depend on demographic change to explain income decline should be discounted.

The numbers in Table 1.21 show the percent changes in real household income from 1969 to 1998, along with the changes due to the specific demographic factors. For example, the first section shows that, among families in the lowest fifth of the income scale, the shift to lower-income family types led to a 15.3% decline in income during 1969-79. Note also that this effect fades further up the income scale; the negative effect of family type in the top fifth was 3.6% over this period. As expected, however, educational upgrading lifted incomes between 4.5% and 5.8%. The penultimate row of the section, which sums the impact of each demographic factor, shows that, on net, the impact of demographic change was negative for all but the highest income group (implying that demographic change helped to foster inequality over this period).

Note, however, that the average incomes of all but the second fifth grew significantly from 1969 to 1979 (top row). This means that, despite the downward pressure of the negative factors (primarily family type), incomes *within* each demographic group grew enough to offset these losses. The last row of each panel, which shows the percent of income growth within each demographic group, by income fifth, quantifies this point. These changes are net of demographic effects and thus represent the impact of economic changes such as real wage trends or the growth of income inequality on household incomes.

During the 1970s, household incomes within demographic groups grew strongly, and were also equalizing in nature. Net of demographic change, the income of the bottom fifth of households grew 15.9%, while that of the top fifth grew 9.8%. Thus, over the period when demographic pressure was exerting its strongest negative effects, favorable economic growth among low-income households was great enough to more than offset the unfavorable demographic trends. (Chapter 5 finds similar dynamics regarding the impact of demographic change on poverty rates over this period.)

Over the 1980s, the impact of family type, though still negative, was less a factor than in the previous period for each income group, particularly for the least well-off. For example, while shifts in family structure lowered the average income of the bottom fifth by 15.3% over the 1970s, continuing shifts lowered that group's average income by 5.6% in the 1980s. For the middle fifth, the comparable changes were -8.8% in the 1970s and -4.1% in the 1980s. Conversely, the positive impact of educational upgrading fell only slightly, from 5.5% in the 1970s for the bottom fifth to 5.0% in the 1980s, with similarly small declines for each income group. Thus, in the 1980s, the net impact of demographics were notably smaller than that of the previous period, with incomes for the bottom lowered by 1% and raised for the top by 3%.

Unlike the prior period, however, income growth net of demographic change (i.e., within demographic groups) slowed considerably for all but the wealthiest households. For example, the last row of the middle panel shows that, holding demographics constant, incomes grew by 3.3% for the bottom fifth, 3.7% for the middle fifth, and 16.0% for those at the top of the income scale. Thus, despite the smaller negative impact of changes in family type over the 1980s, economic growth shifted in such a way as to dampen the growth of income for low-income households within each demographic category.

Over the most recent period, 1989-98, the impact of changes in family type has continued to decline. Thus, in this period, net changes in demographics were actually *positive* for each group, though only marginally so at the bottom of the income scale. In the bottom quintile, the negative impacts of family type and race were essentially reversed by the positive impact of education. Within-group (non-demographic) factors (bottom row), such as the wage increases that prevailed in the latter part of the period, led to real average income gains for all households, with larger gains at the bottom than in the middle. Accordingly, both net demographic and within-group trends were reinforcing in the 1990s.

In sum, the message from Table 1.21 is that demographic factors, including education, cannot account for the scope of income problems we have seen thus far. Nor do they help explain why income trends were slower and more unequal after 1979 compared to earlier periods. Over the 1970s, while the shift to less well-off family types was putting significant downward pressure on income growth, incomes grew at a strong pace both at the top (10.2%) and the bottom (7.1%) of the income scale. Over the next two decades, however, when changes in family type had a much smaller negative impact, income growth was highly unequal, growing 35% at the top and 6% at the bottom. Additionally, while the negative impact of changes in family type was tapering off, the positive effect of educational upgrading persisted at similar levels in each time period.

Growth in inequality narrows pathways to prosperity

Another dimension of income growth is the proportion of the population that has low, middle, and high incomes. Two factors determine the distribution of the population at various income levels—the rate of growth of average income and changes in income equality. As long as average income growth (holding inequality constant) is faster than inflation, there will be a greater proportion of the population at higher income levels over time. For example, the share of families with incomes under $25,000 (adjusted for inflation) will fall under this scenario. However, if inequality grows such that the low-income population receives an unusually low proportion of the income growth and the high-income population obtains an unusually large proportion, then a rise in average income

TABLE 1.22 Distribution of persons, households, and families by income level, 1969-99

	1969	1979	1989	1999	Percentage-point change 1969-79	1979-89	1989-99
Family incomes							
Under $25,000	25.6%	24.5%	24.3%	22.5%	-1.1	-0.2	-1.8
$25,000 to $50,000	40.7	33.8	30.6	28.4	-6.9	-3.2	-2.2
$50,000 to $100,000	29.3	34.2	33.7	33.9	4.9	-0.5	0.2
Over $100,000	4.5	7.5	11.5	15.2	3.0	4.0	3.7
Total	100.0	100.0	100.0	100.0			
Household incomes							
Under $25,000	34.0%	33.9%	32.3%	30.6%	-0.1	-1.6	-1.7
$25,000 to $50,000	37.1	32.0	30.2	28.5	-5.1	-1.8	-1.7
$50,000 to $100,000	25.2	28.1	28.3	28.7	2.9	0.2	0.4
Over $100,000	3.9	6.0	9.2	12.3	2.1	3.2	3.1
Total	100.0	100.0	100.0	100.1			
Persons (income relative to the median)							
Less than 50% of median	18.0%	20.1%	22.1%	22.3%	2.1	2.0	0.2
50-200% of median	71.2	68.0	63.2	61.2	-3.2	-4.8	-2.0
Over 200% of median	10.8	11.9	14.7	16.6	1.1	2.8	1.9
Total	100.0	100.0	100.0	100.0			

Source: Authors' analysis of March CPS data.

is unlikely to translate into a general upward movement of the population to higher income levels. The following table reveals that, as expected, economic growth has led to a larger share of families with higher incomes, both in absolute and relative terms. However, the post-1979 growth of inequality has mitigated that progress, meaning that fewer families reside in the middle class than would have been the case had inequality grown less.

The first two panels of **Table 1.22** show the proportion of families and households (recall that households include one-person units) with low, low-middle ($25,000 to $50,000), high-middle ($50,000-$100,000), and high incomes in 1969, 1979, 1989, and 1999. Over the 1969-79 period, when income inequality grew relatively little, average income growth lifted significant proportions of families and households from low and low-middle incomes to the two highest categories. Focusing on families (top panel), there was an 8.0 percentage point shift out of the bottom two income categories. Over the 1980s and 1990s, however, the share of families moving out of the lowest category was much smaller, as was the share moving into the high-middle group, which fluctuated around

34% from 1979 to 1999. A somewhat similar pattern prevailed for households, though the share in the lowest category fell more than it did for families.

Meanwhile, the share of families and households with incomes over $100,000 grew consistently, from 4.5% (1969) to 15.2% for families and from 3.9% to 12.3% for households. This increase in the share of higher-income households is, of course, a positive development and one that should be expected to prevail in a growing economy. But the fact that the shift from low/low-middle to high/high-middle slowed so dramatically over the last 20 years, while the share in the lowest category has fallen only slightly, means that the upward path to prosperity has been made considerably steeper by the growth in inequality.

The third section of Table 1.22 examines the incomes of individuals—single and in families—according to the per capita incomes of their families (size-adjusted), with single persons given their individual incomes. In this analysis, the income of persons is measured relative to the median. Thus, unlike the above sections, which fix the income brackets in real dollar terms, the brackets for the income categories in this section move with the median income. This approach provides more important insights into inequality, because it measures the relative, as opposed to the absolute, changes in family incomes. Thus, in the first section, the absolute income level of a low-income family may grow such that it crosses from the $25,000 category into the middle group. But if its income grows more slowly than that of the median, the family will still fall behind relative to more affluent families. The bottom panel shows evidence of precisely this pattern.

From 1979 forward, more than one-fifth of the population lived in households with income below half of the median income. Over both the 1970s and 1980s, this share grew by about two percentage points, and remained at about that level in 1999. Meanwhile, the share at the top of the income distribution (above 200% of the median) also grew consistently. Since these shares must sum to 100 in each year, and therefore the changes in each of the last three columns must sum to zero, this pattern indicates a declining share in the middle of the income distribution, from half of to two times the median, which fell from 71.2% in 1979 to 61.2% in 1999. By this measure, America's broad middle class has been shrinking, with shares shifting upward and downward.

Expanding capital incomes

The fortunes of individual families depend heavily on their reliance upon the particular sources of their incomes: labor income, capital income, or govern-

TABLE 1.23 Sources of household income by income type, 1999

| Income group | Share of each group's income | | | | Share of income type by group | | | |
	Wage and salary	Capital*	Government transfer and other	Total	Wage and salary	Capital*	Government transfer and other	Total
Bottom								
four-fifths	76.5%	10.0%	13.5%	100.0%	45.7%	19.7%	83.6%	42.5%
First	56.6	5.6	37.8	100.0	2.7	0.9	18.3	3.3
Second	71.7	8.0	20.3	100.0	7.4	2.7	21.7	7.3
Middle	76.1	10.9	13.0	100.0	12.9	6.1	23.0	12.1
Fourth	81.8	11.0	7.2	100.0	22.7	10.0	20.6	19.8
Top fifth	67.5%	30.5%	2.1%	100.0%	54.3%	80.9%	16.7%	57.6%
81-90%	82.2	13.5	4.3	100.0	17.2	9.3	9.2	15.0
91-95%	81.9	15.5	2.6	100.0	12.0	7.5	3.9	10.5
96-99%	73.6	24.8	1.6	100.0	14.7	16.3	3.2	14.3
Top 1%	41.6	58.2	0.2	100.0	10.4	47.8	0.4	17.8
All	71.4%	21.7%	6.9%	100.0%	100.0%	100.0%	100.0%	100.0%

* Includes rent, dividends, interest income, and realized capital gains.

Source: Institute on Economic and Tax Policy (ITEP).

ment assistance. For instance, one significant reason for the unequal growth in family incomes since 1979 was an increase in the share of capital income (such as rent, dividends, interest payments, and capital gains) and a smaller share earned as wages and salaries. Since most families receive little or no capital income, this shift generated greater income inequality.

Table 1.23 presents data that show estimates of the sources of income for families in each income group in 1999. These data are from a different source than that used for our analysis of income trends presented above (which used the CPS) but are comparable to the CBO data used to analyze tax trends. The top fifth received a larger share of its income (30.5%) from financial assets (capital) compared to the other 80% of the population. For instance, the top 1% received 58.2% of its income from capital-based income. The other income groups in the upper 10% received 13.5% to 24.8% of their income from capital. In contrast, the bottom 80% of families relied on capital income for 11% or less of their income in 1999. Obviously then, a fast growth of capital income will disproportionately benefit the best-off income groups. Another way of demonstrating this is to note, as Table 1.23 shows, that the top fifth receives 80.9% of all capital income with nearly half (47.8%) of all capital income accruing to the top 1%.

Those with less access to capital income depend either on wages (the broad middle) or on government transfers (the bottom) as their primary source of income. As a result, any cutback in government cash assistance primarily affects the income prospects of the lowest 40% of the population, but particularly the bottom fifth. For instance, roughly 40% of the income of families in the bottom fifth is drawn from government cash assistance programs (e.g., welfare benefits, unemployment insurance, Social Security, Supplemental Security Income) or other income (pensions, alimony). The income prospects of families in the 20th to 99th percentiles, on the other hand, depend primarily on their wages and salaries (which make up at least 70% of their income). Thus, changes in the level and distribution of wages are key to understanding changes in the incomes of the broad middle class.

The shift in the composition of personal income toward greater capital income is shown in **Table 1.24**. Over the 1979-89 period, capital income's share of market-based income (personal income less government transfers) shifted sharply upward, from 16.4% to 21.9%, as interest income expanded. This shift toward capital income was slightly reversed by 1998 and 1999 as interest rates and, therefore, interest income fell. However, dividend income has expanded in the 1990s. Unfortunately, these data (drawn from the GDP accounts) do not capture realized capital gains as a source of income, and therefore provide an increasingly partial picture of income trends. Therefore, the table supplements the data with Internal Revenue Service data on realized capital gains. As the table shows, this does not affect any conclusions about the 1970s or 1980s since capital gains were comparably important in 1973, 1979, and in 1989. However, capital gains grew to be 6.3-6.9% of income in 1998-99, a significant growth from 1989. Thus capital income, inclusive of realized capital gains, was clearly a larger share of income in the 1998-99 period than in 1989 despite the drop in interest income's role. We conclude that there was an expansion of capital income's role in both the 1980s and the 1990s. Correspondingly, there was a smaller share of income being paid out to wages and benefits, with the compensation share falling from 74.0% in 1979 to 70.5% in 1999 (not counting any impact of capital gains).

This shift away from labor income and toward capital income is unique in the postwar period and is partly responsible for the ongoing growth of inequality since 1979. Since the rich are the primary owners of income-producing property, the fact that the assets they own have commanded an increasing share of total income automatically leads to income growth that is concentrated at the top.

It is difficult to interpret changes in proprietor's income (presented in Table 1.24) because it is a mixture of both labor and capital income. That is, the in-

TABLE 1.24 Shares of market-based personal income by income type, 1959-99

Income type	Shares of income					
	1959	1973	1979	1989	1998	1999
Total capital income	13.5%	14.5%	16.4%	21.9%	20.7%	20.3%
Rent	4.0	2.2	1.3	1.0	2.1	2.1
Dividends	3.4	2.9	3.0	3.6	5.2	5.1
Interest	6.1	9.4	12.2	17.3	13.4	13.1
Total labor income	72.7%	74.4%	74.0%	69.6%	70.3%	70.5%
Wages and salaries	69.1	68.3	65.5	61.1	62.6	62.9
Fringe benefits	3.6	6.1	8.5	8.5	7.7	7.5
Proprietor's income*	13.8%	11.1%	9.6%	8.5%	9.1%	9.3%
Total market-based personal income **	100.0%	100.0%	100.0%	100.0%	100.0%	100.0%
Realized capital gains	n.a.	3.3%	3.6%	3.4%	6.3%	6.9%

* Business and farm owners' income.
** Total of listed income types.

Source: Authors' analysis of NIPA and IRS data.

come that an owner of a business (or farmer) receives results from his or her work effort (labor income) and his or her ownership (capital income) of the business or farm. To the extent that the shrinkage of proprietor's income results from a shift of people out of the proprietary sector (e.g., leaving farming) and into wage and salary employment, there will be a corresponding increase in labor's share of income (e.g., as farm income is replaced by wage income). This shift out of proprietor's income thus helps to explain a rising labor share in some periods, such as from 1959 to 1973. However, there has not been much of a shift in proprietor's income over the last few decades, so it has not been a factor that has shifted the income distribution.

From the point of view of national income (incomes generated by the corporate, proprietor, and government sectors), one can also discern a clear shift away from labor income toward capital income (**Table 1.25**). For instance, labor's share of national income fell from 73.5% in 1979 to 72.1% in 1989 and then fell further to 71.1% in 1998. A closer look at the underlying data, however, suggests an even more significant shift away from labor income. First, labor's share of national income rose steadily from 1959 to 1979. One reason for the expand-ing share of labor income was the steady expansion of the government/non-profit sector. When the government/nonprofit sector grows, there is a tendency for labor's share of income to grow because this sector generates *only* labor income and no capital income. For example, Table 1.25 shows that the growth of the government/nonprofit sector, from 18.4% to 19.4% of national income between 1979 and 1989, necessarily added 1.0 percentage points to labor's share of national income (other things remaining equal). On the other hand, the shrink-age of the government/nonprofit sector over the 1989-98 period led to a smaller labor share of income. Thus, the growth of the government sector over the 1980s led to an understatement of the decline of labor's share in that decade; in the 1990s, the decline in the government/nonprofit sector had the opposite effect.

Labor's share of national income also grows as the proprietary sector (farm and non-farm unincorporated businesses) shrinks, as it did from 1959 to 1979, because labor's share of income in that sector is relatively low (about one-third in 1979). When resources shift from a sector with a low labor share of income, such as the proprietor's sector, to sectors with a higher labor share (all of the other sectors), the share of labor income in the economy necessarily rises. Thus, the changing composition of income across organizational sectors (expanding government, shrinking proprietorships) helped to increase labor's share of na-tional income somewhat since 1979 but less so than in the 1959-73 period. So it is all the more impressive that, despite these compositional shifts, labor's share of national income fell from 73.5% in 1979 to 71.1% in 1998.

The clearest way to examine the changes in income shares is to focus on the corporate sector, which accounted for 61% of national income in 1999. Such an analysis is useful because it is not muddied by income shifts among sectors (such as expanding or shrinking government or proprietors' sectors) or the diffi-culty in defining "proprietor's" income as either labor or capital income. The division of incomes in the corporate sector are shown in the bottom panel of Table 1.25 and in **Figure 1L.** Labor's share fell from 82.3% in 1979 to 81.8% in 1989 and then to 79.5% in 1999. These data suggest that there has been a strong shift away from labor income in the private corporate sector.

How important is the shift in the shares of labor and capital income? Be-tween 1979 and 1999, labor's share in the corporate sector fell 2.8 percentage points. A return to the 1979 labor share would require average hourly compen-sation to be 3.5% greater (82.3 divided by 79.5, less 1). Similarly, the shift of income from labor to capital lowered compensation growth by 2.9% over the 1989-99 period. These calculations illustrate that the shift toward greater capital income shares has had non-trivial implications for wage and compensation growth.

TABLE 1.25 Shares of income by type and sector, 1959-99

Sector	Shares of domestic national income							
	1959	1969	1973	1979	1989	1997	1998	1999
National income all sectors								
Labor	68.8%	72.5%	72.8%	73.5%	72.1%	70.5%	71.1%	n.a.
Capital	18.6	17.6	16.9	17.5	19.6	20.7	20.2	n.a.
Proprietor's profit	12.7	9.9	10.3	9.0	8.3	8.7	8.6	n.a.
Total	100.0	100.0	100.0	100.0	100.0	99.9	99.9	n.a.
Corporate and business sector								
Labor	44.4%	47.9%	48.3%	50.4%	48.3%	47.3%	48.2%	n.a.
Capital	18.3	17.0	15.9	16.1	17.4	19.5	19.0	n.a.
Total	62.7	64.9	64.1	66.5	65.8	66.8	67.2	n.a.
Proprietor's sector								
Labor	9.1%	6.0%	5.2%	4.7%	4.3%	4.4%	4.5%	n.a.
Capital	0.3	0.6	1.0	1.4	2.2	1.2	1.2	n.a.
Proprietor's profit	12.7	9.9	10.3	9.0	8.3	8.7	8.6	n.a.
Total	22.0	16.6	16.6	15.1	14.8	14.4	14.3	n.a.
Government/ nonprofit sector								
Labor	15.2%	18.6%	19.3%	18.4%	19.4%	18.8%	18.4%	n.a.
Capital	0.0	0.0	0.0	0.0	0.0	0.0	0.0	n.a.
Total	15.2	18.6	19.3	18.4	19.4	18.8	18.4	n.a.
ADDENDUM Shares of corporate sector income*								
Labor	78.1%	80.3%	81.8%	82.3%	81.8%	78.7%	79.4%	79.5%
Capital	21.9	19.7	18.2	17.7	18.2	21.3	20.6	20.5
Total	100.0	100.0	100.0	100.0	100.0	100.0	100.0	100.0

* Does not include sole proprietorships, partnerships, and other private non-corporate business. The corporate sector, which includes both financial and non-financial corporations, accounted for 61% of national income in 1999.

Source: Authors' analysis of NIPA data.

An examination of factor (labor or capital) income shares, however, cannot fully determine whether there has been a redistribution of income from labor to capital, or vice versa. This type of analysis assumes that if factor shares remain constant then there has been no redistribution. Such an analysis is too simple for several reasons. First, in contrast to most topics in econom-

FIGURE 1L Income shares in the corporate sector, 1947-99

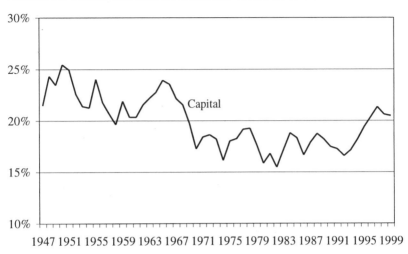

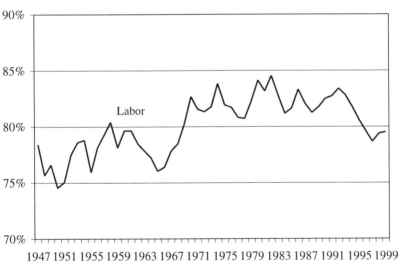

Source: Authors' analysis of NIPA data.

ics, such an analysis makes no comparison of actual outcomes relative to what one might expect given a model of what drives factor income shares. This means we need to look at the current period relative to earlier periods and examine variables that affect income shares. Several trends suggest that, other things being equal, capital's share might have been expected to decline and

TABLE 1.26 Profit rates and shares at business cycle peaks, 1959-99

Corporate sector	Business cycle peaks							
	1959	1969	1973	1979	1989	1997	1998	1999
Profit rates*								
Pre-tax	12.0%	12.5%	10.9%	9.2%	10.0%	12.4%	12.2%	12.1%
After-tax	6.4	6.8	6.0	4.9	5.7	8.4	8.3	8.1
Income shares								
Profit share**	21.9%	19.7%	18.2%	17.7%	18.2%	21.3%	20.6%	20.5%
Labor share	78.1	80.3	81.8	82.3	81.8	78.7	79.4	79.5
Total corporate income	100.0	100.0	100.0	100.0	100.0	100.0	100.0	100.0
Capital-output ratio	1.83	1.57	1.67	1.93	1.83	1.72	1.69	1.69

* "Profit" is all capital income. This measure, therefore, reflects the returns to capital per dollar of assets.
** "Profit share" is the ratio of capital income to all corporate income.

Source: Authors' analysis of NIPA and BEA data.

labor's share to rise over the last two decades. One reason for this expectation is that there has been a rapid growth in education levels and labor quality that would tend to raise labor's share. The primary trend, however, that would tend to lessen capital's share (and increase labor's share) is the rapid decline in the capital-output ratio since the early 1980s (see **Table 1.26**). For instance, in 1979 there was $1.93 of corporate capital assets (building and equipment) for every dollar of corporate income generated, a ratio that fell to $1.69 by 1999. This fall in the ratio of the capital stock to private-sector output implies that capital's role in production has lessened, suggesting that capital's income share might have been expected to fall in tandem.

Rather than fall, the share of capital income has risen, due to the rapid growth in the return to capital, before- and after-tax, starting in the late 1980s and continuing steadily through 1999 (Table 1.26 and **Figure 1M**). That is, the amount of before-tax profit received per dollar of assets (i.e., the capital stock) has grown to its highest levels since the mid-1960s, while the after-tax return on capital is also at historically high levels: since 1929, the only years of comparably high after-tax returns on capital were the booming years of the mid-1960s and the years at the end of World War II. The relationship between

RISING PROFIT RATES, CONSTANT PROFIT SHARE

There has been some confusion as to the difference between a rise in the *profit rate*, or return to capital (which has risen dramatically in the last 15 years), and a rise in *capital's share of income*, which has grown less. The following exercise is designed to show how these two rates differ and how each can rise or fall at its own pace.

Income is the sum of the returns to capital and labor. It can be expressed in the following equation:

$$(K * r) + (W * L) = Y$$

where K is the capital stock, r is the rate of return on capital (the profit rate), W is the average hourly wage, L is the number of labor hours, and Y is income.

Capital's share of income can be calculated by dividing capital income, K * r, by total income, Y. If the capital share remains constant, then the quantity (K * r)/Y doesn't change (nor does the labor share, (W * L)/Y). Capital's share, (K * r)/Y, can also be written as (K/Y) * r, where the quantity K/Y is equal to the ratio of the capital stock to total income. If K/Y falls, as it has over the last 10 years, then r can rise a great deal, even if capital's share remains constant.

For example, if K = $2,000, r = .05, and Y = $1,000, then the capital share of income would be 10%:

$$(K * r)/Y = (\$2,000 * .05)/\$1,000 = \$100/\$1,000 = .10$$

If the capital stock fell to $1,000 (so that K′= $1,000), the profit rate rose to 10% (so that r′ = .10), and income remained unchanged (Y′ = $1,000), the capital share would still be 10%:

$$(K′ * r′)/Y′ = (\$1,000*.10)/\$1,000 = \$100/\$1,000 = .10$$

In this example, the profit rate doubles, but the capital share of income remains the same because the capital stock has fallen 50%.

Over the last 15 years, the fall in the capital-output ratio has muted the rise in capital's share of income. From 1979 to 1997 the capital-output ratio fell 25% (from 2.23 to 1.68) while the "profit rate," or return to capital, rose from 6.4% to 10.4% (a 62.5% rise). The combined effect of these two trends was to raise capital's income share from 17.4% to 21.6%.

---

the return to capital and capital's share of income is illustrated in the accompanying box.

This growth in profitability has left less room for wage growth, or it might be considered the consequence of businesses successfully being able to restrain wage growth as sales and profits grew in recent years, even in years of low unemployment. If the after-tax return to capital in the 1997-99 period (8.3%) had been at the average of the postwar period (1946-99), or 6.3%, then hourly compensation would have been 4.3% higher in the corporate sector in 1999. This is a large loss, comparable or greater in size to the loss of wages for the

FIGURE 1M Pre- and post-tax return to capital, 1947-99

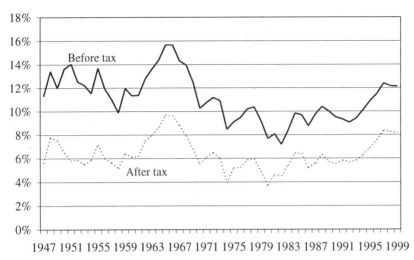

Source: Authors' analysis of NIPA and FRB data.

typical worker due to factors such as the shift to services, globalization, deunionization, or any of the other prominent causes of growing wage inequality discussed in Chapter 2.

The 'time crunch:' married-couple families with children working harder than ever

Family-earnings growth over the past few decades has not only been unequal, it has also come increasingly from greater work effort—from a rise in the number of earners per family and in the average weeks and weekly hours worked per earner. In this section we examine this phenomenon from the perspective of married-couple families with children. The sample also focuses exclusively on families headed by someone 25-54 years of age, thus excluding families whose time spent in the paid labor market would be affected by retirement or schooling. (The exception is the first figure in the section, which looks at all married-couple families with working wives.)

As the following set of tables reveals, these families have greatly increased their labor supply, giving rise to an important theme in living standards research: the 'time-crunch' experienced by many working families who are spending more time than ever at work. As will be detailed in Chapter 3, during the 1980s this increased work effort occurred at the same time as a fall in real hourly wages for men and for some groups of women. While this pattern changed in the 1990s as husbands' wages rebounded, the fact remains that over the 19-year period (from 1979 to 1998) increases in annual earnings were primarily achieved through more work rather than through higher hourly wages.

Much of this increased work effort has, of course, come from the contribution of wives joining the paid labor force and working outside the home. This trend also stems from the fact that historical conventions and gender discrimination, which formerly served to reduce female economic independence, have lessened, though they have not disappeared. These changes represent a positive social and economic evolution of women's integration into the labor force.

At the same time, for many families the increased work effort of their female members, who were either out of the paid labor force or working few hours, has been the main way to keep their incomes growing. ("Work" in this section refers exclusively to labor market work—of course, women have long been the major contributors to non-market work.) In this regard, families are clearly worse off if their primary means to obtain higher incomes is more hours of work rather than regular pay increases.

Figure 1N tracks the median percent of total family income contributed by wives' earnings for all families with working wives from 1970 to 1998. Table 1.6 emphasized the increase in the share of working wives; this figure complements that trend by showing the growing importance of wives' earnings since 1970. The median percent contribution of working wives, after remaining relatively constant over the 1970s, grew from around 26% of family income in 1979 to over 32% in 1992. Since then, the trend has been much flatter, but clearly, wives' contributions to family income have become increasingly important over time.

Table 1.27 shifts the focus to married-couple families with children, headed by someone age 25-54. The table shows the average incomes of these families by income fifth and measures working wives' contributions to these incomes. The percent changes in the bottom panel simulate the effect on average family income for the quintile if wives' earnings had not grown from the earlier year of comparison. For example, to arrive at the percent changes in the first row of the bottom panel, we subtracted the 1979-89 growth in wives' earnings from the actual 1989 income levels and calculated the change in income between this lower simulated value for 1989 and the actual value for 1979.

The top section of the table shows that incomes of low-income prime-age families fell by 5.8% during the 1980s. The bottom section reveals, however, that in the absence of wives' earnings, the decline would have been a much

FIGURE 1N Contribution of wives' earnings to family income, 1970-98

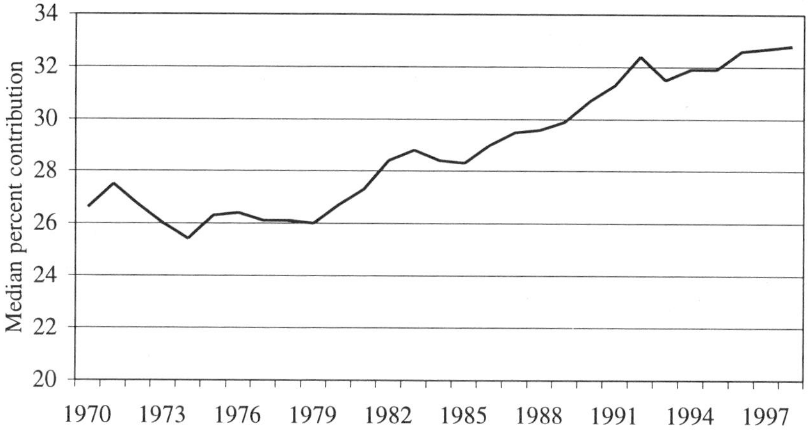

Source: Hayghe (1993) and unpublished updates.

TABLE 1.27 Average income, married-couple families with children, head of household age 25-54, 1979-98 (1998 dollars)

	First fifth	Second fifth	Middle fifth	Fourth fifth	Top fifth	Average
1979	$22,220	$39,569	$51,670	$65,935	$109,643	$57,820
1989	20,922	39,389	53,703	71,355	118,447	60,775
1998	21,936	42,159	58,659	79,624	148,413	70,160
1979-89	-5.8%	-0.5%	3.9%	8.2%	8.0%	5.1%
1989-98	4.8	7.0	9.2	11.6	25.3	15.4
1979-98	-1.3	6.5	13.5	20.8	35.4	21.3
Without increased wives earnings						
1979-89	-10.4%	-7.4%	-4.3%	0.1%	-0.3%	-2.8%
1989-98	2.8	1.9	3.6	4.6	15.5	8.3
1979-98	-7.8	-5.6	-0.7	5.1	16.4	5.9

Source: Authors' analysis of March CPS data.

steeper 10.4%. For middle-income families, incomes would have fallen 4.3% were it not for wives' contributions; instead, they grew 3.9%. Gains were significantly higher across the income scale over the 1990s, with wives' earnings continuing to play a key role. As shown in a later table, husband's earnings also grew in real terms over this period, and thus both partners contributed to family income growth. Note, for example, that on average, even if wives' earnings had failed to grow in the 1990s, average income still would have increased by 8.3%, thanks in part to the increase in husband's earnings over the period (other, non-labor income sources also played a role).

Over the full period, wives' earnings made a notable difference in the growth of family incomes. Low-income families ended the period 1.3% less well-off than in 1979, but in the absence of wives' earnings the average income of the bottom fifth would have been 7.8%. Middle-income families would have seen no income gain had wives' earnings not increased; instead, the average income of middle-fifth families grew 13.5%. And the growth of income for married-couple families in the top fifth would have been less than half of its actual value in the absence of wives' contributions.

These additions to income came from more weeks and hours worked, along with significant wage growth for working wives, particularly in the 1990s. In the following tables, we examine these factors in some detail.

Table 1.28 shows the average annual weeks worked, summed across the family, by income fifth. As might be expected, particularly among prime-age families who depend primarily on earnings, weeks worked in any given year increase with income level. The average family added over 10 weeks of work during the 29-year period covered by the table, but there was variation among the income fifths and over different time periods. The number of weeks worked varied slightly among the lowest- and highest-income workers (as noted earlier, there is a "ceiling effect" in this type of analysis, i.e., family members cannot work more than full year). Families in the middle three-fifths added between 5.0 and 8.8 weeks per year during the 1970s.

The 1980s, the decade when real wage decline was most pervasive, saw the most significant growth in weeks worked. The average family added 3.9 weeks over the period, with the largest percentage gains among lower-income families. Families in the bottom 60% increased their average weeks by about 10%. Middle-income families added 8.9 weeks, more than that of any other income fifth.

The increase in weeks worked continued to grow in the 1990s, but at a slower rate than in the 1980s. Middle-income families increased their average weeks by 4.9% (4.5 weeks), while most other families experienced slightly lower percent increases. It is too soon to tell whether this deceleration reflects a pause

TABLE 1.28 Average weeks worked per year by income quintile, 1969-98, married-couple families with children, head of household age 25-54

Year	First fifth	Second fifth	Middle fifth	Fourth fifth	Top fifth	Average
1969	60.5	68.1	78.2	87.9	107.2	80.4
1979	58.9	75.4	83.2	96.7	109.2	84.7
1989	64.5	83.5	92.1	98.3	104.6	88.6
1998	66.5	87.3	96.6	102.3	102.9	91.1
Weeks added						
1969-79	-1.6	7.3	5.0	8.8	2.0	4.2
1979-89	5.6	8.1	8.9	1.7	-4.6	3.9
1989-98	1.9	3.8	4.5	3.9	-1.6	2.5
1969-98	5.9	19.2	18.4	14.4	-4.3	10.7
Percent change						
1969-79	-2.7%	10.7%	6.4%	10.0%	1.8%	5.3%
1979-89	9.6	10.8	10.6	1.7	-4.2	4.6
1989-98	3.0	4.5	4.9	4.0	-1.5	2.8
1969-98	9.8	28.1	23.5	16.4	-4.0	13.3

Source: Authors' analysis of March CPS data.

in a longer-term trend or a real shift in the work patterns of families. The slowing trend may reflect a "topping out" of weeks worked by over-burdened families, or possibly a cutting back of work caused by the wage and income gains of the latter part of the 1990s. At any rate, the increase in weeks worked over the full period is significant, and it is by no means concentrated among the most wealthy. Note that by 1998, the number of weeks worked by the middle and fourth fifths were much closer to those worked by the highest-income families than in 1969.

Another way to think about these results is to compare them to the total weeks per year that married parents can spend either in or out of the labor market, i.e., 104 (52 weeks for each parent). Thirty years ago, middle-income parents spent three-quarters of their weeks in the labor market (78.2/104; of course, some of these weeks represent part-time work). By 1998, that share had increased to 92%. Clearly, the share of their time that parents are spending in the labor market has expanded.

Table 1.29 shows annual hours for these same families (hours data are not

TABLE 1.29 Average annual hours worked per year by income quintile, 1979-98, married-couple families with children, head of household age 25-54

	First fifth	Second fifth	Middle fifth	Fourth fifth	Top fifth	Average
All						
1979	2,354	3,013	3,272	3,757	4,256	3,331
1989	2,553	3,330	3,639	3,914	4,231	3,534
1998	2,612	3,512	3,885	4,142	4,271	3,685
1979-89	8.5%	10.5%	11.2%	4.2%	-0.6%	6.1%
1989-98	2.3	5.5	6.8	5.8	1.0	4.3
1979-98	11.0	16.6	18.7	10.3	0.4	10.6
Head of family *high school or less*						
1979	2,349	3,114	3,387	4,031	4,865	3,325
1989	2,517	3,397	3,801	4,159	4,889	3,451
1998	2,599	3,623	4,156	4,546	4,917	3,601
1979-89	7.1%	9.1%	12.2%	3.2%	0.5%	3.8%
1989-98	3.3	6.6	9.3	9.3	0.6	4.3
1979-98	10.6	16.3	22.7	12.8	1.1	8.3
Head of family *some college or more*						
1979	2,366	2,835	3,133	3,489	3,980	3,337
1989	2,652	3,228	3,481	3,768	4,071	3,610
1998	2,639	3,394	3,712	3,976	4,169	3,741
1979-89	12.1%	13.9%	11.1%	8.0%	2.3%	8.2%
1989-98	-0.5	5.1	6.6	5.5	2.4	3.6
1979-98	11.6	19.7	18.5	13.9	4.8	12.1

Source: Authors' analysis of March CPS data.

available for 1969), again by income fifth. As would be expected, the pattern for hours is similar to that of weeks, with smaller increases in the 1990s relative to the 1980s. While the number of hours worked by married couples in the lowest fifth is consistently lower than those of better-off fifths, their increase in hours over the 1980s—11%—was greater than that of higher-income families. Middle-income families experienced the greatest percent growth of hours in both periods: 11.2% over the 1980s and 6.8% in the 1990s. Combining the information from the previous table on weeks with these data on hours reveals that middle-income families have added 12.5 weeks (over three months) and 613 hours since 1979.

Some critics have argued that the increase in inequality has been generated simply by those with higher incomes working harder, while other, less well-off families did not increase their work effort. Clearly, these weeks and hours data belie this claim. The increases in hours and weeks cannot be solely claimed by those at the top; they are spread throughout the income distribution.

The next two sections examine a similar sample of families (married couples with children, headed by someone aged 18-54; we expand the age range here to generate a larger sample), but do so separately for those families headed by someone with a high school education or less and those headed by someone with a college education or more. The income cutoffs are the same as for the income fifths in the top section. Thus, the definitions of low, middle, and high income are the same in each section. This means that, unlike the top section, there is no longer 20% in each fifth. In fact, as would be expected given their higher income levels, the families headed by someone with at least some college are more likely to be in the top income brackets and vice versa. In 1989, for example, 31% of families headed by someone with a high school education or less were in the bottom fifth, compared to 10% of those with at least some college. In the top fifth, the shares were reversed, at 8% (high school) and 31% (college), respectively.

In the spirit of the critique just mentioned, much discussion of labor market trends has stressed the increase in demand for more highly educated workers in the new economy, suggesting that we should see significantly larger increases in hours worked among the "some college or more" group. While this was the case on average in the 1980s, it was not the case for middle-income families in that time period, nor was it the case in general over the 1990s. In fact, increases in time spent at work have occurred among both groups shown in the table.

Annual hours worked by middle-income families headed by those with at most a high school degree grew by 12.2%, or 414 hours, from 1979 to 1989. Their hours grew another 9.3% in the 1990s so that, over the full period, their hours increased by 22.7%, well over the average increase of 8.3% and above the full-period increase of 18.5% by middle-income families headed by someone with at least some college. As shown in **Figure 10**, in both 1979 and 1998 the hours worked by these families surpassed those of families headed by someone with at least some college in the same income bracket, and the difference grew larger over time, amounting to 444 hours in 1998. Making the same type of comparison for the next highest fifth (the fourth fifth) shows comparable growth in hours by those families headed by at most a high school graduate compared to the similar group with some college (12.8% vs. 13.9% from 1979 to 1998).

On the low end of the income scale, however, hours clearly increased more for families headed by more highly educated persons during the 1980s. But this

FIGURE 10 Average family work hours, middle-income, married-couple families with children, 1979 and 1998, by education level

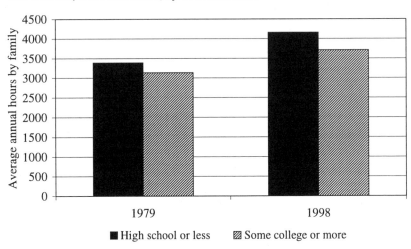

Source: Authors' analysis of March CPS data.

trend reversed in the 1990s, and the full period increases were similar. There has also been little growth among the top income fifth in both education groups, but this is again due to the fact that these families were already hitting the labor supply "ceiling," i.e., their hours already sum to more than full-time, full-year work for two persons, especially for the group headed by someone with a high school degree or less, whose hours far surpassed those in the top fifth of the more highly educated group. In these families, it is likely that members other than the spouses were contributing hours as well.

Thus, there is no evidence of broad-based decline in labor market activity among families with either lower levels of income or fewer years of education. These families continue to work harder than ever and, in some cases, have experienced more growth in hours worked than more highly educated families.

Table 1.30 examines hours of work by race and ethnicity. We continue to look at prime-age, married-couple families with children, and, as above, we maintain the same income fifth cutoffs for all families in each panel. Thus, the income cutoffs for African Americans in the top section, for example, do not divide black families into five equal groups; they are the same cutoffs used for all families in the top section of the previous table. In fact, in 1998, 25% of black families were in the lowest fifth of the overall distribution, and 14%

TABLE 1.30 Average annual hours worked by income quintile, 1979-98, married-couple families with children, household head age 18-54, by race of household head

	First fifth	Second fifth	Middle fifth	Fourth fifth	Top fifth	Average
Black						
1979	2,078	3,147	3,636	3,964	4,708	3,227
1989	2,409	3,509	3,944	4,239	4,780	3,556
1998	2,682	3,698	4,278	4,371	4,785	3,843
1979-89	15.9%	11.5%	8.5%	6.9%	1.5%	10.2%
1989-98	11.3	5.4	8.5	3.1	0.1	8.1
1979-98	29.0	17.5	17.6	10.3	1.6	19.1
Hispanic						
1979	2,178	3,160	3,385	4,087	4,563	3,082
1989	2,385	3,559	3,916	4,271	4,898	3,302
1998	2,574	3,791	4,050	4,590	4,896	3,415
1979-89	9.5%	12.6%	15.7%	4.5%	7.3%	7.1%
1989-98	7.9	6.5	3.4	7.5	0.0	3.4
1979-98	18.2	20.0	19.6	12.3	7.3	10.8
White						
1979	2,320	2,925	3,203	3,655	4,198	3,302
1989	2,552	3,266	3,553	3,852	4,163	3,529
1998	2,543	3,376	3,789	4,074	4,222	3,689
1979-89	10.0%	11.7%	10.9%	5.4%	-0.8%	6.9%
1989-98	-0.4	3.4	6.6	5.8	1.4	4.5
1979-98	9.6	15.4	18.3	11.5	0.6	11.7

Source: Authors' analysis of March CPS data.

were in the top fifth; for white families, the comparable shares were 15% and 23%. Here again, we structure the analysis this way to compare the work effort of middle- and low-income families using consistent income definitions across racial groups.

Both the levels and the trends reveal interesting patterns. Hours of work have grown especially quickly among black families, particularly among those in the lowest fifth. In fact, average work effort of African American married-couple families with children grew more than that of either whites or Hispanics in both the 1980s and the 1990s. Although they started out the period working fewer hours, by 1998 low-income black families worked more hours than either white or Hispanic families.

Figure 1P focuses on middle-income families with children, showing higher levels of hours worked by African American families relative to both whites and Hispanics in 1979 and 1998. By the end of the period, these families were working 489 more hours than whites and 228 more hours than Hispanics. Taking the first comparison, this means that an average middle-income black family with children needed over 12 more weeks of work than the average white family in order to reach the middle-income ranks. These increased work hours for blacks may also help to partially explain the relative gains of black families in the 1990s (see Figure 1E).

High-income minority families consistently had hours of work above 4,500, suggesting full-time work by both parents with contributions by other family members as well. Thus, one message from this table is that, due to their lower wage levels, minority families have to put in extremely long hours relative to whites to make it to the top of the overall income distribution. By 1998, the highest-income minority families were working at least 500 hours more per year than white families.

Across education and racial groups, and across the income scale, hours spent in the labor market have clearly increased for prime-age, married-couple families with children. By 1998, the average middle-income family was spending 87 weeks and 3,600 hours at work, compared to 75 weeks and 3,041 hours in 1979. Clearly, the time crunch is a real phenomenon, and it is one experienced not just by the elite lawyers, money managers, or "knowledge workers" of the new economy but by families working harder to keep their living standards rising.

Where have these extra hours come from? As shown in **Table 1.31** they came mostly from working wives and mostly during the 1980s. Between 1979 and 1989, wives' hours in the paid labor market increased on average by 28.7%, an increase of 249 hours, compared to an average 2.2% increase for husbands (who were, for the most part, already working full year). Middle- and lower-income wives experienced above-average growth rates. The growth in hours for middle-income wives over the 1980s was 36.6% (324 hours, or eight more weeks of full-time work); that of wives in the lowest fifth was 35.2% (though from a relatively low base of 507 annual hours in 1979).

Hours growth decelerated quite sharply in the 1990s, particularly for families in the lowest fifth. It is difficult to account for this sharp deceleration—it may stem from the sharp reversal of real wages (shown below) for wives in the lowest fifth, or perhaps from the relatively large increase in the growth of hours worked by husbands in the income group. Nevertheless, hours continued to grow for wives in other quintiles, and, even with the deceleration, the annual hours

FIGURE 1P Average family work hours, by race/ethnicity, 1979 and 1998, middle-income, married-couple families with children

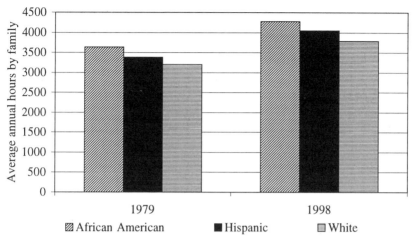

Source: Authors' analysis of March CPS data.

TABLE 1.31 Hours of work by husbands and wives, couples with children, 1979-98, head of household age 25-54

	First fifth	Second fifth	Middle fifth	Fourth fifth	Top fifth	Average
Husbands						
1979	1,743	2,098	2,172	2,232	2,355	2,120
1989	1,754	2,158	2,218	2,285	2,416	2,167
1998	1,820	2,182	2,269	2,316	2,448	2,205
1979-89	0.7%	2.9%	2.1%	2.4%	2.6%	2.2%
1989-98	3.8	1.1	2.3	1.3	1.3	1.8
1979-98	4.5	4.0	4.5	3.7	3.9	4.0
Wives						
1979	507	736	884	1,094	1,086	870
1989	686	1,008	1,208	1,319	1,340	1,119
1998	684	1,169	1,363	1,507	1,436	1,235
1979-89	35.2%	36.9%	36.6%	20.6%	23.3%	28.7%
1989-98	-0.3	16.0	12.8	14.3	7.1	10.4
1979-98	34.8	58.8	54.2	37.8	32.2	42.0

Source: Authors' analysis of March CPS data.

worked by wives in the middle three fifths grew between 12.8% and 16.0%. By 1998, wives' hours in the paid labor force had grown by 42%, on average, since 1979, and by more than half for women in the second and third income fifths. Middle-income wives with children added 479 hours over this 19-year period, close to three months of full-time work. Recall that this analysis focuses exclusively on families with children; in that light, these added work hours come at the expense of time for family activities.

Table 1.32 shows that husbands' and wives' real wage trends help to explain the movements in hours worked. The table provides hourly inflation-adjusted wage data by income fifth for husbands and wives in prime-age families with children (these wage levels are calculated by dividing annual earnings by annual hours—see table note for how this method differs from that used throughout the most of the book). Over the 1980s, when weeks and hours grew the most, husbands' wages fell the fastest, by 14.2% for husbands in the bottom fifth to 1.7% for those in the fourth income quintile; only husbands in the top fifth experienced positive real wage growth. Outside of the lowest income group, however, wives' earnings grew significantly over the 1980s, by 17.1% on average. The wages of middle-income wives grew by 11.0%, while those of higher-income wives grew much faster. Among married-couple families in the fourth quintile, for example, while average husbands' wages fell slightly over the 1980s, those of wives in this income fifth grew just under 20%. These very divergent patterns of growth between men and women suggest a plausible explanation for the increase in hours and weeks worked. Wives' extra earnings were needed in the 1980s to make up the ground lost by falling husbands' wages.

The 1990s saw a continuation of the same wage patterns for wives, with the addition of significant wage gains for those in the lowest income fifth (recall that wages among families in this group fell over the 1980s). For all but the middle fifth, husbands' wages reversed course, and grew slightly over the 1990s. In tandem with the "ceiling effect"—working parents with children have a limit on how much time they can devote to paid work—these trends may partially explain the fairly sharp deceleration of hours growth over the 1990s. By 1989, the two parents in an average middle-income family with children were working 3,426 hours (summing the average hours of wives' and husbands' hours from Table 1.31). This is full-year work for one parent (husbands) and roughly two-thirds of a year's work for the other. It is possibly the case that continued wage gains for wives in the 1990s, the generalized reversal of wage losses of husbands, and the fact that these families were already "topped-out" in terms of the amount of time they could spend at work played a role in slowing the growth of hours in the 1990s.

But despite higher wives' earnings, families continue to work more than ever. Combining the annual hours of husbands and wives, middle-income spouses

TABLE 1.32 Hourly earnings (1998 dollars) by husbands and wives, couples with children, 1979-98, head of household age 25-54

	First fifth	Second fifth	Middle fifth	Fourth fifth	Top fifth	Average
Husbands						
1979	$9.32	$14.83	$18.28	$21.35	$30.35	$19.46
1989	7.99	12.99	16.93	21.00	32.07	18.96
1998	8.19	13.04	16.89	21.51	41.04	20.97
1979-89	-14.2%	-12.4%	-7.4%	-1.7%	5.7%	-2.6%
1989-98	2.5	0.4	-0.2	2.4	28.0	10.6
1979-98	-12.1	-12.1	-7.6	0.7	35.2	7.7
Wives						
1979	$5.80	$7.63	$9.36	$11.00	$14.16	$10.37
1989	5.78	8.31	10.40	13.18	18.32	12.14
1998	6.43	8.91	11.45	14.83	25.17	14.53
1979-89	-0.4%	8.9%	11.0%	19.8%	29.4%	17.1%
1989-98	11.3	7.2	10.1	12.6	37.3	19.6
1979-98	10.9	16.7	22.3	34.9	77.8	40.1

Source: Authors' analysis of March CPS data.

worked 577 more hours in 1998 than in 1979, an added 14.4 weeks of full-time work. Most importantly, were if not for this added effort, the average income of the bottom 60% of prime-age, married-couple families with children would have been lower in 1998 than it was in 1979. These trends in incomes, weeks, hours, and wages go a long way toward explaining the stress faced by working families with children in the "new economy."

Have the growing earnings of wives contributed to the growth of income inequality? The notion that the growth of "two-earner" families has contributed to growing inequality is intuitively plausible if one thinks that (1) there has been a growth of high-wage employed women marrying high-wage men, and (2) the increase in the hours worked and earnings of these women has been greater than that of their lower-income counterparts. It is true, in fact, that wives in higher-income families earn more than those in other families and that their hourly wages have grown the quickest (Table 1.32). However, the fastest growth in work hours has been among the wives in the bottom three-fifths (Table 1.31). The data discussed so far, however, indirectly relate only to whether the pattern of growth of wives' earnings led to greater inequality and do not address whether inequality would be higher or lower without any earnings from wives. The following table addresses this omission.

The data in **Table 1.33** allow a direct examination of the effect of wives' earnings on income inequality of prime-age, married-couple families from 1979 to 1998 and on the growth of inequality over that period. The numbers in the table are the shares of total income going to each income group, calculated with and without wives earnings (note that, in this analysis, the top fifth is broken down into the 80-95th percentile and the top 5%). The difference between shares calculated in this manner reveals the contribution of wives' earnings to inequality. For example, in 1979, wives' earnings led to a more equal distribution of income, since without wives' earnings the lowest fifth would have had a 6.9% share of total income instead of the 7.7% share it had with wives' earnings. Overall in 1979, wives' earnings increased the income shares of the bottom four-fifths and decreased the share of income of the top fifth by 1.9 percentage points. In 1989, wives' earnings had a larger effect on raising the income shares of the lowest 80% of families and on lessening the income share of the top fifth, which fell by 2.7 points, with the largest share decline (1.9 percentage points) in the top 5%. This pattern continued in 1998, as the size of wives' contributions to the income shares of the bottom 80% continued to grow while that of the top fifth fell further.

The bottom section ("changes in income shares") reveals that between 1979 and 1989 the income shares of the bottom 60% of prime-age, married-couple families with children fell, with the largest declines among the bottom two-fifths. In the absence of wives' earnings, however, income shares would have been slightly (0.2 points) lower in the first fifth and 0.3 points lower in the second fifth. Conversely, they would have been 0.8 points higher in the top fifth. This pattern shows that the shifts in wives' hours and wages were equalizing over the 1979-89 period.

In the latter period—1989-98—only the top 20% gained income share, with fairly uniform losses among the bottom 80% of families. Note, however, that wives' earnings had little effect in the bottom two fifths and were equalizing in the middle and fourth fifths. Thus, the slowdown in wives' hours had little impact on inequality in the 1990s. Among the top 20%, there is evidence that the pattern of wives' earnings dampened the growth of income share, from an increase of 4.0 points without wives' earnings to an actual increase of 3.3 points.

The last panel shows that, over the entire period (1979-98), wives' contributions to family income were equalizing. Wives' work increased the income share of the bottom 80% by 1.4 percentage points, and thus lowered the share going to the top fifth by the same amount.

In sum, the results from this section have both positive and negative impli-

TABLE 1.33 Effect of wives' earnings on income shares of prime-age, married-couple families with children

	Lowest fifth	Second fifth	Middle fifth	Fourth fifth	Top fifth	80-95%	Top 5%
Family income shares							
1979							
Actual	7.7%	13.7%	17.9%	22.8%	37.9%	23.5%	14.4%
Without wives' earnings	6.9	13.2	17.5	22.6	39.9	24.0	15.8
Effect of wives' earning	0.7	0.5	0.4	0.3	-1.9	-0.5	-1.4
1989							
Actual	6.9%	12.9%	17.7%	23.5%	39.0%	25.1%	13.9%
Without wives' earnings	6.0	12.1	17.0	23.1	41.7	25.9	15.8
Effect of wives' earning	0.9	0.8	0.7	0.3	-2.7	-0.8	-1.9
1998							
Actual	6.3%	12.0%	16.7%	22.7%	42.3%	24.9%	17.4%
Without wives' earnings	5.5	11.1	15.7	22.0	45.7	25.9	19.8
Effect of wives' earning	0.8	0.9	1.0	0.7	-3.4	-0.9	-2.4
Changes in income shares							
1979-89							
Actual	-0.8	-0.8	-0.2	0.7	1.1	1.6	-0.5
Without wives' earnings	-1.0	-1.1	-0.4	0.6	1.9	1.9	0.0
Effect of wives' earning	0.2	0.3	0.2	0.1	-0.8	-0.3	-0.5
1989-98							
Actual	-0.6	-0.9	-1.0	-0.8	3.3	-0.2	3.5
Without wives' earnings	-0.5	-1.0	-1.3	-1.1	4.0	0.0	4.0
Effect of wives' earning	-0.1	0.1	0.4	0.3	-0.6	-0.1	-0.5
1979-98							
Actual	-1.4	-1.7	-1.2	-0.1	4.4	1.4	3.0
Without wives' earnings	-1.5	-2.1	-1.8	-0.5	5.8	1.8	4.0
Effect of wives' earning	0.1	0.4	0.6	0.4	-1.4	-0.4	-1.0

Source: Authors' analysis of March CPS data.

cations. On the plus side, there is clear evidence of increased economic progress for female workers. Since 1979, wives have increased their hours of market work; for most wives, wages have also risen. To a large extent, these increases have offset widespread declines in their husbands' earnings. Furthermore, the pattern of these changes in wives' contributions to family income have been equalizing, i.e., the income distribution for prime-age, married-couple families would have been more skewed toward the wealthy in the absence of wives' increased contributions.

On the negative side, the evidence also shows that, over the long term, families have been working longer for less. Particularly in the 1980s, family work hours needed to increase sharply to compensate for negative male wage trends, which we explore in detail in Chapter 2. The increase in hours slowed in the 1990s, particularly for wives, and this may in part represent a response to the reversal of male wage losses and continued gains for wives. But this possibility reminds us that more work is a self-limiting strategy, and the average middle-income, married-couple family with children is already working a combined 87 weeks and 3,600 hours per year. If the pattern of wage growth were to return to that of the 1980s, families would be hard pressed to further increase their time spent in the labor force.

Conclusion

One of the most important developments regarding contemporary income trends is the slow and unequal growth that has prevailed since the mid-1970s. Between 1947 and 1979, median family income grew 2.4% per year; since then, it has grown at 0.5% annually. Moreover, growth has been much more unequal over the past two decades, particularly in the 1980s, when rapid income growth among upper-income families and stagnant or falling incomes for the bottom 60% of families led to sharp increases in inequality. Inequality has continued to grow in the 1990s, though its pace has decelerated.

These results clearly do not stem from a lack of effort on the part of working families. In fact, our focus on married-couple families with children reveals that they are spending more time than ever in the paid labor market. And it is not just the economic elites of the new economy that are driving this result: there is evidence of more work across all education and racial groups.

The other important development revealed above is the dual nature of income trends in the 1990s, with the latter half of the decade representing one of the most positive and broad-based growth periods since the slowing of income growth in the mid-1970s. Clearly, a number of positive labor market developments, especially full employment and faster productivity growth, have made a positive contribution to the incomes of working families.

What does the future hold? For one, the strategy of working more to keep a family's living standards rising is self-limiting, and families may be approaching the limit. While hours and weeks worked by most families continued to grow in the 1990s, the rate of increase slowed over prior years. Part of this deceleration is attributable to the increase in hourly wages over the latter part of the decade, enabling families to raise their incomes without adding more hours. But, should the tight labor market unwind and wages reverse course, it is reasonable to speculate that many families will have difficulty working too many more hours. They may already be bumping up against the ceiling of available time to spend at work.

Income inequality is a continuing concern. While the positive economic conditions that prevailed over the mid- to late 1990s have slowed the growth of inequality, as of 1999 these conditions—especially the tight labor market—have not reversed inequality's two-decade climb. To do so unquestionably calls for sustaining the gains of the late 1990s and, after the next recession, making sure we return to full employment as quickly as possible.

The remainder of this book elaborates on the themes established in this chapter. The next two chapters examine the labor-market trends (wages and employment) that are at the heart of the growth in inequality and sluggish income growth. Chapters 4 and 5 broaden the income analysis by examining trends in wealth and poverty. Chapter 6 examines the impact of wage and income trends from a regional perspective, and Chapter 7 compares trends in the United States to those in other advanced countries.

Wages: turnaround in the late 1990s

Because wages and salaries make up roughly three-fourths of total family income (the proportion is even higher among the broad middle class), wage trends are the primary determinant of income growth and income inequality trends. This chapter examines and explains the wage growth and wage inequality of the last few decades.

The wage story of the past quarter century has two predominant themes. First, from the early-1970s to 1995, wages were stagnant overall, and median wages fell. After 1995 wages changed course, rising strongly in response to the persistent low unemployment and faster productivity growth of recent years. Second, in the 1980s wage inequality widened dramatically and, coupled with stagnant average wages, brought about a widespread erosion of real wages. Wage inequality continued its growth in the 1990s but took a different shape: a continued growth in the wage gap between top and middle earners but a shrinking wage gap between middle and low earners. Understanding and explaining these trends is the task of this chapter.

The trends in average wage growth—the slowdown in the 1970s and the speed-up in the mid-1990s—can be attributed to corresponding changes in productivity growth. As reviewed in the Introduction, the recent acceleration of productivity growth is not yet fully understood, but it probably relates to both a surge in computer investment driven by technological change and the fast growth in demand while at low unemployment. It is noteworthy that average wage (and average compensation) growth has significantly lagged behind productivity growth throughout the entire 1973-99 period.

Explaining the shifts in wage inequality requires attention to several factors that affect low-, middle-, and high-wage workers differently. The experience of the late 1990s should remind us of the great extent to which low unemployment benefits workers, especially low-wage earners. Correspondingly, the high levels of unemployment in the early and mid-1980s disempowered wage earners and provided the context in which other forces—specifically, a weakening of labor market institutions and globalization—could drive up wage inequality. Significant shifts in the labor market, such as the severe drop in the minimum wage and deunionization, can explain one-third of the growing wage inequality in the 1980s. Similarly, the increasing globalization of the economy—immigration, trade, and capital mobility—and the employment shift toward lower-paying service industries (such as retail trade) and away from manufacturing can explain, in combination, another third of the total growth in wage inequality.

The shape of wage inequality shifted in the late 1980s as the wage gap at the bottom—i.e., the 50/10 gap between workers at the 50th percentile and those at the 10th—began to decline; by 1999 this dimension of wage inequality had returned to its level of the early 1970s. The greatest increase in wage inequality at the bottom occurred among women and corresponds to the fall in the minimum wage over the 1980s, the high unemployment of the early 1980s, and the expansion of retail jobs. The positive trend in the wage gap over the 1990s owes much to the rise in the minimum wage, the low unemployment, and the slight, relative contraction in low-paying retail jobs in the late 1990s. The wage gap at the top—the 90/50 gap between high- and middle-wage earners—continued its steady growth in the 1990s but at a somewhat slower pace than in the 1980s. The continuing influence of globalization, deunionization, and the shift to lower-paying service industries ("industry shifts") can explain the continued 1990s growth of wage inequality at the top. Among women, though, industry shifts actually became "equalizing" in the recent recovery as retail trade jobs became relatively less important.

There is a popular notion that the growth of wage inequality reflects primarily a technology-driven increase in demand for "educated" or "skilled" workers. Yet we find that the overall impact of technology on the wage and employment structure was no greater in the 1980s or 1990s than in the 1970s. Moreover, skill demand and technology have little relationship to the growth of wage inequality within the same group (i.e., workers with similar levels of experience and education), which was responsible for half of the overall growth of wage inequality in the 1980s and 1990s. Technology has been and continues to be an important force, but there was no "technology shock" in the 1980s or 1990s, and no ensuing demand for "skill," that was not satisfied by the continuing expansion of the educational attainment of the workforce.

The conventional story about technology leading to increased demand for skills and the erosion of wages among the less-skilled does not readily explain the pattern of growth in wage inequality. In particular, the 1990s are seen as a period of rapid technological change, yet during that decade wage inequality diminished at the bottom. Similarly, education differentials grew slowly among men during most of the 1990s, a trend incompatible with rapid technological change driving up demand for skills. Moreover, it was the growth of wage inequality among workers of similar education and experience, not easily linked to technology, that kept male wage inequality at the top growing in the 1990s.

Moreover, the high-tech sector has not been a wage leader. The wage premium for so-called information technology (IT) workers grew hardly at all in the 1990s, and it fell among women. The wages offered college graduates with computer science degrees fell from the mid-1980s to the mid-1990s, and the upturn in their wage offers in the late 1990s paralleled higher offers to all college graduates, particularly business majors. These trends do not easily fit with a story in which information technology transforms the workplace so that those equipped to participate enjoy prosperity while those lacking skills lag behind.

Despite the strong wage improvements in the late 1990s, it was not until 1999 that the wage level for middle-wage workers (the median hourly wage) returned to its 1979 level. Yet productivity was 37.7% higher in 1999 than in 1979. One reason for this divergence is increased corporate profitability (discussed in Chapter 1), which drove a wedge between productivity and compensation growth.

Another noteworthy trend is the decline in benefits in the late 1990s. Although health insurance coverage increased, after falling for more than a decade, employer costs for health insurance dropped in recent years. Employer pension contributions also fell.

As wages fell for the typical worker, corporate pay soared. From 1989 to 1999, the wage of the typical (i.e., median) chief executive officer grew 62.7%. In 1965 CEOs made 20.3 times more than a typical worker; this ratio had risen to 55.9 by 1989 and to 106.9 by 1999. U.S. CEOs make about two-and-half times as much as their counterparts abroad.

The turnaround of the late 1990s has been a boon for workers' wages and incomes, but will these trends continue? If productivity growth continues to be strong (say, 0.5 to 1.0 percentage points better than in the 1979-95 period), even if not as strong as in recent years, then real wages may continue to expand for most of the workforce. A more rapid shift to more-skilled jobs than has already occurred seems unlikely, but continuing pressures from globalization and deunionization, a rise in unemployment, or a fall in the real value of the minimum wage could weaken wages and exacerbate inequality.

The chapter's wage analysis proceeds in the following fashion: The first half of the chapter documents changes in the various dimensions of the wage structure, i.e., changes in average wages and compensation and changes by occupation, gender, wage level, education level, age, and race and ethnicity. These shifts in the various dimensions of wage inequality are then assessed and explained by focusing on particular factors such as industry shifts, deunionization, the value of the minimum wage, globalization and immigration, and technology. The chapter ends with an assessment of the future.

Contrasting hours and hourly wage growth

To understand changes in wage trends, it is important to distinguish between trends in annual, weekly, and hourly wages. Trends in annual wages, for instance, are driven by changes in both hourly wages and the amount of time spent working (weeks worked per year and hours worked per week). Likewise, weekly wage trends reflect changes in hourly pay and weekly hours. In this chapter we focus on the hourly pay levels of the workforce and its sub-groups. We do this to be able to distinguish changes in earnings resulting from more (or less) work rather than more (or less) pay. Also, the hourly wage can be said to represent the "true" price of labor (exclusive of benefits, which we analyze separately). Chapter 3 goes on to address employment, unemployment, underemployment, and other issues related to changes in work time and opportunities.

Table 2.1 illustrates the importance of distinguishing between annual, weekly, and hourly wage trends. The annual wage and salary of the average worker in inflation-adjusted terms grew twice as fast as the average hourly wage in each of the last two decades. Thus, hourly wages grew 0.4% each year over both the 1979-89 and 1989-98 periods. Yet annual wages grew at 0.8% or 0.9%, reflecting the hourly wage growth and the 0.4% growth in annual hours worked. The most remarkable story in Table 2.1, however, is the sharp acceleration in hourly wage growth (to 1.9%) in the 1995-98 period relative to the negative growth (-0.4%) of the earlier part of the business cycle from 1989 to 1995 and the slow growth (0.4%) of the prior business cycle of 1979-89. This pickup in wage growth, along with an even stronger pickup of wage growth at the bottom end of the wage scale (detailed below), is the main factor behind the better family income growth of the late 1990s, discussed in Chapter 1. This strong post-1995 wage growth is a prominent theme of our discussion throughout this chapter.

The main reason for the faster wage growth in the late 1990s—faster productivity growth—is also shown in Table 2.1. Productivity growth in 1996 and later years (2.4% annual growth from 1995 to 1998) was substantially higher than the productivity growth earlier in the business cycle (1.5% in 1989-95) or

TABLE 2.1 Trends in average wages and average hours, 1967-98 (1999 dollars)

Year	Productivity per hour (1992=100)	Wage levels			Hours worked		
		Annual wages	Weekly wages	Hourly wages	Annual hours	Weeks per year	Hours per week
1967	64.6	$22,660	$520.85	$13.24	1,758	43.5	39.3
1973	75.2	26,358	607.46	15.75	1,720	43.4	38.6
1979	81.3	26,552	606.22	15.62	1,745	43.8	38.8
1989	93.5	28,909	636.76	16.20	1,823	45.4	39.3
1995	102.4	28,810	627.67	15.81	1,868	45.9	39.7
1998	110.2	31,123	667.51	16.74	1,898	46.6	39.9
Annual growth rate*							
1967-73	2.5%	2.5%	2.6%	2.9%	-0.4%	0.0%	-0.3%
1973-79	1.3	0.1	0.0	-0.1	0.2	0.2	0.1
1979-89	1.4	0.9	0.5	0.4	0.4	0.4	0.1
1989-98	1.8	0.8	0.5	0.4	0.4	0.3	0.2
1989-95	1.5	-0.1	-0.2	-0.4	0.4	0.2	0.2
1995-98	2.4	2.6	2.1	1.9	0.5	0.5	0.1

*   Log growth rates.

Source: Authors' analysis of CPS data and Murphy and Welch (1989). For detailed information on table sources, see Table Notes.

in the two prior business cycles (roughly 1.4% to 1.8%). Thus, productivity growth was 1% faster each year in the late 1990s than in the prior 22 years and comparable to the growth of the late 1960s (2.5% from 1967 to 1973). Recent productivity growth, however, is still below the pace of the 1950s and 1960s (3.0% from 1947 to 1967).

The fact that the acceleration of wage growth in the late 1990s (from -0.4% to 1.9% a year) exceeds that of the 1% productivity acceleration requires an explanation as well. One part of it is that the 0.4% annual fall in average hourly wages over the 1989-95 period may be too pessimistic, since the wage measures more closely associated with the productivity data (in **Table 2.2**) show a higher wage growth of 0.6% over this same period. Other wage measures discussed below, however, do indicate falling average wages in the early 1990s. A better explanation is probably that the persistent low unemployment of the late 1990s allowed workers to achieve faster wage gains and share in productivity growth— after all, productivity was growing 1.5% yearly in the early 1990s while average wages were falling. Thus, there are two parts to an explanation for the faster wage growth in the late 1990s: first, persistent low unemployment enabled work-

TABLE 2.2 Growth of average hourly wages, benefits, and compensation, 1948-98 (1999 dollars)

Year	Wages and salaries	Benefits*	Total compensation	Benefit share of compensation
*Hourly pay***				
1948	$8.16	$0.44	$8.60	5.1%
1967	13.42	1.66	15.08	11.0
1973	15.51	2.54	18.05	14.1
1979	15.69	3.43	19.12	17.9
1989	16.89	3.81	20.70	18.4
1995	17.56	3.91	21.47	18.2
1999	19.50	3.59	23.09	15.6
Annual dollar change				
1948-73	$0.29	$0.08	$0.38	
1973-79	0.03	0.15	0.18	
1979-89	0.12	0.04	0.16	
1989-99	0.26	-0.02	0.24	
1989-95	0.11	0.02	0.13	
1995-99	0.49	-0.08	0.41	
1979-99	0.19	0.01	0.20	
Annual percent change				
1948-73	2.6%	7.2%	3.0%	
1973-79	0.2	5.1	1.0	
1979-89	0.7	1.1	0.8	
1989-99	1.4	-0.6	1.1	
1989-95	0.6	0.4	0.6	
1995-99	2.7	-2.1	1.8	
1979-99	1.1	0.2	0.9	

*   Includes payroll taxes, health, pension, and other non-wage benefits.
** Deflated by Personal Consumption Expenditure (PCE) index for all items, except health, which is deflated by PCE Medical Index.

Source: Authors' analysis of BEA and NIPA data.

ers to attain a rising wage that more closely reflected productivity growth, and, second, productivity growth accelerated (which itself requires explanation, as discussed in the Introduction). It is also worth noting that the 1.9% wage growth of the late 1990s still lags significantly behind the 2.9% growth of the late 1960s and early 1970s.

The other important story in Table 2.1 is the continuing growth in annual hours worked. For instance, the average worker worked 1,898 hours in 1998, 75 more—nearly an additional hour and a half more each week, or nearly two additional 40-hour weeks each year—than the 1,823 hours worked in 1989. This growth in hours worked was evident both in the 1989-95 and 1995-98 parts of the current business cycle, reflecting the long-term growth in weeks worked per year and a modest growth in weekly hours.

The 1979-89 period was also characterized by growing annual hours of work (up 78, from 1,745 to 1,823). The 0.4% yearly growth in hours worked was driven by the increase in the average work year to 45.4 weeks from 43.8 weeks, a 0.4% annual growth, and a slight increase in the hours of the average workweek, to 39.3 hours. In the 1973-79 period, annual hours grew more slowly, at 0.2% annually.

Contrasting compensation and wage growth

A worker's pay is made up of both non-wage payments, referred to as "fringe benefits," and wages. Together, wages and fringe benefits make up compensation. This section examines the growth of compensation using the only two available data series and finds that, in the 1980s, hourly compensation grew at the same pace as wages, while in the 1990s it grew more slowly. One implication of compensation and wages growing in tandem is that analyses (such as ours below) that focus on wage trends are using an appropriate proxy for compensation. If anything, analyses of wage growth overstate the corresponding growth of compensation, especially in the late 1990s.

Table 2.2 examines the wage and compensation data that are developed as a major part of the National Income and Product Accounts (NIPA), the Commerce Department's effort to measure gross domestic product, or the size of the national economy. Compensation levels exceed wage levels because they include employer payments for health insurance, pensions, and payroll taxes (primarily payments toward Social Security and unemployment insurance).

Benefits grew faster, if not much faster, than wages in the 1960s, 1970s, and 1980s. For instance, over the 1979-89 period benefits grew 1.1% annually, while wages grew at a 0.7% pace. Yet total compensation (wages and benefits) grew at relatively the same rate as wages, 0.8% versus 0.7% per year. This apparent contradiction is readily explained: non-wage compensation in 1979 totaled just 18.0% of total compensation. Thus, even a faster growth of a small part of compensation (benefits) did not lead to growth in total compensation much greater than that of wages.

Another way of portraying the limited role of benefits growth is to note that 1.1% annual growth over the 1979-89 period translated to a $0.04 per year growth in hourly benefits, boosting benefits from $3.42 an hour in 1979 to $3.80 in 1989.

Over the 1989-98 period, benefits actually fell 0.6% per year. In contrast, the annual growth in average hourly wages accelerated to 1.4% per year. Consequently, the benefits share of compensation fell sharply, from 17.9% to 15.6%, and compensation grew more slowly than wages, 1.1% versus 1.4%. As Table 2.2 shows, there was a slowdown in benefits over the 1989-95 period; growth dropped to 0.4%, substantially less than the 1.1% growth in the 1979-89 period. However, there was a *reduction* in benefits over the 1995-98 period. As shown in a later section, this benefit decline reflects a fall in employer pension contributions and a fall in employer health care costs (relative to medical inflation).

This slowdown and then fall in benefits in the 1990s tells a richer story than one that is limited to wages. According to the wage data in Table 2.2, wage growth accelerated from 0.6% to 2.7% a year between the 1989-95 and 1995-98 periods, a rise of 2.1 percentage points. The comparable acceleration of compensation growth, however, was a 1.2 percentage-point rise (from 0.6% to 1.8%). Taking account of the benefit reductions of the late 1990s, therefore, shows an acceleration of compensation (of 1.2%) that more closely corresponds to the 1% productivity acceleration than does the 2.0% wage acceleration.

The data in **Table 2.3** take a different look at the role of benefit growth in driving total compensation growth. These data are drawn from the Bureau of Labor Statistics' Employment Cost Index (ECI) program, which provides the value of wages and employer-provided benefits for each year since 1987. These ECI data corroborate the earlier finding that benefits, defined as pension, insurance (health and life), and payroll taxes dropped sharply in the mid-1990s. In fact, these ECI data are somewhat more pessimistic than those in Table 2.2, since they show fairly stable benefits from 1989 to 1994 and then a 1.6% annual *decline* in benefits from 1995 to 2000. These numbers vary from the ones presented earlier because they describe only the private sector (government employment is excluded), and the definition of "hours worked" is different. Nevertheless, neither source of data provides much support for the view that increased benefits made up the difference for disappointing wage growth in the 1980s and early 1990s. More importantly, both data sources indicate that compensation growth lagged behind wage growth in the late 1990s, with Table 2.3 suggesting compensation grew at half the pace of wages over 1995-2000, 0.5% versus 1.0% a year. We return to a discussion of benefit growth below when we examine specific benefits, such as health insurance and pensions.

Although studies of labor market trends should examine both wages and benefits, those that focus on long-term wage trends alone (usually because of a lack of benefit data) are not misleading. Taking account of payroll taxes or pen-

TABLE 2.3 Growth in private-sector average hourly wages, benefits, and compensation, 1987-2000 (1999 dollars)

Year*	Wages and salaries	Benefits**	Total compensation***	Benefit share of compensation
Hourly pay				
1987	$16.39	$3.75	$20.14	18.6%
1988	16.10	3.80	19.90	19.1
1989	15.90	3.74	19.64	19.0
1990	15.77	3.76	19.53	19.3
1991	15.36	3.70	19.05	19.4
1992	15.55	3.78	19.33	19.6
1993	15.57	3.78	19.35	19.5
1994	15.42	3.85	19.27	20.0
1995	15.12	3.61	18.73	19.3
1996	15.10	3.52	18.62	18.9
1997	15.20	3.40	18.60	18.3
1998	15.48	3.36	18.83	17.8
1999	15.65	3.35	19.00	17.6
2000	15.89	3.34	19.23	17.6
Annual dollar change				
1989-2000	-$0.01	-$0.40	-$0.42	
1989-95	-0.78	-0.13	-0.91	
1995-2000	0.77	-0.28	0.49	
Annual percent change				
1989-2000	0.0%	-1.0%	-0.2%	
1989-95	-0.8	-0.6	-0.8	
1995-2000	1.0	-1.6	0.5	

*   Data are for March.
**   Includes payroll taxes, health, pension, and other non-wage benefits.
***   Deflated by CPI, except health deflated by CPI Medical Care Index.

Source: Authors' analysis of BLS ECI levels data.

sion and insurance costs (including both health and life insurance), given their small size and slow growth, would not substantively alter the picture emerging from analyses of the 1980s and early 1990s that use the conventional government wage data frequently used to track labor market trends (such as we employ). The sharp divergence of compensation and wage trends in the late 1990s, however, marks a new trend and merits watching.

TABLE 2.4 Hourly and weekly earnings for production and non-supervisory workers, 1947-99* (1999 dollars)

Year	Real average hourly earnings	Real average weekly earnings
1947	$7.78	$313.79
1967	12.30	467.40
1973	13.91	513.18
1979	13.87	495.09
1982	13.38	465.75
1989	12.98	449.07
1992	12.55	431.77
1995	12.50	431.08
1999	13.24	456.78
Business cycles	Annual growth rate	
1947-67	2.3%	2.0%
1967-73	2.1	1.6
1973-79	0.0	-0.6
1979-89	-0.7	-1.0
1989-99	0.2	0.2
1989-95	-0.6	-0.7
1995-99	1.5	1.5
1979-99	-0.2	-0.4

* Production and non-supervisory workers account for more than 80% of wage and salary employment.

Source: Authors' analysis.

Wages by occupation

We now turn to the pattern of growth or decline in wages for the various segments of the workforce since 1973. In general, the workers who experienced the greatest fall in real wages since then were likely to be men, workers who initially had lower wages, workers without a college degree, blue-collar or service workers, or younger workers. In the early 1990s, however, there was also real wage erosion among male white-collar and college-educated workers. As seen earlier, however, there has been an impressive across-the-board growth in real wages since 1995.

The data in **Table 2.4** and **Figure 2A** show wage trends for the 80% of the workforce who are production and non-supervisory workers. This category includes factory workers, construction workers, and a wide variety of service-

FIGURE 2A Hourly wage and compensation growth for production/non-supervisory workers, 1959-99

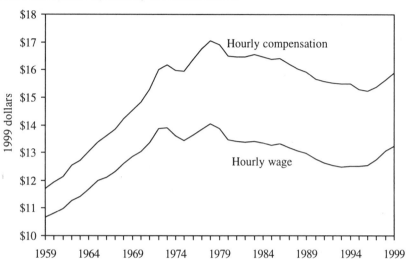

Source: Authors' analysis.

sector workers ranging from restaurant and clerical workers to nurses and teachers; it leaves out higher-paid managers and supervisors. Between 1989 and 1999, average hourly earnings for these workers rose $0.26, or 0.2% annually. As we have seen earlier, the differences in trends between the early and latter part of this period are striking: hourly wages fell 0.6% a year from 1989 to 1995 and then grew 1.5% a year from 1995 to 1999, a turnaround of 2.1 percentage points. Over the longer term, from 1979 to 1999, wages are down, from $13.87 in 1979 to $13.24 in 1999, due to the sharp fall in wages over the 1979-95 period. Figure 2A also tracks an estimate of the hourly compensation of production/non-supervisory workers that shows compensation growing far faster than wages in the 1970s, when wages stagnated, but otherwise shows a similar trend in compensation and wage growth.

The trends in weekly earnings correspond closely to that of hourly earnings, with a decline in the 1980s and early 1990s and a shift to strong positive growth after 1995. Still, the weekly earnings of production and non-supervisory workers in 1999 were $456.78 per week (in 1999 dollars), $38 less than in 1979 and still below the $467 level in 1967.

Table 2.5 presents post-1973 wage trends by occupation for men and women.

TABLE 2.5 Changes in hourly wages by occupation, 1979-99 (1999 dollars)

Occupation*	Percent of employment 1999	Hourly wage					Annual percent change			
		1973	1979	1989	1995	1999	1973-79	1979-89	1989-99	1995-99
Males										
White collar	46.8%	$19.91	$19.91	$19.99	$19.68	$21.47	0.0%	0.0%	0.7%	2.2%
Managers	13.6	22.05	22.17	23.68	23.26	25.49	0.1	0.7	0.7	2.3
Professional	13.6	22.09	21.58	22.69	22.86	24.57	-0.4	0.5	0.8	1.8
Technical	3.3	18.77	18.51	19.03	18.43	20.04	-0.2	0.3	0.5	2.1
Sales	10.1	17.30	17.53	16.36	15.71	17.42	0.2	-0.7	0.6	2.6
Admin., clerk	6.3	15.14	15.23	13.98	13.08	13.35	0.1	-0.8	-0.5	0.5
Service	10.4%	$12.47	$11.45	$10.43	$10.09	$10.57	-1.4%	-0.9%	0.1%	1.2%
Protective	3.2	16.10	14.54	14.59	14.38	15.23	-1.7	0.0	0.4	1.4
Other	7.3	10.69	10.02	8.63	8.19	8.53	-1.1	-1.5	-0.1	1.0
Blue collar	40.2%	$15.00	$15.07	$13.68	$12.70	$13.26	0.1%	-1.0%	-0.3%	1.1%
Craft	18.8	17.16	16.83	15.50	14.57	15.16	-0.3	-0.8	-0.2	1.0
Operatives	7.6	13.45	13.92	12.74	11.64	12.09	0.6	-0.9	-0.5	1.0
Trans. op.	7.4	14.12	14.43	12.83	12.06	12.44	0.4	-1.2	-0.3	0.8
Laborers	6.4	12.33	12.22	10.42	9.57	10.02	-0.1	-1.6	-0.4	1.2
Females										
White collar	73.2%	$12.09	$11.90	$13.00	$13.42	$14.41	-0.3%	0.9%	1.0%	1.8%
Managers	14.0	13.92	13.66	15.81	16.17	17.66	-0.3	1.5	1.1	2.2
Professional	18.8	16.15	15.09	17.10	17.88	18.48	-1.1	1.3	0.8	0.8
Technical	4.0	12.73	13.32	14.26	14.06	14.34	0.8	0.7	0.1	0.5
Sales	11.6	8.32	9.62	9.59	9.71	10.89	2.4	0.0	1.3	2.9
Admin., clerk	24.8	10.84	10.58	11.01	10.78	11.15	-0.4	0.4	0.1	0.9
Service	15.3%	$7.88	$8.13	$7.61	$7.59	$7.90	0.5%	-0.7%	0.4%	1.0%
Protective	0.8	10.77	10.50	11.37	11.95	11.68	-0.4	0.8	0.3	-0.6
Other	14.6	7.83	8.08	7.45	7.39	7.70	0.5	-0.8	0.3	1.0
Blue collar	9.7%	$9.17	$9.74	$9.37	$9.14	$9.62	1.0%	-0.4%	0.3%	1.3%
Craft	2.1	10.52	11.02	11.17	10.88	11.77	0.8	0.1	0.5	2.0
Operatives	4.8	8.99	9.49	8.80	8.61	9.08	0.9	-0.7	0.3	1.3
Trans. op.	0.9	10.60	10.77	10.54	10.37	10.07	0.3	-0.2	-0.5	-0.7
Laborers	1.8	9.05	9.64	8.68	8.08	8.31	1.1	-1.0	-0.4	0.7

* Data for private household and farming, forestry, and fishing occupations not shown and not included in wage calculations.

Source: Authors' analysis.

There was a decline in hourly wages from 1989 to 1995 among men in every occupational category except professionals, and the decline was greater among blue-collar workers than managers. For blue-collar men, who made up 40.2% of male employment in 1999, the wage setbacks in the early 1990s followed the deep, 1.0% annual real wage declines of the 1979-89 period. Men in the higher-paid white-collar occupations, on the other hand, enjoyed real wage growth in the 1980s, so their early 1990s experiences represented a turnaround. White-collar men in 1995 earned less, $19.68, than their counterparts did in 1973 or 1979.

The big story of the 1990s was the strong wage growth of the 1995-99 period, which Table 2.5 shows occurred among men in every occupation. White-collar men, however, enjoyed roughly double the wage growth of men in blue-collar and service occupations.

Nearly three-fourths (73.2%) of women workers were white-collar workers in 1999, and their annual 1.0% wage growth over the 1989-99 period was comparable to that of the prior decade. Women in every occupation (except those in which women make up less than 1% of the workforce) also enjoyed strong wage growth, following a period of slow growth from 1989 to 1995.

Wage trends by wage level

For any given trend in average wages, there will be different outcomes for particular groups of workers if wage inequality changes, as it has in recent years: it grew pervasively in the 1980s, and grew at the top and fell at the bottom in the 1990s. Wage trends can be described by examining groups of workers by occupation, education level, and so on, but doing so omits the impact of changes such as increasing inequality within groups. The advantage of an analysis of wage trends by wage level or percentile (the 60th percentile, for instance, is the wage at which a worker earners more than 60% of all earners but less than 40% of all earners), as in **Table 2.6**, is that it captures all of the changes in the wage structure. Table 2.6 provides data on wage trends for workers at different percentiles (or levels) in the wage distribution, thus allowing us to characterize wage growth for low-, middle-, and high-wage earners. The data are presented for the cyclical peak years 1973, 1979, and 1989 and for the most recent year for which we have a complete year of data, 1999, along with data for the 1995-99 period (so we can examine the character of the rebound in wage growth over this period). The data show that the deterioration in real wages from 1979 to 1995 was both broad and uneven. The breadth of recent wage problems is clear from the fact that real wages fell for the bottom 70% of wage earners over the 1979-89 and 1989-95 periods. Wages grew modestly for high-wage workers—4.8%—at the 90th percentile over the 16 years from 1979 to 1995. Workers with the very highest wages, at the 95th percentile, saw the most wage growth in this period.

However, there was a different pattern of wage decline in the 1980s and early 1990s. In the 1980s, the decline was greater the lower the wage, with the lowest-wage workers losing 8.5% to 16.1% and the 60th and 70th percentile wages

TABLE 2.6 Wages for all workers by wage percentile, 1973-99 (1999 dollars)

	Percentile*									
Year	10	20	30	40	50	60	70	80	90	95
Real hourly wage										
1973	$6.30	$7.60	$9.04	$10.51	$12.05	$13.80	$16.05	$18.35	$23.06	$28.94
1979	6.67	7.61	8.93	10.51	11.89	13.78	16.29	18.99	23.31	28.28
1989	5.60	6.97	8.35	9.98	11.60	13.55	16.12	19.28	24.35	29.91
1995	5.53	6.76	8.08	9.51	11.07	13.10	15.62	18.91	24.43	30.64
1999	6.05	7.35	8.72	10.10	11.87	13.93	16.45	19.93	26.05	33.25
Dollar change										
1973-79	$0.37	$0.00	-$0.10	$0.00	-$0.16	-$0.05	$0.24	$0.64	$0.25	-$0.65
1979-89	-1.07	-0.64	-0.58	-0.53	-0.29	-0.23	-0.17	0.29	1.04	1.62
1989-99	0.45	0.39	0.36	0.12	0.27	0.39	0.33	0.65	1.70	3.34
1989-95	-0.06	-0.20	-0.27	-0.47	-0.53	-0.45	-0.50	-0.37	0.08	0.74
1995-99	0.51	0.59	0.64	0.59	0.80	0.83	0.83	1.02	1.62	2.61
1979-99	-0.62	-0.25	-0.22	-0.41	-0.02	0.16	0.16	0.94	2.73	4.97
Percent change										
1973-79	5.8%	0.1%	-1.1%	0.0%	-1.3%	-0.3%	1.5%	3.5%	1.1%	-2.3%
1979-89	-16.1	-8.5	-6.5	-5.0	-2.4	-1.7	-1.0	1.5	4.5	5.7
1989-99	8.1	5.6	4.3	1.2	2.4	2.9	2.1	3.4	7.0	11.2
1989-95	-1.1	-2.9	-3.3	-4.7	-4.6	-3.3	-3.1	-1.9	0.3	2.5
1995-99	9.3	8.8	7.9	6.2	7.3	6.4	5.3	5.4	6.6	8.5
1979-99	-9.3	-3.3	-2.4	-3.9	-0.2	1.1	1.0	4.9	11.7	17.6

* The Xth percentile wage is the wage at which X% of wage earners earn less and (100-X)% earn more.

Source: Authors' analysis.

falling by 1.7% and 1%, respectively. In the early 1990s, however, wages fell among the bottom 80% but fell less at the bottom than in the middle. Explaining this changing pattern of wage growth is the subject of later sections of this chapter.

Table 2.6 also shows the emergence of strong across-the-board real wage growth from 1995 to 1999. Remarkably, the strongest wage growth was the 7.9% to 9.3% gain for the lowest-wage workers, who fared better than middle- and upper-middle-wage workers (growth of roughly 5% to 7% over the 40th to 90th percentiles). Only the best paid workers, earning $30.64 per hour at the 95th percentile in 1995, saw their wages grow as fast as low-wage workers over the 1995-99 period.

This overall picture, however, masks somewhat different outcomes for men and women. First, consider the 1979-89 and 1989-95 periods. Among men in

TABLE 2.7 Wages for male workers by wage percentile, 1973-99 (1999 dollars)

Year	Percentile* 10	20	30	40	50	60	70	80	90	95
1973	$7.43	$9.54	$11.25	$12.89	$14.62	$16.57	$18.23	$20.98	$26.72	$32.21
1979	7.34	9.32	11.21	13.04	14.93	16.95	19.01	22.08	26.92	32.21
1989	6.41	8.02	9.85	11.66	13.57	15.97	18.47	21.64	27.11	33.64
1995	6.00	7.58	9.01	10.83	12.71	14.85	17.44	20.86	27.19	34.01
1999	6.59	8.12	9.85	11.50	13.40	15.63	18.42	22.23	29.17	37.99
Dollar change										
1973-79	-$0.10	-$0.22	-$0.04	$0.15	$0.32	$0.38	$0.78	$1.10	$0.19	$0.01
1979-89	-0.93	-1.30	-1.36	-1.38	-1.37	-0.98	-0.54	-0.44	0.19	1.43
1989-99	0.18	0.10	0.00	-0.16	-0.16	-0.33	-0.05	0.58	2.06	4.34
1989-95	-0.41	-0.44	-0.84	-0.83	-0.86	-1.12	-1.03	-0.78	0.09	0.37
1995-99	0.59	0.55	0.84	0.67	0.70	0.79	0.98	1.37	1.98	3.98
1979-99	-0.75	-1.20	-1.36	-1.54	-1.53	-1.31	-0.59	0.15	2.25	5.77
Percent change										
1973-79	-1.3%	-2.3%	-0.3%	1.2%	2.2%	2.3%	4.3%	5.2%	0.7%	0.0%
1979-89	-12.7	-13.9	-12.1	-10.6	-9.1	-5.8	-2.9	-2.0	0.7	4.4
1989-99	2.8	1.3	0.0	-1.4	-1.2	-2.1	-0.3	2.7	7.6	12.9
1989-95	-6.4	-5.5	-8.5	-7.1	-6.3	-7.0	-5.6	-3.6	0.3	1.1
1995-99	9.8	7.2	9.3	6.1	5.5	5.3	5.6	6.6	7.3	11.7
1979-99	-10.2	-12.8	-12.1	-11.8	-10.2	-7.8	-3.1	0.7	8.4	17.9

* The Xth percentile wage is the wage at which X% of wage earners earn less and (100-X)% earn more.

Source: Authors' analysis.

the 1980s, wages fell at nearly all parts of the wage distribution (**Table 2.7** and **Figure 2B**). In the middle, for instance, the median male hourly wage fell 9.1% between 1979 and 1989, while low-wage men lost roughly 13%. There was an across-the-board wage decline of roughly 6% in the early 1990s affecting the bottom 70% of male earners. Over the entire 1979-95 period the wage declines were substantial, amounting to about 15%, for instance, for the median male worker. Even high-wage men at the 90th percentile, who earn about $29 per hour, did well only in relative terms, since their wage was just 1% higher in 1995 than in 1979.

As with the overall trend, the pattern of male wage deterioration shifted between the 1980s and the early 1990s. In the 1980s, wages fell most the lower the wage, while in the 1990s there was comparable wage erosion in the middle and at the bottom. Thus, the wage gap between middle- and low-wage men was

FIGURE 2B Change in hourly wages for men by wage percentile, 1973-99

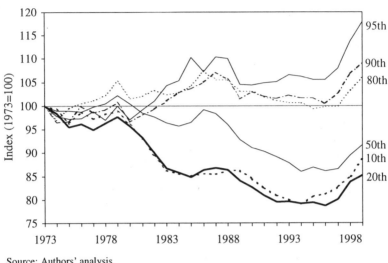

Source: Authors' analysis.

stable in the early 1990s, although the gap between high-wage men (at the 90th percentile) and middle- and low-wage men continued to grow.

The wage recovery among men in the 1995-99 period corresponds to the pattern among all workers discussed earlier: strong across-the-board wage growth, with low-wage workers faring better than middle-wage workers. Among men, however, the highest-wage workers—at the 95th percentile—clearly fared better than either low- or middle-wage workers.

The only significant and persistent wage growth between 1979 and 1995 appears to have been among the highest-wage women (**Table 2.8** and **Figure 2C**). For instance, wages grew 16.3% for women at the 90th percentile from 1979 to 1989 and another 4.4% over 1989-95. In contrast, low-wage women, particularly the lowest paid at the 10th percentile, saw their wages fall in the 1980s. In contrast, middle-wage women saw modest wage growth over that same period. Women's wages grew more slowly in the early 1990s than in the 1980s, with the wages in the middle actually falling. The one positive development was that wages for 10th percentile women actually rose in the early 1990s, in contrast to the sharp decline in the 1980s. As we will discuss below, minimum-wage trends—falling in real value in the 1980s and rising in the 1990s—can explain this pattern.

As with men, women's wages rose strongly across the board in the 1995-99 period. It is remarkable that this wage growth was fairly even, from about 6% to 9%, among all women.

TABLE 2.8 Wages for female workers by wage percentile, 1973-99 (1999 dollars)

	Percentile*									
Year	10	20	30	40	50	60	70	80	90	95
1973	$5.24	$6.51	$7.32	$8.19	$9.23	$10.39	$11.70	$13.49	$16.68	$19.71
1979	6.36	6.89	7.49	8.35	9.38	10.66	11.89	13.82	17.25	20.25
1989	5.21	6.41	7.43	8.53	9.92	11.33	13.34	15.99	20.07	24.19
1995	5.29	6.31	7.38	8.49	9.75	11.23	13.35	16.31	20.95	26.04
1999	5.77	6.83	7.89	9.05	10.31	12.03	14.30	17.40	22.63	28.07
Dollar change										
1973-79	$1.12	$0.38	$0.17	$0.17	$0.15	$0.28	$0.19	$0.33	$0.57	$0.54
1979-89	-1.16	-0.48	-0.07	0.18	0.54	0.67	1.45	2.17	2.82	3.94
1989-99	0.57	0.42	0.47	0.52	0.39	0.70	0.96	1.41	2.56	3.87
1989-95	0.08	-0.10	-0.05	-0.04	-0.17	-0.10	0.00	0.32	0.88	1.85
1995-99	0.48	0.52	0.51	0.57	0.56	0.80	0.95	1.09	1.67	2.03
1979-99	-0.59	-0.06	0.40	0.70	0.93	1.37	2.41	3.58	5.38	7.82
Percent change										
1973-79	21.3%	5.9%	2.3%	2.0%	1.6%	2.7%	1.6%	2.5%	3.4%	2.8%
1979-89	-18.2	-7.0	-0.9	2.1	5.7	6.2	12.2	15.7	16.3	19.5
1989-99	10.9	6.5	6.3	6.1	4.0	6.2	7.2	8.8	12.7	16.0
1989-95	1.6	-1.6	-0.7	-0.5	-1.7	-0.8	0.0	2.0	4.4	7.6
1995-99	9.1	8.2	7.0	6.7	5.8	7.1	7.2	6.7	8.0	7.8
1979-99	-9.3	-0.9	5.3	8.4	9.9	12.8	20.2	25.9	31.2	38.6

* The Xth percentile wage is the wage at which X% of wage earners earn less and (100-X)% earn more.

Source: Authors' analysis.

The male/female wage gap

As we have seen, from 1979 to 1989 the median hourly wage fell $1.37 for men and rose $0.54 for women (**Table 2.9**). Consequently, the ratio of women's to men's median hourly wages grew by 10.3 percentage points, from 62.8% in 1979 to 73.1% in 1989, representing a sizable reduction in gender wage inequality. The gender wage gap closed further, but more slowly, in the 1990s, with the ratio rising to 76.9% in 1999. However, women still earned nearly one-fourth less than men in 1999.

This narrowing of the male/female wage gap in the 1980s was the result of both improvements in real hourly wages for women and real wage reductions for men. If real wages among men had not fallen by 1989 but had remained at their 1979 level (at $14.93), the wage gap would have been 66.4%, or just 3.6 percentage points higher rather than the actual 10.3. Thus, falling real wages

127

FIGURE 2C Change in hourly wages for women by wage percentile, 1973-99

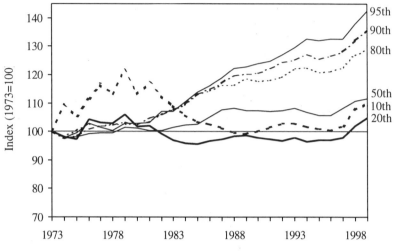

Source: Authors' analysis.

TABLE 2.9 Changes in the gender wage differential, 1973-99 (1999 dollars)

	Median hourly wage			Women's share of
Year	Male	Female	Ratio	employment
1973	$14.62	$9.23	63.1%	38.5%
1979	14.93	9.38	62.8	41.7
1989	13.57	9.92	73.1	45.2
1999	13.40	10.31	76.9	46.5
Change				
1979-89	-$1.37	$0.54	10.3	
1989-99	-0.16	0.39	3.8	

Source: Authors' analysis.

among men can explain 64.9% of the closing of the gender wage gap between 1979 and 1989; correspondingly, only 35.1% (3.6% divided by 10.3%) was due to women's rising real wages.

Between 1989 and 1999, the median wage of men fell slightly ($0.16), and the median wage of women grew by only $0.39. The smaller wage gains for

FIGURE 2D The gender earnings gap, 1973-99

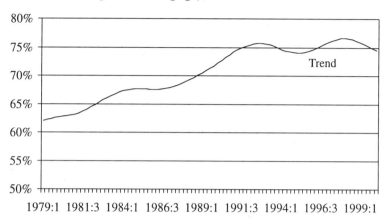

Source: Authors' analysis.

women in the 1990s and the smaller wage declines for men explain the smaller shrinkage of the gender wage gap in the 1990s than in the 1980s. **Figure 2D**, which illustrates the trend-adjusted, year-by-year gender wage gap, shows that the gap has been relatively stable for the last seven years.

Shifts in low-wage jobs

Another useful way of characterizing changes in the wage structure is to examine the trend in the proportion of workers earning low, middle, and high wages. These trends are presented in **Table 2.10** for all workers and for men and women. The workforce is divided into six wage groups based on multiples of the "poverty-wage level," or the hourly wage that a full-time, year-round worker must earn to sustain a family of four at the poverty threshold, which was $8.19 in 1999 (in 1999 dollars). Thus, workers are assigned to a wage group according to the degree to which they earned more (or less) than poverty-level wages.

As we have seen with other dimensions of the wage structure, there is a sharp change in the trend before and after 1995. As shown in **Figure 2E**, the share of workers earning far less than poverty-level wages expanded significantly between 1979 and 1989, and again until 1995. In 1979, only 4.2% of the workforce were "very low earners," with wages at least 25% below the poverty-level wage (labeled "0-75"). By 1989, 13.4% of the workforce earned such wages,

TABLE 2.10 Distribution of total employment by wage level, 1973-99

	Share of employment by wage multiple of poverty wage*							
	Poverty-level wages:							
Year	0-75	75-100	Total**	100-125	125-200	200-300	300+	Total
All								
1973	8.0%	15.6%	23.6%	13.6%	34.3%	19.9%	8.6%	100%
1979	4.2	19.5	23.7	15.3	31.4	21.0	8.6	100
1989	13.4	15.1	28.5	13.5	29.2	19.1	9.7	100
1999	10.8	15.9	26.8	14.5	28.6	18.2	12.0	100
Change								
1973-79	-3.7	3.9	0.1	1.7	-3.0	1.1	0.0	
1979-89	9.2	-4.3	4.8	-1.8	-2.2	-1.9	1.1	
1989-99	-2.6	0.8	-1.7	1.0	-0.6	-0.9	2.3	
Men								
1973	3.8%	9.0%	12.8%	9.9%	36.5%	27.9%	12.9%	100%
1979	2.4	11.1	13.5	11.3	32.1	29.6	13.5	100
1989	9.1	12.1	21.2	11.3	29.7	23.7	14.1	100
1999	7.8	12.9	20.7	13.1	29.1	21.3	15.8	100
Change								
1973-79	-1.4	2.1	0.6	1.4	-4.4	1.7	0.6	
1979-89	6.8	1.0	7.8	0.0	-2.4	-5.9	0.6	
1989-99	-1.3	0.8	-0.5	1.8	-0.6	-2.4	1.7	
Women								
1973	14.0%	25.2%	39.2%	19.0%	31.2%	8.3%	2.3%	100%
1979	6.7	30.4	37.1	20.5	30.5	9.7	2.3	100
1989	18.3	18.5	36.8	16.0	28.7	13.8	4.7	100
1999	14.1	19.3	33.4	16.0	28.0	14.8	7.8	100
Change								
1973-79	-7.3	5.2	-2.2	1.5	-0.8	1.4	0.0	
1979-89	11.6	-11.9	-0.3	-4.5	-1.8	4.1	2.5	
1989-99	-4.2	0.8	-3.4	0.0	-0.6	1.0	3.1	

*   The wage ranges are equivalent in 1999 dollars to: $6.14 and below (0-75), $6.14-$8.19 (75-100), $8.19-$10.24 (100-125), $10.24-$16.38 (125-200), $16.38-$24.57 (200-300), and $24.57 and above (300+).

** Combines lowest two categories and represents the share of wage earners earning poverty-level wages.

Source: Authors' analysis.

FIGURE 2E Share of workers earning poverty-level wages, 1973-99

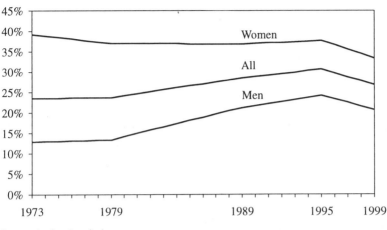

Source: Authors' analysis.

a shift of 9.2% of the workforce into this low-wage group. Looking at the total group earning poverty-level wages, Table 2.10 shows that, in 1989, 28.5% of the workforce earned poverty-level wages, a rise from 23.7% in 1979. Thus, over the 1979-89 period, there was not only a sizable growth (4.8% of the workforce) in the proportion of workers earning poverty-level wages, but also a shift within this group to those earning very low wages.

The share of workers earning poverty-level wages continued to expand, though more slowly, in the 1989-95 period, but then, not surprisingly, given other trends discussed earlier, contracted in the 1995-99 period (as seen in Figure 2E). The result was a fall in the poverty-wage employment share to 26.8% in 1999, down 1.7 percentage points from 1989 but still 3.1 points above its 1979 level. Those earning very low wages still represented 10.8% of the workforce in 1999, 6.6% more of the workforce than in 1979.

Over the 1979-89 period, the entire wage structure shifted downward, with proportionately fewer workers in the middle- and high-wage groups in 1989 than in 1979. The only exception is the modest expansion of the share of the workforce at the very highest earnings level (exceeding three times the poverty-level wage). In the 1989-99 period there was a somewhat larger shift to the highest-wage jobs and a small, 1% shift upward into lower middle-wage jobs paying $8.19 to $10.24.

Among women workers, 11.6% shifted into the very-low-wage category during the 1979-89 period, while at the same time the two highest-wage groups grew by 6.6 percentage points. The shift downward among women appears to be an enlargement of the workforce earning very low wages, while the proportion earning poverty-level wages was stable, remaining at about 37%. In the 1989-99 period, the very bottom of the wage structure shrank as the proportion of women earning poverty-level wages diminished. There was a corresponding shift to the top two wage categories among women in the 1990s, although less of a shift than in the 1980s.The improvements, as Figure 2E shows, emerged in the 1995-99 period.

Among men, the overall changes in the wage structure between 1979 and 1989 meant proportionately fewer middle-wage workers and more low-wage workers, with essentially no growth of very high earners. For instance, 7.8% of the male workforce shifted into the group earning less than the poverty-level wage, and the proportion of men in the second- and third-highest wage groups contracted. Over the 1989-99 period the share of men earning poverty-level wages declined, but only by 0.5%. The shrinkage of upper-middle jobs among men was due to a slight shift to the highest paid but also to a comparable shift down. Regardless of the recent trends, the share of poverty-level earners among men was 20.7% in 1999, still 7.2% more of the male workforce than in 1979.

Women are much more likely to earn low wages than men. In 1999, 33.4% of women earned poverty-level wages or less, significantly more than the share of men (20.7%). Women are also much less likely to earn very high wages. In 1999, only 7.8% of women, but 15.8% of men, earned at least three times the poverty-level wage.

Tables 2.11, 2.12, and **2.13** (and **Figure 2F**) present an analysis similar to the one in Table 2.10 for white, black, and Hispanic employment. The proportion of minority workers earning low wages is substantial—35.6% of black workers and 45.1% of Hispanic workers in 1999. Minority women are even more likely to be low earners—40.7% of black women and 51.8% of Hispanic women in 1999. The wage structure for each race/gender group has shifted over the last few decades.

Table 2.11 shows the modest shift downward in the wage structure for whites in the 1970s, followed by a larger downward shift in the 1979-89 period. In the 1989-99 period, however, whites moved from lower-paid to middle-wage jobs and into very-high-wage jobs. By 1999, the poverty-wage share among white workers had nearly returned to its 1979 level, all due to progress in the late 1990s. Over the entire period from 1979 to 1999, however, white workers shifted toward both the very bottom and the very top. The white male and white female wage structures have moved in different directions. In the 1980s, white women shifted substantially into the lowest and highest earnings groups. In contrast, the share of white men eroded in the middle-wage range in the 1980s, grew only

TABLE 2.11 Distribution of white employment by wage level, 1973-99

	Share of employment by wage multiple of poverty wage*							
	Poverty-level wages:							
Year	0-75	75-100	Total**	100-125	125-200	200-300	300+	Total
All								
1973	6.9%	14.5%	21.4%	13.2%	34.6%	21.2%	9.5%	100%
1979	3.9	18.0	21.8	14.8	31.8	22.1	9.5	100
1989	11.9	13.8	25.6	13.1	29.8	20.5	10.9	100
1999	8.9	13.7	22.6	13.8	29.6	20.2	13.9	100
Change								
1973-79	-3.0	3.5	0.5	1.5	-2.8	0.9	0.0	
1979-89	8.0	-4.2	3.8	-1.7	-1.9	-1.6	1.4	
1989-99	-3.0	0.0	-3.0	0.6	-0.2	-0.3	2.9	
Men								
1973	3.1%	7.6%	10.7%	9.2%	36.0%	29.6%	14.4%	100%
1979	2.0	9.4	11.5	10.4	32.0	31.2	14.9	100
1989	7.4	10.2	17.6	10.5	30.0	25.7	16.2	100
1999	5.9	10.2	16.1	11.8	29.8	23.7	18.6	100
Change								
1973-79	-1.0	1.8	0.8	1.2	-4.0	1.6	0.5	
1979-89	5.4	0.8	6.1	0.1	-2.0	-5.5	1.3	
1989-99	-1.5	0.0	-1.5	1.3	-0.2	-1.9	2.4	
Women								
1973	12.6%	24.7%	37.2%	19.3%	32.5%	8.7%	2.3%	100%
1979	6.3	29.3	35.6	20.7	31.4	10.0	2.3	100
1989	16.9	17.8	34.7	16.1	29.6	14.6	5.0	100
1999	12.1	17.6	29.7	16.0	29.4	16.3	8.7	100
Change								
1973-79	-6.2	4.6	-1.6	1.4	-1.1	1.2	0.0	
1979-89	10.6	-11.5	-0.9	-4.6	-1.8	4.6	2.7	
1989-99	-4.8	-0.2	-5.0	-0.1	-0.2	1.7	3.7	

*   The wage ranges are equivalent in 1999 dollars to: $6.14 and below (0-75), $6.14-$8.19 (75-100), $8.19-$10.24 (100-125), $10.24-$16.38 (125-200), $16.38-$24.57 (200-300), and $24.57 and above (300+).

** Combines lowest two categories and represents the share of wage earners earning poverty-level wages.

Source: Authors' analysis.

TABLE 2.12 Distribution of black employment by wage level, 1973-99

| | Share of employment by wage multiple of poverty wage* | | | | | | | |
| | Poverty-level wages: | | | | | | | |
Year	0-75	75-100	Total**	100-125	125-200	200-300	300+	Total
All								
1973	14.8%	22.0%	36.8%	15.0%	32.7%	12.3%	3.2%	100%
1979	6.3	26.5	32.8	17.8	29.9	15.7	3.8	100
1989	19.2	19.4	38.5	15.7	27.0	14.4	4.3	100
1999	14.0	21.6	35.6	17.3	27.8	13.6	5.7	100
Change								
1973-79	-8.5	4.5	-4.0	2.9	-2.8	3.4	0.6	
1979-89	12.8	-7.1	5.7	-2.2	-2.9	-1.2	0.6	
1989-99	-5.2	2.3	-2.9	1.6	0.8	-0.8	1.4	
Men								
1973	7.4%	17.4%	24.8%	14.0%	39.5%	17.6%	4.1%	100%
1979	4.3	19.2	23.4	16.2	32.9	21.8	5.7	100
1989	15.0	18.2	33.2	15.3	28.9	17.4	5.3	100
1999	10.7	18.8	29.5	17.3	30.4	16.2	6.6	100
Change								
1973-79	-3.1	1.8	-1.3	2.1	-6.6	4.2	1.6	
1979-89	10.7	-1.0%	9.7	-0.9	-4.0	-4.4	-0.4	
1989-99	-4.2	0.6	-3.7	2.1	1.5	-1.3	1.3	
Women								
1973	23.3%	27.4%	50.8%	16.1%	24.8%	6.1%	2.2%	100%
1979	8.5	34.3	42.8	19.6	26.7	9.1	1.7	100
1989	23.2	20.5	43.6	16.1	25.3	11.6	3.5	100
1999	16.7	24.0	40.7	17.3	25.6	11.5	4.9	100
Change								
1973-79	-14.8	6.9	-8.0	3.6	1.9	3.0	-0.5	
1979-89	14.7	-13.8	0.8	-3.6	-1.4	2.5	1.7	
1989-99	-6.5	3.6	-2.9	1.2	0.3	-0.1	1.5	

*   The wage ranges are equivalent in 1999 dollars to: $6.14 and below (0-75), $6.14-$8.19 (75-100), $8.19-$10.24 (100-125), $10.24-$16.38 (125-200), $16.38-$24.57 (200-300), and $24.57 and above (300+).

** Combines lowest two categories and represents the share of wage earners earning poverty-level wages.

Source: Authors' analysis.

TABLE 2.13 Distribution of Hispanic employment by wage level, 1973-99

Year	Share of employment by wage multiple of poverty wage*							
	Poverty-level wages:							
	0-75	75-100	Total**	100-125	125-200	200-300	300+	Total
All								
1973	12.2%	22.2%	34.4%	17.0%	33.9%	11.5%	3.2%	100%
1979	5.4	28.2	33.6	18.0	29.8	14.8	3.8	100
1989	20.9	22.8	43.8	14.7	26.1	11.6	3.9	100
1999	20.3	24.8	45.1	17.0	23.3	9.9	4.7	100
Change								
1973-79	-6.8	6.0	-0.8	1.1	-4.2	3.3	0.6	
1979-89	15.6	-5.4	10.2	-3.3	-3.7	-3.2	0.0	
1989-99	-0.6	2.0	1.3	2.3	-2.8	-1.7	0.8	
Men								
1973	8.9%	16.2%	25.1%	14.3%	40.4%	15.8%	4.4%	100%
1979	3.5	19.9	23.4	17.1	33.8	20.3	5.3	100
1989	17.5	21.5	39.0	14.3	27.7	14.1	4.9	100
1999	16.7	23.6	40.3	18.1	24.6	11.4	5.7	100
Change								
1973-79	-5.4	3.7	-1.7	2.9	-6.6	4.5	0.9	
1979-89	13.9	1.6	15.6	-2.8	-6.1	-6.2	-0.4	
1989-99	-0.8	2.1	1.3	3.7	-3.1	-2.7	0.8	
Women								
1973	17.8%	32.6%	50.4%	21.6%	22.7%	4.0%	1.2%	99%
1979	8.2	41.0	49.1	19.4	23.6	6.4	1.5	100
1989	26.1	24.8	50.9	15.2	23.8	7.9	2.3	100
1999	25.3	26.5	51.8	15.5	21.6	7.8	3.3	100
Change								
1973-79	-9.7	8.4	-1.3	-2.2	0.9	2.3	1.5	
1979-89	17.9	-16.2	1.7	-4.2	0.1	1.5	0.8	
1989-99	-0.8	1.7	0.9	0.3	-2.1	0.0	1.0	

* The wage ranges are equivalent in 1999 dollars to: $6.14 and below (0-75), $6.14-$8.19 (75-100), $8.19-$10.24 (100-125), $10.24-$16.38 (125-200), $16.38-$24.57 (200-300), and $24.57 and above (300+).

** Combines lowest two categories and represents the share of wage earners earning poverty-level wages.

Source: Authors' analysis.

FIGURE 2F Share of workers earning poverty-level wages, by race/ethnicity, 1973-99

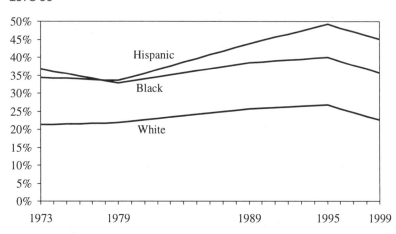

Source: Authors' analysis.

slightly in the very-high-wage category, and shifted (although less than women) to the very bottom. Similarly, the improvements in the 1990s were far greater for white women than white men. Over the longer term, in fact, white women have seen their share of poverty-level earners decline and their share of high and very high earners grow.

Blacks (Table 2.12) in the 1980s saw a dramatic downward shift out of better-paying and middle-wage employment into very low-wage employment, a trend that was partially reversed in the 1990s. By 1999, the share of poverty-wage earners was still 6.1% higher among men than in 1979 but was at a historic low among women (Figure 2F).

However, in 1999, 35.6% of black workers (29.5% of black men and 40.7% of black women) were in jobs paying less than poverty-level wages. The post-1979 trends, despite the recent improvement, have left black men with far fewer middle-wage jobs and more low-earning jobs. The "hollowing" of the middle among black women has meant a modest shift up and a larger shift to the very lowest-earning jobs.

Since 1979, despite the recent turnaround, the Hispanic wage structure has generally shifted downward, for both men and women, with modest growth in the highest-wage jobs (Table 2.13). Both Hispanic women and men shifted in large numbers into the lowest-wage jobs between 1979 and 1989, and saw little improvement over the 1990s. The growth in the percentage of Hispanic males earning poverty-level wages was substantial, up from 23.4% in 1979 to 40.3% in 1999. More than half of Hispanic women earned poverty-level wages in 1999, just as they did in 1973.

Trends in benefit growth and inequality

The data already reviewed show that real wages have declined for a wide array of workers over both the 1980s and the early 1990s, with strong real wage growth since 1995. We have also seen, in Tables 2.2 and 2.3, that total compensation, the real value of both wages and fringe benefits, grew at the same pace as wages over the 1979-95 period. Benefits grew faster than wages during much of that time, but since they make up a small (18-20%) share of compensation, their growth did not generate fast compensation growth overall. A new trend has emerged in the 1990s, however. Benefit growth was slightly slower than that of wages in the early 1990s and then actually fell in the middle and late 1990s. The result has been a sizable divergence between compensation and wage growth. In this section we explore these issues further and examine changes in benefits by type of benefit and changes in health and pension coverage for different groups of workers; this analysis allows us to determine whether there has been growing inequality of benefits. We are not able to examine the benefit of stock options, because there are no reliable, comprehensive data on the extent and quality of stock option programs. What evidence is available suggests that stock options are mostly provided to top managerial workers and that a growing, but still small, share of employers provide them.

Table 2.14 provides a breakdown of growth in non-wage compensation, or benefits, using the two available data series (the "aggregates" were shown already in Tables 2.2 and 2.3). The NIPA data provide a long-term perspective. In the 1948-73 and 1973-79 periods, the inflation-adjusted value of benefits grew by $0.08 and $0.15 each year, respectively, translating into annual growth rates of 7.2% and 5.1%. In contrast, the average value of non-wage compensation, including employer-provided health insurance, pension plans, and payroll taxes, grew just $0.04 per year over the 1979-89 period and were lower in 1999 than in 1989, translating into annual growth rates of 1.1% in 1979-89 and a 0.6% decline from 1989 to 1998. The 1990s decline of benefits took place in the late 1990s and reflects a fall in both health insurance and pension costs. The ECI data in the bottom panel of Table 2.14 confirm the slowing of annual benefits growth in the early 1990s. In fact, the ECI data show an actual decline in benefits, from $3.78 starting in 1992 to $3.34 in 2000. Both data sources show a steep annual decline in benefits after 1995.

TABLE 2.14 Growth of specific fringe benefits, 1948-99 (1999 dollars)

Year	Voluntary benefits			Payroll taxes	Total benefits and non-wage compensation
	Pension	Health*	Subtotal		
BEA NIPA**					
1948	$0.12	$0.09	$0.21	$0.23	$0.44
1967	0.51	0.50	1.01	0.65	1.66
1973	0.80	0.75	1.55	0.98	2.54
1979	1.13	1.07	2.22	1.21	3.43
1989	0.96	1.35	2.33	1.48	3.81
1992	0.97	1.51	2.52	1.57	4.10
1995	0.95	1.39	2.36	1.55	3.91
1999	0.74	1.27	2.03	1.56	3.59
Annual dollar change					
1948-73	$0.03	$0.02	$0.05	$0.03	$0.08
1973-79	0.06	0.05	0.11	0.04	0.15
1979-89	-0.02	0.02	0.01	0.03	0.04
1989-99	-0.02	-0.15	-0.03	0.01	-0.02
1989-95	0.00	-0.04	0.00	0.01	0.02
1995-99	-0.05	-0.32	-0.08	0.00	-0.08
1979-99	-0.02	-0.07	-0.01	0.02	0.01
Annual percent change					
1948-73	7.8%	9.0%	8.3%	6.0%	7.2%
1973-79	6.0	6.1	6.1	3.5	5.1
1979-89	-1.6	2.3	0.5	2.0	1.1
1989-99	-2.6	-0.6	-1.4	0.5	-0.6
1989-95	-0.2	0.5	0.2	0.8	0.4
1995-99	-6.1	-2.1	-3.7	0.1	-2.1
1979-99	-2.1	0.9	-0.4	1.3	0.2
BLS ECI levels*					
1987	$0.71	$1.37	$2.08	$1.67	$3.75
1989	0.57	1.45	2.02	1.72	3.74
1992	0.55	1.49	2.04	1.75	3.78
1995	0.57	1.31	1.88	1.74	3.61
2000	0.57	1.15	1.72	1.62	3.34
Annual dollar change					
1989-2000	$0.00	-$0.30	-$0.30	-$0.10	-$0.40
1989-95	0.00	-0.14	-0.14	0.02	-0.13
1995-2000	0.00	-0.16	-0.16	-0.12	-0.28
Annual percent change					
1989-2000	0.0%	-2.1%	-1.5%	-0.6%	-1.0%
1989-95	0.0	-1.7	-1.2	0.2	-0.6
1995-2000	0.1	-2.6	-1.7	-1.4	-1.6

*   Deflated by medical care price index.
**   National Income and Product Accounts (NIPA).
*** Employment Cost Index (ECI) levels data for March of each year.

Source: Authors' analysis of BLS and BEA data.

How can it be that benefits grew so slowly in the 1980s, a time when health insurance costs rose rapidly (relative to other products) and the payroll tax spiked upward? One reason is that, in Table 2.14, health insurance costs are converted to "real" dollars by a medical care price index and reflect the degree to which more health care was being bought (e.g., if medical care prices rise by 10% and health insurance expenditures rise 10%, then health care purchases did not rise). Even if health costs were adjusted by the general consumer price index, however, the results would not change significantly. More important, health care costs have been contained because many workers (about a third of the workforce) receive no health insurance coverage from their employers. Furthermore, the share of workers covered fell in the 1980s and is still below its 1989 or 1979 levels (as discussed below). Thus, even rapid increases in health costs among a small group of workers with good health plans does not necessarily mean that health costs for the workforce as a whole rose rapidly. Last, the efforts of employers to shift the costs of health care to employees has probably helped to contain the growth of benefits paid by employers. Overall, health care costs per hour worked rose from $1.07 in 1979 to $1.35 in 1989 to as high as $1.51 in 1992 before falling to $1.27 in 1999, $0.08 below their 1989 level.

The drop in pension costs over the 1980s partially offset the rise in health care costs in that time period. In 1979, employers paid $1.13 an hour for various pension and retirement schemes; by 1989 hourly pension costs were down to $0.96, and they fell to $0.74 by 1999. In the 1979-89 period this drop in pension costs offset $0.17 of the $0.28 hourly increase in health costs, as reflected in the minimal rise in total "voluntary benefits" from $2.22 to $2.33. In the 1990s, the drop in pension costs coupled with declining health care costs led to the overall drop in benefit costs.

Employers pay payroll taxes for their employees into a variety of social insurance programs: unemployment insurance, Medicare, Social Security, and workers compensation insurance. These costs grew 2.0% annually in the 1980s but by only 0.5% in the post-1989 period. Payroll taxes grew much more rapidly—6.0% a year—over the 1948-73 period, reflecting faster wage growth and tax rate increases.

The data in Table 2.14 reflect "average" benefit costs. Given the rapid growth of wage inequality in recent years, it should not be surprising to find a growing inequality of benefits. **Tables 2.15** and **2.16** examine changes in health and pension insurance coverage for different demographic groups between 1979, 1989, 1995, and 1998. The share of workers covered by employer-provided health care plans dropped a steep 7.1 percentage points, from 70.2% to 63.1%, in the 1980s (Table 2.15). As **Figure 2G** shows, health care coverage eroded in the 1990s until 1993-94 and then started growing, another reflection of improved

TABLE 2.15 Change in private sector employer-provided health insurance coverage, 1979-98

	Health insurance coverage (%)				Percentage-point change			
Group*	1979	1989	1995	1998	1979-89	1989-98	1995-98	1979-98
All workers	70.2%	63.1%	59.1%	62.9%	-7.1	-0.2	3.8	-7.3
Gender								
Men	75.1%	66.8%	61.6%	66.0%	-8.3	-0.8	4.4	-9.1
Women	62.2	57.9	55.5	58.6	-4.3	0.7	3.1	-3.6
Race								
White	71.6%	65.8%	62.3%	66.4%	-5.7	0.5	4.1	-5.2
Black	64.1	56.9	53.3	58.4	-7.2	1.5	5.1	-5.7
Hispanic	60.9	46.3	42.3	44.6	-14.5	-1.7	2.4	-16.2
Wage fifth								
Lowest	40.7%	29.4%	27.7%	29.6%	-11.3	0.2	1.9	-11.1
Second	62.8	54.7	51.3	56.4	-8.1	1.7	5.1	-6.4
Middle	75.9	69.4	63.6	69.0	-6.5	-0.4	5.4	-6.9
Fourth	84.0	78.6	74.2	77.6	-5.5	-0.9	3.4	-6.4
Top	87.9	83.7	79.1	82.3	-4.2	-1.4	3.2	-5.6

* Private sector, wage and salary workers age 18-64, who worked at least 20 hours per week and 26 weeks per year.

Source: Authors' analysis.

pay in the late 1990s. Still, health insurance coverage in 1998 was roughly at its 1989 level and far below its 1979 level. This growth in coverage in the late 1990s does not contradict the earlier finding of declining health benefit costs; rather, it probably means that the cost of those previously covered are not keeping up with inflation and that newly covered workers have modest benefits. Unfortunately, there are no data available to show the degree to which the quality of coverage has changed, i.e., whether health plans are more inclusive or more restricted.

Over the 1979-98 period, health care coverage has declined more among men than women but similarly among both whites and blacks, with Hispanics suffering by far the largest drop—a 16.2% decline. The pattern in the erosion of health insurance coverage by wage level shows a growth in inequality in the 1980s, with greater erosion the lower the wage. In the 1990s, however, there

TABLE 2.16 Change in private sector employer-provided pension coverage, 1979-98

| | Pension coverage (%) | | | | | | | |
| | | | | | Percentage-point change | | | |
Group*	1979	1989	1995	1998	1979-89	1989-98	1995-98	1979-98
All workers	51.1%	44.3%	45.7%	49.2%	-6.8	4.9	3.5	-1.9
Gender								
Men	56.2%	46.4%	47.4%	50.9%	-9.7	4.5	3.6	-5.2
Women	42.8	41.2	43.5	46.8	-1.5	5.6	3.4	4.1
Race								
White	52.6%	46.7%	49.2%	53.6%	-5.9	6.8	4.4	0.9
Black	46.4	41.3	43.2	42.4	-5.0	1.1	-0.8	-4.0
Hispanic	38.3	26.5	24.6	28.4	-11.8	2.0	3.8	-9.9
Wage fifth								
Lowest	19.5%	14.0%	14.1%	17.9%	-5.5	3.9	3.7	-1.6
Second	38.0	30.8	33.1	36.9	-7.2	6.1	3.8	-1.1
Middle	53.3	46.4	47.6	53.8	-6.9	7.4	6.1	0.5
Fourth	68.9	60.2	62.7	64.9	-8.7	4.7	2.3	-4.0
Top	76.5	70.2	72.0	73.0	-6.3	2.8	1.0	-3.5

* Private-sector, wage and salary workers age 18-64, who worked at least 20 hours per week and 26 weeks per year.

Source: Authors' analysis.

were modest extensions of coverage for the bottom 40% (including a 1.7 percentage-point expansion for the second fifth), while erosion continued for middle- and high-wage workers.

Pension plan coverage (Table 2.16) declined as quickly as health care coverage in the 1980s: it dropped from 51.1% in 1979 to 44.3% in 1989. This decline is perhaps one of the reasons for the lessening of pension costs for employers over that period. In the 1989-95 period, however, pension coverage expanded, easing back to 45.7% in 1995. By 1998, however, coverage had grown to 49.2%, just shy of 1979 coverage. Over the 1979-98 period, lower pension coverage occurred primarily among men, for whom it fell from 56.2% to 50.9%. Women's pension coverage, on the other hand, rose slightly, from 42.8% to 46.8%. Women workers by 1998 were only slightly less likely than men to be

FIGURE 2G Health insurance and pension coverage, 1979-98

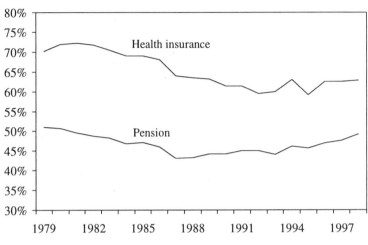

Source: Authors' analysis.

covered by an employer's pension plan. Both black and white workers saw pension coverage erode in the 1980s, but Hispanics experienced a large decline—an 11.8 percentage-point drop from 1979 to 1989. In the late 1990s, however, whites expanded their pension coverage and attained a level, 53.6%, slightly above the 1979 level of 52.6%. Hispanics also increased their coverage in the 1990s but still have coverage—28.4% in 1998—far below the 1979 level. Black workers saw a very modest increase in coverage in the 1990s.

The pattern of decline in pension coverage by wage level shows coverage dropping relatively evenly across wage groups in the 1980s and an across-the-board broadening of coverage in the 1990s, with coverage expanding most in the middle. Nevertheless, lower-wage workers are unlikely to have jobs with employer-provided pension plans (just 17.9% were covered in 1998), and only about half of all workers have pension coverage.

The widening coverage of employer-provided pension plans in the 1990s is most likely due to the expansion of 401(k) and other "defined-contribution" pension plans. These plans need to be distinguished from defined-benefit plans, which guarantee a worker a fixed payment in retirement based on pre-retirement wages and years of service; these are generally considered the best plans from a worker's perspective. In contrast (as shown in **Figure 2H**), a larger share of workers are now covered by defined-contribution plans, in which employers make contributions (to which employees often can add) each year. With this

FIGURE 2H Share of pension participants in defined-contribution plans, 1975-97

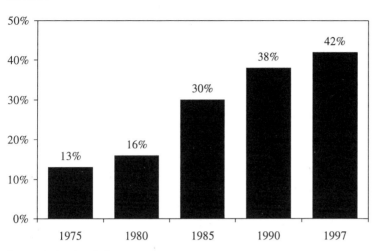

Source: Authors' analysis.

type of plan, a worker's retirement income depends on his or her success in investing these funds, and investment risks are borne by the employee rather than the employer. Therefore, the shift from traditional defined-benefit plans to defined-contribution plans represents an erosion of pension quality. The expenditures data from Table 2.14 suggest a long-term cutback in pension costs, mirroring other indicators of lessened pension quality.

Figure 2H shows the share of active pension plan participants (workers and retirees) who are in defined contribution plans as their primary plan (meaning they are not also in a defined-benefit plan). The share rose from 13% in 1975 to 42% in 1997. These data show the erosion of pension plan quality over time, especially when coupled with data showing lower employer pension contributions.

Explaining wage inequality

In this section we shift the discussion from a presentation of wage and benefit trends overall and for sub-groups to an examination of explanations for the pattern of recent wage growth. It is important to understand the average performance of wage growth (i.e., the stagnation since 1973) and why particular groups fared well or poorly compared to others.

The data presented above have shown the stagnation of wages and overall compensation since 1973 and a strong wage growth after 1995. **Table 2.17** presents indicators of the variety of dimensions (excluding race and gender differentials) of the wage structure that have grown more unequal over the 1973-99 period. Any explanation of growing wage inequality must be able to explain the movement of these indicators. These inequality indicators are computed from our analysis of the Current Population Survey (CPS) Outgoing Rotation Group (ORG) data series. These trends, however, parallel those in the other major data series (the March CPS).

The top panel shows the trends in the 90/10 wage differential and its two components, the 90/50 and 50/10 wage differential (whose annual values are shown in **Figures 2I** and **2J**), over the 1973-99 period. These differentials reflect the growth in overall wage inequality that we are attempting to explain. The 90/10 wage gap, for instance, shows the degree to which the 90th percentile worker—a "high-wage" worker who makes more than 90% but less than 10% of the workforce—fared better than the low-wage worker at the 10th percentile. The growth in the 90/10 differential is frequently broken down into two components: the 90/50 wage gap shows how high earners fared relative to middle earners, and the 50/10 wage gap shows how middle earners fared relative to low earners.

An important theme in the following discussion is that wage inequalities have been growing continuously since 1979. However, among both men and women the shape of growing inequality differed in the 1980s (actually, differing after about 1987-88) and the 1990s. In the 1979-89 period, as we have seen in our decile analysis (Tables 2.6-2.8), there was a dramatic across-the-board broadening of the wage structure, with the top and bottom pulling away from the middle. In the late 1980s, however, the wage inequality in the bottom half of the wage structure, as reflected in the 50/10 differential, began shrinking and has done so through 1999. On the other hand, the 90/50 differential has continued to widen in the 1990s, as it had done in the 1980s. This widening of the top is even stronger if we examine the 95/50 differential (**Figure 2K**) which benchmarks wage growth to the very highest earners (those whose wages are above 95% of the workforce, the highest wage we feel can be tracked in our data with technical precision). Thus, the trends in the 1990s include a continued widening of wage inequality at the top (i.e., between the top and the middle) at the same time as wage inequality was shrinking at the bottom. These disparate trends should motivate explanations that focus on how causal factors affect particular portions of the wage structure—top, middle, or bottom—rather than on how causal factors generally affect inequality.

We now turn to the specifics in Table 2.17. Among men, there was a dra-

TABLE 2.17 Dimensions of wage inequality, 1973-99

	Log wage differentials					Percentage-point change		
	1973	1979	1989	1995	1999	1973-79	1979-89	1989-99
Total wage inequality								
90/10								
Men	127.9%	130.0%	144.3%	151.2%	148.8%	2.1	14.3	4.5
Women	115.7	103.6	134.9	137.6	136.6	-12.1	31.3	1.7
90/50								
Men	60.3%	58.9%	69.2%	76.1%	77.8%	-1.4	10.3	8.5
Women	59.2	61.1	70.5	76.5	78.6	1.9	9.4	8.1
50/10								
Men	67.6%	71.1%	75.0%	75.1%	71.0%	3.5	4.0	-4.0
Women	56.5	42.5	64.4	61.1	58.0	-14.0	21.9	-6.4
Between group inequality*								
College/H.S.								
Men	25.3%	20.1%	33.9%	37.1%	42.4%	-5.2	13.9	8.4
Women	37.7	26.5	41.0	46.7	48.3	-11.2	14.5	7.3
Less than H.S./H.S.								
Men	-20.8%	-17.6%	-20.9%	-23.0%	-22.9%	3.2	-3.3	-2.0
Women	-18.2	-18.0	-18.1	-21.0	-20.9	0.2	0.0	-2.8
*Experience** Middle/young*								
Men	22.0%	21.5%	25.7%	27.0%	24.0%	-0.5	4.1	-1.7
Women	8.0	9.5	17.8	21.8	18.5	1.5	8.3	0.7
Old/middle								
Men	3.4%	8.2%	12.4%	12.7%	9.8%	4.7	4.3	-2.6
Women	-2.0	0.4	2.1	5.4	6.1	2.4	1.7	4.0
Within group inequality*								
Men	0.423	0.428	0.467	0.478	0.476	0.01	0.04	0.01
Women	0.418	0.402	0.447	0.467	0.457	-0.02	0.05	0.01

*   Differentials based on a simple human capital regression of log wages on four education categorical variables: age as a quartic, race, marital status, region and ethnicity (Hispanic).
**   Age differentials between 25- and 35-year-olds and 35- and 50-year-olds.
***   Mean square error from same regressions used to estimate experience and age differentials. Changes measured as percent change.

Source: Authors' analysis.

FIGURE 2I Men's wage inequality, 1973-99

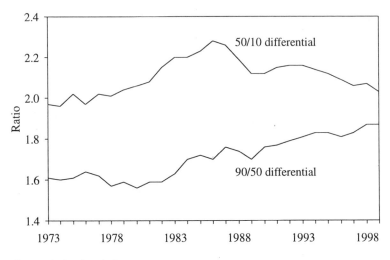

Source: Authors' analysis.

FIGURE 2J Women's wage inequality, 1973-99

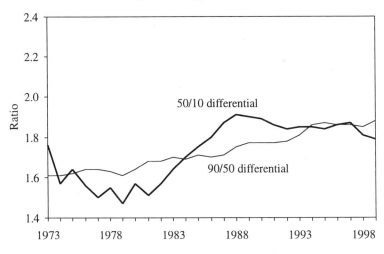

Source: Authors' analysis.

FIGURE 2K 95/50 percentile wage inequality, 1973-99

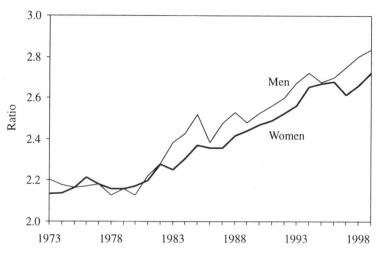

Source: Authors' analysis.

matic growth in wage inequality at the top and bottom in the 1979-89 period that has continued, in terms of the 90/50 differential, as quickly through the 1989-99 period (Figure 2I). Specifically, the 90/50 wage gap grew roughly 10 (log) percentage points in both decades. As discussed above, the character of this growing male wage inequality shifted in the most recent period. In the 1980s there was a growing separation between both the top and the middle and the middle and the bottom (seen in the 50/10 differential). However, in the 1989-99 period, all of the growing wage inequality was generated by a divergence between the top and everyone else: the 90/50 differential grew while the 50/10 differential actually fell continuously. The drop in the 50/10 wage gap actually began in 1986 (Figure 2I).

Among women, the wage inequality trends across time periods correspond to those of men. The 90/10 ratio dropped significantly between 1973 and the late 1970s, primarily because of the strong equalization in the 50/10 wage gap. In the 1980s, however, there was a tremendous growth in the 50/10 wage gap that reversed the 1970s compression and increased the gap another 8 percentage points over 1973. One conclusion that can be reached about women's wage inequality is that it has been driven much more than was the change for men by what happened at the bottom—the 10th percentile. This is likely due to the importance of the legal minimum wage to low-wage women, as we will discuss in a later section. Among women, the growth of the 90/50 differential was compa-

147

rable to that of men in the 1980s and in the 1990s. As with men, there was an actual decline of the 50/10 wage gap in the 1990s (which Figure 2J shows started about 1987).

The 95/50 wage gap among women followed approximately the same track as for men (Figure 2K). Wage inequality between the very top earners and those in the middle has been growing strongly, and steadily, since about 1980, confirming the continuous widening of wages at the top over the last two decades.

Analysts have tended to decompose, or break down, growing wage inequality into two types of inequality—"between group" and "within group." The former is illustrated in Table 2.17 in two ways: the growing wage differentials between groups of workers defined either by their education levels or by their labor market experience. The "college wage premium"—the wage gap between college and high school graduates—fell in the 1970s among both men and women but exploded in the 1980s, growing about 14 percentage points for each. The growth of the college wage premium in the post-1989 period, however, was only half as much. The pattern of growth of this key education differential within the 1990s, however, differed between men and women (see **Figure 2L**). Among men there was only modest growth in the education premium in the early 1990s, which year-by-year trends (discussed below) show to be relatively flat between 1987 and 1997. Thus, the 1990s growth in the male education premium primarily occurred in the last few years. Among women, however, there was a relatively steady but modest growth of the college wage premium throughout the period after 1989.

Table 2.17 also presents the trends in another education differential—between those completing high school and those without high school degrees; this differential would be expected to affect the wage distribution in the bottom half, as about 10% of the workforce is in the "no high school degree" category and high school graduates make up about a third of the workforce (see discussion of Tables 2.18-2.21). In 1973, those without a high school degree earned about 20% less than those with a degree. Perhaps surprisingly, this wage differential has grown very modestly over the last 26 years, suggesting that changing wage differentials at the bottom have had only a weak relationship to changing education differentials.

The growth of experience differentials reflect the wage gap between older and middle-age and younger workers. The wage gap between middle-age and younger workers grew in the 1980s but not in the 1990s, particularly because the 1995-99 wage boom, characterized by relatively faster wage growth among younger workers, reduced this differential. The wage gap between older and middle-age women workers grew over the entire 1973-99 period; it grew as well for men until 1995, then declined.

FIGURE 2L College/high school wage premium, 1973-99

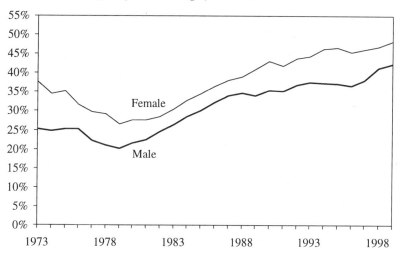

Source: Authors' analysis.

Within-group wage inequality—wage dispersion among workers with comparable education and experience—has been a major dimension of growing wage inequality. The growth of within-group wage inequality is presented in the last section of Table 2.17, with changes measured in percent. These data show that within-group wage inequality grew slightly among men in the 1970s and 1990s, but grew by 9% over the 1980s. Among women, within-group wage inequality fell in the 1970s, grew by 11.4% in the 1980s, and then grew a modest 2.2% in the 1990s.

This measure of within-group wage inequality is a "summary measure" describing changes across the entire wage distribution. Unfortunately, such a measure does not help us understand changes in particular measures of wage inequality, such as the 90/50 and 50/10 differentials presented in Table 2.17. This is particularly troublesome for an analysis of the 1989-99 period in which inequalities were expanding at the top (i.e., the 90/50) but shrinking at the bottom (i.e., the 50/10). A summary measure of inequality by definition reflects the net effect of the two shifts in wage inequality in the 1990s, and explains the small change of within-group wage inequality from 1989 to 1999.

Since changes in within-group wage inequality have been a significant factor in various periods, it is important to be able to explain and interpret these trends. In a later section, we show that about half of the growth of wage inequality since 1979 has been from growing within-group wage inequality. Unfortunately, the interpretation of growing wage inequality among workers with similar "human capital" has not been the subject of much research. Some analysts suggest it reflects growing premiums for skills that are not captured by traditional human capital measures available in government surveys. Others suggest that changing "wage norms," employer practices, and institutions are responsible. We turn to these trends next.

Productivity and the compensation-productivity gap

The most commonly mentioned reason for the wage stagnation of the 1970s and 1980s is slow productivity growth (i.e., changes in output per hour worked) since 1973. As the data in Table 2.1 showed, productivity grew about 1.4% annually over the entire 1973-95 period. This is a slower growth in productivity than occurred in the pre-1973 period, and so this period has been marked by a "productivity slowdown."

Slow productivity growth was a major problem, but it provides only a partial explanation for the slow average wage trends in this period, since productivity grew significantly more than wages or compensation. At the same time, the pickup of productivity growth after 1995 provides a major explanation for the much stronger real wage growth in recent years.

The relationship between hourly productivity and compensation growth is portrayed in **Figure 2M**, which shows the growth of each relative to 1973 (i.e., each is indexed so that 1973 equals 100). As the figure shows, productivity grew 48.4% from 1973 to 1998, enough to generate broadly shared growth in living standards and wages. But growth in both average and median compensation lagged behind productivity growth, and, likewise, median hourly compensation grew less than average compensation, reflecting growing wage and benefit inequality. Thus, a major reason why median compensation (or wages) lags behind productivity is that growing inequality creates a "wedge" that prevents the typical worker from enjoying the average growth of national output or income.

There are several possible interpretations of the gap between average compensation and productivity. One is that prices for national output have grown more slowly than prices for consumer purchases. Therefore, the same growth in nominal, or current dollar, wages and output yields faster growth in real (inflation-adjusted) output (which is adjusted for changes in the prices of investment goods, exports, and consumer purchases) than in real wages (adjusted for changes in consumer purchases only). That is, workers have suffered a worsening "terms of trade," in which the prices of things they buy (i.e.,

FIGURE 2M Productivity and hourly compensation growth, 1973-98

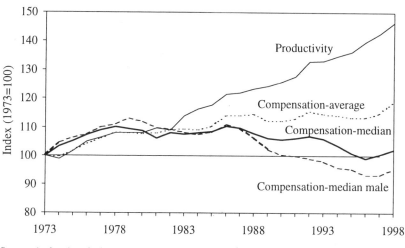

Source: Authors' analysis.

consumer goods) have risen faster than the items they produce (consumer goods but also capital goods).

This "terms of trade" explanation is actually more of a description than an explanation. A growing gap between output and consumer prices has not been a persistent characteristic of the U.S. economy, and the emergence of this gap requires an exploration of what economic forces are driving it. Once the causes of the price gap are known (not simply accounted for), it can be interpreted. In the meantime, there are two ways to look at the divergence of compensation and productivity created by the "terms of trade" shift of prices. One is to note that, regardless of cause, the implication is that the "average" worker is not benefiting fully from productivity growth. Another is to note that the price divergence does not simply reflect a redistribution from labor to capital; the gap between compensation and productivity growth reflects, at least in part, differences in price trends rather than a larger share of productivity growth going to capital incomes.

This leaves open the question of whether wages are being squeezed by higher profits. In other words, has the growth in rates of profit (defined broadly as profits and interest per dollar of assets) meant that wages have grown less than they would have otherwise? As discussed in Chapter 1, the share of income going to capital has grown significantly, driven by a large increase in "profitability," or the return to capital per dollar of plant and equipment. Labor's share of corporate sector income has dropped correspondingly, thus providing evidence of a redistribution of wages to capital incomes. As discussed in Chapter 1, had growth in profitability been more modest up to the 1997-99 period, hourly compensation would have been 4.3% higher in 1999.

Rising education wage differentials

Changes in the economic returns to education affect the structure of wages by changing the wage gaps between different educational groups. The growth in "education–wage differentials" has led to greater wage inequality in the 1980s and 1990s (see Table 2.17) and helps explain the relatively faster wage growth among high-wage workers. This section examines wage trends among workers at different levels of education and begins the discussion, carried on through the remainder of the chapter, of the causes of rising education–wage differentials.

Table 2.18 presents the wage trends and employment shares (percentage of the workforce) for workers at various education levels over the 1973-99 period. It is common to point out that the wages of "more-educated" workers have grown faster than the wages of "less-educated" workers since 1979, with the real wages of less-educated workers falling sharply (or rising more slowly in the 1995-99 period). This pattern of wage growth is sometimes described in terms of a rising differential, or "premium," between the wages of the college-educated and high-school-educated workforces (as shown earlier in Table 2.17).

The usual terminology of the less educated and more educated is misleading. Given that workers with some college education (from one to three years) also experienced falling real wages (down 8.8% from 1979 to 1995), it is apparent that the "less-educated" group—those with less than a four-year college degree—makes up nearly three-fourths of the workforce. Moreover, it is notable that the "college-educated" group consists of two groups: one, with just four years of college, enjoyed a minimal 3.2% wage gain over the 1979-95 period, while the other, the more-educated ("advanced degree") but smaller group (8.6% of the workforce in 1999), enjoyed 11.5% wage growth.

Table 2.18 also shows, however, that the strong real wage growth of the 1995-99 period was evident among all education groups, with faster wage growth among the college-educated and advanced degree workers.

The increased wage differential between college-educated and other workers is frequently ascribed to a relative increase in employer demand for workers with greater skills and education. This interpretation follows from the fact that the wages of college-educated workers increased relative to others despite an increase in their relative supply, from 12.7% of the workforce in 1979 to 18.6%

TABLE 2.18 Change in real hourly wage for all by education, 1973-99
(1999 dollars)

Year	Less than high school	High school	Some college	College	Advanced degree
Hourly wage					
1973	$11.64	$13.34	$14.37	$19.46	$23.53
1979	11.58	12.99	13.89	18.21	22.24
1989	9.73	11.86	13.32	18.68	24.08
1995	8.57	11.33	12.67	18.80	24.80
1999	8.83	11.83	13.37	20.58	26.44
Annual percent change					
1973-79	-0.1%	-0.4%	-0.6%	-1.1%	-0.9%
1979-89	-1.7	-0.9	-0.4	0.3	0.8
1989-99	-1.0	0.0	0.0	1.0	0.9
1989-95	-2.1	-0.8	-0.8	0.1	0.5
1995-99	0.8	1.1	1.4	2.3	1.6
1979-99	-1.1	-0.5	-0.3	0.2	0.5
Share of employment					
1973	28.5%	38.3%	18.5%	10.1%	4.5%
1979	20.1	38.5	22.8	12.7	6.0
1989	13.7	36.9	26.0	15.6	7.9
1995	10.8	33.3	30.5	17.3	8.0
1999	10.8	32.3	29.6	18.6	8.6

Source: Authors' analysis.

in 1999. That is, given the increased supply of college-educated workers, the fact that their relative wages were bid up implies a strong growth in employer demand for more-educated workers, presumably reflecting technological and other workplace trends.

Yet an increased relative demand for educated workers is only a partial explanation, especially if ascribed to a benign process of technology or other factors leading to a higher value for education, thus bidding up the wages of more-educated workers. Note, for instance, that the primary reason for an increased wage gap between college-educated and other workers is the precipitous decline of wages among the non-college-educated workforce and not any strong growth in the college wage. Moreover, as discussed below, there are many important factors (that may not reflect changes in demand for skill), such as the shift to low-wage industries, deunionization, a falling minimum wage, and import competition, that can also lead to a wage gap between workers with more and less education. Below, we present direct evidence that technological change has not been the driving force behind growing wage inequality.

Tables 2.19 and 2.20 present trends in wage and employment shares for the various education groups for men and women. Among men, the wages of non-college-educated workers fell steadily from 1979 to 1995. The decline in wages was sizable even among men with "some college"—12.4% from 1979 to 1995. The wage of the average high-school-educated male fell more, 18.3% from 1979 to 1995, while the wages of those without a high school degree fell 29.4%. By contrast, the wages of male college graduates actually rose just 0.7% from 1979 to 1989 and fell 1.3% over the 1989-95 period. Year-by-year data show male college wages in the 1979-95 period peaked in 1987. The period from 1995 to 1999 was one of strong real wage growth among men in every education category, although stronger for the higher-education groups.

This 1979-95 pattern of stagnant wages for college men and declining wages for non-college-educated men has meant a rise in the relative wage or premium for male college graduates. As shown in Table 2.17, the estimated college/high school wage premium (where experience, race, and other characteristics are controlled for) grew from 20.1% in 1979 to 33.9% in 1989 and to 42.4% in 1999. As Figure 2L shows, however, there was a flattening of the male college/high school premium over the 1988-95 period, particularly in the early 1990s. Since there has not been an acceleration of the supply of college-educated men (as shown in a later section), this implies, within a conventional demand-supply framework, that there was a slowdown in the growth of relative demand for college workers in that period. Since 1995, however, the persistent low unemployment has led to a sharp growth in this key education differential.

A somewhat different pattern has prevailed among women (Table 2.20). In the 1979-89 period wages fell modestly (2.6%) among high-school-educated women but significantly among those without a high school degree (10.6%). Women with some college, unlike their male counterparts, saw wage gains in the 1980s (5.0%), but not as high as college-educated women (12.3%). This pattern of wage growth, however, still resulted in an equivalent growth of the college/high school wage differential from 26.5% in 1979 to 41.0% in 1989 (Table 2.17). Thus, the education–wage gap grew as quickly among women as among men in the 1979-89 period but the relative losers—non-college-educated women—saw a slight, not large, decline in wages.

The pattern of wage growth among women shifted in the early 1990s; wages

TABLE 2.19 Change in real hourly wage for men by education, 1973-99 (1999 dollars)

Year	Less than high school	High school	Some college	College	Advanced degree
Hourly wage					
1973	$13.61	$16.14	$16.50	$22.26	$24.72
1979	13.36	15.65	16.28	21.28	24.21
1989	11.03	13.77	15.18	21.42	26.64
1995	9.43	12.78	14.26	21.14	27.50
1999	9.78	13.34	15.12	23.52	29.66
Annual					
percent change					
1973-79	-0.3%	-0.5%	-0.2%	-0.8%	-0.4%
1979-89	-1.9	-1.3	-0.7	0.1	1.0
1989-99	-1.2	-0.3	0.0	0.9	1.1
1989-95	-2.6	-1.2	-1.0	-0.2	0.5
1995-99	0.9	1.1	1.5	2.7	1.9
1979-99	-1.3	-0.7	-0.3	0.2	0.7
Share of employment					
1973	30.6%	34.4%	19.2%	10.3%	5.4%
1979	22.3	35.0	22.4	13.2	7.1
1989	15.9	35.2	24.4	15.7	8.8
1995	12.6	33.2	28.3	17.3	8.6
1999	12.5	32.6	27.6	18.3	9.0

Source: Authors' analysis.

were stagnant or fell among women with less than a college degree. Wages among college-educated women continued to grow in the 1989-95 period but at a slower pace. In contrast with men, the college/high school differential among women continued to grow in the early 1990s (Figure 2L).

Wage growth was strong over the 1995-99 period among women at all education levels. As with men, wage growth was strongest among those with a bachelor's or advanced degree.

Even though the wages of college-educated women have grown rapidly since 1979, a female college graduate in 1999 still earned only a dollar more than a male with only some college earned in 1973 ($17.50 versus $16.50) and about six dollars less than a male college graduate in 1999.

TABLE 2.20 Change in real hourly wage for women by education, 1973-99 (1999 dollars)

Year	Less than high school	High school	Some college	College	Advanced degree
Hourly wage					
1973	$8.21	$10.16	$10.98	$15.20	$20.13
1979	8.57	10.16	10.92	13.82	17.70
1989	7.66	9.90	11.47	15.52	20.23
1995	7.19	9.73	11.15	16.22	21.35
1999	7.39	10.17	11.75	17.50	22.61
Annual percent change					
1973-79	0.7%	0.0%	-0.1%	-1.6%	-2.1%
1979-89	-1.1	-0.3	0.5	1.2	1.3
1989-99	-0.3	0.3	0.2	1.2	1.1
1989-95	-1.0	-0.3	-0.5	0.7	0.9
1995-99	0.7	1.1	1.3	1.9	1.4
1979-99	-0.4	0.0	0.3	0.5	0.4
Share of employment					
1973	25.6%	44.0%	17.5%	9.9%	3.1%
1979	17.2	43.0	23.4	12.0	4.4
1989	11.2	38.8	27.8	15.4	6.8
1995	8.8	33.6	32.8	17.4	7.4
1999	9.0	32.0	31.9	19.0	8.2

Source: Authors' analysis.

Table 2.21 shows a breakdown of the workforce in 1999 by the highest degree attained. Only about one-fourth (27.3%) of the workforce has at least a four-year college degree (18.6% have no more than a college degree and 8.6% also have a graduate or professional degree). Roughly two-thirds (64.1%) of the workforce has no more than a high school degree, with 10.8% never completing high school, 32.3% completing high school, and another 21.0% having attended college but earning no degree beyond high school. An additional 8.6% hold associate degrees. These data reinforce our earlier discussion that the wage reductions experienced by the "less educated" (frequently defined by economists as those without a college degree) between 1979 and 1995 affected roughly 73% of the workforce.

TABLE 2.21 Educational attainment of workforce, 1999

| Highest | Percent of workforce | | |
degree attained	All	Men	Women
Less than high school	10.8%	12.5%	9.0%
High school/GED	32.3	32.6	32.0
Some college	21.0	19.9	22.3
Assoc. college	8.6	7.7	9.6
College B.A.	18.6	18.3	19.0
Advanced degree*	8.6	9.0	8.2
Total	100.0	100.0	100.0
Memo			
High school or less	43.1%	45.1%	40.9%
Less than B.A. degree	72.7	72.7	72.8
College B.A. or more	27.3	27.3	27.2
Advanced degree	8.6	9.0	8.2

* Includes law degrees, Ph.D.s, M.B.A.s, and similar degrees.

Source: Authors' analysis.

Young workers' wages

The most dramatic erosion of wages since 1973 has been among young workers. However, young workers experienced the fastest wage growth over the 1995-99 period. As a result, there have been significant changes—up and down—in the wage differentials between younger and older workers, as shown earlier in Table 2.17. Since the wages of both younger and non-college-educated workers fell most rapidly in the 1979-95 period, it should not be surprising that entry-level wages for high school graduates in 1999 were far below their levels in 1979 or 1973.

The adverse wage trends among young workers in the 1979-95 period were strongest among men. **Table 2.22** presents trends in wages for entry-level (one to five years of experience) high school and college graduates. The entry-level hourly wage of a young male high school graduate in 1995 was 28.5% less than that for the equivalent worker in 1979, a drop of $3.47 per hour. Among women, the entry-level high school wage fell 17.5% in this period. Entry-level wages for high school graduates rebounded strongly after 1995, growing over 6% among both men and women. The dramatic decline in entry-level wages among high school graduates and the recent recovery is illustrated in **Figure 2N**.

TABLE 2.22 Hourly wages of entry-level and experienced workers by education, 1973-99 (1999 dollars)

Education/ experience	Hourly wage					Percent change			
	1973	1979	1989	1995	1999	1973-79	1979-89	1989-99	1995-99
High school									
Men									
Entry*	$12.42	$12.19	$9.66	$8.72	$9.27	-1.8%	-20.8%	-4.0%	6.3%
34-40	17.74	17.45	14.93	13.93	14.28	-1.6	-14.4	-4.4	2.5
49-55	18.70	18.62	16.84	15.74	15.69	-0.4	-9.5	-6.8	-0.3
Women									
Entry*	$9.09	$9.01	$7.90	$7.43	$7.89	-0.9%	-12.3%	-0.2%	6.2%
34-40	10.44	10.52	10.36	10.19	10.71	0.8	-1.6	3.4	5.1
49-55	10.88	10.83	10.90	10.69	11.22	-0.4	0.6	2.9	4.9
College									
Men									
Entry**	$16.46	$16.07	$16.16	$14.57	$16.74	-2.4%	0.6%	3.6%	14.9%
34-40	26.57	24.97	23.91	23.83	26.43	-6.0	-4.2	10.5	10.9
49-55	27.38	27.67	26.88	26.41	26.49	1.1	-2.9	-1.5	0.3
Women									
Entry**	$13.80	$12.71	$14.07	$13.39	$14.65	-7.9%	10.7%	4.2%	9.4%
34-40	16.46	14.56	16.24	17.81	19.06	-11.5	11.5	17.3	7.0
49-55	15.70	14.74	15.77	17.97	18.74	-6.1	7.0	18.8	4.3

* Entry-level wage measured as wage of those from 19 to 25 years of age.
** Entry-level wage measured as wage of those from 23 to 29 years of age.

Source: Authors' analysis.

Entry-level wages among male college graduates were stagnant over the 1973-89 period and fell 9.9% from 1989 to 1995, as shown in **Figure 2O**. Thus, new male college graduates earned $1.89 less per hour in 1995 than their counterparts did in 1973. A sharp decline in entry-level wages of college graduates also took place among women in the early 1990s, when the wage fell 5.0%. Wages for young college graduates grew strongly—14.9% among men and 9.4% among women—in the 1995-99 wage boom. This solid wage growth boosted entry-level male college graduates to a higher wage than in 1989, offsetting the early 1990s decline; however, their wage in 1999 was only $0.28, or 1.7%, greater than that of their counterparts in 1973. Young women college graduates attained wages in 1999 that were 4.2% higher than in 1989, having made up the ground lost in the early 1990s.

The fact that entry-level wages for college graduates remain higher than for high school graduates means that it makes economic sense for individuals to

FIGURE 2N Entry-level wages of male and female high school graduates, 1973-99

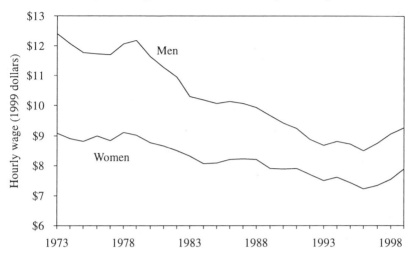

Source: Authors' analysis.

FIGURE 2O Entry-level wages of male and female college graduates, 1973-99

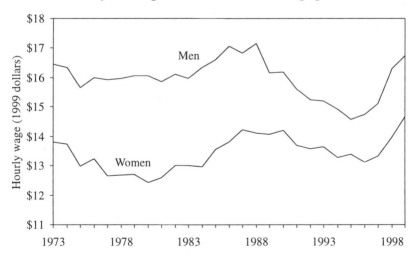

Source: Authors' analysis.

complete college. Nevertheless, men who obtain a college degree will have wages similar only to those obtained by an earlier generation of male college graduates, despite a large productivity gain in the economy over this time period. For instance, the wage of a college-educated male in his late thirties was $26.43 per hour in 1999, comparable to the $26.57 wage paid to an equivalent worker in his late thirties in 1973. Women college graduates, on the other hand, have had a remarkable growth in wages over the last 20 years. For instance, a woman college graduate in her late thirties earned 30.9% more in 1999 than her counterpart did in 1979, although she earned 28% less than her male counterpart in 1999 ($26.43 versus $19.06).

The importance of within-group wage inequality

The data presented so far illustrate the various dimensions of wage inequality. The "between-group" inequality for workers by both education and experience (or age) can be characterized as a growth in education and experience differentials, which is sometimes labeled as an increase in the "returns to education and experience" or as a shift in the rewards or price of "skill." We now examine in greater depth the growth of "within-group" wage inequality, the inequality among workers with similar education and experience.

This growth in within-group wage inequality was shown earlier in Table 2.17. The analysis in **Table 2.23** illustrates the growth of this type of inequality by presenting wage trends of high-, middle-, and low-wage workers among high school and college graduates. In other words, the data track the wages of 90th, 50th (median), and 10th percentile high-school-educated and college-educated workers by gender and show a growing wage gap among college graduates and high school graduates.

Because of rising within-group inequality, the wage growth of the median or "typical" worker within each group has been less than that of the "average" worker. For instance, the wage of the median male high school graduate fell 18.6% over the 1979-99 period, compared to the 14.8% wage drop of the "average" male high school graduate (Table 2.19). Similarly, the wage growth of male college graduates in the 1979-99 period was 10.6% at the average (Table 2.19) but only 4.8% at the median.

The growing disparity of wages within groups is amply demonstrated in Table 2.23. While the high (90th percentile) wage among female college graduates grew 38.5% from 1979 to 1999, the low (10th percentile) wage in this group rose 13.2%, a 25 percentage-point divergence. Similarly, there was a large divergence between wage trends at the top of the college male wage ladder

TABLE 2.23 Hourly wages by decile within education groups, 1973-99 (1999 dollars)

Education/ gender decile	Hourly wage					Percent change				
	1973	1979	1989	1995	1999	1973-79	1979-89	1989-99	1995-99	1979-99
High school										
Men										
Low*	$8.24	$7.63	$6.46	$6.10	$6.54	-7.4%	-15.4%	1.2%	7.2%	-14.3%
Median	14.86	14.55	12.54	11.24	11.84	-2.1	-13.9	-5.5	5.4	-18.6
High	24.28	23.75	22.10	20.67	21.33	-2.2	-7.0	-3.5	3.2	-10.2
Women										
Low	$5.58	$6.37	$5.13	$5.20	$5.59	14.0%	-19.5%	9.0%	7.4%	-12.3%
Median	9.22	9.01	8.86	8.49	8.95	-2.3	-1.6	1.0	5.4	-0.6
High	15.26	15.38	15.97	15.69	16.02	0.8	3.8	0.3	2.1	4.2
College										
Men										
Low	$10.18	$9.84	$9.15	$8.51	$9.62	-3.3%	-7.1%	5.1%	13.1%	-2.3%
Median	19.11	18.56	18.97	18.22	19.45	-2.9	2.2	2.5	6.8	4.8
High	35.63	34.10	34.40	35.59	40.74	-4.3	0.9	18.4	14.5	19.5
Women										
Low	$7.83	$7.07	$7.22	$7.16	$8.01	-9.6%	2.0%	11.0%	11.9%	13.2%
Median	13.52	12.28	13.94	14.42	15.26	-9.2	13.6	9.4	5.8	24.2
High	21.36	20.87	24.29	26.76	28.90	-2.3	16.4	19.0	8.0	38.5

* "Low," "median," and "high" earners refer to, respectively, the 10th, 50th, and 90th percentile wage.

Source: Authors' analysis.

(19.5% growth) and the bottom (a 2.3% drop) over the 1979-99 period.

The question remains, however, as to how much the growth in overall wage inequality in particular time periods has been driven by changes in between-group versus within-group wage inequality. It would also be useful to know the role of the growth of between- and within-group inequality on growing wage inequality at the top (the 90/50 differential) versus the bottom (the 50/10 differential), but measurement techniques for answering this question are not readily available.

Table 2.24 presents the trends in overall wage inequality, as measured by the standard deviation of log hourly wages, and the trends in within-group wage inequality. These measures allow us to examine how much of the change in overall wage inequality in particular periods was due to changes in within-group wage inequality and between-group wage inequality (primarily changes in education and experience differentials).

TABLE 2.24 Decomposition of total and within-group wage inequality, 1973-99

	Women				Men			
Year	Overall wage inequality* (1)	Between-group inequality*** (2)	Within-group inequality** (3)	Contribution of within-group inequality (3)/(1)	Overall wage inequality* (1)	Between-group inequality*** (2)	Within-group inequality** (3)	Contribution of within-group inequality (3)/(1)
1973	0.478	0.061	0.418		0.506	0.083	0.423	
1979	0.446	0.044	0.402		0.506	0.078	0.428	
1989	0.529	0.082	0.447		0.579	0.112	0.467	
1995	0.562	0.095	0.467		0.595	0.118	0.478	
1999	0.553	0.096	0.457		0.595	0.119	0.476	
Change								
1973-79	-0.033	-0.017	-0.016	49%	0.000	-0.005	0.006	n.a
1979-89	0.083	0.038	0.046	55	0.073	0.034	0.038	53%
1989-99	0.024	0.014	0.010	40	0.016	0.007	0.009	55
1989-95	0.033	0.013	0.019	59	0.016	0.006	0.011	65
1995-99	-0.008	0.001	-0.010	n.a	0.000	0.002	-0.002	n.a
1979-99	0.108	0.052	0.055	51	0.089	0.042	0.047	53

* Measured as standard deviation of log wages.

** Measured as mean square error from a standard (log) wage regression.

*** Reflects changes in education, experience, race/ethnicity, marital status, and regional differentials.

n.a. not applicable because denominator is zero or too small.

Source: Authors' analysis.

The data in Table 2.24 indicate that half or more of the growth of wage inequality since 1979 has been due to the growth of within-group wage inequality. Among women, for instance, overall wage inequality grew 0.108 over the 1979-99 period, of which 0.055 was due to the growth of within-group wage inequality. Similarly, 0.047 of the 0.089 increase in overall male wage inequality over the 1979-99 period was due to growing within-group inequality.

Within-group wage inequality drove half of the overall growth in wage inequality in both the 1980s and the early 1990s. Wage inequality over the 1995-99 period was essentially unchanged, the result of a decline in within-group wage inequality offsetting growth in between-group inequality. Thus, Table 2.24 makes clear that any explanation of growing wage inequality must go beyond explaining changes in skill, education, experience, or other wage differentials and be able to explain growing inequalities within each of these categories.

It is also noteworthy that between-group wage inequality did not rise appreciably in the 1995-99 technology-related productivity and wage boom. This finding is inconsistent with a story that technology has generated greater wage inequalities by expanding skill differentials—primarily by education and experience. These data show that, while it is true that the college/high school wage differential grew in the 1995-99 period, experience differentials fell and education differentials between high school and less-than-high-school workers were stable (see Table 2.17).

School quality and tests

One potential explanation for the poor performance of wages for the non-college-educated workforce over the 1979-95 period is a deterioration in school quality. That is, if schools have worsened, then the lower wages of high school graduates might simply reflect that they are less knowledgeable. Several studies have rejected this explanation on the grounds that a significant growth in wage inequality and in education premiums has occurred in every age group. If "school deterioration" were the driving force behind wage inequality, then one would expect these wage developments to be limited to recent entrants to the workforce and not affect the graduates of the 1970s, 1960s, and 1950s. The data in Table 2.22, for instance, show that wages for high school men fell over the 1980s and 1990s not only among recent high school graduates but also for those who had graduated roughly 20 to 35 years earlier.

Another reason for skepticism is that there is not much evidence of a deterioration in school quality, although there is not much evidence of overall improvement either, as evidenced by the historical trends in mathematics and reading test scores for 17-year-olds shown in **Figure 2P**. Among whites, test scores have been fairly constant since the early 1970s. In contrast, black and Hispanic 17-year-olds in 1994 scored higher in math and reading than their counterparts did in the early or late 1970s. So, test trends do not readily correspond to the pattern of wage decline for less-skilled workers—or even for entry-level high school graduates, whose wages might be expected to parallel 17-year-olds' test scores. Their wages fell in the 1980s relative to the 1970s even though test scores improved, and the better wage performance of the 1990s did not follow any test score improvement.

Wage growth by race and ethnicity

Race and ethnicity have long played an important role in shaping employment opportunities and labor market outcomes. As the United States has become more diverse, it becomes useful to review trends among the various race/ethnic subgroups. **Tables 2.25** and **2.26** present the wage trends by gender for key indicators of the wage structure (the median wage and the high school wage) for four populations: white, black, Hispanic, and Asian. (A finer breakdown of groups was not possible in the 1990s because of sample size limitations and, for the same reason, the trends for the 1980s are not available. Also, note that our definitions of race/ethnicity categories exclude Hispanics from the white, black, and Asian groups.)

The male median wage trends show that all groups, except Hispanics, experienced declining wages during the 1989-95 period, followed by strong wage growth between 1995 and 1999 (Table 2.25 and **Figure 2Q**). Despite the strong wage growth after 1995, however, it was not until 1999 that the median male wage among whites, blacks, and Asians returned to its 1989, pre-recession level. In contrast, the median Hispanic male's wage in 1999 was still 2.5% below its 1989 level. A similar pattern is evident among high-school-educated male workers: wages declined significantly over the 1989-95 period, then grew in 1995-99. However, even by 1999, the wages of high-school-educated men in each group were just at or below their 1989 levels.

Wage trends among women correspond to those of men except for slightly faster wage growth. For instance, the median or typical white, black, Hispanic, and Asian woman worker lost ground in 1989-95 but recovered during 1995-99. As **Figure 2R** shows, women's median wages returned to their 1989 levels in 1997 for whites, Asians, and Hispanics, but it was not until 1998 that the wages of black women recovered. Wage growth among high-school-educated women showed a similar pattern, with whites, blacks, and Hispanics having persistent wage erosion from 1989 to 1995. Wages rebounded strongly, however, after 1995.

FIGURE 2P Reading and mathematics proficiency by race

READING PROFICIENCY, 1971-98

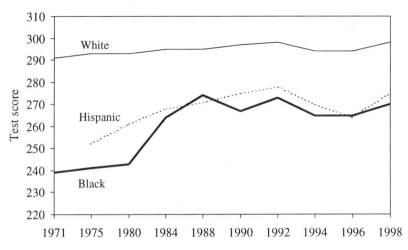

MATHEMATICS PROFICIENCY, 1973-96

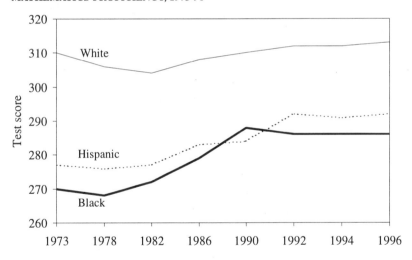

Source: Authors' analysis.

TABLE 2.25 Hourly wage growth among men by race/ethnicity, 1989-99 (1999 dollars)

	Hourly wage (1999 dollars)			Changes		
	1989	1995	1999	1989-99	1989-95	1995-99
Medians						
White	$13.89	$13.09	$13.90	0.1%	-5.7%	6.2%
Black	10.55	9.97	10.78	2.3	-5.4	8.1
Hispanic	11.31	11.43	11.03	-2.5	1.1	-3.5
Asian	13.62	13.12	14.67	7.7	-3.7	11.8
By education						
*High school**						
White	$14.13	$13.14	$13.69	-3.1%	-7.0%	4.1%
Black	11.46	10.69	11.40	-0.5	-6.7	6.6
Hispanic	12.47	12.83	12.37	-0.8	2.9	-3.6
Asian	12.52	11.90	12.24	-2.3	-5.0	2.8

* Average wage.

Source: Authors' analysis.

TABLE 2.26 Hourly wage growth among women by race/ethnicity, 1989-99 (1999 dollars)

	Hourly wage (1999 dollars)			Changes		
	1989	1995	1999	1989-99	1989-95	1995-99
Medians						
White	$10.03	$9.93	$10.57	5.4%	-1.1%	6.5%
Black	9.11	8.74	9.23	1.3	-4.0	5.5
Hispanic	8.80	8.37	9.06	2.9	-4.9	8.2
Asian	10.55	10.44	11.39	8.0	-1.0	9.1
By education						
*High school**						
White	$10.01	$9.88	$10.32	3.1%	-1.2%	4.4%
Black	9.29	8.97	9.36	0.8	-3.4	4.4
Hispanic	9.02	9.11	9.84	9.1	1.0	8.1
Asian	9.57	9.41	10.14	6.0	-1.7	7.8

* Average wage.

Source: Authors' analysis.

FIGURE 2Q Index of median hourly wages for men by race and ethnicity

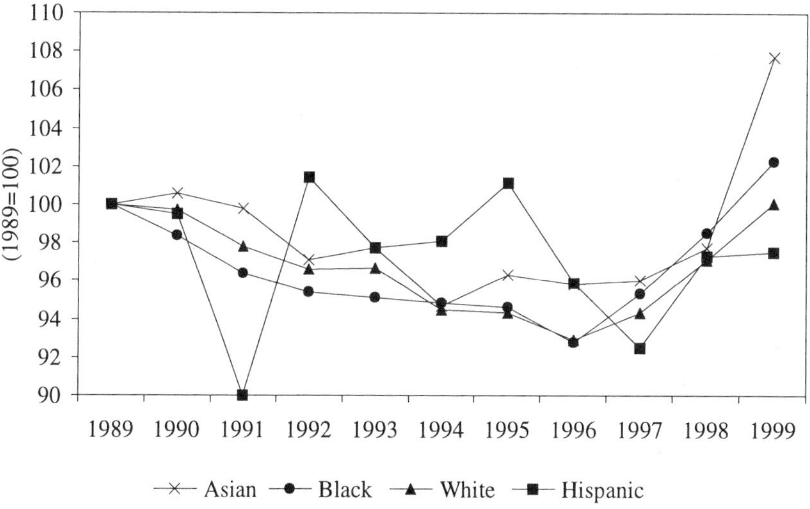

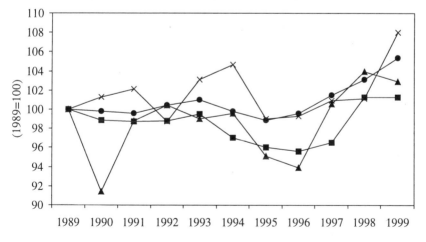

Source: Authors' analysis.

FIGURE 2R Index of median hourly wages for women by race and ethnicity

Source: Authors' analysis.

The shift to low-paying industries

One causal factor that is frequently considered in any analysis of growing inequality is a changing mix of industries in the economy. Such changes include the continued shift from goods-producing to service-producing industries. The consequence for the labor market results from the consequent shift in the mix of employment among industries, which matters because some industries pay more than others (for workers of comparable skill).

These industry employment shifts are a consequence of trade deficits and deindustrialization as well as stagnant or falling productivity growth in service sector industries. This section examines the significant erosion of wages and compensation for non-college-educated workers that resulted from an employment shift to low-paying industries in the 1980s. The smaller impact of industry shifts in the 1990 is one of the reasons that low-wage workers saw some economic gains in the 1990s.

Despite a common perception, this industry shift effect is not the simple consequence of some natural evolution from an agricultural to a manufacturing to a service economy. For one thing, a significant part of the shrinkage of manufacturing is trade related. More important, industry shifts would not provide a downward pressure on wages if service sector wages were more closely aligned with manufacturing wages, as is the case in other countries. Moreover, since health coverage, vacations, and pensions in this country are related to the specific job or sector in which a worker is employed, the sectoral distribution of employment matters more in the United States than in other countries. An alternative institutional arrangement found in other advanced countries sets health, pensions, vacation, and other benefits through legislation in a universal manner regardless of sector or firm. Therefore, the downward pressure of industry shifts on pay can be said to be the consequence of the absence of institutional structures that lessen inter-industry pay differences.

Trends in employment growth by major industry sector and the hourly compensation of each sector are presented in **Table 2.27**. The 18.1 million (net) jobs created between 1979 and 1989 involved a loss of manufacturing (1.6 million) and mining (266,000) jobs and an increase (19.3 million jobs) in the service sector. The largest amount of job growth (14.2 million) was in the two lowest-paying service sector industries—retail trade and services (business, personnel, and health). In fact, these two industries accounted for 79% of all the net new jobs over the 1979-89 period.

The shift toward low-paying industries continued in the 1990s, although at a much slower pace. Low-wage retail jobs have played a smaller role in overall job creation, contributing 15.9% of the new jobs, but the services industry (pri-

TABLE 2.27 Employment growth by sector, 1979-99 (in thousands)

Industry sector	Employment (thousands)			Job growth		Industry share of job growth		Hourly compensation 1997 (ECI)
	1979	1989	1999	1979-89	1989-99	1979-89	1989-99	
Goods producing	26,461	25,254	25,482	-1,207	228	-6.7%	1.1%	$21.86
Mining	958	692	535	-266	-157	-1.5	-0.8	n.a.
Construction	4,463	5,171	6,404	708	1,233	3.9	5.9	21.47
Manufacturing	21,040	19,391	18,543	-1,649	-848	-9.1	-4.1	21.84
Durable goods	12,760	11,394	11,103	-1,366	-291	-7.6	-1.4	23.49
Nondurable goods	8,280	7,997	7,440	-283	-557	-1.6	-2.7	19.48
Service producing	63,363	82,642	103,304	19,279	20,662	106.7%	98.9%	$16.73
Trans., comm., util.	5,136	5,625	6,826	489	1,201	2.7	5.7	n.a.
Wholesale	5,204	6,187	6,924	983	737	5.4	3.5	19.98
Retail	14,989	19,475	22,788	4,486	3,313	24.8	15.9	9.92
Fin., ins., real est.	4,975	6,668	7,569	1,693	901	9.4	4.3	23.01
Services	17,112	26,907	39,027	9,795	12,120	54.2	58.0	17.84
Government	15,947	17,779	20,170	1,832	2,391	10.1	11.4	n.a.
Total	89,823	107,895	128,786	18,072	20,891	100.0%	100.0%	$17.97

Source: Authors' analysis.

marily health and temporary services) became somewhat more important, supplying 58.0% of the net new jobs. Together, these low-wage industries accounted for 73.9% of all new jobs in 1989-99. Manufacturing job loss was just half as great in the 1990s as in the 1980s, and higher-wage industries such as construction and transportation/communications expanded more in the 1990s than in the 1980s. Thus, industry shifts were less adverse in the 1990s.

The extent of the shift to low-wage industries in the 1980s is more evident in an analysis of changes in the shares of the workforce in various sectors (**Table 2.28**). Several high-wage sectors, such as construction, transportation, wholesale, communications, and government, increased employment in the 1980s but ended up providing a smaller or similar share of overall employment over time. A lower share of employment in these high-wage sectors puts downward pressure on wages. Overall, the share of the workforce in low-paying services and in retail trade was 7.3 percentage points higher in 1989 than in 1979. The parallel trend was the roughly 8 percentage-point drop in the share of the workforce in high-paying industries, such as manufacturing, construction, mining, government, transportation, communications, and utilities.

The data in Table 2.28 illustrate the different, and less adverse, shifts in

TABLE 2.28 Changes in employment share by sector, 1979-99

Industry sector	Employment shares			Percentage-point change	
	1979	1989	1999	1979-89	1989-99
Goods producing	29.5%	23.4%	19.8%	-6.1	-3.6
Mining	1.1	0.6	0.4	-0.4	-0.2
Construction	5.0	4.8	5.0	-0.2	0.2
Manufacturing	23.4	18.0	14.4	-5.5	-3.6
Durable goods	14.2	10.6	8.6	-3.6	-1.9
Nondurable goods	9.2	7.4	5.8	-1.8	-1.6
Service Producing	70.5%	76.6%	80.2%	6.1	3.6
Trans., comm., util.	5.7	5.2	5.3	-0.5	0.1
Wholesale	5.8	5.7	5.4	-0.1	-0.4
Retail	16.7	18.0	17.7	1.4	-0.4
Fin., ins., real est.	5.5	6.2	5.9	0.6	-0.3
Services	19.1	24.9	30.3	5.9	5.4
Government	17.8	16.5	15.7	-1.3	-0.8
Total	100%	100%	100%		

Source: Authors' analysis.

industry employment in the 1990s relative to the 1980s. Although durable manufacturing's share of employment declined in the 1990s (by 1.9 percentage points), this was roughly half the decline of the 1980s (3.6 percentage points). The low-wage retail trade sector expanded by 1.4 percentage points in the 1980s but shrank in the 1990s. Similarly, higher-wage sectors such as construction and transportation/communications expanded in the 1990s but contracted in the 1980s. In general, high-wage sectors fared better in terms of employment growth in the 1990s than the 1980s. Correspondingly, the 1990s contraction of retail trade, by far the lowest wage sector, helped wages grow. Thus, one reason that median wages eroded less and low wages did better in the early 1990s than in the 1980s might be related to this different pattern of industry employment growth.

Table 2.29 presents an analysis of the impact of the shift in the industry mix of employment on the growth of the college/high school wage premium, providing some systematic evidence of how industry shifts affect the growth of wage inequality, at least on this one wage premium. The analysis uses wage data on individuals to determine the growth of the college/high school wage premium when one does and does not control for industry shifts—the "constant" and "actual" under "industry composition." Comparing the growth of the education

TABLE 2.29 The effect of industry shifts on the growth of the college/high school differential, 1973-99

| | College/high school wage differential industry composition: | | Industry shift: | |
	Actual* (1)	Constant** (2)	Effect (3) = (1) - (2)	Share*** (3) / (1)
Men				
1973	25.3%	30.3%		
1979	20.1	24.8		
1989	33.9	36.2		
1992	36.9	38.2		
1999	42.4	43.3		
Percentage-point change				
1979-89	13.9	11.4	2.5	18.0
1989-99	8.4	7.0	1.4	16.5
1989-92	2.9	2.0	0.9	31.6
1992-99	5.5	5.0	0.5	8.6
Women				
1973	37.7%	35.2%		
1979	26.5	25.2		
1989	41.0	37.1		
1992	43.7	39.5		
1999	48.3	45.0		
Percentage-point change				
1979-89	14.5	11.9	2.7	18.4
1989-99	7.3	8.0	-0.7	-9.7
1989-92	2.7	2.5	0.3	9.8
1992-99	4.5	5.5	-1.0	-21.5

*   Estimated with controls for experience as a quartic, marital status, race, and four regions.
**   Adds 12 industry controls to the regression reported in first column, thereby holding industry constant.
*** Share of the rise in "actual" that is explained by industry shifts, calculated from the difference between actual and constant relative to actual.

Source: Authors' analysis.

premium in the first two columns provides information on the impact of changes in the industry composition of employment, or industry shifts. This analysis suggests that the employment shift to low-wage industries accounted for almost 20% of the growth of education premiums over the 1979-89 period among men and women. Among men, for instance, the college/high school wage premium grew 13.9 percentage points from 1979 to 1989, but would have grown by 11.4 percentage points had industry composition not changed. Therefore, 2.5 percentage points (13.9 less 11.4) of the 13.9 percentage-point growth, equivalent to 18% of the total growth in the college/high school differential in the 1980s, can be accounted for by industry shifts.

Among men, the industry shift effect was smaller in 1989-99 than in 1979-89, 2.5% versus 1.4%, and was especially slow during the 1992-99 recovery. Among women, industry shifts were actually inequality-reducing in the 1990s due to the trends over the 1992-99 recovery. Thus, the industry shift effect went from inducing a 2.7% increase in the college wage premium in the 1980s to reducing this premium by 0.7% in the 1990s, a 3.4% turnaround in trend. It is likely that this reversal is due to the corresponding reversal of retail trade employment (heavily female intensive) in the 1990s—its employment share contracted rather than expanded, as it had in the 1980s.

Trade and wages

The process of globalization in the 1980s and 1990s has been an important factor in both slowing the growth rate of average wages and reducing the wage levels of workers with less than a college degree. The increase in international trade and investment flows affects wages through several channels. First, increases in imports of finished manufactured goods, especially from countries where workers earn only a fraction of what U.S. workers earn, reduces manufacturing employment in the United States. While increases in exports create employment opportunities for some domestic workers, imports mean job losses for many others. Large, chronic trade deficits over the last 17 years suggest that the jobs lost to import competition have outnumbered the jobs gained from increasing exports. Given that export industries tend to be less labor intensive than import-competing industries, even growth in "balanced trade" (where exports and imports both increase by the same dollar amount) would lead to a decline in manufacturing jobs.

Second, imports of intermediate manufactured goods (used as inputs in the production of final goods) also help to lower domestic manufacturing employment, especially for production workers and others with less than a college education. The expansion of export platforms in low-wage countries has induced many U.S. manufacturing firms to outsource part of their production processes to low-wage countries. Since firms generally find it most profitable to outsource the most labor-intensive processes, the increase in outsourcing has hit non-college-educated production workers hardest.

Third, low wages and greater world capacity for producing manufactured goods can lower the prices of many international goods. Since workers' pay is tied to the value of the goods they produce, lower prices internationally can lead to a reduction in the earnings of U.S. workers, even if imports themselves do not increase.

Fourth, in many cases the mere threat of direct foreign competition or of the relocation of part or all of a production facility can lead workers to grant wage concessions to their employers.

Fifth, the very large increases in direct investment (i.e., plant and equipment) flows to other countries have meant reduced investment in the domestic manufacturing base and significant growth in the foreign manufacturing capacity capable of competing directly with U.S.-based manufacturers.

Finally, the effects of globalization go beyond those workers exposed directly to foreign competition. As trade drives workers out of manufacturing and into lower-paying service jobs, not only do their own wages fall, but the new supply of workers to the service sector (from displaced workers plus young workers not able to find manufacturing jobs) also helps to lower the wages of those already employed in service jobs.

This section briefly examines the role of international trade and investment in recent changes in the U.S. wage structure. Since even the preceding list of channels through which globalization affects wages is not complete and not yet quantified, this analysis will *understate* the impact of globalization on wages in the 1980s and 1990s. This topic is a relatively new area of inquiry in empirical labor economics and international trade; as befits a new area of investigation, it is beset with considerable controversy and confusion. Unfortunately, no studies are yet available that analyze trade's impact on the wage structure over the 1990s, although some do analyze the early 1990s.

Table 2.30 provides information on the growth of the manufacturing trade deficit (the excess of imports over exports) from 1973 to 1993 by region and by type of industry—industries that heavily use unskilled labor, skilled labor, or capital. The trade deficit grew to $130.7 billion in 1993 (and has grown further since), whereas U.S. manufacturing trade was balanced in 1973 and mildly unbalanced in the late 1970s. This growing trade deficit reflects the fast growth of imports in the 1980s and 1990s and the much slower growth of exports.

A sizable deterioration in the U.S. trade balance with Asian developing countries (Singapore, Taiwan, Korea, and Hong Kong), China (in "other Asia"), and

TABLE 2.30 Net trade in U.S. manufactures by skill intensity and trading partner, 1973-93 ($ millions)

Country/Region	Skilled-intensive manufactures			Unskilled-intensive manufactures			Capital-intensive manufactures			Total		
	1973	1984	1993	1973	1984	1993	1973	1984	1993	1973	1984	1993
Advanced	$2,648	-$8,249	-$27,531	-$5,863	-$26,078	-$18,728	-$3,941	-$36,550	-$45,746	-$7,156	-$70,877	-$92,006
Japan	-2,088	-19,999	-45,284	-1,903	-10,772	-4,703	-2,005	-17,596	-26,076	-5,997	-48,367	-76,063
Other	4,736	11,750	17,753	-3,960	-15,306	-14,026	-1,936	-18,955	-19,671	-1,159	-22,510	-15,943
OPEC	1,207	5,029	6,070	206	79	-2,044	718	2,921	5,847	2,131	8,030	9,872
Eastern Europe	285	174	1,587	-236	-469	-1,355	101	19	496	149	-276	728
Developing	3,375	337	-17,407	-2,713	-24,971	-57,812	3,594	8,643	25,918	4,256	-15,991	-49,301
Latin America	2,422	4,420	6,136	-41	-2,656	-872	2,091	4,178	8,981	4,472	5,942	14,245
Asia-Four Tigers	-311	-8,699	-23,431	-2,322	-18,640	-33,013	354	788	7,900	-2,278	-26,551	-48,545
Other Asia	464	2,167	-2,603	-244	-3,148	-20,854	344	1,773	6,148	564	792	-17,309
Other	799	2,449	2,491	-106	-527	-3,073	804	1,904	2,889	1,498	3,826	2,308
Total	7,515	-2,709	-37,281	-8,606	-51,438	-79,940	471	-24,968	-13,486	-620	-79,114	-130,708

Source: Cline (1997).

Japan has driven the rising trade deficit. In contrast, the deficit with other advanced (and higher-wage) countries grew less than $15 billion over this period.

Much of the growth in the trade deficit from 1973 to 1993 occurred in industries that intensively use unskilled labor, about $70 billion of the $130 billion growth. However, there was also a roughly $45 billion deterioration (from $7.5 to -$37.3 billion) in skill-intensive industries and a $14 billion erosion in capital-intensive industries. More recent data would show a large deterioration with China, Canada, and Mexico fueling a historically high trade deficit.

These data suggest not only a large increase in the trade deficit but a growing exposure of a broad range of industries to foreign competition from the most advanced, developing countries. This growth in the trade deficit and increased global competition can, and would be expected to, adversely affect the wages of non-college-educated workers relative to others. In fact, any potential gains from trade would be created precisely through such a mechanism—a redeployment of workers and capital into more highly skilled or capital-intensive industries, which lessens the need for non-college-educated workers.

We now turn to an examination of the types of jobs that were lost as the trade deficit grew, as job losses in import-sensitive industries exceeded job gains in export industries. In periods of low unemployment, it may be the case that a trade deficit does not cause actual job loss because workers displaced by rising imports have found employment in non-traded sectors such as services. Nevertheless, even at low unemployment a trade deficit will affect the composition of jobs (less manufacturing, more services), thereby affecting wage inequality. In this light, **Table 2.31** indicates how trade flows affect the composition of employment by wage level and education relative to a situation in which the ratios of imports and exports to output remained at 1979 levels.

Of the 2,366,000 jobs lost over the 1979-94 period, college-educated workers lost 290,000 and high-wage workers lost 230,000. The impact of the growing trade deficit, nevertheless, was disproportionately borne by non-college-educated workers, especially those with no more than a high school degree. Likewise, trade-deficit-related job losses fell disproportionately on the lowest-wage workers and lower-middle-wage workers, the 62.5% of the workforce with the lowest pay. Consequently, non-college-educated and middle- and lower-wage workers disproportionately bear the costs and pressures due to trade deficits and the global competition they reflect.

Taken together, Tables 2.30 and 2.31 suggest that trade, particularly with low-wage developing countries, accelerated the long-term decline in manufacturing employment. The data also suggest that the fall in employment opportunities was especially severe for non-college-educated manufacturing production workers. Since production workers in manufacturing on average earn

TABLE 2.31 Trade-deficit-induced job loss by wage and education level, 1979-94

Job characteristic	Share of total employment, 1989	Trade-deficit related job loss (thousands)		
		1979-89	1989-94	1979-94
Education level				
College graduate*	18.6%	-215	-31	-290
Non-college	81.4	-1,550	-356	-2,076
Some college	31.3	-403	-55	-519
High school	31.2	-653	-148	-867
Less than high school	18.9	-495	-153	-690
	100.0			
Wage level**				
Highest wage	9.7%	-163	-34	-230
High wage	11.2	-186	-27	-244
Upper-middle	16.6	-269	-36	-345
Lower-middle	26.4	-478	-96	-631
Lowest wage	36.1	-670	-194	-916
	100.0			
Total		-1,765	-387	-2,366

*   Four years of college or more.
** Corresponding to jobs that paid in the following wage percentile ranges in 1979: 90-99; 75-89; 50-74; 21-49; 0-20.

Source: Scott et al. (1997), Tables 1 and 2.

substantially more than workers with similar skills in non-manufacturing jobs, these trade-induced job losses contributed directly to the deterioration in the wage structure. Since millions of trade-displaced workers sought jobs in non-manufacturing sectors, trade also worked to depress wages of comparable workers employed outside manufacturing.

As discussed earlier, international trade can also affect U.S. wages through the prices of internationally traded manufactured goods without any change in the quantity of exports or imports. The expansion of manufacturing capacity in low-wage countries since the 1970s has significantly increased the supply of less-skill-intensive manufactured goods, inducing a reduction in the U.S. price of these goods. Since workers' earnings reflect changes in the prices of the goods they produce, a lower price for less-skill-intensive goods drives down the wages of less-skilled workers. **Table 2.32** presents results from some simple calcula-

TABLE 2.32 Effect of changes in prices of internationally traded manufactured goods on wage inequality

Industry price changes*	1959-69	1969-79	1979-89
College weighted	12.9%	159.5%	61.4%
Non-college weighted	15.1	142.8	58.5
Difference	-2.2	16.7	2.9
Non-production weighted	16.1%	13.7%	62.0%
Production weighted	16.2	137.5	56.6
Difference	-0.1	-0.5	5.4
Labor share in value-added			70.0%
Implied decline in wages**			
Noncollege			4.1%
Production			7.7
Actual change in relative wages			
College/non-college***			13.9%
Non-production/production			7.7
Share of change in relative wages **caused by change in relative prices**			
College/non-college			29.8%
Non-production/production			110.2

*   Change in value-added producer price indexes over the period.
**   Assuming no change in the real wage of non-production and college workers.
*** Change between 1979 and 1989 in regression-based college/non-college wage differential, controlling for workers' experience and region of residence.

Source: Authors' analysis of Schmitt and Mishel (1996).

tions designed to estimate the effect of trade-induced price changes on U.S. wages. It examines whether prices grew more slowly in the manufacturing industries most reliant on non-college-educated or unskilled and semi-skilled workers—the industries most affected by low-wage imports. Two measures of skill intensity are shown. The first section shows that between 1979 and 1989 the prices in college-worker-intensive industries increased by 2.9% relative to non-college-worker-intensive industries. The second section shows that the prices in non-production-intensive industries rose by 5.4% relative to those in production-worker-intensive industries over the same period.

These relative price changes require the wages of non-college-educated and production workers to fall. The size of the wage declines depends on the importance of labor costs in overall manufacturing costs. If labor were a small share of total manufacturing costs, say 10%, then a 1% decline in the relative prices of less-skill-intensive goods would require a large fall (10%) in the less-skilled workers' wage in order to leave the overall industry costs unchanged (a 10% fall in something that is 10% of total costs represents a 1% savings on overall costs). If labor were a large share of total manufacturing costs, or value-added (say, 100%), then a 1% decline in the relative prices of less-skill-intensive industries would require a much smaller (1%) decline in the costs of less-skilled labor (a 1% fall in the costs of something that is 100% of total costs represents a 1% savings on overall costs). Since labor costs are, on average, 70% of total manufacturing value-added, then a 1% fall in the relative less-skill-intensive industry price requires about a 1.4% fall in the wage of the relatively less-skilled worker. If we assume that the average real wage for college-educated and non-production workers was unchanged between 1979 and 1989 (as was generally the case), then the 2.9% fall in the relative prices in non-college-educated-intensive industries should have lowered the non-college wage by 4.1% over the period. The 5.4% relative fall in production-worker-intensive prices should have lowered production worker wages by 7.7%. Since the wages of non-college-educated relative to college-educated workers actually fell 13.9% over the period, trade appears to have contributed about 30% of the decline in the college/non-college wage over the 1979-89 period. By this measure, trade was entirely responsible for the 7.7% fall in production worker wages relative to those of non-production workers.

The preceding tables document the rise in trade deficits and the decline in prices of less-skill-intensive, internationally traded manufactured goods. These channels have contributed to the long-term decline in manufacturing employment and directly and indirectly to the deterioration in the U.S. wage structure. Little concrete evidence is available on the other channels discussed at the beginning of this section—the "threat effect" of imports and plant relocation on U.S. manufacturing wages and the reality of large-scale international direct investment flows. Nevertheless, these effects are likely to be as large or larger than those that are more readily quantifiable.

Another aspect of globalization is immigration. After six decades of decline in the percentage of immigrants in the total population of the United States, the immigrant share began to grow in the 1970s (**Table 2.33**). The annual increase in legal immigrants (no data are available on undocumented, or "illegal," immigrants) has grown significantly, now nearly 1 million each year in the 1990s, up from less than half that much in the 1970s (449,000 annually). As a result, the foreign-born share of the population rose to 9.8% in 1998, with legal immigrants making up 37.5% of the population growth in the 1990s.

Holding all else constant, a rise in immigration increases the available labor

TABLE 2.33 Legal immigrant flow to the United States, 1881-1998

Decade	Number (thousands)		As percentage of change in population	Foreign-born as share of population*
	Total	Annual		
1881-1890	5,246.6	524.7	41.0%	14.7%
1891-1900	3,687.6	368.8	28.3	13.6
1901-1910	8,795.4	879.5	53.9	14.6
1911-1920	5,735.8	573.6	40.8	13.2
1921-1930	4,107.2	410.7	24.6	11.6
1931-1940	528.4	52.8	5.9	8.8
1941-1950	1,350.0	135.0	5.3	6.9
1951-1960	2,515.5	251.6	8.7	5.4
1961-1970	3,321.7	332.2	13.7	4.7
1971-1980	4,493.3	449.3	20.7	6.2
1981-1990	7,338.1	733.8	33.1	7.9
1991-1998	7,605.1	950.6	37.5	9.8

* At end of period.

Source: Borjas (1999) and Camarota (2000).

supply in the United States and thus tends to reduce wages. **Table 2.34** shows that a large share of recent immigrants have less than the equivalent of a high school education (although immigrants, at least until 1990, also were more likely than natives to have a college degree). These numbers suggest that immigrants compete disproportionately with the least-skilled U.S. workers and therefore have contributed to lower wages for those without a high school degree since the end of the 1970s.

Given this downward pressure on low-wage workers from increased immigration, it is surprising that wages at the bottom have done better in the 1990s than in the 1980s, and that the 50/10 wage gap has been stable or declining since the late 1980s. However, the 1990s have also seen two increases in the minimum wage and several years of persistent low unemployment. These factors may have offset the impact of immigration.

The union dimension

The percentage of the workforce represented by unions was stable in the 1970s but fell rapidly in the 1980s and continued to fall in the 1990s, as shown in **Figure 2S**. This falling rate of unionization has lowered wages, not only be-

TABLE 2.34 Educational attainment of immigrant and native men, 1960-98

	Less than high school		College educated	
Year	Native	Immigrants	Native	Immigrants
1960	53.0%	66.0%	11.4%	10.1%
1970	39.7	49.0	15.4	18.6
1980	23.3	37.5	22.8	25.3
1990	11.9	31.4	26.4	26.6
1998	9.0	33.6	29.8	28.3

Source: Authors' analysis of Borjas (1999).

FIGURE 2S Union coverage in the United States, 1973-99

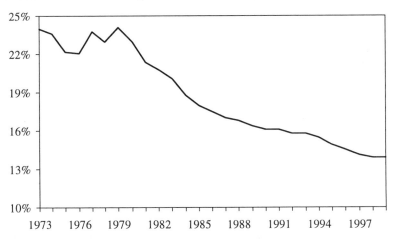

Source: Hirsch and Macpherson (1997) and BLS.

cause some workers no longer receive the higher union wage but also because there is less pressure on non-union employers to raise wages (a "spillover" or "threat effect" of unionism). There are also reasons to believe that union bargaining power has weakened, adding a qualitative shift to the quantitative decline. This erosion of bargaining power is partially related to a harsher economic context for unions because of trade pressures, the shift to services, and ongoing technological change. However, analysts have also pointed to other factors, such as employer militancy and changes in the application and administration of labor law, that have helped to weaken unions.

TABLE 2.35 Union wage and benefit premium, 1997 (1997 dollars)

	Hourly pay			
	Wages	Insurance	Pension	Compensation
All workers				
Union	$17.60	$2.19	$1.33	$23.48
Non-union	14.29	0.94	0.44	17.28
Union premium				
Dollars	$3.31	$1.25	$0.89	$6.20
Percent	23.2%	133.0%	202.3%	35.9%
Blue collar				
Union	$17.73	$2.35	$1.48	$24.07
Non-union	11.84	0.91	0.32	14.75
Union premium				
Dollars	$5.89	$1.44	$1.16	$9.32
Percent	49.7%	158.2%	362.5%	63.2%
Regression-adjusted union effect*				
Union effect, total	21.0%	51.3%	20.3%	27.8%
Incidence		16.0	26.7	
Expenditure		44.2	16.0	

* Controlling for full-time, industry (74), occupation (47), public sector, region (9), and establishment size in 1994.

Source: Authors' analysis of BLS data and Pierce (1998).

Table 2.35 shows the union wage premium—the degree to which union wages exceed non-union wages—by type of pay (benefits or wages) for all workers and for blue-collar workers in 1997. The union premium is larger for total compensation (35.9%) than for wages alone (23.2%), reflecting the fact that unionized workers are provided insurance and pension benefits that are more than double those of non-union workers. For blue-collar workers (where the comparison is more of an "apples to apples" one), the union premium in insurance and benefits is even larger: union blue-collar workers receive 158.2% and 362.5% more in health and pension benefits than do their non-union counterparts.

The bottom section provides a more refined analysis of the union wage premium by comparing the pay in unionized occupations compared to non-union pay in comparable occupations and establishments (factories or offices). Specifically, the estimated union premium controls for the sector (public or private) in which the establishment is located, the establishment's size, full-time or part-time status of its employees, and its detailed industry and region. In this analysis, the union wage premium is 21.0%, while the union compensation premium (combining the effect on wages and benefits) is 27.8%. Similarly, the employers of unionized workers pay 51.3% more in insurance costs (health and life) per hour and 20.3% more for retirement/savings/pension plans

This analysis also shows that unionized workers are 16.0% more likely to be in an employer-provided insurance plan (the "incidence" effect); among workers who are in employer-provided insurance plans, unionized employers pay 44.2% more per hour for the plan (the "expenditure" effect). Similarly, unionized workers are 26.7% more likely to be in a pension plan, and unionized employers pay 16.0% more into these plans than do comparable non-union employers who provide pension plans.

Table 2.36, using a different data source and methodology (and year), presents another set of estimates of the union wage premium. Specifically, the premium is computed so as to reflect differences in hourly wages between union and non-union workers who are otherwise comparable in experience, education, region, industry, occupation, and marital status. This methodology yields a lower but still sizable union premium of 15.1% overall—15.7% for men and 12.8% for women. The differences in union wage premiums across demographic groups are relatively small, ranging from 12.8% to 21.0%. Hispanic and black union members tend to reap the greatest wage advantage from unionism.

The effect of the erosion of unionization on the wages of a segment of the workforce depends on the degree to which deunionization has taken place and the degree to which the union wage premium among that segment of the workforce has declined. **Table 2.37** shows both the degree to which unionization and the union wage premium have declined by occupation and education level over the 1978-97 period (1979 data were not available). These data, which are for men only (some data on women are in a later table), are used to calculate the effect of weakened unions (less representation and a weaker wage effect) over the 1978-97 period on the wages of particular groups and the effect of deunionization on occupation and education wage differentials.

Union representation fell dramatically among blue-collar and high-school-educated male workers from 1978 to 1997. Among the high-school-graduate workforce, unionization fell from 37.9% in 1978 to 20.8% in 1997, almost by half. This obviously weakened the effect of unions on the wages of both union and non-union high-school-educated workers. Because unionized high school graduates earned about 21% more than equivalent non-union workers (a pre-

TABLE 2.36 Union wage premium by demographic group, 1997

Demographic group	Percent union*	Union premium** Dollars	Percent
Total	16.1%	$1.42	15.1%
Men	18.3	1.59	15.7
Women	13.8	1.24	12.8
Whites	15.9%	$1.41	14.9%
Men	18.6	1.54	15.0
Women	13.1	1.28	12.8
Blacks	20.5%	$1.57	15.1%
Men	22.5	1.74	17.0
Women	18.7	1.48	13.1
Hispanics	13.8%	$1.73	18.7%
Men	14.5	2.20	21.0
Women	12.6	0.87	13.1

* Union member or covered by a collective bargaining agreement.
** Regression-adjusted union premium advantage controlling for experience, education, region, industry, occupation, and marital status.

Source: Authors' analysis.

mium that did not change over the 1978-97 period), unionization raised the wage of the average high school graduate by 8.2% in 1978 (the "union effect"). Unions had a 0.9% impact on male college graduate wages in 1978, leaving the net effect of unions to narrow the college/high school gap by 7.3 percentage points in that year. The decline in union representation from 1978 to 1997, however, reduced the union effect for high school male workers to 4.3% in 1997 while hardly affecting college graduates; thus, unions closed the college/high school wage gap by only 3.8 percentage points in 1997. The lessened ability of unions to narrow this wage gap (from a 7.3% to a 3.8% narrowing effect) contributed to a 3.5 percentage-point rise in the college/high school wage differential, an amount equal to 22.5% of the total rise in this wage gap.

The weakening of unionism's wage impact had an even larger effect on blue-collar workers and on the wage gap between blue-collar and white-collar workers. The 43.1% unionization rate among blue-collar workers in 1978 and their 26.6% union wage premium boosted blue-collar wages by 11.5%, thereby closing the blue-collar/white-collar wage gap by 11.3 percentage points in that

TABLE 2.37 Effect of deunionization on male wage differentials, 1978-97

Effect of union decline on wages

	Percent union			Union wage premium*			Union effect**		
	1978	1989	1997	1978	1989	1997	1978	1989	1997
By occupation									
White collar	14.7%	12.1%	10.4%	1.1%	-0.3%	2.2%	0.2%	0.0%	0.2%
Blue collar	43.1	28.9	23.6	26.6	23.3	22.2	11.5	6.7	5.3
Difference	-28.4	-16.7	-13.2	-25.6	-23.6	-20.1	-11.3	-6.8	-5.0
By education									
College	14.3%	11.9%	11.6%	6.3%	4.2%	5.1%	0.9%	0.5%	0.6%
High school	37.9	25.5	20.8	21.7	21.5	20.8	8.2	5.5	4.3
Difference	-23.6	-13.6	-9.2	-15.3	-17.3	-15.8	-7.3	-5.0	-3.8

Contribution of union decline on wage differentials

	Change in wage differential***			Change in union effect			Contribution of lower union effect		
Differential	1978-89	1989-97	1978-97	1978-89	1989-97	1978-97	1978-89	1989-97	1978-97
White collar/ blue collar	9.3%	2.4%	11.6%	4.6%	1.7%	6.3%	49.2%	74.3%	54.3%
College/ high school	13.4	2.3	15.8	2.3	1.2	3.5	17.2	52.8	22.5

*   Estimated with a simple human capital model plus industry and occupation controls.
**   Calculated as the product of percent union and the union wage premium.
*** Estimated with a simple human capital model.

Source: Authors' update of Freeman (1991).

year. The union impact on this differential declined as unionization and the union wage premium declined, such that unionism reduced the blue-collar/white-collar differential by 5.0 rather than 11.3 percentage points in 1997, a 6.3 percentage-point weakening. This lessened effect of unionism can account for about half (54.3%) of the 11.6 percentage-point growth of the blue-collar/white-collar wage gap over the 1978-97 period.

Table 2.38 presents the results of a study that examines the effect of lower unionization on workers at various wage levels. It thus analyzes the impact of deunionization on overall wage inequality (between low-, middle-, and high-wage workers), not just between groups (e.g., high school versus college educated). The data show that unions have their largest effect on the wages of lower-

TABLE 2.38 Effect of unions on wages, by wage fifth, 1973-87

	Lowest fifth	Second fifth	Middle fifth	Fourth fifth	Top fifth	Average
Percent union						
1973	39.9%	43.7%	38.3%	33.5%	12.5%	33.7%
1987	23.5	30.3	33.1	24.7	17.7	26.4
Change, 1973-87	-15.4	-13.4	-5.2	-8.8	7.2	-7.3
Effect of union on:						
Union wage, 1987	27.9%	16.2%	18.0%	0.9%	10.5%	15.9%
Average wage, 1987	6.6	4.9	6.0	2.1	2.1	4.2
Wage effect of deunionization						
1973-87	-4.3%	-2.2%	-0.9%	-0.1%	0.8%	-1.1%

Source: Card (1991).

wage workers, raising the wages of union members in the lowest and second-lowest fifths by 27.9% and 16.2%, respectively. Because workers in the bottom three-fifths have higher unionization rates and higher union wage premiums, the effect of unions on average wages for these groups is largest, increasing the average wage from 4.9% to 6.6%.

Unionization declined more among low-wage than high-wage workers from 1973 to 1987, at the same time that unionization actually increased among the top fifth. The impact was to increase the wage gap between high- and low-wage workers. For instance, an increase in union representation lifted the wages of the top fifth by 0.8%, but deunionization lowered the wages in the bottom fifth by 4.3%, creating a roughly 5 percentage-point divergence between high- and low-wage earners.

Table 2.39 displays the results of three studies of the effect of the drop in unionization on overall male wage inequality. These data show that wage inequality grew substantially between the 1970s and the late 1980s. Remarkably, all three studies found that lower unionization can account for the same proportion of overall higher wage inequality—21%—even though they employ radically different methodologies. Unfortunately, these studies do not examine women's wages. Another study, discussed below (Table 2.44), shows deunionization playing a smaller role among women than men.

As the analysis presented below (Table 2.44) will show, the decline of union coverage and power affects men more than women and adversely affects middle-

TABLE 2.39 Effect of deunionization on male wage inequality

	Wage inequality		
Item	1973-87*	1978-88**	1979-88***
Early year	0.227	0.235	n.a.
Later year	0.284	0.269	n.a.
Change in inequality	0.057	0.034	0.066
Change due to lower unionization	0.012	0.007	0.014
Deunionization contribution to total rise in inequality	21%	21%	21%

*   Change in variance of log earnings among men age 25-64.
**   Change in variance of log earnings among men age 25-65.
*** Change in standard deviation of log earnings among men age 25-65.

Sources: Card (1991); DiNardo, Fortin, and Lemieux (1994); Freeman (1991).

wage men more than lower-wage men. Consequently, deunionization has its greatest impact on the growth of the 90/50 wage gap among men. In this light, it is not surprising that the period of rapid decline of union coverage from 1979 to 1984 (during a deep recession, and at a time that the manufacturing sector was battered by the trade deficit) was also one where the male 90/50 wage gap grew the most. Recall from Table 2.37 that male blue-collar unionization fell from 43.1% in 1978 to just 28.9% in 1989, contributing to the rapid growth of male wage inequality in the 1980s. The decline of unionization in the 1990s put continued downward pressure on middle-wage men and contributed to the continued growth of the 90/50 wage gap.

An eroded minimum wage

The real value of the minimum wage has fallen considerably since its high point in the late 1960s (**Figure 2T**). The decline was particularly steep and steady between 1979 and 1989, when inflation whittled it down from $6.53 to $4.50 (in 1999 dollars), a fall of 31.1% (**Table 2.40**). Despite the legislated increases in the minimum wage in 1990 and 1991 and again in 1996 and 1997, the value of the minimum wage in 1999 was still 21% less than in 1979. The increases in the 1990s raised its 1999 value 14.4% over 1989.

It has been argued that the minimum wage primarily affects teenagers and

FIGURE 2T Real value of the minimum wage, 1960-2001

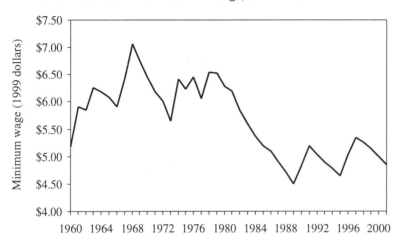

Source: Authors' analysis.

others with no family responsibilities. **Table 2.41** examines the demographic composition of the workforce that benefited from the recent increases in the minimum wage. In fact, only 28.6% of the affected 9,886,158 minimum wage workers were teenagers, suggesting that many minimum wage workers have important economic responsibilities. The information at the bottom of the table shows that minimum wage earners contribute 54% of their family's weekly earnings. Although the majority work part time (less than 35 hours weekly), 46.0% in 1993 worked full time and another 33.3% worked more than 20 hours each week. While minorities are disproportionately represented among minimum wage workers, almost two-thirds are white. These workers also tend to be women (58.2% of the total). Table 2.42 also shows that minimum wage and other low-wage workers are heavily concentrated in the retail trade industry but are underrepresented in manufacturing industries and among unionized employers.

An analysis of only those earning between the old and the new minimum wage would be too narrow, however, since a higher minimum wage affects workers who earn more than but close to the minimum; they will receive increases when the minimum wage rises. For these reasons, Table 2.41 also presents the demographic breakdown of those workers who earned within a dollar of the new minimum wage level ($5.15-$6.14), a group labeled "other low-wage workers." This more broadly defined minimum wage workforce includes an additional 9.6 million workers, or an additional 8.7% of the total workforce. Thus,

TABLE 2.40 Value of the minimum wage, 1960-99

	Minimum wage	
Year	Current dollars	1999 dollars
1960	$1.00	$5.18
1967	1.40	6.43
1973	1.60	5.65
1979	2.90	6.53
1989	3.35	4.50
1990	3.80	4.84
1991	4.25	5.20
1996	4.75	5.04
1997	5.15	5.35
1999	5.15	5.15
Period average		
1960s	$1.29	$6.16
1970s	2.07	6.25
1980s	3.33	5.37
1990s	4.53	5.02
Percent change		
1979-89		-31.1%
1989-99		14.4
1979-99		-21.1

Source: Authors' analysis.

any significant change in the minimum wage would affect a substantial group, as much as 18% of the workforce. The demographic breakdown of "other low-wage workers" is more inclusive of full-time and adult workers but has proportionately fewer minority workers compared to the group of directly affected minimum wage earners.

Table 2.42 assesses the impact of the lowering of the real value of the minimum wage on key wage differentials. The analysis is limited to women, who are affected most by the minimum wage. As the bottom of Table 2.42 shows, 20.1% of women workers in 1989 earned less than the real value of the minimum wage in 1979; in other words, they were directly affected by its erosion in value after 1979. Women without a high school degree were hit hardest, with 43.4% and 53.7% earning below the 1979 minimum wage level in 1989 and 1997, respectively.

TABLE 2.41 Characteristics of minimum wage and other workers, Oct. '95-Sep. '96

Characteristic	Workers directly affected by new minimum ($4.25-$5.14)	Other low-wage workers ($5.15-$6.14)	Workers above minimum wage ($6.15+)	All workers
Average wage	$4.73	$5.72	$14.64	$12.73
Employment	9,886,158	9,610,926	89,079,931	110,999,085
Share of total	8.9%	8.7%	80.3%	100.0%
Demographics				
Male	41.8%	41.9%	54.9%	52.3%
16-19	13.7	8.1	1.0	2.9
20+	28.2	33.8	53.9	49.4
Female	58.2	58.1	45.1	47.7
16-19	14.9	7.9	0.7	2.8
20+	43.2	50.2	44.	44.9
White	62.8	67.7	77.9	75.4
Male	24.6	26.2	42.8	39.4
Female	38.2	41.5	35.1	36.0
Black	16.1	13.8	10.4	11.3
Male	6.4	5.5	5.1	5.3
Female	9.8	8.3	5.3	6.0
Hispanic	17.5	14.8	7.9	9.5
Male	9.3	8.6	4.9	5.7
Female	8.2	6.2	3.0	3.8
Teens (16-19)	28.6%	16.0%	1.7%	5.6%
Work hours				
Full time (35+)	46.0%	62.7%	87.7%	81.1%
Part time				
20-34 hours	33.3%	25.4%	9.0%	13.0%
1-19 hours	20.7	11.9	3.3	5.9
Industry				
Manufacturing	8.8%	12.7%	19.7%	17.8%
Retail trade	42.6	35.8	12.2	17.3
Union*				
Union	4.4%	6.3%	19.1%	16.4%
Non-union	95.6	93.7	80.9	83.6

Addendum: The share of weekly earnings contributed by minimum wage workers, 1997

	Average	Median
All families with an affected worker	54%	41%
excluding one-person families	44	27

* Includes both union members and non-members covered by union contracts.

Source: Bernstein and Schmitt (1998).

TABLE 2.42 Impact of lower minimum wage on key wage differentials among women, 1979-97

Wage differential	Actual wage differentials			Simulated wage differentials at 1979 minimum wage		1979-89				1979-97			
						Change in wage differential			Minimum wage effect	Change in wage differential			Minimum wage effect
	1979	1989	1997	1989	1997	Actual	Simulated	Difference		Actual	Simulated	Difference	
Wage ratios (logs)													
50/10	0.39	0.64	0.63	0.41	0.41	0.26	0.02	0.23	91.1%	0.24	0.02	0.21	89.5%
90/10	1.00	1.35	1.39	1.12	1.18	0.35	0.12	0.23	66.4	0.39	0.18	0.21	54.3
Education differentials													
College/high school	0.31	0.46	0.51	0.42	0.48	0.15	0.11	0.04	28.1%	0.20	0.17	0.03	15.8%
College/less than high school	0.49	0.69	0.75	0.60	0.67	0.20	0.11	0.09	44.2%	0.26	0.18	0.08	29.4
Memo:													
Percent earning less than 1979 minimum													
Less than high school	43.4%		53.7%										
High school	23.6		26.2										
College	6.1		7.0										
All	20.1		21.5										

Source: Authors' analysis.

The analysis in Table 2.42 of the impact of a lower minimum wage on the wage structure is based on a simple simulation. Data on individual workers' wages in recent years are used to construct what the wage structure would have been in 1989 and 1997 if the 1979 minimum wage (again, inflation-adjusted) had still prevailed. Drawing on these simulated counterfactuals, the analysis compares the actual growth in wage differentials to the growth that would have occurred if the 1979 minimum wage had been maintained. The difference between "actual" and "simulated" is a measure of the impact of the lowering of the real value of the minimum wage on particular wage differentials.

The minimum wage most affects women at the 10th percentile and women with the least education, so it should not be surprising that wage differentials between middle- and low-wage women (the 50/10 differential) and college/less-than-high-school wage differentials are greatly affected by a decline in the minimum wage. For instance, the 50/10 differentials (in logs, which approximate percentage differences) would have grown from 0.39 in 1979 to only 0.41, rather than to 0.64, in 1989 if the minimum wage had been maintained. Thus, 0.23 of the 0.26 rise in the 50/10 differential in the 1980s among women, or 91.1% of the rise, can be attributed to a change in minimum wage policy. Similarly, the devaluing of the minimum wage can explain 44.2% of the growth in the college/less-than-high-school wage gap among women in the 1980s. A lower minimum wage also greatly affected the college/high school wage gap, explaining 28.1% of its growth in the 1980s. This analysis confirms the importance of the erosion of a key labor market institution, the minimum wage, on the growth of women's wage inequality at the bottom of the wage scale.

Because there is substantial evidence (with some controversy, of course) that a moderately higher minimum wage does not significantly lower employment (or reduce it at all), there has been an increased focus on which groups of low-wage workers benefit from a higher minimum wage. In other words, because a higher minimum may not have much of an effect on efficiency or output, the merit of such a policy will depend greatly on its fairness.

Table 2.43 presents a computation of which families benefited from the higher minimum wage legislated over the 1996-97 period. The analysis calculates the annual gain to each worker based on the amount of his or her wage increase (i.e., based on the distance to the new minimum) and annual hours worked. Given this information, it is possible to calculate the share of the aggregate wage gain generated from the higher minimum wage that accrues to each household income fifth. As shown in Table 2.43, 35.3% of the gains generated by the higher minimum wage were received by the poorest 20% of working households; 58.1% of the gains were received by the poorest 40%.

TABLE 2.43 Distribution of minimum wage gains and income shares by fifth for various household types

Income fifth	Share of gain from increase	Share of income	Average income
Prime-age working households,* 1997			
Lowest	35.3%	5.4%	$15,728
Second	22.8	11.0	32,547
Middle	15.2	15.9	47,699
Fourth	14.5	22.3	66,104
Highest	12.2	45.3	134,128
All prime-age households (including non-working), 1997			
Lowest	28.0%	3.8%	$10,518
Second	22.8	9.8	26,965
Middle	20.2	15.6	42,848
Fourth	15.8	22.7	62,502
Highest	13.3	48.0	131,991

* Prime-age households are headed by a person age 25-54. One-person households are included. Panel A excludes households with no earners.

Source: Bernstein and Schmitt (1997).

The minimum wage generates the most help to those with the least income and the least help to those with the most income. For instance, as Table 2.43 also shows, the poorest fifth of working households had 5.4% of all income but received 35.3% of the gains from the higher minimum wage. In contrast, the best-off families received 45.3% of all income but received only 12.2% of the benefits of the higher minimum wage. The results are comparable when the analysis is repeated for all households, including those with no workers.

What happens to the minimum wage level strongly affects the wage gains of low-wage workers, particularly low-wage women whose wage is essentially set by the legislated minimum. Thus, the erosion of the minimum wage's value led to a precipitous drop in the wages of low-wage women in the 1980s and to a large increase in the 50/10 wage gap. The level of women's low wages (i.e., the 10th percentile) stabilized in the late 1980s when the wage level descended to its lowest possible level (at which employers could still hire) and as unemployment dropped. Thereafter, the 50/10 gap was flat or declined as unemployment fell to low levels in the late 1990s and as two increases in the minimum wage were implemented.

TABLE 2.44 The impact of labor market institutions on wage differentials, 1973-92

	Men			Women		
Period	90/10	90/50	50/10	90/10	90/50	50/10
1973-79						
Total change	-0.4	-1.8	1.5	-1.7	-1.6	-0.1
Change in min. wage	-0.2	0.1	-0.3	-4.4	0.3	-4.6
Deunionization	-0.9	-1.0	0.2	0.7	0.1	-0.5
1979-88						
Total change	19.5	11.9	7.6	32.8	8.5	24.3
Change in min. wage	4.9	0.0	5.0	14.8	-0.2	15.0
Deunionization	2.1	4.0	-1.9	0.4	1.4	-1.0
1988-92						
Total change	2.0	2.5	-0.5	1.9	3.7	-1.9
Change in min. wage	-0.1	0.0	-0.1	-0.4	-0.1	-0.3
Deunionization	0.9	1.0	-0.1	0.2	0.2	0.0

Contribution to growing wage inequality
1979-92

Total change	100%	100%	100%	100%	100%	100%
Change in min. wage	22	0	69	42	-2	66
Deunionization	14	35	-28	2	13	-5

Source: Fortin and Lemieux (1996).

Summarizing the role of labor market institutions

The analysis in **Table 2.44**, which examines the impact of changes in labor market institutions on wage differentials, adds several new dimensions to this discussion. First, it looks at the effect of specific factors (increases and decreases in the minimum wage, deunionization) on different dimensions of the overall wage structure—the 90/50 and 50/10 differentials. The analysis, therefore, permits a more refined discussion that allows some factors to affect the bottom of the wage structure while other factors might affect the top. Second, the analysis covers several sub-periods (1973-79, 1979-88, 1988-92), so one can observe how a factor's impact can shift over time. Unfortunately, there is no analysis for recent years.

Over the 1973-79 period there was a growth in the minimum wage and stability of union representation. The result of the strong minimum wage was a sizable lowering of the 50/10 differential among women (4.6 percentage points) and a slight lowering of the wage gap at the bottom among men (0.3 percentage points). Changes in unionization in this period enhanced wage equality among men but diminished it among women.

The results for the 1979-88 period make clear that deunionization was an important factor in the growth of male wage inequality at the top; it contributed 4.0 of the 11.9-percentage-point growth in the 90/50 differential. The reduction of the minimum wage over the 1979-88 period, however, generated 15.0 of the 24.3 percentage-point growth in the 50/10 differential among women and a large part (5.0) of the 7.6 percentage-point growth in the male 50/10 differential. Thus, a lower minimum wage was a major factor in lowering the wages of low-wage men and women relative to the median. Deunionization, in contrast, primarily lowered the wages of middle-wage men relative to high-wage men.

In the 1988-92 period, a modest rise in the minimum wage tightened the wage structure at the bottom, and continued deunionization helped to widen the male wage structure at the top.

Looking at the 1979-92 period as a whole, deunionization was a major factor driving wage inequality at the top of the wage structure, responsible for 5.0 of the 14.4 percentage-point rise of the 90/50 differential (contributing 35% of the total growth). The erosion of the minimum wage, on the other hand, was the major factor generating inequality at the bottom among women (contributing 66% of the growth) and men (69% of the growth). Together, the shifts in labor market institutions—deunionization and a lower minimum wage—over the 1979-92 period can explain 36% and 44% of the growth of overall wage inequality (the 90/10 differential), respectively, among men and women.

The technology story of wage inequality

Technological change can affect the wage structure by displacing some types of workers and by increasing demand for others. Given the seemingly rapid diffusion of microelectronic technologies in recent years, many analysts have considered technological change a major factor in the recent increase in wage inequality. Unfortunately, because it is difficult to measure the extent of technological change and its overall character (whether it requires less skill from workers or more, and by how much), it is difficult to identify the role of technological change on recent wage trends. More than a few analysts, in fact, have simply assumed that whatever portion of wage inequality is unexplained by measurable factors can be considered to be the consequence of technological change. This type of analysis, however, only puts a name to our ignorance.

It is easy to understand why people might consider technology to be a major factor in explaining recent wage and employment trends. We are often told that the pace of change in the workplace is accelerating, and there is a widespread visibility of automation and robotics; computers and microelectronics provide a visible dimension evident in workplaces, such as offices, not usually affected by technology. Perhaps even more important is that technology has provided advances in products used by consumers, including home computers, CD players, VCRs, microwaves, electronic games, advanced televisions, cell phones, and so on. Equally visible is the use of the Internet among both consumers and business people. Given these advances, it is not surprising for non-economists to readily accept that technology is transforming the wage structure. It needs to be noted, however, that technological advances in consumer products are not related to changes in labor market outcomes—it is the way goods and services are produced and changes in the relative demand for different types of workers that affect wage trends. Since many high-tech products are made with low-tech methods, there is no close correspondence between advanced consumer products and an increased need for skilled workers. Similarly, ordering a book over the Internet rather than at a downtown bookstore does not necessarily change the types of jobs available in the economy—truckers, warehouse workers, and so on still do the work of getting the book to the buyer.

The economic intuition for a large role for technology in the growth of wage inequality is that the growth of wage inequality and the employment shift to more-educated workers has occurred within industries and has not been caused primarily by shifts across industries (i.e., more service jobs, fewer manufacturing jobs). Research has also shown that technological change has traditionally been associated with an increased demand for more-educated or "skilled" workers. As we have noted, the wage premium for "more-educated" workers, exemplified by college graduates, has risen over the last two decades. This pattern of change suggests, to some analysts, an increase in skill-biased technological change driving large changes within industries.

Because wages have risen the most for groups whose supply expanded the fastest (e.g., college graduates), most economists have concluded that non-supply factors (i.e., shifts in demand or institutional factors, such as those discussed in earlier sections) are the driving force behind growing wage inequality. These economists reason that those groups with the relatively fastest growth in supply would be expected to see their wages depressed relative to other groups unless there were other factors working strongly in their favor, such as rapid expansion in demand. Rapid technological change favoring more-educated groups could logically explain demand side shifts leading to wider wage differences.

There are many reasons to be skeptical of a technology-led increase in demand for "skill" as an explanation for growing wage inequality. Unfortunately, the "skills/technology" hypothesis frequently is presented as if evidence that technological change is associated with a greater need for skills or education is sufficient to show that technological change has led to the growth in wage inequality since 1979. This is not the case, since the impact of technology must have "accelerated" in order to explain why wage inequality started to grow in the 1980s and 1990s and did not grow in the prior decades. For instance, it is generally true that investment and technological change are associated with the need for more workforce skill and education—but this has been true for the entire 20th century, and it therefore does not explain why wage inequality began to grow two decades ago. Moreover, the skills and education level (and quality) of the workforce have been continually improving. Thus, the issue is whether technology's impact on skill demand was significantly greater in the 1980s and 1990s than in earlier periods. We explore this "acceleration" issue in greater detail below and provide evidence that it had no role in the 1980s or 1990s.

The skills/technology story is also, unfortunately, frequently presented as a uni-causal explanation of the growth in wage inequality. On this account, however, it fails to explain the pattern and timing of the growth in wage inequality over the last two decades. Specifically, there seems to be no consistent technology explanation for the relationship over time between productivity (presumably technologically driven) and wage inequality; the shifts over time in the various dimensions of wage inequality—within-group wage inequality, education differentials, and experience differentials; or the shifts in wage inequality at various parts of the wage structure, such as between the 90th and 50th or 90th and 10th percentiles. We now turn to an exploration of the various patterns documented earlier in this chapter and whether a technology story can explain them.

First consider the correspondence, or lack thereof, between productivity growth and wage inequality. It is plausible to assume that technological change that is radically shifting the demand for skills in the workplace would also raise productivity growth. Yet the greatest period of rising wage inequality, the early and mid-1980s, was a period in which productivity growth (measured as multifactor or labor productivity growth) was no faster than in the "stagnant" 1970s. Overall, wage inequality continued to grow through the mid-1990s, but productivity continued its slow pace. However, when productivity accelerated after 1995, there was no accompanying growth of wage inequality (see Table 2.24). Perhaps a process began in the 1979-95 period that led to a radical restructuring of skill demand and that ultimately led to the post-1995 productivity growth. But we are not aware of any such explanation.

Second, as we discussed below, there are two dimensions of wage inequality—the between-group wage differentials, such as those relating to education and experience, and the within-group wage inequality that occurs among workers of similar education and experience— and the technology story does not readily fit either pattern. The growth of within-group inequality, which accounts for half the growth of overall wage inequality in both the 1980s and 1990s, may be related to technological change if it is interpreted as a reflection of growing economic returns to worker skills (motivation, aptitudes for math, etc.) that are not easily measured. However, there are no signs that the growth of within-group wage inequality has been fastest in those industries where the use of technology grew the most. It is also unclear why the economic returns for measurable skills (e.g., education) and unmeasured skills (e.g., motivation) should not grow in tandem. In fact, between-group and within-group inequality have failed to move together in the various sub-periods since 1973.

The timing of the growth of within-group wage inequality does not easily correspond to a technology story. For instance, within-group wage inequality actually declined, among both men and women, in the 1995-99 period associated with a technology-led productivity boom. In the early 1990s, the so-called early stages of the new economy, within-group wage inequality grew slightly, whereas it grew rapidly in the 1980s.

Nor does the pattern of growth of education and experience differentials correspond easily to a technology story. Before reviewing these patterns, however, it is worth noting that these skill differentials are affected by much more than technology. For instance, we have shown in earlier sections that changes in labor market institutions such as the minimum wage and unionization are responsible for some of the rise in education wage differentials. Other factors, such as trade and industry shifts, also affect education and other skill differentials, and so, of course, there is not a complete correspondence of technology with skill differentials.

Again, the timing of change in skill differentials does not easily match the simple technology story. Among men, for instance, the college/high-school wage gap grew most rapidly in the early 1980s but grew hardly at all in the early and mid-1990s, when technological change is thought to have been more rapid. The college wage premium did, however, grow faster in the 1995-99 period, which is consistent with a "new economy" story (but also consistent with other stories, such as low unemployment). Among women, the growth in the college wage premium has been relatively steady since 1979, with some slowing in the late 1990s.

The education differential pattern most in conflict with a technology story is the one between high school graduates and those without a high school degree. This wage gap (Table 2.17) rose modestly over the 1979-95 period and was stable thereafter. Thus, if those without a high school degree can be considered "unskilled," then the wage structure has not shifted much against these unskilled workers, especially during the 1995-99 technology-led boom. It is apparent, therefore, that shifts in education differentials do not drive the changes in wage inequality at the bottom, since the 50/10 wage gap rose markedly in the 1980s and has fallen since, all while the education gap at the bottom was relatively stable.

The wage gap by age—experience differentials—is frequently considered a skill gap driven by technological change. And it is true that experience and education differentials both grew in the 1980s, giving the impression they both were affected by the same factor, such as technology. Among men, experience differentials grew only modestly in the early 1990s, as did the college wage premium, but they *fell* after 1995 as the college premium grew faster (Table 2.17). The consequence is that overall between-group inequality grew hardly at all in the 1995-99 period—a pattern true among women as well. How can technology be driving wage inequality when between-group wage inequality (the dimension of inequality most closely corresponding to a technology-related skill) was flat during the 1995-99 technology-led boom?

The experience since the mid- to late 1980s does not accord with the conventional technology story, whose imagery is of computer-driven technology bidding up the wages of more-skilled and more-educated workers, leaving behind a small group of unskilled workers with inadequate abilities. The facts are hard to reconcile with the notion that technological change grew as fast or faster in the 1990s than in earlier periods. If technology were adverse for unskilled or less-educated workers, then we would expect a continued expansion of the wage differential between middle-wage and low-wage workers (the 50/10 differential). Yet, the 50/10 differential has been stable or declining among both men and women from 1986 or 1987 to 1997. Instead, we are seeing the top earners steadily pulling away from nearly all other earners—reflected in the 90/50 or 95/50 wage gap. Therefore, there seem to be factors driving a wedge between the top 10% and everyone else, rather than a skill-biased technological change aiding the vast majority but leaving a small group of unskilled workers behind. Further confirmation of the breadth of those left behind is that wages were stable or in decline for the bottom 80% of men and the bottom 70% of women over the 1989-95 period, with wages falling for the entire non-college-educated workforce (roughly 73% of workers).

Finally, the notion that technology has been bidding up the wages of the skilled relative to the unskilled does not accord with many of the basic facts presented earlier. Or, it holds true in a relative but not an absolute sense. The wages of skilled men, defined as white-collar, college-educated, or 90th percentile workers, were flat or in decline from the mid-1980s to the mid-1990s. As described in Chapter 3, white-collar men were increasingly becoming displaced and beset by employment problems in the early 1990s. High-wage women have continued to see their wages grow, but is it likely that technology is primarily affecting skilled women but not skilled men? Moreover, as discussed below, the wages of new college graduates working in information technology occupations were stagnant or falling from the mid-1980s to the mid-1990s, suggesting technology was not raising the wages of those most directly connected to it, at least until recently (see next section). The dramatic fall of entry-level wages for all college graduates, both men and women, reinforces this point.

We now turn to other challenges to the technology story by examining which occupations are driving up education differentials and whether there has been an acceleration of technology's impact on the labor market.

One way of gaining insight into the role of technology in generating a widening of the education wage gap is to examine which occupations, in terms of their employment expansion and relative wage improvements, have contributed to the growth of education differentials. Such an analysis is presented in **Tables 2.45** and **2.46** for men and women, respectively. In these analyses, the workforce is divided into 11 specific white-collar occupations (from among the aggregate managerial, professional, technical, and sales groups) and three more aggregate, lower-paid occupations (blue-collar, service, and clerical). This breakdown permits an examination of which occupations within the white-collar workforce experienced the greatest growth in demand in the 1980s and 1990s, as reflected by their fast growth in employment and wages.

As Table 2.45 shows, the wage premium of college-educated male workers (excluding those with degrees beyond college) relative to non-college-educated males (including those with some college, a high school degree, or less) rose 7.9 percentage points from 1979 to 1989. This wage premium grew because of a 6.3 percentage-point "relative wage" effect (the wages of college graduates within particular occupations growing relatively faster than those of non-college-educated workers) and a 1.6 percentage-point "relative employment" effect (the occupations in which college graduates expanded their employment relatively faster). The analysis in Table 2.45 identifies the "relative wage" effect and "relative employment" effect overall and for specific occupations, thus allowing a computation of the share of the aggregate change in the premium associated with trends in each occupation.

The results show that it was the fast growth in the wages and employment of managers and sales workers ("other sales" and "financial sales") that drove up the education wage differential among men; it accounted for all of the increase. In contrast, engineers, scientists, mathematicians, and computer science professionals (and associated technical workers) played a very small role in driving up education differentials.

TABLE 2.45 Decomposition of growth of male college/non-college wage premium by occupation, 1979-97

| | 1979-89 | | | | 1989-97 | | | | 1979-97 | | | |
| | Growth due to: | | | | Growth due to: | | | | Growth due to: | | | |
Occupation	Higher relative wage*	Increased relative employment**	Combined effect	Share of aggregate change	Higher relative wage*	Increased relative employment**	Combined effect	Share of aggregate change	Higher relative wage*	Increased relative employment**	Combined effect	Share of aggregate change
Managers	2.9	1.7	4.6	58.3%	1.2	-0.2	0.9	27.6%	4.1	1.5	5.6	49.2%
Engineers	1.0	-0.1	0.8	10.5	0.1	-0.4	-0.3	-7.6	1.1	-0.5	0.6	5.1
Math/computer	0.5	-0.4	0.1	1.5	0.2	1.0	1.2	34.9	0.6	0.6	1.3	11.5
Nat. science	0.1	0.0	0.0	0.5	0.0	0.1	0.1	2.8	0.1	0.1	0.1	1.2
Health prof.	0.2	0.0	0.2	3.1	0.2	0.3	0.5	14.1	0.4	0.3	0.7	6.3
Soc. sci./law	0.0	0.0	0.0	-0.6	0.0	0.0	0.0	-0.5	0.0	0.0	-0.1	-0.5
Other professional	-0.4	-2.5	-2.9	-36.2	1.0	0.4	1.4	42.6	0.6	-2.0	-1.4	-12.7
Hlth., eng., sci. tech.	0.1	0.0	0.1	1.4	0.1	0.0	0.1	4.2	0.2	0.0	0.3	2.2
Other tech.	-0.1	1.4	1.3	16.7	0.3	-0.2	0.1	3.4	0.2	1.2	1.4	12.7
Other sales	1.1	1.5	2.6	32.7	0.1	-0.3	-0.1	-3.5	1.3	1.2	2.5	21.9
Sales, fin.	0.6	0.1	0.7	9.4	-0.2	-0.2	-0.4	-11.3	0.4	-0.1	0.4	3.2
Clerks	0.1	0.0	0.1	0.9	0.2	-0.1	0.1	4.4	0.3	-0.1	0.2	2.0
Service	0.1	0.0	0.1	1.2	0.2	-0.1	0.2	4.5	0.3	-0.1	0.2	2.2
Blue collar, farm	0.1	-0.1	0.1	0.7	-0.4	-0.1	-0.5	-15.7	-0.3	-0.2	-0.5	-4.2
Growth of college/non-college wage premium***	6.3	1.6	7.9	100.0%	3.1	0.2	3.4	100.0%	9.4	1.9	11.3	100.0%

* Measures whether college graduates (four-year only) in this occupation had a greater (than other college graduates) increase in wages relative to non-college-educated workers, controlling for other human capital characteristics.

** Measures whether college graduates in this occupation had a greater growth in employment relative to other college graduates.

*** Sample excludes those with more than four years of college.

Source: Authors' analysis.

TABLE 2.46 Decomposition of growth of female college/non-college wage premium by occupation, 1979-97

| | 1979-89 | | | | 1989-97 | | | | 1979-97 | | | |
| | Growth due to: | | | | Growth due to: | | | | Growth due to: | | | |
Occupation	Higher relative wage*	Increased relative employment**	Combined effect	Share of aggregate change	Higher relative wage*	Increased relative employment**	Combined effect	Share of aggregate change	Higher relative wage*	Increased relative employment**	Combined effect	Share of aggregate change
Managers	1.6	4.0	5.6	67.7%	1.6	1.4	3.0	53.8%	3.2	5.4	8.6	62.1%
Engineers	0.1	0.6	0.7	8.4	-0.1	0.0	-0.1	-1.9	0.0	0.6	0.6	4.2
Math/computer	0.1	-0.1	0.0	-0.1	0.2	0.4	0.5	9.4	0.2	0.3	0.5	3.7
Nat. science	0.1	0.0	0.1	1.4	0.0	0.0	0.0	0.6	0.1	0.0	0.1	1.1
Health prof.	1.9	0.5	2.4	29.2	0.6	-0.3	0.3	4.6	2.4	0.2	2.7	19.3
Soc. sci./law	0.0	0.0	0.0	0.5	0.0	0.1	0.1	1.7	0.1	0.1	0.1	1.0
Other prof.	0.2	-4.8	-4.6	-55.5	1.8	0.2	2.0	35.0	2.0	-4.6	-2.6	-18.9
Hlth., eng., sci. tech.	0.1	0.1	0.3	3.1	0.0	-0.2	-0.2	-3.6	0.1	-0.1	0.1	0.4
Other tech.	0.1	1.0	1.2	14.1	0.1	-0.3	-0.2	-4.0	0.2	0.7	0.9	6.8
Other sales	0.8	1.1	1.8	22.2	0.5	0.0	0.5	9.5	1.3	1.0	2.4	17.0
Sales, fin.	0.1	0.0	0.0	0.5	0.3	0.0	0.3	5.7	0.4	0.0	0.4	2.6
Clerks	0.8	-0.3	0.5	5.7	-0.1	-0.3	-0.4	-7.8	0.7	-0.7	0.0	0.2
Service	0.0	0.1	0.1	1.0	-0.1	0.1	0.0	-0.9	-0.1	0.2	0.0	0.3
Blue collar, farm	0.2	0.0	0.2	1.8	-0.1	0.0	-0.1	-2.1	0.1	0.0	0.0	0.2
Growth of college/non-college wage premium***	5.9	2.3	8.2	100.0%	4.7	0.9	5.6	100.0%	10.6	3.2	13.8	100.0%

* Measures whether college graduates (four-year only) in this occupation had a greater (than other college graduates) increase in wages relative to non-college-educated workers, controlling for other human capital characteristics.

** Measures whether college graduates in this occupation had a greater growth in employment relative to other college graduates.

*** Sample excludes those with more than four years of college.

Source: Authors' analysis.

As we have noted, the college wage premium grew only modestly over the 1989-97 period (and hardly at all in 1990-97). Table 2.45 suggests this small growth was due to white-collar occupations increasing their employment relative to other occupations only slightly; white-collar wage gains were smaller as well.

Over the entire 1979-97 period, managers were responsible for half (49.2%) of the entire 11.3 percentage-point rise in the college/non-college wage premium among men, with another fourth (25.1%) associated with sales workers.

Table 2.46, which presents the occupational decomposition of the growth of the education wage gap among women, generally shows the same pattern as among men: increased wages and employment of managers and sales workers accounting for more than 80% of the 13.8 percentage-point growth in the education wage premium, with very little role for scientists, engineers, computer professionals, or technical workers. Again, this pattern seems hard to reconcile with the conventional technology story.

What does this analysis tell us about a technology story of wage inequality? Basically, if technology is responsible for bidding up the education wage gap by increasing the demand for skilled or educated workers, then the particular skills associated with technological change in this period were those of managers and sales workers. Such a portrait of technology's role is at odds with the conventional one, which tends to focus on the role of computers and microelectronics. It may be that information-age technology transforms workplaces by generating fast wage and employment growth for managers and sales workers. Nevertheless, managers and sales workers are not the usual occupations associated with the mastery of the new skills associated with an information technology era. The next section further explores the role of information technology workers on labor market trends.

We now turn to the issue of whether technology's impact accelerated in the 1980s and 1990s so as to increase the demand for skills much faster than the ongoing expansion of college graduates in the workforce. The rhetoric in the discussion of technology's role in growing wage inequality presumes that we have entered a new era of technological change, signified by the computer revolution. In this scenario, either the rate of introduction of new technologies or the types of technologies being introduced is creating a new situation in today's workplace and an enhanced demand for cognitive skills. Some analysts have explicitly talked in terms of a "technology shock." This widely expressed view assumes an *acceleration* of technology's impact on relative demand, suggesting that one test of the technology hypothesis is whether technology had a greater impact on skill demand in the 1980s or 1990s than in the 1970s or earlier periods.

That a technology explanation requires an acceleration of technology's impact on workplace skills is implicit in the conventional demand-and-supply framework used to explain wage differentials. As discussed earlier, most analysts have concluded that the growth of wage inequality since 1979 must be primarily explained by demand side factors (or non-supply side factors, including institutional shifts) rather than supply side factors (i.e., fewer college graduates). Thus, the focus has turned to trade, industry shifts, and technological change, all factors that could explain shifts in relative demand. However, it would not make sense to be seeking the source of relative-demand shifts in the 1980s and 1990s if demand trends were essentially the same over the last few decades. Similarly, demand side shifts seem relevant to explaining a wage inequality originating in the 1980s only if there were something new and different about recent demand trends. In fact, if the relative demand for skill grew at the same pace over the last three decades—at a smooth, secular, or historic rate—then the only factors that could be different in the 1980s and 1990s and explain growing wage inequality are those affecting the supply of "skills," a context with no possible special role for trade, technology, or other factors shaping relative demand.

In this light, a technology explanation makes sense only if there is a greater growth in the demand for skills in the 1980s and 1990s than in earlier periods and if these demand side changes can be attributed to technological change. This motivates our efforts to test for an acceleration of technology's impact on the use of more-educated and higher-paid workers.

It is also useful to distinguish between the role of technology in the growth of wage inequality and the issue of "skill complementarity," the concept that there is a positive relationship between capital (e.g., computers) and worker skill. The existence of skill complementarity is one of the main explanations of the growing need for workers with more education and skills: as investment or capital per worker has grown, the need for more skills has grown commensurately. The explanation of growing wage inequality, on the other hand, requires an analysis that separates out the *growth* of the relative supply and demand for education and skill. To show that relative demand for skill is accelerating (as is necessary, as argued above), it is not enough to simply cite the existence of skill complementarities, since such complementarities have long been associated with the need for greater skills and education. That is, technological change has been a force for increasing employers' demand for more-skilled and more-educated workers for a long time. The issue regarding wage inequality is whether technological change has increased demand for skill faster than the supply of skill has been growing.

We do not question that technological change and capital accumulation have been historically associated with the need for greater skills and education. Technology and investment have been major forces driving the long-term growth of demands for skill.

But is there reason to believe that technology's impact *accelerated* in the 1980s or 1990s? Technological change is inherently difficult to quantify. The analysis in **Table 2.47** examines technology's impact on the utilization of different types of workers, such as high-wage (therefore, presumably high-skill) or college-educated workers. Specifically, Table 2.47 presents quantitative estimates of the impact of technological change on the rate at which there were within-industry shifts toward the use of more-educated workers (i.e., the effect of technology on relative demand within industries in different time periods). These estimates reflect whether there was a faster rate of introduction of new technology (proxied by increased equipment investment, computerization, and research and development) and changes in the degree to which new technology was associated with higher skill requirements (a tighter complementarity of skill and technology). The estimate of technology's impact on utilization, therefore, reflects new investment; research and development innovations; and any associated technical, work organization, or work-process changes.

Table 2.47 presents estimates in four periods, 1963-73, 1973-79, 1979-89, and 1989-94. The critical issue to be addressed is whether technology's impact was greater in the 1980s or 1990s than in the 1970s. Unfortunately, neither this nor any other analysis addresses the trends in the late 1990s.

Consider, first, technology's impact on the increased utilization of college-educated workers, as shown in the bottom section. The data show that in the 1970s, 1980s, and 1990s technology was indeed associated with an increased utilization of college-educated workers, as seen by the positive estimates (e.g., technology led to a 0.217 annual change in the male employment share of workers with a college degree in the 1973-79 period). However, there was no sizable (and statistically significant) growth, or acceleration, of technology's impact on the utilization of more-educated workers in the 1980s and 1990s relative to the 1970s (e.g., the difference between the 1980s and 1970s was 0.004, a statistically insignificant change). Therefore, although technology may have played an important role in each period, its impact did not grow in such a way as to be able to explain why wage inequality (or education differentials) began to grow after 1979. These estimates do show an acceleration of technology's impact on the use of college-educated men in the 1970s relative to the 1960s, but this hardly corresponds to the onset of information-age technology.

Table 2.47 also examines a broader measure of technology's impact by estimating the effect on the utilization of high-wage workers (earning in the upper 25% of the wage distribution) or low-wage workers (earning in the bottom half of the wage distribution). These estimates are extremely inhospitable to a tech-

TABLE 2.47 Utilization[a] of workers by technology's impact on wage and education level, 1963-94

Within-industry change in use of:	Technology's impact on utilization of:	
	Men	Women
Low-wage workers		
1963-73	-.088	-.135
1973-79	-.498**	-.362**
1979-89	-0.152	-.176**
1989-94	.237	.221**
Differences		
'70s less '60s	-.411**	-.228*
'80s less '70s	.346**	.187*
'90s less '70s	.735**	.583**
'90s less '80s	.389**	.396**
Highest-wage workers		
1963-73	.185	.107
1973-79	.603**	.148**
1979-89	.227**	.061
1989-94	-.187*	-.098**
Differences		
'70s less '60s	.418**	.041
'80s less '70s	-.376**	-.087
'90s less '70s	-.790**	-.246**
'90s less '80s	-.414**	-.159**
College-educated workers		
1963-73	-.032	.046
1973-79	.217**	.050
1979-89	.220**	.117**
1989-94	.359**	.181**
Differences		
'70s less '60s	.249*	.003
'80s less '70s	.004	.067
'90s less '70s	.142	.131**
'90s less '80s	.138	.064

* Statistically significant change at the 10% level.
** Statistically significant change at the 5% level.

[a] Utilization refers to annual increase in the employment share of particular type of worker.

Source: Mishel, Bernstein, and Schmitt (1997).

nology story of wage inequality, since technology is associated with a declining use of high-wage workers both in the 1980s relative to the 1970s and in the 1990s relative to the 1980s (most of the declines being statistically significant). Correspondingly, technology was associated with a declining utilization of low-wage men and women in the 1970s, but this association was less strong in the 1980s and 1990s. In fact, these estimates show that technology was less adverse for low-wage workers in the 1980s and 1990s relative to the 1970s. These estimates, using the broadest measure of skill (a worker's wage level), therefore, run directly counter to a technology story of an ever-accelerating technology-driven growth in demand for skill.

Information technology workers

There has been much attention paid recently to the assertions of high-technology companies that they are facing a labor shortage of information technology workers. This complaint has raised a series of issues, such as whether these firms should be able to recruit more IT workers via immigration or whether these firms need to reform their own human resource systems by raising pay, ending age discrimination, and offering more regular, full-time positions (rather than temporary ones). Such issues are beyond the scope of this inquiry. We do address, however, whether employment and wage trends suggest an information technology worker shortage and, if so, its character. Equally important, we examine whether high-tech or IT occupations and industries are wage leaders. As a first step, **Table 2.48** presents occupational employment shares in the 1989-98 period for two groups of workers, all workers and young college graduates, the latter presumably being the chief beneficiaries of any IT worker shortage. These data allow us to gauge the increased importance of occupations among college graduates and the workforce generally.

The employment shares presented in Table 2.48 show a steady rise in relative employment among math and computer science professionals until 1995 and a quicker growth through 1998. There was no relative employment expansion among engineers. Among young college graduates engineering employment has declined, offset, though, by an upward movement of mathematics and computer science employment. Thus, there does seem to be an increased growth in relative demand for some segments of information technology workers (computer science) but not others (engineers). Whatever growth there has been, however, seems to be recent, since most of the expansion of employment occurred in 1995-98. The overall significance of this increased relative demand for computer workers is unclear, since there is a nearly comparable,

TABLE 2.48 Changes in employment shares by occupation for all workers and young college graduates, 1989-97

Occupation	Shares of employment by occupation				Change
	1989	1992	1995	1998	1989-98
All workers					
Managers	11.9%	11.9%	12.9%	13.6%	1.7
Engineers, architects, surveyors	1.8	1.7	1.9	1.9	0.0
Math/computer science	0.8	0.9	1.0	1.5	0.7
Natural scientists	0.4	0.4	0.5	0.4	0.1
Health professionals	2.4	2.8	3.0	3.0	0.5
Other professionals	7.9	8.2	8.5	8.7	0.8
Technicians	3.5	4.1	3.6	3.7	0.2
Sales	10.5	10.6	10.9	11.0	0.5
Other occupations	60.8	59.4	57.8	56.3	-4.5
Total	100.0	100.0	100.0	100.0	
Young college graduates					
Managers	22.7%	21.9%	23.0%	23.4%	0.6
Engineers, architects, surveyors	6.3	5.5	5.3	4.7	-1.6
Math/computer science	2.7	2.9	3.2	4.1	1.4
Natural scientists	0.9	1.2	1.5	1.2	0.3
Health professionals	5.6	5.6	5.1	5.1	-0.5
Other professionals	15.8	17.3	19.2	20.3	4.5
Technicians	6.4	6.4	5.4	5.3	-1.0
Sales	15.0	14.6	13.9	13.6	-1.4
Other occupations	24.7	24.6	23.5	22.3	-2.4
Total	100.0	100.0	100.0	100.0	

* College graduates (four-year) with 1 to 10 years of experience.

Source: Authors' analysis.

or greater, expansion of employment among other professional or white-collar occupations, just as there has been for decades. All in all, therefore, nothing spectacular seems to be taking place, although the last few years may anticipate large changes ahead.

Are IT worker wages being bid up, as one would expect if a shortage exists? Are IT workers wage leaders? We can track IT worker wage trends by estimating their wage premium—the amount they earn above workers with comparable education and experience and in similar broad occupational (i.e., professional) and industrial (i.e., communications/transportation) settings. We do so for IT occupations (computer program analysts, computer programmers, and operations and system researchers/analysts) and a set of IT industries. **Figures 2U** and **2V** present the wage premiums for IT occupations and industries for men and women. Figure 2U indicates that men in IT occupations earned 16.6% more in 1984 than other professional men with comparable education and experience working in similar industries. Interestingly, this IT occupation wage premium has had no strong discernable trend since 1984 (the earliest year we can estimate this). Similarly, the male wage premium for working in an IT industry was similar in the late 1990s (except the very last year, 1999) to what it was in the mid-1980s. Among women, however, IT wage premiums were lower in the late 1990s than they were in the 1980s. These data, therefore, provide no evidence of wage leadership among IT workers, industries, or employers, especially among women. Without any noticeable increase in the IT worker wage premium, it is also evident that there is no IT worker shortage, except insofar as there might be one for all professionals.

Another way to gauge the market for IT workers is to examine the wages offered to new college graduates in computer science relative to graduates in other majors, as shown in **Figure 2W**. These data, collected by college placement officers, show that computer science graduates saw their wage offers steadily decline from 1986 through 1994. Wage offers rose after 1994, but not until 1998 were computer science majors offered as much as in 1986. Interestingly, the wage offer trends for business majors and all majors parallel those of computer science majors. This, again, shows that there has been nothing particularly unique about the computer science, or IT, labor market.

Executive pay soars

Another cause of greater wage inequality has been the enormous pay increases received by chief executive officers (CEOs) and the spillover effects (the pay of other executives and managers rising in tandem with CEO pay) of these increases. These large pay raises go far beyond those received by other white-collar workers.

The 1980s and 1990s have been prosperous times for top U.S. executives. **Table 2.49** presents the trends in CEO pay over the 1989-99 period. For instance, the median wage (cash payments including bonuses of CEOs) grew 62.7% from 1989 to 1999, far exceeding the growth in any other occupation. These CEO wages grew 53.6% in just the recovery years from 1992 to 1999. In contrast, the median hourly wage for all workers grew just 2.4% from 1989 to 1999 (Table 2.6). These CEO wage increases were probably larger if measured as averages rather than at the median.

FIGURE 2U Information technology wage premium, men, 1984-99

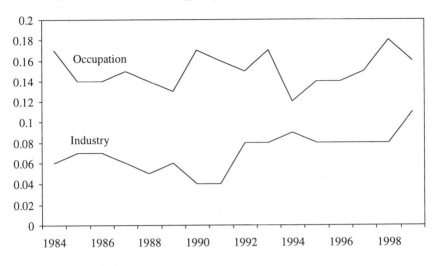

Source: Authors' analysis.

FIGURE 2V Information technology wage premium, women, 1984-99

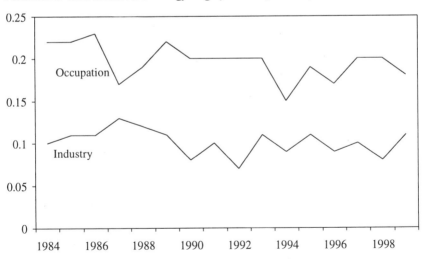

Source: Authors' analysis.

FIGURE 2W Wage offers to new college graduates by major, 1979-99

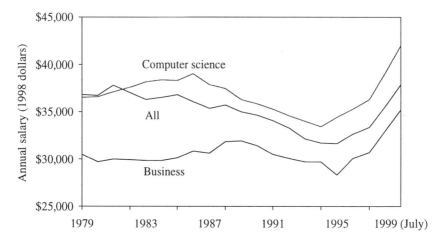

Source: EPI analysis of National Association of College and Employers data.

TABLE 2.49 Executive pay growth, 1989-99 (1999 dollars)

Pay category and percentile	($ thousands)				Change	Percent change		
	1989	1992	1995	1999	1992-99 ($000)	1989-99	1992-99	1995-99
Realized direct compensation *								
25th	n.a.	$1,141	$1,327	$1,454	$313	n.a.	27.4%	9.6%
Median	n.a.	1,841	2,178	2,788	947	n.a.	51.5	28.0
75th	n.a.	3,510	3,907	6,343	2,833	n.a.	80.7	62.3
Average	1,851	2,164	2,471	3,528	1,364	90.6%	63.1	42.8
Cash compensation ** Index, 1989 = 100								
Median	100	105.9	129.6	162.7	n.a.	62.7%	53.6%	25.5%

* Sum of salary, bonus, gains from options exercised, value of restricted stock at grant, and other long-term incentive award payments.
** Salary and cash bonuses.

Source: Authors' analysis of *Wall Street Journal*/Mercer Survey.

FIGURE 2X Ratio of CEO to average worker pay, 1965-99

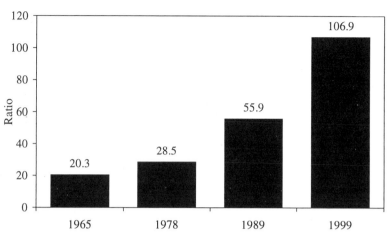

Source: Authors' analysis.

The growth in CEO pay can also be measured by including all of the components of direct compensation: salaries, bonuses, incentive awards, stock options exercised, stock granted, and so on. By this measure, the full compensation of CEOs nearly doubled over the 1989-99 period, growing 90.6% and increasing 63.1% in the 1992-99 recovery. Even lesser-paid CEOs at the 25th percentile saw a 27.4% compensation growth in the recovery. Higher paid executives at the 75th percentile saw their compensation grow by 80.7% in the recovery.

The increased divergence between the growth of CEO pay and an average worker's pay is captured in the growth of the ratio of CEO to worker pay, shown in **Figure 2X**. In 1965, U.S. CEOs in major companies earned 20.3 times more than an average worker; this ratio grew to 28.5 in 1978, to 55.9 in 1989, and then to 106.9 in 1999. In other words, in 1999, a CEO worked half a week to earn what an average worker earned in 52 weeks. In 1965, by contrast, it took a CEO two and a half weeks to earn a worker's annual pay.

Not only are U.S. executives paid far better than U.S. workers, they also earn substantially more than CEOs in other advanced countries. **Table 2.50** presents CEO pay in 12 other countries in 1999 and an index (in the last two columns) that sets U.S. compensation equal to 100 (any index value less than 100 implies that that country's CEOs earn less than U.S. CEOs). The index shows that U.S. CEOs earn more than double the average of the 12 other advanced

TABLE 2.50 CEO pay in advanced countries, 1988-99 (1999 dollars)

Country	CEO compensation ($ thousands) 1988	1999	Percent change 1988-99	Ratio of CEO to worker pay, 1999*	Foreign pay relative to U.S. pay, 1999 U.S. = 100 CEOs	Workers
Australia	$160.5	$518.8	223.1%	23.3	38.4%	56.3%
Belgium	340.8	662.0	94.3	18.4	49.0	91.3
Canada	376.0	666.0	77.1	20.0	49.3	84.6
France	359.1	571.6	59.2	15.1	42.3	95.7
Germany	366.2	533.7	45.8	13.3	39.5	101.7
Italy	304.2	568.0	86.7	19.8	42.1	72.7
Japan	446.4	486.7	9.0	10.8	36.0	114.2
Netherlands	352.1	576.4	63.7	16.6	42.7	88.2
Spain	312.6	426.1	36.3	17.2	31.6	62.7
Sweden	208.4	425.3	104.1	13.0	31.5	82.9
Switzerland	453.5	498.3	9.9	10.9	36.9	115.8
United Kingdom	402.8	667.6	65.8	24.0	49.4	70.4
United States	715.4	1,350.6	88.8	34.2	100.0	100.0
Non-U.S. average	$340.2	$550.0	61.7%	16.9	40.7%	86.4%

* Ratio of CEO compensation to the compensation of manufacturing production workers.

Source: Authors' analysis of Towers Perrin (1988 and 1999).

countries for which there are comparable data (note the non-U.S. average of 40.7). In fact, there is no country listed whose CEOs are paid even as much as 50% that of U.S. CEOs. This international pattern does not hold true for the pay of manufacturing workers, for whom an index is also presented in Table 2.50. Workers in other advanced countries earn 86.4% of what U.S. workers earn. Not surprisingly, the ratio of CEO to worker pay was far larger in the United States in 1999 than in other countries, 34.2 versus 16.9. Note that these cross-country comparisons employ different data (and definitions) than those used for historical U.S. trends in Table 2.49 and therefore yield a different CEO/worker pay ratio. Last, Table 2.50 shows that CEO pay in other countries has tended to grow rapidly over the 1988-99 period, but for most countries not as rapidly as the 88.8% growth in the U.S.

What does the future hold?

This section examines future trends in wages and job quality by analyzing the projected trends of the key forces that will shape the wage structure—demand (skill requirements), labor supply factors (education, age, immigration), and various institutional factors. We do not attempt to predict wages in the future, but our assessment of wage trends over the current business cycle and the forces at work over the next decade lead us to believe that wage inequality will continue to grow between the top and the middle, as it has for the last two decades. If unemployment returns to more familiar levels and the minimum wage is not increased, then we will probably see a growing wage gap at the bottom again. The recent improvement in productivity growth will likely continue, although perhaps at a lower level (1.5% to 2.0%). If so, then real wage growth will probably continue for most workers, although at a rate below that of the late 1990s.

The first dimension of change we consider are shifts in demand for skills. The greater the increase in employer demand for workers with more skill and education, the greater is the economy's ability to shift people into better-paying jobs (although there is not necessarily a one-to-one relationship between skill and pay).

An analysis of recent trends and future projections suggests that the jobs of the future will not be markedly different from the jobs available today. Future jobs will have somewhat greater educational and skill requirements, primarily the need for basic literacy and numeracy, but the job structure will not shift markedly toward higher-paying jobs. Most important, the skill and education requirements of jobs are expected to grow more slowly than they did in the 1970s, 1980s, and early 1990s.

This view of future jobs is based on an analysis of labor market trends anticipated by the Bureau of Labor Statistics in its employment projections to the year 2008. The data in **Table 2.51** allow us to assess the effect of occupational upgrading (e.g., the rising importance of white-collar professional/technical jobs) on education requirements. Specifically, the data show the effect of changes in the distribution of employment among occupations on the education levels required and on the pay received for jobs. The analysis examines trends over the last three decades to provide a point of comparison.

The analysis shows that job education requirements have been increasing since 1973 and are projected to increase through 2008. Rather than the skills explosion projected by some analysts, however, future growth in education requirements will be historically modest. For instance, the new distribution of jobs across occupations in 2008 will require a worker's average years of schooling to grow at a 0.7% rate over the 1998-2008 period, slower than in any of the three periods since 1973. Thus, occupation shifts are not expected to generate

TABLE 2.51 Demand shifts: changes in pay and education requirements, 1973-2008*

Job characteristic	1973-79	1979-89	1989-99 1989-95	1995-99	1989-99	BLS projections 1998-2008
Pay			Annual growth			
Hourly compensation	1.6%	2.3%	1.4%	2.7%	1.9%	1.2%
Hourly wages	2.0	2.9	1.8	3.1	2.3	1.0
Education requirements						
Years of schooling	0.9%	1.4%	0.9%	1.0%	0.9%	0.7%
Shares of employment requiring:			Percentage-point change per decade			
Less than high school	-1.57	-1.33	-0.57	-1.06	-0.77	-0.38
High school	-1.03	-1.51	-1.40	-1.78	-1.55	-0.61
Some college	0.61	0.38	-0.29	-0.23	-0.24	0.01
College (4-year)	1.21	1.69	1.25	1.60	1.39	0.64
Advanced degree	0.73	0.99	0.95	1.23	1.07	0.54

* Based on a shift-share analysis using the shares of employment by occupation and the 1995 education distributions of 13 occupation groups and their relative pay structure over the 1979-93 period.

Source: Authors' analysis.

a large growth in the demand for education, at least by historical standards. This can also be seen in the analysis of the effects of occupation shifts on the need for workers at various education levels. For instance, projected changes in the occupational composition of employment imply an extra growth of 0.64% of the workforce needing a college degree every 10 years, a growth less than half of that generated by the actual employment shifts in the 1970s, 1980s, or 1990s. The ultimate conclusion to be drawn from these analyses is that demand shifts in the future will not be a powerful force for improving overall job quality and pay, absent some change in government policies and employer strategies.

The most optimistic trend is the possibility of a continued higher rate of productivity growth in the future. To the extent that higher productivity leads to higher average wage growth (they are closely related but, as we have shown, less so than in the past), wages can be expected to grow more for every type of worker. Put another way, a productivity-related acceleration of average wage

TABLE 2.52 Future labor supply trends

Characteristic	1979	1989	1996	2009
College education				
College full-time enrollment rate				
Men	n.a.	n.a.	22.7%	22.2%
Women	n.a.	n.a.	26.9	28.3
College-age population (thousands)				
18-24 years	30,048	27,378	24,982	29,890
Bachelor's degrees awarded (thousands)				
Men	477	483	522	531
Women	444	535	642	725
Degrees awarded				
as share of employment				
Men	0.90%	0.79%	0.81%	0.73%
Women	1.08	1.01	1.16	1.10
	1979	1988	2005	
Immigrant share of labor force				
Men	7.0%	9.9%	13.3–14.8%	
Women	6.8	8.6	10.9–13.4	
	1980	1990	1998	2008
Labor force age (median)	34.6	36.6	38.7	40.7

Source: Authors' analysis.

growth can partially offset any further growth of wage inequality. Of course, it is not known whether the current productivity growth will continue. To the extent it is technologically driven (by the arrival of new technologies and the consequent faster growth of investment), there will be a continuation of fast productivity growth. If unemployment returns to the 5% level or higher, then productivity growth will slow down. However, in our opinion, productivity growth will probably stay above the rate prevailing over the 1973-95 period, by somewhere between 0.5% and 1.0%. Therefore, wage growth will remain stronger than during the 1973-95 period, and even with a continued rise in wage inequality there will be real wage growth for most workers, although not as much as over the 1995-99 period.

Table 2.52 presents data on future labor supply trends that affect the wage structure. One major factor is how fast the supply of more-educated workers, or college graduates, will expand. If the supply outpaces the demand for college graduates, then the college premium will fall, creating a tendency toward less wage inequality. The data in Table 2.54 show that college enrollment rates are expected to rise by 2009, but only among women and even then only slightly. This suggests that the supply of college-educated workers may expand somewhat, although maybe not as fast as in the last few decades.

What matters, however, is not how many attend college but how many people earn degrees. As Table 2.52 shows, the number of bachelor's degrees awarded annually is not expected to rise much among men but to rise by 12.9%, or 83,000, among women. This expected growth in the numbers completing college, however, is less than the expected growth rate of the labor force, as seen in the trend of degrees awarded as a share of employment. For instance, nearly 7.5 million more men will be employed in 2009 but only 6,000 more bachelor's degrees will be awarded to men that year. The 19% expected employment growth among women is greater than the 11.6% expected growth in women's college degrees. Thus, new entrants will not be driving up the relative supply of "educated workers," even among women. In fact, as Table 2.52 and **Figure 2Y** show, the amount of new college degrees relative to the size of adult employment is expected to be stable or falling over the 1996-2009 period (down for men, stable for women). A surge in the supply of college graduates, therefore, is not likely to be a strong force for restoring a lesser college wage premium.

Immigration trends imply a further growth of immigrants as a share of the labor force. If future immigrants are proportionately less educated, in accordance with recent trends, then future immigration will also serve to depress low-end wages and be a force for a further widening of wage inequality—unless, of course, persistently low unemployment and increases in the minimum wage offset immigration pressures.

The workforce is expected to have a significantly higher age in 2009 than in recent years. The move by the youngest of the baby boomers into their forties and fifties should put upward pressure on average wages (wage trajectories are relatively rapid for these age groups) and may serve to narrow the wage gap between younger and older workers. How powerful a force this will be is uncertain. Note that the age of the workforce grew considerably over the 1980-90 period (from 34.6 to 36.6 years), when experience differentials actually widened.

Other trends will also affect the wage structure. The continued expansion of international trade's role in the economy and the continued shrinkage of employment in goods production will act to depress wages for the non-college-educated workforce, as they have in recent years. If union coverage rates stabilize and grow (in response to a renewed union effort at organizing), some of the pressure for greater inequality may lessen or reverse itself. Likewise, if the minimum wage rises relative to inflation in the next few years, then there will be less

FIGURE 2Y College degrees as share of employment, 1961-2009*

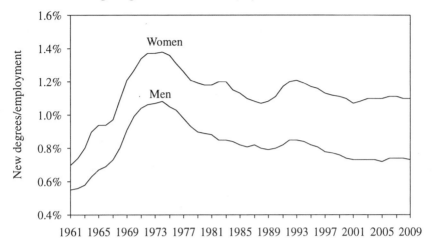

* 1996-2009 projected.

Source: Authors' analysis.

pressure for wage inequality at the bottom to grow, especially among women. This mix of trends suggests some continuation of the growth of wage inequality, but perhaps not as quickly as in the recent past.

To conclude, the forces that drove wage inequality in the past can be expected to have a similar, although possibly lesser, effect in the future. And if productivity growth persists along its recent (1980s and 1990s) trajectory, then wages over the long term will continue to deteriorate for most men, rise modestly only among high-wage women, and stagnate for women at the median. However, if low unemployment persists (i.e., the business cycle is repealed) or productivity growth accelerates, then future wage trends can continue the positive trends of the last few years.

Conclusion

There have been dramatic changes in the wage structure over the last two decades or so. From 1979 to 1995, the real hourly wages of most workers fell, with non-college-educated workers, especially new entrants to the labor force, experiencing the greatest wage decline. Given that three-fourths of the workforce has not earned a four-year college degree, the wage erosion of high school graduates (whose wages fell somewhat less than those of high school dropouts but somewhat more than those of workers with some college) meant that the vast majority of men and many women were working at far lower wages in 1995 than their counterparts did a generation earlier. In the early 1990s, wages were falling or stagnant, even among college graduates and white-collar workers, especially men. New college graduates in the mid-1990s earned less than their counterparts did in the late 1980s.

Since 1995, however, there has been a very different, and far better, wage performance as real wages grew rapidly for nearly all segments of the workforce. Wage growth at the bottom, in particular, has been strong, and wage inequality at the bottom has continued to decline, as it has since the late 1980s. Faster productivity growth, persistent low unemployment, and increases in the minimum wage are responsible for this turnaround. Whether these beneficial wage trends continue will depend on the future of these three indicators.

CHAPTER 3 ————————————————————————————

Jobs: sustained low unemployment key to recent progress

Since the middle of the 1990s, rapid economic growth—and especially sustained low unemployment—have had a large, positive effect on the economic prospects of American workers. Employment opportunities have expanded considerably, especially for historically disadvantaged groups, including women, blacks, and Hispanics. The long-term rise in job instability and job insecurity, which continued well into the current economic recovery, finally appeared to have abated at the end of the last decade. Even the share of workers in nonstandard—often substandard—work arrangements, such as temporary work and part-time work, has declined as opportunities for regular full-time employment have grown.

Problems remain, however. Large pockets of the population still have employment rates far below—and unemployment rates far above—the national average. Even more importantly, many of the employment gains described in this chapter, and at least a portion of the wage and income gains described in earlier chapters, depend on continued low unemployment rates. Many of the positive developments of the late 1990s described in this and other chapters could fade in the next recession.

This chapter first examines developments in unemployment, underemployment, and job creation over the entire postwar period. Next, it looks at a variety of objective and subjective evidence on job security, and then analyzes the growth and current state of nonstandard work arrangements.

Unemployment and underemployment

Table 3.1 gives a broad overview of unemployment rates by sex and race during the various peak years in the business cycles since World War II and for 1999, the most recent year for which complete data are available. The economy is at its strongest in peak years, and therefore unemployment is at its lowest. In 1999, the national unemployment rate (column 1) was 4.2%, lower than at any cyclical peak in the last three decades and close to the 3.8% rate achieved in 1967. The separate unemployment rates for men, women, whites, blacks, and Hispanics were all lower in 1999 than they were during any peak year since the early 1970s.

The low unemployment rate in 1999 reflects the strong economic performance of the U.S. economy since about 1996. As discussed earlier, this low unemployment boosts workers' bargaining power with respect to their employers because it suggests that new jobs are relatively easy to find. Perhaps even more important for bargaining power, however, is that the unemployment rate has remained at relatively low levels for over four years. As illustrated in **Figure 3A**, the overall unemployment rate has been below 5.5% since 1996. At no other time since 1970 has the unemployment rate remained below 5.5% for more than two consecutive years.

Even in good times, workers' experiences with unemployment differ markedly by race (or ethnicity) and sex. Unemployment rates for black workers, for example, are consistently more than double the rates for white workers. In 1999, the black unemployment rate was 8.0%, compared to 3.7% for whites. Unemployment rates for Hispanic workers tend to lie between those for whites and blacks. Even in 1999, however, the Hispanic unemployment rate (6.4%) stood at a level that few would consider indicative of prosperity if it were applied to the labor force as a whole. Before 1979, women workers generally had an unemployment rate substantially higher than the rate for men, but since then women have seen their unemployment rates converge on the men rates.

Table 3.1 also shows the unemployment rate in 1992, which marked the most recent high point for unemployment. A comparison of the unemployment rates in the recession year of 1992 and the boom year of 1999 illustrates that the low unemployment rates of the late 1990s strongly benefited the most disadvantaged workers. While the white unemployment rate, for example, fell 2.8 percentage points over the 1992-99 recovery, the unemployment rate dropped 6.1 percentage points for blacks and 5.0 percentage points for Hispanics.

Table 3.2 presents data on "underemployment," a broader measure than unemployment of lack of success in the labor market. This alternative measure includes unemployed workers as well as: (1) those working part time but who

TABLE 3.1 Unemployment rates, 1947-99

	Total	Male	Female	White	Black	Hispanic*
1947	3.9%	4.0%	3.7%	n.a.	n.a.	n.a.
1967	3.8	3.1	5.2	3.4%	n.a.	n.a.
1973	4.9	4.2	6.0	4.3	9.4%	7.7%
1979	5.8	5.1	6.8	5.1	12.3	8.3
1989	5.3	5.2	5.4	4.5	11.4	8.0
1992	7.4	7.0	6.3	6.5	14.1	11.4
1999	4.2	4.1	4.3	3.7	8.0	6.4
Annual averages						
1947-67	4.7%	4.5%	5.0%	n.a.	n.a.	n.a.
1967-73	4.6	4.0	5.7	4.1%	n.a.	n.a.
1973-79	6.5	5.8	7.5	5.8	12.5%	9.5%
1979-89	7.1	7.0	7.3	6.2	14.7	10.3
1992-99	5.6	5.7	5.5	4.9	10.9	9.0
1989-99	5.7	5.8	5.6	4.9	11.1	8.9

* Persons of Hispanic origin may be of any race.

Source: Authors' analysis of BLS data.

FIGURE 3A Unemployment rate, 1947-99

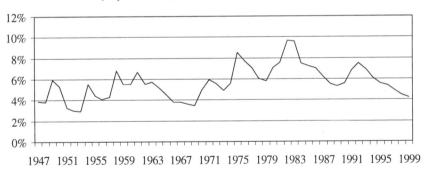

Source: Authors' analysis of BLS data.

TABLE 3.2 Underemployment, 1999

	In thousands
Civilian labor force	139,368
Unemployed	5,880
Discouraged*	331
Other marginally attached*	979
Involuntary part time	3,357
Total underemployed	10,547
Underemployment rate**	7.5%
Unemployment rate	4.2%

* Marginally attached workers are persons who currently are neither working nor looking for work, but who indicate that they want and are available for a job and have looked for work in the last 12 months. Discouraged workers are the subset of the marginally attached who have given a job-market-related reason for not currently looking for a job.
** Total underemployed workers divided by the sum of the labor force plus discouraged and other marginally attached workers.

Source: Authors' analysis of BLS data.

want to work full time ("involuntary" part-timers); (2) those who want to work but have been discouraged from searching by their lack of success ("discouraged" workers); and (3) others who are neither working nor seeking work at the moment but who indicate that they want and are available to work and have looked for a job in the last 12 months. (The second and third categories together are described as "marginally attached" workers.) At 7.5%, the 1999 underemployment rate (see Table 3.2 and **Figure 3B**) was substantially higher than the 4.2% unemployment rate, primarily because of the more than 3.4 million involuntary part-time workers. Discouraged and other marginally attached workers added another 1.3 million to the number underemployed.

Unemployment and the earnings distribution

The prolonged economic recovery, which has brought steep declines in unemployment, has largely (and disproportionately) benefited the bottom 60% of families. **Table 3.3** shows the effect of a 1% decrease in unemployment on the number of weeks unemployed and employed in a year and on the annual earnings for families in each income group (estimated over the 1967-91 period). The last

FIGURE 3B Underemployment, 1999

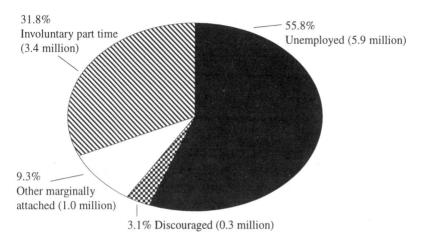

31.8%
Involuntary part time
(3.4 million)

55.8%
Unemployed (5.9 million)

9.3%
Other marginally
attached (1.0 million)

3.1% Discouraged (0.3 million)

Source: Authors' analysis of BLS data.

TABLE 3.3 Effect of a 1% lower unemployment rate on weeks unemployed and employed and on annual earnings, 1967-91

	Lowest fifth	Second fifth	Middle fifth	Fourth fifth	Highest fifth	All
Weeks unemployed						
Household head	-0.49	-0.33	-0.23	-0.15	-0.06	-0.25
Other adults	-0.13	-0.16	-0.22	-0.27	-0.25	-0.21
All persons	-0.63	-0.50	-0.45	-0.42	-0.31	-0.46
Weeks employed						
All persons	0.51	0.89	0.61	0.57	0.46	0.62
Annual earnings (1991 dollars)						
Household head	$75	$334	$292	$278	$435	$288
Other adults	5	29	89	232	488	169
All persons	80	362	381	511	924	457
Increase in annual earnings						
All persons	3.7%	3.7%	1.8%	1.4%	1.4%	1.7%

Source: Authors' analysis of Blank and Card (1993).

223

column shows the effect of a 1% decline in the unemployment rate on the "average" family. Among all persons, time in unemployment falls an average of (0.46) per year; weeks worked per year rises 0.62; and annual income increases $457 (in 1991 dollars), or about 1.7% of the corresponding family's total income. (Weeks worked in a year rises by more than the fall in weeks spent unemployed because some people enter employment from outside the labor force, without spending any time "unemployed.")

The disproportionate benefits of low unemployment for lower-income families are most apparent for weeks unemployed among household heads. A 1% decrease in the national unemployment rate leads to a half-a-week (0.49) decline in the time that household heads in the lowest-income group spend unemployed; by contrast, for household heads in the highest fifth the effect is very small (0.06 weeks per year).

The total impact of unemployment on families depends not just on the effect on the head of household but also on the effect on other earners in the family. Since low-income families tend to have fewer earners, the impact of falling unemployment on "other adult workers" is not as great as it is for upper-income groups, where two-earner families are more prevalent. Thus, the effect of lower unemployment on "all persons" is not as unequal as for heads of households. Nevertheless, falling unemployment still benefits middle- and low-income families relative to the best-off families.

Finally, Table 3.3 shows the earnings gain to each income group as unemployment falls. Although the increase in income for better-off families is larger than it is for middle- or lower-income families, as a percentage of each group's income the rise is greatest for the lowest-income families.

Employment

In an economy with a growing population and rising labor force participation, employment growth is one of the key determinants of unemployment and underemployment. **Table 3.4** looks at employment growth over the last three business cycles (1973-79, 1979-89, and the period since 1989) relative to the earlier postwar period. The table presents four measures of employment growth. The first two examine job creation—nonfarm payroll employment (from a national survey of business establishments) and civilian employment (from a national survey of households). The second two indicators track the total "volume" of work—measured as the total number of hours worked in the economy in a year and the total number of full-time equivalent jobs (which combines part-time and full-time according to practices in each industry).

TABLE 3.4 Employment growth, 1947-99 (annual percentage rates of growth)

	Measures of employment				Working-age population	Labor-force participation rate**
	Non-farm payroll	Civilian employment	Hours of work*	Full-time equivalent employment*		
1947-67	2.0%	1.3%	1.7%	1.8%	1.2%	0.07
1967-73	2.6	2.3	1.7	1.9	2.1	0.20
1973-79	2.6	2.5	1.9	2.3	1.9	0.48
1979-89	1.8	1.7	1.6	1.7	1.2	0.28
1989-99	1.8	1.3	1.5	1.6	1.1	0.06

* Figure for 1947-67 refers to 1948-1967; for 1989-99, to 1989-98.
** Average annual percentage-point change.

Source: Authors' analysis of BLS and NIPA data.

The current business cycle differs in important ways from the earlier postwar period. Job creation rates in 1989-99, whether measured using non-farm payrolls or counts of civilian employment based on household surveys, were slow compared to earlier periods. Non-farm payrolls grew at a 1.8% annual rate between 1989 and 1999, equal to the annual rate for 1979-89 but well below the rates for 1967-73 and 1973-79 (both 2.6% per year). Civilian employment grew 1.3% per year in the 1990s, about two-thirds the rate for 1979-89 and just over half the rates achieved in 1967-73 (2.3%) and 1973-79 (2.5%).

Despite these lower job creation rates in the 1990s, the growth in the "volume" (total hours) of work has been almost as rapid in the current business cycle as it was during the 1960s, 1970s, and 1980s. The average growth in annual hours worked was 1.5% per year in the period 1989-98, not far below the rates in the three preceding business cycles. Between 1989 and 1998, full-time-equivalent employment grew 1.6% per year, close to its 1.7% rate for 1979-89 but lower than the 2.3% rate in 1973-79 and 1.9% rate in 1967-73. Given the deceleration in job creation rates, the relatively constant growth rate in total hours worked implies that, on average, Americans are working more hours per year. This is consistent with the finding in Chapter 1 that families' total hours worked have been rising in the 1980s and 1990s, and the finding in Chapter 2 that annual hours per worker have been growing. In the earlier postwar period, American workers and their families appear to have taken some of the benefits of higher productivity growth in the form of more hours of leisure. Slower growth and rising inequality since the mid-1970s, however, seem to have pushed more workers to work longer hours.

The data on decelerating job growth rates in the 1990s raise an important question: how can unemployment rates be falling below those of the 1970s and 1980s if job creation rates in the 1990s are below those achieved in the earlier two decades? The last two columns of Table 3.4 provide the answer. Slower job creation rates can still produce lower unemployment rates because the portion of the population seeking employment is growing much more slowly than before. The first reason is that, in the 1990s, the working-age population grew at only about half the rate of the late 1960s and 1970s. The current generation entering the labor force is smaller in numbers than the baby boomers that preceded them, and immigration rates, which grew in the 1980s and again in the 1990s, were not sufficient to offset a deceleration in the growth of the native working-age population.

The second factor affecting the supply of available workers is a slowdown in the rate at which women join the paid labor force. The last column of Table 3.4 shows the change in the overall labor force participation rate (the share of the population that is in work or seeking work) over the postwar period. Since the labor force participation rate for men was falling continuously over this period (in part because of increased schooling and early retirement), the rise in the overall labor force participation rate in the 1960s, 1970s, and 1980s reflects the large increase in women's work outside the home (see Chapter 1). The U.S. economy had to produce many more jobs in the 1960s, 1970s, and 1980s to accommodate the large influx of women, but, with much slower rates of growth in labor force participation in the 1990s, job creation rates can decelerate and unemployment rates can fall at the same time.

The various employment measures in Table 3.4 tell only part of the employment story. Another important, though complicated, gauge of employment opportunities is the share of the working-age population that has a job at any particular time. Rising employment rates generally indicate rising opportunities, as, for example, was the case for women in the postwar period. Nevertheless, employment rates can differ over time and across age, sex, and race for many reasons. Declining employment rates, for example, could reflect a rise in the share of young people staying in school or an increase in the share of older workers deciding to take early retirement, both developments that presumably reflect improvements in the economic circumstances of workers and their families. Alternatively, rising employment rates might respond to declining real wages: families facing declining real wages for current workers might send additional family members to the labor market to make up for lost earnings. So, higher employment rates may or may not indicate greater economic well-being.

Table 3.5 shows the share of the working-age population in work in selected years from 1973 to 1999. (**Figures 3C, 3D,** and **3E** graph the data for

TABLE 3.5 Employment rates, 1973-99

| | 1973 | 1979 | 1989 | 1992 | 1999 | Percentage-point change | | | | |
						1973-99	1973-79	1979-89	1989-99	1992-99
All										
(16 and over)	57.8%	59.9%	63.0%	61.5%	64.3%	6.5	2.1	3.1	1.3	2.8
Adults										
(age 20 and over)										
Men	78.6%	76.5%	74.5%	72.1%	74.0%	-4.6	-2.1	-2.0	-0.5	1.9
White	79.2	77.3	75.4	73.1	74.8	-4.4	-1.9	-1.9	-0.6	1.7
Black	73.7	69.1	67.0	64.3	67.5	-6.2	-4.6	-2.1	0.5	3.2
Hispanic	81.3	80.3	79.4	75.2	79.6	-1.8	-1.0	-1.0	0.2	4.3
Women	42.2%	47.7%	54.9%	54.8%	58.5%	16.3	5.5	7.2	3.6	3.7
White	41.6	47.3	54.9	54.9	58.0	16.4	5.7	7.6	3.1	3.1
Black	47.2	49.3	54.6	53.6	61.5	14.3	2.1	5.3	6.9	7.9
Hispanic	38.3	43.7	50.5	48.8	53.9	15.5	5.3	6.9	3.3	5.1

Source: Authors' analysis of BLS data.

FIGURE 3C Employment rates, ages 20 and over, 1973-99

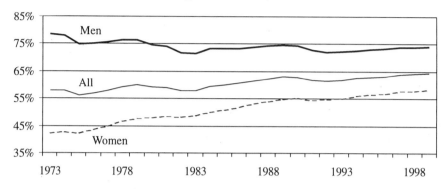

Source: Authors' analysis of BLS data.

FIGURE 3D Employment rates, men 20 and over, 1973-99

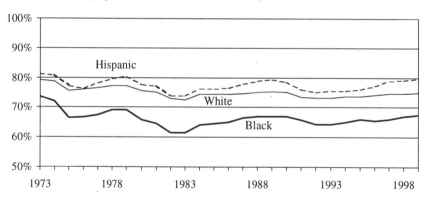

Source: Authors' analysis of BLS data.

every year over the same period.) These employment rates vary considerably across different groups. In 1999, for example, men had much higher employment rates (74.0%) than did women (58.5%). Among men, Hispanics had the highest employment rate (79.6%), followed by whites (74.8%), with blacks trailing considerably (67.5%). Among women, however, blacks had the highest employment rate (61.5%), followed by whites (58.0%), and then Hispanics (53.9%). Trends in employment rates across groups differ as well. Employment rates for men fell between 1973 and 1999 across all racial and ethnic groups, with the largest de-

FIGURE 3E Employment rates, women 20 and over, 1973-99

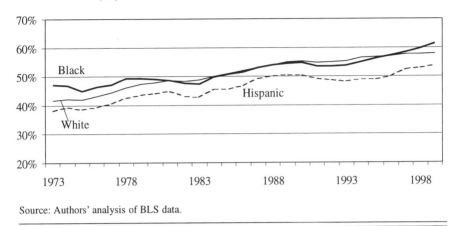

Source: Authors' analysis of BLS data.

clines in the periods 1973-79 and 1979-89. In the 1990s, however, the long-term decline in male employment rates decelerated noticeably—and rates even rose over the period for black and Hispanic men. For women, employment rates climbed steadily over the business cycle peaks between 1973 and 1999, with whites, blacks, and Hispanics all experiencing roughly equal increases.

Table 3.5 also allows us to look at changes in employment rates over the current economic expansion. As with unemployment, traditionally disadvantaged groups benefited more from the expansion of 1992-99 than did generally better-off groups. In 1992-99, the employment rate for white men, for example, increased 1.7 percentage points, well below the increases experienced by black men (3.2 percentages points), Hispanic men (4.3), white women (3.1), black women (7.9), and Hispanic women (5.1).

The evidence on the number of jobs created in the 1980s and 1990s, however, tells us little about the changing characteristics of new and existing jobs. In Chapter 2, we saw that the hourly wages for most men and many women have been declining over most of the last two decades. In the remainder of this chapter, we look at other aspects of job quality, including job stability and security and "nonstandard" or "contingent" work arrangements.

Job stability and job security

Widespread economic anxiety, which persisted well into the current economic recovery, has often been linked to the feeling that job security and long-term-employment prospects declined considerably in the 1980s and 1990s. In this section, we examine the available data on job stability and job security. First, we look at data for the periods 1966-81 and 1979-94 on changes in male workers' attachment to their jobs. In many respects, this first set of data is ideal because it tracks the employment and earnings of sets of the same workers over the two decades, allowing a measure of changes in job stability as well as the earnings costs associated with diminished long-term attachments. Unfortunately, no comparable data cover women's job stability over the same period, nor are more recent data available. We, therefore, turn next to a broader set of measures of job stability. These include data on the duration of a typical job, the share of workers in "long-term jobs," the tendency of workers to stay in a particular job once they have established a relationship with an employer, the rate of involuntary job loss (i.e., not for cause), and workers' perceptions of job security. Each measure has its problems, but taken together they paint a comprehensive picture of the changing nature of job stability and security over the last two decades. Unfortunately, little of the data that are currently available on job stability and job security cover the last several years of the 1990s, when the economy's performance improved markedly. What evidence that is available suggests that job stability and job security increased along with wages and job opportunities, but that job stability remains high given 30-year lows in the level of unemployment.

Throughout the review of these data, it is important to keep in mind the distinction between *job stability*—what economists Daniel Aaronson and Daniel Sullivan have called "the tendency of workers and employers to form long-term bonds"—and *job security*—"workers' ability to remain in an employment relationship for as long as their job performance is satisfactory." From a social perspective, our primary concern should be with job security. We would not be worried, for example, if job stability had declined primarily because workers found that they could improve wages, benefits, and working conditions by frequently changing jobs.

Unfortunately, much of the available evidence—the number of job changes in a period of time, the duration of the typical job, and the share of workers in long-term jobs—deals more directly with job stability than job security. Still, the data on job stability are potentially instructive. Given the well-documented tendency of wages to rise with a worker's tenure (the time spent with a particular employer), and given the apparently widespread anxiety over the perceived decline in long-term jobs, any evidence of declining job stability would tend to support the view that job security is falling. Moreover, in some cases, we can link declining job stability with falling earnings for affected groups. While workers could be trading their old, better-paying jobs for new, lower-paying jobs that these workers prefer for other reasons, we believe that these kinds of job changes

TABLE 3.6 Job stability of men, age 16-36, 1979-94

Cohort	Two-year job separation rate	Median hourly wage increase between age 16 and age 36 (1997 dollars)
1966-81	46.4%	$9.90
1979-94	52.7	7.65
Change	13.6%	-22.7%

Source: Bernhardt, Morris, Handcock, and Scott (1998) analysis of the National Longitudinal Surveys (NLS).

are the exception, not the rule. We therefore feel comfortable interpreting declining job stability in the presence of falling earnings as evidence of diminished job security. Finally, we note that job stability need not decline for job security to do so. When job insecurity rises, workers may become less likely to quit their current jobs to accept or seek new ones. This reluctance to change would contribute to rising job stability even as job security was falling.

Declining job stability

Table 3.6 presents the results of a unique analysis of job stability among young, white men during two periods: 1966-81, which mostly predates stagnating wages and incomes, and 1979-94, which covers most of the period when economic inequality grew sharply. Researchers followed two groups of men. The first group, which researchers followed in 1966-81, was born between 1944 and 1952; the second, which researchers tracked in 1979-94, was born between 1957 and 1965. The choice of years meant that the first group of men was the same age during the first period as the second group of men during the second period. The researchers measured job instability for the two groups by counting the share of workers in a given year that were no longer with the same employer two years later. In the 1966-81 period, an average of 46.4% of young men were not with the same employer two years later; in 1979-94, the average rose to 52.7%, an increase of about 13.6%. The rise in instability coincided with a steep decline in real wage growth. The young men in the first group saw their after-inflation wages rise an average of $9.90 during 1966-81; those in the later, less stable group saw their wages rise only $7.65 in 1979-94. Wage gains in the later period

231

TABLE 3.7 Median years with same employer, by age, 1963-96

					Change	
Group	1963	1981	1987	1996	1963-96	1987-96
Age 25-34						
All	3.0	3.1	2.9	2.8	-0.2	-0.1
Men	3.5	3.1	3.1	3.0	-0.5	-0.1
Women	2.0	3.0	2.6	2.7	0.7	0.1
Age 35-44						
All	6.0	5.1	5.5	5.3	-0.7	-0.2
Men	7.6	7.1	7.0	6.1	-1.5	-0.9
Women	3.6	4.1	4.4	4.8	1.2	0.4
Age 45-54						
All	9.0	9.1	8.8	8.3	-0.7	-0.5
Men	11.4	11.1	11.8	10.1	-1.3	-1.7
Women	6.1	6.1	6.8	7.0	0.9	0.2

Source: Aaronson and Sullivan (1998).

were 22.7% below those in the first period.

As mentioned above, no comparable data exist for women over the same period, nor are more recent, comparable data yet available for men. For a more comprehensive and up-to-date picture of job stability, therefore, we now turn to a broader set of measures. Unlike the data in Table 3.6, which followed the same workers over time, these data are "snapshots" of the employment circumstances of different workers at different points in time.

Table 3.7 and **Figure 3F** provide the most basic information on job stability—the median number of years of tenure for men and women from the early 1960s through 1996 (tenure data are not available for the standard business cycle years we use elsewhere in this book, so we use the years closest to them). Since the tenure distribution is sensitive to the age distribution in the population (young workers can't have long job tenure no matter how stable underlying employment relationships are at a particular time), we present the data separately for 25-34-year-olds, 35-44-year-olds, and 45-54-year-olds.

Several features of the tenure distribution stand out. First, tenure for men in all age groups fell between 1963 and 1996, with much of the decline between 1987 and 1996. Declines in male tenure were largest for the middle and older age groups. For 35-44-year-old men, median tenure dropped 1.5 years, from 7.6

FIGURE 3F Median years with same employer, by age, 1963-96

AGES 25-34

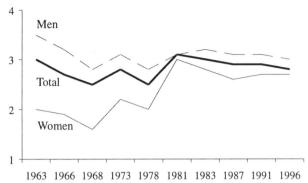

AGES 35-44

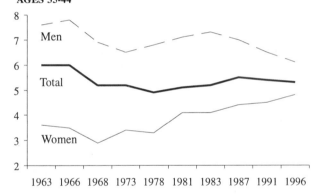

AGES 45-54

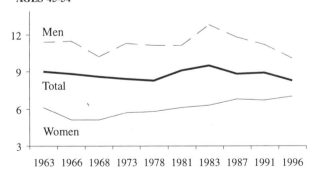

Source: Aaronson and Sullivan (1998).

years in 1963 to 6.1 years in 1996; most of the decline (nine-tenths of a year) occurred between 1987 and 1996. The pattern is similar for 45-54-year-old men, who saw median tenure fall 1.3 years between 1963 and 1996, with an even steeper decline between 1987 and 1996. Tenure fell only slightly for the youngest group of men, about half a year (0.5) between 1963 and 1996, with a minimal one-tenth of a year fall between 1987 and 1996.

Second, women consistently have lower tenure than men of the same age. In 1996, for example, 35-44-year-old women had a median tenure of 4.8 years, while the median man in the same age range had 6.1 years with his current employer. Third, while women still have lower tenure than men, a combination of rising tenure for women and declining tenure for men allowed women to narrow the tenure gap between 1963 and 1996. Finally, the declining tenure for men and the rising tenure for women have come close to canceling each other out. The overall distribution at all three age levels generally changes much less than either of the corresponding male or female distributions.

Median job tenure sheds important light on job stability, but the share of jobs that are "long-term" may be more relevant to workers' perceptions of job security. "Long-term" jobs (ones that last, say, at least 10 years) typically are the kinds of employment situations that provide workers with the best potential for sustained wage growth, good fringe benefits, and a feeling of employment security. **Table 3.8** reports the share of workers in 1979, 1988, and 1996 that had been in their jobs for 10 or more and 20 or more years. The data show a significant decline during the 1980s and 1990s in the share of men in long-term jobs and little change in the share of women in such jobs. In 1979, just under half (49.8%) of all men had been in their jobs for 10 years or longer; by 1996, the share had fallen 9.8 percentage points to 40.0%. In 1979, far fewer women (29.1%) than men had tenure of 10 years or more, and that share had increased only slightly by 1996 (to 30.3%). The data for men and women with 20 years on the job tell a similar story. The share of men with these very-long-tenure jobs fell 6.8 percentage points between 1979 and 1996, from 33.8% to 27.0%. Meanwhile, the share of women in these long-term jobs rose 1.2 percentage points, from 13.1% to 14.3%. The data by education, which include both men and women, suggest that the declines in job tenure cut across all education levels. Declines in 10-year-tenure jobs between 1979 and 1996, for example, were almost as large among college-educated workers (-6.9 percentage points) as they were for those with less than a high school degree (-7.3 percentage points).

Another important feature of job stability is the probability that a worker's current job will continue into the future. **Table 3.9** shows the results of an analysis that asks how likely it is that a worker with a given number of years on his or her current job will be holding the same job in four years (the time period is

TABLE 3.8 Share of employed workers in long-term jobs, 1979-96

	1979	1988	1996	Percentage-point change		
				1979-88	1988-96	1979-96
More than 10 years on current job						
All	41.0%	39.1%	35.4%	-1.9	-3.7	-5.6
Male	49.8	45.7	40.0	-4.1	-5.7	-9.8
Female	29.1	31.2	30.3	2.1	-0.9	1.2
Less than high school	38.6%	39.8%	31.3%	1.2	-8.5	-7.3
High school	41.9	40.2	37.2	-1.7	-3.0	-4.7
Some college	38.8	34.8	33.3	-4.0	-1.5	-5.5
College and beyond	43.6	40.4	36.7	-3.2	-3.7	-6.9
More than 20 years on current job						
All	25.1%	23.7%	20.9%	-1.4	-2.8	-4.2
Male	33.8	31.4	27.0	-2.4	-4.4	-6.8
Female	13.1	14.5	14.3	1.4	-0.2	1.2
Less than high school	22.5%	21.8%	19.8%	-0.7	-2.0	-2.7
High school	26.3	23.8	22.0	-2.5	-1.8	-4.3
Some college	25.5	21.5	19.2	-4.0	-2.3	-6.3
College and beyond	26.6	26.7	21.7	0.1	-5.0	-4.9

Source: Farber (1997).

forced by the nature of the underlying data). The data presented here allow us to look separately at men, women, whites, and blacks and, within each of these groups, at workers with zero to two, two to nine, nine to 15, and 15 or more years of tenure. The time period covered begins in the mid-1980s (1983-87) and ends in the first half of the 1990s (1991-95). While the data tell a complicated story, the main results are consistent with those provided by earlier indicators: during the first half of the 1990s, job stability fell for men while it simultaneously rose for women (though women still experience lower levels of job stability than do men).

The data for men show that, on average, the probability that a worker's current job will continue for four more years changed relatively little between the mid-1980s and the first half of the 1990s. In 1983-87, 58.5% of current male jobs lasted at least four more years. By 1991-95, the share of male jobs lasting at least four more years fell 2.1 percentage points to 56.4%. The average, however,

TABLE 3.9 Four-year job retention* rates, 1983-95

				Percentage-point change		
Years of tenure	Mid-1980s (1983-87)	Late 1980s (1987-91)	Early 1990s (1991-95)	Mid-80s to late 80s	Late 80s to early 90s	Mid-80s to early 90s
Male	58.5%	56.5%	56.4%	-2.0	-0.1	-2.1
0-2	35.2	36.1	39.4	0.9	3.3	4.2
2-9	63.7	56.6	58.4	-7.1	1.8	-5.3
9-15	86.1	84.6	78.6	-1.5	-6.0	-7.5
15+	66.0	70.5	63.3	4.5	-7.2	-2.7
Female	48.4%	50.3%	52.1%	1.9	1.8	3.7
0-2	30.5	33.1	38.8	2.6	5.7	8.3
2-9	53.4	52.9	54.4	-0.5	1.5	1.0
9-15	78.2	78.0	70.5	-0.2	-7.5	-7.7
15+	55.7	69.7	63.3	14.0	-6.4	7.6
White	53.2%	53.5%	54.2%	0.3	0.7	1.0
0-2	32.2	34.7	38.4	2.5	3.7	6.2
2-9	57.9	54.6	56.4	-3.3	1.8	-1.5
9-15	81.8	81.9	74.0	0.1	-7.9	-7.8
15+	62.8	69.5	64.0	6.7	-5.5	1.2
Black	60.5%	55.4%	55.3%	-5.1	-0.1	-5.2
0-2	38.3	34.2	41.8	-4.1	7.6	3.5
2-9	64.4	56.9	54.9	-7.5	-2.0	-9.5
9-15	89.2	79.9	85.2	-9.3	5.3	-4.0
15+	66.1	75.7	59.4	9.6	-16.3	-6.7

*Share of workers with given characteristics who work with same employer for the four-year period beginning and ending in the years indicated.

Source: Neumark, Polsky, and Hansen (1997).

masks two offsetting trends in the data. The share of short-tenure jobs (up to two years) that lasted at least four more years rose from 35.2% in 1983-87 to 39.4% in 1991-95. Over the same period, however, the share of longer-tenure jobs that survived for four or more years fell 5.3 percentage points in the case of two-to-nine-year jobs; 7.5 percentage points for nine-to-15-year jobs; and 2.7 percentage points for 15-or-more-year jobs. Since the share of employment in jobs lasting up to two years is larger than the other four categories, the 4.2 percentage-point rise in four-year retention rates for this group counteracted much of the larger decline in retention rates for longer-tenure workers. Since workers' perceptions of job security probably weigh the fate of longer-tenure jobs more heavily than shorter-tenure jobs, the relatively large decline in job retention rates for longer-tenure jobs may have a bigger influence on workers' perceptions of job security than the smaller decline in average retention rates, which includes the effects of improvements on the shortest-tenure jobs.

The job retention rates for women generally show a steady convergence toward those of men. Retention rates for women are all below those of men in 1983-87 but are, overall, much closer in 1991-95. For example, the 10 percentage-point gap between the male and female average four-year retention rates in 1983-87 (58.5% for men compared to 48.4% for women) fell to only a little over 4 percentage points by 1991-95 (56.4% compared to 52.1%). This convergence reflects both the decline in most male retention rates and the increase in most female retention rates.

Displacement

Job stability can decline because workers change jobs more frequently in order to take advantage of other opportunities, or it can fall because employers lay off or fire workers in greater numbers. The evidence on the poor wage-growth prospects of those with weak job stability (see Table 3.6) argues that much of the increase in job instability was probably involuntary. This section focuses special attention on involuntary job loss.

Table 3.10 reports data for the 1980s and 1990s on the share of workers that have experienced involuntary job loss during four different three-year periods. The data show that, in any given three-year period over the last two decades, 8 to 12% of workers suffered at least one involuntary job loss. The 12.3% job loss rate for 1981-83, a period that included the 1982 recession and had an average unemployment rate of 9.1%, was the highest level of the last two decades. The job loss rate fell to 7.9% during the economic recovery years of 1987-89, when the average unemployment rate was a much lower 5.7%. Job displacement rates rose in the 1990s, to 10.9% in 1991-93 (the average unemployment rate was 7.3%) and then increased again to 11.4% in 1993-95, despite the economic recovery that lowered the average unemployment rate to 6.2%. The rise in the job loss rate between 1991-93, a period of relatively high unemployment, and 1993-95, a period of relatively low unemployment, suggests that the underlying rate of job loss (that is, the component of job loss that is independent of the rise and fall of the business cycle) accelerated in the 1990s.

Table 3.10 also summarizes how the reasons for job loss have changed over time. Plant closings and "slack work" both declined between the recessionary periods in 1981-83 and 1991-93, reflecting in part the much lower unemploy-

TABLE 3.10 Rate of job loss by reason,* 1981-95

					Percentage-point change		
Reason	1981-83	1987-89	1991-93	1993-95	1981-83– 1991-93	1987-89– 1993-95	1991-93– 1993-95
Plant closing	4.5%	3.6%	3.6%	3.2%	-0.9	-0.4	-0.4
Slack work	5.4	2.4	3.7	3.8	-1.7	1.4	0.1
Position abolished	1.4	1.1	2.2	2.4	0.8	1.3	0.2
Other	1.0	0.8	1.4	2.0	0.4	1.2	0.6
All reasons	12.3%	7.9%	10.9%	11.4%	-1.4	3.5	0.5
Unemployment rate	9.1%	5.7%	7.3%	6.2%	-1.8	0.5	-1.1

* Data are adjusted for change in recall period, and the "other" response has been discounted in all years.

Source: Farber (1998).

ment rates in the second recession and the steeper manufacturing downturn in the 1980s recession. Over the same period, however, "position abolished," a term that may reflect the "downsizing" phenomenon, rose sharply, from 1.4% to 2.2%. Displacements due to "position abolished" continued to rise through 1993-95 (to 2.4%), despite the economic recovery.

Table 3.11 examines differences in job loss by occupation. The data presented here examine only the three principal reasons for involuntary job loss because the survey that generated these data did not ask workers about their occupation if they lost their job for "other" reasons. The first striking feature is the high rate of job loss for blue-collar workers (craftsmen, operatives, and laborers) relative to workers in other professions. The job loss rate for blue-collar workers over the 1981-83 period was 21.2%, almost three times higher than the next most heavily affected group (sales and administration workers, with 8.5%). By 1993-95, the job loss rate for blue-collar workers had fallen to 13.5%, but it still exceeded the rates for all other broad occupational categories.

The second feature of the displacement data is the significant increase during the 1990s in the risk of job loss for white-collar workers (managers, professional and technical workers, and sales and administrative workers). Between the recessionary periods 1981-83 and 1991-93, the share of managers whose positions were abolished more than doubled, from 1.4% to 3.0%; over the same period, the proportion of professional and technical workers whose positions were abolished increased from 1.1% to 1.7%; and for sales and administrative workers the share grew from 1.3% to 2.4%. Between the two periods of economic recovery, 1987-89 and 1993-95, the rise in the incidence of job loss from

TABLE 3.11 Rate of job loss by occupation and reason,* 1981-95

					Percentage-point change		
Occupation/reason	1981-83	1987-89	1991-93	1993-95	1981-83– 1991-93	1987-89– 1993-95	1991-93– 1993-95
Managers							
All reasons	8.2%	6.4%	9.7%	7.8%	1.5	1.4	-1.9
Plant closing	4.2	3.9	3.9	3.4	-0.3	-0.5	-0.5
Slack work	2.6	1.2	2.7	2.0	0.1	0.8	-0.7
Position abolished	1.4	1.3	3.0	2.4	1.6	1.1	-0.6
Professional, technical workers							
All reasons	5.1%	3.5%	5.5%	5.8%	0.4	2.3	0.3
Plant closing	1.8	1.4	1.6	1.7	-0.2	0.3	0.1
Slack work	2.3	1.1	2.1	1.9	-0.2	0.8	-0.2
Position abolished	1.1	1.0	1.7	2.2	0.6	1.2	0.5
Sales, administrative workers							
All reasons	8.5%	6.9%	9.1%	9.3%	0.6	2.4	0.2
Plant closing	4.1	3.8	3.8	3.9	-0.3	0.1	0.1
Slack work	3.1	1.8	3.0	2.8	-0.1	1.0	-0.2
Position abolished	1.3	1.3	2.4	2.7	1.1	1.4	0.3
Service workers							
All reasons	5.9%	4.8%	6.5%	7.3%	0.6	2.5	0.8
Plant closing	3.0	3.0	3.1	3.4	0.1	0.4	0.3
Slack work	2.3	1.3	2.4	2.8	0.1	1.5	0.4
Position abolished	0.6	0.5	1.0	1.1	0.4	0.6	0.1
Crafts, operatives, and laborers							
All reasons	21.2%	11.1%	13.7%	13.5%	-7.5	2.4	-0.2
Plant closing	7.7	5.1	5.2	4.2	-2.5	-0.9	-1.0
Slack work	12.1	5.1	7.0	7.6	-5.1	2.5	0.6
Position abolished	1.5	0.9	1.5	1.7	0.0	0.8	0.2
Unemployment rate	9.1%	5.7%	7.3%	6.2%	-1.8	0.5	-1.1

*Data are adjusted for change in recall period and exclude "other" category.

Source: Farber (1997).

"position abolished" was just as dramatic: from 1.3% to 2.4% for managers; 1.0% to 2.2% for professional and technical workers; and 1.3% to 2.7% for sales and administrative workers.

When workers leave their jobs voluntarily, they generally move on to better circumstances in a new job with better pay or working conditions. (They may also choose to leave work to pursue other activities such as education, child rearing, or retirement.) When workers lose their jobs involuntarily, however, they typically pay a large economic price. **Table 3.12** provides estimates of some of the principal economic costs associated with involuntary job loss. The first obvious cost of job loss is that displaced workers often experience difficulty finding a new job. Among all workers who reported losing their jobs in the previous three years (the data cover the period 1981-95), 35.1% (see last column) were out of work at the time they were interviewed about their experience of job loss. While not all of these displaced, out-of-work workers were looking for a job at the time they were interviewed, if they were, then the 35.1% out-of-work rate would translate to an unemployment rate that was five times the average unemployment rate for the 1981-95 period (6.9%). Among the 65% or so of workers who did manage to find new jobs, the new job paid less on average than the old one. Specifically, among the workers who moved from full-time to full-time work, the new positions paid, on average, 9.2% less than the old job. Many previous full-timers, however, were not able to find full-time work (though some displaced part-timers did manage to find new full-time positions). Therefore, the average decline in hourly wages for all workers, including those who went from full-time to part-time work and vice versa, was even steeper (-14.2%). With both lower wages and fewer hours, workers who lost full-time jobs and managed only to find part-time replacement jobs were especially badly off.

The preceding figures for wage loss compare displaced workers' wages on their new jobs with those earned on their old jobs. These estimates of the wage costs of job loss, however, almost certainly underestimate the true wage loss. Some of these workers lost their jobs as many as three years before they were asked about the wages at their new job. If they had not lost their old jobs and had been able to continue at that same job for one to three years longer, many would have received further nominal pay increases. When we compare displaced workers with similar workers who did not lose their jobs, the average decline in wages for those who went from full-time to full-time jobs grows from 9.2% to 13.0% (see row 4).

Moreover, wages are only part of the story. Many displaced workers also lose the non-wage benefits provided through their previous employers. Of those workers who had health benefits on the job they lost, 28.7% (see row 5) had no employer-provided health benefits on their new jobs. Some displaced workers, of course, had no health insurance coverage at their old jobs but found new jobs that did provide insurance. When we include these workers in the calculation, job displacement reduced health insurance coverage by 14.0% (see row 6). Both health insurance figures paint an overly rosy picture, however, because, as we noted above, many displaced workers have difficulty finding new work.

TABLE 3.12 The costs of job loss, averages for 1980s and 1990s

	Reason for job loss				
Post-loss outcome	Plant closing	Slack work	Position abolished	Other	All
Out of work*	30.2%	40.9%	29.7%	37.2%	35.1%
Average wage change					
Full time to full time	-9.3%	-8.7%	-12.0%	-6.5%	-9.2%
All job changes	-13.0	-14.3	-19.2	-11.4	-14.2
Average wage loss, compared to continuously employed	-13.2%	-13.0%	-16.3%	-9.2%	-13.0%
Health benefits before loss, no health benefits after loss	n.a.	n.a.	n.a.	n.a.	28.7%
No health benefits after loss, including those with no coverage at lost job	n.a.	n.a.	n.a.	n.a.	14.0%

* Of those who lost job in the last three years, the share out of work at time of interview.
** Full-time to full-time job changes only.

Sources: Authors' analysis of Farber (1997) and Gardner (1995).

Job security

The preceding sections on job stability and job displacement examined statistical measures of the economy's tendency to create and destroy long-term employment relationships. We began that discussion by emphasizing the importance of differentiating between objective measures of job stability and more subjective, and probably more important, measures of "job security"—workers' perceptions of their ability to remain in their current job as long as they perform satisfactorily. Much of the evidence presented on job stability and displacement suggests that the underlying level of employment instability is higher in the 1990s than it was in the 1980s and earlier periods. Since the decline in job stability and the rise in job displacement appear to be linked to worsening economic circumstances for affected workers, we believe that this evidence on instability supports the conclusion that job insecurity has also increased in the 1990s. In this section, we turn to direct evidence on job security, based on workers' reported evaluation of the security of their current jobs.

TABLE 3.13 Perceptions of job security, 1978-96

	1978*	1989	1996	Percentage-point change 1978-89	1989-96
How likely to lose your job or be laid off in next 12 months?					
Very or fairly likely	8.0%	8.0%	11.2%	0.0	3.2
Not at all likely	71.0	69.2	60.3	-1.8	-8.9
How easy to find a job with another employer with about the same income and benefits?					
Not easy at all	38.7%	37.8%	39.4%	-0.9	1.6
Very easy	28.1	34.2	27.1	6.1	-7.1
National unemployment rate	6.1%	5.3%	5.4%	-0.8	0.1

* No data available for 1979.

Source: Aaronson and Sullivan (1998) analysis of GSS data.

Table 3.13 presents results on reported levels of job security from a nationally representative survey of workers in the years 1978, 1989, and 1996 (no survey data exist for 1979, our normal comparison year). The share of workers who said they thought they were very or fairly likely to lose their jobs in the next 12 months was 8.0% in both 1978 and 1989 (despite a slight decline in the national unemployment rate between the two years). Between 1989 and 1996, however, the share of workers who thought they faced a significant chance of losing their jobs in the next year rose 3.2 percentage points to 11.2%. Perceived job security fell over the period even though the national unemployment rate was essentially identical in the two years (5.3% in 1989 compared to 5.4% in 1996). The same polling data also show a large drop between 1978 and 1996 in the share of workers who thought that they were not at all likely to lose their jobs in the next 12 months. In 1978, 71.0% of workers thought that they faced little chance of losing their jobs; by 1996, the figure had fallen 10.7 percentage points to 60.3%. As before, most of the decline in perceived job security took place in the 1990s, with 8.9 percentage points of the decline occurring between 1989 and 1996, compared to only a 1.8 percentage-point drop between 1978 and 1989.

Workers also appear less optimistic about their employment prospects in the event of job loss. In all three years, just under 40% of workers thought that it

FIGURE 3G Job leavers, 1967-99

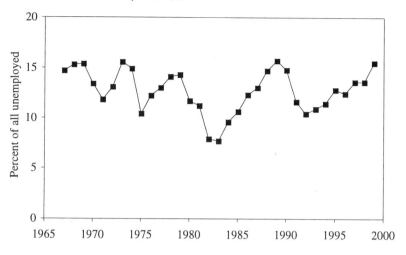

Source: Authors' analysis of BLS data.

would not be at all easy to find other jobs with the same pay and benefits as their current jobs. The share of pessimists increased slightly (1.6 percentage points) between 1989 and 1996, from 37.8% to 39.4%. Over the same period, the share of optimists—those who thought it would be very easy to find a new job with the same pay and benefits—fell sharply (7.1 percentage points), from 34.2% to 27.1%.

The data on workers' perceptions show a high and growing level of job insecurity in the 1990s. These subjective impressions are consistent with the increases in job instability over the last two decades. They also support the conclusion that rising job instability does not respond to workers' desires to enter more "flexible" employment relationships, but rather represents an additional psychological and financial burden on workers.

As mentioned earlier, little information is available on job stability and job security after the mid-1990s. **Figure 3G** presents one imperfect indicator of job security that is available through 1999. The data in the figure show the share of all unemployed workers who are unemployed because they quit their previous jobs to look for new ones. When times are good and unemployment falls, the share of job leavers among all unemployed workers rises, reflecting both lower levels of layoffs and workers' greater confidence about their ability to find new, better jobs. When times are bad and the unemployment rate rises, the share of job leavers in total unemployment falls, reflecting both an influx of involuntarily displaced workers and the general unwillingness of workers to give up their current jobs to search for new ones. As has historically been the case, the decline in the unemployment rate during the current economic recovery led to a rise in the share of job-leavers, suggesting that workers' insecurity abated during the recovery. At the same time, the job-leavers data also suggest that underlying job insecurity may have been higher at the end of the 1990s than it was in earlier periods. In 1999, with the national unemployment rate at 4.2%, the job-leavers rate had risen only to the same level it reached in 1989, when the unemployment rate was 5.3%, more than a full percentage point higher. If the historical relationship between unemployment and the job-leavers rate held at the end of the 1990s, we would expect to have seen a higher job-leavers rate than we actually observed. The economic developments of the 1980s and 1990s appear to have raised the level of insecurity that workers feel at any given level of unemployment.

The contingent workforce

The preceding analysis of job stability, job displacement, and direct measures of job security suggests that underlying job security fell markedly between the 1970s and the 1990s. One important reason that workers may have felt less secure in their jobs in the middle of the 1990s than they did in earlier periods with comparable or even higher unemployment rates is that a large and growing part of the workforce holds "nonstandard" or "contingent" jobs.

Broadly defined, nonstandard employment arrangements are all jobs that are not regular, full-time employment; these include temporary, part-time, on-call, and self-employed workers. Businesses hire contingent workers on a temporary basis in a variety of ways. Some firms put workers directly on their payrolls but assign them to an internal temporary worker pool. Others hire on-call workers and day laborers. Employers also use temporary help agencies and contracting firms to obtain workers on a temporary basis, sometimes for long periods. Some businesses hire independent contractors to perform work that would otherwise be done by employees.

In this section, we report results from three special analyses of nonstandard work arrangements: the 1995, 1997, and 1999 Contingent Work Supplements to the Current Population Survey (the monthly government household survey that has provided much of the information on wages and employment presented in this book). These data allow us to examine the different types of nonstandard work, their prevalence, and their associated pay and working conditions. While

TABLE 3.14 Employed workers by work arrangement, 1995-99

Work arrangement	Percent of all employed		
	1995	1997	1999
Regular part-time	16.5%	16.0%	15.5%
Temporary help agency	1.0	1.0	0.9
On call	1.7	1.6	1.5
Independent contractors	6.7	6.7	6.3
Contract firms	0.5	0.6	0.6
All nonstandard	26.4%	25.9%	24.8%
Regular full-time	73.6%	74.1%	75.1%

Source: Authors' analysis of BLS (1995, 1997, 1999). All data are for February.

the surveys provide a comprehensive look at nonstandard work arrangements in the mid- to late 1990s, no comparable, earlier surveys exist. After reviewing the most recent data, therefore, we will turn to other, less comprehensive data that can give some indication of longer-term trends in the growth of nonstandard work arrangements.

Nonstandard work: widespread and often substandard

Table 3.14 shows the distribution of employment in 1995, 1997, and 1999 by type of work arrangement. In 1999, about 75% of all workers held regular full-time jobs, leaving almost 25% of workers in different nonstandard work arrangements (these figures exclude some self-employed workers). The largest nonstandard category was regular part-time work (15.5%), followed by independent contracting (6.3%). Some workers held nonstandard jobs through temporary help agencies (0.9%) and contract companies (0.6). Others were "on call" with their regular employers (1.5%). The table also shows that the share of nonstandard workers fell as the economy improved between 1995 and 1999. The share of workers in all forms of nonstandard work declined from 26.4% of the workforce in 1995 to 24.8% in 1999. Nearly every type of nonstandard arrangement experienced some decline: regular part-time work fell from 16.5% in 1995 to 15.5% in 1999, and independent contractors from 6.7% to 6.3%; even temporary work, which we will see later grew rapidly through most of the 1980s and 1990s, was essentially flat over the last half of the 1990s.

TABLE 3.15 Characteristics of nonstandard workers, 1999

	Temporary help agency	On call	Independent contractors	Contract firms	Standard work
Men	42.2%	48.8%	66.2%	70.5%	52.4%
Women	57.8	51.2	33.8	29.5	47.6
White	74.3%	84.2%	90.6%	79.2%	84.0%
Black	21.2	12.7	5.8	12.6	11.4
Hispanic*	13.6	11.6	6.1	6.0	10.4
Age					
16-24	26.7%	18.8%	4.0%	16.1%	15.0%
25-64	70.5	73.0	89.2	82.1	82.5
65 and older	2.8	8.2	6.8	1.8	2.5
Education					
Less than high school	14.6%	13.4%	7.5%	6.4%	9.2%
High school	30.5	29.6	29.7	22.7	31.4
Some college	33.7	29.1	28.5	31.9	28.3
College or more	21.2	27.9	34.3	38.9	31.1

* Hispanics can be of any race; other racial and ethnic categories not shown.

Source: Authors' analysis of BLS (1999).

Table 3.15 compares the characteristics of nonstandard workers (the first four columns) with those of workers in standard arrangements (the last column) in 1999. Women made up less than half (47.6%) the standard work force, but were well over half (57.8%) of temporary workers and just over half (51.2%) of on-call workers. Women, however, were strongly underrepresented (33.8%) among independent contractors, the category of nonstandard workers that consistently appears to offer the highest pay and benefits as well as the greatest reported satisfaction rates. Black, Hispanic, and younger (16- to 24-year-old) workers are also overrepresented in typically substandard temp and on-call work and underrepresented in independent contracting.

Nonstandard workers generally earn less and receive fewer fringe benefits than workers with similar skills in regular full-time jobs. **Table 3.16** reports the results of a statistical analysis of wages of workers in different work arrangements in 1995. The findings presented in the top panel control for key worker

TABLE 3.16 Wages of nonstandard workers compared to regular full-time workers, by gender and work arrangement, 1995

Work arrangement	Women	Men
Controlling for personal characteristics		
Regular part time	-20%	-24%
Temporary help agency	-17	-21
On call	-21	-9
Self-employed	-25	-13
Independent contracting	-14	-5
Contract company	—	7
Controlling for personal and job characteristics		
Regular part time	-5%	-10%
Temporary help agency	—	-8
On call	-6	—
Self-employed	-6	8
Independent contracting	7	12
Contract company	11	9

— indicates that the difference is not statistically significant. All other differences are statistically significant.

Source: Kalleberg et al. (1997) analysis of CWS data.

characteristics such as the level of education and years of work experience. The analysis demonstrates that women and men in nonstandard work arrangements earn substantially less than their counterparts with similar skills and backgrounds but who are in regular full-time jobs. For example, regular part-time women workers—who make up about one-fifth of the female workforce—earned 20% less on average than similar women in full-time employment. The gap between men and women who worked as temps and their regular part-time counterparts was also about 20%. Not all nonstandard workers, however, earn less than regular full-timers. Men working with contract companies, for example, earn about 7% more than comparable standard workers.

One reason that the nonstandard wages in the top panel of Table 3.16 are so much lower than those for regular full-time work is that nonstandard workers tend to be concentrated in low-paying industries and occupations. In the second panel of the table, we present further results that control for both workers' personal characteristics and the characteristics of the jobs they perform. In this analysis, the wage "penalty" for working in nonstandard jobs is smaller than when we ignore job characteristics. In half the cases, nonstandard workers appear to earn more than "standard" workers with similar personal skills in the same kinds of jobs. This evidence supports the view that nonstandard workers tend to work in less-well-paid industries and occupations.

At the same time, one reason that some nonstandard workers may earn wages above those of comparable full-timers in similar jobs is that nonstandard workers are much less likely to receive fringe benefits than are regular employees. In other words, employers may have to pay a slightly higher cash wage to compensate for the lack of health or pension benefits. (Employers may also have to pay a slightly higher hourly wage to help offset the higher level of job insecurity associated with nonstandard work.) **Table 3.17** shows the share of workers, by work arrangement, with health and pension coverage through their employer in 1999. About 57.9% of standard workers had employer-provided health benefits in 1999. Employer-provided health coverage rates were generally far lower for nonstandard workers: among temps it was 8.5%, and among on-call workers it was 21.1%. Only workers with contract firms came close (56.1%) to the level of benefits among standard workers. Some defenders of nonstandard work arrangements argue that nonstandard workers receive health insurance through other sources, typically a spouse. The data in the second column, which show the share of workers with health insurance from any source, demonstrate that many nonstandard workers, in fact, have no health insurance from any source. Among temp workers, for example, only 41.0% have any form of health insurance. In fact, across all categories of nonstandard work, nonstandard workers are less likely to have health insurance than are standard workers. The story for pension benefits is similar: nonstandard workers are generally far less likely than are their counterparts in standard arrangements to have employer-provided pension benefits or to be eligible for pensions from other sources.

Clearly, many workers appreciate the flexibility that nonstandard work arrangements provide, but most of the evidence on nonstandard arrangements suggests that these nonstandard jobs are substandard. **Table 3.18** reports nonstandard workers' own preferences. In 1999, over half (57%) of temp workers and almost half (46.7%) of on-call workers said that they would have preferred to have a standard job. Independent contractors, who, we saw earlier, generally enjoy pay and benefits comparable to standard workers, are the only group of nonstandard workers that strongly prefer their nonstandard arrangements to standard work. Table 3.18 provides additional indirect evidence of workers' preferences for standard work. As the economy improved between 1995 and 1999, the share of workers in each category that prefers standard work declined, suggesting that, as the economy improved, many nonstandard workers unhappy with

TABLE 3.17 Health and pension coverage by nonstandard work arrangement, 1999

	Share with health insurance		Share eligible for pension**	
	Employer-provided*	All sources	Included in pension plan	All sources
Temporary help agency	8.5%	41.0%	5.8%	11.8%
On call	21.1	67.3	22.5	29.0
Independent contractors	n.a.	73.3	1.9	2.8
Contract firms	56.1	79.9	40.2	53.9
Standard arrangements	57.9%	82.8%	48.3%	54.1%

* Excludes incorporated and unincorporated self-employed and independent contractors.
** Percent eligible for employer-provided pension plan; excludes incorporated and unincorporated self-employed, but includes self-employed independent contractors.

Source: Authors' analysis of BLS (1999).

TABLE 3.18 Satisfaction with work arrangement, by type of arrangement, 1995-99

	Percent preferring standard work		
	1995	1997	1999
Temporary help agency	63.3%	59.2%	57.0%
On call	57.9	50.0	46.7
Independent contractors	9.8	9.3	8.5
Contract firms	n.a.	n.a.	n.a.

Source: BLS (1995, 1997, 1999).

their arrangements were able to leave their nonstandard arrangements. Those left in nonstandard arrangements as the economy boomed were those who most enjoyed the flexibility and other benefits of nonstandard arrangements. Another possible explanation for the decline in dissatisfaction with nonstandard arrangements is that the abundance of work at the end of the 1990s reduced the inherent uncertainty of nonstandard arrangements.

The most recent evidence on nonstandard work shows that such arrangements are widespread, varied, and generally substandard. Nonstandard work pays less, is much less likely to provide health or pension benefits, and, almost by definition, provides far less job security than regular full-time employment. Unfortunately, the kind of detailed survey that has allowed us to sketch the main features of nonstandard work in the mid-1990s does not exist for earlier periods. As a result, we have some difficulty gauging the growth in nonstandard work over the last two decades of substantial economic change. In the remainder of this chapter, we look at the data that do exist on the growth of some kinds of nonstandard work: regular part-time employment, temporary work, self-employment, and multiple job holding.

Part-time work

The most important form of nonstandard work is part-time work. Many workers prefer a part-time schedule because it allows time to pursue education, leisure, or family responsibilities. Nevertheless, part-timers generally have lower pay, less-skilled jobs, poor chances of promotion, less job security, inferior benefits (such as vacation, health insurance, and pension), and lower status overall within their places of employment. Large numbers of part-timers would prefer to work full time, and even those who work part-time schedules by choice would prefer to receive the same compensation (hourly pay rate and prorated benefits) in exchange for performing work done by their full-time coworkers.

According to the data in **Table 3.19**, 17.1% of employees worked part-time in 1999. Of these, 85% (14.6 percentage points of the 17.1%) voluntarily chose part-time work, while 15% (2.6 percentage points) were working part-time jobs because they could not find full-time work. The pattern of part-time work has changed over time. Between 1973 and 1989, part-time work increased 1.5 percentage points, from 16.6% to 18.1% of all employees. (The definition of part time used here differs from the earlier analysis of nonstandard work. See the note in the table.) This increase in part-time work from 1973 to 1989 resulted almost entirely from the rise in *involuntary* part-time employment, which expanded 1.2 percentage points, from 3.1% to 4.3% of employment. By 1989, nearly one-fourth of all part-time workers were involuntary part-timers. The rise in part-time work over the 1970s and 1980s, therefore, did not reflect workers' preferences for shorter hours.

Part-time employment declined between 1989 and 1999. Overall part-time employment fell a full percentage point over the period, with the share of involuntary part-time employment falling even more (1.7 percentage points). In fact, by 1999, in response to the expanded employment opportunities available in the 1990s, the share of involuntary part-time workers was below its 1973 level. That *voluntary* part-time work also fell with the recovery suggests that at least some

TABLE 3.19 Employment (non-farm) by full-time and part-time status,* 1973-99

| | | Percent part time | | Percent | |
Year	Total	Involuntary	Voluntary	full time	Total
1973	16.6%	3.1%	13.5%	83.4%	100.0%
1979	17.6	3.8	13.8	82.4	100.0
1989	18.1	4.3	13.8	81.9	100.0
1999**	17.1	2.6	14.6	82.9	100.0

* The definition of part time used here differs from the earlier analysis of nonstandard work. Here, part-time workers include any of the work types in the earlier table, including temps and the self-employed who work part-time schedules. In the earlier tables a temp or self-employed worker who generally worked part time would have been classified as a temp or as self-employed regardless of hours. This explains the much smaller share of part-timers in Table 3.14.
** Data for 1999 not strictly comparable with earlier years because of survey changes.

Source: Authors' analysis of BLS data.

of the workers classified as voluntary part-timers may still prefer full-time work: when given the chance to work full-time, many voluntary workers appear willing to take it. (Of course, voluntary part-time workers may also take full-time jobs reluctantly and only at the prompting of employers facing rising demand for the goods and services that they sell.)

The economic expansion of the late 1990s has reduced both the level of part-time work and, more importantly, the level of involuntary part-time work. Nevertheless, in 1999, about 3.3 million part-time workers who wanted full-time work could not find it.

Temping

As we saw earlier, temps and workers with contract agencies are an important part of the nonstandard workforce. Unfortunately, the government did not gather data on temporary work before 1982, and even the data that the government has collected on a regular basis since then is not directly comparable to the detailed information in Table 3.14. **Table 3.20**, however, reports the number of workers employed in personnel services industries, which include temporary help agencies, between 1973 and 1999. The last three columns of the table show employment as a percent of the total workforce. In 1999, 2.6% of all workers were employed in the personnel services industry, a large increase from the 0.3%

TABLE 3.20 Employment in personnel services industry, 1973-99

	Number (thousands)			As share of total employment		
Year	All	Men	Women	All	Men	Women
1973	247	118	128	0.3%	0.2%	0.2%
1979	508	210	298	0.6	0.2	0.3
1989	1,455	581	874	1.3	0.5	0.8
1992	1,629	676	954	1.5	0.6	0.9
1999	3,405	1,584	1,821	2.6	1.3	1.5

Source: Authors' analysis of BLS data.

employed in the industry in 1973. During the 1990s, the share of workers in the personnel services industry more than doubled. Data from 1982 onward for temporary help agencies (**Table 3.21** and **Figure 3H**) show that employment there doubled between 1982 and 1989 and doubled again between 1989 and 1997.

The data in Tables 3.20 and 3.21 suggest that temporary and related employment arrangements were more important in 1999 than they were at any earlier time. Earlier, more detailed information on temps from the Contingent Work Survey indicated that temporary employment had flattened out during the economic recovery of 1995-99, but the long-term trend captured in these two tables suggests that long-term economic forces may be pushing the economy toward ever greater use of temporary workers.

Self-employment

A significant portion of all employment consists of self-employed workers, whose primary job is working in their own business, farms, crafts, or professions. Independent contracting, mentioned earlier, is one form of self-employment.

In 1999, about 6.7% of all workers were self-employed (see **Table 3.22**), representing the lowest level of self-employment during a business-cycle peak since 1973 (also 6.7%). As the table shows, self-employment was substantially higher (8.1%) in the middle of the last recession than it was during the boom year of 1999. The decline in the self-employment rate between 1992, when the unemployment rate was high (7.5%), and 1999, when the unemployment rate was much lower (4.2%), suggests that self-employment is a refuge from unemployment for workers who are not able to find regular employment. The data

TABLE 3.21 Employment in temporary help industry, 1982-99

	Number (thousands)			As share of total employment		
Year	All	Men	Women	All	Men	Women
1982*	417	158	259	0.5%	0.2%	0.3%
1989	1,216	494	722	1.1	0.5	0.7
1992	1,411	594	817	1.3	0.5	0.8
1999	3,017	1,437	1,580	2.3	1.1	1.2

* Earliest data available.

Source: Authors' analysis of BLS data.

FIGURE 3H Employment in temporary help industry, 1982-99

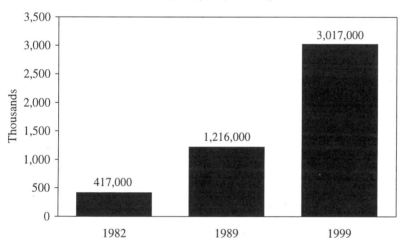

Source: Authors' analysis of BLS data.

also show that men are consistently more likely to be self-employed than are women. Research suggests that one factor in the different rates of self-employment is that women often lack the kinds of access that men have to the capital necessary to start and sustain small businesses.

TABLE 3.22 Self-employment, 1948-99 (percent of total employment*)

Year	All	Men	Women
1948	12.1%	n.a.	n.a.
1967	7.3	8.8%	4.4%
1973	6.7	8.2	4.9
1979	7.1	8.8	5.8
1989	7.5	9.0	6.0
1992	8.1	9.1	5.6
1999	6.7	7.8	5.6

*Non-farm industries.

Source: Authors' analysis of BLS data.

More than one job

A final aspect of nonstandard work, which we have not yet addressed, is the prevalence of multiple job holding—people working in at least two jobs. In part, multiple job holding reflects the deterioration in hourly wages in workers' primary jobs and the rise, at least during the 1980s, in the share of workers working part time because they were not able to find full-time work.

Table 3.23 summarizes the available data on multiple job holding for selected years between 1973 and 1999. In 1999, about 5.9% of workers—almost 8 million people—held two or more jobs. Between 1979 and 1989, the share of multiple job holders jumped from 4.9% to 6.2% of the total workforce. Most of this increase occurred in the economic recovery years of 1985-89 (0.8 percentage points compared to a 0.5 percentage-point increase for 1979-85.) Over the current business cycle, however, multiple job holding has fallen slightly.

For the 1979-89 period, the Current Population Survey (the underlying source of the data presented here) also asked multiple job holders why they held more than one job. In 1989, just under half (2.8 percentage points of the 6.2% of multiple job holders) cited economic hardship (to meet regular household expenses or to pay off debts) as the reason they were working more than one job. Workers citing economic hardship for their multiple jobs accounted for most (1.0 percentage points) of the 1.3 percentage-point increase in multiple job holders between 1979 and 1989. These data support the view that multiple job holding was one method for coping with declining real wages. Unfortunately, no data on the reasons people work multiple jobs exist after 1991. We speculate, however, that improvements in wages and employment opportunities since 1996 have been an important reason for the fall in multiple job holding in the 1990s.

TABLE 3.23 Multiple job holding, 1973-99

Year	Number of multiple job holders (000)	Multiple-job-holding rate	Percent of workforce who hold multiple jobs because of:	
			Economic hardship*	Other reasons**
1973	4,262	5.1%	n.a.	n.a.
1979	4,724	4.9	1.8%	3.1%
1985	5,730	5.4	2.2	3.2
1989	7,225	6.2	2.8	3.4
1999	7,895	5.9	n.a.	n.a.
Change				
1973-79	462	-0.2%	n.a.	n.a.
1979-85	1,006	0.5	0.4%	0.1%
1985-89	1,495	0.8	0.6	0.2
1989-99***	670	-0.3	n.a.	n.a.

*   To meet regular household expenses or pay off debts.
**   Includes savings for the future, getting experience, helping a friend or relative, buying something special, enjoying the work, and so on.
*** Data for 1999 not strictly comparable with data for earlier years because of survey design changes.

Source: Authors' analysis of BLS data.

Conclusion

In the last half of the 1990s, strong employment growth—and especially sustained low unemployment—significantly improved the economic circumstances of American workers, especially those who have traditionally suffered most in the labor market. Job creation, while slower over the current business cycle than it was in earlier cycles, has been sufficient to lower the overall unemployment rate to 4%. Perhaps most importantly, economic growth has been steady enough to keep unemployment below 5.5% for more than four straight years. The advantages of this sustained period of prosperity are evident. Black and Hispanic unemployment rates are at record lows. Employment rates for women of all races are at all-time highs, while employment rates for men have halted their long-term slide and have even risen somewhat for blacks and Hispanics. In the second half of the 1990s, job stability and job security appeared to improve. The long-term rise in nonstandard work arrangements also appeared to have ended and even to have reversed itself somewhat. After a period in the 1970s and 1980s when part-time work (especially involuntary part-time work) and multiple job holding were on the rise, in the 1990s all forms of part-time work and the share of workers with more than one job fell.

Nevertheless, many workers have still not felt the full benefits of strong employment growth. Black and Hispanic unemployment rates are still high, and underemployment rates are roughly double the rosier unemployment figure. Black men and women of all races continue to trail far behind white men when it comes to employment rates, suggesting that these traditionally disadvantaged groups still don't have the same economic opportunities as white men. While the available evidence suggests that job security improved at the end of the 1990s, a large body of evidence supports the view that underlying levels of job instability and job insecurity remain higher than in earlier periods. Almost one in four workers was still in a nonstandard work arrangement in 1999. While many of these workers prefer nonstandard jobs, a large portion say that they would prefer a standard job, with the better pay, benefits, and opportunities for advancement that standard work usually implies. A final concern is that many positive changes in employment may reflect not so much long-term structural improvements in the economy, but rather the old-fashioned improvements that we would expect from the boom phase of an economic cycle. If these improvements are purely cyclical, the next recession could erase these gains in employment, job security, and work arrangements.

CHAPTER 4

Wealth: deeper in debt

The main focus of the preceding chapters has been on the wages and incomes of American families. In this chapter, we turn our attention to the distribution of wealth. Like wages and incomes, wealth has an important impact on a family's standard of living. Checking account balances, stocks, bonds, and other liquid assets can help families cope with financial emergencies related to unemployment or illness. Wealth can also make it easier for families to invest in education and training, to buy a house, or to start a small business. More tangible forms of wealth, such as cars, computers, and homes, can directly affect families' abilities to participate fully in work and broader economic and community life.

In the United States today, the wealth distribution is highly unequal. The wealthiest 1% of households control about 38% of national wealth, while the bottom 80% of households control only 17%. The ownership of stocks is particularly unequal. The top 1% of stock owners hold almost half (47.7%) of all stocks, by value; by contrast, the bottom 80% of stock owners own just 4.1% of total stock holdings.

The total wealth of the typical American household improved only marginally during the 1990s. The net worth of the typical household rose about $2,200 in the 1990s—from $58,800 in 1989 to $61,000 in 1998. While this household's assets grew modestly—stock assets were up by $5,500 and non-stock assets by $8,500—its debt rose as well, by $11,800. Thus, the relatively modest gains in stock and non-stock assets combined with the offsetting rise in household debt meant that the 1990s were far less generous to typical households than business-page headlines often suggest.

Indeed, the top financial story of the 1990s was probably the booming stock market, yet most Americans have no economically meaningful stake in stocks.

The most recent government data show that less than half of households hold stock in any form, including mutual funds and 401(k)-style pension plans. The same data reveal that 64% of households have stock holdings worth just $5,000 or less.

For the typical household, rising debt, not a rising stock market, was the big story of the 1990s. Household debt grew much more rapidly than household income in the 1990s so that, by 1999, total household debt, for the first time in history, exceeded total household disposable income. Households in the middle of the wealth distribution absorbed the largest share of this run-up in debt. While low nominal interest rates have made it easier for households to carry the greatly expanded debt, many households appear to be straining. The most recent government data show that 14% of middle-income households have debt service obligations that exceed 40% of their income; 9% have at least one bill that is more than 60 days past due. Meanwhile, despite the robust state of the economy, personal bankruptcy rates reached all time highs in the late 1990s.

Wealth and worth

The concept of wealth used in this chapter is net worth, i.e., the sum of all of a family's assets—house, checking and savings account balances, stock holdings, retirement funds (such as 401(k) plans and individual retirement accounts), and other assets—minus the sum of all of the family's liabilities—mortgage, credit-card debt, student loans, and other debts. This analysis excludes assets in defined-benefit pension plans, since workers do not legally own the assets held in these plans and therefore typically do not benefit from improvements in the value of assets used to pay the defined benefit (rather, their companies do, because higher asset values reduce the contributions companies have to pay to meet future defined benefits). Nor do workers suffer financially if the underlying assets underperform expectations. For similar reasons, our analysis also excludes another important source of retirement support : Social Security and Medicare.

A key feature of the wealth distribution is that it is much more unequal than either the distribution of wages or incomes. **Table 4.1** shows income and wealth data from the most recent Survey of Consumer Finances (SCF), conducted by the Federal Reserve Board. The first column shows that, in 1998, the 1% of households with the highest incomes received 16.6% of all income. By comparison, the wealthiest 1% of households, in the same year, owned 38.1% of all wealth. At the other end of the distribution, the 90% of households with the lowest incomes received 58.8% of all income, but the corresponding share of households with the lowest net worth held only 29.0% of all wealth.

TABLE 4.1 Distribution of income and wealth, 1998 (percent)

	Distribution of:		
	Household income	Net worth	Net financial assets
All	100.0%	100.0%	100.0%
Top 1%	16.6	38.1	47.3
Next 9%	24.6	32.9	32.4
Bottom 90%	58.8	29.0	20.2

Source: Unpublished analysis of 1998 Survey of Consumer Finance data by Wolff.

Net worth

As noted earlier, the distribution of wealth in the United States is highly unequal. **Table 4.2** summarizes data from the six SCF surveys conducted since 1962. In 1998, the wealthiest 1% of households controlled 38.1% of all wealth, the top fifth controlled 83.4%, and the middle fifth a mere 4.5%; the bottom fifth of households actually had negative net worth, that is, they owed more than they owned.

Table 4.3 puts dollar figures to the wealth shares in Table 4.2. In 1998, the average net worth of the top 1% of households was about $10.2 million. Moving down from this group, wealth holdings drop off sharply. The 4% of households right below the top 1%, for example, had an average net worth of $1.4 million, and the next 5% had an average net worth of just over $600,000. In the same year, the average wealth of the middle fifth of households was $61,000 (consisting primarily of home equity, as discussed later).

The data in Tables 4.2 and 4.3 and data from other sources tell a complicated story about trends in wealth concentration over time. Over a fairly long time horizon, the distribution of wealth appears to be growing more equal. **Figure 4A** graphs historical estimates of the share of total wealth held by the top 1% of individuals from 1922 through 1981. By this measure, inequality was generally higher before World War II than it was after the war, with the concentration of wealth reaching its lowest points in 1976 and 1981. The data on wealth shares in Table 4.2, however, show a sharp rise in the wealth held by the top 1% of households between 1983 (33.8% of all wealth) and 1989 (37.4%). The concentration of wealth continued after 1989, but at a slower pace than in the 1980s, with the share of wealth owned by the top 1% rising from 37.4% in 1989 to 38.1% in 1998.

TABLE 4.2 Changes in the distribution of household wealth,* 1962-98 (percent)

							Percentage-point change		
Wealth class	1962	1983	1989	1992	1995	1998	1962-83	1983-89	1989-98
Top fifth	81.0%	81.3%	83.5%	83.8%	83.9%	83.4%	0.4	2.2	-0.1
Top 1%	33.4	33.8	37.4	37.2	38.5	38.1	0.3	3.6	0.7
Next 4%	21.2	22.3	21.6	22.8	21.8	21.3	1.2	-0.8	-0.2
Next 5%	12.4	12.1	11.6	11.8	11.5	11.5	-0.2	-0.5	-0.1
Next 10%	14.0	13.1	13.0	12.0	12.1	12.5	-0.9	-0.1	-0.5
Bottom four-fifths	19.1%	18.7%	16.5%	16.2%	16.1%	16.6%	-0.4	-2.2	0.1
Fourth	13.4	12.6	12.3	11.5	11.4	11.9	-0.8	-0.3	-0.4
Middle	5.4	5.2	4.8	4.4	4.5	4.5	-0.2	-0.4	-0.3
Second	1.0	1.2	0.8	0.9	0.9	0.8	0.2	-0.3	-0.1
Lowest	-0.7	-0.3	-1.5	-0.5	-0.7	-0.6	0.4	-1.2	0.9
Total	100.0%	100.0%	100.0%	100.0%	100.0%	100.0%			

* Wealth defined as net worth (household assets minus debts).

Source: Unpublished analysis of Survey of Consumer Finance data by Wolff.

TABLE 4.3 Change in average wealth* by wealth class, 1962-98 (thousands of 1998 dollars)

							Annualized growth (percent)		
Wealth class	1962	1983	1989	1992	1995	1998	1962-83	1983-89	1989-98
Top fifth	$587.4	$864.5	$1,017.1	$991.9	$917.8	$1,126.7	1.9%	2.7%	1.1%
Top 1%	4,851.8	7,175.1	9,101.7	8,796.4	8,422.5	10,203.7	1.9	4.0	1.3
Next 4%	768.1	1,186.8	1,313.4	1,351.4	1,192.9	1,441.2	2.1	1.7	1.0
Next 5%	359.1	516.2	565.5	559.3	504.5	623.5	1.7	1.5	1.1
Next 10%	202.9	278.7	315.9	283.9	263.9	344.9	1.5	2.1	1.0
Bottom four-fifths	$34.6	$49.6	$50.2	$48.0	$44.0	$56.1	1.7%	0.2%	1.3%
Fourth	97.2	133.6	150.0	135.7	124.9	161.3	1.5	1.9	0.8
Middle	39.4	55.5	58.8	51.9	49.1	61.0	1.6	1.0	0.4
Second	6.9	12.5	10.2	10.5	9.6	11.1	2.9	-3.3	0.9
Lowest	-5.3	-3.2	-18.4	-6.0	-7.6	-8.9	n.a.	n.a.	n.a.
Average	$145.1	$212.6	$243.6	$236.8	$218.8	$270.3	1.8%	2.3%	1.2%
Median	38.8	54.6	58.4	49.9	48.8	60.7	1.6	1.1	0.4

* Wealth defined as net worth (household assets minus debts).

Source: Unpublished analysis of Survey of Consumer Finance data by Wolff.

FIGURE 4A Share of total household wealth held by richest 1% of individuals, 1922-81

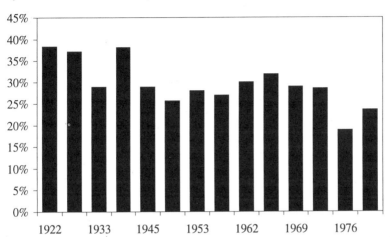

Source: Wolff (1992).

Other data, however, suggest that wealth inequality may have risen faster in the 1990s than in the 1980s. **Figure 4B** shows the minimum, average, and maximum levels of wealth of the members of the *Forbes 400*, an annual, unscientific, but carefully constructed list of the 400 wealthiest people in the United States. The graph shows wealth holdings on a log scale, which compresses large differences and helps fit the three lines on the same graph. The figure indicates that the gap between the wealthiest and the "poorest" member of the *Forbes 400* grew significantly in the 1990s, especially after 1995. This suggests that inequality at the very top (above the level captured by the SCF, which, by design, excludes members of the Forbes 400) grew more rapidly in the 1990s than it did in the 1980s.

The data in Table 4.3 also illustrate how the absolute level of wealth changed over time for households at different points in the distribution. During the 1990s, the average wealth of the top 1% of households grew over $1 million, from $9.1 million in 1989 to $10.2 million in 1998. Meanwhile, the average wealth of the middle 20% of households grew only marginally, from $58,800 in 1989 to $61,000 in 1998. Wealth levels among the poorest households did improve considerably in the 1990s, but the poorest 20% of households still finished the decade with negative net worth (-$8,900 in 1998, up from -$18,400 in 1989).

Across almost all levels of wealth, wealth grew more slowly in the period

FIGURE 4B Net worth of the "Forbes 400"

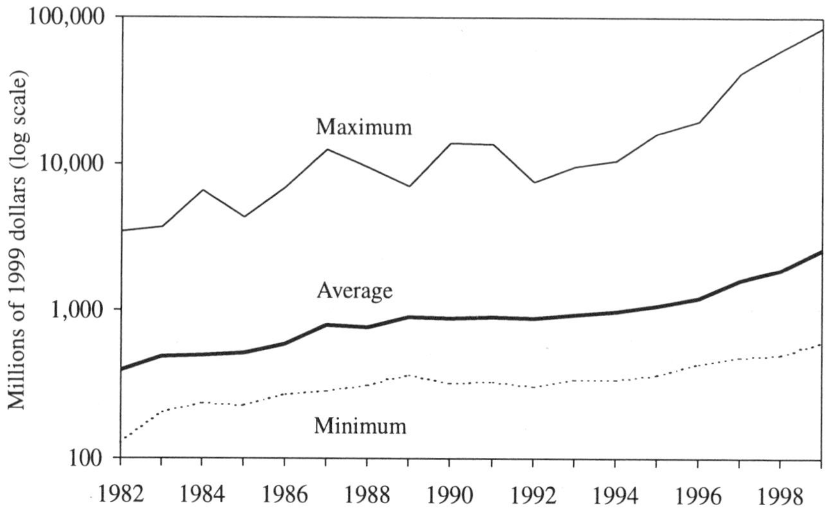

Source: Broom and Shay (2000).

1989-98 than it did in the periods 1962-83 and 1983-89. Average wealth grew at a 1.2% annual rate between 1989 and 1998, below the 1.8% rate for 1962-83 and the 2.3% rate for 1983-89. The same was true for the median household, whose wealth grew at only a 0.4% annual rate in the 1990s, less than half the rate for 1962-83 (1.6%) or 1983-89 (1.1%). The apparent slowdown in wealth accumulation in the 1990s, however, blurs the very different experience between 1989 and 1995—when net worth fell across most of the wealth distribution—and 1995-98, when wealth grew rapidly by historical standards.

Racial divide

The data presented so far mask an important feature of the wealth distribution: wealth is very unequally distributed by race. **Table 4.4** presents SCF wealth data separately for blacks and whites. The first section shows average wealth by race. In 1998, the average black household had a net worth equal to about 18% of the average white household. This ratio has remained relatively constant over the period 1983-98, suggesting economic growth over the past two decades has done little to narrow the wealth gap between the two races.

TABLE 4.4 Wealth* by race, 1983-98 (thousands of 1998 dollars)

	1983	1989	1992	1995	1998
Average wealth					
Black	$46.8	$49.3	$52.9	$43.6	$58.3
White	248.4	293.9	284.4	259.2	320.9
Ratio	0.19	0.17	0.19	0.17	0.18
Median wealth					
Black	$4.8	$2.2	$12.0	$7.9	$10.0
White	71.5	84.9	71.3	65.2	81.7
Ratio	0.07	0.03	0.17	0.12	0.12
Households with zero or negative net wealth (%)					
Black	34.1%	40.7%	31.5%	31.3%	27.4%
White	11.3%	12.1%	13.8%	15.0%	14.8%
Ratio	3.01	3.38	2.28	2.09	2.09
Average financial wealth					
Black	$23.6	$24.1	$30.1	$22.7	$37.6
White	183.0	222.2	219.0	201.5	254.8
Ratio	0.13	0.11	0.14	0.11	0.15
Median financial wealth					
Black	$0.0	$0.0	$0.2	$0.2	$1.2
White	19.9	26.9	21.9	19.3	37.6
Ratio	0.00	0.00	0.01	0.01	0.03

* Wealth defined as net worth (household assets minus debts).

Source: Unpublished analysis of Survey of Consumer Finance data by Wolff.

The second section of Table 4.4 gives the median wealth holdings for blacks and whites. The most striking aspect of this panel is the extremely low level of median wealth of black households. In 1998, the median black household had a net worth of $10,000, about 12% of the corresponding figure for whites. Since the median wealth of black families is so low, relatively small dollar movements have a large impact on the ratio of the black median to the white median. The 12% figure in 1998 was far better than the 3% ratio in 1989, but below the 17% figure for 1992. (In fact, the absolute level of wealth in the median black household was $2,000 lower in 1998 ($10,000) than it had been in 1992 ($12,000)).

Low net worth

Another important feature of the wealth distribution is the large share of house-holds that have low, zero, or negative net worth. **Table 4.5** reports the share of all households with zero or negative net worth (the first line) or net worth of less than $10,000 (the second line). In 1998, 18% of all households had a net worth that was zero or negative; just over 30% had a net worth that was less than $10,000. As before, the experience of black households differs significantly from that of white households. Returning to Table 4.4 (see the third section), the SCF data reveal that, in 1998, almost twice as many black households (27.4%) as white house-holds (14.8%) had zero or negative net worth. Half of black households had a net worth of $10,000 or less, compared to 30% for the population as a whole.

The overall share of households with low net worth remained relatively con-stant over the 1990s. The circumstances of black households, however, appeared to improve substantially over the period, with the share of black households with zero or negative net worth falling from 40.7% in 1989 to 27.4% in 1998.

To summarize, the data on net worth reveal the highly unequal distribution of wealth. A large share of the population has little or no net worth, while, since the end of World War II at least, the wealthiest 20% of the population has con-sistently held over 80% of all wealth and the top 1% has consistently held close to 40%. Wealth inequality increased sharply during the 1980s and showed no signs of improving over the 1990s.

Assets

The preceding section summarized the overall distribution of net worth—the sum of each household's assets and liabilities. This section focuses on the first major component of net worth, assets. (An examination of liabilities follows in the next section.) Households hold a variety of assets, from houses and boats to stocks and bonds. The distributions of assets, however, differs significantly by asset. Some assets, such as stocks and bonds, are highly concentrated; other assets, such as houses, are more widely held. The differences in these distribu-tions are strongly related to overall wealth. Wealthy households, for example, tend to have much of their wealth in stocks and bonds, while the less well-to-do typically hold most of their wealth in housing equity.

Table 4.6 shows the distribution of several types of household assets in 1998. The top 0.5% of stock-owning households held 37.0% of all stock, while the bottom 80% of stock-owning households owned just 4.1% of all stock. By contrast, the top 0.5% of home-owning households held only 10.2% of total

TABLE 4.5 Households with low net wealth, 1962-98 (percent of all households)

						Percentage-point change		
Net worth	1962	1983	1989	1995	1998	1962-83	1983-89	1989-98
Zero or negative	23.6%	15.5%	17.9%	18.5%	18.0%	-8.1	2.4	0.1
Less than $10,000*	34.3	29.7	31.8	31.9	30.3	-4.6	2.1	-1.5

* Constant 1998 dollars.

Source: Unpublished analysis of Survey of Consumer Finance data by Wolff.

TABLE 4.6 Distribution of asset ownership across households, 1998

	Percentage of all holdings of each asset:				
Percentage of owners	Common stock excluding pensions	All common stock	Non-equity financial assets	Housing equity	Net worth
Top 0.5 percent	41.4%	37.0%	24.2%	10.2%	25.6%
Next 0.5 percent	11.8	10.7	7.8	4.6	8.4
Next 4 percent	27.7	27.2	26.2	20.5	23.4
Next 5 percent	10.3	11.3	14.0	15.4	11.4
Next 10 percent	7.2	9.8	13.9	20.1	12.8
Bottom 80 percent	1.7	4.1	14.0	29.3	18.5

Source: Poterba (2000) analysis of Survey of Consumer Finances data.

housing equity, leaving the bottom 80% of home owners with 29.3% of all housing equity. While housing equity is unequally distributed, its distribution is much more equal than is that of stocks.

The rest of this section takes a closer look at the distribution of three important household assets: stocks, houses, and computers.

Stocks

The last decade or so has witnessed a breathtaking run up in the price of stocks. As **Figure 4C** illustrates, the inflation-adjusted value of the Standard & Poor's 500 index of stocks tripled between the beginning and the end of the 1990s.

FIGURE 4C Growth of U.S. stock market, 1955-99 (1999 dollars)

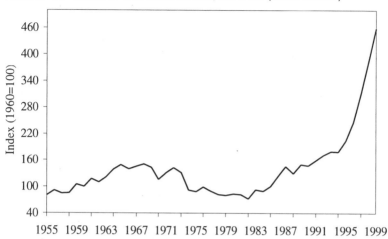

Source: Authors' analysis of data from ERP.

These increases have focused enormous media and public attention on the stock market. While a small number of individuals have ridden the stock market boom to great personal wealth, data on stock ownership establish that the stock market, in practice, is of little or no financial importance to the vast majority of U.S. households.

Even well into the stock market boom of the 1990s, a majority of U.S. households had no stock holdings of any form, direct or indirect. (Households own stock directly when they buy shares in a particular company. Households own stock indirectly when they buy shares through a mutual fund that, in turn, holds a portfolio of stocks, or when household members make contributions to a 401(k)-style, defined-contribution pension plan that holds stocks for its beneficiaries.) **Table 4.7** summarizes data from the SCF on the share of households with direct or indirect stock holdings. In 1998, just under half (48.2%) of households owned stock in any form. Only about one-third (36.3%) of households held stock worth $5,000 or more.

Black households were especially unlikely to hold financial assets such as stocks and bonds (government and corporate debt) in the 1990s. In 1998, the average financial wealth of black households (see the fourth section of Table 4.4) was only about 15% of the average for white households. The median financial wealth for blacks (see the last section of Table 4.4) was just $1,200, about 3% of the corresponding figure for whites.

TABLE 4.7 Share of households owning stock (percent)

	1962	1983	1989	1992	1995	1998	Percentage-point change 1989-98
Any stock holdings							
Direct holdings	10.7%	13.7%	13.1%	14.8%	15.2%	19.2%	6.1
Indirect holdings			24.7	28.4	30.2	43.4	18.7
Total			31.7	37.2	40.4	48.2	16.5
Stock holdings of $5,000 or more*							
Direct holdings			10.0%	11.4%	12.3%	13.6%	3.6
Indirect holdings			16.9	21.5	22.7	32.2	15.3
Total			22.6	27.3	28.8	36.3	13.7

* Constant 1998 dollars.

Source: Unpublished analysis of Survey of Consumer Finance data by Wolff.

The first section of **Table 4.8** provides a more detailed description of the distribution of stock ownership. In 1998, the wealthiest 1% of households owned an average of $2.5 million in stocks. The holdings of the next 9% of households averaged $291,500. By comparison, the average direct and indirect stock holdings of the middle 20% of households were small, at $9,200, and the average for the bottom 40% of households was just $1,700. The value of stock holdings did grow across the board in the 1990s, but in dollar terms—and relative to the typical household's needs during retirement—the increases were small for 80% of households. The total value of stocks owned by the middle 20% of households, for example, grew only $5,500 between 1989 and 1998—less than the average $11,800 rise in indebtedness for the same group over the same period (see the third section).

Stocks are also highly concentrated by household income. **Table 4.9** shows the share of all stock owned by households at different income levels. In 1998, the 1.6% of all households with annual incomes of $250,000 or more owned 36.1% of all stocks (see the bottom section). Households with annual incomes of $100,000 or more—about 8.5% of all households—controlled 63.9% of all stock. By contrast, the 29% of households with annual incomes in the $25-50,000 range owned just 8.5% of all stocks by value. The high degree of concentration of stocks across income levels holds true even for stocks in pension plans, such as 401(k)s. The main difference between stock holdings in pension plans and other (direct) stock holdings is that pension assets are more evenly

TABLE 4.8 Household assets and liabilities by wealth class
(thousands of 1998 dollars)

Assets and liabilities	Top 1.0%	Next 9%	Next 10%	Next 20%	Middle 20%	Bottom 40%	Average
Stocks*							
1962	$2,409.0	$123.2	$13.7	$4.4	$1.1	$0.3	$38.3
1983	1,564.2	100.9	12.1	4.6	1.6	0.4	27.7
1989	1,180.7	129.7	25.4	8.9	3.7	0.6	29.2
1992	1,350.0	185.1	37.2	13.8	4.2	0.8	38.4
1995	1,772.1	197.9	35.2	14.1	5.6	1.1	43.9
1998	2,525.2	291.5	79.5	27.6	9.2	1.7	71.8
All other assets							
1962	$2,620.7	$452.5	$215.0	$119.5	$64.7	$15.4	$130.7
1983	6,020.1	781.4	315.9	162.5	80.0	16.8	217.0
1989	8,367.1	859.0	339.6	185.5	89.1	19.3	257.0
1992	7,978.7	849.4	298.3	164.3	81.5	19.1	242.4
1995	7,037.1	710.0	275.2	153.2	88.0	20.6	217.3
1998	7,961.1	826.2	331.3	181.1	97.6	23.8	246.0
Total debt							
1962	$177.9	$34.8	$25.8	$26.7	$26.4	$14.8	$23.8
1983	409.1	68.1	49.2	33.5	26.1	12.5	32.1
1989	446.1	90.8	49.1	44.4	34.0	24.0	42.7
1992	532.2	123.2	51.6	42.5	33.9	17.6	44.0
1995	386.8	90.2	47.5	42.5	44.6	20.7	42.5
1998	282.6	104.9	66.0	47.4	45.8	24.4	47.5
Net worth							
1962	$4,851.8	$540.9	$202.9	$97.2	$39.4	$0.8	$145.1
1983	7,175.1	814.2	278.7	133.6	55.5	4.7	212.6
1989	9,101.7	897.9	315.9	150.0	58.8	(4.1)	243.6
1992	8,796.4	911.3	283.9	135.7	51.9	2.2	236.8
1995	8,422.5	817.7	262.8	124.8	49.1	1.0	218.8
1998	10,203.7	1,012.7	344.9	161.3	61.0	1.1	270.3

* All direct and indirect stock holdings.

Source: Unpublished analysis of Survey of Consumer Finance data by Wolff.

distributed *among high-income households*. While the highest-income group, households with an annual income above $250,000, controls 48.1% of all publicly traded stock, these high earners own only 16.7% of stocks in pension plans, leaving a bigger share for households in the $100,000-250,000 range. At the same time, the bottom two-thirds of households—those with annual incomes of

TABLE 4.9 Concentration of stock ownership by income level, 1998 (percent)

Income level	Share of households	Percent who own	Percent of stock owned Shares	Percent of stock owned Cumulative
Publicly traded stock				
250,000 and above	1.6%	73.8%	48.1%	48.1%
100,000-249,999	6.9	53.0	24.7	72.8
75,000-99,999	7.7	31.4	8.2	81.0
50,000-74,999	17.4	25.9	8.4	89.4
25,000-49,999	29.0	17.7	7.0	96.5
15,000-24,999	16.1	8.6	2.5	98.9
Under 15,000	21.3	4.3	1.1	100.0
Total	100.0	19.2	100.0	0.0
Stocks in pension plans*				
250,000 and above	1.6%	44.3%	16.7%	16.7%
100,000-249,999	6.9	51.7	29.7	46.4
75,000-99,999	7.7	51.2	18.4	64.8
50,000-74,999	17.4	41.5	22.2	87.0
25,000-49,000	29.0	28.0	12.0	99.1
15,000-24,999	16.1	10.2	0.8	99.9
Under 15,000	21.3	3.6	0.1	100.0
Total	100.0	26.0	100.0	0.0
All stock**				
250,000 and above	1.6%	93.3%	36.1%	36.1%
100,000-249,999	6.9	89.0	27.7	63.9
75,000-99,999	7.7	80.7	10.8	74.7
50,000-74,999	17.4	70.9	13.1	87.8
25,000-49,999	29.0	52.0	8.5	96.3
15,000-24,999	16.1	29.2	2.6	98.9
Under 15,000	21.3	10.6	1.1	100.0
Total	100.0	48.2	100.0	0.0

* All defined contribution stock plans including 401(k) plans.
** All stock directly or indirectly held in mutual funds, IRAs, Keogh plans, and defined-contribution pension plans.

Source: Unpublished analysis of Survey of Consumer Finance data by Wolff.

$50,000 or less—still hold only 13.0% of all stocks in pension plans (compared to 11.6% of publicly traded stock).

The high concentration of stock ownership means that the gains associated with the recent stock boom have also been highly concentrated. **Figure 4D** uses the information in Table 4.9 to illustrate the distribution of growth in stock mar-

FIGURE 4D Distribution of growth in stock market holdings, by wealth class, 1989-98

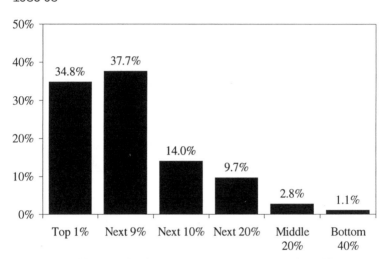

Source: Unpublished analysis of Survey of Consumer Finance data by Wolff.

ket holdings between 1989 and 1998. Almost 35% of the growth over the period went to the wealthiest 1% of households, and almost 38% of the total increase went to the next 9% of households. The middle 20% of households received only 2.8% of the rise in the overall value of stock holdings over the period.

Home ownership

While most media analyses of wealth focus on stocks, housing equity is actually a far more important form of wealth for most households. The second panel of Table 4.8, which shows the distribution of all non-stock assets by overall household wealth, makes this point indirectly. In 1998, the total value of all non-stock assets held by the middle 20% of households—overwhelmingly housing equity—was $97,600, more than ten times larger than the average stock holdings for the same group ($9,200).

Census data graphed in **Figure 4E** indicate that, in 1999, about two-thirds (66.7%) of households owned their own homes. More detailed data collected through the biennial American Housing Survey, however, show that home ownership rates vary considerably by income and race. In 1997 (the most recent year for which data are available), 86.5% of household in the top 25% of the

FIGURE 4E Average rate of homeownership, 1965-99

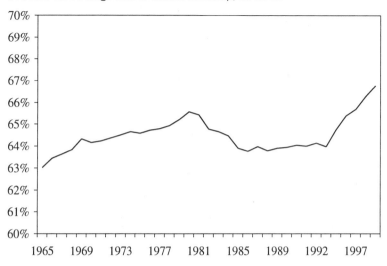

Source: U.S. Bureau of the Census analysis of Current Population Survey.

income distribution were homeowners, compared to just 48% among those households in the bottom 25% (see **Table 4.10** and **Figure 4F**). White households were also much more likely (72.5%) than were black households to own their own homes (45.2%).

As Figure 4E illustrates, home ownership rates have fluctuated in a fairly narrow band—63-67%—since the mid-1960s. Within this range, however, home ownership rates rose sharply at the end of the 1990s. The home ownership data by income and race in Table 4.10 demonstrate that the rise in home ownership was broad based and included black, Hispanic, and lower-income households.

Computers

IBM sold the first personal computer in 1981. While no official data are yet available, by 2000 more than half of all households almost certainly owned at least one personal computer. Compared to housing equity or even the stock holdings of the typical household, the money value of computers is small. Nevertheless, access to computers may have an important impact on a household's ability to participate in the "new economy." The impact of computers may be even greater for households with school-age children, whose school performance

TABLE 4.10 Home ownership rates, by race and income

	Home ownership rate				Percentage-point change	
	1973	1979	1989	1997	1979-89	1989-97
All	64.4%	65.4%	64.0%	65.8%	-1.4	1.8
White	67.1%	68.4%	69.4%	72.5%	1.0	3.1
Black*	43.4	44.4	42.9	45.2	n.a.	2.2
Hispanic	n.a.	n.a.	40.3	42.8	n.a.	2.5
Income						
Top 25%	81.1%	87.0%	84.5%	86.5%	-2.5	1.9
Next 25%	69.2	72.3	68.6	71.4	-3.6	2.8
Next 25%	55.9	56.2	56.3	57.5	0.0	1.2
Bottom 25%	51.3	46.2	46.4	48.0	0.2	1.6

* Black includes all non-white in 1973 and 1977.

Source: Authors' analysis of published American Housing Survey data.

FIGURE 4F Average rate of homeownership, by income quartile, 1997

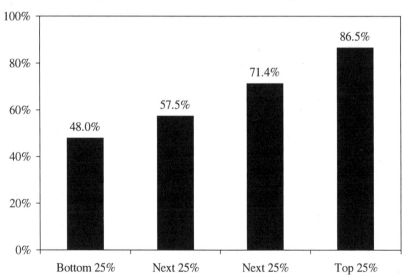

Source: Authors' analysis of published American Housing Survey data.

TABLE 4.11 Computer ownership (percent)

	1984	1989	1993	1998
All	7.9%	14.4%	22.8%	42.1%
Education				
College+	16.4%	30.6%	46.9%	68.7%
Some college	11.3	18.1	27.7	49.3
High school	5.9	9.1	13.5	31.2
Some high school	2.3	4.5	5.4	15.7
Elementary	0.9	1.9	3.0	7.9
Race				
White	8.8%	16.0%	25.1%	46.6%
Black	3.8	6.6	11.3	23.2
Hispanic	4.3	7.1	12.1	25.5
Other	8.4	17.6	30.3	50.9
Income*				
75,000 and above	22.1%	43.8%	60.2%	79.9%
50,000-74,999	22.4	31.6	45.2	66.3
35,000-49,999	17.0	22.5	30.8	50.2
25,000-34,999	11.7	14.6	20.8	35.8
20,000-24,999	8.1	9.7	15.0	25.7
15,000-19,999	5.3	8.0	11.7	21.2
10,000-14,999	3.3	4.5	8.0	15.9
5,000-9,999	1.7	3.7	5.1	12.3
Less than 5,000	1.6	5.8	6.8	15.9

* Current dollars.

Source: Authors' analysis of data from Kominski and Newburger (1999) and NTIA (1999).

and subsequent economic circumstances may be tied to familiarity and facility with computers.

Table 4.11 summarizes data from a periodic government survey designed to measure computer ownership. In 1998, 42.1% of all households owned a personal computer. Ownership rates, however, varied significantly by income, education, and race. Households with the highest incomes, not surprisingly, had the highest rates of computer ownership. In 1998, for example, 79.9% of households with annual incomes of $75,000 or more owned computers, compared to just 25.7% of households in the $20,000-24,999 range. Among households where the head of household had a college degree or more, over two-thirds (68.7%)

owned a computer, compared to just 31.2% among households headed by a high school graduate. Almost half (46.6%) of white households owned computers, while less than one-fourth (23.2%) of black households did.

Unfortunately, the rapid growth in computer ownership has been uneven and the gap in computer ownership along education and race lines appears to have grown markedly in the 1990s. The data on education and race in **Figures 4G** and **4H** (drawn from Table 4.11) show small gaps in ownership rates across education and racial groups in 1984. These gaps, however, increased dramatically by 1998. (Unfortunately, the publicly available data for ownership by income in Table 4.11 use income categories in current, rather than inflation-adjusted, values, making comparisons over time difficult.)

In many respects, the patterns of computer ownership in 1998 and trends over the 1980s and 1990s appear to mirror inequalities that pre-dated the era of the personal computer. To the extent that access to computers does affect children's performance in school and, later, in work, the current inequities in the distribution of computer ownership could end up reinforcing the existing pattern of economic inequality in the future.

Whether looking at stocks, homes, or computers, the distribution of assets is highly unequal. The wealthy own a disproportionate share of all assets, especially financial assets such as stocks. While the stock market has received a great deal of attention over the last decade, housing equity is, by far, the most important form of wealth held by typical American households. While home ownership rates have improved somewhat in the 1990s, inequalities in housing ownership remain high across income and race.

Liabilities

An examination of the other side of the balance sheet—liabilities—reveals the sizeable scale of household debt in 1999. As **Table 4.12** shows, in 1999 the total value of all forms of outstanding household debt was greater than the total disposable income of all households. Mortgage debt accounted for about two-thirds, and consumer debt (mostly credit card debt) for about one-fifth, of the total debt owed.

The debt levels in 1999 were at historic highs. **Figure 4I** first graphs all debt, and then mortgage debt alone, as a share of disposable personal income from 1947 to 1999. All debt rose from about 20% of disposable personal income at the end of World War II to over 60% by the early 1960s. Overall debt levels then remained roughly constant through the early 1980s, when they began to increase rapidly again. By 1999, overall debt was more than 100% of annual

FIGURE 4G Percentage of households with a computer, by education, 1984-98

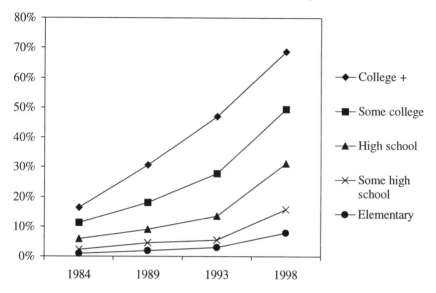

Source: Authors' analysis of data from Kominski and Newburger (1999) and NTIA (1999).

FIGURE 4H Percentage of households with a computer, by race, 1984-98

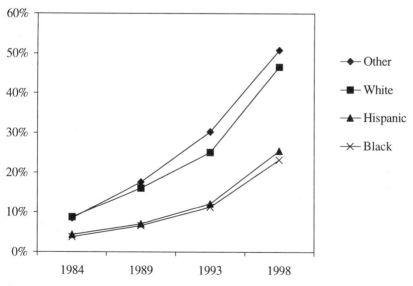

Source: Authors' analysis of data from Kominski and Newburger (1999) and NTIA (1999).

TABLE 4.12 Household debt, by type, 1949-99 (percent)

	As a share of disposable personal income				As a share of assets**	
	All debt	Mortgage	Home equity loans*	Consumer credit	All debt	Mortgage
1949	31.9%	18.5%	n.a.	10.2%	5.9%	14.2%
1967	66.9	40.3	n.a.	18.8	11.7	29.2
1973	65.2	37.9	n.a.	19.7	12.3	25.2
1979	71.9	44.7	n.a.	19.5	13.5	26.7
1989	84.6	55.3	7.0%	19.8	14.4	30.4
1995	91.9	60.0	5.8	20.7	15.3	38.6
1999	103.0	67.5	7.7	21.5	14.1	40.1
Annual percentage-point change						
1949-67	1.9	1.2	n.a.	0.5	0.3	0.8
1967-73	-0.3	-0.4	n.a.	0.1	0.1	-0.7
1973-79	1.1	1.1	n.a.	0.0	0.2	0.3
1979-89	1.3	1.1	n.a.	0.0	0.1	0.4
1989-99	1.8	1.2	0.1	0.2	0.0	1.0
1995-99	2.8	1.9	0.2	0.2	-0.3	0.4

* Data for 1989 refer to 1990.
** All debt as a share of all assets; mortgage debt as a share of real estate assets.

Source: Authors' analysis of Flow of Funds Account and other data.

disposable income.

At the aggregate level, debt is a more important feature of the household economy than at any time in modern history. The aggregate data, however, don't tell anything about the distribution of the debt: that can be seen in Table 4.8. The debt distribution (see the third section) has several striking features. First, debt is more equally distributed than are either assets or net worth. In 1998, for example, the average household in the top 1% had a net worth 167 times greater than that of the average household in the middle 20%. In the same year, however, the average debt held by the top 1% was only six times greater than the average for the middle 20%. Second, for typical households, debt levels are high compared to the value of assets. In 1998, the average outstanding debt of households in the middle 20% was $45,800 (typically mortgage debt plus credit card debt). This debt level is about nine times greater than the corresponding $9,200 average for stock holdings and about half the total value of other assets (overwhelmingly the family home). Third, as noted earlier, the increase between

FIGURE 4I Debt as a percentage of disposable personal income, 1947-99

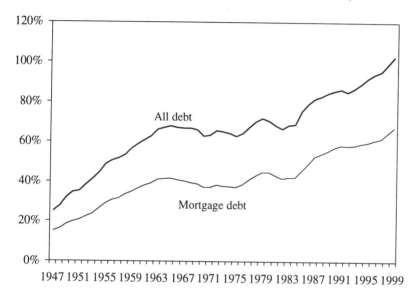

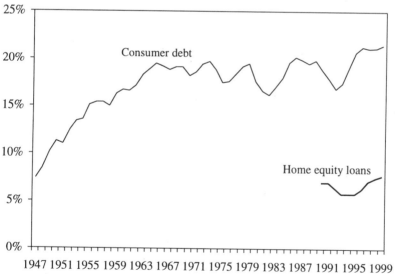

Source: Authors' analysis of Federal Reserve Board (2000).

1989 and 1998 in average household debt held by the middle 20% (up $11,800) was much larger than the corresponding increase in stocks (up $5,500). The run-up in debt at the middle was also larger than the corresponding increase in the value of all non-stock assets (up $8,500). These data suggest that, as far as the wealth of typical households is concerned, the real story of the 1990s was not the stock market boom, but the debt explosion.

The debt data in Table 4.8 also illustrate how the run-up in household debt during the 1990s was shared among households at different wealth levels. **Figure 4J** divides the total increase in debt between 1989 and 1998 among households at different points in the wealth distribution. (The approach here is identical to that used in Figure 4D, which looked at the distribution of growth in stock holdings.) As overall household debt ballooned during the 1990s, the share of debt held by the top 1% of households actually fell; the decline in debt held by the top 1% of households was equal to about 27% of the total growth in debt over the period. The middle 20% of households absorbed the largest share (38.8%) of the increase in debt. The top fifth of households (excluding the top 1%) also bore a large share of the overall increase in debt. The "next 9%" group accounted for 21% of the total rise in debt; the "next 10%" almost 28%.

Debt service

In and of itself, debt is not a problem for households. In fact, credit generally represents a tremendous economic opportunity for households, since they can use it to buy houses, cars, and other big-ticket consumer goods that provide services over many years; to cope with short-term economic setbacks such as unemployment or illness; or to make investments in education or small businesses. Debt becomes a burden only when required debt payments begin to crowd out other economic obligations.

Table 4.13 reproduces estimates from the Federal Reserve Board on the average household debt service burden from 1980 through 1999. The figures in the table are the Federal Reserve Board's estimates of the minimum required payments on outstanding debt, as a share of household disposable income. In 1999, minimum debt payments totaled about 13.4% of all household disposable income. Mortgage payments were, on average, 7.6% of disposable personal income (note that many households rent and many have paid off their mortgages, so the burden on mortgage holders alone would be higher). Minimum consumer debt payments were another 5.8% of disposable income. Over the full 1980-99 period, the debt service burden varied by only a small margin, a surprising finding given that household debt levels rose so much over the same period. The

FIGURE 4J Distribution of growth in debt, 1989-98

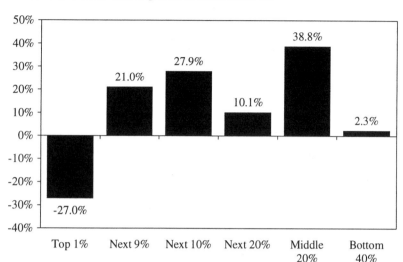

Source: Unpublished analysis of Survey of Consumer Finance data by Wolff.

TABLE 4.13 Household debt service burden,* 1980-99
(percent of disposable personal income)

	All debt	Mortgage	Consumer
1980	12.8%	8.4%	4.4%
1989	13.4	7.6	5.8
1995	12.5	6.8	5.6
1999	13.4	7.6	5.8
Percentage-point change			
1980-89	0.6	-0.9	1.5
1989-99	0.0	0.0	0.0
1995-99	1.0	0.8	0.2

* Federal Reserve Board's estimate of minimum required payments on outstanding mortgage and consumer debt.

Source: Federal Reserve Board (2000a).

main reason for the relatively constant debt service burden is that nominal interest rates were much lower at the end of the 1990s than they had been at the beginning of the 1980s. For a given level of debt, debt service will be lower the lower the interest rate. With debt levels substantially higher at the turn of the century than they were 20 years earlier, the household sector is much more vulnerable to high interest rates than in the past.

Of course, the aggregate debt service figures in Table 4.13 do not show how debt service varies across households. **Table 4.14** shows household debt payments as a share of income for households at different income levels. (These numbers, also from the Federal Reserve Board, use a different underlying source of data than that used in Table 4.13. The definitions of payments and incomes also differ slightly. As a result, the aggregate numbers in Tables 4.13 and 4.14 don't match exactly.) The data in Table 4.14 demonstrate that debt service takes the biggest share of income from lower-income households. In 1998, households with annual incomes of $100,000 or more spent 10% of their income meeting minimum-required debt payments, compared to 19.4% of income for those in households with less than $10,000 in annual income. Household debt service consumed 17.4% of the income of middle-income groups (those in the $25,000-49,999 and $50,000-99,999 range). The Federal Reserve Board data also show that debt service payments rose during the 1990s, especially among lower-income households. Between 1989 and 1998, for example, debt service payments by households in the $10,000-24,999 income range increased by 3.7 percentage points of total income.

Hardship

Table 4.15 takes a slightly different look at the distribution of debt service payments by showing the share of each household income group that has debt service payments equal to more than 40% of household income, a level that is generally considered to represent economic hardship. In 1998, 13.8% of households in the middle-income range ($25,000-49,999) were making debt service payments in excess of 40% of their income, as were almost 20% of those in the $10,000-24,999 range and almost one-third of those with incomes below $10,000. Despite the strong recovery of 1995-99, the share of households with high debt service payouts increased significantly in the 1990s. Between 1989 and 1998, for example, the share of households in the $25,000-49,999 range facing high debt burdens increased 4.7 percentage points; the share among households in the $10,000-24,999 range rose 4.9 percentage points.

Table 4.16 shows another measure of the impact of debt on economic hard-

TABLE 4.14 Household debt service as a share of income, by income level, 1989-98 (percent)

Household income*	1989	1992	1995	1998	Percentage-point change 1989-98	Percentage-point change 1995-98
$100,000 or more	8.0%	10.7%	8.7%	10.0%	2.0	1.3
$50,000 - 99,999	16.5	15.3	16.0	17.4	0.9	1.4
$25,000 - 49,999	16.0	16.5	16.2	17.4	1.4	1.2
$10,000 - 24,999	12.5	14.8	16.1	16.2	3.7	0.1
Less than $10,000	16.2	16.8	19.5	19.4	3.2	-0.1
Average	12.7%	14.1%	13.6%	14.5%	1.8	0.9

* In 1998 dollars.

Source: Federal Reserve Board (2000b).

TABLE 4.15 Households with high debt burdens, by income level, 1989-98 (percent of households)

Household income*	1989	1992	1995	1998	Percentage-point change 1989-98	Percentage-point change 1995-98
$100,000 or more	1.8%	2.2%	1.7%	2.1%	0.3	0.4
$50,000 - 99,999	4.9	4.4	4.2	5.7	0.8	1.5
$25,000 - 49,999	9.1	9.6	8.0	13.8	4.7	5.8
$10,000 - 24,999	15.0	15.5	17.3	19.9	4.9	2.6
Less than $10,000	28.6	28.4	27.6	32.0	3.4	4.4
Average	10.1%	10.9%	10.5%	12.7%	2.6	2.2

* Constant 1998 dollars.

Source: Federal Reserve Board (2000b).

ship: the share of households, by income, that are late paying bills. In 1998, 8.1%—about one in 12—of all households were 60 days or more late in paying at least one bill. Not surprisingly, the share of households behind on their bills is strongly related to income. Very few (1.5%) of the highest income group were late in paying bills. About one in 11 (9.2%) of those in the middle-income range, however, were behind on at least one bill and about 15% of those with the low-

TABLE 4.16 Households late paying bills, by income level, 1989-98
(percent of households)

Household income*	1989	1992	1995	1998	Percentage-point change	
					1989-98	1995-98
$100,000 or more	1.2%	0.5%	1.3%	1.5%	0.3	0.2
$50,000 - 99,999	4.5	2.2	2.7	4.5	0.0	1.8
$25,000 - 49,999	4.8	6.3	8.6	9.2	4.4	0.6
$10,000 - 24,999	12.2	9.4	11.3	12.3	0.1	1.0
Less than $10,000	20.9	11.6	8.4	15.1	-5.8	6.7
Average	7.3%	6.0%	7.1%	8.1%	0.8	1.0

* Constant 1998 dollars.

Source: Federal Reserve Board (2000).

est incomes were having trouble with their bills. Another troubling feature of the data in Table 4.16 is the large rise during the 1990s in the share of middle-income households falling behind on their bills. Between 1989 and 1998, the share of middle-income households behind on their bills rose 4.4 percentage points, from an initial level of just 4.8%.

The ultimate indicator of debt-related difficulties is personal bankruptcy. **Figure 4K** graphs the rate of personal bankruptcies from 1980 through 1999. In 1999, about six out of every 1,000 adults declared personal bankruptcy, a rate almost twice as high as the rate reached in the last business cycle peak in 1989. Despite the strong economic recovery during the second half of the 1990s, personal bankruptcies grew almost continuously throughout the last half of the 1990s.

Household debt grew rapidly in the 1990s, reaching historically high levels by the end of the century. This growth in debt was disproportionately concentrated in the middle of the wealth distribution. Thanks, however, to low nominal interest rates throughout most of the 1990s, debt service did not rise as much as debt levels, and the debt burden has remained lighter than it otherwise would have been. Nevertheless, many households still experienced difficulties. The share of households—especially low- and middle-income households—experiencing real economic hardships, including excessive debt service burdens and problems paying bills, have increased substantially. By the end of the 1990s, personal bankruptcy rates stood at historically high levels, despite the strong recovery.

FIGURE 4K Consumer bankruptcies per 1,000 adults, 1947-99

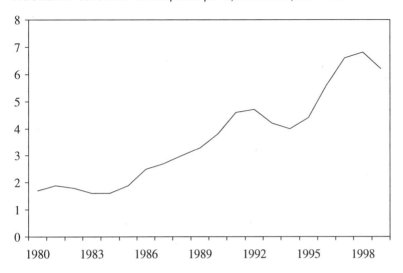

Source: Authors' analysis of American Bankruptcy Institute data.

Conclusion

The data presented here establish that the distribution of wealth is highly unequal, much more so than the distribution of wages and income that were the main focus of earlier chapters. Stocks and other financial assets are particularly concentrated, but even housing equity and computer ownership vary substantially by income and race.

The media casts much attention on the stock market. But for most households, rising debt—not a rising stock market—is the real story of the 1990s. Burgeoning debt has squeezed the net worth of the typical household, which saw only small gains in wealth in the 1990s. This growth in debt has put real economic strains on a significant number of low- and middle-income families, leading, in extreme cases, to personal bankruptcy. The unprecedented levels of household debt suggest caution in evaluating the state of the economy at the turn of the century: part of our current prosperity is borrowed against the future.

CHAPTER 5

Poverty: the roles of measurement, growth, family structure, and work

Previous chapters have focused on the incomes, jobs, and wealth holdings of working families. We now turn to families who have the least of all of these economic assets: the poor.

Many who followed the pronouncements about the new economy and the broad-based wage and income gains of the latter 1990s would be surprised to learn that it wasn't until 1999 that the poverty rate finally fell to a level below that of the last business cycle peak (1989). This chapter examines these trends in some detail, focusing both on the role of the overall economy in determining the rate of poverty and on the poor themselves, with emphases on their demographic status, their educational gains, and their increases in hours worked in the 1990s.

By definition, poor persons are those who live in families whose income before taxes and after government cash transfers leaves them below the poverty line for a family of their size (cash transfers come from various government programs, such as welfare and Social Security). Thus, a family with two parents, two children, and income below $16,895 in 1999 would be considered poor. This threshold is adjusted each year by the growth of inflation.

After using this official measure to present a portrait of the poor and discussing the basic facts regarding poverty trends, we look closely at this definition of poverty. A variety of social scientists have evaluated the official poverty line and found that it is no longer up to the task of reliably determining who is poor. We present some of this research, showing that updated definitions lead to poverty rates that were, on average, 3.6 percentage points above the official rate in the 1990s.

We then examine the factors that have driven poverty trends, paying special attention to the 1970s, 1980s, and 1990s. These decades make for useful comparisons, because, as regards the poor, they differ in demographic, economic, and policy terms. Demographic change, as in the shift to single-parent families, has been held to be a major determinant of poverty since the 1970s, when this shift was occurring most quickly. But this conventional wisdom is incorrect. While family structure changes have led to higher poverty rates over the years, their role has diminished over time, and other factors, such as more education (which has led to less poverty) and the growth in inequality (which has increased poverty rates over time) have been quantitatively more important than changes in family structure in determining the rate of poverty.

Economic trends have, of course, played a primary role in poverty trends. Over the 1980s, growth was slower, the labor market never tightened up as it did in the 1990s, and, most importantly, inequality grew quickly relative to earlier periods. As a result, poverty rates never responded to the growing economy as much as might have been expected given the growth that did occur in the 1980s and early 1990s. In the latter 1990s, however, the labor market moved toward full employment, creating upward pressure on wages that was felt by even the lowest wage workers. At the same time, welfare reform, with its emphasis on work, was passed, and together these two factors led to a notable increase in labor supply from poor families.

The gains against poverty in the latter 1990s were particularly impressive for minorities. Poverty among minorities remains well above that of white families, but the decline in the poverty rates for blacks and Hispanics in the 1990s was far steeper than the decline for whites. In the four years between 1995 and 1999, for example, African American and Hispanic poverty rates fell 5.7 and 7.5points, respectively, while those of whites fell 1.4 points. For minority children the gains were even more impressive—over that same four-year period, minority child poverty rates fell by about nine percentage points, while white child poverty rates fell by about three points. These gains, however, only reduced the racial poverty gap—they were far too small to close it.

Part of the gains for minorities come from the significant increase in hours they spent in the paid labor market over this period. There is compelling evidence that the poorest families are working much more than in the past, and that their poverty rates have fallen in response (overall, the percent of families in poverty fell from 10.3% in 1989 to 9.3% in 1999). Yet, given the strength of the late 1990s economy, wage gains at the bottom of the wage scale, and the increase in hours worked by minorities, one might have hoped for larger declines in poverty rates. Several factors seem to have kept poverty from falling further. First, even with their increased annual hours of work in the 1990s, most poor families work few hours compared to the non-poor. Second, even with the gains in the latter 1990s, the wages of low-wage workers remain below a level that would lift them out of poverty, even were they to double their hours worked. Finally, the loss of welfare benefits over this period has made the poor more dependent on these low earnings. For example, for the average poor family with children headed by a working-age person, the share of income from earnings rose from 58% to 71% from 1989 to 1998, while the share from public assistance (mostly welfare benefits) fell from 25% to 11%.

The fact that work in the paid labor market has become the premiere anti-poverty strategy in the United States no doubt reflects American values regarding the integrity of work and public distaste for dependence on government support by low-income families. The analysis that follows, however, shows that the poor will need further supports if they are to increase their earnings and their hours of work. The 1990s have demonstrated that tight labor markets and minimum wage increases can help to raise the income of the working poor, as did the expansion in the Earned Income Tax Credit (or EITC, a wage subsidy targeted at low-income workers). But making it possible for the poor to significantly increase their hours of work will require expanded subsidies—for child care, transportation, and job training—that facilitate and encourage work. Unless we maintain tight labor markets and significantly expand these policies, the following evidence suggests that we cannot realistically expect the poor to work their way out of poverty.

Who are the poor?

Figure 5A shows the trend in the poverty rate for individuals from 1959 to 1999, the last year for which data of this type are available. **Table 5.1** shows the rates at peaks in the business cycle since 1959 and for the most recent observation, 1999. Compared to the levels that have prevailed since the 1970s, poverty rates at the beginning of this period, 22.4% in 1959, were much higher. They began falling in the 1960s in response to economic growth and more generous government transfers. By 1967 poverty had dropped to 14.2%, and it continued to fall during the early 1970s, hitting a low of 11.1% in 1973. Poverty rose steeply during the recession of the early 1980s and, despite the long recovery that followed, was higher at the end of the 1980s than in the late 1970s. As the bottom section of the table shows, average poverty rates over the 1980s business cycle were two percentage points higher than over the 1970s.

As in Chapter 1, we divide our analysis into the early and late 1990s. Despite the fact that unemployment did not rise as much as in prior recessions, the early 1990s downturn generated a sustained increase in poverty rates that lasted through 1993. Poverty rates began to respond to the recovery at that point, but by 1997 were still above their 1989 level. By 1999, the poverty rate fell to 11.8%,

FIGURE 5A Poverty rate, 1959-99

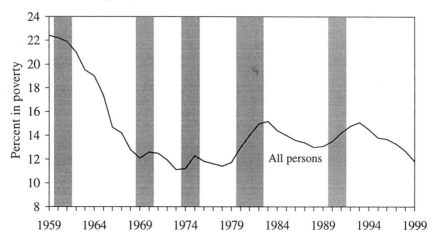

Note: Periods of recession are shaded.

Source: U.S. Bureau of the Census, P60-210.

TABLE 5.1 Percent and number of persons in poverty, 1959-99

Year	Poverty rates	Number in poverty (thousands)
1959	22.4%	39,490
1967	14.2	27,769
1973	11.1	22,973
1979	11.7	26,072
1989	12.8	31,528
1995	13.8	36,425
1999	11.8	32,258
Averages over peak cycles		
1959-67	19.0%	
1967-73	12.4	
1973-79	11.6	
1979-89	13.6	
1989-99	13.7	
1989-95	14.1	
1995-99	13.1	

Source: U.S. Bureau of the Census, P60-198.

TABLE 5.2 Persons in poverty, by race/ethnicity, 1959-99

Year	Total	White	Black	Hispanic
1959	22.4%	18.1%	55.1%	n.a.
1967	14.2	11.0	39.3	n.a.
1973	11.1	8.4	31.4	21.9%
1979	11.7	9.0	31.0	21.8
1989	12.8	10.0	30.7	26.2
1995	13.8	11.2	29.3	30.3
1999	11.8	9.8	23.6	22.8
Percentage-point changes				
1959-73	-11.3	-9.7	-23.7	n.a.
1973-79	0.6	0.6	-0.4	-0.1
1979-89	1.1	1.0	-0.3	4.4
1989-99	-1.0	-0.2	-7.1	-3.4
1989-95	1.0	1.2	-1.4	4.1
1995-99	-2.0	-1.4	-5.7	-7.5

Source: U.S. Bureau of the Census, P60-198.

about the same level as in 1979. Thus, in both the 1980s and the 1990s poverty rates reacted quite slowly to the recoveries that followed the recessions. In other words, it took quite a few years before the benefits of growth "trickled down" to the poor.

Given the fact that minority incomes are generally lower than those of whites, it is not surprising that minority poverty rates are higher. In fact, as **Table 5.2** shows, minority poverty rates are typically two to three times those of whites. The rates for blacks were historically the highest, though Hispanic rates (unavailable for 1959 and 1967) rose more quickly than the other groups over the 1980s, in part due to increased immigration of low-income Hispanic families over this period.

In the 1990s, minorities, and blacks in particular, made significant gains relative to whites (this pattern was also evident in the income data in Chapter 1). While white and Hispanic poverty increased from 1989 to 1995, African American poverty fell by 1.4 percentage points. And while each group's poverty rates fell during 1995-99, the rates of decrease were many times faster for minorities. For example, Hispanic poverty fell 7.5 percentage points, while white poverty fell 1.4 points. (Recall that in these data Hispanics can be in any racial group; thus, some Hispanics are also counted in the white rates. The decrease in poverty for non-Hispanic whites during 1995-99 was 0.8 points—8.5% to 7.7%). Thus, by 1999, black poverty rates were well below their 1989 level, while rates for whites where about the same. Of course, these relative gains do not nearly erase the large gap between minority and white poverty levels.

As pointed out in the discussion of similar trends regarding income (Chapter 1), it is not clear what precisely accounts for the relative gains of blacks and Hispanics in the latter half of the 1990s. The discussion in Chapter 1 of hours of work suggests that relative gains in hours worked may play a role, an impression confirmed by later analysis of this issue in the context of poverty.

Given the importance of adequate income during formative years, the high poverty rates among children in the U.S. have long been considered an important socioeconomic problem here, much more so than in other nations (see Chapter 7 for international poverty comparisons). **Table 5.3** shows that, in 1999, child poverty rates were 16.9% for all children and 18.4% for children under 6. After increasing by 3.2 percentage points during the 1980s, overall child poverty rates fell 2.7 points in the 1990s, with all the decline occurring after 1995. As expected, given the relative gains in family income among African Americans, these data also reveal the relative progress of black children, as black child poverty rates were 10.6 percentage points lower in 1999 than in 1989. For young black and Hispanic children (less than 6 years old), the gains have been particularly strong; their child poverty rates fell 12.6 and 12.0 percentage points, respectively, through 1999. Yet, in terms of levels, black child poverty rates were still more than double those of white children.

Of course, child poverty rates are fully a function of family income. **Table 5.4** shifts the unit of observation from persons to families, which in Census terminology refers to two or more persons related through blood, marriage, or adoption (i.e., one-person units are excluded). In general, family poverty rates are lower than poverty rates for persons, reflecting both the relatively high number of poor children and unrelated individuals included in the person counts. Despite consistent overall economic growth, the family poverty rate was successively higher at the business cycle peaks of 1979 and 1989. The better conditions of the latter 1990s, however, helped to return family poverty rates to their 1979 levels by 1999.

Between 1973 and 1989, the poverty rates of African American families were essentially unchanged at about 28% for each cyclical peak shown in the table. They fell, however, by 5.9 percentage points in the 1990s, with most of the progress coming between 1995 and 1999. Unlike the rates for blacks, Hispanic family poverty grew sharply through 1995, but fell even more quickly than the rate for blacks after that. By 1999, Hispanic poverty was 3.2 points below its 1989 level, while white rates were only half a percentage point lower. Thus, here

TABLE 5.3 Percent of children in poverty, by race, 1979-99

	Total	White	Black	Hispanic
Children under 18				
1979	16.4%	11.8%	41.2%	28.0%
1989	19.6	14.8	43.7	36.2
1995	20.8	16.2	41.9	40.0
1999	16.9	13.5	33.1	30.3
Percentage-point change				
1979-89	3.2	3.0	2.5	8.2
1989-99	-2.7	-1.3	-10.6	-5.9
1989-95	1.2	1.4	-1.8	3.8
1995-99	-3.9	-2.7	-8.8	-9.7
Children under 6				
1979	18.1%	13.3%	43.6%	29.2%
1989	22.5	16.9	49.8	38.8
1995	24.1	18.6	49.2	42.8
1999	18.4	14.9	36.6	30.8
Percentage-point change				
1979-89	4.4	3.6	6.2	9.6
1989-99	-4.1	-2.0	-13.2	-8.0
1989-95	1.6	1.7	-0.6	4.0
1995-99	-5.7	-3.7	-12.6	-12.0

Source: U.S. Bureau of the Census, various years.

again the data show minorities gaining in both absolute and relative terms.

The last two columns show the poverty rates of two family types with very different probabilities of being poor: married couples with children and female-headed families with children (we exclude the other family type—male heads with children—as they represent a small share of families with children (6% in 1998)). Single-mother families are most vulnerable to poverty: about three-fifths of such families were poor in 1959. As we saw in Chapter 1, many married-couple families have increased their time spent in the paid labor market since the late 1970s, mostly through the sharp increase in wives' work outside the home, a strategy unavailable to single parents. They can, of course, increase their own hours, and they have done so, but they have no other adult to make a major contribution to family income.

Nevertheless, thanks to the expansion of cash transfers over the 1960s, the increased labor force participation of women (including single mothers, 71% of

TABLE 5.4 Family poverty, by race/ethnicity of family head of household and for different family types, 1959-99

| | Race/ethnicity of family head: | | | | Families with children: | |
	All	White	Black	Hispanic	Married couples	Female heads
1959	18.5%	15.2%	n.a.	n.a.	n.a.	59.9%
1967	11.4	9.1	33.9%	n.a.	n.a.	44.5
1973	8.8	6.6	28.1	19.8%	n.a.	43.2
1979	9.2	6.9	27.8	20.3	6.1%	39.6
1989	10.3	7.8	27.8	23.4	7.3	42.8
1995	10.8	8.5	26.4	27.0	7.5	41.5
1999	9.3	7.3	21.9	20.2	6.3	35.7
Percentage-point changes						
1959-73	-9.7	-8.6	n.a.	n.a.	n.a.	-16.7
1973-79	0.4	0.3	-0.3	0.5	n.a.	-3.6
1979-89	1.1	0.9	0.0	3.1	1.2	3.2
1989-99	-1.0	-0.5	-5.9	-3.2	-1.0	-7.1
1989-95	0.5	0.7	-1.4	3.6	0.2	-1.3
1995-99	-1.5	-1.2	-4.5	-6.8	-1.2	-5.8

Source: U.S. Bureau of the Census, P60-210.

whom now work), and the expansion of this family type among more affluent women, the poverty rate for single-mother families fell through 1979 to about 40%. Like all families, including married couples, the poverty rates of female-headed families increased in the 1980s, from 39.6% to 42.8%. In the 1990s, however, poverty rates for single mothers and their children fell 7.1 percentage points, more than for any other family type shown. While there are numerous factors responsible for this change, increased work and wage gains provide part of the answer. As shown below, however, due to their loss of welfare benefits over the late 1990s and the low wages they typically earn, single mothers have not found an economic panacea in the labor market.

Race, age, family type, and education level of the family head (a factor on which we focus below) all affect the probability of poverty. And, as **Table 5.5** shows, various combinations of minority status, family type, and low educational attainment lead to poverty rates well above the average. The rates in the table refer exclusively to women 25 years and over in 1998.

The first line of Table 5.5 reinforces the importance of race, as black and

TABLE 5.5 High-risk factors for poverty, females 25 and over, 1998

	White	Black	Hispanic*
All females	11.8%	28.7%	28.0%
(1) Single heads of households	24.9	40.8	43.7
(2) Less than a high school degree	41.4	53.6	53.8
(1) and (2) with children	62.6	65.1	64.8

* Hispanics can be of any race.

Source: U.S. Bureau of the Census, unpublished tables (http://ferret.bls.census.gov/macro/031999/pov/new7_002.htm).

Hispanic women had poverty rates about two and a half times those of white women. The second line reveals that single-head-of-household family type leads to significantly higher poverty rates for women, regardless of race. Note, for example, that in this category alone the poverty rates for white women climb from 11.8% to 24.9%. Lack of a high school degree further drives up poverty rates; over half of black and Hispanic females meeting these criteria were poor in 1998. Adding children to the mix further strains the scant resources of many families within these categories; the poverty rates here rise to 62.6% for white women, 65.1% for blacks, and 64.8% for Hispanics. Note that combining all these characteristics leads to similar levels of poverty, regardless of race.

Alternative approaches to measuring poverty

The method for measuring poverty in the United States is widely viewed as inaccurate, for a variety of reasons. In general, an accurate measure of poverty requires a reliable and representative measure of how much income it takes for a family to meet its most basic needs. A second prerequisite is a comprehensive measure of a family's resources. If the former is higher than the latter, then the family is poor. Of course, determining and assembling the data for this simple equation is nowhere near as easy as it sounds, and any approach to measuring poverty is sure to be fraught with many choices.

Unfortunately, the current measure fails on both of the above counts. The thresholds are outdated, and a substantial number of studies (which form the basis for much of what follows—see table notes for references) find that the U.S. poverty thresholds no longer accurately represent what even poor families need to make ends meet. On the income side, the current approach fails to accurately take account of the resources available to families. Alternative measures almost unanimously raise the level of poverty rates at a point in time compared to the official measure, but they tend to show the same trends in poverty as do the official series. In terms of the composition of poverty, the most important finding is that when the costs associated with working are subtracted from available family resources, the share of the poor who work and are in poverty increases (and conversely, the share that does not work falls).

The current approach to measuring poverty—that which underlies the rates shown in Tables 5.1-5.5—is based on a comparison of each family's income before taxes and after cash transfers (e.g., unemployment insurance, Social Security, and public assistance payments) against the official Census poverty thresholds, adjusted for family size and price changes. These thresholds were originally derived in the early 1960s, based on consumption data collected in the mid-1950s, when it was assumed that poor families spent one-third of their income on food (thus assuming that families could purchase all other necessities for twice what they spent on food). The poverty lines were then constructed by multiplying the Department of Agriculture's minimum food budgets for different-sized families by three. However, consumption patterns and the relative prices of goods have changed since 1955. For example, since food costs have fallen relative to the costs of housing, the proportion of income spent on food has fallen over time, with the average family spending a smaller proportion of the family budget on this necessity and, in turn, a larger proportion on other necessities. Therefore, if the poverty lines were recalculated today, they would be higher (as would poverty rates), since the food budget would be multiplied by a number larger than three.

A panel of poverty experts examined these issues and released a study in 1995 under the aegis of the National Research Council (NRC). The panel found that changes in consumption, work patterns, taxes, and government benefits all suggested the need for an updated measure of poverty. The panel's alternative measure incorporates these factors. It reflects contemporary consumption patterns, adds the cash value of food stamps and housing benefits, and subtracts out-of-pocket medical, child care, and work-related expenses. The next step in this evolution was undertaken by analysts at the Census Bureau and the Bureau of Labor Statistics, who implemented the panel's recommendations, added a few of their own variations, and presented a detailed analysis of the implications of the panel's approach.

The data in **Figure 5B** and **Table 5.6** use one of the Census Bureau's alternative definitions. This measure differs considerably from the current approach on both the threshold and income sides. The threshold is updated using actual expenditure on basic items (food, clothing, housing, and utilities) along with a

FIGURE 5B Official vs. alternative poverty measures

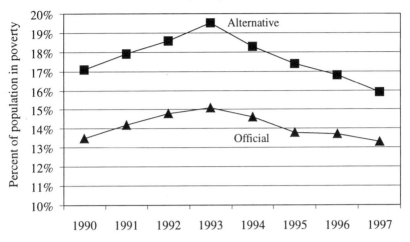

Source: U.S. Bureau of the Census, P60-205, Tables B6A and B6C.

bit more for other necessities such as household supplies and personal care items. It also adjusts the thresholds for the difference in housing costs across the country. On the resource side, it adds various cash and near-cash benefits (such as the value of food stamps) to income, and subtracts out-of-pocket medical costs. It also adjusts income for federal and state taxes, including both tax liabilities and tax credits, such as the Earned Income Tax Credit. Finally, for working parents, this measure subtracts work-related expenses such as child care and transportation.

Figure 5B plots this alternative against the current measure for the years included in the Census analysis: 1990-97 (the most recent year of available data of this type). The alternative measure is higher than that of the current, official measure in each year. On average, the difference is 3.6 percentage points, though the gap is larger at the beginning than at the end of the series, perhaps due to the inclusion of taxes—and thus the poverty reduction effect of the increased EITC over this period—in the alternative measure. Thus, while both series peak in 1993, the official measure falls 1.8 percentage points through 1997 and the alternative rate falls 3.6 points. Nevertheless, by 1997, 7 million more persons were classified as poor under the alternative measure.

Table 5.6 shows the impact of the alternative measure on poverty rates for various individuals, groups, and regions (top section) and for the composition of the poor within those categories (bottom section). The top section shows the

TABLE 5.6 Distribution of the poor, official and alternative measures, 1997

	Official	Census Bureau alternative	Difference (alt.-official)
Poverty rates			
Children	19.9%	21.4%	1.5
Non-elderly adults	10.9	13.2	2.3
Elderly	10.5	17.4	6.9
Persons in:			
Married-couple families	6.4%	9.7%	3.3
Female-headed families	31.5	32.5	1.0
Male-headed families	16.1	18.0	1.9
No workers	36.3%	38.4%	2.1
One or more workers	9.5	12.2	2.7
Regions			
Northeast	12.6%	16.6%	4.0
Midwest	10.4	12.0	1.6
South	14.6	16.0	1.4
West	14.6	19.2	4.6
Distribution of the poor			
Children	39.7%	35.7%	-4.0
Non-elderly adults	50.8	51.3	0.5
Elderly	9.5	13.0	3.5
Persons in:			
Married-couple families	31.5%	40.1%	8.6
Female-headed families	54.4	46.8	-7.6
Male-headed families	14.1	13.1	-1.0
No workers	38.8%	34.2%	-4.6
One or more workers	61.2	65.8	4.6
Regions			
Northeast	18.2%	19.9%	1.7
Midwest	18.3	17.5	-0.8
South	38.7	35.3	-3.4
West	24.9	27.2	2.3

Source: U.S. Bureau of the Census, P60-205, Table B2A and B2B.

two rates and their differences, while the bottom panel shows the share of the poor in the categories listed (note that each sub-section in the bottom section sums to 100%). Poverty rates are higher for all categories under the alternative rates, especially for the elderly (mostly due to the subtraction of out-of-pocket medical costs from their income), married couples (medical costs and work expenses), and persons in the Northeast and West (higher housing prices relative to the other regions). Regarding the composition of the poor, the largest differences are for family structure, where the alternative measure leads to a smaller share of poor single-mother families, and work status, where the alternative measure generates a larger share of working poor. The former result is due to the addition of more transfer income to the resources of single-mother families relative to the official measure. The larger share of workers under the alternative measure is due to the subtraction of work-related expenses, especially child care, from resources.

There is no perfect way to measure poverty, and reasonable persons could find arguments with the experimental alternatives presented by the Census Bureau. And there is room for improvement in these measures in the way price differences, child care costs, and medical costs are estimated (note that the value of publicly provided health insurance is excluded, primarily because it remains unclear how to appropriately value this component). Nevertheless, the alternative measures represent a vast improvement in poverty measurement, successfully addressing and correcting the range of inadequacies embedded in the current measure.

Examining some other alternative ways of measuring poverty can yield additional insights.

As noted above, the official poverty lines are indexed for inflation. However, some analysts claim that the price index used to adjust the poverty lines overstated inflation in the 1970s and early 1980s and thereby overestimated real poverty rates. **Figure 5C** tracks poverty rates from 1968 to 1999 using an alternative consumer price index, the CPI-U-X1, which is considered a more conservative measure of inflation (see the Methodology section for a discussion of the differences in these deflators). As would be expected, the more conservative price index leads to lower measured poverty rates. However, Figure 5C also shows that, regardless of the price index chosen to adjust the poverty lines for price changes, there has been a rise in poverty since 1979 despite overall income growth.

Another important way of measuring poverty is to examine relative economic well-being. A conceptual shortcoming of the official poverty lines is that they are adjusted only for inflation; they do not reflect overall income growth and thus fail to capture changing standards of what is an acceptable poverty threshold. This shortcoming results from the fact that, as average income grows

FIGURE 5C Poverty rates by price index, 1968-99

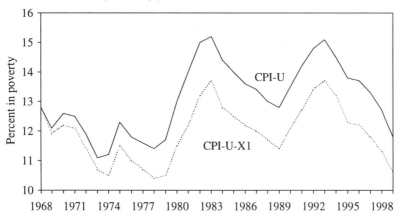

Source: U.S. Bureau of the Census, P60-210.

over time and standards of living rise, the economic "distance" between the officially poor and the rest of society expands. While the earliest poverty income threshold (1959) for a family of four was 55% of the median family income, that ratio has fallen to 36%. A relative measure of poverty accounts for this change by measuring poverty relative to the median family income (which changes yearly). As seen in Chapter 7, most international comparisons use just such a metric, with a poverty threshold typically set at 50% of median family income.

Table 5.7 presents this measure by race. As would be expected (since median family income usually grows faster than prices), the poverty rates at one-half the median are substantially higher than the official (absolute) rates shown in column 4. For example, whereas 12.7% of the population were poor according to the official poverty measure in 1998, 22.3% of all persons were in families with incomes below one-half of the median family income. As with absolute poverty rates, relative rates have increased since 1979, with the bulk of the increase derived from the increased relative poverty of the poorest group: those with incomes less than one-quarter of the median.

As shown in Table 5.2, absolute poverty rates for minorities are higher than those of whites. The bottom three panels of Table 5.7 reveal that the same relationship holds for relative poverty rates of minorities (Hispanics in these data can be of any race). In addition, the gap between relative and absolute rates (the last column of Table 5.7) is higher for minorities than whites, suggesting that

TABLE 5.7 Percent of persons with low relative income, by race, adjusted for family size, 1969-98

	Relative income poverty measures				
	Less than 1/4 the median	1/4 to 1/2 of the median	Less than 1/2 of the median	Official rate	Difference (official-1/2 median)
All					
1969	5.5%	12.4%	17.9%	12.1%	5.8
1979	6.7	13.3	20.0	11.7	8.3
1989	8.3	13.7	22.0	12.8	9.2
1998	8.7	13.6	22.3	12.7	9.6
Whites					
1969	4.3%	10.4%	14.7%	9.5%	5.2
1979	5.0	11.7	16.7	9.0	7.7
1989	6.3	12.5	18.8	10.0	8.8
1998	7.0	12.4	19.4	10.5	8.9
Blacks					
1969	15.3%	27.3%	42.6%	32.2%	10.4
1979	18.8	25.3	44.1	31.0	13.1
1989	21.8	22.1	43.9	30.7	13.2
1998	18.3	21.9	40.2	26.1	14.1
Hispanics *(any race)*					
1969	n.a.	n.a.	n.a.	n.a.	
1979	11.6%	22.6%	34.2%	21.8%	12.4
1989	16.3	23.8	40.1	26.2	13.9
1998	16.7	24.7	41.4	25.6	15.8

Source: U.S. Bureau of the Census (McNeil), various years.

minorities are, in general, further below the absolute poverty line than whites. In 1998, the relative poverty rates for blacks were 40.2% (14.1 points above the absolute rate), and blacks were fairly equally divided between zero to one-quarter of the median and one-quarter to one-half. Relative poverty rates for whites in that year were about half those of blacks (19.4%, 8.9 points above the absolute rate) and fell mostly in the one-quarter to one-half category.

Chapter 1 pointed out the income gains made by African Americans relative to whites over the 1990s. Though these relative gains were at the median, Table

TABLE 5.8 Average poverty gap, 1967-99 (1999 dollars)

Years	Families	Persons not in families
1959	$6,608	$4,390
1967	5,901	3,631
1973	5,910	3,499
1979	6,188	3,428
1989	6,574	3,813
1995	6,601	4,113
1999	6,687	4,206
Annual growth rates		
1959-67	-1.4%	-2.3%
1967-73	0.0	-0.6
1973-79	0.8	-0.3
1979-89	0.6	1.1
1989-99	0.2	1.0
1989-95	0.1	1.3
1995-99	0.3 .	0.6

Source: Center for Budget and Policy Priorities (1998), updated with U.S. Bureau of the Census P60s.

5.7 shows relative gains in poverty as well. Back in 1969, black relative poverty rates (using less than half median income) were close to three times those of whites. By 1998, they were closer to two times higher. Hispanic relative rates (to whites) changed little over the 1979-98 period.

The depth of poverty at a point in time is another useful gauge of how the poor are faring. Since poverty is a fixed income level, families are considered poor whether they are one dollar or $1,000 below the poverty line. **Figure 5D** and **Table 5.8** examine the poverty gap: the distance in the average dollar amount of a person or family from the poverty line. Although family poverty fell slightly in the 1990s, the poverty gap has actually also expanded slightly, suggesting that, while there are fewer poor families (as a share of the population), their poverty is deeper than in prior years.

The figure shows that from the 1960s through the mid-1970s both the rate of poverty and the poverty gap declined, meaning that fewer families were poor and, of those that were, they were on average less poor over time. The strong labor market, along with the expansion of cash transfers over this period, including both Social Security (which significantly reduced the poverty of the elderly) and welfare benefits, contributed to these trends. As shown in the table,

FIGURE 5D Family poverty gap and poverty rates, 1959-99

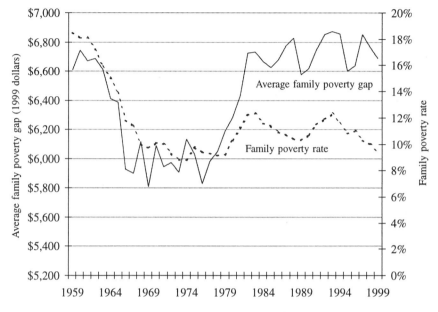

Source: U.S. Bureau of the Census.

the average family poverty gap fell by 1.4% annually over this period.

Both family poverty and the poverty gap rose steeply over the recessionary period in the early 1980s, and, as shown in the figure, the gap has not closed. In fact, the growth rates in the bottom panel of the table reveal that the family poverty gap has risen consistently over business cycle peaks (the gap for individuals fell 0.3% annually from 1973 to 1979 but has risen, albeit very slightly in the 1990s, since).

Table 5.9 and **Figure 5E** show another measure of the depth of poverty: the percentage of the poor below 50% of the poverty line, which in 1999 meant a pre-tax income of about $8,450 for a family of four. In 1979, close to one-third (32.8%) of the poor were in "deep poverty." By 1983, following the deep recession of the early 1980s, this proportion had approached two-fifths (38.5%), where it essentially held throughout the decade.

In the late 1990s, deep poverty was less responsive to growth as was the overall rate. Table 5.1 showed that poverty rates fell 2 percentage points from 1995 to 1999, but, as shown in Table 5.9, deep poverty grew by 1.2 percentage points. Thus, while the share of the population that was poor was falling, the

TABLE 5.9 Persons below 50% of poverty level, 1975-99

Year	Percent of all poor	Number of persons (thousands)
1975	29.9%	7,733
1979	32.8	8,553
1983	38.5	13,590
1989	38.0	11,983
1995	38.1	13,892
1999	39.3	12,681

Source: U.S. Bureau of the Census, various years.

FIGURE 5E Percent of poor persons below 50% of poverty level, 1975-99

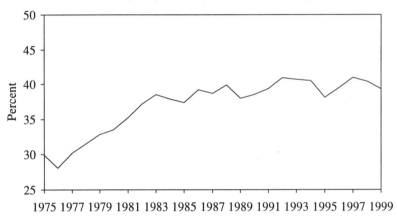

Source: U.S. Bureau of the Census web site.

share of the poor that was deeply poor was rising. Research on this pattern has identified welfare reform as one causal factor. The welfare-to-work component of reform, in tandem with the strong labor market of the late 1990s, has meant that some of the most able of the poor have been able to cross the poverty line, leaving behind those with weaker economic prospects.

In sum, the official poverty measure is clearly outdated and in need of repair. Furthermore, the most carefully designed alternative measures show higher levels of poverty than the official approach. Both, however, show the same trends. No matter how they are measured, poverty rates were slow to respond to economic growth in the 1980s and for much of the 1990s, a phenomenon we examine in the next section. In the latter years of the 1990s, poverty rates have responded to growth, and, by many of the measures above, they are now back to their 1979 levels. Yet the remaining poor are poorer than those who have left the poverty rolls.

Poverty, overall growth, and inequality

Several decades ago, economists thought that poverty would continually diminish (and virtually disappear) as the economy expanded. But if economic growth is unequally distributed, as shown in prior chapters, the inverse relationship between growth and poverty is weakened. When the fruits of growth are concentrated at the top of income and wealth distributions, those at the bottom are less likely to benefit from overall growth, and poverty rates are thereby less responsive to the growing economy.

In many ways, this scenario describes the relationship between growth and poverty over the 1980s and early 1990s. But, as emphasized throughout the book, income inequality grew considerably slower in the 1990s. Thus, the above reasoning would suggest that poverty rates would have begun to respond more readily to overall growth during this period. The following analysis reveals this to be the case, supporting the connection between more equally distributed growth and less poverty.

Table 5.10 shows changes in poverty rates along with changes in various indicators of overall growth and inequality. These broad indicators show quite different relationships between the macroeconomy, poverty, and inequality (as measured by the Gini coefficient (see Chapter 1)) in the different time periods. In the 1960s, growth was relatively fast, unemployment and inequality fell, and poverty rates fell sharply (as has been emphasized, part of this decline was due to increased transfers over that decade). Over the 1970s and 1980s, however, the macroeconomic disconnect is evident. Productivity and per capita income growth slowed progressively in each period, and unemployment grew in the 1970s. Inequality expanded somewhat in the 1970s and accelerated strongly in the 1980s. Partly as a result of these developments, poverty's declining trend of the 1960s was slowed almost to a halt in the 1970s and reversed in the 1980s.

Over the 1990s, some important improvements began to occur, particularly in the latter part of the period. These developments are illustrated in the last two rows, which show the annualized changes in the indicators between the beginning and end of the 1990s. Most notably, from 1995 to 1999, productivity and per capita income accelerated and unemployment fell. Inequality grew more

TABLE 5.10 Changes in poverty rates and growth indicators

	Poverty rates	Productivity*	Per capita income	Unemployment	Gini coefficient
1959-69	-10.3	32.6%	34.6%	-2.0	-3.3%
1969-79	-0.4	21.4	23.9	2.3	4.6
1979-89	1.1	14.3	22.1	-0.5	9.9
1989-99	-1.0	20.4	21.6	-1.1	4.0**
Annualized changes					
1989-95	0.2	1.5%	1.2%	0.05	0.4%
1995-99	-0.5	2.5	2.3	-0.35	0.4

* Non-farm business sector.
** This percent change in the Gini coefficient includes a downward adjustment for the effect of the topcode change in 1993. Without the adjustment, the change would be 6.7%. See table note.

Source: Poverty rates and Gini coefficients from U.S. Bureau of the Census, P60-206 and P60-207. All else from ERP (2000).

slowly in the 1990s than in the 1980s, and below we show how important this trend was to the decline in poverty rates. Thus, each of these important aggregate statistics moved in such a way as to reduce poverty rates. Income grew more quickly overall, and the slowing of inequality growth meant that more of these benefits were likely to accrue to low-income families over the 1990s relative to earlier periods. Productivity accelerated and unemployment fell, translating into more employment opportunities at higher wages for low-wage workers. In these ways, the latter 1990s stand in stark contrast to the previous 15 years.

Three main explanations have been offered for this phenomenon of unresponsive poverty rates over the 1980s and early 1990s: a decline in government assistance for the poor, changing family demographics, and negative labor market changes such as falling real wages and declining employment opportunities for low-wage workers. While each one of these has played an important role, their respective roles have not been constant over time. For example, while the shift toward family types more susceptible to poverty, like female-headed families, has consistently led to higher poverty rates, this factor was less important in the 1980s and 1990s than in earlier periods. Regarding employment opportunities, the 1990s provides a good "laboratory" to examine the relationship between poverty and the labor market, since the relevant variables follow distinct patterns over the period. In the next section we examine the relative contributions of these factors.

The role of demographics and inequality

Table 5.11 shows the percent of persons in three different family types in the period 1959-98, along with the poverty rates of persons in those families. Clearly, there has been a shift over time into family types more vulnerable to poverty. For instance, the percentage of persons in married-couple and male-headed families, which have the lowest poverty rates, has consistently fallen, from 85.9% in 1959 to 69.9% in 1998. Conversely, there has been a consistent expansion of female-headed families and an even faster growth of households consisting of single individuals.

By itself, we would expect this pattern of family-structure changes to increase poverty rates. However, changes in poverty rates within these groups also play a determining role. Growth in vulnerable family types as a share of all families would put upward pressure on poverty rates. But rising relative incomes concurrent with this growth would be a countervailing factor. In fact, the poverty rates for persons by family type show that all family types saw their poverty rates fall over the 1960s and 1970s, with single persons showing the largest drop (12 percentage points in both decades). Note also the decline in the poverty rates of persons in female-headed families of 11.2 points over the 1960s and another 3.3 points over the 1970s. This trend then reversed, and between 1979 and 1989 poverty rates grew comparably for persons in female-headed families (1.0 points) and in married-couple families (0.9 points), while falling much more slowly for individuals. Between 1989 and 1998, poverty again fell for female-headed families, but was little changed for persons in other family types.

What does Table 5.11 reveal about the relationship between demographic shifts and changes in poverty rates? The evidence is mixed. On the one hand, it is clear that there has been a compositional shift to families more vulnerable to poverty. However, when the demographic shifts were occurring most rapidly, in the 1969-79 period, the overall poverty rate declined from 12.1% to 11.7%, with declines occurring for each family type, and most quickly for those with the highest poverty rates: individuals and those in female-headed families. Conversely, when demographic forces diminished over the 1980s, the poverty trend reversed. Moreover, poverty also grew among the family type least vulnerable to poverty: persons in married-couple families. Thus, while demographic shifts to family types with higher poverty rates have played a role in the high poverty rates of the 1980s, such shifts are clearly only part of the story. The question is: how large a part relative to other factors?

To answer this question, we use two "decomposition" techniques, i.e., analyses that estimate the extent to which different factors contribute to a particular outcome. The first, in **Table 5.12**, focuses exclusively on family structure by

TABLE 5.11 Changing family structure and poverty, 1959-98

	Percent of persons in:				Poverty rate of persons in:			
Year	Female-headed families	Married-couple and male-headed families*	Not living in families	Total	Female-headed families	Married-couple and male-headed families*	Not living in families	All persons
1959	8.0%	85.9%	6.1%	100%	49.4%	18.2%	46.1%	22.4%
1969	9.0	83.7	7.3	100	38.2	7.4	34.0	12.1
1979	12.1	76.2	11.7	100	34.9	6.4	21.9	11.7
1989	13.2	72.5	14.3	100	35.9	7.3	19.2	12.8
1998	14.4	69.9	15.7	100	33.1	6.9	19.9	12.7
Percentage-point changes								
1959-69	1.0	-2.2	1.2	0.0	-11.2	-10.8	-12.1	-10.3
1969-79	3.1	-7.5	4.4	0.0	-3.3	-1.0	-12.1	-0.4
1979-89	1.1	-3.7	2.6	0.0	1.0	0.9	-2.7	1.1
1989-98	1.2	-2.6	1.4	0.0	-2.8	-0.4	0.7	-0.1
1959-98	6.4	-16.0	9.6	0.0	-16.3	-11.3	-26.2	-9.7

* From 1979 forward, this group includes a small residual number of persons in unrelated sub-families.

Source: U.S. Bureau of the Census, P60-198.

TABLE 5.12 The impact of changes in family structure on poverty rates, 1959-98

	Changes in poverty due to:		
	Family structure	Other factors	Total
1959-69	0.6	-10.9	-10.3
1969-79	1.8	-2.3	-0.5
1979-89	0.7	0.4	1.1
1989-98	0.5	-0.6	-0.1
1959-98	3.7	-13.3	-9.7

*   Change in poverty rates due to changes in the percent of persons in each of the three family types shown in the previous table.

**   Change in poverty rates due to changes in factors other than family structure, most notably, changes in incomes within the various family types.

*** 10-year growth rate so as to be comparable to other rows.

Source: U.S. Bureau of the Census, P60-198.

separating it from all the other factors (the most important of which are economic changes). The second technique adds the important component of education to the demographic side of the ledger, and inequality growth to the economic side.

Column 3 of Table 5.12 shows the total change in poverty rates over the various time periods of interest. Columns 1 and 2 divide these changes into the portions due to demographic change and those due to other factors. While the shift to more vulnerable family types has clearly played its expected poverty-increasing role, other than in the 1970s that role has been remarkably consistent. In the 1960s, 1980s, and 1990s, family structure changes added at most 0.7 percentage points to poverty rates. Only in the 1970s did this value accelerate, and even then its contribution was overtaken by other factors.

In the 1960s, family structure changes were quite unimportant relative to the other factors (for the most part, equally distributed growth and the expansion of government transfers) that lowered poverty by 10.3 percentage points. In the 1980s and 1990s, family structure changes increased poverty by 0.7 and 0.5 percentage points, but the other factors—income changes that occurred within each family type—reinforced this family structure effect in the 1980s, and counteracted it in the 1990s. These interesting dynamics will be examined more carefully below, but these findings suggest that the role played by the shift to families more vulnerable to poverty has been a relatively small one compared to income changes within family types. Only in the 1970s were family structure changes the key determinant of poverty's growth, accounting for 1.8 percentage points. This contribution, however, was outpaced by other changes, which led to a 2.3 percentage-point decline in the 1970s. And since the 1970s, the role of family structure has decelerated swiftly.

This analysis is not intended to dismiss the role of demographic change, only to give it its proper context. And since that context is of a small magnitude compared to other factors, we must look beyond family structure changes for these other factors.

One important factor, and one which is often overlooked, is the countervailing trend of educational upgrading of heads of families. As Americans from all walks of life become more highly educated, they and their families are less likely to be poor (holding all else equal). This relationship can be seen in **Table 5.13**, which shows the family poverty rates for families with children in the 1969-98 period by the education level of the family head (top section), along with the shares of families in each category (bottom section). Clearly, families headed by persons with higher levels of education are less likely to be poor. Note, for example, that families with children headed by a college graduate have poverty rates between 2% and 3.3%. On the other end of the scale, the rate for families headed by someone with less than a high school degree reveals the increased importance of education as an antipoverty tool. Those with the least education were always most likely to be poor, but in 1969 their rates were less than twice the overall average and about ten times that of families headed by a college graduate. By 1998, the rate for the families headed by high school dropouts was about two-and-a-half times the overall rate and 17 times the college rate. The increasing importance of education as a poverty-reducer is highlighted in the decomposition that follows.

The bottom panel of the table shows the persistent shift toward higher levels of educational attainment by poor families. For instance, over the full period for which we have these types of data, 1969-98, there was a 26.4 percentage-point shift out of the bottom two education categories into the "some college" and college graduate categories.

So far we have shown that, while family structure changes have played a role in increasing poverty rates, education has played a countervailing role. We have also emphasized the role played by other factors, including the increase in economic inequality. While we have lumped the non-demographic factors (such as overall economic growth and growing inequality) together in the above de-compositions, we need now to account for these factors separately as well. **Table 5.14** provides a decomposition of poverty's growth that separately accounts for these factors.

TABLE 5.13 Educational level of family heads and poverty,
families with children, 1969-98

Educational level of family heads	Poverty rates					Changes			
	1969	1979	1989	1995	1998	1969-79	1979-89	1989-98	1969-98
Less than high school	19.4%	26.8%	38.0%	41.6%	39.1%	7.3	11.3	1.1	19.7
High school	6.6	10.4	15.4	17.2	17.7	3.8	5.0	2.4	11.2
Some college	5.4	6.8	9.0	11.2	10.3	1.4	2.2	1.3	4.9
College +	2.0	2.5	2.6	3.3	2.3	0.4	0.1	-0.3	0.3
Total	10.5	12.5	15.5	16.3	15.1	2.0	2.9	-0.4	4.6
	Percent of families					Changes			
Less than high school	37.0%	26.2%	18.9%	16.5%	15.5%	-10.8	-7.3	-3.3	-21.4
High school	36.4	38.1	38.7	32.1	31.4	1.7	0.5	-7.3	-5.0
Some college	12.1	16.3	19.9	28.1	28.1	4.2	3.6	8.2	16.0
College +	14.5	19.4	22.6	23.3	25.0	4.9	3.2	2.4	10.4
Total	100.0	100.0	100.0	100.0	100.0				

Source: Authors' analysis of March CPS data.

This table separates the growth in person-level poverty rates into three demographic factors—the race of the family head, the education level of the family head, and family structure—and two economic components—the poverty-reducing effect of overall economic growth and the poverty-increasing effect of growing inequality (these changes are slightly different in some periods than those in previous tables due to rounding). Thus, it highlights the relative importance of these different factors in the growth of poverty in each time period. If the conventional wisdom is correct—that family structure changes are the key factor driving a wedge between economic growth and poverty—then this decomposition should reveal a consistent increase in this factor's role over time. Similarly, the role of economic factors, such as the overall growth of the economy and the increase in inequality in particular, should have diminished.

In fact, as Table 5.14 shows, the opposite is the case, reinforcing the earlier results. Family structure changes played the largest role in poverty's growth in the 1970s; however, in the 1980s and 1990s, the higher poverty associated with changes in their family structure component of demographic change was more than offset by the poverty-reducing impact of educational upgrading. In fact, in the most recent period, the education effect was twice that of the family structure effect (-1.0 vs. 0.5).

TABLE 5.14 The impact of demographic and education changes
on family poverty rates

	1969-79	1979-89	1989-98	1969-98
Actual change	-0.5	1.2	-0.1	0.5
Total demographic effect	0.5	-0.3	-0.4	-0.2
Race	0.3	0.4	0.3	1.0
Education	-1.6	-1.2	-1.0	-3.9
Family structure	1.9	0.7	0.5	3.1
Interaction	-0.2	-0.1	-0.1	-0.4
Economic change	-1.0	1.4	0.3	0.8
Growth	-1.5	-1.3	-1.5	-4.3
Inequality	0.5	2.7	1.8	5.1

Source: Authors' analysis of March CPS data.

In the 1970s, poverty rates fell by 0.5 percentage points, thanks to economic growth that was only partially offset by increasing income inequality (which grew little in this period relative to later periods) and demographic change. As shown in Table 5.11 above, the 1970s saw an accelerated shift toward female-headed families, leading to a relatively large 1.9 percentage-point increase in poverty. However, the educational upgrading described in Table 5.13 was an important countervailing factor (lowering poverty by 1.6 percentage points), and this decomposition shows this effect to almost reverse the poverty-increasing impact of family structure in the 1970s.

Family structure plays a lesser role in the next two time periods, accounting for 0.7 and 0.5 points in the 1980s and 1990s, respectively. Education levels of family heads continued to reduce poverty rates, by 1.2 points in the 1980s and 1.0 points in the 1990s. Since the role of race (the racial composition of family heads) was barely changed over the period, the impact of all demographic change, including education, on post-1979 poverty rates was actually negative.

Given that demographic shifts (including educational upgrading), fully considered, actually reduced poverty over the 1980s and 1990s, the explanation for increasing poverty in the 1980s and unchanging rates in the 1990s must lie with the economic factors. Since overall economic growth was a relatively constant factor in lowering poverty since the late 1960s, the increased role of inequality is the most likely suspect. In fact, over the 1980s, when income inequality was increasing faster than in any other postwar decade, it led to a 2.7 percentage-point increase in poverty rates. Notice that this role continued into the 1990s, but was significantly reduced, contributing 1.8 percentage points. Since the role of the other factors in the decomposition were about the same magnitude as the 1980s (education was slightly less poverty-reducing, but family structure was less poverty-increasing), the main difference in poverty outcomes was the slower growth of inequality over the 1990s. In the absence of this important change, even with the same level of growth that we enjoyed in the 1990s, poverty would have expanded much as it did over the 1980s, instead of holding steady.

In sum, a full accounting for the scope of demographic change over the last 30 years does not support a simple story where the increased share of female-headed families is the sole, or even the most important, determinant of increased poverty. Family structure changes were most "influential" over the 1970s, when poverty rates actually fell slightly due to strong and fairly balanced economic growth. After that, though such changes continued to put upward pressure on poverty rates, their role decelerated. Also, the usual demographic story fails to take account of the successively higher levels of education of heads of families over time. Over the full period, this factor alone reduced poverty by 3.9 points.

The changing effects of taxes and transfers

As we have stressed throughout the chapter, the poverty-reducing role of cash transfers has fluctuated over time. Such benefits, by providing cash and near-cash resources to low-income persons and families, are an important determinant of the poverty rate. The impact of this determinant over time is a function of two forces: changes in market-driven poverty rates and changes in the magnitude of benefits. If the pre-tax, pre-transfer distribution delivers up less poverty (say, due to stronger and more equal growth), the transfer system has less work to do to reduce poverty rates. Conversely, when inequality rises and incomes fall, the transfer system must expand if poverty levels are to be maintained, let alone further reduced.

Table 5.15 examines both the changes in market poverty and the impact of taxes and transfers for various family types from 1979 to 1999 (earlier data are not available). The first column of the top section (all persons) shows the poverty rate before taxes and transfers; these rates represent the degree of poverty that would exist in the absence of any government intervention. Moving left to right, the table introduces different transfers and taxes and shows how poverty would be affected by each. In column 2, for example, the poverty rate for all persons fell slightly, by 0.9 percentage points, once taxes (and tax credits) were taken into account, from 19.2% to 18.3%, in 1999. This represents both the poverty-reducing effects of the EITC and the poverty-increasing effects of state

TABLE 5.15 The poverty-reducing effects of transfers, 1979-99

All persons	(1) Before taxes and transfers	(2) After taxes	(3) Plus non- means tested (including Medicare)*	(4) Plus means tested (including Medicaid)*	(5) Reduction in poverty due to taxes and transfers (1)-(4)	(6) Reduction effectiveness rate (5)/(1)
1979	19.5%	19.3%	12.4%	8.9%	10.6%	54%
1989	20.0	20.3	13.5	10.4	9.6	48
1999	19.2	18.3	11.3	8.8	10.4	54
Persons 65 and over						
1979	54.2%	54.1%	15.4%	12.3%	41.9%	77%
1989	47.6	48.1	11.4	8.6	39.0	82
1999	47.7	47.6	9.4	7.8	39.9	84
Persons in female- *headed families* *with children under 18*						
1979	53.4%	52.3%	47.3%	28.1%	25.3%	47%
1989	51.4	51.1	47.0	34.9	16.5	32
1999	43.6	39.1	35.0	25.7	17.9	41
Persons in married- *couple families* *with children under 18*						
1979	9.4%	9.1%	7.3%	5.2%	4.2%	45%
1989	10.3	10.5	9.0	6.6	3.7	36
1999	9.0	7.6	6.1	4.4	4.6	51

* Includes fungible value of Medicare and Medicaid benefits; see table note.

Source: EPI analysis of U.S. Bureau of the Census data, P60s, No. 182-RD and No. 198.

taxes, which tend to be regressive (see Chapters 1 and 6). The addition of non-means-tested benefits, including Medicare (i.e., that portion of Medicare estimated to increase a family's resources), lowered the rate to 11.3% in 1999 (column 3). Column 5 totals the effects of government tax and transfer policies, showing, for example, that in 1999 they reduced market-generated poverty by 10.4 points. The final column, "reduction effectiveness rate," is the previous column divided by column 1. It represents the share of market poverty reduced by government tax and transfer policy.

Note first that market outcomes were slightly worse (about half a percentage point) for all persons in 1989 than in 1979, meaning that the tax and transfer system would have had to work a bit harder to keep poverty from rising. In fact, as seen in column 4, for all persons, poverty rates after taxes and transfers were significantly higher in 1989 than in 1979 (10.4% vs. 8.9%). Since transfers reduced poverty less in 1989 than in 1979 (column 5), and market poverty was also slightly higher in the later year, the reduction effectiveness rate (the share of market poverty reduced by taxes and transfers) fell from 54% to 48%.

Between 1989 and 1999, market poverty rates fell by 0.8 percentage points 20.0% vs. 19.2%), and the offsetting effect of transfers expanded. Note, for example, that while taxes raised market poverty 0.3 points in 1989, in 1998, they lowered market poverty by 0.9 points (mostly due to the expansion of the EITC). Thanks in part to this expansion, the reduction effectiveness rate returned to its 1979 level.

The second panel of Table 5.15 shows the importance of transfers for persons over 65, who have the highest rates of poverty reduction by far. Note that market outcomes (column 1) became less poverty-inducing over the 1980s and that the reduction effectiveness of transfers increased in each period for the elderly. By 1999, 84% of pre-transfer elderly poverty had been reduced by the tax and transfer system.

Relative to the elderly, taxes and transfers were significantly less effective at reducing the poverty of persons in female-headed families with children. Over the 1979-89 period, market outcomes actually reduced their poverty by 2.0 percentage points, but a fall in benefits led to a post-tax and -transfer poverty rate in 1989 that was 6.8 points higher than that of 1979 (column 4), leading to a 15 percentage-point decline in the reduction effectiveness rate, from 47% to 32%. Due to their increased work effort and the favorable trends shown in Table 5.10, female-headed families with children had a significantly lower rate of market poverty in 1999 than in 1989 and—as with all persons—experienced an expansion of the poverty-reducing effect of taxes. At the same time as this poverty-reducing tax effect, however, these families benefited less from means-tested benefits than in prior years. These two effects offset each other to some degree, though the combination of better market outcomes and the EITC effect led to an increase in the reduction effectiveness relative to 1989, although the rate remained 6 percentage points less than in 1979.

Persons in married-couple families with children have the lowest market poverty rates, less than half that of all persons in 1999 (9.0% vs. 19.2%). The expansion of the EITC in the early 1990s clearly reached them as well. In 1989, their rates in columns 1 and 2 are about the same, meaning that, on net, federal and state taxes had little effect on their market poverty rates that year. In 1999, however, their market poverty rate was lowered by 1.4 percentage points. Thus, relative to 1989, persons in these families in 1999 started out with lower poverty rates and were lifted further by favorable tax changes. This pattern more than made up for the decrease in the reduction effectiveness rate that occurred over the 1980s. By 1999, the effectiveness rate for these families rose 15 percentage points, ending up 6 points above its 1979 level.

The increasing prevalence of working poverty

While work in the paid labor market has always been central in debates over poverty policy, this role was reinforced with the passage of welfare reform in 1996. The framers of this policy clearly viewed work as a path out of poverty. Time limits on welfare receipt were introduced so that such benefits would be relegated to a temporary role. Some transitional benefits have been introduced, such as extended health care for parents moving from welfare to work, but, in most cases, receipt of these benefits has been tied to working. Without doubt, the labor market has been cast as the central solution to the problem of poverty.

How realistic is this strategy? How much do the poor work? What do they tend to earn? How have these trends evolved over time? Have the poor responded to welfare reform by increasing their time spent at work? These are the questions we address in this section, and the findings show that the poor have clearly responded to the policy shift toward work. They are working more in the 1990s, and their income is much more dependent on earnings, relative to welfare benefits, than in years past.

We set the context for the analysis by first examining the income of prime-age (family head of household age 25-54), low-income families—those in the bottom 20% of the income distribution—and comparing them to the poor, a subset of this larger group. Through much of this section, we focus on prime-age families, since these are the families we typically expect to be in their working years. Our motivation for looking at both low-income and poor families is because there is much crossover between these two groups. The income of many poor and near-poor families hovers about the poverty threshold, and thus poverty is episodic among those in the bottom fifth.

For most low-income prime-age families, the primary source of family income is the earnings of family members. Government transfers such as welfare benefits and housing subsidies are also important, but, particularly in the era of welfare reform, paid work in the labor market is key to economic well-being. For prime-age poor families, transfers play a larger role. Yet, even for these families, earnings are still the largest component of income, and, with the decline in public assistance benefits in the 1990s, earnings have become significantly more important over time.

Table 5.16 shows the average income, by component, for such families, with public assistance income shown as a sub-component of unearned income. The top two sections refer to families whose incomes place them in the bottom 20%, and the bottom two refer to poor families. In each case, families with children are shown separately. Turning first to all prime-age families in the bottom fifth, note that average family income fell 10.6% over the 1980s and rose 1.4% in the 1990s. Clearly, earnings were the key factor in this reversal of trend over the two decades, as average earnings grew by 7.0% in the 1990s after falling by 10.1% in the 1980s. The public assistance component fell in both periods, but much faster in the 1990s. Thus, the income shares shifted accordingly. In both 1979 and 1989, earnings made up about 75% of the income of those in the bottom fifth. By 1998, that share had grown by about 4 percentage points, which is explained by the 5 point decline in public assistance as a share of income. (Other unearned income sources, such as other cash transfers and interest income, also increased in the 1990s.)

The story is much the same for families with children, though due to their larger earnings gains in the 1990s they experienced an even larger increase (7.3 percentage points) in earnings as a share of total family income.

For poor prime-age families, earnings, as might be expected, are much lower than for all low-income families, and unearned income plays a much larger role (bottom two sections, Table 5.16). However, that role has diminished significantly over time. In 1979, earnings made up 53.6% of income, and unearned income comprised 46.4%. By 1998, by dint of strong earnings gains and the loss of welfare benefits, these shares had shifted to 69.1% from earned income and 30.9% from unearned income. The patterns are similar for poor, prime-age families with children, but while their earnings grew more than for all poor families (20.1% vs. 17.4%), their unearned income fell further, such that their overall income was slightly lower, on average, in 1998 than in 1989.

Figure 5F portrays the significant shift in the composition of income for poor, prime-age families with children. Each bar stacks the three income components shown in the table, and thus each sums to 100%. Note that the earnings share grows slightly from 1979 to 1989, but is much higher still in 1998. Since the "other unearned income" share is relatively constant, the public assistance segment of each bar is successively "squeezed" in each period. This shift is especially notable in the 1998 bar. As the hours data shown next reveal, these earnings gains came largely from working more hours, although poor workers also benefited from the wage gains to low-wage workers in the latter half of the 1990s, as shown in Chapter 2.

We now turn to the question of how much the poor work, and how this has evolved over time. The question is not as simple as is sometimes thought, be-

315

TABLE 5.16 Average income by components, prime-age families, bottom 20% and in poverty, 1979-98 (1998 dollars)

				Change	
	1979	1989	1998	1979-89	1989-98
Low-income (bottom 20%)					
prime-age families				Percent change	
Total	$16,177	$14,461	$14,667	-10.6%	1.4%
Earnings	12,049	10,832	11,589	-10.1	7.0
Unearned income	4,128	3,630	3,078	-12.1	-15.2
Public assistance	1,545	1,294	573	-16.2	-55.7
Other	2,583	2,335	2,505	-9.6	7.3
Shares of total	100.0%	100.0%	100.0%	Percentage-point change	
Earnings	74.5	74.9	79.0	0.4	4.1
Unearned income	25.5	25.1	21.0	-0.4	-4.1
Public assistance	9.6	8.9	3.9	-0.6	-5.0
Other	16.0	16.1	17.1	0.2	0.9
Low-income (bottom 20%)					
prime-age families with children				Percent change	
Total	$14,841	$12,607	$12,615	-15.1%	0.1%
Earnings	10,611	8,797	9,724	-17.1	10.5
Unearned income	4,230	3,809	2,891	-9.9	-24.1
Public assistance	1,960	1,750	785	-10.7	-55.2
Other	2,270	2,059	2,106	-9.3	2.3
Shares of total	100.0%	100.0%	100.0%	Percentage-point change	
Earnings	71.5	69.8	77.1	-1.7	7.3
Unearned income	28.5	30.2	22.9	1.7	-7.3
Public assistance	13.2	13.9	6.2	0.7	-7.7
Other	15.3	16.3	16.7	1.0	0.4
Prime-age poor families				Percent change	
Total	$10,332	$9,651	$9,526	-6.6%	-1.3%
Earnings	5,539	5,608	6,583	1.3	17.4
Unearned income	4,794	4,042	2,943	-15.7	-27.2
Public assistance	2,837	2,267	1,004	-20.1	-55.7
Other	1,956	1,775	1,939	-9.2	9.2
Shares of total	100.0%	100.0%	100.0%	Percentage-point change	
Earnings	53.6	58.1	69.1	4.5	11.0
Unearned income	46.4	41.9	30.9	-4.5	-11.0
Public assistance	27.5	23.5	10.5	-4.0	-12.9
Other	18.9	18.4	20.4	-0.5	2.0

(cont.)

TABLE 5.16 *(cont.)* Average income by components, prime-age families, bottom 20% and in poverty, 1979-98 (1998 dollars)

	1979	1989	1998	Change 1979-89	1989-98
Prime-age poor					
families with children				Percent change	
Total	$10,591	$9,945	$9,821	-6.1%	-1.3%
Earnings	5,668	5,797	6,962	2.3	20.1
Unearned income	4,923	4,148	2,858	-15.7	-31.1
Public assistance	3,018	2,448	1,082	-18.9	-55.8
Other	1,904	1,700	1,777	-10.7	4.5
Shares of total	100.0%	100.0%	100.0%	Percentage-point change	
Earnings	53.5	58.3	70.9	4.8	12.6
Unearned income	46.5	41.7	29.1	-4.8	-12.6
Public assistance	28.5	24.6	11.0	-3.9	-13.6
Other	18.0	17.1	18.1	-0.9	1.0

Source: Authors' analysis of CPS data.

FIGURE 5F Earnings and public assistance as a share of income, poor families with children,* 1979-98

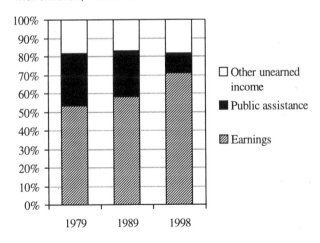

* Families headed by person 25-54 years of age.

Source: Authors' analysis of CPS data.

cause many of the poor are children and elderly and thus typically not expected to work. As we show below, a majority of the able-bodied, prime-age poor do tend to work in a given year, but they also tend to work much less than the comparable non-poor. On the other hand, their work effort, as measured by family work hours (as in Chapter 1), has increased considerably over time, such that the poor are averaging more hours in the workforce in 1998 than in 1979 or 1989. Nevertheless, even with these recent gains, given the wages they command in the low-wage sector (which also rose in the 1990s), poor families will have to vastly expand their hours and earnings if they are to leave working poverty.

In 1998, 49% of the poor were either children (under 18) or elderly (65 and up). As shown in **Table 5.17**, which focuses again on prime-age workers, numerous others were unable to work due to disability or illness. Despite the popular notion that few of the poor work, the table shows that, in 1998, 75.6% of the employable, prime-age poor either worked (70.3%) or sought work (5.3%). But the table also shows that only a minority worked full-time, year-round (25.9% in 1998). The table shows that, of the 11.1 million prime-age poor persons in 1998, 26.5% were not employable due to illness, disability, school, or retirement. Among the rest of the prime-age poor, termed "employable" in the table, slightly less than one-quarter (24.4%) neither sought nor found work in the most recent year, a share that has continuously fallen since 1979. It is true, however, that while the majority of the prime-age poor work, they are significantly more likely to work part time or part year than full time. Here too, though, the trend over time has been toward an increase in the share of full-time, full-year work, from 16.8% in 1979 to 25.9% in 1998.

Table 5.18 turns from the incidence to the intensity of work among the poor, examining the trends in hours worked by poor families. The table examines the trend in annual hours worked by poor families from 1979 to 1998 by summing hours of work across poor families and looking at the share of families in each of four hours categories: no work, 1-999 hours, 1,000-1,999, and 2,000 or more. In addition, we provide the average hours worked (including zeros for families with no time in the paid labor market), the average "family wage" (the average of family earnings divided by family hours for families with positive values of both variables), and the family poverty rate. The so-called "family wage" is not a typical hourly wage measure—unlike the measures shown in Chapter 2, it applies not to a specific person but to a family, wherein one or more persons may have worked at some point during the year in question. We use it here to get a sense of how much more work an average poor family would need to lift its earnings above the poverty threshold.

Some important findings emerge from the analysis. First, a clear minority

TABLE 5.17 Work experience of the poor, 1979-98

	1979*	1989	1998
Number of poor aged 25-54 (thousands)	7,659	9,674	11,108
Not employable (percent)	17.6%	18.4%	26.5%
Ill or disabled	11.7	11.6	19.0
Going to school	5.5	6.3	6.0
Retired	0.4	0.4	1.4
Employable poor aged 25-54	82.4%	81.6%	73.5%
Unable to find work	4.4	6.0	5.3
Employable poor who worked	64.8	65.0	70.3
Year round, full time	16.8	18.0	25.9
Part time or part year	48.0	47.0	44.3
Employable poor who either worked or sought work	69.2	71.0	75.6
Employable poor who neither sought nor found work	30.8	29.0	24.4

*Includes persons 22-54.

Source: U.S. Bureau of the Census, various years.

of poor families works full-time, and, second, the work effort of poor families has increased significantly over the 1990s. Third, the family wage increased in the 1990s, but is still well below the level needed to lift most family types above the poverty threshold. In fact, increased work effort and low-wage gains led to small declines in poverty for most families relative to 1989. However, the long-term decline in low wages has taken its toll on the working poor. Despite considerably more work effort since 1979, the rate of family poverty remains higher than its 1979 level.

The first panel examines all poor families. In 1979, 41.6% did not work at all over the course of the year and 21.3% worked at least 2,000 hours (remember that these hours are pooled across family members, so this could represent one full-time, full-year worker, or some combination of fewer hours by different family members). These shares changed little by 1989, but family poverty rates grew to 10.3% (from 9.2% in 1979). At the same time, average hours grew and the average family wage fell, from $6.76 in 1979 to $5.70 in 1989. At that wage, a family of four would need to work over 2,900 hours to reach the poverty line.

By 1998, however, a new trend had emerged as the distribution of hours worked among the poor families shifted upwards. The share of families working

TABLE 5.18 Family work hours and wages among poor families, 1979-98
(percent of poor families in each category)

	No work	1-999	1,000-1,999	2,000+	Total	Average family hours	Average family wage* (1998 dollars)	Poverty rate
All								
1979	41.6%	21.3%	15.8%	21.3%	100.0%	961	$6.76	9.2%
1989	40.6	19.3	17.6	22.5	100.0	1,002	5.70	10.3
1998	33.7	19.7	19.0	27.6	100.0	1,112	6.16	10.0
Family head 25-54								
1979	32.6%	22.4%	18.6%	26.4%	100.0%	1,169	$6.51	9.0%
1989	34.3	19.4	19.6	26.7	100.0	1,161	5.66	10.5
1998	27.1	19.4	21.0	32.5	100.0	1,273	6.28	10.2
Families with children								
All								
1979	36.1%	22.8%	18.1%	23.0%	100.0%	1,032	$7.07	12.6%
1989	36.5	20.0	18.9	24.5	100.0	1,070	5.83	15.5
1998	26.8	21.4	21.2	30.6	100.0	1,213	6.18	15.1
Female headed								
1979	49.5%	27.3%	15.5%	7.7%	100.0%	515	$6.62	39.6%
1989	50.8	22.7	17.0	9.5	100.0	577	5.55	42.9
1998	34.7	27.3	21.9	16.1	100.0	808	6.45	38.7
By race of family head								
White								
1979	39.1%	20.4%	15.8%	24.7%	100.0%	1,124	$6.31	6.1%
1989	36.9	19.4	18.6	25.1	100.0	1,143	5.40	6.4
1998	34.0	20.7	18.6	26.7	100.0	1,146	6.07	6.2
Black								
1979	46.0%	23.7%	15.6%	14.8%	100.0%	685	$7.60	27.8%
1989	48.1	20.1	16.2	15.6	100.0	723	5.85	27.9
1998	38.0	21.7	20.0	20.3	100.0	875	6.11	23.2
Hispanic								
1979	42.5%	18.7%	15.8%	23.0%	100.0%	943	$6.81	20.3%
1989	36.2	16.8	17.2	29.7	100.0	1,155	6.10	23.4
1998	27.9	15.2	18.7	38.2	100.0	1,331	6.48	22.7

* "Family wage" is the average of family earnings divided by family hours, calculated only for those families with positive values of both variables. The "average family hours" tabulations include zeros.

Source: Authors' analysis of CPS data.

no hours fell by 6.9 percentage points, and the share working at least 2,000 hours grew by 5.1 points. Average hours worked increased by over 100. At the same time, the family wage increased and poverty fell slightly, from 10.3% to 10.0%. However, compared to 1979, the share of poor families was larger yet working harder and earning less. Prime-age poor families were more likely to work more hours in any of the time periods in the table (their share with no hours is smaller than that for all families in each year), and their shift toward more work was larger as well. In 1979, 45.0% of poor, prime-age families worked at least 1,000 hours; by 1998, that share had climbed to 53.5%. Yet, here again, poverty rates were higher in 1998 than in 1979.

The next two sections of the table are for families with children, with single-mother families shown separately. In 1979 and 1989, more than a third of poor families with children did not work at all, but this share fell to about one-fourth in 1998. Conversely, the share of families with children working at least 2,000 hours grew from 24.5% in 1989 to 30.6% in 1998. Average hours and the family wage also increased significantly.

The lack of work effort in the paid labor market is quite conspicuous for single-mother families—in 1979, only 7.7% worked at least 2,000 hours. This is not unexpected, given their lack of resources and the fact that single mothers bear sole child care responsibilities. Poverty rates are highest for this group, hovering about 40% over the three years shown in the table, and their average hours are by far lowest. Yet, in response to the tight labor market and to welfare reform, these poor mothers have seen large decreases in the "no work" category and large increases in the other three categories. Note that in 1979 and 1989, half of these families did not work at all. By 1998, that share had fallen to 34.7%, the share in the 2,000+ category had more than doubled (relative to 1979), and the poverty rate had fallen as well. Nevertheless, given the average family wage of $6.45 in 1998, and the fact that the poverty threshold that year for a single-parent with two children was $13,133, family work hours would need to reach 2,036 for the family to climb over the poverty line. (Including the value of the EITC would reduce the needed number of hours worked, but, even with the wage subsidy, a single mother with two children would still have to double her hours worked in 1998 to reach the poverty line.)

The next three sections of the table examine hours of work by the race/ethnicity of the head of the family. While poor white and Hispanic families clearly have the highest levels of hours worked, the increase in hours in the 1990s and the decline in family poverty rates were greatest among minority families. The share of families in the "no work" category fell 5.1 percentage points for white families, compared to 7.9 and 14.7 percentage points for black and Hispanic families. At the other end of the distribution, the shift into at least

2,000 hours was highest among poor minorities. Here again it is clear that, despite consistent gains over the 1990s, the family wage for each of the three groups is poverty level.

The low-wage labor market: workers' characteristics and earnings

The above analysis, along with the thrust in poverty policy toward work in the paid labor market, have raised the visibility and importance of the low-wage labor market. As poor families increase their labor supply, this is where they will start out. And given the relatively low rates of mobility that analysts have found to prevail in this sector for workers who lack a college education, this is where many will remain for at least part of their careers. In this final section, we examine the characteristics of those working in the low-wage labor market in 1999 and how the wages and annual earnings of low-wage workers have evolved over time.

The next two figures show that even some workers with full-time, year-round labor force attachment earn poverty-level wages. The figures, derived from analysis done by the Census Bureau, focus on prime-age persons who spent at least 50 weeks of the year at work or looking for work (i.e., in the labor force). They must have worked full time or else part time but involuntarily, yet their annual earnings were not high enough to reach the poverty line for a family of four, which in 1998 was $15,208 (this threshold is based on the CPI-U-X1).

Figure 5G charts the share of these workers, by sex, for the period 1974-98. The trend shows a secular increase in the proportion earning poverty-level wages. This is particularly the case for men, whose share has grown by 5 percentage points since 1974. Although the proportion of male low-wage workers grew over the full period, the figure shows that the steepest growth was post-1979, when the wages of males with low earnings fell most steeply (see Chapter 2). For women, the share of low earners hovered around 25% for the full period; by 1998, 23.7% of prime-age female workers (8.1 million) earned poverty-level wages.

Since the wages of low-wage workers increased significantly in the latter half of the 1990s, we would expect to see improvement in this indicator as well. In fact, after rising through 1995, the share of prime-age, low earners fell for both men and women by 1998. For female workers (and job seekers), these gains returned their share back to its level at the last business cycle peak (23.8%), but males still remained 0.8 percentage points above their 1989 level.

Figure 5H focuses on low earners (again, with full labor-force attachment) in families with children; female-headed families are shown separately. Note

FIGURE 5G Prime-age workers with low earnings
and full-time/year-round attachment, 1974-98

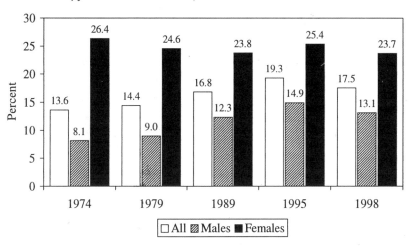

Source: U.S. Bureau of the Census (1992) and unpublished data.

that this group of workers is worse off than those shown in the previous figure (compare the levels in the bars marked "All"), suggesting that families with children have a lower standard of living than the population of all prime-age workers. Families with children that are headed by a female are particularly likely to face low earnings; in 1998, close to two-fifths of fully attached workers in these families earned poverty-level wages. Between 1974 and 1979, the share of low-earner single mothers fell, from 37.5% to 34.4%. This share remained flat over the 1980s and then rose through 1995. Unlike the groups examined in the prior graph, these women did not see much improvement over the latter 1990s.

Table 5.19 looks at the demographic characteristics of low-wage workers compared to those of the overall workforce in 1999. Low-wage workers, in column 1, are defined as those whose hourly wage is less than the wage that would lift a family of four just up to the poverty line in 1999: $8.19 per hour.

This group's average wage in 1999 was $6.41, slightly above the family wage earned by poor families in 1998 but still 22% below the poverty-level wage. Comparing the percentages in the two columns reveals categories in which low-wage workers are overrepresented. Such workers are disproportionately female, minority, non-college educated, and young. They also are more likely to work in low-wage industries such as retail trade and less likely to work in manu-

FIGURE 5H Workers in families with children, with low earnings and full-time/year-round attachment, 1974-98

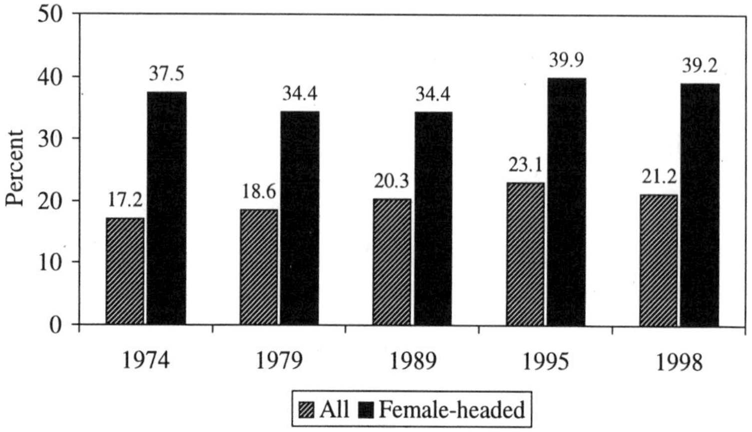

Source: U.S. Bureau of the Census (1992) and unpublished data.

facturing, transportation and utilities, finance, and government (interestingly, the share of low-wage workers in the services industry is about the same as the overall share, due to the varied nature of the occupations within this industry, such as security guards and lawyers). By occupation, low-wage workers are overrepresented in services, where they staff the low-paying jobs, such as cashiers in the retail sector, or home health aides in health services. They are least likely to be managers and professionals. Finally, they are significantly less likely to either be union members or covered by union contracts.

Table 5.20 examines the annualized percentage changes in inflation-adjusted hourly wage levels of the poorest male and female workers (those in the bottom 30% of the hourly earnings distribution). Here again we break the 1990s into two parts with distinctly different trends, 1989-95 and 1995-99. Male low wages fell considerably before 1989 and increased little over the 1990s overall. As shown below, by 1999 even the 20th percentile male wage ended up slightly below the poverty-level wage for a family of four. With the exception of the 10th percentile in the 1980s (due mostly to the sharp fall in the minimum wage over this period—see Chapter 2), female low wages increased more than men's, though women's wage levels were consistently lower. Only in the 1990s did the female 20th percentile wage surpass the male 10th percentile.

For low-wage men between 1973 and 1979, there were small negative

TABLE 5.19 Characteristics of low-wage workers, 1999

	Low wage*	Total
Share of total	26.8%	100.0%
Number	30,302,348	113,093,330
Average wage	$6.41	$14.86
Gender		
Male	40.2%	52.1%
Female	59.8	47.9
Race		
White	61.4%	72.7%
Black	15.7	11.9
Hispanic	18.5	11.0
Other	4.4	4.4
Education		
Less than high school	23.9%	10.8%
High school	38.8	32.3
Some college	24.2	21.0
Associate degree	5.7	8.6
College or more	7.5	27.3
Age		
18-25	36.3%	17.1%
26-35	22.8	26.0
35 and older	40.9	56.9
Industry		
Services	36.4%	36.2%
Retail trade	32.1	15.8
Manufacuring	11.5	16.8
Construction	4.0	5.8
Transportation, utilities	4.0	7.7
Finance	3.7	6.6
Other	3.3	1.9
Wholesale trade	3.0	3.9
Government	1.9	5.1
Occupation		
Services	30.2%	13.4%
Blue collar	25.3	25.6
Technical, sales	17.0	14.5
Clerical	15.0	15.1
Managers, professionals	9.1	29.9
Others	3.4	1.5
Union		
*Union***	6.7%	15.8%
Non-union	93.3	84.2

* Low wage refers to hourly wage rate necessary to lift a family of four above the poverty line with full-time, full-year work. In 1999, this comes to $8.19.
** Union includes members and workers covered by union contracts.

Source: Authors' analysis of CPS ORG data.

TABLE 5.20 Changes in hourly wages of low-wage workers, 1973-99

	10th	20th	30th
Males			
1973-79	-1.3%	-2.3%	-0.3%
1979-89	-12.7	-13.9	-12.1
1989-99	2.8	1.3	0.0
1989-95	-6.4	-5.5	-8.5
1995-99	9.8	7.2	9.3
Females			
1973-79	21.3%	5.9%	2.3%
1979-89	-18.2	-7.0	-0.9
1989-99	10.9	6.5	6.3
1989-95	1.6	-1.6	-0.7
1995-99	9.1	8.2	7.0

Source: Authors' analysis of CPS ORG data.

changes in the bottom three-tenths. For low-wage women, 1973-79 was a period of strong growth, particularly among the lowest-wage female workers, as the 10th percentile female wage grew 21.3%. This pattern of gains or small losses reversed, however, between 1979 and 1989, as all groups in the bottom 30% experienced real wage declines. Men in particular (and the lowest-earning women) experienced the steepest losses, 12.7%, 13.9%, and 12.1% in the first, second, and third deciles.

In the 1990s, however, these trends reversed, and, as shown in the last two rows, the gains came almost exclusively in the latter part of the decade. In fact, as pointed out in Chapter 2, the wage gains of the latter 1990s were particularly strong at the low end of the labor market. Note, for example, the 9.8% and 9.1% gains from 1995 to 1999, in the hourly wage of 10th percentile male and female workers. What's more, the rates of increase were fairly uniform across the bottom three deciles for both genders.

Figure 5I shows the trend in the 20th percentile wage, in 1999 dollars, relative to the 1999 poverty-level wage ($8.19; see Table 5.19), and it puts the late 1990s positive trend in historical context. Clearly, female wages at the 20th percentile have at no time in the period been near the poverty-level wage. Male 20th percentile wages, however, were well above the poverty-level wage at the beginning of the period, though their erosion over the 1980s has left them slightly below it by the end of the period, even with the recent growth. Nevertheless, this

FIGURE 5I Real hourly wages of low-wage workers (1999 dollars)

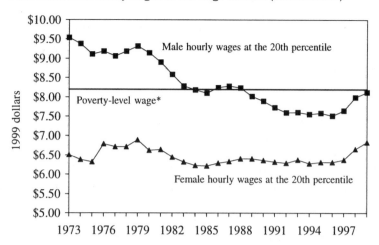

* $8.19 is the wage level that, at full-time, full-year work, would lift a family of four above the poverty line ($17,028 in 1999 dollars).

Source: Authors' analysis of CPS data.

reversal of wage decline experienced by low-wage workers in the latter 1990s, along with the increase in work, certainly helps explain the decline in poverty rates over this period.

Conclusion

Despite long economic recoveries over the 1980s and 1990s, it was not until 1999 that the poverty rate finally fell below its 1989 level. This chapter examines a variety of explanations as to why it took so long for poverty rates to respond to the recoveries of the 1980s and 1990s. In doing so, we paid particular attention to the latter half of the 1990s, since various changes in both the economic and policy landscapes have made this a unique period. In these years, the labor market tightened up, finally giving a boost to the earnings of low-wage workers. At the same time, the poor significantly expanded their hours of work in the paid labor market, due both to the strong economy and the welfare-to-work component of welfare reform. The result was some diminution of the poverty rate, both overall and particularly for minorities.

Yet it took many years for these gains against poverty to materialize as the progress of the poor was held back by numerous factors. First, though there was a clear increase in hours worked by poor families, their level of hours remains low compared to non-poor families, such as those highlighted in Chapter 1. Second, even with the growth rates in low wages generated by the tight labor market and minimum wage increases of the 1990s, the wage levels of the poor are still too low to lift them above the poverty threshold, even were they to vastly increase their hours of work. And it is equally important to note that, due to policy changes that have reduced cash welfare benefits, the income of the poor is much more dependent on earnings now than in the past.

Thus, antipoverty policy has clearly emphasized the importance of work as a pathway out of poverty, and the poor have responded. While this policy emphasis no doubt reflects American values regarding the integrity of work and public distaste for dependence on government support by low-income families, it is clear that the poor will need further supports to increase their pre-tax wages, their post-tax earnings, and their hours of work. The latter 1990s have demonstrated that tight labor markets and minimum wage increases help, as did the expansion in the EITC. Regarding hours, the expansion of subsidies that facilitate and encourage work, such as child care, transportation, and job training, are also needed. In the absence of these policies, we cannot realistically expect the poor to work their way out of poverty alone.

CHAPTER 6

Regional analysis: variation across the country

Most of the analysis up to this point has looked at the nation as a whole. This chapter looks specifically at regions, divisions (i.e., groups of states within regions), and states, a focus that is particularly important given the recent devolution of some important economic and social policies to the state and local level. The most prominent example is welfare reform, but other wage and income policies, such as state-level earned income tax credits, state minimum wages, and municipal living wage ordinances have also become much more common in recent years. As policy decisions and analyses have devolved to the state and local levels, geographically specific data are needed to better understand and evaluate the impact of these changes.

In general, the trends in states and regions mirror those at the national level: many states have experienced lower unemployment and higher real wage growth in the mid- to late 1990s compared to earlier periods. But there is a great deal of regional variation as well.

For example, Midwesterners and Southerners experienced many of the positive economic developments of the 1990s more so than did people in the Northeast and West, where median family incomes were slightly lower and poverty was considerably higher in 1998 than in 1989. Similarly, while national unemployment rates fell more quickly in the 1990s than in the 1980s, the largest declines were concentrated in the Midwest and South. Unemployment rates in the nation's most populous states, California and New York, were higher in 1999 than 1989. Moreover, in the 1990s wage growth for middle- and low-wage workers in these two states, where about 20% of the population resides, started later and was smaller than for similar workers in the rest of the country.

Due to the limited nature of the regional data, some of this examination will cover slightly different time periods than the discussions in earlier chapters. Also, in cases where sufficient data is not available for each and every state, we restrict the examination to the region or division level.

Median family income grows in Midwest and South

As discussed in Chapter 1, the income of the median family (the family at the midpoint of the family income distribution) is a key indicator of the economic well-being of the typical family. **Figure 6A** and **Table 6.1** show the levels (in 1998 dollars) and growth rates, in every region, of the income of the median family. The analysis shows that, over the past 25 years, income growth has slowed overall and become somewhat more varied between regions.

Between 1953 and 1973, inflation-adjusted median family income for the nation grew 2.8% annually. Most regions experienced similar growth rates over this period, with the exception of the South, where median family income grew 3.5% annually, outpacing the national growth rate by 0.7 percentage points. As Figure 6A shows, the level of the median family's income has been consistently lower in the South, and (as shown in tables that follow) the South has lower wage levels and higher poverty levels than other regions. Nevertheless, the median income gap between the South and the nation closed considerably over the 1953-73 period, from 22% to 12%. Since then this gap has remained roughly constant, with the South about 10% below the national level. (Note also that these dollars are deflated using a national deflator; since the cost of living is lower in the South, a regional-specific deflator would reduce the differences between the South and other regions.)

As the figure and table show, the Northeast region pulled away from the pack over the 1980s, due at least in part to the boom in the financial sector, which is most heavily concentrated in the Northeast. During that decade, while the income of the median family in the other regions was growing at historically moderate rates, the income of families in the Northeast was growing more than three times faster. By the peak of the 1980s business cycle, the income of the median Northeast family was 29% higher than that of the median family in the South and 11% above that of the median family in the West.

However, the median family in the Northeast lost ground the fastest during the recession of the early 1990s (although the West was a close second). As noted in Chapter 2, the fact that white-collar workers were uncharacteristically vulnerable in that recession is probably to blame for the sharp Northeastern decline. While median family income began to trend upward for other regions in about 1993, income growth was falling or flat in the Northeast through 1995.

TABLE 6.1 Median family income by region (1998 dollars)

Year	U.S.	Northeast	Midwest	South	West
1953	$23,843	$25,715	$25,765	$18,593	$25,850
1973	41,617	44,376	44,310	36,699	43,064
1979	43,144	45,424	45,312	38,657	45,572
1989	44,974	51,902	45,499	40,091	46,926
1998	46,737	50,567	49,552	42,711	46,819
Annual growth rates					
1953-73	2.8%	2.8%	2.7%	3.5%	2.6%
1973-79	0.6	0.4	0.4	0.9	0.9
1979-89	0.4	1.3	0.0	0.4	0.3
1989-98	0.4	-0.3	1.0	0.7	0.0

Source: U.S. Bureau of the Census, income web site.

FIGURE 6A Median family income growth, by region, 1953-98

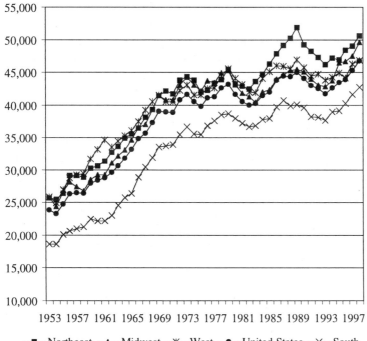

Source: U.S. Bureau of the Census, income web site.

331

By 1998, the last year of available data, the median family in the Northeast was still $1,335 dollars (2.6%) below its 1989 peak. The median Western family also failed to regain its 1989 level.

While families in the Northeast and West experienced declining and flat income growth, respectively, in the 1990s, the Midwest rebounded, with median income growing more quickly over this 1990s business cycle than over the prior two periods. The strong growth of jobs, many of which were in relatively high-paying sectors like manufacturing, was partly responsible for this turnaround in the Midwest, although this trend in manufacturing job growth reversed in the later 1990s. Income growth in the South also accelerated.

Table 6.2 shows the trend in median family income for four-person families by state for the period 1974-98. (This data series is unavailable prior to 1974.) By controlling for family size, the data in this table address the argument advanced by some analysts that, since family size has declined over time, income trends overstate recent income losses (see Chapter 1 for a discussion of this issue).

Income growth for the median four-person family was fairly uniform across states in the 1970s, although some of the oil-rich states in the West South Central division appear to have benefited from the rise in energy prices. Growth was both slower and less uniform in the 1980s: as suggested by the regional results above, a number of Northeastern states experienced faster-than-average income growth, while some of the Southwestern states saw their fortunes reverse as the growth in energy prices tapered off.

Nationally, the median income of four-person families grew a total of 4.6% from 1989 to 1998. Annualized, family income grew 0.3 percentage points more slowly in the 1990s than in the 1980s. Real median income actually fell in the largest coastal states in the 1990s—by 0.1% per year in New York and 0.2% in California—and grew slowly in some other populous states (e.g., Massachusetts, at 0.1% per year). Most Midwestern states, such as Indiana, Illinois, Minnesota, and Iowa, experienced an acceleration of income growth in the 1990s over the previous decade. Many Southern states also experienced growth rates that outpaced the national growth rate of 0.5%. Texas experienced a notable turnaround in the 1990s, with incomes growing at an annual rate of 1.2% and making up much (though not all) of the ground lost over the 1980s.

In the context of some of the analysis that follows, Arizona is an interesting case. Median family income fell slightly there over the 1990s and, as shown below, inequality grew steeply, yet at the same time job growth was robust and unemployment fell. Demographic trends probably played a role, as both low-wage immigrants and higher income seniors have increased as a share of the population there. But this disparate pattern of positive job growth, negative median income growth, and increases in inequality underscores the importance of using a variety of economic criteria to evaluate a state's economic progress. In the case of Arizona, these data suggest that job growth is not the only criterion by which to judge a state or locality's labor market; job *quality* also matters.

The growth of income inequality by state

While Chapter 1 focused on the growth of family income inequality at the national level, here we examine the same phenomenon at the state level. The metric we use is the ratio of the average income of the most well-off families to that of the least well-off. Specifically, we compare the average income of the top fifth to that of the bottom fifth (**Table 6.3**) and, for 11 states for which data are available, the top 5% to the bottom fifth (Table 6.4). In order to generate large enough samples to make reliable comparisons, we pooled three years of data from successive economic peak periods: 1978-1980, 1988-1990, and 1996-1998.

As shown in Chapter 1, national family income inequality increased over the 1980s and 1990s. The data in Table 6.3 show that, in the late 1970s, families in the top fifth earned, on average, 7.4 times that of families in the bottom fifth. By the end of the period covered in the table—the late 1990s—that ratio had increased to 10.6. Comparing the top 5% to the bottom fifth at the national level (Table 6.4), the ratio grew from 11.0 to 18.3.

Inequality grew in almost every state in the 1980s and in most states in the 1990s (note that for most states changes in these ratios of less than 1 are statistically insignificant; for larger states, changes greater than 0.5 points tend to be significant). By 1997, the midpoint of the last group of years, only one state (Alaska, which is frequently a statistical outlier) had a lower inequality ratio than in 1979.

National trends tend to be driven by the most populous states. Over the 1980s, the top-fifth/bottom-fifth ratio grew 2.6 points in New York and 2.3 points in California. In two large Midwestern states, Illinois and Michigan, inequality also grew by more than 2 points over the 1980s.

Among Southern states, inequality grew considerably faster than the national average in the District of Columbia (which also tends to be an outlier in this type of research) and Louisiana.

Nationally, this measure of inequality grew a bit more slowly in the 1990s (on a per-year basis, the growth rates were 0.19 in the 1980s and 0.16 in the 1990s). Inequality continued to grow in most states in the 1990s, with faster growth in New York (especially considering the shorter time period). By the end of the period, the average income of the richest fifth of New York families was

TABLE 6.2 Median income for four-person families, by state, 1974-98 (1998 dollars)

	1974	1979	1989	1998	Annual growth rates 1974-79	1979-89	1989-98
NORTHEAST							
New England							
Maine	$39,422	$39,812	$50,393	$51,059	0.2%	2.4%	0.1%
New Hampshire	43,925	49,197	63,074	61,014	2.3	2.5	-0.4
Vermont	41,284	42,543	53,103	53,691	0.6	2.2	0.1
Massachusetts	49,088	52,393	68,091	68,958	1.3	2.7	0.1
Rhode Island	45,238	47,658	56,890	62,339	1.0	1.8	1.0
Connecticut	51,745	53,768	70,081	75,534	0.8	2.7	0.8
Middle Atlantic							
New York	$47,641	$46,437	$57,435	$57,142	-0.5%	2.1%	-0.1%
New Jersey	52,534	54,275	69,970	70,983	0.7	2.6	0.2
Pennsylvania	45,505	49,151	53,112	58,507	1.6	0.8	1.1
MIDWEST							
East North Central							
Ohio	$47,490	$49,622	$54,512	$60,169	0.9%	0.9%	1.1%
Indiana	45,470	49,812	50,216	55,284	1.8	0.1	1.1
Illinois	51,350	53,449	56,010	61,672	0.8	0.5	1.1
Michigan	50,797	53,794	56,294	59,019	1.2	0.5	0.5
Wisconsin	48,360	51,803	53,313	57,890	1.4	0.3	0.9
West North Central							
Minnesota	$49,597	$53,766	$55,689	$67,140	1.6%	0.4%	2.1%
Iowa	45,134	49,708	48,290	53,230	1.9	-0.3	1.1
Missouri	43,247	46,904	50,580	54,190	1.6	0.8	0.8
North Dakota	47,126	42,997	45,753	51,002	-1.8	0.6	1.2
South Dakota	40,276	42,312	43,154	49,702	1.0	0.2	1.6
Nebraska	41,972	45,704	49,823	56,692	1.7	0.9	1.4
Kansas	45,210	50,327	49,870	55,341	2.2	-0.1	1.2
SOUTH							
South Atlantic							
Delaware	$ 47,835	$46,662	$56,248	$65,157	-0.5%	1.9%	1.6%
Maryland	52,292	54,376	65,916	71,404	0.8	1.9	0.9
District of Columbia	47,402	46,940	53,335	60,674	-0.2	1.3	1.4
Virginia	47,518	50,609	59,272	60,860	1.3	1.6	0.3
West Virginia	39,475	41,578	41,816	43,239	1.0	0.1	0.4
North Carolina	41,403	43,279	50,041	54,331	0.9	1.5	0.9
South Carolina	41,001	44,393	47,471	52,111	1.6	0.7	1.0
Georgia	42,920	47,530	52,606	55,989	2.1	1.0	0.7
Florida	46,444	45,722	49,162	52,581	-0.3	0.7	0.7
East South Central							
Kentucky	$39,302	$42,155	$45,206	$49,108	1.4%	0.7%	0.9%
Tennessee	40,163	42,814	45,853	50,310	1.3	0.7	1.0
Alabama	40,216	40,999	45,916	51,156	0.4	1.1	1.2
Mississippi	36,312	38,926	42,459	43,907	1.4	0.9	0.4

(cont.)

TABLE 6.2 *(cont.)* Median income for four-person families, by state, 1974-98 (1998 dollars)

	1974	1979	1989	1998	1974-79	1979-89	1989-98
					Annual growth rates		
SOUTH *(cont.)*							
West South Central							
Arkansas	$37,342	$40,735	$41,871	$44,471	1.8%	0.3%	0.7%
Louisiana	39,572	44,420	45,227	49,037	2.3	0.2	0.9
Oklahoma	39,714	45,931	45,311	47,436	3.0	-0.1	0.5
Texas	43,730	51,578	45,979	51,148	3.4	-1.1	1.2
WEST							
Mountain							
Montana	$42,983	$44,166	$44,538	$44,737	0.5%	0.1%	0.0%
Idaho	44,205	44,999	44,211	49,174	0.4	-0.2	1.2
Wyoming	46,585	49,942	46,823	50,989	1.4	-0.6	1.0
Colorado	49,085	55,570	52,929	63,428	2.5	-0.5	2.0
New Mexico	38,137	46,327	40,955	43,829	4.0	-1.2	0.8
Arizona	47,832	50,662	50,408	49,397	1.2	-0.1	-0.2
Utah	43,979	46,807	48,061	54,946	1.3	0.3	1.5
Nevada	48,231	56,074	52,235	53,054	3.1	-0.7	0.2
Pacific							
Washington	$48,369	$53,768	$54,852	$61,059	2.1%	0.2%	1.2%
Oregon	47,151	52,933	50,902	55,892	2.3	-0.4	1.0
California	50,034	55,308	56,278	55,209	2.0	0.2	-0.2
Alaska	60,828	68,365	63,637	59,726	2.4	-0.7	-0.7
Hawaii	53,608	54,147	59,137	61,838	0.2	0.9	0.5
TOTAL U.S.	$46,315	$49,330	$53,584	$56,061	1.3%	0.8%	0.5%

Source: Authors' analysis of U.S. Bureau of the Census, income web site.

14.1 times that of the poorest families in that state. The Southwestern states of New Mexico and Arizona also saw relatively fast growth in inequality over the 1990s, and ended the period with ratios of 12.8 and 13.1, respectively, among the highest in the country. As noted above, the migration into these states of low-wage immigrants and wealthy seniors may have played a role in these patterns of inequality.

Table 6.4 looks at the gap between the income of the top 5% of families and those in the bottom 20% for the most populous states (for which these data can be most reliably computed). Even before family inequality began its upward climb over the 1980s and 1990s, the average income of the top 5% was at least nine times that of the bottom 20% in most of these states. Over the 1980s, this measure of disparity grew by 3.5 points nationally, led by California (4.4), New

335

TABLE 6.3 Income inequality by state: average income of top 20% relative to bottom 20%

	Income ratio, top 20%/lowest 20%			Changes (top 20%/lowest 20%)	
	1978-80	1988-90	1996-98	Late 1970s-Late 1980s	Late 1980s-Late 1990s
NORTHEAST					
New England					
Maine	6.6	7.6	8.1	1.0	0.5
New Hampshire	5.6	6.9	8.8	1.3	1.9
Vermont	6.4	7.4	8.4	1.0	1.0
Massachusetts	7.0	8.6	10.2	1.6	1.6
Rhode Island	6.3	7.2	11.8	0.9	4.6
Connecticut	6.1	6.2	9.9	0.1	3.7
Middle Atlantic					
New York	7.8	10.4	14.1	2.6	3.7
New Jersey	7.0	8.1	9.5	1.1	1.4
Pennsylvania	6.4	7.9	9.4	1.5	1.6
MIDWEST					
East North Central					
Ohio	6.4	8.3	9.7	1.9	1.4
Indiana	5.8	7.9	7.3	2.1	-0.5
Illinois	7.5	9.6	9.6	2.1	0.0
Michigan	6.6	8.9	9.2	2.3	0.3
Wisconsin	6.1	6.4	8.2	0.3	1.8
West North Central					
Minnesota	6.1	7.7	8.8	1.7	1.1
Iowa	5.7	6.5	7.4	0.8	0.9
Missouri	6.9	8.9	9.0	1.9	0.1
North Dakota	7.3	6.8	7.9	-0.4	1.1
South Dakota	7.3	7.3	9.0	0.0	1.7
Nebraska	6.6	7.0	8.4	0.4	1.3
Kansas	6.0	7.0	9.8	1.0	2.8
SOUTH					
South Atlantic					
Delaware	6.6	6.7	8.7	0.1	1.9
Maryland	6.9	7.8	9.2	0.8	1.4
District of Columbia	12.1	16.4	27.1	4.3	10.6
Virginia	7.4	9.1	10.7	1.8	1.5
West Virginia	6.5	8.8	10.4	2.4	1.6
North Carolina	7.2	8.4	10.0	1.2	1.7
South Carolina	7.9	9.3	8.7	1.4	-0.7
Georgia	8.1	10.3	10.6	2.2	0.3
Florida	7.9	9.1	10.6	1.2	1.5
East South Central					
Kentucky	7.1	9.1	11.1	1.9	2.0
Tennessee	8.1	10.3	9.3	2.2	-1.1
Alabama	9.0	9.8	10.6	0.8	0.8
Mississippi	8.9	10.9	10.3	2.1	-0.7

(cont.)

TABLE 6.3 *(cont.)* Income inequality by state: average income of top 20% relative to bottom 20%

	Income ratio, top 20%/lowest 20%			Changes (top 20%/lowest 20%)	
	1978-80	1988-90	1996-98	Late 1970s-Late 1980s	Late 1980s-Late 1990s
SOUTH *(cont.)*					
West South Central					
Arkansas	8.6	9.3	9.2	0.7	-0.1
Louisiana	9.1	15.6	12.0	6.5	-3.6
Oklahoma	7.7	9.4	10.0	1.7	0.5
Texas	8.6	10.3	11.6	1.7	1.3
WEST					
Mountain					
Montana	7.7	7.2	9.3	-0.5	2.1
Idaho	6.3	7.1	8.5	0.9	1.3
Wyoming	5.6	6.9	8.2	1.3	1.3
Colorado	6.8	8.5	8.1	1.8	-0.5
New Mexico	8.5	10.5	12.8	2.0	2.2
Arizona	7.3	9.2	13.1	1.9	3.9
Utah	6.0	6.0	6.9	0.0	0.9
Nevada	6.5	6.9	8.5	0.5	1.5
Pacific					
Washington	7.2	7.0	9.2	-0.2	2.2
Oregon	6.4	7.0	11.2	0.6	4.2
California	7.6	9.8	11.9	2.3	2.1
Alaska	9.3	9.6	8.1	0.4	-1.5
Hawaii	7.0	9.1	9.8	2.1	0.7
TOTAL U.S.	7.4	9.3	10.6	1.9	1.3

Source: Economic Policy Institute/Center on Budget and Policy Priorities' analysis of data from the U.S. Census Bureau's Current Population Survey.

York (4.3), and Illinois (4.1). In contrast to the trends observed in the previous table, this measure of extreme inequality grew faster in the 1990s than in the 1980s, suggesting that income became more concentrated among the very top-earning families in the 1990s relative to the 1980s. By the end of the period the wealthiest families in New York, Texas, and California had average incomes at least 20 times that of the lowest-income families.

TABLE 6.4 Inequality ratio: top 5% to bottom 20%, 11 most populous states

| | Income ratio, top 5%/lowest 20% | | | Changes (top 5%/lowest 20%) | |
	1978-80	1988-90	1996-98	Late 1970s-late 1980s	Late 1980s-late 1990s
Massachusetts	10.2	13.0	16.8	2.8	3.7
New York	11.8	16.1	25.0	4.3	8.9
New Jersey	10.0	12.4	15.7	2.4	3.3
Pennsylvania	9.1	12.0	16.4	2.9	4.3
Ohio	9.4	12.8	16.6	3.5	3.8
Illinois	11.1	15.2	15.9	4.1	0.7
Michigan	9.4	13.0	15.3	3.6	2.3
North Carolina	11.1	13.5	16.9	2.3	3.4
Florida	11.7	14.6	18.2	2.9	3.6
Texas	13.5	15.6	20.1	2.1	4.5
California	11.2	15.5	20.5	4.4	4.9
TOTAL U.S.	11.0	14.5	18.3	3.5	3.8

Source: Economic Policy Institute/Center on Budget and Policy Priorities' analysis of data from the U.S. Census Bureau's Current Population Survey.

Trends in employment and unemployment and their impact on wage growth

The relationship between falling unemployment and wage growth, examined throughout the book, can be investigated in detail by looking at the differing patterns of growth between states. Various findings emerge from the data that follow. First, the regional pattern of job growth was different in the 1990s than in the 1980s, with the most recent period favoring the Midwest. Second, though unemployment fell in many states in the 1980s, few states experienced positive wage growth for low- or middle-wage workers. In the 1990s, however, falling unemployment rates were much more closely associated with real wage gains, particularly for low-wage workers. The difference is in part attributable to (1) the deeper fall in unemployment in most states in the 1990s than in the 1980s, and (2) the two minimum wage increases implemented in the 1990s, compared to none in the 1980s.

Employment and unemployment: When analysts seek to characterize a state or local labor market, two of the most commonly referenced indicators are the unemployment rate and the rate of job growth. This section examines the trends in these key variables and the extent to which these indicators correlate with wage growth. The data reveal that, while falling unemployment rates and strong job growth are positively correlated with rising wages, the relationship is more complex than that, with other factors, such as the real value of the minimum wage and the quality of new jobs, playing a role as well.

Table 6.5 shows non-farm payroll employment (in thousands) by state for the 30-year period 1969-99, along with the percent change in employment growth for the three decades. Employment grew by about 58 million jobs over the full period, but growth rates varied considerably by region and time period. As noted in Chapter 3, employment growth was fastest in the 1970s, particularly in the West, where payrolls grew by almost half (47.7%). Employment growth in the relatively large Pacific states of California (39.4%) and Washington (41.2%) was notably faster than the average national growth rate (27.6%). At the same time, the experience of some of the large Eastern states, like New York (no growth), New Jersey (17.8%), and Massachusetts (15.7%), was below average.

During the 1980s, employment growth slowed in each region except the Northeast. The loss of manufacturing jobs in the Midwest slowed job growth by half—from 20.3% to 10.0%—in that region relative to the prior business cycle (manufacturing payrolls fell by 16% in Michigan and 18% in Illinois over the 1980s—data not shown). Job growth was less than 10% in Michigan and Illinois, and, relative to the 1970s, job growth in Wisconsin slowed by 14.4 percentage points. Growth accelerated, however, in New York and New Jersey as the service sector expanded in those states. A number of Southern states experienced above-average employment growth, but (as shown below) most did not experience corresponding wage growth.

The nation's payrolls added 21 million jobs between 1989 and 1999 and employment grew by 19.2%. Employment growth in the 1990s was relatively flat, however, in the Northeast. After growing by 15.9% over the 1980s, Northeastern payrolls grew by 4.1% in the 1990s, less than one-fourth the growth rate of the nation. The largest state in this region, New York, did not begin to add jobs until 1994, and, over the 1989-99 period, jobs grew there at a rate of 1.6%.

Job growth picked up steam in the 1990s in the Midwest, as manufacturing employment expanded in the early part of the recovery and services grew throughout the decade. Growth rates roughly doubled in most states in the larger East North Central division, e.g., in Illinois and Michigan. Some Western states, particularly those in the Mountain division, enjoyed particularly strong rates of growth. Other than Wyoming, each state in that division experienced growth rates far faster than the national rate of 19.2%.

State unemployment rates for 1979-99 are shown in **Table 6.6**. Over the 1980s, national unemployment rates fell by one-half a percentage point, from 5.8% to 5.3%. The largest declines occurred in the Northeast region, particu-

TABLE 6.5 Non-farm payroll employment, by state, 1969-99, in thousands

	1969	1979	1989	1999	Percentage change 69-79	79-89	89-99
NORTHEAST	18,651	20,407	23,644	24,612	9.4%	15.9%	4.1%
New England	4,525	5,394	6,569	6,829	19.2	21.8	4.0
Maine	330	416	542	584	26.0	30.3	7.8
New Hampshire	259	379	529	598	46.0	39.8	13.0
Vermont	146	198	262	291	36.0	32.3	11.3
Massachusetts	2,249	2,604	3,109	3,222	15.7	19.4	3.7
Rhode Island	346	400	462	464	15.5	15.5	0.5
Connecticut	1,194	1,398	1,666	1,669	17.1	19.1	0.2
Middle Atlantic	14,127	15,013	17,075	17,783	6.3%	13.7%	4.1%
New York	7,182	7,179	8,247	8,381	0.0	14.9	1.6
New Jersey	2,570	3,027	3,690	3,866	17.8	21.9	4.8
Pennsylvania	4,375	4,806	5,139	5,536	9.9	6.9	7.7
MIDWEST	20,087	24,172	26,580	31,452	20.3%	10.0%	18.3%
East North Central	14,750	17,198	18,669	21,745	16.6	8.6	16.5
Ohio	3,887	4,485	4,817	5,518	15.4	7.4	14.5
Indiana	1,880	2,236	2,479	2,953	18.9	10.9	19.1
Illinois	4,376	4,880	5,214	5,966	11.5	6.8	14.4
Michigan	3,081	3,637	3,922	4,566	18.0	7.8	16.4
Wisconsin	1,525	1,960	2,236	2,743	28.5	14.1	22.6
West North Central	5,337	6,973	7,911	9,707	30.7%	13.4%	22.7%
Minnesota	1,300	1,767	2,087	2,611	35.9	18.1	25.1
Iowa	873	1,132	1,200	1,483	29.6	6.0	23.6
Missouri	1,672	2,011	2,315	2,706	20.3	15.1	16.9
North Dakota	158	244	260	319	54.8	6.6	22.4
South Dakota	173	241	276	366	39.6	14.3	32.6
Nebraska	474	631	708	880	33.1	12.2	24.3
Kansas	686	947	1,064	1,342	37.9	12.4	26.1
SOUTH	19,867	28,571	35,989	45,227	43.8%	26.0%	25.7%
South Atlantic	10,176	14,392	19,433	23,979	41.4	35.0	23.4
Delaware	212	257	345	412	21.1	34.2	19.5
Maryland	1,272	1,691	2,155	2,372	32.9	27.4	10.1
District of Columbia	575	613	681	618	6.5	11.1	-9.3
Virginia	1,436	2,115	2,862	3,383	47.2	35.3	18.2
West Virginia	512	659	615	726	28.6	-6.7	18.2
North Carolina	1,747	2,373	3,074	3,837	35.8	29.5	24.8
South Carolina	820	1,176	1,500	1,835	43.4	27.5	22.3
Georgia	1,532	2,128	2,941	3,866	38.9	38.2	31.4
Florida	2,070	3,381	5,261	6,930	63.4	55.6	31.7
East South Central	3,779	5,223	6,121	7,523	38.2%	17.2%	22.9%
Kentucky	896	1,245	1,433	1,789	39.1	15.1	24.8
Tennessee	1,310	1,777	2,167	2,669	35.7	21.9	23.1
Alabama	1,000	1,362	1,601	1,932	36.2	17.6	20.7
Mississippi	573	838	919	1,134	46.3	9.7	23.3

(cont.)

TABLE 6.5 *(cont.)* Non-farm payroll employment, by state, 1969-99, in thousands

	1969	1979	1989	1999	Percentage change		
					69-79	79-89	89-99
SOUTH *(cont.)*							
West South Central	5,912	8,957	10,436	13,725	51.5%	16.5%	31.5%
Arkansas	534	749	893	1,139	40.4	19.2	27.5
Louisiana	1,033	1,517	1,539	1,918	46.9	1.4	24.7
Oklahoma	748	1,088	1,164	1,475	45.4	7.0	26.8
Texas	3,597	5,602	6,840	9,193	55.7	22.1	34.4
WEST	11,694	17,276	21,845	27,168	47.7%	26.4%	24.4%
Mountain	2,571	4,414	5,621	8,147	71.7	27.4	44.9
Montana	196	284	291	381	45.2	2.5	31.0
Idaho	201	338	366	534	67.8	8.2	46.0
Wyoming	107	201	193	231	87.7	-3.9	19.6
Colorado	721	1,218	1,482	2,098	69.0	21.7	41.6
New Mexico	288	461	562	731	60.3	22.0	30.0
Arizona	517	980	1,455	2,151	89.5	48.4	47.9
Utah	348	548	691	1,051	57.5	26.0	52.0
Nevada	194	384	581	970	98.3	51.5	66.9
Pacific	9,123	12,863	16,224	19,020	41.0%	26.1%	17.2%
Washington	1,120	1,581	2,047	2,650	41.2	29.4	29.5
Oregon	709	1,056	1,206	1,587	49.0	14.2	31.6
California	6,932	9,665	12,239	13,975	39.4	26.6	14.2
Alaska	87	167	227	278	92.3	36.0	22.4
Hawaii	276	394	506	530	42.8	28.3	4.9
TOTAL U.S.	70,384	89,823	107,884	128,616	27.6%	20.1%	19.2%

Note: Regional sums do not add to U.S. totals due to: (1) separate estimation techniques by states, and (2) different timing in benchmarking procedures between the state and national estimates.

Source: Authors' analysis of BLS data.

larly in the Mid-Atlantic states. Unemployment also fell in numerous Southern states, but this trend was generally reversed from the East South Central division on down through Oklahoma and Texas, where unemployment rates grew by more than two percentage points. Jobless rates also fell in the Pacific region, including California, where unemployment fell by 1.1 points between 1979 and 1989.

Over the 1990s, national unemployment fell twice as far as it had in the previous decade (it dropped 1.1 percentage points in the 1990s versus 0.5 in the 1980s), as labor markets tightened up considerably throughout the country. In

TABLE 6.6 Unemployment rates by state and division, 1979-99

	1979	1989	1999	Percentage-point change 1979-89	Percentage-point change 1989-99
NORTHEAST	6.6	4.5	4.4	-2.1	-0.1
New England	5.5	3.8	3.3	-1.7	-0.5
Maine	7.2	4.1	4.1	-3.1	0.0
New Hampshire	3.1	3.5	2.7	0.4	-0.8
Vermont	5.3	3.7	3.0	-1.6	-0.7
Massachusetts	5.5	4.0	3.2	-1.5	-0.8
Rhode Island	6.7	4.1	4.1	-2.6	0.0
Connecticut	5.1	3.7	3.2	-1.4	-0.5
Middle Atlantic	7.0	4.7	4.8	-2.3	0.1
New York	7.1	5.1	5.2	-2.0	0.1
New Jersey	6.9	4.1	4.6	-2.8	0.5
Pennsylvania	6.9	4.5	4.4	-2.4	-0.1
MIDWEST	5.5	5.4	3.6	-0.1	-1.8
East North Central	6.1	5.7	3.8	-0.4	-1.9
Ohio	5.9	5.5	4.3	-0.4	-1.2
Indiana	6.4	4.7	3.0	-1.7	-1.7
Illinois	5.5	6.0	4.3	0.5	-1.7
Michigan	7.8	7.1	3.8	-0.7	-3.3
Wisconsin	4.5	4.4	3.0	-0.1	-1.4
West North Central	4.0	4.5	3.0	0.5	-1.5
Minnesota	4.2	4.3	2.8	0.1	-1.5
Iowa	4.1	4.3	2.5	0.2	-1.8
Missouri	4.5	5.5	3.4	1.0	-2.1
North Dakota	3.7	4.3	3.4	0.6	-0.9
South Dakota	3.6	4.2	2.9	0.6	-1.3
Nebraska	3.1	3.1	2.9	0.0	-0.2
Kansas	3.3	4.0	3.0	0.7	-1.0
SOUTH	5.4	5.7	4.1	0.3	-1.6
South Atlantic	5.5	4.8	3.7	-0.7	-1.1
Delaware	8.2	3.5	3.5	-4.7	0.0
Maryland	5.9	3.7	3.5	-2.2	-0.2
District of Columbia	7.3	5.0	6.3	-2.3	1.3
Virginia	4.7	3.9	2.8	-0.8	-1.1
West Virginia	6.7	8.6	6.6	1.9	-2.0
North Carolina	4.8	3.5	3.2	-1.3	-0.3
South Carolina	5.1	4.7	4.5	-0.4	-0.2
Georgia	5.1	5.5	4.0	0.4	-1.5
Florida	6.0	5.6	3.9	-0.4	-1.7

(cont.)

TABLE 6.6 *(cont.)* Unemployment rates by state and division, 1979-99

	1979	1989	1999	Percentage-point change	
				1979-89	1989-99
SOUTH *(cont.)*					
East South Central	6.1	6.3	4.5	0.2	-1.8
Kentucky	5.6	6.2	4.5	0.6	-1.7
Tennessee	5.8	5.1	4.0	-0.7	-1.1
Alabama	7.1	7.0	4.8	-0.1	-2.2
Mississippi	5.8	7.8	5.1	2.0	-2.7
West South Central	4.7	6.8	4.5	2.1	-2.3
Arkansas	6.2	7.2	4.5	1.0	-2.7
Louisiana	6.7	7.9	5.1	1.2	-2.8
Oklahoma	3.4	5.6	3.4	2.2	-2.2
Texas	4.2	6.7	4.6	2.5	-2.1
WEST	6.0	5.3	4.9	-0.7	-0.4
Mountain	5.0	5.5	4.2	0.5	-1.3
Montana	5.1	5.9	5.2	0.8	-0.7
Idaho	5.6	5.1	5.2	-0.5	0.1
Wyoming	3.1	6.3	4.9	3.2	-1.4
Colorado	4.8	5.8	2.9	1.0	-2.9
New Mexico	6.6	6.7	5.6	0.1	-1.1
Arizona	5.0	5.2	4.4	0.2	-0.8
Utah	4.3	4.6	3.7	0.3	-0.9
Nevada	5.0	5.0	4.4	0.0	-0.6
Pacific	6.4	5.2	5.2	-1.2	0.0
Washington	6.8	6.2	4.7	-0.6	-1.5
Oregon	6.8	5.7	5.7	-1.1	0.0
California	6.2	5.1	5.2	-1.1	0.1'
Alaska	9.3	6.7	6.4	-2.6	-0.3
Hawaii	6.4	2.6	5.6	-3.8	3.0
Total U.S.	5.8	5.3	4.2	-0.5	-1.1

* Unemployment rates for 1994 and beyond are not directly comparable to those from earlier years, due to changes in BLS survey methodology.

Source: Authors' analysis of BLS data from Labstat web site.

fact, in only four states (five, counting the District of Columbia) did unemployment fail to decline, although three of those states—California, New York, and New Jersey—were among the most populous. The fact that these large states moved against the national trend in the 1990s helps to explain the slower income growth in their regions.

After remaining at about the same level in 1989 as in 1979, Midwestern unemployment fell by 1.9 percentage points over the 1990s, with broad-based declines occurring throughout the region. The Michigan rate, after staying above 7% in both prior business-cycle peaks, fell 3.4 percentage points in the 1990s. Most states in this region ended the decade with unemployment rates below 4% and even 3%. Southern states also experienced significant declines in unemployment, though levels ended up higher there, on average, than in the Midwest.

Wage trends: Chapter 2 revealed that wages nationwide began to grow in real terms in the mid-1990s after falling for many workers over the prior two decades. At the state level, falling unemployment in the 1990s benefited most low-wage and many middle-wage workers. (Note that, unlike in Chapter 2, the tables in this section combine data for males and females in order to generate large enough sample sizes.)

Table 6.7 compares the level of the 20th percentile wage in 1979, 1989, and 1999 (80% of the workforce earns a higher wage than these workers; 20% earns less). As the last two columns reveal, low-wage workers clearly lost ground in most states in the 1980s but experienced real wage growth in the 1990s. Nationally, low wages fell 8.5% in real terms during the 1980s, with most of the losses occurring outside the Northeast. Low-wage workers in many states experienced wage losses considerably greater than the national trend; losses in numerous states exceeded 15%. By the end of the 1980s, low-wage levels ranged from $5.40 in Mississippi, where real wages had fallen 19.7% over the decade, to $9.40 in Connecticut, where wages had increased by 15.1% over the same period.

By contrast, in the 1990s low wages grew strongly throughout most of the country, except in the Northeast. Nationally, 20th percentile wages grew 5.6% over the decade, although, as Chapter 2 revealed, all of the growth came in the second half of the decade. Particularly large gains occurred in the Midwest, where inflation-adjusted low-wage rates grew by 13.1%. Conversely, inflation-adjusted low-wage levels were essentially unchanged in the West, yet wage growth varied throughout the region. Wages rebounded sharply in some Western states, such as Idaho, Colorado, and New Mexico, but fell by 7.5% in California. **Figure 6B** shows the trend in low wages over the 1990s for a populous state in each region. In each case, real 20th percentile wages were flat or falling

FIGURE 6B Trends in 20th percentile real wages for four states, 1989-99

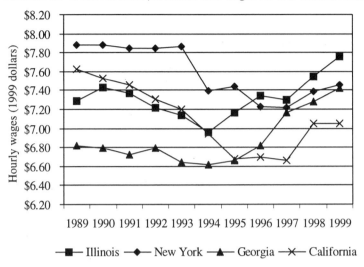

Source: EPI analysis of CPS ORG data; see data appendix.

in each state through 1994. (The sharp drop in New York in 1994 probably resulted from survey changes introduced in that year, particularly the recognition that Hispanic workers had been previously undercounted. In this regard, the one-year change was not incorrect per se, but the effect of the reweighting would ideally have been phased in over a number of years.) At or near that point, wage trends in Illinois and Georgia began to move up. California and New York, however, did not start to see wage gains until 1997.

Note that by the end of the 20-year period, the growth in low-wages in the 1990s did not fully reverse the losses of the 1980s. The 20th[th] percentile wage ended the period 3.3%, or $0.26 per hour, lower than in 1979. For a full-time, year-round worker, this translates into over $500 less in annual earnings.

Table 6.8 shifts the focus to median (i.e., 50th percentile) hourly wages. The pattern here is roughly similar to that of the previous table, but less dramatic: median wages fell less steeply in most states over the 1980s and grew less in the 1990s. There was, however, extensive variation between states in both periods.

Over the 1980s the national median hourly wage declined 2.4%. Median wages fell in every Midwestern and most Western states, with the notable exception of California, where the median remained essentially unchanged. In Utah, for example, the median wage was $0.20 higher than the national level in

TABLE 6.7 Low wages (20th percentile) by state, 1989-99 (1999 dollars)

	1979	1989	1999	Percent changes	
				1979-89	1989-99
NORTHEAST	$7.87	$8.03	$7.85	2.0%	-2.3%
Maine	7.06	7.56	7.48	7.1	-1.0
New Hampshire	7.61	8.48	8.32	11.3	-1.9
Vermont	7.01	7.78	7.75	11.0	-0.4
Massachusetts	7.81	9.07	8.35	16.1	-7.9
Rhode Island	7.61	7.92	7.76	4.1	-2.0
Connecticut	8.17	9.40	8.92	15.1	-5.2
New York	7.92	7.88	7.45	-0.5	-5.4
New Jersey	7.96	8.69	8.32	9.1	-4.2
Pennsylvania	7.94	7.20	7.52	-9.4	4.4
MIDWEST	$7.88	$6.85	$ 7.74	-13.1%	13.1%
Ohio	7.90	6.97	7.57	-11.8	8.6
Indiana	7.60	6.60	7.80	-13.2	18.1
Illinois	8.44	7.29	7.75	-13.7	6.4
Michigan	8.45	7.00	7.87	-17.1	12.3
Wisconsin	7.85	6.74	7.89	-14.1	17.1
Minnesota	7.85	7.43	8.44	-5.3	13.6
Iowa	7.46	6.40	7.77	-14.1	21.3
Missouri	7.37	6.54	7.77	-11.2	18.8
North Dakota	7.04	6.18	6.66	-12.2	7.7
South Dakota	6.83	5.82	7.10	-14.8	21.9
Nebraska	7.25	6.33	7.22	-12.6	14.1
Kansas	7.59	6.63	7.12	-12.6	7.3
SOUTH	$7.14	$6.57	$7.06	-8.0%	7.5%
Delaware	8.03	7.70	7.85	-4.1	1.9
Maryland	8.13	8.16	8.25	0.4	1.0
District of Columbia	8.88	8.20	8.48	-7.7	3.4
Virginia	7.29	7.35	7.72	0.8	5.0
West Virginia	7.48	5.61	6.32	-25.0	12.8
North Carolina	7.05	6.73	7.38	-4.5	9.6
South Carolina	6.92	6.46	7.46	-6.5	15.5
Georgia	7.15	6.82	7.42	-4.6	8.8
Florida	7.00	6.79	6.95	-3.0	2.4
Kentucky	7.28	6.03	7.06	-17.2	17.0
Tennessee	7.06	6.30	7.06	-10.8	12.1
Alabama	6.97	6.22	6.80	-10.8	9.4
Mississippi	6.72	5.40	6.50	-19.7	20.4
Arkansas	6.89	5.83	6.47	-15.4	11.0
Louisiana	7.12	5.84	6.20	-18.0	6.3
Oklahoma	7.42	6.43	6.74	-13.3	4.9
Texas	7.19	6.27	6.87	-12.7	9.4

(cont.)

TABLE 6.7 *(cont.)* Low wages (20th percentile) by state, 1989-99 (1999 dollars)

	1979	1989	1999	Percent changes 1979-89	1989-99
WEST	$8.14	$7.27	$7.25	-10.7%	-0.2%
Montana	7.26	6.20	6.33	-14.5	2.1
Idaho	7.28	6.11	6.92	-16.1	13.3
Wyoming	8.08	6.40	6.65	-20.8	3.8
Colorado	7.83	6.83	8.37	-12.8	22.4
New Mexico	7.14	5.94	6.80	-16.8	14.5
Arizona	7.54	6.86	7.10	-9.1	3.6
Utah	7.63	6.86	7.47	-10.0	8.9
Nevada	7.91	7.50	7.61	-5.2	1.5
Washington	8.76	7.57	8.14	-13.6	7.5
Oregon	8.45	7.38	7.70	-12.6	4.2
California	8.31	7.62	7.05	-8.3	-7.5
Alaska	11.83	9.85	8.72	-16.8	-11.5
Hawaii	7.28	7.83	7.71	7.6	-1.5
TOTAL U.S.	$7.61	$6.97	$7.35	-8.5%	5.6%

Source: EPI analysis of CPS ORG data; see data appendix.

1979, but by 1989, after falling 9.3%, it was $0.64 below. Keeping with the general regional trend over the 1980s, Northeastern states, particularly in New England, enjoyed relatively large real wage gains over the period.

As with low-wage trends, median wages also grew in most states over the 1990s, though most of the growth was concentrated in the Midwest and South, where median wages grew by 4.9% and 4.7%, respectively. The median declined by 4.2% in New York and by 6.6% in California. **Figure 6C** shows the timing of some of these state trends over the 1990s. Median wages fell fairly consistently through 1996 in both New York and California, not reversing course until 1998. Wages in Georgia and Illinois fell less steeply and began growing earlier, in 1996 and 1997, respectively.

Table 6.9 looks at the wage trends for higher-wage, 80th percentile workers. Nationally, these wages grew 1.5% over the 1980s, but regional growth rates varied greatly, from an 8.5% rise in the Northeast to a 2.8% drop in the Midwest. While most Western high-wage trends were negative, in California, the dominant regional state, the 80th percentile wage grew by 2.8%.

TABLE 6.8 State hourly median wages (50th percentile), 1979-99 (1999 dollars)

	1979	1989	1999	Percent changes 1979-89	1989-99
NORTHEAST	$12.16	$13.16	$12.84	8.2%	-2.4%
Maine	9.70	10.76	11.01	10.9	2.3
New Hampshire	11.03	12.83	12.78	16.3	-0.5
Vermont	10.35	11.21	11.61	8.3	3.6
Massachusetts	11.63	13.62	13.45	17.1	-1.2
Rhode Island	11.15	11.89	12.18	6.6	2.4
Connecticut	12.36	14.20	15.12	14.9	6.5
New York	12.42	13.33	12.77	7.4	-4.2
New Jersey	12.73	14.15	14.08	11.2	-0.5
Pennsylvania	12.36	11.59	11.96	-6.2	3.2
MIDWEST	$12.62	$11.46	$12.02	-9.2%	4.9%
Ohio	12.92	11.67	12.06	-9.7	3.4
Indiana	11.78	10.66	11.69	-9.5	9.7
Illinois	13.33	12.39	12.43	-7.0	0.3
Michigan	13.87	12.32	12.51	-11.2	1.5
Wisconsin	12.43	11.07	11.84	-11.0	6.9
Minnesota	12.39	11.92	13.45	-3.7	12.8
Iowa	11.59	10.35	11.01	-10.7	6.4
Missouri	11.53	10.73	11.89	-7.0	10.8
North Dakota	10.82	9.57	9.92	-11.6	3.7
South Dakota	9.54	8.92	10.05	-6.5	12.6
Nebraska	10.89	9.78	10.43	-10.2	6.7
Kansas	11.34	10.90	10.89	-3.9	-0.1
SOUTH	$10.90	$10.54	$11.03	-3.3%	4.7%
Delaware	12.13	12.27	12.33	1.2	0.5
Maryland	13.08	13.23	14.06	1.2	6.2
District of Columbia	13.53	13.40	13.76	-1.0	2.7
Virginia	11.50	12.20	12.24	6.0	0.3
West Virginia	12.73	9.84	9.95	-22.7	1.0
North Carolina	9.90	10.13	11.15	2.4	10.0
South Carolina	9.58	10.09	11.25	5.3	11.5
Georgia	10.66	10.90	11.31	2.2	3.7
Florida	10.10	10.47	10.64	3.6	1.7
Kentucky	11.50	10.43	10.82	-9.3	3.8
Tennessee	10.38	9.67	10.33	-6.9	6.8
Alabama	10.88	10.00	10.88	-8.1	8.8
Mississippi	9.21	8.67	10.12	-5.9	16.7
Arkansas	9.31	8.88	9.84	-4.6	10.8
Louisiana	11.21	9.71	10.02	-13.4	3.2
Oklahoma	11.60	10.38	10.35	-10.5	-0.3
Texas	11.27	10.52	10.82	-6.7	2.8

(cont.)

TABLE 6.8 *(cont.)* State hourly median wages (50th percentile), 1979-99
(1999 dollars)

	1979	1989	1999	Percent changes 1979-89	Percent changes 1989-99
WEST	$13.09	$12.59	$12.13	-3.9%	-3.6%
Montana	11.84	10.04	9.77	-15.2	-2.7
Idaho	11.36	9.85	10.39	-13.3	5.5
Wyoming	13.38	11.04	10.41	-17.5	-5.7
Colorado	12.76	11.61	12.99	-9.0	11.9
New Mexico	11.41	9.69	10.76	-15.1	11.0
Arizona	11.58	11.22	10.96	-3.1	-2.3
Utah	12.09	10.96	11.08	-9.3	1.0
Nevada	11.92	11.81	11.16	-0.9	-5.6
Washington	13.90	12.82	13.33	-7.8	4.0
Oregon	13.21	12.27	11.98	-7.1	-2.4
California	13.26	13.29	12.41	0.2	-6.6
Alaska	18.85	15.90	13.90	-15.7	-12.6
Hawaii	11.94	12.63	11.96	5.8	-5.3
TOTAL U.S.	$11.89	$11.60	$11.87	-2.4%	2.4%

Source: EPI analysis of CPS ORG data; see data appendix.

FIGURE 6C Trends in median real wages for four states, 1989-99

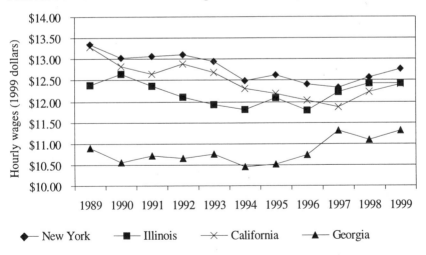

Source: EPI analysis of CPS ORG data; see data appendix.

TABLE 6.9 State hourly high wages (80th percentile), 1979-99 (1999 dollars)

	1979	1989	1999	Percent changes 1979-89	Percent changes 1989-99
NORTHEAST	$18.95	$20.57	$21.70	8.5%	5.5%
Maine	15.33	16.39	17.18	6.9	4.9
New Hampshire	16.57	20.02	20.07	20.9	0.2
Vermont	15.63	16.72	17.92	7.0	7.2
Massachusetts	18.08	21.52	22.41	19.1	4.2
Rhode Island	16.95	19.37	20.17	14.3	4.1
Connecticut	18.97	21.94	24.16	15.6	10.1
New York	19.42	21.48	22.02	10.6	2.5
New Jersey	20.19	23.02	23.94	14.0	4.0
Pennsylvania	18.58	18.26	19.58	-1.7	7.3
MIDWEST	$19.22	$18.68	$19.87	-2.8%	6.3%
Ohio	18.95	18.49	19.88	-2.4	7.6
Indiana	18.12	17.19	18.78	-5.1	9.3
Illinois	20.97	20.17	21.15	-3.8	4.9
Michigan	20.32	20.09	21.18	-1.1	5.4
Wisconsin	18.57	17.71	18.79	-4.6	6.1
Minnesota	19.20	20.07	21.75	4.6	8.4
Iowa	18.04	16.29	17.35	-9.7	6.5
Missouri	18.84	17.72	18.85	-5.9	6.3
North Dakota	17.67	16.29	16.01	-7.9	-1.7
South Dakota	15.68	14.25	15.93	-9.1	11.8
Nebraska	16.86	16.25	16.95	-3.6	4.3
Kansas	17.37	17.54	18.05	1.0	2.9
SOUTH	$17.60	$17.52	$18.59	-0.5%	6.1%
Delaware	20.37	19.70	20.91	-3.3	6.2
Maryland	22.00	20.89	23.37	-5.0	11.9
District of Columbia	22.07	21.65	23.15	-1.9	6.9
Virginia	18.64	20.38	21.72	9.3	6.6
West Virginia	19.55	16.82	17.16	-14.0	2.0
North Carolina	14.97	16.33	18.11	9.1	10.9
South Carolina	14.96	16.25	17.67	8.6	8.7
Georgia	16.84	18.18	18.67	7.9	2.7
Florida	16.37	17.03	18.22	4.0	7.0
Kentucky	18.36	16.80	17.66	-8.5	5.1
Tennessee	16.66	15.78	17.49	-5.3	10.9
Alabama	17.52	16.83	17.71	-3.9	5.2
Mississippi	15.13	14.73	16.48	-2.6	11.9
Arkansas	13.94	14.20	15.58	1.9	9.7
Louisiana	18.00	17.12	17.28	-4.9	0.9
Oklahoma	18.39	17.00	17.33	-7.6	2.0
Texas	18.38	18.01	18.63	-2.0	3.5

(cont.)

TABLE 6.9 *(cont.)* State hourly high wages (80th percentile), 1979-99 (1999 dollars)

	1979	1989	1999	Percent changes 1979-89	1989-99
WEST	$20.73	$20.43	$20.91	-1.5%	2.4%
Montana	18.02	16.39	16.12	-9.0	-1.6
Idaho	18.14	15.95	17.78	-12.1	11.4
Wyoming	20.93	18.79	17.80	-10.2	-5.3
Colorado	20.17	19.70	21.32	-2.3	8.2
New Mexico	18.78	16.49	18.33	-12.2	11.2
Arizona	19.26	18.61	18.26	-3.4	-1.9
Utah	18.37	17.83	18.76	-3.0	5.2
Nevada	19.81	18.79	18.73	-5.1	-0.3
Washington	21.60	19.93	21.58	-7.7	8.3
Oregon	20.04	18.41	19.95	-8.1	8.4
California	21.24	21.83	22.26	2.8	2.0
Alaska	30.16	26.48	22.99	-12.2	-13.2
Hawaii	19.33	20.21	19.68	4.6	-2.7
TOTAL U.S.	$18.99	$19.28	$19.93	1.5%	3.4%

Source: EPI analysis of CPS ORG data; see data appendix.

In the 1990s, the 80th percentile wage grew by 3.4% nationally. An interesting contrast emerges in the Northeast. While median- and low-wage workers there generally lost ground in the 1990s, the hourly earnings of high-wage workers continued to grow, although at a slower rate than in the 1980s. As shown in Chapter 2, this pattern of wage growth led to the continuation of growing wage inequality between workers at the top of the wage scale relative to those at the middle and low end.

The share of workers by state earning poverty-level wages (the wage level needed to lift a family of four above the poverty line with full-time, full-year work) is shown in **Table 6.10**. These state-level comparisons of the low-wage sector serve two purposes: first, they identify states with above-average shares of low-wage workers at a point in time, and, second, they measure the extent to which the low-wage sector has grown or contracted over time. In this regard, this poverty-wage measure is a proxy for the change in the quality of low-wage jobs, at least in terms of hourly pay, in the lower end of a state's labor market.

Due to lower wage levels in the South overall, low-wage shares are typically largest there. In 1999, for example, the shares in the East and West South

TABLE 6.10 Poverty-level wage shares by state, 1979-99

	1979	1989	1999	Percentage-point change 1979-89	1989-99	1979-99
NORTHEAST	21.6%	21.3%	23.0%	-0.3	1.7	1.4
New England	23.1	17.4	20.0	-5.7	2.6	-3.1
Maine	34.1	27.3	27.4	-6.8	0.1	-6.7
New Hampshire	24.9	17.9	19.2	-7.0	1.3	-5.7
Vermont	32.5	24.2	25.5	-8.3	1.3	-7.0
Massachussetts	22.0	15.7	19.3	-6.3	3.6	-2.7
Rhode Island	25.2	22.7	23.9	-2.5	1.2	-1.4
Connecticut	19.4	14.3	16.8	-5.2	2.5	-2.6
Middle Atlantic	21.1%	22.7%	24.1%	1.7	1.4	3.1
New York	21.1	22.2	25.6	1.1	3.4	4.6
New Jersey	21.1	17.0	19.4	-4.1	2.4	-1.7
Pennsylvania	21.0	27.4	25.4	6.4	-2.1	4.3
MIDWEST	21.6%	29.6%	24.3%	8.0	-5.3	2.7
East North Central	20.0	28.4	24.0	8.4	-4.4	4.0
Ohio	21.4	28.4	25.4	7.0	-2.9	4.1
Indiana	24.2	34.8	24.3	10.5	-10.4	0.1
Illinois	17.6	25.5	23.9	7.8	-1.6	6.3
Michigan	17.9	27.2	22.9	9.3	-4.3	5.0
Wisconsin	21.6	30.3	22.7	8.7	-7.5	1.1
West North Central	25.6%	32.5%	25.0%	7.0	-7.5	-0.6
Minnesota	21.9	26.2	18.7	4.3	-7.5	-3.2
Iowa	25.7	35.4	25.1	9.6	-10.3	-0.7
Missouri	26.2	33.0	24.7	6.8	-8.4	-1.5
North Dakota	31.6	39.3	37.0	7.8	-2.4	5.4
South Dakota	37.4	43.5	32.2	6.1	-11.3	-5.2
Nebraska	28.4	38.4	30.6	10.0	-7.8	2.2
Kansas	24.6	32.1	29.9	7.5	-2.2	5.3
SOUTH	29.4%	33.7%	30.3%	4.3	-3.4	1.0
South Atlantic	28.8	30.4	27.7	1.5	-2.6	-1.1
Delaware	19.9	24.3	23.5	4.4	-0.7	3.7
Maryland	19.7	20.1	20.0	0.4	-0.1	0.3
District of Columbia	13.7	19.9	18.9	6.3	-1.0	5.2
Virginia	27.2	25.9	24.6	-1.3	-1.2	-2.5
West Virginia	25.7	39.6	36.6	13.9	-3.0	10.8
North Carolina	32.1	33.8	27.4	1.7	-6.3	-4.7
South Carolina	35.0	35.3	27.4	0.4	-7.9	-7.6
Georgia	29.5	31.7	27.4	2.2	-4.3	-2.1
Florida	33.1	33.0	32.4	-0.1	-0.6	-0.7
East South Central	32.0%	38.9%	32.5%	6.9	-6.4	0.5
Kentucky	26.8	36.5	31.4	9.6	-5.1	4.5
Tennessee	31.6	37.9	32.0	6.3	-5.9	0.4

(cont.)

TABLE 6.10 *(cont.)* Poverty-level wage shares by state, 1979-99

	1979	1989	1999	1979-89	1989-99	1979-99
				Percent point change		
SOUTH *(cont.)*						
East South Central *(cont.)*						
Alabama	32.2	38.3	32.3	6.2	-6.0	0.1
Mississippi	41.0	45.7	35.7	4.8	-10.1	-5.3
West South Central	28.6%	36.6%	33.5%	8.0	-3.1	4.9
Arkansas	37.8	43.5	38.4	5.7	-5.1	0.5
Louisiana	28.6	38.9	37.3	10.3	-1.6	8.7
Oklahoma	24.8	34.6	34.3	9.8	-0.2	9.6
Texas	28.0	35.5	32.0	7.5	-3.5	4.0
WEST	19.6%	26.1%	27.2%	6.5	1.0	7.5
Mountain	24.4	32.2	27.6	7.8	-4.6	3.2
Montana	27.1	37.5	39.3	10.4	1.8	12.2
Idaho	27.2	38.2	32.5	11.0	-5.7	5.3
Wyoming	19.8	32.8	34.3	13.0	1.5	14.5
Colorado	21.9	30.0	18.8	8.0	-11.2	-3.2
New Mexico	28.8	40.3	33.0	11.5	-7.3	4.2
Arizona	25.9	31.0	30.2	5.1	-0.8	4.3
Utah	23.7	31.8	28.7	8.1	-3.1	5.0
Nevada	20.9	25.5	25.8	4.7	0.3	4.9
Pacific	18.1%	24.1%	27.0%	5.9	2.9	8.9
Washington	16.2	24.6	20.5	8.4	-4.1	4.3
Oregon	17.8	26.1	24.6	8.4	-1.5	6.8
California	18.4	24.0	28.7	5.6	4.7	10.3
Alaska	6.5	12.9	17.5	6.5	4.6	11.1
Hawaii	24.5	23.0	24.8	-1.5	1.8	0.3
U.S. AVERAGES	23.7%	28.5%	26.8%	4.9	-1.7	3.1

Source: Authors' analysis of CPS data.

Central divisions were about 33%, compared to 26.8% for the nation. The lowest shares are typically in the Northeast. (Note that these data use the national poverty line and do not make any adjustments for price differences between the relatively high-cost Northeast and the low-cost South. However, even with such adjustments, the share of low-wage workers in the South would still surpass that of most of the nation.)

The national analysis in Chapter 2 revealed that the low-wage share expanded 4.9 percentage points in the 1980s (driven by male wage decline) and fell 1.7 points in the 1990s. The regional analysis shows that, outside of the Northeast, low-wage shares in the 1980s grew most quickly in the Midwest, the deep South, and the Mountain division of the West. In the 1990s, however, many of these trends reversed. The share of low-wage jobs in the Northeast expanded faster over the 1990s than it declined over the 1980s, such that over the full period the low-wage share was up by 1.4 percentage points in this region. In the Midwest, low-wage shares contracted in every state over the 1990s, with particularly large declines in Indiana, Iowa, and South Dakota. Some of the lowest-wage Southern states (e.g., Mississippi) also got a boost in the 1990s, in part from the increases in the federal minimum wage, which tends to reach more workers in this part of the country due to the lower level of wages there. Finally, while some Western states, such as Colorado and New Mexico, saw significant declines in their low-wage shares, California's low-wage share expanded only slightly less in the 1990s than it had over the 1980s (4.7 versus 5.6 points). Thus, the West went from having a below-average share of low-wage workers at the beginning of the 20-year period to a slightly above-average share by 1999.

Are there any general conclusions that can be drawn from the proceeding analysis of wages and job trends, beyond the general connection between tighter labor markets and overall wage growth? One important piece of information that can be drawn from these state-level data is the extent to which a change in unemployment affects different wage levels. Of course, there are many other factors besides employment that drive state-level wage trends, but this approach can provide a rough proxy for the effect of this one important factor.

Table 6.11 shows estimates of the impact of a 1 percentage-point decline in the unemployment rate on 20th, 50th, and 80th percentile wages and on the share of workers earning poverty-level wages, in both the 1980s and 1990s. (Note that these results are unweighted, i.e., each state is weighted equally. In a sense, then, the results address questions about the relationship between employment and wages for an average state, not for an average worker.)

The first column shows that a one-point fall in the unemployment rate would have led to a 3.5% gain in the 20th percentile wage in the 1980s. The second column multiplies the wage gain in column 1 by the actual fall in national unemployment in each time period (0.5 percentage points in the 1980s and 1.1 points in the 1990s). The result represents the impact of falling unemployment in each period on wage growth. However, since this simple model focuses only on one factor affecting wage growth—the change in unemployment—the actual wage changes, given in the third column, can be quite different from the estimate.

The relationship between unemployment and wages was quite robust in both decades, particularly for 20th percentile workers, for whom a one-percentage-point fall (increase) in the unemployment rate was associated with a 3.5%-

TABLE 6.11 The impact of a one-percentage-point decline in the unemployment rate on real wage trends

	Estimated wage impact of 1% decline in unemployment*	Impact on wages**	Actual national change
1980s			
20th percentile wage	3.5%	1.8%	-8.5%
50th percentile wage	3.0	1.5	-2.4
80th percentile wage	1.9	1.0	1.5
Share of low-wage workers	-1.8	-0.9	4.9
1990s			
20th percentile wage	3.5%	3.9%	5.6%
50th percentile wage	2.1	2.3	2.4
80th percentile wage	0.7	n.a.	3.4
Share of low-wage workers	-1.6	-1.8	-1.7

* All coefficients are signficant at the 1% level except the 80th percentile result for the 1990s.
** Entries in the column are the product of the coefficient for the time period and the national decline in the unemployment rate over the period (0.5 percentage points in the 1980s and 1.1 in the 1990s).

Source: Authors' analysis.

4% rise (decline) in wages. The impact on wages (column 2) was smaller in the 1980s, however, because unemployment fell half as much as in the 1990s. Also, as seen in the last column, other factors (including the decline in the real value of the minimum wage, the fall in union bargaining power, the shift to poorer-quality jobs) overpowered the unemployment effect and led to falling wages for low- and middle-wage workers. For example, for low-wage workers the 30% fall in the real minimum wage over the decade certainly played a role in the 8.5% fall in wages at the 20th percentile and the 4.9 percentage-point growth in the share of workers earning poverty-level wages.

Other research of this type has shown that the benefits from lower unemployment become more pronounced the further the unemployment level falls. That is, the wage gains that result from a decline in unemployment from 6% to 5% tend to be smaller than those that result from a decline from 5% to 4%. By 1989, 23 states had an unemployment rate less than 5%, and nine states were below 4%. Ten years later, 42 states had unemployment rates below 5%, and 25 were below 4%. Thus, the effect of tight labor markets on wages was accentuated in the 1990s relative to the 1980s because unemployment fell further in more states.

FIGURE 6D Changes in the low-wage share and the unemployment rate

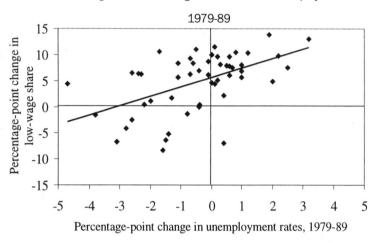

Percentage-point change in unemployment rates, 1979-89

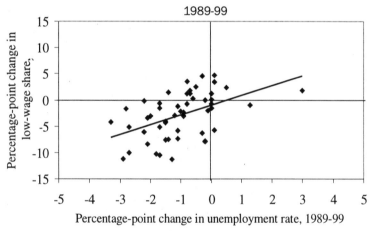

Percentage-point change in unemployment rate, 1989-99

Source: Authors' analysis of CPS data.

Figure 6D looks at the relationship between changes in unemployment and the share of workers earnings poverty-level wages. For each decade, the percentage-point changes in unemployment rates and poverty-level wages are plotted in a scatter diagram; the line passing through them indicates whether the relationship between unemployment rates and poverty-level wage shares is generally positive or negative. One would expect the relationship between these two variables to be a positive one, with falling unemployment leading to fewer workers earning poverty-level wages. This relationship will be diminished, however, if other factors, such as those that played a role in falling wages in the 1980s (see the discussion of Table 6.11 above), dominate the unemployment effect.

In fact, the regression line is positive in both time periods, confirming the relationship between falling unemployment and rising wages. But interestingly, the scatter of dots is quite different in each period. Over the 1980s, only nine states were in the lower-left quadrant, meaning falling unemployment accompanied a decline in the low-wage share. Over the 1990s, however, most states are clustered in this region of the graph, meaning they experienced the decline in both unemployment and low-wage work. This reflects the fact that more states experienced larger, and more sustained, declines in unemployment in this decade relative to the 1980s. As shown in column 1 of Table 6.11, the slope (upward slant) of the line is essentially the same for low-wage workers in both periods, meaning that a 1-percentage point fall in unemployment had the same impact on wages in the 1980s and the 1990s. Thus, the more impressive outcomes in the 1990s primarily reflect a deeper, widespread drop in unemployment (along with some of the factors noted above) rather than a significant change in the relationship between unemployment and wage growth.

The wages of the median worker are also responsive to changes in the unemployment rate, although, unlike the case for lower-wage workers, the median wage was somewhat less responsive to unemployment in the 1990s than in the 1980s (2.1% versus 3.0%). However, the fact that unemployment fell further in the 1990s led to a larger wage effect in that decade (2.3% versus 1.5%). For 80th percentile workers, the wage impact of falling unemployment was smaller than other factors in the 1980s and insignificant in the 1990s, implying that, unlike the wages of the low-wage workforce, the wages of these better-off workers are not particularly responsive to the change in unemployment.

These data reveal that falling unemployment benefited most low- and many middle-wage workers in the 1980s and 1990s, although more so in the 1990s when unemployment fell further in many states and in the nation. Another boost to low-wage workers in the 1990s was delivered by two national increases and numerous state-level increases in the minimum wage. These increases were especially important in low-wage states, where they reached more workers.

The overall unemployment rate masks considerable variation in the rates faced by persons with differing demographic characteristics. **Table 6.12** examines the rates of unemployment and underemployment (this latter concept adds discouraged job seekers and marginally employed persons to the unemployed; see table note) among those typically at a disadvantage in the labor market: young persons (18-35 years old), with at most a high school degree. The table pools data across three years (1997-99) in order to generate large enough samples.

TABLE 6.12 Unemployment and underemployment, 18-35-year-olds, by gender, education, and race, 1996-99 (pooled)

	Female				Male			
	Unemployment		Underemployment*		Unemployment		Underemployment*	
ALL	LTHS	HS	LTHS	HS	LTHS	HS	LTHS	HS
NORTHEAST								
New England								
Maine	—	6.7%	32.0%	17.1%	14.8%	6.7%	27.2%	12.3%
New Hampshire	—	5.1	19.2	10.5	9.5	3.6	17.6	6.7
Vermont	—	6.1	27.4	14	—	6.7	15.3	11.6
Massachusetts	11.6%	6.5	20.2	12.5	11.3	5.7	17.3	10.3
Rhode Island	15.8	7.0	25.3	16.3	11.8	7.6	20.3	13.3
Connecticut	—	—	21.5	10.8	17.2	6.6	29.3	12.4
Middle Atlantic								
New York	21.8%	9.7%	34.1%	18.4%	15.3%	8.6%	24.9%	15%
New Jersey	16.3	7.4	26.0	13.4	12.6	7.2	19.9	11.4
Pennsylvania	21.0	7.6	33.2	15.5	14.8	7.7	22.6	12.8
MIDWEST								
East North Central								
Ohio	17.5%	6.8%	28.6%	12.3%	15.7%	7.2%	24.6%	11.9%
Indiana	13.2	5.7	23.0	11.8	—	3.9	10.6	7.6
Illinois	18.0	7.5	27.8	13.6	12.4	8.4	20.0	14.0
Michigan	16.4	6.5	28.5	13.9	13.7	6.5	21.8	11.8
Wisconsin	14.4	5.6	25.1	12.2	14.3	4.9	24.4	8.9
West North Central								
Minnesota	—	4.3%	21.4%	11.0%	10.1%	6.0%	20.2%	10.7%
Iowa	—	4.9	18.5	12.2	8.1	4.0	13.4	7.0
Missouri	13.1%	7.8	24.5	13.9	16.6	5.9	25.6	10.6
North Dakota	—	5.2	19.9	12.6	10.4	5.0	19.6	9.8
South Dakota	9.0	5.9	17.8	11.7	8.4	6.1	13.9	10.0
Nebraska	—	5.3	20.7	11.8	—	4.1	13.4	7.8
Kansas	14.3	6.8	29.0	11.7	9.8	5.0	18.4	9.5
SOUTH								
South Atlantic								
Delaware	—	5.9%	20.6%	13.6%	11.8%	6.4%	18.2%	12.3%
Maryland	21%	7.5	35.0	13.5	17.7	6.4	26.3	11.4
District of Columbia	42.4	22.3	60.0	33.5	23.8	16.2	33.9	25.9
Virginia	13.8	5.8	24.8	11.3	6.9	4.0	14.3	8.0
West Virginia	19.8	11.0	35.6	23.5	22.2	10.3	34.5	19.2
North Carolina	12.7	7.2	23.5	12.2	8.1	4.8	16.1	8.7
South Carolina	17.0	10.1	28.0	16.0	13.6	5.9	24.6	9.9
Georgia	20.7	6.7	32.3	11.4	10.5	5.7	18.4	9.7
Florida	15.0	6.5	26.7	12.1	9.8	5.5	18.5	10.6
East South Central								
Kentucky	20.2%	9.1%	35.2%	18.3%	14.3%	7.1%	25.0%	13.0%
Tennessee	16.1	7.2	28.8	13.3	15.7	6.1	23.7	10.5
Alabama	16.1	10.6	28.9	18.8	13.3	7.1	21.1	11.3
Mississippi	19.4	10.8	32.7	19.6	16.2	7.9	25.2	13.1

(cont.)

TABLE 6.12 *(cont.)* Unemployment and underemployment, 18-35-year-olds, by gender, education, and race, 1996-99 (pooled)

	Female				Male			
	Unemployment		Underemployment*		Unemployment		Underemployment*	
ALL	LTHS	HS	LTHS	HS	LTHS	HS	LTHS	HS
SOUTH *(cont.)*								
West South Central								
Arkansas	20.9%	9.8%	32.6%	17.6%	17.1%	7.9%	24.9%	12.4%
Louisiana	26.5	8.6	40.2	17.2	16.8	7.6	26.3	11.5
Oklahoma	16.3	7.3	26.4	14.4	11.4	5.8	20.2	10.4
Texas	14.5	8.9	24.8	16.1	9.0	7.1	16.4	11.7
WEST								
Mountain								
Montana	18.8%	9.2%	35.6%	21%	16.8%	9.7%	28.4%	16.0%
Idaho	16.6	6.4	28.0	16.2	13.3	6.7	21.0	13.2
Wyoming	14.2	10.0	28.7	20.4	12.2	9.5	22.3	15.8
Colorado	13.4	4.7	22.5	11.8	9.0	5.0	15.3	9.2
New Mexico	23.0	10.1	38.4	18.0	14.6	9.0	25.3	15.4
Arizona	13.2	7.0	22.6	11.4	8.3	4.9	14.2	10.5
Utah	11.6	4.8	23.1	9.9	6.9	4.6	13.8	8.2
Nevada	11.7	6.9	23.4	11.9	9.4	4.8	15.5	10.0
Pacific								
Washington	15.3%	7.5%	30.3%	16%	11.8%	7.4%	22.3%	14.2%
Oregon	14.3	8.8	26.4	17.0	13.5	6.9	23.5	13.7
California	16.8	9.4	30.1	18.4	10.9	8.2	20.2	14.7
Alaska	—	7.7	36.6	17.3	19.4	11.5	33.8	21.0
Hawaii	—	8.7	29.0	20.4	—	13.2	25.1	23.6
BLACK								
New York	37.1%	15.4%	52.8%	26.6%	32.1%	16.1%	47.9%	26.%
New Jersey	—	14.9	42.8	23.6	24.7	17.3	38.9	22.9
Pennsylvania	37.3	16.2	54.1	28.0	—	21.3	47.7	30.8
Ohio	21.8	12.5	33.3	21.0	—	11.6	37.1	21.7
Illinois	32.3	16.7	46.1	27.7	30.3	22.4	42.7	32.5
Michigan	25.5	11.7	44.3	19.7	28.1	13.7	43.3	22.0
Maryland	—	11.7	55.2	20.2	45.3	12.1	57.0	20.2
District of Columbia	51.2	23.6	67.2	34.5	38.6	18.4	50.7	29.4
Virginia	—	14.8	38.0	21.9	—	—	—	11.5
North Carolina	23.5	11.1	34.1	18.8	17.3	11.2	27.2	15.7
South Carolina	—	16.5	42.1	25.8	—	—	42.9	15.0
Georgia	36.2	10.6	50.5	17.7	21.9	10.5	34.0	16.1
Florida	20.9	12.0	35.4	19.3	20.4	11.0	30.4	17.7
Alabama	18.6	18.0	35.3	28.3	—	12.8	41.0	19.2
Mississippi	28.3	15.8	42.5	26.9	28.1	15.0	39.5	22.3
Arkansas	46.9	20.8	59.0	32.0	—	18.8	57.0	28.6
Louisiana	37.5	11.5	51.9	25.1	31.7	12.1	46.8	18.8
Texas	27.1	12.9	41.4	22.7	20.1	11.5	29.7	18.6
California	39.1	20.0	50.9	31.7	43.2	20.3	58.0	27.8

(cont.)

359

TABLE 6.12 *(cont.)* Unemployment and underemployment, 18-35-year-olds, by gender, education, and race, 1996-99 (pooled)

ALL	Female				Male			
	Unemployment		Underemployment*		Unemployment		Underemployment*	
STATE	LTHS	HS	LTHS	HS	LTHS	HS	LTHS	HS
HISPANIC								
New York	18.9%	13.3%	31.2%	21.9%	10.2%	7.3%	17.2%	12.8%
New Jersey	18.6	7.8	26.9	14.6	—	—	14.5	10.2
Illinois	10.9	—	19.5	11.0	7.4	6.8	13.8	10.9
Florida	14.3	8.1	26.1	13.9	6.8	5.2	15.5	10.8
Texas	14.0	10.6	25.0	18.9	7.6	7.0	14.7	12.1
New Mexico	23.5	8.9	41.0	15.3	16.5	9.2	26.7	15.3
Arizona	16.8	—	27.2	15.3	7.9	—	14.3	9.5
California	15.8	9.6	29.4	20.2	9.3	7.7	17.8	14.1

ADDENDUM: Un- and underemployment rates for all persons (all education levels), 18-35, 1997-99.

U.S.	Unemployment			Underemployment		
	All	Black	Hispanic	All	Black	Hispanic
Females	6.2%	12.2%	9.4%	11.8%	20.1%	17.7%
Males	5.9	12.3	6.9	10.4	19.5	12.8

* Underemployment refers to persons who are either unsuccessfully seeking work (i.e., unemployed), not seeking work due to discouragement about their job prospects, involuntarily part-time workers, or have sought work in the past year but are not currently looking for other reasons, such as lack of child care.

Source: Authors' analysis of monthly CPS data.

Even so, many states did not have large enough samples to generate reliable estimates, particularly for minorities.

While the national unemployment rate for all females age 18-35 over this time period was 6.2% (see addendum, Table 6.12), women this age with less than high school degrees had rates ranging from 9.0% in South Dakota to 26.5% in Louisiana (rates were highest in the District of Columbia, as is common in urban areas). For black females with less than a high school degree, rates of unemployment were as high as 46.9% in Arkansas, while underemployment rates ranged from about 35% to 65%.

For young Hispanic females, these indicators were less negative. In California their unemployment rate was 15.8% for those with less than a high school education and 9.6% for high school graduates; both of these rates were close to the levels for all young women in the state (this is partly due to the fact that these young Hispanic women constitute a large share of the overall group in California). Even so, these rates, especially those for African American women, suggest that, despite recent tightening in the overall labor, the low-wage labor market is still characterized by high levels of un- and underemployment.

For male workers age 18-35, the national unemployment rate was 5.9% in 1997-99. As with females, the unemployment rate for young, non-college-educated males was two to three times this overall rate. Here again, large differences are evident between black and Hispanic young male job seekers. In New York, for example, among high school dropouts, unemployment rates for young Hispanic males were one-third the rate of young African American males (10.2% as opposed to 32.1%). The gap was smaller among blacks and Hispanics with high school degrees, due to the large difference in unemployment rates by education in New York.

Poverty rates vary greatly by region and area

Figure 6E shows the trend in the percent of people who are poor—the poverty rate—by region for the period 1971-98; **Table 6.13** presents the regional rates at various economic peaks.

While the trend in regional rates follows the familiar cyclical pattern—rising over economic downturns and falling over recoveries—some interesting differences emerge in the figure, particularly toward the end of the period. Following the deep recession of the early 1980s, poverty rates in the Northeast fell steeply; by the 1989 peak, this was the only region where the poverty rate—10.0%—was below its 1979 level of 10.4%. Over the much milder (from a national perspective) recession of the early 1990s, however, poverty rates increased most steeply in the Northeast and West, and, as of 1998, they had yet to fall back to their 1989 levels. These trends led to some shifts in terms of regional poverty rankings. For example, although Midwestern poverty was roughly equal to that of the Northeast prior to 1979, from the mid-1990s forward Northeastern poverty was 2 percentage points higher than the Midwest. Similarly, Southern poverty rates were far and away the highest in the nation throughout most of the period in the figure, yet by 1998 Western and Southern rates were about equal (14.0% and 13.7%, respectively). The differing trends in wages, unemployment, and job growth just examined explain part of the convergence of these regional trends. Immigration of low-income families into Western states is probably another relevant factor.

Table 6.14, which combines two years of data from the most recent business cycle peak (1988-89) and for the most recent data (1997-98), examines

FIGURE 6E Poverty rates by region, 1971-98

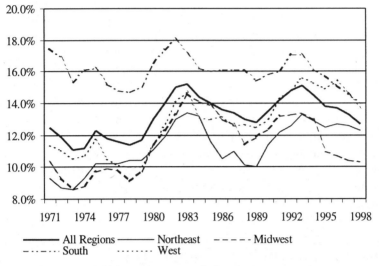

Source: U.S. Bureau of the Census, poverty web site.

TABLE 6.13 Poverty rates for persons by region

Year	U.S.	Northeast	Midwest	South	West
1973	11.1%	8.6%	8.6%	15.3%	10.5%
1979	11.7	10.4	9.7	15.0	10.0
1989	12.8	10.0	11.9	15.4	12.5
1998	12.7	12.3	10.3	13.7	14.0
Percentage-point changes					
1973-79	0.6	1.8	1.1	-0.3	-0.5
1979-89	1.1	-0.4	2.2	0.4	2.5
1989-98	-0.1	2.3	-1.6	-1.7	1.5

Source: U.S. Bureau of the Census, poverty web site.

recent developments in state-level poverty rates. **Figure 6F** shows selected trends for some larger states for 1989-98.

The Northeastern trends just discussed were driven by broad-based increases in poverty throughout the region in the 1990s. The only state in the region to experience falling poverty was Maine, one of the least populous Northeastern states. In some of the larger states, like New York and Massachusetts, poverty rates grew by 3.6 and 1.8 percentage points, respectively. The decline in Midwestern poverty rates was driven mostly by the larger states in the East North Central division, as Indiana, Illinois, and Michigan all experienced declines of at least 2 percentage points. Southern poverty rates fell especially steeply in some of the poorest states. For example, in 1988-89, Mississippi had the highest rate in the nation, at 24.6%. By 1997-98, the rate had fallen 7.5 percentage points—the largest decline in the nation—to 17.2%. Western trends were dominated by California, where poverty grew by 3 percentage points. California ended the last business cycle in 1989 with poverty rates close to that of the nation; by 1997-98, the state poverty rate was well-above that of the U.S.

Figure 6G and **Table 6.15** shift the geographical focus on poverty from regions and states to residence. Census data allow for the comparison of poverty rates in metropolitan and non-metropolitan (or rural) areas. Within metropolitan areas, poverty rates in central cities can be compared with those in surrounding areas. The last column in the table compares city and rural poverty rates.

In 1959, national poverty rates were dominated by very high levels of rural

FIGURE 6F Poverty rates for four states, 1989-98

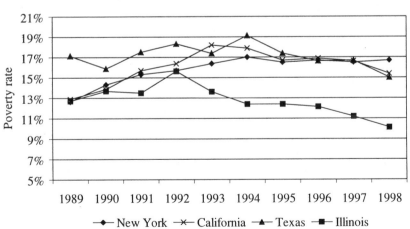

Source: U.S. Bureau of the Census, poverty web site.

TABLE 6.14 Poverty by state, two-year averages, 1988-98

	1988-89	1997-98	Percentage-point change (1988/89)-(1997/98)
NORTHEAST			
New England			
Maine	11.8%	10.3%	-1.6
New Hampshire	7.2	9.5	2.3
Vermont	8.1	9.6	1.6
Massachusetts	8.7	10.5	1.8
Rhode Island	8.3	12.2	3.9
Connecticut	3.5	9.1	5.6
Middle Atlantic			
New York	13.0%	16.6%	3.6
New Jersey	7.2	9.0	1.8
Pennsylvania	10.4	11.2	0.8
MIDWEST			
East North Central			
Ohio	11.5%	11.1%	-0.4
Indiana	11.9	9.1	-2.8
Illinois	12.7	10.7	-2.1
Michigan	12.7	10.7	-2.0
Wisconsin	8.1	8.5	0.4
West North Central			
Minnesota	11.4%	10.0%	-1.4
Iowa	9.9	9.4	-0.5
Missouri	12.7	10.8	-1.9
North Dakota	11.9	14.4	2.5
South Dakota	13.7	13.7	0.0
Nebraska	11.6	11.1	-0.5
Kansas	9.5	9.7	0.2
SOUTH			
South Atlantic			
Delaware	9.3%	10.0%	0.6
Maryland	9.4	7.8	-1.6
District of Columbia	16.6	22.1	5.5
Virginia	10.9	10.8	-0.1
West Virginia	16.8	17.1	0.3
North Carolina	12.4	12.7	0.3
South Carolina	16.3	13.4	-2.9
Georgia	14.5	14.1	-0.4
Florida	13.1	13.7	0.6

(cont.)

TABLE 6.14 *(cont.)* Poverty by state, two-year averages, 1988-98

	1988-89	1997-98	Percentage-point change (1987/88)-(1997/98)
SOUTH *(cont.)*			
East South Central			
Kentucky	16.9%	14.7%	-2.2
Tennessee	18.2	13.9	-4.4
Alabama	19.1	15.1	-4.0
Mississippi	24.6	17.2	-7.5
West South Central			
Arkansas	20.0%	17.3%	-2.7
Louisiana	23.1	17.7	-5.4
Oklahoma	16.0	13.9	-2.1
Texas	17.6	15.9	-1.7
WEST			
Mountain			
Montana	15.1%	16.1%	1.0
Idaho	12.5	13.9	1.4
Wyoming	10.3	12.1	1.8
Colorado	12.3	8.7	-3.6
New Mexico	21.3	20.8	-0.5
Arizona	14.1	16.9	2.8
Utah	9.0	9.0	-0.1
Nevada	9.7	10.8	1.1
Pacific			
Washington	9.2%	9.1%	-0.1
Oregon	10.8	13.3	2.5
California	13.1	16.0	3.0
Alaska	10.8	9.1	-1.7
Hawaii	11.2	12.4	1.2
TOTAL U.S.	12.9%	13.0%	0.1

Source: U.S. Bureau of the Census, poverty web site.

poverty. But, as shown in the figure, rural poverty rates fell by more than half over the 1960s and 1970s. Poverty in urban areas, after falling in the 1960s, began to increase at rates well above the national average. By the end of the period, this growth pattern left urban poverty back at its 1959 level. As the last column of Table 6.15 shows, the urban poverty rate was about half that of rural areas in 1959, but by the end of the period urban poverty rates were 4.1 points above rural rates. Nevertheless, it would be a mistake to envision poverty as an

FIGURE 6G Poverty rates by metro/nonmetro area, 1959-98

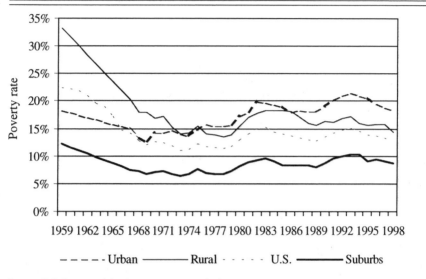

Source: U.S. Bureau of the Census, poverty web site.

TABLE 6.15 Poverty rates by metro/nonmetro areas

Year	City	Suburbs	Rural	U.S.	City/rural difference
1959	18%	12%	33%	22%	-14.9
1973	14.0	6.4	14.0	11.1	0.0
1979	15.7	7.2	13.8	11.7	1.9
1989	18.1	8.0	15.7	12.8	2.4
1998	18.5	8.7	14.4	12.7	4.1
Percentage-point changes					
1959-73	-4.3	-5.8	-19.2	-11.3	-14.9
1973-79	1.7	0.8	-0.2	0.6	1.9
1979-89	2.4	0.8	1.9	1.1	0.5
1989-98	0.4	0.7	-1.3	-0.1	1.7

Source: U.S. Bureau of the Census, poverty web site.

inner-city problem, since rural poverty rates remain 1.7 points above the national average. The suburbs have consistently been the area with the lowest rates of poverty, although poverty has increased there slightly (by less than 1 percentage point) in each business cycle since 1973.

The regressivity of state tax liabilities

State and local taxes are significantly more regressive than federal taxes, meaning that tax liability as a share of income falls as income increases. Most of state tax revenue is derived from sales taxes—a highly regressive revenue source—and property taxes, which, though less so than sales taxes, are also regressive. Evidence of state-tax regressivity is shown in **Table 6.16**, which presents state-level effective tax rates (liability as a share of income) by income quintile in 1995 (the most recent available analysis of this sort).

Note that in each state effective tax rates decline as income grows. For example, in the state of Washington, one of the most regressive, families in the bottom fifth paid 17% of their income in 1995 in state and local taxes, while the wealthiest families—those in the top 1%—paid 3.6%. In Nevada, families in the top 1% paid less than 2% of their income in state and local taxes, while families in the bottom fifth paid 8.9%. Delaware has a relatively flat tax structure; low-income families pay only a slightly larger share of their income in taxes than families in the top fifth. But, as shown in the final row ("U.S. Average"), most states and localities have a more regressive tax structure, as the average effective rate falls from 12.4% for the bottom fifth to 5.8% for the top 1%.

Conclusion

The data from individual regions and states show a high degree of variation, but a few general points emerge: (1) although unemployment fell in many states in the 1980s, regional labor markets did not tighten up sufficiently to generate geographically broad-based wage gains in that period; (2) while the states of the Northeast and California did relatively well during the expansion of the 1980s, compared to other states, they lost relatively more, or gained less, in terms of income, wages, employment, and poverty in the 1990s—in fact, median family income was lower and poverty was higher in the Northeast in 1998 than in 1989; and (3) in the 1990s, low- and middle-wage workers in most states, particularly those in the South and Midwest, benefited from a tightening labor market and the increases in the minimum wage.

TABLE 6.16 State and local taxes in 1995, effective rates*

	Lowest 20%	Second 20%	Middle 20%	Fourth 20%	Top 20% Next 15%	Top 20% Next 4%	Top 20% Top 1%
NORTHEAST							
New England							
Maine	11.6%	9.7%	9.9%	10.1%	9.4%	8.2%	7.2%
New Hampshire	9.0	6.7	5.7	5.6	4.7	3.8	3.2
Vermont	9.4	8.5	9.6	8.4	8.0	7.0	6.9
Massachussetts	11.4	10.2	9.6	8.7	8.0	7.0	6.0
Rhode Island	12.8	10.9	9.9	9.4	8.7	7.6	7.5
Connecticut	11.3	9.5	9.5	8.8	7.8	6.1	4.9
Middle Atlantic							
New York	16.1%	13.9%	13.5%	12.6%	11.4%	9.8%	8.9%
New Jersey	15.6	10.0	9.1	8.	8.0	7.0	6.2
Pennsylvania	13.2	10.7	9.8	8.9	7.7	6.2	4.5
MIDWEST							
East North Central							
Ohio	11.6%	10.0%	9.6%	9.1%	8.1%	7.2%	6.3%
Indiana	12.6	10.3	9.4	8.3	7.3	6.0	4.9
Illinois	13.5	10.3	9.4	8.3	7.3	5.7	4.9
Michigan	13.2	11.4	10.2	9.1	7.8	6.5	5.0
Wisconsin	13.6	12.1	12.0	11.1	9.8	8.1	6.4
West North Central							
Minnesota	10.9%	10.9%	10.4%	9.7%	8.7%	8.0%	7.8%
Iowa	12.3	11.0	10.2	9.7	8.7	7.5	6.1
Missouri	11.5	10.2	9.6	8.8	7.7	6.5	5.5
North Dakota	10.6	8.7	7.8	7.3	6.5	5.7	5.2
South Dakota	11.7	8.9	7.8	6.6	5.7	4.0	2.6
Nebraska	10.8	10.1	9.7	9.1	8.3	7.2	6.4
Kansas	10.9	9.7	9.3	8.8	7.8	6.6	5.9
SOUTH							
South Atlantic							
Delaware	6.3%	6.5%	6.2%	6.0%	5.8%	5.2%	4.9%
Maryland	10.8	10.7	9.8	9.0	8.2	6.7	5.6
District of Columbia	10.5	10.0	9.5	9.1	8.0	6.4	6.4
Virginia	9.6	8.8	8.3	7.6	6.8	5.9	5.0
West Virginia	10.6	9.4	8.6	8.2	7.8	6.9	5.7
North Carolina	9.6	9.7	9.1	8.7	7.7	6.7	6.0
South Carolina	8.0	7.0	7.8	7.8	7.0	6.3	5.6
Georgia	11.1	9.9	9.3	8.4	7.4	6.3	5.7
Florida	14.0	9.8	7.6	6.4	5.3	4.1	3.2

(cont.)

TABLE 6.16 *(cont.)* State and local taxes in 1995, effective rates*

	Lowest 20%	Second 20%	Middle 20%	Fourth 20%	Top 20% Next 15%	Next 4%	Top 1%
SOUTH *(cont.)*							
East South Central							
Kentucky	10.4%	10.5%	10.2%	9.9%	8.7%	7.4%	5.7%
Tennessee	12.3	9.3	7.6	6.4	5.3	3.9	3.2
Alabama	11.5	10.3	9.0	7.8	6.5	5.2	3.6
Mississippi	12.1	9.7	9.6	9.1	7.7	6.4	5.4
West South Central							
Arkansas	12.0%	10.5%	9.6%	9.0%	8.1%	6.8%	5.7%
Louisiana	13.4	11.2	10.4	8.8	7.4	5.6	4.8
Oklahoma	9.9	10.0	9.4	8.9	7.6	6.1	5.0
Texas	13.8	10.4	8.5	7.3	6.1	4.9	4.0
WEST							
Mountain							
Montana	7.6%	6.5%	6.6%	6.9%	6.6%	5.9%	5.5%
Idaho	9.2	9.2	9.0	8.8	8.2	7.1	6.8
Wyoming	8.2	6.5	5.7	4.7	3.8	3.0	2.7
Colorado	9.9	9.0	8.4	7.7	6.6	5.6	5.1
New Mexico	15.0	12.6	11.0	10.0	8.9	7.5	6.7
Arizona	11.3	9.5	8.5	7.7	6.5	5.7	5.3
Utah	12.0	11.2	10.6	9.8	8.4	7.0	5.7
Nevada	8.9	5.6	4.7	4.1	3.4	2.5	1.6
Pacific							
Washington	17.0%	12.2%	10.4%	8.9%	7.2%	5.4%	3.6%
Oregon	10.8	9.1	9.2	9.2	8.5	7.6	7.0
California	12.0	9.0	8.5	8.1	7.8	7.4	8.1
Alaska	6.9	3.7	2.7	2.4	2.0	2.0	2.1
Hawaii	11.0	10.1	9.7	8.6	7.9	6.9	6.2
U.S. AVERAGES	12.4%	10.3%	9.4%	8.6%	7.7%	6.5%	5.8%

* The rates are the ratio of average tax liability to pre-tax family income by income class, after
  deducting the federal offset from state tax liability (since taxpayers can deduct state and local
  income and property taxes from their federal liability).

Source: Citizens for Tax Justice and Institute on Taxation and Economic Policy.

CHAPTER 7

International comparisons:
less-than-model behavior

In the preceding chapters, we judged current economic outcomes using historical data for the United States as a benchmark. In this chapter, we compare the
economic performance of the United States to that of 19 other rich, industrialized countries belonging to the Paris-based Organization for Economic Cooperation and Development (OECD). The comparison provides an independent
yardstick for gauging the strengths and weaknesses of the U.S. economy, allowing a comparison of the U.S. economy with similar economies facing the same
global conditions with respect to trade, investment, technology, the environment, and other factors that shape economic opportunities. The international
comparisons also shed light on an important debate about the advisability of
exporting the "U.S. model" to other economies. In particular, with unemployment rates in the late 1990s low in the United States and generally high in Europe, many have argued that Europe should emulate key features of the U.S.
economy, including weaker unions, lower minimum wages, less-generous social benefit systems, and lower taxes.

The international comparisons underline several features of postwar economic development in the United States and the rest of the OECD. First – despite improvements in the last years of the decade – the 1990s were a period of
slow growth in national income and productivity in all of the OECD economies,
including the United States. Income and productivity growth over the last decade have generally trailed the rates obtained in the 1970s and 1980s and are far
below those of the "Golden Age" from the end of World War II through the first
oil shock in 1973. Second, the United States has consistently ranked in the middle
or near the bottom of the OECD countries with respect to income and productivity growth. Third, the U.S. economy has consistently produced the highest

levels of economic inequality, including the highest poverty rate, among the rich, industrialized economies. Moreover, inequality in the United States (along with the United Kingdom) has shown a strong tendency to rise, even as inequality was relatively stable or declining in most of the rest of the OECD. Fourth, economic mobility for those at the bottom, a factor that in principle could counteract the effects of inequality, is actually *lower* in the United States than in other OECD economies.

Incomes and productivity: United States loses edge

For the entire postwar period, the United States has provided an average standard of living that is among the highest in the world. **Tables 7.1** and **7.2** summarize data from 1960 through 1998 on the most common measure of average living standards: per capita income, or the total value of goods and services produced in the domestic economy per member of the population. Table 7.1 converts the value of foreign goods and services, measured in foreign currency, to U.S. dollars using the market-determined exchange rate in each year. By this measure, in 1960, the United States had one of the highest standards of living among the 20 countries in the table, trailing only Switzerland, Sweden, and Denmark, but well ahead of most of the European economies that were still rebuilding themselves after World War II. Per capita income grew rapidly in the United States in the 1960s and 1970s, but rose even more rapidly in almost all the other economies. As a result, almost all of the OECD economies narrowed the income gap with the United States. In the 1980s and again in the 1990s, growth in per capita income decelerated sharply throughout most of the OECD, including the United States. In these last two sluggish decades, growth in U.S. per capita income was about average for the rich countries. By 1998, the slower relative U.S. growth overall had left per capita income in the United States at $32,051 per year. This was above the average – $27,237, excluding the United States and weighted by population – but below that of Norway ($43,375), Switzerland ($41,361), Denmark ($38,785), Finland ($36,804), and Sweden ($35,042), and about equal to that of Japan ($32,043).

Using market exchange rates to convert the cost of goods and services in other countries to a U.S. value can, in some cases, give a misleading picture of the relative standards of living. If the citizens of every country faced the same prices for the goods and services they purchased with their incomes, then a simple conversion using market exchange rates would be sufficient for making comparisons. In reality, however, prices vary considerably across countries. For example, land and housing prices are generally much lower in the wide-open

TABLE 7.1 Per capita income, using market exchange rates,* 1960-98 (1998 dollars)

Country	Per capita income				Annual growth rates (%)		
	1960	1979	1989	1998	1960-79	1979-89	1989-98
United States	$15,413	$23,936	$27,676	$32,051	2.3%	1.5%	1.6%
Japan	6,418	21,008	28,630	32,043	6.4	3.1	1.3
Germany**	11,234	20,889	25,183	28,483	3.3	1.9	1.4
France	11,161	22,107	25,806	28,649	3.7	1.6	1.2
Italy	8,789	18,764	23,550	25,924	4.1	2.3	1.1
United Kingdom	11,134	16,955	21,128	23,681	2.2	2.2	1.3
Canada	12,183	22,019	26,021	27,227	3.2	1.7	0.5
Australia	$11,055	$18,166	$21,673	$25,452	2.6%	1.8%	1.8%
Austria	9,937	20,503	24,840	29,229	3.9	1.9	1.8
Belgium	9,920	19,776	23,903	27,471	3.7	1.9	1.6
Denmark	15,449	26,847	32,020	38,785	3.0	1.8	2.2
Finland	12,453	24,650	33,863	36,804	3.7	3.2	0.9
Ireland	5,860	11,459	14,913	26,965	3.6	2.7	6.8
Netherlands	11,361	20,071	22,889	27,715	3.0	1.3	2.1
New Zealand	10,917	14,321	16,238	15,848	1.4	1.3	-0.3
Norway	13,235	26,579	33,404	43,375	3.7	2.3	2.9
Portugal	2,484	6,247	8,312	10,488	5.0	2.9	2.6
Spain	5,164	12,142	15,245	18,369	4.6	2.3	2.1
Sweden	16,437	27,851	33,285	35,042	2.8	1.8	0.6
Switzerland	24,154	35,001	40,841	41,361	2.0	1.6	0.1
Average excluding U.S.	$9,219	$19,305	$24,149	$27,237	4.1%	2.2%	1.4%

* At the price levels and exchange rates for 1990.
** Eastern and Western Germany.

Source: Authors' analysis of OECD (1999) data.

United States, Canada, and Australia than they are in more crowded European countries. Market exchange rates can also fluctuate widely in response to short-term international capital flows and other macroeconomic factors, and thus they may not accurately reflect long-term differences in national prices. To correct for this shortcoming, Table 7.2 uses an alternative set of criteria for converting the value of each country's goods and services into U.S. dollars. These alternative exchange rates, known as purchasing-power parities (PPPs), are not based on international currency market exchange rates but, rather, on the price of buying the same "basket" of goods and services in all countries. While calculation of PPPs presents many practical and conceptual problems, PPPs are probably a reasonable indicator of the relative price of consumption and arguably a better measure of relative living standards than market exchange rates.

TABLE 7.2 Per capita income, using purchasing-power-parity exchange rates,*
1960-98 (1998 dollars)

Country	Per capita income				Annual growth rates (%)		
	1960	1979	1989	1998	1960-79	1979-89	1989-98
United States	$13,414	$22,254	$27,312	$32,413	2.7%	2.1%	1.9%
Japan	4,672	14,812	20,201	24,170	6.3	3.2	2.0
Germany**	9,842	17,769	20,961	24,868	3.2	1.7	1.9
France	8,546	17,064	20,495	22,255	3.7	1.8	0.9
Italy	7,286	15,369	18,998	22,234	4.0	2.1	1.8
United Kingdom	9,974	15,202	18,903	21,502	2.2	2.2	1.4
Canada	10,503	19,099	22,587	25,496	3.2	1.7	1.4
Australia	—	—	—	—	—	—	—
Austria	$7,666	$15,817	$19,163	$23,930	3.9%	1.9%	2.5%
Belgium	8,069	16,016	19,318	24,239	3.7	1.9	2.6
Denmark	9,793	16,807	20,042	26,176	2.9	1.8	3.0
Finland	—	—	—	—	—	—	—
Ireland	—	—	—	—	—	—	—
Netherlands	9,351	16,736	19,085	24,008	3.1	1.3	2.6
New Zealand	—	—	—	—	—	—	—
Norway	8,120	16,244	20,414	27,581	3.7	2.3	3.4
Portugal	—	—	—	—	—	—	—
Spain	—	—	—	—	—	—	—
Sweden	9,894	16,765	20,035	21,218	2.8	1.8	0.6
Switzerland	—	—	—	—	—	—	—
Average excl. U.S.	$7,891	$16,179	$20,128	$23,547	3.8%	2.2%	1.8%

* 1996 benchmark EKS.
** Western Germany only.

Source: Authors' analysis of BLS (2000) data.

When per capita income is measured on a PPP basis, the United States appears to provide an average standard of living that is well above that of most of the rest of the OECD economies. This suggests that consumption goods (housing, food, transportation, clothing) are generally cheaper in the United States than in the other economies, helping to raise the national standard of living relative to other "more expensive" economies. The pattern of *growth* in per capita income, however, differs little when PPPs are used instead of market exchange rates. Across almost all of the economies in Table 7.2, including the United States, growth in per capita income decelerated sharply in the 1980s and again in the 1990s. Throughout the period 1960-98, the U.S. growth rate was consistently in the middle or the bottom of the pack.

TABLE 7.3 Relative productivity levels, 1960-97 (U.S. = 100)

Country	1960	1973	1987	1997
United States	100	100	100	100
Japan	21	45	58	68
Germany	—	—	—	88
Western Germany*	52	69	84	101
France	54	73	96	103
Italy	40	64	78	88
United Kingdom	58	66	79	83
Canada	79	79	86	81
Australia	73	70	77	80
Austria	44	64	79	85
Belgium	49	68	89	107
Denmark	48	63	68	77
Finland	37	55	64	78
Ireland	31	42	59	90
Netherlands	58	77	95	101
New Zealand	—	—	—	58
Norway	48	56	76	106
Portugal	22	37	40	47
Spain	23	44	57	70
Sweden	58	73	78	78
Switzerland	71	76	76	78
Average excl. U.S.	47	61	73	82

* Figure in column for 1997 refers to 1995.

Source: Conference Board (1999).

The main determinant of an economy's current and future standard of living is the level and rate of growth of productivity – the value of goods and services that the economy can produce on average in an hour of work. Productivity is, therefore, the starting point in any explanation of differences in the level and growth of income across countries. **Table 7.3** presents data on the productivity level of the same economies examined in Tables 7.1 and 7.2. In each of the four years covered, each country's productivity level is expressed as a percentage of the corresponding productivity level in the United States. In 1960, the U.S. economy was far more productive than the others, producing almost five times more goods and services in an hour than Japan and almost twice as much in an hour as Germany, France, or the United Kingdom. The nearest competitors were

TABLE 7.4 Labor productivity growth per year, 1960-97

	1960*-73	1973-79	1979-97**
United States	2.6%	0.3%	0.9%
Japan	8.4	2.8	2.3
Germany***	4.5	3.1	2.2
France	5.3	2.9	2.2
Italy	6.4	2.8	2.0
United Kingdom	4.0	1.6	2.0
Canada	2.5	1.1	1.0
Australia	3.0%	2.5%	1.5%
Austria	5.9	3.1	2.3
Belgium	5.2	2.7	1.9
Denmark	3.9	2.3	2.1
Finland	5.0	3.2	3.5
Ireland	4.8	4.3	4.1
Netherlands	4.8	2.6	1.5
New Zealand	2.1	-1.1	1.3
Norway	3.8	2.7	1.8
Portugal	7.5	0.5	2.4
Spain	5.9	2.8	2.7
Sweden	3.7	1.4	2.0
Switzerland	3.3	0.8	0.6

*   Business sector.
**   Or closest available year.
*** First two columns refer to western Germany. The third column is calculated as the weighted average of West German productivity growth between 1979 and 1991 and total German productivity growth between 1991 and 1997.

Source: OECD (1998).

other economies that had escaped massive dislocation during World War II: Canada (79% of the U.S. level), Australia (73%), and Switzerland (71%). Between 1960 and 1995, all of the economies narrowed the productivity gap with the United States. By 1997, five of the economies – Belgium (107%), France (103%), western Germany (101%), the Netherlands (101%), and Norway (106%) – had essentially attained or exceeded U.S. productivity levels.

Table 7.4 and **Figure 7A** summarize the international trends in productivity growth rates. The pattern of productivity growth closely resembles that of per capita income, which is not surprising given the close connection between the two concepts. The first key feature of productivity growth is the dramatic slowdown after the mid-1970s: productivity across the OECD economies was much more

FIGURE 7A Productivity growth rates, 1960-97

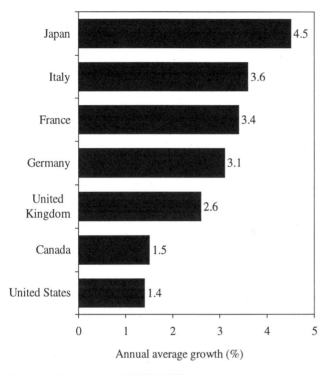

Annual average growth (%)

Source: Authors' analysis of OECD (1999).

rapid in the 1960s than in the 1980s and 1990s. A second feature of international productivity growth is that the United States has been among the poorest performers over the whole period. (The estimate for the United States for the period 1979-97, taken from the OECD, is slightly lower than the official U.S. government rate because the estimates in Table 7.4 do not take into account recent changes in the method that the Bureau of Labor Statistics uses to calculate labor productivity. The figures here, however, are comparable across countries.)

Traditionally, economists have excused the poor U.S. performance by arguing that it is much harder to lead than to follow, to innovate than to imitate. In this view, productivity growth is faster outside the United States because other economies are engaged in a constant game of catch-up that involves the rapid assimilation of technological improvements pioneered in the United States. While this view may have made sense as late as the 1960s or 1970s, the data on productivity levels in Table 7.3 suggest that, by the mid-1990s, several European economies had matched or exceeded U.S. productivity levels, and many others had narrowed the gap considerably. If U.S. productivity growth rates continue to lag behind those in other OECD economies, economists may have to allow that features intrinsic to European economies provide them with an important edge over the United States when it comes to productivity growth. Certainly, the ability of Belgium, France, western Germany, the Netherlands, and Norway to reach U.S. productivity levels in the 1990s suggests that these countries' comprehensive welfare and collective-bargaining systems have not stymied income growth or improvements in economic efficiency relative to the more free-market-oriented United States.

Some economists have also dismissed the evidence of high European productivity levels as simply a by-product of high European unemployment rates. These economists argue that low-productivity workers find jobs in the low-unemployment United States, thus pulling down the average productivity level of the economy. In Europe, which generally has higher unemployment rates than the United States, low-productivity workers are less likely to work and therefore don't pull down average productivity levels. This argument, however, has several flaws. First, two of the European economies in Table 7.3 with productivity levels above the U.S. level – the Netherlands and Norway – actually have *lower* unemployment rates than does the United States. (See Table 7.21, which indicates that, in 1999, the unemployment rate was 3.3% in the Netherlands and 3.2% in Norway.) The very low unemployment rates in these countries did not prevent them from achieving high productivity levels. Second, in the European economies that do have high unemployment rates, an important share of unemployed workers have mid- to high levels of formal education. (See, for example, Table 7.22 and the related discussion.) These levels of education suggest that, if unemployed workers in Europe did find work, they would not have a significant negative impact on average productivity. Even if currently unemployed workers had zero productivity, however, their inclusion in the workforce would not substantially alter the picture in Table 7.3. Take the case of Belgium, with a 1997 productivity level 107% of that in the United States. In that same year, the unemployment rate in Belgium was 9.4%, about 4.5 percentage points above the 4.9% rate in the United States. Lowering the Belgian unemployment rate by 4.5 percentage points—to be equal to that of the United States—and assigning these formerly unemployed workers to jobs with zero productivity would reduce the relative productivity level in Belgium from 107% of the U.S. level to roughly 102.5%. Even under these unrealistic assumptions, Belgium would maintain its productivity advantage over the United States, despite Belgium's much higher unemployment rate. Furthermore, conducting a similar exercise with all the countries in Table 7.3 does not significantly alter the earlier conclusions.

TABLE 7.5 Real compensation growth per year,* 1979-98

Country	1979-89	1989-98
United States	-0.3%	0.6%
Japan	1.4	0.4
Germany*	1.2	1.2
France	1.0	1.0
Italy	1.4	0.5
United Kingdom	2.1	1.3
Canada	0.5	0.8
Australia	0.3%	1.3%
Austria	1.9	1.4
Belgium	0.9	1.5
Denmark	0.2	1.6
Finland	3.0	2.3
Ireland	1.6	1.7
Netherlands	0.0	0.4
New Zealand	0.1	-0.3
Norway	0.4	1.7
Portugal	0.1	3.2
Spain	0.1	1.5
Sweden	1.3	1.3
Switzerland	1.5	0.0
Average excl. U.S.	1.2%	0.9%

*   Compensation per employee in business sector.
** Growth rate for western Germany, 1979-91; eastern and western Germany, 1992-98.

Source: Authors' analysis of OECD data.

Workers' wages and compensation: slow, unequal growth

Wages and other work-related benefits are by far the most important source of income for the vast majority of people in the United States and the other comparison countries. The level, growth, and distribution of wages and benefits are therefore important starting points for international economic comparisons.

Table 7.5 shows the annual growth rate of total compensation (wages plus fringe benefits) in the private sector for 20 countries in the 1980s and 1990s. In both decades, growth rates have varied considerably across countries. In the 1980s, the United States put in the worst performance, with average compensation falling about 0.3% per year; compensation grew most in Finland (3.0% per year) and the United Kingdom (2.1% per year). In the 1990s, average compensa-

TABLE 7.6 Relative hourly compensation of manufacturing production workers, 1979-98 (using market exchange rates, U.S. = 100)

Country	Hourly compensation (U.S. = 100)		
	1979	1989	1998
United States	100%	100%	100%
Japan	60	88	97
Germany*	124	123	151
France	85	88	98
Italy	78	101	92
United Kingdom	63	74	89
Canada	87	103	85
Australia	83%	87%	80%
Austria	88	99	119
Belgium	131	108	125
Denmark	116	101	122
Finland	83	118	116
Ireland	54	67	72
Netherlands	126	105	111
New Zealand	52	54	50
Norway	114	128	128
Portugal	19	21	30
Spain	59	63	65
Sweden	125	122	119
Switzerland	117	117	131
Average excl. U.S.	82%	93%	101%

* Western Germany.

Source: Authors' analysis of BLS data.

tion in the United States recovered somewhat, with an annual growth rate of 0.6%. Over the same period, compensation growth was the worst in New Zealand (-0.3% per year) and Switzerland (0.0% per year). Nevertheless, in most economies in the 1990s, total compensation grew more rapidly than in the United States.

The most extensive international data on compensation covers the narrower group of workers in manufacturing. **Tables 7.6** and **7.7** compare hourly compensation in manufacturing in 19 OECD countries to the corresponding levels in the United States in 1979, 1989, and 1998. In Table 7.6, national compensation rates are converted into U.S. dollars using market exchange rates. Since market exchange rates reflect the relative value of American goods, services

TABLE 7.7 Relative hourly compensation of manufacturing production workers, 1979-98 (using purchasing power parities, U.S. = 100)

Country	Hourly compensation (U.S. = 100)		
	1979	1989	1998
United States	100%	100%	100%
Japan	49	61	78
Germany*	86	111	132
France	66	86	87
Italy	87	100	96
United Kingdom	62	76	81
Canada	81	92	107
Australia	71%	79%	97%
Austria	72	92	109
Belgium	91	107	120
Denmark	71	78	96
Finland	59	80	101
Ireland	50	65	73
Netherlands	87	101	107
New Zealand	55	56	62
Norway	70	90	105
Portugal	31	34	43
Spain	58	70	76
Sweden	78	88	97
Switzerland	75	87	96
Average excl. U.S.	67%	82%	93%

* Western Germany.

Source: Authors' analysis of BLS and OECD data.

(including labor), and assets in international markets, the compensation figures here capture the relative costs to an employer of hiring U.S. labor. In 1998, nine of the 19 countries had total compensation levels in manufacturing that were higher than those in the United States; two other countries (Japan and France) provided compensation to their manufacturing workers that was almost identical to rates in the United States. Those countries offering compensation above that paid in the United States generally paid well above the U.S. rates, from 11% more in the Netherlands (111) to 51% more in western Germany (151). At least among the rich, industrialized countries, the United States has become something of a low-wage country.

In Table 7.7, national compensation rates are converted into U.S. dollars using purchasing-power parities. As with the per capita income figures calculated using PPPs in Table 7.2, these compensation figures probably better reflect the ability of the compensation levels in each country to guarantee a specific standard of living. When PPPs are used to adjust national compensation, U.S. workers fare better in the international comparison. In 1979, manufacturing compensation on a PPP basis was higher in the United States than in every other country examined here; only one country, Belgium (91), was within 10% of the U.S. level. All of the economies, however, closed the compensation gap between 1979 and 1998. By 1998, manufacturing compensation in the United States (100) had fallen behind that of western Germany (132), Belgium (120), Austria (109), the Netherlands (107), Canada (107), Norway (105), and Finland (101).

Table 7.8 looks more carefully at growth in manufacturing compensation, on a PPP basis, over the periods 1979-89 and 1989-98. The table examines growth in compensation over the two periods separately for all employees (i.e., both production, or non-supervisory, workers and non-production, or supervisory, workers) and for production workers only. During the 1980s, the United States had one of the lowest rates of growth in hourly compensation in manufacturing, just 0.2% per year. Over the same period, hourly compensation for production workers in the United States actually fell 0.8% per year, compared to an average growth in the other advanced economies of 1.5% per year. Production worker compensation also fell in New Zealand (-0.7% per year) and Denmark (-0.1% per year), but rose in every other country examined here. In the 1990s, the United States turned in the worst performance in compensation rates for all manufacturing employees, with a 0.6% per year growth rate. At the same time, compensation for production workers in the United States fell 0.2% per year. Outside the United States, hourly compensation for production workers grew, on average, 1.4% per year. The positive growth rates in hourly compensation for all manufacturing employees and the negative growth rates for production workers in the United States are another manifestation of growing inequality in the United States over the 1980s and 1990s. In short, the hourly compensation data suggest that manufacturing compensation is growing more slowly and more unequally in the United States than it is in other OECD countries.

Table 7.9 takes a broader look at international earnings inequality, using data on full-time employees in all sectors of the economy. The table measures inequality as the ratio of earnings of high-wage workers (those making more than 90% of the total workforce) to the earnings of low-wage workers (those making more than only 10% of the workforce). By this measure, in the early 1980s, Canada and the United States were the most unequal of the OECD countries. The ratio of earnings of the 90th-percentile worker to those of the 10th-

TABLE 7.8 Real hourly compensation growth in manufacturing, 1979-98

Country	1979-89		1989-98	
	All employees	Production workers	All employees	Production workers
United States	0.2%	-0.8%	0.6%	-0.2%
Japan	1.8	1.4	2.2	2.2
Germany*	2.5	2.0	2.1	1.7
France	2.0	2.3	1.1	1.0
Italy	1.0	1.7	1.4	0.3
United Kingdom	2.9	1.8	1.7	1.0
Canada	0.2	0.2	1.1	1.0
Australia	—	0.5%	—	2.1%
Austria	—	2.0	—	1.7
Belgium	1.3%	1.0	1.1%	1.3
Denmark**	0.0	-0.1	2.4	2.0
Finland	—	3.1	—	3.0
Ireland	—	1.9	—	1.3
Netherlands	0.9	0.5	0.7	0.3
New Zealand	—	-0.7	—	0.6
Norway	1.0	1.0	1.7	1.5
Portugal	—	1.5	—	2.3
Spain	—	1.4	—	1.7
Sweden	1.0	0.9	1.0	1.2
Switzerland	—	1.3	—	0.4
Average excl. U.S.	1.8%	1.5%	1.7%	1.4%

* Western Germany.
** Figure for all workers in second period is 1989-93.

Source: Authors' analysis of BLS and OECD data.

percentile worker (the "90-10 ratio") was 4.01 in Canada and 3.65 in the United States, well above most of the rest of the economies in the table. As the last two columns of the table indicate, inequality grew steadily in the United States throughout the 1980s and 1990s. As a result, by the mid-1990s, the United States had surpassed Canada as the OECD country with the greatest degree of earnings inequality among full-time workers.

The pattern of changes in inequality in the rest of the OECD economies was complex. In the 1980s, inequality grew in the United Kingdom (4.9 points per year), Canada (4.4), Japan (1.5), Australia (1.3), and Finland (1.2); was rela-

TABLE 7.9 Earnings inequality growth, 1979-97

Country	Earnings inequality*			Annual point change x 100	
	Early 1980s	Late 1980s	Mid-1990s	Early 1980s to late 1980s	Late 1980s to mid-1990s
United States	3.65	4.14	4.43	5.0	3.6
Japan	3.01	3.16	3.02	1.5	-2.4
Germany**	2.69	2.46	2.32	-3.8	-3.5
France	3.24	3.28	3.06	0.4	-3.2
Italy	2.94	2.16	2.80	-7.8	16.0
United Kingdom	2.79	3.28	3.37	4.9	1.1
Canada	4.01	4.40	4.20	4.4	-5.2
Australia	2.74	2.87	2.92	1.3	0.8
Austria	3.45	3.51	3.66	0.6	2.9
Belgium***	—	1.99	2.07	—	1.4
Denmark	2.14	2.18	—	0.4	—
Finland	2.46	2.57	2.34	1.2	-3.7
Ireland	—	—	—	—	—
Netherlands	—	2.61	2.59	—	-0.3
New Zealand	—	2.92	3.40	—	5.3
Norway	2.06	1.98	—	-0.7	—
Portugal	—	3.49	4.05	—	13.9
Spain	—	—	—	—	—
Sweden	2.04	2.12	2.21	0.9	1.5
Switzerland	—	2.70	2.75	—	0.9

* Measured as the ratio of the earnings of the 90th-percentile worker to the 10th-percentile worker, i.e., the 90-10 ratio.
** Western Germany.
*** Data are for the 80-10 ratio.

Source: Authors' analysis of OECD data.

tively flat in Sweden (0.9), Austria (0.6), France (0.4), Denmark (0.4), and Norway (-0.7); and fell sharply in Italy (-7.8) and Germany (-3.8). In the 1990s, inequality grew sharply in Italy (16.0) and Portugal (13.9) and less in New Zealand (5.3), Austria (2.9), Sweden (1.5), Belgium (1.4), and the United Kingdom (1.1, a significant deceleration from the 4.9 points of the 1980s). Over the same period, inequality changed relatively little in Switzerland (0.9), Australia (0.8), and the Netherlands (-0.3), and actually declined in Canada (-5.2), Finland (-3.7), Germany (-3.5), France (-3.2), and Japan (-2.4). In short, since the end of the 1970s, earnings inequality has grown substantially in the United States, the United Kingdom, and New Zealand, but has fluctuated within a much narrower band in most of the rest of the more regulated OECD economies.

One of the most troubling aspects of U.S. inequality is that it can imply a

FIGURE 7B Hourly wages at 10th percentile, indexed to U.S., based on purchasing-power parities, 1991

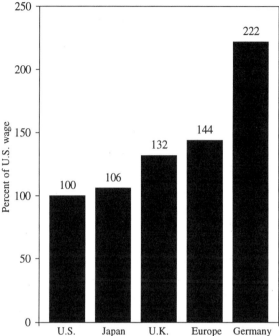

Source: Freeman (1995).

low standard of living for those at the bottom, despite the generally high average living standards for the U.S. economy as a whole. **Figure 7B** shows that, despite relatively high levels of average productivity in the U.S. economy, workers at the 10th percentile of the earnings distribution make considerably less in absolute terms than workers at a similar position in the earnings distribution of other rich, industrialized countries. (While more recent internationally comparable data are not available, wage trends over the 1990s almost certainly would have only a minor impact on the relative numbers in the figure.) On a purchasing-power basis (which, compared to market exchange rates, tends to raise the earnings of U.S. workers relative to workers in other countries), a low-wage worker in Germany, for example, makes more than twice as much as a low-wage worker in the United States. The typical low-wage worker in an advanced European economy earns 44% more than in the United States. The large dispersion of earnings in the United States relative to other countries leaves U.S. low-wage

TABLE 7.10 Earnings mobility of low-paid workers

Country	1991 earnings status of 1986 low-paid* workers			
	No longer employed full time	Still low paid*	Moved to second fifth	Moved to upper 60%
United States	41.4	30.6	16.7	11.3
Germany**	39.3	27.4	16.8	16.6
France	22.5	35.7	23.8	18.0
Italy	8.3	43.8	25.1	22.8
United Kingdom	12.9	35.8	27.8	23.6
Denmark	26.7	32.1	20.5	20.7
Finland	26.3	28.8	20.1	24.8
Sweden	27.6	35.5	18.4	18.4

* The bottom 20% of workers.
** Western Germany.

Source: Authors' analysis of OECD (1996).

workers with very low earnings, despite living in the country with one of the world's highest average income levels.

Boosters of the U.S. labor-market model often argue that greater economic mobility in the United States counteracts any negative effects of higher U.S. inequality in any given year. **Table 7.10** reproduces results from an OECD analysis of this claim. For each of eight countries, including the United States, the OECD identified workers from national surveys whose earnings placed them among the poorest 20% of full-time workers in 1986. The OECD used the same surveys to examine how these same workers were faring five years later, in 1991. In the United States, 41.4% were no longer employed full time, 30.6% still had earnings in the bottom 20% of all full-time workers, 16.7% had moved up to the second fifth of the earnings distribution, and 11.3% had joined the top 60% of earners. This U.S. record for mobility compares poorly to those of the other seven economies. The United States had the lowest share of workers moving to the second fifth of earners and the lowest share moving into the top 60%; it also had the highest share of workers no longer employed full time. By these figures, the United States economy appears to offer *less mobility* than those of Germany, France, Italy, the United Kingdom, Denmark, Finland, and Sweden, all economies known for a much greater degree of government intervention in the labor market than the United States.

Household income: slow, unequal growth

The per capita income figures in Tables 7.1 and 7.2 were economy-wide, annual averages. Since individuals make many important decisions about consumption as part of a family or broader household, and since, as we have seen, averages can be deceiving, we now turn to international comparisons of the distribution of household income. Since labor compensation accounts for the largest share of household income, the basic pattern of inequality that we observed with earnings repeats itself here: income inequality is high (and rising) in the United States compared to the rest of the OECD. U.S. inequality yields poverty rates that are higher, and living standards that are lower at the bottom, than those in comparable economies. As with earnings, income mobility appears to be *lower* in the United States than in other OECD countries.

Table 7.11 uses two measures of household income inequality for 19 OECD countries. The first measure is the "90-10 ratio" for household income, which is calculated using the same procedure as employed in Table 7.9. The 90-10 ratio gives the ratio of income received by the 90th-percentile household (receiving income greater than 90% of all households) to the income received by the 10th-percentile household (receiving more than 10%, but less than 90%, of all households). The second inequality measure is the Gini coefficient, a special inequality scale ranging from zero (perfect equality of income across households) to one (all income is concentrated at the very top of the income distribution). The United States has the most unequal household income by both measures (see also **Figure 7C**). In the United States, a household in the 10th percentile of the income distribution receives just 36% of the income of the median household (the household exactly in the middle of the income distribution). In the other 18 economies, the 10th percentile household receives between 44% (United Kingdom) and 58% (Belgium) of the median national income. At the other extreme, the 90th percentile household in the United States makes 208% of the median national income, a level matched only by Ireland (209%) and the United Kingdom (206%), with most other countries finding themselves somewhere between 155% (Denmark) and 185% (Switzerland). (The data in this figure and in some of the later figures and tables that deal with international comparisons of income distributions and poverty rates are the most recent internationally comparable data available. As is often the case when making international comparisons, however, some of the data are available only after a long lag. Data on the experiences of individual countries that cover more recent periods suggest that in most of the countries studied here income and poverty change only slowly over time—the United States and the United Kingdom are unusual in this respect—and the broad trends outlined here hold throughout the 1990s.)

TABLE 7.11 Household income inequality, relative to national median income

| Country | Year | Percent of national median | | Ratio of 90th to 10th percentile | Gini coefficient** |
		10th percentile*	90th percentile*		
United States	1991	36%	208%	5.78	0.343
Japan	1992	46	192	4.17	0.315
Germany***	1989	54	172	3.21	0.261
France	1984	55	193	3.48	0.294
Italy	1991	56	176	3.14	0.255
United Kingdom	1991	44	206	4.67	0.335
Canada	1991	47	183	3.90	0.285
Australia	1989	45%	193%	4.30	0.308
Austria	1987	56	187	3.34	—
Belgium	1992	58	163	2.79	0.230
Denmark	1992	54	155	2.86	0.239
Finland	1991	57	158	2.75	0.223
Ireland	1987	50	209	4.18	0.328
Netherlands	1991	57	173	3.05	0.249
New Zealand	1987-88	54	187	3.46	—
Norway	1991	56	158	2.80	0.233
Portugal	—	—	—	—	—
Spain	1990	49	198	4.04	0.306
Sweden	1992	57	159	2.78	0.229
Switzerland	1982	54	185	3.43	0.311
Average excluding U.S.	—	51%	186%	3.73	0.290

*   The 10th percentile household receives a higher income than 10% of the population, but less than 90% of the population; the 90th percentile household receives a higher income than 90% of the population, but less than 10% of the population.

**   The Gini coefficient equals 0 when income is perfectly equally distributed; it equals 1 when all income is concentrated at the top of the income distribution.

*** Western Germany.

Source: Gottschalk and Smeeding (1997).

The income inequality in Table 7.11 compares the position of low- and high-income households relative to the median income in each country. We can also compare the incomes of low- and high-income households to the median in the United States, thereby illustrating the absolute standard of living of low- and high-income households across countries (**Table 7.12** and **Figure 7D**). Despite the high median income in the United States, inequality in this country is so severe that low-income households in the United States are actually worse off

FIGURE 7C Household income inequality, national median income = 100

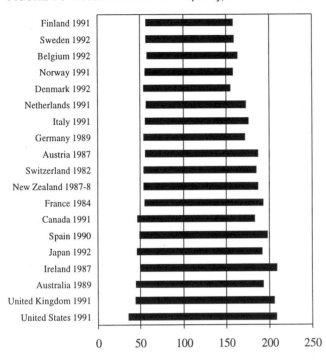

Source: Gottschalk and Smeeding (1997).

than in every other country in the table except the United Kingdom (which has a lower median household income and a high level of income inequality). Not surprisingly, high-income households are much better off in the United States (208% of the median income) than in the rest of the countries (except Canada, which trails only slightly behind the United States at 201% of the U.S. median).

Table 7.13 shows that, since the end of the 1970s, income inequality has been growing in most rich, industrialized countries. In absolute terms (see the last column of Table 7.13), the annual increase in income inequality has been strongest in Sweden, the United States, Australia, Japan, the Netherlands, and the United Kingdom. Income inequality has grown more slowly in Germany, France, and Norway and has been basically unchanged in Canada and Finland. Income inequality has fallen over the same period in Italy (though the more recent earnings data in Table 7.9 suggest that subsequent income data may show a large jump in inequality by the mid-1990s). Given the lower initial levels of inequality in most countries other than the United States, the absolute increases

TABLE 7.12 Household income inequality, relative to U.S. median income

| Country | Year | Percent of U.S. median | | Ratio of real national median to real U.S. median |
		10th percentile*	90th percentile*	
United States	1991	36%	208%	1.00
Japan	1991	43	176	0.92
Germany**	1989	41	133	0.77
France	1984	39	137	0.71
Italy	—	—	—	—
United Kingdom	1991	33	156	0.76
Canada	1991	52	201	1.10
Australia	1989	38%	165%	0.86
Austria	1987	—	—	—
Belgium	1992	43	120	0.74
Denmark	1992	46	131	0.85
Finland	1991	50	138	0.88
Ireland	—	—	—	—
Netherlands	1991	44	133	0.77
New Zealand	—	—	—	—
Norway	1991	51	143	0.91
Portugal	—	—	—	—
Spain	—	—	—	—
Sweden	1992	47	132	0.83
Switzerland	—	—	—	—
Average excluding U.S.	—	41%	155%	0.84

* The 10th percentile household receives a higher income than 10% of the population, but less than 90% of the population; the 90th percentile household receives a higher income than 90% of the population, but less than 10% of the population.
** Western Germany.

Source: Gottschalk and Smeeding (1997).

in other economies represent much larger relative increases in inequality than they would in the United States.

Since most studies of international poverty use relative income inequality to measure national poverty rates, higher inequality translates almost directly into higher levels of poverty in these international studies. **Table 7.14** summarizes international data from the 1990s on poverty rates for the population as a whole, for the elderly (65 and older), and for children (17 and under). Following

FIGURE 7D Household income inequality, U.S. median income = 100

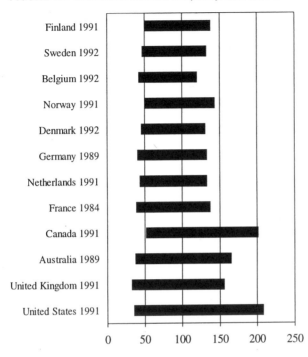

Source: Gottschalk and Smeeding (1997).

the standard methodology for international comparisons, the table defines the poverty rate as the share of households receiving 50% or less of the median household income in each country. In the United States, this threshold amounts to an income that is close to the official U.S. poverty line (see Chapter 6). (The data in Table 7.12, which compare the incomes of the 10th-percentile households in each country to the U.S. median income, provide an indication of the absolute standard of living of low-income families across the OECD countries.) Like the official U.S. definition, the poverty rates in Table 7.14 take into account cash transfers and are adjusted for family size, but, unlike the U.S. definition, they also account for taxes and the value of food stamps.

The United States, with 19.1% of its total population living in poverty in 1994 (this poverty rate, used for international comparison purposes, is higher than the official U.S. poverty rate for the same year), had the highest level of overall poverty among the 16 countries examined here. The next closest was the United Kingdom, with a 14.6% poverty rate. Nine of the 16 countries had pov-

TABLE 7.13 Change in income inequality after 1979

Country	Period	Annual change in Gini coefficient*	
		Relative (percent)	Absolute (point change)
United States	1979-95	0.79	0.35
Japan	1979-93	0.84	0.25
Germany**	1979-95	0.50	0.13
France	1979-89	0.40	0.12
Italy	1980-91	-0.64	-0.58
United Kingdom	1979-95	1.80	0.22
Canada	1979-95	-0.02	0.00
Australia	1981-89	1.16	0.34
Austria	—	—	—
Belgium	—	—	—
Denmark	1981-90	1.20	—
Finland	1979-94	-0.10	-0.02
Ireland	—	—	—
Netherlands	1979-94	1.07	0.25
New Zealand	—	—	—
Norway	1979-92	0.22	0.05
Portugal	—	—	—
Spain	—	—	—
Sweden	1979-94	1.68	0.38
Switzerland	—	—	—

*   Measured as the relative change in the Gini coefficient, where growth reflects more inequality.
** Western Germany.

Source: Authors' analysis based on Gottschalk and Smeeding (1997).

erty rates below 8%—less than half the U.S. rate. The United States did a little better with respect to poverty among the elderly. About 19.6% of Americans age 65 and older were living in poverty by this international definition, a smaller share than in the United Kingdom (23.9%) and Australia (21.6%), but the U.S. rate was still above those in the remaining 13 economies. The United States also suffers from the highest rate of child poverty, with almost one in four children (24.9%) under the age of 18 living in poverty by the international definition. Rates in the rest of the countries ranged from 2.7% (Finland) to 18.5% (United Kingdom).

International differences in labor market institutions such as minimum wages and unions explain a large part of the differences in international poverty rates,

TABLE 7.14 Poverty rates*

Country	Year	Percentage in poverty			Rank		
		Total	Elderly	Children	Total	Elderly	Children
United States	1994	19.1%	19.6%	24.9%	1	3	1
Japan	1992	11.8	18.4	12.2	4	4	7
Germany**	1989	7.6	7.5	8.6	8	10	9
France	1984	7.5	4.8	7.4	9	15	11
Italy	1991	6.5	4.4	10.5	14	16	8
United Kingdom	1991	14.6	23.9	18.5	2	1	2
Canada	1991	11.7	5.7	15.3	5	14	4
Australia	1989	12.9%	21.6%	15.4%	3	2	3
Austria	—	—	—	—	—	—	—
Belgium	1992	5.5	11.9	4.4	16	8	15
Denmark	1992	7.5	11.3	5.1	9	10	13
Finland	1991	6.2	14.4	2.7	15	5	17
Ireland	1987	11.1	7.6	13.8	6	11	5
Netherlands	1991	6.7	4.1	8.3	11	17	10
New Zealand	—	—	—	—	—	—	—
Norway	1991	6.6	13.5	4.9	13	6	14
Portugal	—	—	—	—	—	—	—
Spain	1990	10.4	11.4	12.8	7	9	6
Sweden	1992	6.7	6.4	3.0	11	13	16
Switzerland	—	—	—	—	—	—	—
Average excluding U.S.	—	9.8%	12.2%	11.3%	—	—	—

* Measured as share below 50% of the median adjusted disposable personal income for individuals.
Elderly are 65 and older; children are 17 and under.
** Western Germany.

Source: Smeeding (1997).

but variations across countries in tax and transfer programs for low-income households are also important. **Table 7.15** illustrates the net effect of national tax and transfer programs on poverty rates for the population as a whole, the elderly, and children in 15 countries. For the population as a whole, the "Pre" column gives the poverty rate determined by the workings of the labor market, that is, before taxes on gross incomes and before income received from government assistance programs. The United States, which has the highest overall poverty level in Table 7.14, has, at 26.7%, a lower "market-determined" poverty level than do Sweden (34.1%), Ireland (30.3%), the United Kingdom (29.2%), Belgium (28.4%), Spain (28.2%), and Denmark (26.9%). The U.S. tax and transfer

TABLE 7.15 The impact of taxes and transfers on poverty rates*

	Year	All persons Pre**	Post**	Change (%)	Elderly Pre**	Post**	Change (%)	Children Pre**	Post**	Change (%)
United States	1994	26.7	19.1	-28.5	58.7	19.6	-66.6	28.7	24.9	-13.2
Japan	.	.	.	.	.	.	.	.	.	.
Germany***	1989	22.0	7.6	-65.5	65.8	7.5	-88.6	11.7	8.6	-26.5
France	1984	21.6	7.5	-65.3	79.9	4.8	-94.0	27.4	7.4	-73.0
Italy	1991	18.4	6.5	-64.7	55.7	4.4	-92.1	11.0	10.5	-4.5
United Kingdom	1991	29.2	14.6	-50.0	68.5	23.9	-65.1	28.7	18.5	-35.5
Canada	1991	23.4	11.7	-50.0	58.2	5.7	-90.2	22.7	15.3	-32.6
Australia	1989	23.2	12.9	-44.4	70.2	21.6	-69.2	20.5	15.4	-24.9
Austria	—	—	—	—	—	—	—	—	—	—
Belgium	1992	28.4	5.5	-80.6	88.9	11.9	-86.6	17.2	4.4	-74.4
Denmark	1992	26.9	7.5	-72.1	69.9	11.3	-83.8	17.1	5.1	-70.2
Finland	1991	15.6	6.2	-60.3	43.8	14.4	-67.1	11.6	2.7	-76.7
Ireland	1987	30.3	11.1	-63.4	54.9	7.6	-86.2	30.3	13.8	-54.5
Netherlands	1991	22.8	6.7	-70.6	65.5	4.1	-93.7	15.2	8.3	-45.4
New Zealand	—	—	—	—	—	—	—	—	—	—
Norway	1991	21.8	6.6	-69.7	68.0	13.5	-80.1	12.7	4.9	-61.4
Portugal	—	—	—	—	—	—	—	—	—	—
Spain	1990	28.2	10.4	-63.1	68.2	11.4	-83.3	20.7	12.8	-38.2
Sweden	1992	34.1	6.7	-80.4	91.6	6.4	-93.0	18.4	3.0	-83.7
Switzerland	—	—	—	—	—	—	—	—	—	—
Average excluding U.S.	—	23.8	9.2	-61.7	67.5	10.1	-84.9	19.2	11.0	-38.1

* Measured as share below 50% of the median adjusted disposable personal income for individuals. Elderly are 65 and older; children are 17 and under.
** "Pre" refers to pre-tax, pre-transfer income; "post" refers to post-tax, post-transfer income.
*** Western Germany.

Source: Smeeding (1997).

system, however, reduces this market-determined poverty rate only to 19.1% (a 28.5% reduction in the number of persons in poverty). But the tax and transfer systems in all the other countries in the table reduce poverty by substantially higher margins, from 44.4% in Australia to 80.6% in Belgium. The U.S. tax and transfer system works best at reducing poverty among the elderly, due primarily to the workings of the Social Security program, which along with these other programs reduces poverty among the elderly by 66.6%. This sizable reduction, however, is the second smallest in the table, just better than the United Kingdom, which achieved only a 65.1% reduction in poverty among the elderly.

TABLE 7.16 Poverty rates and transitions into and out of poverty (% of population)

Country*	Average poverty rate**	Share poor for entire period	Share poor at least once over period	Avg. annual exit rate from poverty (% of poor)	Probability of re-entry into poverty after	
					1 Year	5 Years
Canada	11.4%	1.8%	28.1%	41.8%	16.0%	4.0%
Germany***	10.2	1.8	19.9	37.0	17.0	7.0
Netherlands	6.1	0.8	12.1	43.7	—	—
Sweden	7.4	1.1	11.9	36.3	20.0	1.0
United Kingdom	20.0	6.1	38.4	29.1	23.0	2.0
United States	14.2	4.6	26.0	28.6	18.0	8.0

*   Periods covered are: Canada, 1990-95; Germany, Netherlands, Sweden, and the United Kingdom, 1991-96; and United States, 1988-93.

**   Measured as percent of individuals with less than 50% of median equivalent disposable income, after taxes and transfers.

***   Western Germany.

Source: Oxley, Dang, and Antolin (1999).

The U.S. tax and transfer system does far worse in reducing poverty among children, managing to lower the market-determined poverty rate only from 28.7% to 24.9%, a mere 13.2% reduction in child poverty rates. Only Italy, with a final child poverty rate of 10.5%, produced a smaller reduction (4.5%) in child poverty. The tax and transfer systems in the rest of the OECD countries reduced child poverty between 24.9% (Australia) and 83.7% (Sweden).

As with earnings, some have argued that, while inequality in the United States may be higher than in other economies, the U.S. economy also offers greater opportunities for low-income households to improve their economic circumstances. **Table 7.16** presents the results of a study of income mobility in six countries in the mid-1990s that assesses this claim. The study offers a unique perspective on economic mobility because it followed the same families in each country for five consecutive years.

The first column of Table 7.16 gives the average poverty rate over a five-year period in each of the six countries studied. The United States had the second highest average poverty rate (14.2%), after the United Kingdom (20.0%). The U.S. rate was well above those in the remaining economies, which ranged from 6.1% in the Netherlands to 11.4% in Canada. The second column in the table shows the share of each country's population that remained in poverty for the entire five-year period under study. Again, the United States had the second highest rate (4.6%) after the United Kingdom (6.1%), with long-term poverty

FIGURE 7E Average annual exit rate from poverty

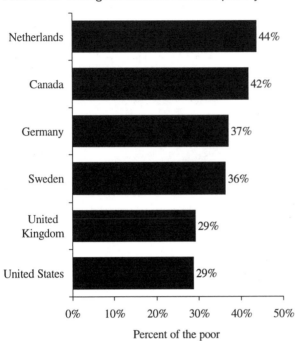

Source: Oxley, Dang, and Antolin (1999).

rates in the remaining countries less than half what they were in the United States. The third column reports the share of the national populations that were poor at least once in the five-year period. Just over one in four Americans (26.0%) were poor in at least one of the five years studied; one-time poverty rates were higher in the United Kingdom (38.4%) and Canada (28.1%), but lower in Germany (19.9%), the Netherlands (12.1%), and Sweden (11.9%). Together, these results suggest that, relative to other rich countries, the United States has a high and persistent poverty rate, with a large portion of its population finding itself in poverty at one point or another.

The last three columns of Table 7.16 provide further evidence of relatively low economic mobility in the United States. The fourth column displays the average annual exit rate (the share of the poor in one year that have left poverty by the following year) from poverty for each of the countries (see also **Figure 7E**). The data indicate that the poor in the United States are less likely than the poor in other countries to leave poverty from one year to the next. On average, about 28.6% of the poor in the United States escape poverty each year. The share of the poor leaving poverty in the other countries in the table ranges from 29.1% in the United Kingdom to 43.7% in the Netherlands. The poor in the United States are also more likely than the poor in other countries to fall back into poverty once they make it out. The last two columns in the table show that about 18% of those who escape poverty in the United States fall back into poverty one year later. This performance falls in the middle of the table, with the United Kingdom (23%) and Sweden (20%) doing worse, but Canada (16%) and Germany (17%) doing better. Five years after leaving poverty, however, about 8% of the previously poor in the United States find themselves poor again, a higher rate than in the other countries studied.

Employment and hours worked: strength of the U.S. model?

The per capita income figures in Tables 7.1 and 7.2 appear, at face value, to be at odds with the international estimates of productivity levels in Table 7.3. Per capita income in the United States – the value of goods and services produced in one year per person in the population – is generally much higher relative to the other OECD economies than is the U.S. productivity level – the value of goods and services produced in an hour of work. These differences between per capita income and productivity levels (gross national product per hour worked) stem from two important differences across countries: the share of the total population in employment, and the average number of hours worked each year by those with jobs.

The U.S. economy employs a greater share of its working-age population, and its workers work, on average, more hours per year, than is the case in any other rich, industrialized economy. These work practices raise per capita income in the United States relative to other economies with roughly similar productivity levels but lower levels of employment and lower average annual hours worked. Supporters of the U.S. model have long argued that the U.S. ability to generate a greater volume of work, whether measured in terms of number of jobs or hours of work, is a major feature of the U.S. model. In this section, we take a closer look at international employment rates, average hours worked, and unemployment rates.

The United States does indeed employ a greater share of its working-age population (men and women together) than any of the 10 economies in **Table 7.17** for which comparable data are available. In 1998, the United States employed 71.6% of its male working-age population (second only to Japan's 73.9%) and ranked first in female employment, with 57.1% of women employed. Em-

TABLE 7.17 Employment rates

	Employment rate*			Percentage-point change	
	1979	1989	1998	1979-89	1989-98
Men					
United States	73.8%	72.5%	71.6%	-1.3	-0.9
Japan	78.2	75.1	73.9	-3.1	-1.2
Germany**	69.8	65.9	61.4	-3.9	—
France	69.6	61.2	57.3	-8.4	-3.9
Italy	66.3	59.9	55.6	-6.4	-4.3
United Kingdom***	74.5	70.4	66.6	-4.1	-3.8
Canada	73.4	71.4	66.2	-2.0	-5.2
Australia	75.3%	71.9%	67.8%	-3.4	-4.1
Netherlands	74.3	65	70.8	-9.3	5.8
Sweden****	73.7	70.9	62.2	-2.8	-8.7
Women					
United States	47.5%	54.3%	57.1%	6.8	2.8
Japan	45.7	47.4	47.4	1.7	0
Germany**	38.4	39.7	43.6	1.3	—
France	40.5	41.2	41.6	0.7	0.4
Italy	27.3	28.6	29.3	1.3	0.7
United Kingdom***	45.3	49.1	50.6	3.8	1.5
Canada	45.3	53.7	53.4	8.4	-0.3
Australia	40.7%	48.6%	50.8%	7.9	2.2
Netherlands	29.2	37.4	48.7	8.2	11.3
Sweden****	57.2	61.7	53.6	4.5	-8.1

* Total employment as a percentage of working-age population.
** 1979 and 1989 data are for western Germany, while 1998 are for unified Germany.
*** Data in 1998 column refer to 1997.
**** Data for 1998 are preliminary.

Source: Authors' analysis of BLS (2000c).

ployment rates can vary because of differences across economies in school enrollment rates for adults, early retirement rates, and women's non-market responsibilities, especially child care. As we shall see below, however, one of the most important determinants of the differences in employment rates across these 10 economies is the unemployment rate.

Table 7.17 shows a different pattern over time for employment rates of men and women. Among working-age men, employment rates fell in every country during the 1980s and in every country except the Netherlands in the 1990s. The decline in male employment between 1979 and 1998 was smallest in the United States (1.3 percentage points in the 1980s and 0.9 percentage points in the 1990s). Declines in employment over the entire period were much higher in several European economies, most notably France (-12.3 percentage points), Sweden (-11.5 percentage points), Italy (-10.7 percentage points) and the United Kingdom (-7.9 percentage points). Among working-age women, employment rates rose between 1979 and 1998 in every country but Sweden (-3.6 percentage points from a high base in 1979). The largest increases occurred in the Netherlands (19.5 percentage points from a very low base in 1979), Australia (10.1 percentage points), the United States (9.6 percentage points), Canada (8.1 percentage points), and the United Kingdom (5.3 percentage points).

Table 7.18 reports the average number of hours worked per year by employees in 15 OECD countries. In 1998, workers in the United States worked, on average, more hours per year (1,966) than workers in any of the other countries, except Portugal (2,009). In fact, U.S. workers spent more time on the job than even the historic leader in hours worked, Japan (1,898). Between 1979 and 1998, as nearly every other country reduced its average hours worked per year, the United States increased its average by 61 hours. (Sweden also increased its average hours worked, by 100 hours per year, but only to a level that kept it next to the bottom in average hours worked per year – 1,551 hours, or less than 80% of the U.S. level.) **Figure 7F** reveals one important reason for international differences in hours worked: statutory annual vacation policies in European countries that exceed the average days provided, on average, by U.S. employers. The U.S. average, about 16 days per year, is below the legally required minimum in all of the countries in the figure.

The data on employment rates and average hours worked suggest that more U.S. workers (as a share of the U.S. working population) contribute more hours on average to GDP than is the case in most other OECD countries. The calculations in **Table 7.19** help to reconcile the differences between the U.S. and the other economies' productivity levels, on the one hand, and their per capita income, on the other. French productivity rates, for example, are 123% of the average productivity in OECD countries (column 1), but a smaller-than-average share of the French population works, which reduces per capita income there by 9% relative to the OECD average. Those in France who do work, on average, work fewer hours than the OECD average, which further reduces per capita income in France by 17% relative to the OECD average. As a result, even though French workers are 23% more productive than the average worker in the OECD, France has a per capita income that is 3% lower than the OECD average. The basic lesson of the employment and hours data, and the exercise in Table 7.19, is that an important portion of the apparently higher standard of living in the United

TABLE 7.18 Average annual hours worked, 1979-98

	1979	1990	1998	Change 1979-98
United States	1,905	1,943	1,966	61
Japan*	2,126	2,031	1,898	-228
Germany**	1,764	1,616	1,562	-202
France*	1,813	1,668	1,634	-179
Italy	1,788	—	—	—
United Kingdom	1,821	1,773	1,737	-84
Canada*	1,802	1,738	1,777	-25
Australia	1,904	1,869	1,861	-43
Austria	—	—	—	—
Belgium	—	—	—	—
Denmark	—	—	—	—
Finland	1,868	1,764	1,761	-107
Ireland	—	—	—	—
Netherlands***	1,591	1,433	1,365	—
New Zealand	—	1,820	1,825	—
Norway	1,516	1,432	1,401	-115
Portugal*	—	—	2,009	—
Spain	1,988	1,829	1,821	-167
Sweden	1,451	1,480	1,551	100
Switzerland*	—	—	1,579	—
Average excl. U.S.	1,900	1,812	1,737	-163

*   Figure in 1998 column refers to 1994 data for Portugal; 1995 data for Japan; and 1997 data for France, Canada, and Switzerland.
** Western Germany.
*** Data refers to dependent employment instead of total employment.

Source: OECD (1999).

States comes not from working smarter than other comparable economies but simply from working longer.

The capacity of the U.S. economy to sustain high employment rates and high volumes of work (measured in the total hours of annual employment) is an important accomplishment of the U.S. economy. **Table 7.20**, nevertheless, attempts to put U.S. job creation into historical and international context. The table shows the annual employment growth rate in 20 OECD economies over two periods, 1979-89 and 1989-98. Two features stand out. First, the U.S. employment growth rate during the incomplete 1990s business cycle (1.3% per

FIGURE 7F Legally mandated paid vacation in European countries

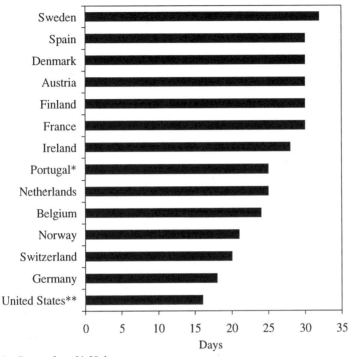

*   Ranges from 21-30 days.
** Average, not legally mandated.

Source: Authors' analysis of Leete-Guy and Schor (1992) and Muñoz de Bustillo and Bonete (2000).

year) was slower than over the 1979-89 business cycle (1.7% per year). Second, the U.S. "jobs machine," while more successful than many European economies, was less effective at creating jobs in the 1990s than Ireland (3.7%, after net job losses in the 1980s), New Zealand (2.1%), the Netherlands (2.0%), Australia (1.4%), and Norway (1.4%). The U.S. performance is also not substantially better over the 1980s and 1990s than that of Canada.

The employment growth data, therefore, suggest that the current U.S. job creation rate is not particularly high either by its own historical terms or when compared with several other economies with different labor market institutions. These job creation data are consistent with the earlier data on employment rates, which showed that the U.S. was not able to prevent the male employment rate from falling in the 1980s and 1990s (though it did a better job than other economies) and that several economies raised their female employment rates by larger

TABLE 7.19 Impact of productivity, employment,* and hours differences on relative per capita income, 1997

Country	Output per hour worked as % of OECD average	Effect (%) of Employment*	Hours	Per capita income as % of OECD average
United States	120%	-1	10	129%
Japan	82	10	14	106
Germany**	105	-5	-4	96
France	123	-9	-17	97
Italy	106	-11	-5	90
United Kingdom	100	-9	0	91
Canada	97	2	2	101
Australia	96%	0	1	97%
Austria	102	-4	2	100
Belgium	128	-5	-22	101
Denmark	92	0	11	103
Finland	93	0	-5	88
Ireland	108	5	-18	95
Netherlands	121	-26	0	95
New Zealand	69	8	2	79
Norway	126	-17	12	121
Portugal	56	2	2	60
Spain	84	13	-26	71
Sweden	93	-3	-1	89
Switzerland	94	0	17	111

* Combined effects of differences in unemployment rate, labor force participation rate, and age composition of total population.

Source: Van Ark and McGuckin (1999).

margins than did the United States over the same period.

Table 7.21 reports the unemployment rate in 20 OECD countries for 1979, 1989, and 1999. The unemployment rate was low in the United States in 1999 (4.2%), but the United States was not the only country with a low unemployment rate in that year. Many countries had unemployment rates below 6% – Japan (4.7%), Denmark (5.2%), Ireland (5.8%), and Portugal (4.5%) – and several had unemployment rates below that of the United States – Austria (3.7%), the Netherlands (3.3%), Norway (3.2%), and Switzerland (3.5%).

Table 7.22 assesses an important claim about the causes of higher European unemployment – that Europe's labor market institutions, such as strong

TABLE 7.20 Employment, 1979-98

	Employment (thousands)			Employment change (thousands)		Annual growth rate (%)	
	1979	1989	1998	1979-89	1989-98	1979-89	1989-98
United States	98,859	117,265	131,440	18,405	14,175	1.7%	1.3%
Japan	55,640	62,250	65,185	6,610	2,935	1.1	0.5
Germany*	33,633	35,055	36,012	1,422	957	0.4	0.3
France	21,796	22,275	22,866	479	590	0.2	0.3
Italy	20,217	20,560	20,251	343	-309	0.2	-0.2
United Kingdom	24,601	26,160	27,201	1,559	1,041	0.6	0.4
Canada	10,624	12,928	14,325	2,304	1,397	2.0	1.1
Australia	6,006	7,587	8,612	1,580	1,026	2.4%	1.4%
Austria	3,350	3,366	3,447	16	81	0.0	0.3
Belgium	3,675	3,683	3,807	9	124	0.0	0.4
Denmark	2,377	2,507	2,683	129	177	0.5	0.8
Finland	2,046	2,242	2,222	195	-20	0.9	-0.1
Ireland	1,150	1,092	1,521	-58	429	-0.5	3.7
Netherlands	5,142	5,490	6,589	349	1,099	0.7	2.0
New Zealand	1,413	1,429	1,726	16	296	0.1	2.1
Norway	1,841	1,985	2,245	144	261	0.8	1.4
Portugal	3,780	4,318	4,400	538	82	1.3	0.2
Spain	11,997	12,103	13,202	106	1,099	0.1	1.0
Sweden	3,964	4,225	3,979	260	-245	0.6	-0.7
Switzerland	3,112	3,725	3,847	613	122	1.8	0.4
Average excl. U.S.	—	—	—	—	—	0.7%	0.5%

*Growth rate for western Germany, 1979-91; eastern and western Germany, 1992-98.

Source: Authors' analysis of OECD (1999).

unions, high minimum wages, and generous benefits, have priced less-skilled workers out of jobs. If this were the case, we would expect the unemployment rates of less-educated workers and better-educated workers to be relatively close to one another in the United States, where relatively weak unions, low minimum wages, and low levels of benefits would have less of an effect on the employment prospects of less-educated workers (that is, wages can fall so as to promote more jobs for the less skilled). Conversely, we would expect the unemployment rates of less-educated and better-educated workers to be relatively farther apart in Europe, where labor market institutions would, by conventional thinking, disproportionately hurt job creation for less-educated workers. The data in Table 7.22 run completely counter to the conventional expectation. The unemployment rate for less-than-high-school-educated workers in the United

TABLE 7.21 Unemployment rates, 1979-98 (percent of civilian labor force)

Country	Standardized unemployment*		
	1979	1989	1999
United States	5.8%	5.3%	4.2%
Japan	2.1	2.3	4.7
Germany	—	—	8.7
Western Germany**	2.7	5.6	7.2
France	5.3	9.3	11.3
Italy	5.8	10.0	11.4
United Kingdom	4.7	7.3	6.1
Canada	7.5	7.5	7.6
Australia	6.1%	6.2%	7.2%
Austria	—	—	3.7
Belgium	9.1	7.5	9.0
Denmark	—	7.4	5.2
Finland	6.5	3.3	10.3
Ireland	—	14.7	5.8
Netherlands	5.8	6.9	3.3
New Zealand***	—	7.1	7.5
Norway	2.0	5.0	3.2
Portugal	—	4.9	4.5
Spain	7.7	17.2	15.9
Sweden	2.1	1.6	7.2
Switzerland***	—	—	3.5
Average excluding U.S.	4.4%	6.9%	8.1%

* Unemployment based on comparable definitions.
** Western German figure for 1999 is through August 1999.
*** Data in column for 1999 refer to 1998.

Source: OECD (1999, 2000) and unpublished BLS tabulations.

States in 1996 was 4.5 times higher than the rate for college-educated workers and higher than every other country in the table. Thus, it appears that Europe's strong labor market institutions have not priced less-skilled workers out of the market, thereby generating higher unemployment rates among less-educated workers relative to the United States. If anything, the European institutions appear to be associated with substantially *lower* relative unemployment rates for less-educated workers.

TABLE 7.22 Unemployment rates by education level, 1996

| Country | Unemployment rate* | | | Ratio of | |
	Less than high school	High school	College	Less than high school/ college	High school/ college
United States	10.9%	5.1%	2.4%	4.5	2.1
Japan	—	—	—	—	—
Germany**	14.2	8.9	5.2	2.7	1.7
France	14.8	9.7	6.7	2.2	1.4
Italy	9.4	8.2	7.3	1.3	1.1
United Kingdom	10.9	7.1	3.5	3.1	2.0
Canada	13.4	8.9	6.7	2.0	1.3
Australia	8.9%	6.3%	3.9%	2.3	1.6
Austria	6.0	3.3	2.3	2.6	1.4
Belgium	13.4	7.4	3.6	3.7	2.1
Denmark	11.8	7.0	3.9	3.0	1.8
Finland	21.5	15.2	7.1	3.0	2.1
Ireland	16.9	7.4	4.2	4.0	1.8
Netherlands	7.0	4.5	3.5	2.0	1.3
New Zealand	6.8	3.5	2.9	2.3	1.2
Norway	4.9	3.8	2.6	1.9	1.5
Portugal	6.4	5.7	3.2	2.0	1.8
Spain	20.1	17.4	14.3	1.4	1.2
Sweden	10.8	9.6	4.8	2.3	2.0
Switzerland	6.5	3.1	2.7	2.4	1.1
Average excl. U.S.	12.6%	8.8%	6.1%	2.3	1.5

* Standardized rate.
** Eastern and western Germany.

Source: Authors' analysis of OECD (1999).

Evaluating the U.S. model

This chapter places the performance of the U.S. economy in an international context. The data suggest that the United States suffers from greater earnings and income inequality and higher pre- and post-tax-and-transfer poverty rates than almost every other OECD economy. Due to the highly unequal distribution of income in the United States, low-wage workers and low-income households here are almost universally worse off in absolute terms than their low-wage, low-income counterparts in other, less-affluent OECD countries. Moreover, most of these economic indicators have deteriorated in the United States in the 1980s and 1990s relative to the rest of the OECD.

Supporters of the U.S. model generally acknowledge the relative inequality in the United States but argue that the model provides greater mobility, greater employment opportunities, and greater dynamism than do more interventionist economies. The evidence, however, provides little support for this view. First, economic mobility, at least for low-wage workers and poor families, appears to be *lower* in the United States than in most European economies.

Second, U.S. success in employment creation is often exaggerated. U.S. job growth rates in the 1990s were lackluster by its own historical standards and no better than several other OECD countries with very different kinds of labor market institutions. While the U.S. is the only economy to escape rising unemployment over the last two decades, several OECD countries still have unemployment rates near or below that of the United States. Perhaps most importantly, the pattern of unemployment rates in OECD countries is completely inconsistent with the idea that labor market institutions have priced less-educated workers out of jobs: the "flexible" U.S. labor market has the highest relative unemployment rate for less-educated workers among all the OECD countries.

Third, the data on growth rates in per capita income and productivity suggest that the U.S. economy is among the *least* dynamic of the OECD economies. In the 1980s and 1990s, nearly all the OECD economies – including the United States – appear to have suffered a dramatic deceleration in both the growth rates of per capita income and productivity. The especially slow growth rates in the United States, however, have allowed all the OECD countries to narrow the U.S. lead; several have eliminated the productivity gap altogether.

The best interpretation of the available international evidence is that all of the OECD economies are experiencing substantial difficulties. Economic growth and productivity growth rates have fallen across the entire OECD in the last two decades. Inequality has risen sharply, especially in the United States, the United Kingdom, and a few other countries. Simultaneously, despite low unemployment in some OECD countries, joblessness has increased to alarming levels in the majority of OECD economies, especially in parts of Europe. The evidence in this chapter, which underscores the diversity of international experience in providing wage, income, and employment security, suggests that those who look exclusively to the United States for solutions will miss a great deal.

Family income and poverty data

This appendix explains the various adjustments made to the March Current Population Survey data and the methodology used to prepare the data in the tables discussed below.

The data source used for the following tables is the U.S. Bureau of the Census's March Current Population Survey (CPS). Each March, approximately 50,000 households are asked questions about their incomes from a wide variety of sources in the prior year (the income data in the 1999 March CPS refer to 1998). For the national analysis in Chapter 1, we use the data relevant to the year in question. For the state income inequality estimates in Chapter 6 (Tables 6.3-6.4), we pool three neighboring years of data for each time period of interest. Thus, the first time period, centered on 1979, includes the income data from 1978-80. (These tables were developed jointly with the Center on Budget and Policy Priorities, see Bernstein et al. 2000).

In order to preserve the confidentiality of respondents, the income variables on the public use files of the CPS are top-coded, i.e., values above a certain level are suppressed. Since income inequality measures are very sensitive to changes in the upper reaches of the income scale, this suppression poses a challenge to analysts interested in both the extent of inequality in a given time period and the change in inequality over time. We use an imputation technique, described below, that is commonly used in such cases to estimate the value of top-coded cases. Over the course of the 1990s, Census top-coding procedures underwent significant changes, which also must be dealt with to preserve consistency. These methods are discussed below.

For most of the years of data in our study, a relatively small share of the distribution of any one variable is top-coded. For example, in 1989, 0.67% (i.e., two-thirds of the top 1%) of weighted cases are top-coded on the variable earnings from longest job, meaning actual reported values are given for over 99% of the those with positive earnings. Nevertheless, the disproportionate influence of the small group of top-coded cases means their earnings levels cannot be ignored.

Our approach has been to impute the average value above the top-code for the key components of income using the assumption that the tails of these distributions follow a Pareto distribution. (The Pareto distribution is defined as $c/(x^{(a+1)})$, where c and a are positive constants that we estimate using the top 20% of the empirical distribution (more precisely, c is a scale parameter assumed known; a is the key parameter for estimation). We apply this technique to four key variables: earnings from longest job, interest, dividend, and rental income. Since the upper tail of empirical income distributions closely follows the general shape of the Pareto, this imputation method is commonly used for dealing with top-coded data (West, undated). The estimate uses the shape of the upper part of the distribution (in our case, the top 20%) to extrapolate to the part that is unobservable due to the top-codes. Intuitively, if the shape of the observable part of the distribution suggests that the tail above the top-code is particularly long, implying a few cases with very high income values, the imputation will return a high mean relative to the case where it appears that the tail above the top-code is rather short.

Polivka (1998), using an uncensored dataset (i.e., without top-codes), shows that the Pareto procedure effectively replicates the mean above the top-code. For example, her analysis of the use of the technique to estimate usual weekly earnings from the earnings files of the CPS yields estimates that are generally within less than 1% of the true mean.

The imputed mean is then assigned to every case above the top-code. For the regional analysis in Chapter 6, we would like to make these imputations at the state level so as to capture regional variations in the values above the top codes. For example, dividend income in the years 1996-97 is top-coded at $99,999. It is reasonable to suspect that an individual with dividend income above this amount in New York has higher dividend income than a top-coded case in a state where dividend income is less common. However, even with the three years of pooled data there were not enough cases to reliably estimate Pareto means by state; in fact, for unearned income, we were unable to go below the national level. For earnings from longest job (the primary income source for most families), we were able to generate four different Pareto estimates for four groups of states (three groups of 13 states and one of 12), sorted by the share of top-coded cases. Thus, we calculated one Pareto mean for the 13 states with the largest share of top-coded cases, another for the states with the next largest share, etc. We would expect these values to fall monotonically, and this is generally the case. For example, in period three (centered on 1997), the four Pareto means for annual earnings from longest job were $220,454; $213,366; $207,622; and $203,349.

As noted, the Census Bureau has lifted the top-codes over time in order to accommodate the fact the nominal and real wage growth eventually renders the old top-codes too low. For example, the top-coded value for "earnings from longest job" was increased from $50,000 in 1979 to $99,999 in 1989. Given the growth of earnings over this period, we did not judge this change (or any others in the income-component variables) to create inconsistencies in the trend comparisons between these two time periods.

However, a change made in the latter 1990s data did require consistency adjustments. For these years, Census both adjusted the top-codes (some were raised, some were lowered; the new top-codes were determined by using whichever value was higher: the top 3% of all reported amounts for the variable, or the top 0.5% of all persons.), and used "plug-in" averages above the top-codes for certain variables. These are group-specific average values taken above the top-code, with the groups defined on the basis of gender, race, and worker status. Since these averages are essentially what we are trying to estimate with the Pareto (since the Census Bureau still has an internal top-code, they are not exactly the same), the question arises as to why we did not simply use these averages. However, since these averages are not available for earlier years, their use would create another trend inconsistency.

The Pareto approach worked well for 1996-97 (the first two years of the third period in Tables 6.3-6.4). However, in the 1998 data used in the Chapter 1 table discussed below, top-codes were lowered significantly for the three unearned income variables for which we impute: interest income, income from dividends, and rental income. While these were all top-coded at $99,999 in 1996 and 1997, in 1998, the top-codes were $35,000, $15,000, and $25,000, respectively, with plug-ins above these values. While we could have calculated Pareto means above these values, to do so would have created a significant inconsistency, since a much larger share of cases would have been assigned this mean value (e.g., in 1996-97, 0.2% of weighted cases were top-coded on interest income, while in 1998 3.8% of cases were top-coded on this variable).

Instead we used the following procedure. Using the pooled data for 1996-97, we estimated the average values between the new 1998 top-codes and $99,999 (x'). Next, we calculated the difference between the shares above the top-codes in 1998 and that above $99,999 in 1996-97. We assumed this to be the implicit share between the new and old top-code between 1996-97 and 1998. Using these shares as weights, we calculated the Pareto average for 1998 as a weighted average of x' for each of the three unearned income variables and the 1996-97 Pareto values above $99,999. The weights in this calculation were the implied shares of cases between the new 1998 top-code and $99,999, and one minus that value (the implied share above $99,999). Note that this procedure assumes that the upper tail of the distribution had the same shape in 1998 as in 1996-97.

For example, x' for interest income was $59,886. The Pareto imputation for this variable, 1996-97, was $821,046. The implied weights were 0.788 between $35,000 and $99,999 and 0.212 above $99,999. Thus, our plug-in for interest income for 1998 was 220,998.

In order to test the reliability of these estimates, we compared the national averages for the top quintile and top 5% to published Census data (these published data derive from Census Bureau internal files that are not subject to the top-codes that are on the public use files; these files do, however, have internal top-codes that are generally well above the pubic use cutoffs.). In order to ensure comparability, we average the Census data over the three-year period used in our study. These values, shown in the data Appendix of Bernstein et al 1999, verify that our imputations do a good job of replicating the values generated by the Census Bureau's internal files.

Table 1.21: The methodology for this table is presented in Ryscavage et al. (1992). Following these authors, we capture the impact of demographic changes on household incomes by adjusting the weights of household heads to reflect demographic changes over the time periods shown in the table.

We use the following categories: *education:* high school or less, some college, and college or more; *age:* less than 25, 25-44, 45-64, and 65 and older; *family type:* married-couple households, single-headed households, individuals living alone; *race:* white, non-white.

In order to simulate the income effects of changing shares of the population with these characteristics between t_0 and t_1, we multiplied each head-of-household's weight by the ratio of the standardized number of households with a particular characteristic in t_0 to that in t_1. For example, to estimate the effect of the change in the age of household heads over the period 1969-79, we divided the 1979 sample into the age groups noted above, and multiplied the weight of each 1979 householder by the ratio of the weighted number of householders in that cell in 1969 to that in 1979. Both numerator and denominator are standardized by dividing each by the total number of households in their respective years. Finally, to measure the impact of all of the demographic factors taken together, we performed the same exercise but with each representing the intersection of all the variables noted above (e.g., one cell would be non-white, married-couple householders, age 25-34, with four or more years of college).

Two caveats should be noted with this type of analysis. First, due to correlation between some of these characteristics and income levels, there are various interactions between these demographic categories that are not reflected in the table. For example, whites tend to have higher incomes than non-whites, and are also more likely than non-whites to be college educated. Thus, the sum of these two effects—race and education—taken separately are likely to be larger than their combined effect, because the summative approach fails to partial out the correlation.

Second, demographic decompositions such as this one tend to suffer from an endogeneity problem. That is, the exercise assigns causation to the demographic changes under analysis, implying, for example, that the increase in single-parent families led to lower average income levels. It is possible, however, that the causality runs the other way. Say, for example, that income declines stemming from male wage declines have led to an increase in female-headed families. To the extent that this is the case, the contribution of demographic factors will be overstated.

Tables 1.27–1.33: These sample for these tables are married couples, spouse present, where the family head was between 25 and 54 years of age. (One exception is in Table 1.30, where we extend the sample to 18-54 year old family heads; this was necessary to increase the sample size for minorities in the upper quintiles since we are using the income cutoffs from the overall distribution). The distributional analysis places 20% of families, not persons, in each fifth. The methodology closely follows that described in Joint Economic Committee (1992).

Husbands and wives' wages in this analysis (Table 1.32) are constructed differently than in most of the analysis in this book, i.e., they are "hour-weighted" in this section and "person-weighted" elsewhere (this follows the JEC methodology). Whereas we usually calculate averages by summing the wages and dividing by the weighted number of earners, in this case we calculate annual hours by dividing annual earnings by annual hours. Since there is a positive correlation between earnings levels and number of hours worked, hour-weighted wage levels tend to be slightly higher than person-weighted wages.

Finally, note that in the calculation of income shares in the absence of wives' earnings (Table 1.33), we determine a separate set of quintile cutoffs (based on family income minus wives' earnings) than those for actual shares. This approach simulates one choice of a counterfactual distribution.

Table 5.14: The methodology for this decomposition is taken from Danziger and Gottschalk (1995, ch. 5). The change to be explained is the difference in poverty rates between t_0 and t_1. We first isolate the effect of average income growth by assigning the average growth between the two time periods to all families in t_0 and recalculate the poverty rate (we adjust each family's poverty line for the increase in the CPI over this period). This procedure holds the demographic composition and the shape of the income distribution constant in t_0 while allowing incomes to grow equally for all families. Thus, the difference between this simulated poverty rate and the actual t_0 poverty rate is attributable to the growth in average income.

We repeat this exercise for each demographic group in t_0 (we use the three family types in Table 5.11, two races—white and non-white—and three education categories of the family head—less than high school, high school and some college, and college or more). By weighting each of these simulated t_0 rates by their t_1 population shares, we can simulate a t_0 poverty rate that reflects the average income growth and demographic composition of t_1. The difference between this simulated rate and the one discussed in the above paragraph gives the contribution of demographic change over the time period. Finally, since this second simulated rate incorporates the mean growth and demographic change between the two periods, but not the change in the shape of the distribution, the difference between this second simulated rate and the actual rate for t_1 equals the change in poverty rates attributable to changes in inequality over the two periods.

Wage analysis computations

This appendix provides background information on our analysis of wage data from the Current Population Survey (CPS), which is prepared by the Bureau of the Census for the Bureau of Labor Statistics (BLS). Specifically, for 1979 and beyond, we analyze microdata files provided by BLS that contain a full year's data on the outgoing rotation groups (ORG) in the CPS. (For years prior to 1979, we use the CPS May files; our use of these files is discussed below.) We believe that the CPS ORG files allow for a timely, up-to-date, and accurate analysis of wage trends keeping within the familiar labor force definitions and concepts employed by the BLS.

The sampling framework of the monthly CPS is a "rolling panel," in which households are in the survey for four consecutive months, out for eight, and then back in for four months. The ORG files provide data on those CPS respondents in either the fourth or eighth month of the CPS (i.e., in groups four or eight, out of a total of eight groups). Therefore, in any given month the ORG file represents a quarter of the CPS sample. For a given year, the ORG file is equivalent to three months of CPSs (1/4th of 12). For our analysis, we use a sample drawn from the full-year ORG sample, the size of which ranges from 160,000 to 180,000 observations during the 1979 to 1994 period. Due to a decrease in the overall sample size of the CPS, the ORG has been shrinking since 1994, and our current sample comes in at about 145,000 cases.

Changes in annual or weekly earnings can result from changes in hourly earnings or from more working time (either more hours per week or weeks per year). Our analysis is centered around the hourly wage, which represents the pure price of labor (exclusive of benefits), because we are interested in changing pay levels for the workforce and its sub-groups. We do this to be able to clearly distinguish changes in earnings resulting from more (or less) work rather than more (or less) pay. Most of our wage analysis, therefore, does not take into account that weekly or annual earnings may have changed because of longer or shorter working hours or lesser or greater opportunities for employment. An exception to this is Table 2.1, where we present annual hours, earnings, and hourly weighted wages from the March CPS.

In our view, the ORG files provide a better source of data for wage analysis than the traditionally used March CPS files. In order to calculate hourly wages from the March CPS, analysts must make calculations using three retrospective variables: the annual earnings, weeks worked, and usual weekly hours worked in the year prior to the survey. In contrast, respondents in the ORG are asked a set of questions about hours worked, weekly wages, and (for workers paid by the hour) hourly wages in the week prior to the survey. In this regard, the data from the ORG are likely to be more reliable than data from the March CPS. See Bernstein and Mishel 1997 for a detailed discussion of these differences.

Our subsample includes all wage and salary workers with valid wage and hour data, whether paid weekly or by the hour. Specifically, in order to be included in our sub-sample, respondents had to meet the following criteria:

- age 18-64;

- employed in the public or private sector (unincorporated self-employed were excluded);

- hours worked within the valid range in the survey (1-99 per week, or hours vary—see discussion below); and,

- either hourly or weekly wages within the valid survey range (top-coding discussed below).

For those who met these criteria, an hourly wage was calculated in the following manner. If a valid hourly wage was reported, that wage was used throughout our analysis. For salaried workers (those who report only a weekly wage), the hourly wage was their weekly wage divided by their hours worked. Outliers, i.e., persons with hourly wages below 50 cents or above $100 in 1989 CPI-U-X1-adjusted dollars, were removed from the analysis. These yearly upper and lower bounds are presented in **Table B-1**. CPS demographic weights were applied to make the sample nationally representative.

The hourly wage reported by hourly workers in the CPS is net of any overtime, tips, or commissions (OTTC), thus introducing a potential undercount in the hourly wage for workers who regularly receive tips or premium pay. OTTC is included in the usual weekly earnings of hourly workers, which raises the

TABLE B-1 Wage earner sample, hourly wage upper and lower limits, 1973-99

Year	Lower	Upper
1973	$0.19	$38.06
1974	0.21	41.85
1975	0.23	45.32
1976	0.24	47.90
1977	0.25	50.97
1978	0.27	54.44
1979	0.30	59.68
1980	0.33	66.37
1981	0.36	72.66
1982	0.39	77.10
1983	0.40	80.32
1984	0.42	83.79
1985	0.43	86.77
1986	0.44	88.39
1987	0.46	91.61
1988	0.48	95.40
1989	0.50	100.00
1990	0.53	105.40
1991	0.55	109.84
1992	0.57	113.15
1993	0.58	116.53
1994	0.60	119.52
1995	0.61	122.90
1996	0.63	126.53
1997	0.65	129.54
1998	0.66	131.45
1999	0.67	134.35

Source: Authors' analysis.

possibility of assigning an imputed hourly wage to hourly workers based on the reported weekly wage and hours worked per week. Conceptually, using this imputed wage is preferable to using the reported hourly wage because it is more inclusive. We have chosen, however, not to use this broader wage measure, because the extra information on OTTC seems unreliable. We compared the imputed hourly wage (reported weekly earnings divided by weekly hours) to the reported hourly wage; the difference presumably reflects OTTC. This comparison showed that significant percentages of the hourly workforce appeared to receive negative OTTC. These error rates range from a low of 0% of the hourly workforce in the period 1989-93 to a high of 16-17% in 1973 to 1988, and persist across the survey change from 1993 to 1994. Since negative OTTC is clearly implausible, we rejected this imputed hourly wage series and rely strictly on the hourly rate of pay as reported directly by hourly workers, subject to the sample criteria discussed above.

For tables that show wage percentiles, we "smooth" hourly wages to compensate for "wage clumps" in the wage distributions. The technique involves creating a categorical hourly wage distribution, where the categories are 50-cent intervals, starting at 25 cents. We then find the categories on either side of each decile and perform a weighted, linear interpolation to locate the wage precisely on the particular decile. The weights for the interpolation are derived from differences in the cumulative percentages on either side of the decile. For example, suppose that 48% of the wage distribution of workers by wage level are in the $9.26-9.75 wage "bin," and 51% are in the next higher bin $9.76-10.25. The weight for the interpolation (in this case the median or 50th

percentile) is: $\dfrac{(50-48)}{(51-48)}$ or 2/3. The interpolated median equals this weight,

times the width of the bin ($.50), plus the upper bound of the previous bin ($9.75), or $10.08 in this example.

For the survey years 1973-88, the weekly wage is top-coded at $999.00 (an extended top-code value of $1,923 is available in 1986-88). Particularly for the later years, this truncation of the wage distribution creates a downward bias in the mean wage. We dealt with the top-coding issue by imputing a new weekly wage for top-coded individuals. The imputed value is the Pareto-imputed mean for the upper tail of the weekly earnings distribution, based on the distribution of weekly earnings up to the 80th percentile. This procedure was done for men and women separately. The imputed values for men and women appear in **Table B-2**. A new hourly wage, equal to the new estimated value for weekly earnings, divided by that person's usual hours per week, was calculated.

In January 1994, a new survey instrument was introduced into the CPS; many labor force items were added and improved. This presents a significant challenge to the researcher who wishes to make comparisons over time. The most careful research on the impact of the survey change has been conducted by BLS researcher Anne Polivka (1996, 1997). Interestingly, Polivka does not find that the survey changes had a major impact on broad measures of unemployment or wage levels, though significant differences did surface for some sub-groups (e.g., weekly earnings for those with less than a high school diploma and advanced degrees, the unemployment rate of older workers). However, a change in the reporting of weekly hours did call for the alteration of our methodology. In 1994 the CPS began allowing people to report that their usual hours worked per week vary. In order to in-

TABLE B-2 Pareto-imputed mean values for top-coded weekly earnings, and share top coded, 1973-99

Year	Share			Value	
	All	Men	Women	Men	Women
1973	0.11%	0.17%	0.02%	1,365	$1,340
1974	0.16	0.26	0.01	1,385	1,297
1975	0.21	0.35	0.02	1,410	1,323
1976	0.30	0.51	0.01	1,392	1,314
1977	0.36	0.59	0.04	1,384	1,309
1978	0.38	0.65	0.02	1,377	1,297
1979	0.57	0.98	0.05	1,388	1,301
1980	0.72	1.23	0.07	1,380	1,287
1981	1.05	1.82	0.10	1,408	1,281
1982	1.45	2.50	0.18	1,430	1,306
1983	1.89	3.27	0.25	1,458	1,307
1984	2.32	3.92	0.42	1,471	1,336
1985	2.78	4.63	0.60	1,490	1,343
1986	0.80	1.37	0.15	2,435	2,466
1987	1.06	1.80	0.20	2,413	2,472
1988	1.30	2.19	0.29	2,410	2,461
1989	0.48	0.84	0.08	2,710	2,506
1990	0.60	1.04	0.11	2,724	2,522
1991	0.71	1.21	0.17	2,744	2,553
1992	0.77	1.28	0.22	2,727	2,581
1993	0.86	1.43	0.24	2,754	2,580
1994	1.25	1.98	0.43	2,882	2,689
1995	1.34	2.16	0.43	2,851	2,660
1996	1.41	2.27	0.46	2,863	2,678
1997	1.71	2.67	0.65	2,908	2,751
1998	2.04	3.23	0.75	3,008	2,771
1999	2.30	3.66	0.82	3,023	2,776

Source: Authors' analysis.

clude non-hourly workers who report varying hours in our wage analysis, we estimated their usual hours using a regression-based imputation procedure, where we predicted the usual hours of work for "hours vary" cases based on the usual hours worked of persons with similar characteristics. An hourly wage was calculated by dividing weekly earnings by the estimate of hours for these workers. The share of our sample that received such a wage is presented in **Table B-3**. The reported hourly wage of hourly workers was preserved.

TABLE B-3 Share of wage earners assigned an hourly wage from imputed weekly hours, 1994-97

Year	Percent hours vary
1994	2.1%
1995	2.1%
1996	2.5%
1997	2.5%

Source: Authors' analysis.

BLS analysts Ilg and Hauzen (2000), following Polivka (1999), do adjust the 10th percentile wage because "changes to the survey in 1994 led to lower reported earnings for relatively low-paid workers, compared with pre-1994 estimates." We make no such adjustments for both practical and empirical reasons. Practically, BLS has provided no adjustment factors for hourly wage trends that we can use—Polivka's work is for weekly wages. More importantly, the trends in 10th percentile hourly wages differ from those reported by Ilg and Hauzen for 10th percentile weekly earnings. This is perhaps not surprising, since the composition of earners at the "bottom" will differ when measured by weekly rather than hourly wages, with low-weekly earners being almost exclusively part-timers. Empirically, Ilg and Hauzen show the unadjusted 50/10 wage gap jumping up between 1993 and 1994, when the new survey begins. In contrast, our 50/10 wage gap for hourly wages falls between 1993 and 1994. Thus, the pattern of wage change in their data differs greatly from that in our data. In fact, our review of the 1993-94 trends across all of the deciles shows no discontinuities whatsoever. Consequently, we make no adjustments to account for any effect of the 1994 survey change. Had we made the sort of adjustments suggested by Polivka, our measured 1990s' fall in the 50/10 wage gap would be even larger and the overall pattern—falling 50/10, rising 90/50, and especially the 95/50 wage gaps—would remain the same.

Demographic variables are also used in the analysis. Our race variable comprises four mutually exclusive categories:

- white, non-Hispanic;

- black, non-Hispanic;

- Hispanic, any race;

- all others.

Beginning in 1992, the CPS employed a new coding scheme for education, providing data on the respondent's highest degree achieved. The CPS in earlier years provided data on years of schooling completed. The challenge to make a consistent wage series by education level is to either make the new data consistent with the past or to make the old "years of schooling" data consistent with the new, educational attainment measures. In prior versions of *The State of Working America*, we achieved a consistent series by imputing years of schooling for 1992 and later years, i.e., making the "new" consistent with the "old." In this version, however, we have converted the "old" data to the new coding following Jaeger (1997). However, Jaeger does not separately identify four-year college and "more than college" categories. Since the wages of these subgroups of the "college or more" group have divergent trends, we construct pre-1992 wages and employment separately for "four-year college" and "advanced." To do so, we compute wages, wage premiums, and employment separately for those with 16, 17, and 18-plus years of schooling completed. The challenge is to distribute the "17s" to the 16 years (presumably a four-year degree) and 18-plus years (presumably advanced) groups. We do this by using the share of the "17s" that have a terminal four-year college degree, as computed in the February 1990 CPS supplement that provides both education codings: 61.4%. We then assume that 61.4% of all of the "17s" are "college-only" and compute a weighted average of the "16s" and 61.4% of the "17s" to construct "college-only" wages and wage premiums. Correspondingly, we compute a weighted average of 38.6% (or 1 less 61.4%) of the "17s" and the "18s" to construct advanced "wages and wage premiums." Distributing the "17s" affects each year differently depending on the actual change in the wages and premiums for "17s" and the changing relative size of the "17s" (which varies only slightly from 2.5% of men and women from 1979 to 1991).

We employ these education categories in various tables in Chapter 2, where we present wage trends by education over time. For the data for 1992 and later, we compute the "some college" trends by aggregating those "with some college but no degree beyond high school" and those with an associate or other degree that is not a four-year college degree.

Information technology and productivity

Productivity or output growth can accelerate for many different reasons. Improvements in the factors of production—capital and labor—might boost productivity, for example, when firms employ more educated workers or provide workers with better equipment. Productivity can also grow if firms learn how to organize production methods more efficiently, thereby producing more without enlarging their workforce or changing their equipment.

These explanations are all "supply-side" factors based on the characteristics of production. However, a strong growth in demand for goods and services can generate productivity growth by motivating investment and work reorganization at a time when it is hard to increase employment—that is, when low unemployment persists.

Why productivity accelerated in 1996 and later years is not yet fully understood and has not been thoroughly examined. However, we can get some insight into the cause by the data presented in **Table C-1**, which lists the various supply-side factors and their contribution to labor productivity (output per hour of work) in three periods, 1974-90, 1991-95, and 1996-99. Our purpose here is to understand why labor productivity grew faster—2.6% annually—in the period 1996-99 compared to the longer term, primarily the 1.4% growth during the 1974-90 period. That is, why (according to the second-to-last column) was labor productivity growth 1.2% faster in the 1996-99 period than in the 1974-90 period?

Table C-1 isolates the role of information technology (IT) from the impact of other sectors and identifies two ways in which IT can affect labor productivity growth. One is an increase in the purchase and use of IT equipment or software—the "information technology capital investment" line in Table C-1. This

TABLE C-1 Contributions to labor productivity

Productivity factor	Annual growth			Difference between 1996-99 and:	
	1974-90	1991-95	1996-99	1974-90	1991-95
Labor productivity	1.4%	1.5%	2.6%	1.2%	1.0%
Information technology (IT)	0.6%	0.7%	1.5%	0.8%	0.7%
Information technology capital investment**	0.4	0.5	1.0	0.5	0.5
Information technology industry efficiency*	0.2	0.2	0.5	0.3	0.3
Other sectors	0.5%	0.4%	0.8%	0.3%	0.5%
Non-IT capital investment	0.4	0.1	0.1	-0.2	0.0
Other sector efficiency*	0.2	0.3	0.7	0.5	0.4
Increased worker skills	0.2%	0.4%	0.3%	0.1%	-0.1%

* Measured as multifactor productivity growth within industries.
** Includes IT-related hardware and software plus communications equipment.

Source: Authors' analysis of Oliner and Sichel (2000).

category reflects the increased use of IT. The second mechanism for IT affecting overall productivity is for the IT sector to become more efficient in the production of IT equipment and software—the "information technology industry efficiency" line 1. These data show that the IT sector contributed 0.6% of the 1.4% labor productivity growth in the 1974-90 period and 1.5% of the 2.6% labor productivity growth over the 1996-99 period. Thus, 0.8% of the 1.2% acceleration of productivity can be attributed to information technology.

A few caveats on the importance of IT to productivity growth are in order, however. As IT investment has become more important, it has not only added to overall investment but it has also substituted for other equipment investment. Thus, Table C-1 shows a decrease in the role of non-IT capital investment in recent years. In this light, the contribution of IT to labor productivity should be measured as net of the substitution for other investment (which we can not determine from Table C-1). If substitution were taken into account, the IT role would be less than Table C-1 shows. Also, this analysis does not take account of demand-side factors that may have led to faster IT investment, including the value of low unemployment and the debt-driven or stock-market-driven consumption growth that led demand to grow rapidly. Plus, there are some analysts who argue that our estimates of IT prices are falling unrealistically quickly, meaning that we are overstating the growth of IT-related investment, productivity, and growth output. Lastly, IT hardware and software generally depreciate quickly (i.e., they often need replacement) so that the effect of IT on output is smaller when one examines net output (output less depreciation). It is net output growth that actually generates higher wages and living standards (since one needs to replace depleted equipment and outdated software). For a variety of reasons, therefore, the impact of IT on living standards is smaller than that shown in Table C-1, but still explains between a third and a half of the acceleration in productivity growth in the late 1990s relative to the 1974-90 period.

The table also shows that efficiency gains within sectors other than IT have improved markedly in recent years, adding 0.5% more to recent productivity growth compared to the past. Thus, changes in work organization and/or the demand-side effects on productivity within these non-IT sectors have been important.

We conclude that technological change, and particularly the increased use of information technology equipment and software, has been a major reason for the recent acceleration of productivity growth. Our analysis cannot explain the surge in IT investment that started in 1996, and it remains to be explained by other researchers. It is our opinion that the 1995-99 IT surge was driven more by technological developments than by any proximate economic policy (budget or tax policy, interest rates, or deregulation).

Table notes

FREQUENTLY CITED SOURCES
The following abbreviations are used throughout the table notes.

ERP—President of the United States. Economic Report of the President.

P-60 Series—U.S. Department of Commerce, Bureau of the Census, Series P-60, various dates.

SCB—U.S. Department of Commerce, Survey of Current Business, monthly.

Employment and Earnings—U.S. Department of Labor, Employment and Earnings, monthly and historical supplements.

NIPA—U.S. Department of Commerce, National Income and Product Accounts, revisions as of spring 2000.

INTRODUCTION

A   *Pay and Productivity Trends, 1989-99.* Based on data in Tables 2.21, 2.6, and 2.7, and productivity data for the nonfarm business sector from Figure 2M.

CHAPTER 1

1.1   *Median Family Income.* Census homepage, Historical Income Tables, Families, Table F7 (http://www.census.gov/hhes/income/histinc/f07.html).

1.2   *Annual Growth of Median Family Income.* Yearly dollar change is annual average of total dollar change in period from sources listed in Table 1.1. Family-size-adjusted income is average family income of the middle fifth adjusted for family size using the official poverty equivalence scale. Census homepage, Historical Income Tables, Families, Table F14 (http://www.census.gov/hhes/income/histinc/f014.html).

1.3   *Median Family Income by Age of Householder.* Census homepage, Historical Income Tables, Families, Table F11 (http://www.census.gov/hhes/income/histinc/f11.html).

1.4   *Family Median Income Growth by 10-Year Cohorts, Starting in 1948.* Historical Income Tables, Families, Table F11 (http://www.census.gov/hhes/income/histinc/f11.html).

1.5   *Median Family Income by Race/Ethnic Group.* Census homepage, Historical Income Tables, Families, Table F5 (http://www.census.gov/hhes/income/histinc/f05.html).

1.6   *Median Family Income by Family Type.* Census homepage, Historical Income Tables, Families, Table F7 (http://www.census.gov/hhes/income/histinc/f07.html).

1.7   *Shares of Family Income Going to Various Income Groups and to Top 5%.* Census homepage, Historical Income Tables, Families, Table F2 (http://www.census.gov/hhes/income/histinc/f02.html).

1.8   *Real Family Income by Income Group.* Census homepage, Historical Income Tables, Families, Table F1 (http://www.census.gov/hhes/income/histinc/f01.html).

1.9   *Pre- and Post-tax Income and Effective Tax Rates.* Authors' calculations based on pre-tax adjusted family income and effective tax rates from Congressional Budget Office (1998), Table A-1, p. 36 and earlier unpublished CBO data.

1.10   *Shares of After-Federal-Tax Income for All Families.* Authors' calculations based on pre-tax adjusted family income and effective tax rates from CBO (1998) and earlier unpublished data. The sum of the shares is forced to sum to 100%, which is not the case in the original data due to the exclusion of families and persons with zero or negative income from the lowest quintile and the inclusion of these same families and individuals in the "all" category.

1.11   *The Effects of Tax and Income Changes on After-Tax Income Shares.* See notes to Table 1.10.

1.12   *Effective Federal Tax Rate for a Family of Four With One Earner.* Department of Treasury (1998), Table 4.

1.13   *Effective Federal Tax Rates for Selected Federal Taxes.* Data for 1977 from U.S. House of Representatives (1991, 73). Data for 1999 from CBO (1998), Table A-3, pp. 40-1.

1.14   *Effective State and Local Tax Rates in 1995 as Percentage Shares of Income for Non-Elderly Married Couples.* Citizens for Tax Justice and Institute on Taxation & Economic Policy (1996), Appendix I, p. 52.

1.15   *Types of Federal vs. State and Local Taxes.* NIPA Tables 3.2 and 3.3.

1.16   *Federal vs. State and Local Tax Burdens.* NIPA Tables 1.1, 3.2, and 3.3.

1.17   *The Growth of Household Income Inequality Using Different Income Definitions and Inequality Measures.* Census homepage, Experimental Income Measures, Tables RDI 5 and 8 (http://www.census.gov/hhes/income/histinc/incexper.html).

1.18   Same source as Table 1.9.

1.19   *Income Mobility.* Unpublished tabulations of the Panel Study of Income Dynamics by Peter Gottschalk. Family heads are less than 62 years of age over the full period. Quintiles are constructed such that 20% of persons, not 20% of families, are in each group. Quintile cutoffs are income-to-needs ratio, using the official poverty lines, so these rates are adjusted for family-size differences. Family income in 1994 is from the 1995 early release of the PSID, which does not include Social Security income. However, since the sample selection excludes families where the household head is 63 or over, this omission is unlikely to affect the results.

1.20   *Income Mobility Over the 1970s and 1980s.* See note to Table 1.19.

1.21   *The Impact of Demographic Change on Household Income.* See Appendix A.

1.22   *Distribution of Persons, Households, and Families by Income Level.* P-60, No. 197, pp. B-2, B-4, U.S. Bureau of the Census (1991), and, for 1998, unpublished data provided by Jack McNeil of the Census Bureau. For relative incomes, family incomes for different size families are made comparable using equivalence scales as in Ruggles (1990), and single individuals are treated as one-person families.

1.23   *Sources of Household Income by Income Type,* Data provided by Michael Ettlinger of the Institute on Economic and Tax Policy.

1.24   *Shares of Market-Based Personal Income by Type.* From NIPA Table 2.1. Capital gains data are from the Internal Revenue Service Statistics on Income series and inlcude gains as well as losses.

1.25   *Shares of Income by Type and Sector.* Based on NIPA Table 1.15. The "Corporate and Business" sector includes "corporate," "other private business," and "rest of world." The "government/nonprofit" sector includes the household, government enterprise, and government sectors, all of which generate no capital income. Capital income consists of profits, interest, and rental income.

1.26   *Profit Rates and Shares at Business Cycle Peaks.* Christian Weller created this series based on the methodology presented in Baker (1996); capital income and tax data are from NIPA table 1.16. The capital cost data are the current cost net stock of private fixed capital for the financial and non-financial sectors from BEA's table 7KCU. The data series ends in 1998. To obtain a 1999 estimate, it was assumed that non-financial sector assets grew as in the Federal Reserve Board data (Flow of Funds Accounts, table B.102). Financial sector assets were assumed to grow at the average rate of the 1991-98 period.

1.27   *Average Income, Married Couple Families With Children, Household Head Age 25-54,* See Appendix A.

1.28   *Average Weeks Worked per Year by Income Quintile, 1969-98, Married-Couple Families With Children, Household Head Age 25-54.* See Appendix A.

1.29   *Average Annual Hours Worked by Income Quintile, 1979-98, Married-Couple Families With Children, Household Head Age 25-54.* See Appendix A.

1.30   *Average Annual Hours Worked by Income Quintile, 1979-98, Married-Couple Families With Children, Household Head Age 25-54, by Race of Household Head.* See Appendix A.

1.31   *Hours of Work by Husbands and Wives, Couples With Children, 1979-98, Head of Household Age 25-54.* See Appendix A.

1.32   *Hourly Earnings by Husbands and Wives, Couples With Children, 1979-98, Head of Household Age 25-54.* See Appendix A.

1.33   *Effect of Wives' Earnings on Income Shares of Prime-Age, Married-Couple Families With Children.* See Appendix A.

CHAPTER 2

2.1 *Trends in Average Wages and Average Hours.* The 1967-73 and 1973-79 trends are from unpublished tabulations provided by Kevin Murphy from an update of Murphy and Welch (1989). These data are based on the March CPS files. Hours of work were derived from differences between annual, weekly, and hourly wage trends. The Murphy and Welch data include self-employment as well as wage and salary workers. The trends from 1979 on are based on the authors' tabulations of March CPS files using a series on annual, weekly, and hourly wages for wage and salary workers using the same sample definition as used in the CPS ORG wage analysis (see Appendix B). The weekly and hourly wage data are "hour weighted," obtained by dividing annual wages by weeks worked and annual hours worked (weeks worked times hours per week). The Murphy and Welch data were bridged to the 1979 levels. Productivity data are from *ERP* (2000), Table B-47, p. 362, for the nonfarm business sector.

2.2 *Growth of Average Hourly Wages, Benefits, and Compensation.* These data are computed from NIPA data on hours worked and compensation, wages, other labor income, group health insurance, and social insurance for the public and private sectors. These data were inflation-adjusted by the NIPA Personal Consumption Expenditure (PCE, chain-weighted) index, with health insurance adjusted by the PCE medical care (chained) index.

2.3 *Growth in Private-Sector Average Hourly Wages, Benefits, and Compensation.* Based on employment cost levels from the BLS Employment Cost Index series for March 1987 to March 2000 for private industry workers (see 2000 data in U.S. Department of Labor, *Employer Costs for Employee Compensation*). We categorize pay differently than BLS, putting all wage-related items (including paid leave and supplemental pay) into the hourly wage. Benefits, in our definition, include only payroll taxes, pensions, insurance, and "other" benefits. It is important to use the current-weighted series rather than the fixed-weighted series because composition shifts (in the distribution of employment across occupations and industries) have a large effect. Employer costs for insurance are deflated by the medical care component of the CPI. All other pay is deflated by the CPI-UX1 for "all items." Inflation is measured for the first quarter of each year.

2.4 *Hourly and Weekly Earnings for Production and Non-supervisory Workers.* Data from 1959 to 1999 from ERP (2000), Table B-45, p. 360. Data for 1947, supplement to *Employment and Earnings* (March 1985, 5).

2.5 *Changes in Hourly Wages by Occupation.* Based on analysis of CPS wage data described in Appendix B.

2.6 *Wages for All Workers by Wage Percentile.* Based on analysis of CPS wage data described in Appendix B.

2.7 *Wages for Male Workers by Wage Percentile.* Based on analysis of CPS wage data described in Appendix B.

2.8 *Wages for Female Workers by Wage Percentile.* Based on analysis of CPS wage data described in Appendix B.

2.9   *Changes in the Gender Wage Differential.* Based on data from Tables 2.7 and 2.8. Women's employment share derived from data in *ERP* (2000), Table B-34, p. 348.

2.10   *Distribution of Total Employment by Wage Level.* Based on analysis of CPS wage data described in Appendix B. The poverty-level wage was defined as the four-person poverty threshold in 1999 ($17,028) divided by 2,080 hours and deflated by CPI-UX1 to obtain levels for other years. The threshold is from www.census.gov/hhes/poverty/threshold/1999prelim.html. We calculated more intervals than we show but aggregated for simplicity of presentation (no trends were lost).

2.11   *Distribution of White Employment by Wage Level.* See note to Table 2.10. These are non-Hispanic whites.

2.12   *Distribution of Black Employment by Wage Level.* See note to Table 2.10. These are non-Hispanic blacks.

2.13   *Distribution of Hispanic Employment by Wage Level.* See note to Table 2.10. Hispanics may be of any race.

2.14   *Growth of Specific Fringe Benefits.* Based on NIPA data described in note to Table 2.2 and ECI data described in note to Table 2.3.

2.15   *Change in Private Sector Employer-Provided Health Insurance Coverage.* Based on tabulations of March CPS data samples of private wage and salary earners ages 18-64 who worked at least 20 hours per week and 26 weeks per year. Coverage is defined as being included in an employer-provided plan where the employer paid for at least some of the coverage.

2.16   *Change in Private Sector Employer-Provided Pension Coverage.* See note to Table 2.15.

2.17   *Dimensions of Wage Inequality.* All of the data are based on analyses of the ORG CPS data described in Appendix B. The measures of total wage inequality are natural logs of wage ratios (multiplied by 100) computed from Tables 2.6 and 2.7. The exception is that the 1979 data for women are 1978-80 averages. This was done to smooth the volatility of the series, especially at the 10th percentile.

        The education and experience differentials are computed from regressions of the log of hourly wages on education categorical variables (high school omitted), experience as a quartic, marital status, race and region (4). The college/high-school and high-school/less-than-high-school premiums are simply the coefficient on "college" and less than high school. The experience differentials are the differences in the value of age (calculated from the coefficients of the quartic specification) evaluated at 25, 35, and 50 years.

        Within-group wage inequality is measured as the root mean square error from the same log wage regressions used to compute age and education differentials.

2.18   *Change in Real Hourly Wage for All by Education.* Based on tabulations of CPS wage data described in Appendix B. See Appendix B for details on how a consistent measure of education was developed to bridge the change in coding in 1992.

2.19   *Change in Real Hourly Wage for Men by Education.* See note to Table 2.18.

429

2.20   *Change in Real Hourly Wage for Women by Education.* See note to Table 2.18.

2.21   *Educational Attainment of Workforce.* Based on analysis of CPS wage earners. The data are described in Appendix B. The categories are as follows: "Less than high school" is grade 1-12 or no diploma; "high school/GED" is high school graduate diploma or equivalent; "some college" is some college but no degree; "associate college" is occupational or academic associate's degree; "college B.A." is a bachelor's degree; and "advanced degree" is a master's, professional, or doctorate degree.

2.22   *Hourly Wages of Entry-Level and Experienced Workers by Education.* Based on analysis of CPS wage data described in Appendix B. Entry-level high school graduates are ages 19-25, while entry-level college graduates are ages 23-29.

2.23   *Hourly Wages by Decile Within Education Groups.* Based on analysis of CPS wage data described in Appendix B.

2.24   *Decomposition of Total and Within-Group Wage Inequality.* All of the data are from the ORG CPS data sample described in Appendix B. Overall wage inequality is measured as the standard deviation of log wages, and "within-group wage inequality" is the mean square error from a log wage regression (the same ones used for Table 2.17). Between-group wage inequality is the difference between the overall and within-group wage inequalities and reflects changes in all of the included variables: education, age, marital status, race, ethnicity, and region.

2.25   *Hourly Wage Growth Among Men by Race/Ethnicity.* Based on analysis of CPS wage data described in Appendix B.

2.26   *Hourly Wage Growth Among Women by Race/Ethnicity.* Based on analysis of CPS wage data described in Appendix B.

2.27   *Employment Growth by Sector.* Employment data from *Employment and Earnings* (March 1996), Table B-1, p. 51, Table B-12, p. 72, and employment updates from the BLS web site. Hourly compensation data from BLS Employment Cost Levels data for 1997. See note to Table 2.3.

2.28   *Changes in Employment Share by Sector.* Based on data in Table 2.27.

2.29   *The Effect of Industry Shifts on the Growth of the College/High School Differential.* The industry shift effect is calculated from estimated college/high school wage differentials using the model described in the note to Table 2.17 ("industry composition actual") and a model that adds a set of industry controls (12), which gives "industry composition constant." The difference in the growth of these estimates is the industry shift effect.

2.30   *Net Trade in U.S. Manufactures by Skill Intensity and Trading Partner.* Cline (1997), Table 4.3, p. 188.

2.31   *Trade-Deficit-Induced Job Loss by Wage and Education Level.* Scott et al. (1997), Tables 1 and 2.

2.32   *Effect of Changes in Prices of Internationally Traded Manufactured Goods on Wage Inequality.* Schmitt and Mishel (1996), Table 9.

2.33   *Legal Immigrant Flow to the United States.* Borjas (1994), Table 1, p. 1668, updated for the 1990s by Steven A. Camarota of the Center for Immigration Studies based on Immigration and Naturalization Service (1999).

2.34   *Educational Attainment of Immigrant and Native Men.* Borjas (1999), Table 2-1, p. 21.

2.35   *Union Wage and Benefit Premium.* Employment Cost Index pay-level data in U.S. Department of Labor *Employment and Earnings* (1997), Table 13. Regression-adjusted union effect from Pierce (1998), Tables 3, 4, and 5. Wages are defined differently in the top and bottom panels, as Pierce follows the BLS definitions while the upper panel defines wages to include paid leave and supplemental pay (as described in note to Table 2.3). Pierce's estimates are based on regressions on ECI microdata for 1994.

2.36   *Union Wage Premium by Demographic Group.* Regression estimates of union wage differentials using CPS ORG data for 1997. See Appendix B for description of the data. The data in the table are the coefficients on union membership (union member or covered by a collective bargaining agreement) in a model of log hourly wages with controls for education, experience as a quartic, marital status, region, industry (12) and occupation (9), and race/ethnicity and gender where appropriate. Percent union is percent of group that are members or covered by a collective bargaining agreement tabulated from the same CPS ORG sample.

2.37   *Effect of Deunionization on Male Wage Differentials.* This analysis replicates, updates, and expands on Freeman (1991), Table 2. The analysis uses the CPS ORG sample used in other analyses (see Appendix B). The year 1978, rather than 1979, is the earliest year analyzed because we have no union membership data in our 1979 sample. The union wage premium for a group is based on the coefficient on collective bargaining coverage in a regression of hourly wages on a simple human capital model (the same one used for estimating education differentials, as described in note to Table 2.17) with major industry (12) and occupation (9) controls in a sample for that group. The change in union premium across years, therefore, holds industry and occupation composition constant. "Percent union" is the share covered by collective bargaining. Freeman's analysis assumed the union premium was unchanged over time. We allow the union premium to differ across years so changes in the union effect are driven by changes in the unionization rate and the union wage premium. The analysis compares the change in the union effect on relative wages to the actual change in relative wages (regression-adjusted with simple human capital controls plus controls for other education or occupation groups).

2.38   *Effect of Unions on Wages, by Wage Fifth.* From Card (1991), Table 8. The effect of deunionization is the change in union coverage times the union wage premium.

2.39   *Effect of Deunionization on Male Wage Inequality.* From Card (1991), Table 9; Freeman (1991), Table 6; and DiNardo, Fortin, and Lemieux (1994), Table 4.

2.40   *Value of the Minimum Wage.* Historical values of minimum wage from Shapiro (1987), p. 19.

2.41   *Characteristics of Minimum Wage and Other Workers.* Bernstein and Schmitt (1998), Table 1.

2.42 *Impact of Lower Minimum Wage on Key Wage Differentials Among Women.* The impact of the change in the minimum wage since 1979 is based on comparing the actual changes with changes from 1979 to simulated wage distributions in 1989 and 1997 where the real value of the minimum wage in 1979 is imposed on the data. This analysis is based on the CPS ORG data described in Appendix B. The simulated microdata are obtained by setting the hourly wages of those in the "sweep" (earning between the current minimum wage and the 1979 value) at the 1979 value (inflation-adjusted by CPI-UX) of the minimum wage. Those earning less than the legislated minimum wage were assigned a wage at the same proportionate distance to the 1979 level as they were to the existing minimum. In 1997, the existing minimum was based on a weighted average by month of the prevailing minimum of $4.75 for nine months and $5.15 for three months. The counterfactual returns to education were estimated on the simulated microdata with a simple human capital model and compared to the actual change (based on the same model) presented in Table 2.17. The other wage differentials are based on logged differentials computed from the actual and simulated microdata. The shares earning less than the 1979 minimum are computed directly from the data.

2.43 *Distribution of Minimum Wage Gains and Income Shares by Fifth for Various Household Types.* Bernstein and Schmitt (1998), Table 2.

2.44 *The Impact of Labor Market Institutions on Wage Differentials.* Fortin and Lemieux (1996), Table 1.

2.45 *Decomposition of Growth of Male College/Non-College Wage Premium by Occupation.* This decomposition starts from the fact that the college/noncollege wage differential in any year is a weighted average of the college wage premium specific to each occupation (e.g., college-educated scientists relative to all non-college workers) and the weight of the occupation (its college employment) in total college employment. Changes in the college/noncollege wage differential can therefore be decomposed into changes in occupational weights (e.g., the expansion of an occupation with a higher-than-average premium expands the differential) and changes in occupation premiums. This analysis is based on a regression of log hourly wages on a simple human capital model (see note to Table 2.17) with one education categorical variable—college graduate—interacted with a dummy variable for each occupation group. The sample is described in Appendix B of the last version of this book (the main difference being the definition of college graduates). For this analysis, those with more than a college degree are excluded. Estimates for 1979, 1989, and 1997 were used for the decomposition.

2.46 *Decomposition of Growth of Female College/Non-College Wage Premium by Occupation.* See methodology described in note to Table 2.45.

2.47 *Utilization of Workers by Technology's Impact on Wage and Education Level.* Mishel and Bernstein (1998).

2.48 *Changes in Employment Shares by Occupation for All Workers and Young College Graduates.* Based on tabulations of CPS ORG data described in Appendix B of the last version of this book. Young college graduates defined as those with 1 to 10 years experience in order to have a sufficient sample size for each occupation group.

2.49   *Executive Pay Growth.* The 1992-99 trends are based on a series of *Wall Street Journal*/William M. Mercer surveys (of 350 large companies) of CEO compensation. "Realized direct compensation" includes salary, bonus, gains from options exercised, value of restricted stock at grant and other long-term incentive award payments. The "average" is computed as the average of each quartile cutoff (25, 50, and 75), which would understate the growth relative to a true average. Cash compensation data, also from Mercer, goes back to 1989. The average compensation for 1989 is backed out of the 1992 data by extrapolating the 1989-92 trend in the Pearl Meyer/*Wall Street Journal* data.

2.50   *CEO Pay in Advanced Countries.* Total CEO compensation in dollars and the ratio of CEO to production-worker pay are from Towers Perrin (1988 and 1999). The production worker ranking is based on data from Towers Perrin (1999).

2.51   *Demand Shifts: Changes in Pay and Education Requirements.* Update of an analysis presented in Mishel and Teixeira (1991), Tables 2 and 7. It is based on a shift-share analysis of the employment distribution of 13 major occupations and the pay and education characteristics of these occupations. The education levels are from tabulations of the CPS ORG data (as described in Appendix B) for 1995 by occupation. Wage levels are those prevailing over the 1979-93 period (from the CPS ORG data), and compensation is based on computing an occupation-specific compensation/wage ratio from ECI levels data and applying it to the wages data. The historical occupation data are from series available from *Employment and Earnings*. Future trends are based on the occupation shifts from 1998 to 2008 in Braddock (1999), Tables 1 and 2.

2.52   *Future Labor Supply Trends.* Immigration was projected by extrapolating the 1980-88 trends in immigrant employment share of Borjas et al. (1991) to 1992. Data from Census P-25 Series, No 1104, Table 1 were used to project the net immigrant (ages 16-64) increase to 2005 (13 times annual growth). The BLS projections of labor force participation in 1998 were used to translate population growth into labor force growth. This estimate was reduced to account for the aging of the immigrant population beyond age 64, using Tables C-3 and C-4. The Census and BLS projections data for medium and high were matched.

Labor-force median age from Fullerton (1999), Table 7. Historical data on college degrees awarded are from Table 28, p. 63, of U.S. Department of Education (1999) and earlier publications. The projected college degrees awarded are the middle projections from Table 28, p. 63, of Department of Education (1999). Past employment is civilian employment (20 years or more) from Table B34, p. 348, of *ERP* (2000). Future employment is estimated based on the growth in the labor force (age 20 or more) from Fullerton (1999), Tables 1 and 5, and assuming the growth rate from 1998-2008 continues to 2009. The college enrollment rate is the average of those ages 18-24 using the middle alternative projection for 2009 from Table A 1.3 of Department of Education (1999). The college-age population projection is the number of 18- to 24-year-olds from Table B4 of Department of Education (1999).

CHAPTER 3

3.1 *Unemployment Rates.* Data for years before 1997 are from U.S. Department of Labor (1988), Table A-24, pp. 404-61, updated from BLS web page (http://stats.bls.gov/ sahome.html), May 2000.

3.2 *Underemployment.* Civilian labor force and unemployed from BLS, *Employment and Earnings* (January 2000), Table 1, p. 166. Discouraged workers are individuals not in the labor force who wanted a job, had searched for work in the previous year, were available to work, but were not actively searching for work because of "discouragement over job prospects." "Other marginally attached" individuals are in identical circumstances, but are not actively searching for work for reasons other than discouragement, including family responsibilities, school or training commitments, or ill health or disabilities. The source for discouraged and marginal workers is BLS, *Employment and Earnings* (January 2000), Table 35, p. 210. "Involuntary part-time" workers cite "economic reasons for working fewer than 35 hours per week (from BLS, *Employment and Earnings*, January 2000, Table 20, p. 196).

3.3 *Effect of 1% Lower Unemployment Rate on Weeks Unemployed and Employed and on Annual Earnings.* Analysis of Tables 5 and 7 in Blank and Card (1993). These tables are slightly mismatched because the coefficients in their Table 7 are for the 1973-91 period, while the means in their Table 5 are for the 1967-91 period.

3.4 *Employment Growth.* Total employees on non-farm payrolls taken from the BLS establishment survey as reported in BLS, *Employment and Earnings* (January 2000), Table B-1, p. 45. Total civilian employment, civilian non-institutional population, and civilian labor force participation rate from the Current Population Survey of households as reported in BLS, *Employment and Earnings* (January 2000), Table 1, p. 162. Hours worked by full-time and part-time employees from NIPA Table 6.9B and full-time equivalent employees from NIPA Table 6.5B; both from the National Income and Product Accounts (http://www.bea.doc.gov/bea/dn1.htm).

3.5 *Employment Rates.* CPS data from the BLS web page (http://stats.bls.gov/ sahome.html), May 2000.

3.6 *Employment Stability for Men.* Authors' analysis of data presented in Bernhardt, Morris, Handcock, and Scott (1998).

3.7 *Median Job Tenure by Age.* Aaronson and Sullivan (1998), Figure 2, p. 21. Numbers corresponding to figure provided by Daniel Aaronson and Ann Ferris.

3.8 *Share of Employed Workers in Long-Term Jobs.* Farber (1997b), Table 1, p. 29.

3.9 *Four-Year Job Retention Rates.* Neumark, Polsky, and Hansen (1997), Table 5.

3.10 *Rate of Job Loss by Reason.* Farber (1998), Appendix Table 3, p. 12.

3.11 *Rate of Job Loss by Occupation and Reason.* Farber (1997a), Appendix Table 5, p. 69. Table excludes other category because workers in the 1994 and 1996 Displaced Workers Survey, which provides the underlying data for the 1991-93 and 1993-95 periods respectively, do not ask workers who cite "other" reason for displacement about their occupation on the lost job.

3.12　*The Costs of Job Loss, Averages for 1980s and 1990s.* Percent out of work from Farber (1997a), Table 6, p. 49, last row; post-displacement change in earnings from Farber (1997a), Table 10, p. 55; post-displacement change in earnings compared to continuously employed from Farber (1997a), Table 14, p. 62; health insurance coverage from Gardner (1996), Table 6, p. 53.

3.13　*Perceptions of Job Security.* Aaronson and Sullivan (1998) analysis of 1997 General Social Survey data, Figure 6, p. 30. Numbers corresponding to figure provided by Daniel Aaronson and Ann Ferris.

3.14　*Workers by Work Arrangement.* EPI analysis of published BLS analysis (1995, 1997, 1999) of CPS Contingent Worker Survey data for 1995, 1997, and 1999.

3.15　*Characteristics of Nonstandard Workers.* BLS (1999), various tables.

3.16　*Wages of Nonstandard Workers Compared to Regular Full-Time Workers, by Gender and Work Arrangement.* Kalleberg et al. (1997) analysis of 1995 Contingent Work Survey, Table 12, p. 23.

3.17　*Percentage Share of Workers With Employer-Provided Health and Pension Benefits by Work Arrangement.* BLS (1999), Table 9.

3.18　*Nonstandard Workers' Satisfaction with Work Arrangement.* BLS (1995, 1997, 1999), Table 11 in each source.

3.19　*Nonagricultural Employment by Full-Time and Part-Time Status.* Employment and Earnings (January 2000), Table 21, p. 197, and earlier issues.

3.20　*Employment in Personnel Services Industry.* Data on personnel services industry employment (SIC code 736) and total employment from establishment survey data on the BLS web site, May 2, 2000.

3.21　*Employment in Temporary Help Industry.* Data on temporary help industry employment (SIC code 7363) and total employment from establishment survey data on the BLS web site, May 2, 2000.

3.22　*Self-Employment.* Prior to 1989, data taken from U.S. Department of Labor (1989), Table 21, pp. 112-113; for 1989, Employment and Earnings (January 1990), Table 23, p. 189; for 1997, Employment and Earnings (January 2000), Table 15, p. 187.

3.23　*Multiple Job Holding.* All figures are for May of the given year. Data for 1973 and 1989 are from the U.S. Department of Labor (1989); 1979 are from Sekscenski (1980); 1985 from Stinson (1986); and 1999 from Employment and Earnings (June 1999), Table A-37, p. 67.

CHAPTER 4

4.1　*Distribution of Income and Wealth.* Unpublished analysis of Survey of Consumer Finance data prepared in May 2000 by Edward Wolff, of New York University, for the Economic Policy Institute.

4.2　*Changes in the Distribution of Household Wealth.* See note to Table 4.1.

4.3   *Change in Average Wealth by Wealth Class.* See note to Table 4.1.

4.4   *Wealth by Race.* See note to Table 4.1.

4.5   *Households With Low Net Wealth.* See note to Table 4.1.

4.6   *Distribution of Asset Ownership Across Households.* Poterba (2000), Table 2.

4.7   *Share of Households Owning Stock.* See note to Table 4.1.

4.8   *Household Assets and Liabilities by Wealth Class.* See note to Table 4.1.

4.9   *Concentration of Stock Ownership by Income Level.* See note to Table 4.1.

4.10   *Home Ownership Rates by Income and Race.* Authors' analysis of published Bureau of Census data from the American Housing Survey. Average home ownership rates by income quintile estimated using ownership rates and population shares by discrete income categories.

4.11   *Computer Ownership Rates.* Kominski and Newburger (1999), Table 2, p. 16 and National Telecommunications and Information Administration (1999), various tables.

4.12   *Household Debt by Type.* Federal Reserve Board, *Flow of Funds Accounts of the United States: Annual Flows and Outstandings*, June 9, 2000, Table B.100.

4.13   *Household Debt Service Burden.* Federal Reserve web page (http://www.bog.frb.fed.us/releases/housedebt/default.htm), June 2000.

4.14   *Household Debt Service as a Share of Income.* Federal Reserve Board (2000b), Table 14, pp. 24-5.

4.15   *Households With High Debt Burdens.* Federal Reserve Board (2000b), Table 14, pp. 24-5.

4.15   *Households Late Paying Bills.* Federal Reserve Board (2000b), Table 14, pp. 24-5.

CHAPTER 5

5.1   *Percent and Number of Persons in Poverty.* U.S. Bureau of the Census, P60-207, C1.

5.2   *Persons in Poverty, by Race/Ethnicity.* U.S. Bureau of the Census, P60-207, C1.

5.3   *Percent of Children in Poverty, by Race.* U.S. Bureau of the Census, P60-207, C2.

5.4   *Family Poverty, by Race/Ethnicity of Family Head and for Different Family Types.* U.S. Bureau of the Census, P60-207, C3.

5.5   *High-Risk Factors for Poverty, Females 25 and Over.* Unpublished tabulations provided by the Census Bureau, poverty division.

5.6   *Distribution of the Poor, Official and Alternative Measures, 1997.* U.S. Bureau of the Census, P60-205. See note for Figure 5B.

5.7   *Percent of Persons With Low Relative Income, by Race, Adjusted for Family Size.* U.S. Bureau of the Census (1991) and unpublished data provided by Jack McNeil. Family incomes for different size families are made comparable using equivalence scales as in Ruggles (1990). Single individuals are treated as one-person families.

5.8   *Average Poverty Gap.* Center on Budget and Policy Priorities (1998), updated with U.S. Bureau of the Census, P60-207, C1.

5.9   *Persons Below 50% of Poverty Level.* Census homepage, Historical Poverty Tables, Persons, Table 22 (http://www.census.gov/hhes/poverty/histpov/hstpov22.html).

5.10   *Changes in Poverty Rates and Growth Indicators.* Poverty rates: see note to Table 5.1; productivity: *ERP* (2000), Table B-47; per capita income, *ERP* (2000), Table B-29; unemployment, *ERP* (2000), Table B-40; Gini coefficient, U.S. Census Bureau, P60-206 and P60-207. We adjust the trend in the Gini to account for a survey change in the following manner. For the 1989-99 and 1989-95 results, we reduce the 1995 and 1999 reported values by one-half of the coefficient for the 1993-99 dummy variable generated by the model described in the note for Figure 1F. This coefficient (0.0216, highly significant) gives the effect of the survey change in Gini series. In earlier research (Mishel et al, 1999) we show that a conservative estimate of the survey effect on the growth of income inequality through 1996 was one-half (i.e., inequality, consistently measured, would have grown about half as fast as it does in the published data). For the 1995-99 annualized change, we use the published Census data, which are consistently measured over this period.

5.11   *Changing Family Structure and Poverty.* U.S. Bureau of the Census, P60-207, C1.

5.12   *The Impact of Changes in Family Structure on Poverty Rates.* See note to Table 5.11. This conventional shift-share analysis assigns the increase in poverty rates to "between" and "within" factors. To the extent that either of these factors is endogenous to poverty changes, e.g., if increasing poverty rates *led* to family structure changes, this simple decomposition will fail to account for such behavioral changes.

5.13   *Educational Level of Family Heads and Poverty, Families With Children.* Authors' analysis of March CPS data. Education coding changes for 1996 column from highest grade completed to highest level of attainment.

5.14   *Decomposing Changes in Poverty Rates Into Demographic and Economic Factors.* See Appendix A.

5.15   *Poverty-Reducing Effects of Transfers.* P-60, No. 182-RD and No. 198, Table 5 (definitions 2, 8, 10, and 14).

5.16   *Average Income by Components, Prime-Age Families, Bottom 20% and in Poverty.* Authors' analysis of March CPS data. Prime-age families are those headed by a person age 25-54, and exclude single person units and families with negative incomes. Since the analysis focuses on the poor and the bottom 20%, we did not adjust income components for changes in top codes.

5.17   *Work Experience of the Poor.* 1979: P-60, No. 130, p. 58; 1989: P-60, No. 168, p. 65; 1989: P-60, No. 185, p. 89; 1998: unpublished tabulation provided by Census Bureau, poverty division.

5.18   *Family Work Hours and Wages Among Poor Families.* Work hours are pooled across families, and include family members with zero hours. The wage calculation is made only for families with positive values on both variables.

5.19   *Characteristics of Low-Wage Workers.* Authors' analysis of CPS ORG data; see Appendix B.

5.20   *Changes in Hourly Wages of Low-Wage Workers.* See Appendix B.

CHAPTER 6

6.1   *Median Family Income by Region.* Census Homepage, Historical Income Tables, Families, Table F3 (http://www.census.gov/hhes/income/histinc/f06.html).

6.2   *Median Income for Four-Person Families, by State.* Census Homepage, Historical Income Tables (http://www.census.gov/hhes/income/4person.html).

6.3   *Income Inequality by State: Average Income of Top 20% Relative to Bottom 20%.* From Bernstein et al, 1999. See Appendix A for discussion of methods.

6.4   *Inequality Ratio: Top 5% to Bottom 20%, 11 Most Populous States.* Same as previous table.

6.5   *Non-Farm Payroll Employment, by State.* BLS Homepage, Nonfarm Payroll Employment.

6.6   *Unemployment Rates, by State and Division.* BLS Homepage, Statistics from the Household Survey, Unemployment by State.

6.7   *Low Wages (20th Percentile) by State.* Based on analysis of CPS wage data as described in Appendix B.

6.8   *State Hourly Median Wages (50th Percentile).* Based on analysis of CPS wage data as described in Appendix B.

6.9   *State Hourly High Wages (80th Percentile).* Based on analysis of CPS wage data as described in Appendix B.

6.10   *Poverty-Level Wage Shares by State.* Based on analysis of CPS wage data as described in Appendix B. The percentage of workers who earned less than, or equal to, the hourly wage needed to reach the poverty threshold if worked full-time over the course of a year (2080 hours). The poverty threshold for a family of four ($17,028 in 1999) comes from the Census Homepage (http://www.census.gov/hhes/poverty/threshld/99prelim.html).

6.11   *The Impact of a One-Percentage Point Decline in the Unemployment Rate on Real Wage Trends.* The numbers in column one are regression coefficients from the regression of the state-level percent change in the variable listed one the change in state unemployment rates (See table 6.6). Regressions are unweighted, and separate equations were run for each time period.

6.12   *Unemployment and Underemployment, 18-35 Year-Olds, by Gender, Education, and*

Race, 1996-99 (pooled). Authors' analysis of CPS monthly data; three years of data are combined to generate samples large enough for reliable estimation.

6.13　*Poverty Rates for Persons by Region.* Census Homepage, Historical Poverty Tables, Persons, Table 9 (http://www.census.gov/hhes/poverty/histpov/hstpov9.html).

6.14　*Poverty by State, Two Year Averages.* Census Homepage, Historical Poverty Tables, Persons, Table 19, and *P60*, No. 189, p. xix. Two-year averages are used to reduce statistical error induced by the small samples in some states.

6.15　*Poverty Rates by Metro/Non-metro Areas.* Census Homepage, Historical Poverty Tables, Persons, Table 8 (http://www.census.gov/hhes/poverty/histpov/hstpov8.html).

6.16　*State and Local Taxes in 1995, Effective Rates.* Citizens for Tax Justice and Institute on Taxation and Economic Policy (1996).

CHAPTER 7

7.1　*Per Capita Income, Using Market Exchange Rates.* GDP per capita from OECD (1999a), *National Accounts: Main Aggregates, Volume 1,* Table 20, p. 146, converted to 1998 dollars (from 1990 dollars in original). Data for the United States deflated using the CPI-U-X1 from the *Economic Report of the President* (2000), Table B-60, p. 376. Average excluding the United States is weighted using national populations for 1989 (various tables); population data for 1998 were not available for the United States and New Zealand and have been estimated by extrapolating from 1997 populations, using growth rates for the 1992-97 period.

7.2　*Per Capita Income, Using Purchasing-Power-Parity Exchange Rates.* BLS (2000a), Table 1 and http://stats.bls.gov/special.requests/ForeignLabor/flsgdp.pdf. Population (1989) weighted average.

7.3　*Relative Productivity Levels.* Conference Board (1997), Table 1, p. 6. Data for 1997 come from the BLS *International Comparisons of Labor Productivity and Per Capita Income,* (1999), except for western Germany, which is from the Conference Board (1999), Table 5, p. 18.

7.4　*Labor Productivity Growth per Year.* Data in first column begin in 1960 or earliest available year: 1961 for Australia and Ireland; 1962 for Japan and the UK; 1964 for Spain; 1965 for France and Sweden; 1966 for Canada and Norway; 1967 for New Zealand; 1969 for the Netherlands; and 1970 for Belgium. Data in last column end in 1996 or latest available year: 1993 for Portugal; 1994 for Austria and Norway; 1995 for Australia, Italy, New Zealand, and Switzerland; 1996 for Japan, Germany, France, the United Kingdom, Belgium, Denmark, Finland, Ireland, the Netherlands, Spain, and Sweden. *Economic Outlook*, OECD (1998), Annex Table 59, p. 284. Employment (1989) weighted average.

7.5　*Real Compensation Growth per Year.* Nominal compensation per employee in the business sector from OECD (1999a), Annex Table 12, p. 206 deflated by changes in consumer prices from OECD (1999a), Annex Table 16, p. 210. Population (1989) weighted average.

7.6 *Relative Hourly Compensation of Manufacturing Production Workers (Using Market Exchange Rates).* Index of hourly compensation costs for production workers in manufacturing from BLS (2000), Table 1 (ftp://ftp.bls.gov/pub/special.requests/ForeignLabor/supptab.txt). Population (1989) weighted average.

7.7 *Relative Hourly Compensation of Manufacturing Production Workers (Using Purchasing Power Parities).* Hourly compensation costs in national currency for production workers in manufacturing from BLS (2000), Table 3, converted to U.S. dollars using purchasing power parities for GDP from OECD (2000a), p. 261. Population (1989) weighted average.

7.8 *Real Hourly Compensation Growth in Manufacturing.* Compensation for all workers in manufacturing is hourly compensation in manufacturing, on a national currency basis, from BLS (2000a), Table 7; The hourly compensation in manufacturing data refer to employees (wage and salary earners) in Belgium, Denmark, Italy, and the Netherlands, and to all employed persons (employees and self-employed workers) in the other countries. Compensation for production workers is hourly compensation costs in national currency for production workers in manufacturing from BLS (2000b), Table 4. Both are deflated using consumer price indexes derived from OECD (1999a), Table 16, p. A19. Population (1989) weighted average.

7.9 *Earnings Inequality Growth.* Unpublished OECD data, updating OECD (1996), Table 3.1, pp. 61-62. The first column refers to 1979, the second to 1989, and the last to 1997, except: Japan, 1995; Germany, 1983, 1993; France, 1996; Italy, 1993; Canada, 1981, 1990, 1994; Australia, 1995; Austria, 1980, 1994; Belgium, 1995; Denmark, 1980; Finland, 1980, 1995; Netherlands, 1994; New Zealand, 1988; Norway, 1980, 1991; Portugal, 1993; Sweden, 1980, 1995; and Switzerland, 1991, 1996.

7.10 *Earnings Mobility of Low-Paid Workers.* OECD (1996), Table 3.10, pp. 95-6.

7.11 *Household Income Inequality, Relative to National Median Income.* Gottschalk and Smeeding (1997), Figure 2. Population (1989) weighted average.

7.12 *Household Income Inequality, Relative to U.S. Median Income.* From Gottschalk and Smeeding (1997), Figure 4. Population (1989) weighted average.

7.13 *Change in Income Inequality After 1979.* Relative changes in the Gini coefficient taken from Gottschalk and Smeeding (1997), Appendix Table A-1. Absolute changes calculated from relative changes in Gottschalk and Smeeding (1997), Appendix Table A-1 and Gini coefficients in Gottschalk and Smeeding (1997), Figure 2; for Japan, 1992 Gini coefficient estimated using average of 1990 and 1993; for Germany, 1990 coefficient estimated using 1989; for Norway, 1992 coefficient used for 1991.

7.14 *Poverty Rates.* Smeeding (1997), Table 1. Population (1989) weighted average.

7.15 *The Impact of Taxes and Transfers on Poverty Rates.* Smeeding (1997), Table 7. Population (1989) weighted average.

7.16 *Poverty Rates and Transitions Out of Poverty.* Oxley, Dang, and Antolin (1999), various tables.

7.17 *Employment Rates.* BLS (2000), Table 5. pp. 22-3.

7.18 *Average Annual Hours Worked per Person in Employment.* OECD (1999b), Table F, p. 241. Population (1989) weighted average.

7.19 *Impact of Productivity, Employment, and Hours Differences.* Van Ark and McGuckin (1999), Table 1, pp. 33-41. The data in Table 7.19 differ from those in Tables 7.17 and 7.18 and are therefore not directly comparable. In Table 7.19, for example, Japanese employment rates and hours worked appear to be higher than in the United States. Despite some minor inconsistencies, we believe that the exercise in Table 7.19 provides a helpful illustration of the impact of international differences in employment rates and hours worked.

7.20 *Employment.* Calculated from employment indexes in OECD (1999a), Annex Table 20, p. A23. Population (1989) weighted average.

7.21 *Standardized Unemployment Rates.* OECD (2000b). Population (1989) weighted average.

7.22 *Unemployment Rates by Education Level.* OECD describes educational categories as: "Less than upper secondary," "Upper secondary," and "Tertiary." OECD (1999b), Table D, pp. 237-8. Population (1989) weighted average.

APPENDIX C

C-1 *Contributions to Labor Productivity.* Based on a reformulation of data in Oliver and Sichel (2000), Tables 2 and 4.

Figure notes

CHAPTER 1

1A   *Median Family Income.* See note to Table 1.1.

1B   *Annual Growth of Median Family Income.* See note to Table 1.1.

1C   *Average Number of Persons per Family.* Census homepage, Historical Time Series, Households, Table 6 (http://www.census.gov/population/socdemo/hh-fam/htabHH-6.txt).

1D   *Median Family Income by Age of Householder.* See note to Table 1.3.

1E   *Ratio to White Median Family Income by Race/Ethnic Background.* See note to Table 1.5.

1F   *Family Income Inequality, Gini Coefficient.* The steep jump in the figure in 1993 is in part due to the lifting of the Census top codes. In order to discount this change, we ran a time series regression with a dummy variable for the 1993-98 period. The regression uses the state-space model approach, described in Koopman et al, 2000. STAMP 6.0 software was used to run the structural model, with a fixed level, stochastic slope, and AR(1) terms to model the unobserved trend and cycle components. See note to Table 1.7.

1G   *Ratio of Family Income of Top 5% to Lowest 20%.* Census homepage, Historical Income Tables, Families, Table 3 (http://www.census.gov/hhes/income/histinc/f03.html).

1H   *Family Income Growth by Quintile.* See note to Figure 1G.

1I   *Effective Federal Tax rate for Family of Four.* See note to Table 1.12.

1J   *Income and Consumption Inequality, CE Survey.* Johnson and Smeeding, 1998, Table 3.

1K   *Percent Staying in Same Fifth in Each Pair of Years, 1968-69–1990-91.* Gottschalk and Danziger (1998).

1L   *Income Shares in the Corporate Sector.* See note to Table 1.25.

1M   *Pre- and Post-Tax Return to Capital.* See note to Table 1.26.

1N   *Contribution of Wives' Earnings to Family Income.* Hayge (1993) and unpublished updates.

1O   *Average Family Work Hours, Middle-income, Married-couple Families with Children, by Education Level.* See note to Table 1.29.

1P   *Average Family Work Hours, by Race/Ethnicity, Middle-income, Married-couple Families with Children.* See note to Table 1.30.

CHAPTER 2

2A   *Hourly Wage and Compensation Growth for Production/Non-supervisory Workers.* See note to Table 2.4. Hourly compensation was estimated based on multiplying hourly wages by the ratio of compensation to wages for all workers in each year. The compensation/wage ratio is drawn from the NIPA data used in Table 2.2. The compensation/wage ratio for 1999 was an estimate based on the previous three year

2B   *Changes in Hourly Wages for Men by Wage Percentile.* See note to Table 2.7.

2C   *Changes in Hourly Wages for Women by Wage Percentile.* See note to Table 2.8.

2D   *The Gender Earnings Gap.* The female-male wage ratio is based on the medium hourly wage of women and men computed from the CPS ORG data, as described in Appendix B. The trend is extracted using a state-space model as described in Koopman et al. (2000). Both the slope and seasonal terms are modeled with a stochastic component (using STAMP 6.0 software). The model also includes an AR (1) term.

2E   *Share of Workers Earning Poverty-Level Wages.* See note to Table 2.10.

2F   *Share of Workers Earning Poverty-Level Wages, by Race/Ethnicity.* See note to Tables 2.11, 2.12, and 2.13.

2G   *Health Insurance and Pension Coverage.* See note to Table 2.15.

2H   *Share of Pension Participants in Defined-Contribution Plans.* From Employment Benefit Research Institute (1998), Table 4.

2I   *Men's Wage Inequality.* Based on ratios of wages by decile in annual data presented in Table 2.7.

2J   *Women's Wage Inequality.* Based on ratios of wages by decile in annual data presented in Table 2.8.

2K   *95/50 Percentile Wage Inequality.* Based on ratios of wages by decile in annual data presented in Table 2.6.

2L   *College/High School Wage Premium.* Differentials estimated with controls for experience (as a quartic), region (4), marital status, and race/ethnicity, and education is specified as dummy variables for less than high school, some college, college, and advanced degree. Estimates were made on the CPS ORG data as described in Appendix B, and presented in Table 2.17.

2M   *Productivity and Hourly Compensation Growth.* Average hourly productivity and compensation are for the nonfarm business sector from *ERP* (2000), Table B-47, p. 362. The compensation series is deflated by the CPI-UX1. The real average hourly compensation series will, therefore, differ (grow faster) from that published by BLS (which is deflated by the CPI). The median compensation of men and all workers is derived by multiplying the compensation/wage ratio (based on the NIPA data discussed in the note to Table 2.2) and the real median wage series for "all" and for "men" in Tables 2.6 and 2.7.

2N   *Entry-Level Wages of Male and Female High School Graduates.* See note to Table 2.22.

2O   *Entry-Level Wages of Male and Female College Graduates.* See note to Table 2.22.

2P   *Reading and Mathematics Proficiency by Race.* From Department of Education, National Assessment of Educational Progress web site (http://nces.ed.gov/nationsreportcard/site/home.asp).

2Q   *Index of Hourly Wages for Men by Race and Ethnicity.* See note to Table 2.25.

2R   *Index of Hourly Wages for Women by Race and Ethnicity.* See note to Table 2.26.

2S   *Union Coverage in the United States.* Hirsch and Macpherson (1997), Table 1. Data was updated with *Employment and Earnings* (January 2000), Table 40, p. 219.

2T   *Real Value of the Minimum Wage.* See note to Table 2.40.

2U   *Information Technology Wage Premium for Men.* The wage premiums for workers in IT occupations and IT industries are based on log hourly wage regressions, which included basic human capital variables (same as those used for Table 2.17) and 12 industry and nine occupational controls. Regressions were run separately for men and women. The coefficients on a variable for being in an IT industry or an IT occupation is the premium reported in the figure. The coefficients represent the hourly wage premium received by an IT worker comparable to someone with equivalent human capital (e.g. education) and in the same broad occupation (e.g., professional) or industry (e.g., personal services). IT occupations are: Computer systems analysts and scientists; computer programmers; and, operations and system researchers/analysts. IT industries are: computers and related equipment; radio and television broadcasting and cable; telephone communications; and computer and data processing services. We developed this list to correspond as closely as possible to those selected by the Information Technology Association of America in its reports. More detail is available from the authors.

2V   *Information Technology Wage Premium for Women.* See note for Figure 2S.

2W   *Wage Offers to New College Graduates by Major.* Average yearly salary offers by curriculum type are derived from data gathered by the National Association of Colleges and Employers (1999), p. 4. The offers reported are a representative sample of actual job offers made to new college graduates during the previous recruiting year and do not imply all job offers made to all college graduates.

2X   *Ratio of CEO to Average Worker Pay.* The ratio of CEO to average worker pay is based on the CEO pay data presented in Table 2.49 and the production worker wage series (converted to compensation and annualized by multiplying by 2,080 hours) presented in Table 2.4. To obtain the historical data on CEO compensation, the Pearl Meyers/*Wall Street Journal* series was used to extend the William M. Mercer/*Wall Street Journal* series backwards.

2Y   *College Degrees as Share of Employment.* See note to Table 2.52.

CHAPTER 3

3A   *Unemployment.* See note to Table 3.1.

3B   *Underemployment.* See note to Table 3.2.

3C   *Employment Rates.* BLS web page, May 5, 2000.

3D   *Employment Rates, Men.* BLS web page, May 5, 2000.

3E   *Employment Rates, Women.* BLS web page, May 5, 2000.

3F   *Median Job Tenure by Age.* See note to Table 3.7.

3G   *Job Leavers.* Data on job leavers and the total unemployed from BLS web site, May 2000. Following Polivka and Miller (1995), figures for 1994-99 have been divided by 0.866 to make them comparable to earlier years.

3H   *Employment in Temporary Help Industry.* See note to Table 3.21.

CHAPTER 4

4A   *Share of Total Household Wealth Held by Richest 1% of Individuals.* Wolff (1992), Table 1.

4B   *Net Worth of the "Forbes 400."* Broom and Shay (2000), Table 2, p. 15.

4C   *Growth of U.S. Stock Market.* Standard & Poor's Composite Index from *ERP* (2000), Table B-93, p. 414, deflated by the CPI-U-X1.

4D   *Distribution of Growth in Stock Market Holdings.* See note to Table 4.8.

4E   *Average Rate of Home Ownership.* Published Current Population Survey/Housing Vacancy Survey (CPS/HVS) data (http://www.census.gov/hhes/www/hvs.html), June 2000.

4F   *Home Ownership Rates by Income Quintile.* See note to Table 4.10.

4G   *Computer Ownership Rates by Education.* See note to Table 4.11.

4H   *Computer Ownership Rates by Race.* See note to Table 4.11.

4I   *Household Debt as a Share of Disposable Personal Income.* See note to Table 4.12.

4J   *Distribution of Growth in Debt.* See note to Table 4.8.

4K   *Consumer Bankruptcies.* Data on consumer bankruptcies from the American Bankruptcy Institute web page (http://www.abiworld.org); data on adult population from the Economic Report of the President (2000), Table B-33, p. 346.

CHAPTER 5

5A   *Poverty Rate.* See note to Table 5.1.

5B   *Official vs. Alternative Poverty Measures.* U.S. Bureau of the Census, P60-205. Of the numerous experimental measures developed by the Census, we choose to use measure DCM1/U. The main difference between this are some other measures is the method used to value child care expenditures. This method assigns 85% of the median annual child care expenditures to working families with children under 12. The child care costs are based on data from the 1993 SIPP, updated by the CPI for child care and nursery school.

5C   *Poverty Rates by Price Index.* Census Poverty Homepage, Historical Poverty Tables, Experimental Measures, Table 3 (http://www.census.gov/hhes/poverty/histpov/rdp03.html).

5D   *Family Poverty Gap and Poverty Rates.* See notes to Tables 5.4 and 5.8.

5E   *Percent of Poor Persons Below 50% of Poverty Level.* See note to Table 5.9.

5F   *Earnings and Public Assistance as a Share of Income, Poor Families With Children.* See note to Table 5.16.

5G   *Prime-Age Workers With Low Earnings and Full-Time/Year-Round Attachment.* Data for 1974-89 from P60-178, Table 3; data for 1995 and 1998 provided by Jack McNeil of the Census Bureau.

5H   *Workers in Families With Children, With Low Earnings and Full-Time/Year-Round Attachment.* See note to Figure 5G.

5I   *Real Hourly Wages of Low-Wage Workers.* Wages are based on analysis of CPS wage data as described in Appendix B. Poverty level wage is the wage that, at full-time, full-year work, would lift a family of four above the poverty line. This equals $8.19 in 1999 dollars.

CHAPTER 6

6A   *Median Family Income Growth by Region.* See note to Table 6.1.

6B   *Trends in 20th Percentile Real Wages for Four States.* See note to Table 6.7.

6C   *Trends in Median Real Wages for Four States.* See note to Table 6.8.

6D   *Changes in the Low-Wage Share and the Unemployment Rate.* See notes to Tables 6.10 and 6.12.

6E   *Poverty Rates by Region.* See note to Table 6.13.

6F   *Poverty Rates for Four States.* See note to Table 6.14.

6G   *Poverty Rates by Metro/Non-metro Area.* See note to Table 6.15.

CHAPTER 7

7A   *Productivity Growth Rates.* See note to Table 7.4.

7B   *Hourly Wages at Tenth Percentile, Indexed to United States.* Data for the United States, Germany, Advanced Europe, and the United Kingdom taken from Freeman (1998), p. 29; data for Japan from Freeman (1995), p. 66.

7C   *Household Income Inequality, Relative to National Median Income.* See note to Table 7.11.

7D   *Household Income Inequality, Relative to U.S. Median Income.* See note to Table 7.12.

7E   *Average Annual Exit Rate From Poverty.* See note to Table 7.16.

7F   *Legally Mandated Paid Vacation in European Countries.* Leete-Guy and Schor (1992), p. 19 and Muñoz de Bustillo and Bonete (2000), Table 11.3, p. 241.

Bibliography

Aaronson, Daniel, and Daniel G. Sullivan. 1998. The Decline of Job Security in the 1990s: Displacement, Anxiety, and Their Effect on Wage Growth. *Economic Perspectives*, First Quarter, pp. 17-43.

Bajika, Jon, and C. Eugene Steuerle. 1991. Individual Income Taxation Since 1948. *National Tax Journal*, vol. 44, no. 4, pp. 451-75.

Baker, Dean. 1996. "Trends in Corporate Profitability: Getting More for Less?" Technical Paper. Washington, D.C.: Economic Policy Institute.

Bernhardt, Annette, Martina Morris, Mark S. Hancock, and Marc A. Scott. 1998. "Trends in Job Instability and Wages for Young Adult Men." Institute on Education and the Economy, Working Paper No. 8. Columbia University.

Bernstein, Jared, and Elizabeth McNichol. 2000. *Pulling Apart: A State-by-State Analysis of Income Trends*. Washington, D.C.: Center on Budget and Policy Priorities and Economic Policy Institute.

Bernstein, Jared, and John Schmitt. 1998. "Making Work Pay: The Impact of the 1996-97 Minimum Wage Increase." Washington, D.C.: Economic Policy Institute.

Blank, Rebecca M. 1991. "Why Were Poverty Rates So High in the 1980s?" National Bureau of Economic Research, Working Paper No. 3878. Cambridge, Mass.: NBER.

Blank, Rebecca M., and David Card. 1993. Poverty, Income Distribution, and Growth: Are They Still Connected? *Brookings Papers on Economic Activity*, No. 2. Washington, D.C.: Brookings Institution.

Bluestone, Barry M., Edith Rasell, and Lawrence Mishel. 1996. *Living Standards Chartbook*. Washington, D.C.: Economic Policy Institute, forthcoming.

Borjas, George J. 1994. The Economics of Immigration. *Journal of Economic Literature*, Vol. 32, No. 4, pp. 1667-1717.

Borjas, George J. 1999. *Heaven's Door*. Princeton, NJ: Princeton University Press.

Braddock, Douglas. 1999. "Labor Force 2008: Occupational Employment Projections to 2008." *Monthly Labor Review*. Vol. 122, No. 11.

Broom, Leonard, and William Shay. 2000. "Discontinuites in the Distribution of Great Wealth: Sectoral Forces Old and New." Paper prepared for the Conference on "Saving, Intergenerational Transfers, and the Distribution of Wealth" at the Jerome Levy Economics Institute, Bard College, June 7-9, 2000.

Camarota, Steven A. 2000. Unpublished tabulations.

Card, David. 1991. "The Effect of Unions on the Distribution of Wages: Redistribution or Relabelling?" Working Paper No. 287. Princeton, N.J.: Department of Economics, Princeton University.

Center on Budget and Policy Priorities. 1998. *Poverty Tables*. Washington, D.C.: CBPP.

Citizens for Tax Justice and Institute on Taxation & Economic Policy. 1996. *Who Pays? A Distributional Analysis of the Tax Systems in All 50 States*. Washington, D.C.: Citizens for Tax Justice and Institute on Taxation & Economic Policy.

Cline, William R. 1997. *Trade and Income Distribution*. Washington, D.C.: Institute for International Economics.

Conference Board. 1997. "Perspectives on a Global Economy: Understanding Differences in Economic Performance." Report Number 1187-97-RR. New York: Conference Board.

Conference Board. 1999. "Perspectives on a Global Economy: The Euro's Impact on European Labor Markets." Report Number 1236-99-RR. New York: Conference Board.

Congressional Budget Office. 1998. *Estimates of Federal Tax Liabilities for Individuals and Families by Income Category and Family Type for 1995 and 1999*. Washington, D.C.: Congressional Budget Office.

Danziger, Sheldon, and Peter Gottschalk. 1995. *America Unequal*. New York, N.Y.: Harvard/Russell Sage Foundation.

DiNardo, John, Nicole M. Fortin, and Thomas Lemieux. 1994. "Labor Market Institutions and the Distribution of Wages, 1973-1992: A Semiparametric Approach." Unpublished.

DiNardo, John, Nicole M. Fortin, and Thomas Lemieux. 1996. "Labor Market Institutions and Gender Differences in Wage Inequality." Paper presented at the Industrial Relations Research Association Meetings, San Francisco, January.

Duncan, Greg, et al. 1991. "Poverty and Social Assistance Dynamics in the United States, Canada and Europe." Paper presented at the Joint Center for Political and Economic Studies Conference on Poverty and Public Policy, Washington, D.C.

Economic Report of the President. Annual. Washington, D.C.: U.S. Government Printing Office.

Employment Benefit Research Institute. 1998. Agenda background material for "The National Summit on Retirement Savings," Washington, D.C., June 4-5.

Farber, Henry S. 1997a. *The Changing Face of Job Loss in the United States, 1981-95.* Princeton, N.J.: Princeton University.

Farber, Henry S. 1997b. "Trends in Long Term Employment in the United States, 1979-96." Industrial Relations Section Working Paper No. 384. Princeton, N.J.: Princeton University.

Faber, Henry S. 1998. "Has the Rate of Job Loss Increased in the Nineties?" Industrial Relations Section Working Paper No. 394. Princeton, N.J.: Princeton University.

Federal Reserve Board. 2000. "Recent Changes in U.S. Family Finances: Results From the 1998 Survey of Consumer Finances." *Federal Reserve Bulletin.* January 2000, pp. 1-29.

Fortin, Nicole M., and Thomas Lemieux. 1996. "Labor Market Institutions and Gender Differences in Wage Inequality." Presented at the Industrial Relations Research Association Annual Meeting, San Francisco, Calif., January.

Freeman, Richard. 1991. "How Much Has De-unionization Contributed to the Rise in Male Earnings Inequality?" National Bureau of Economic Research, Working Paper No. 3826. Cambridge, Mass.: NBER.

Freeman, Richard. 1995. The Limits of Wage Flexibility to Curing Unemployment. *Oxford Review of Economic Policy*, vol. 11, no. 1, pp. 63-72.

Freeman, Richard. 1997. "Low Wage Employment: Is More or Less Better?" Harvard University, unpublished paper.

Freeman, Richard. 1998. "The Facts About Rising Economic Disparity." In James A. Auerbach and Richard S. Belous, eds., *The Inequality Paradox: Growth and Income Disparity.* Washington, D.C.: National Policy Association.

Fullerton, Howard N., Jr. 1999. Labor Force 2008: Steady Growth and Changing Composition. *Monthly Labor Review.* Vol. 122, No. 11.

Gardner, Jennifer M. 1995. Worker Displacement: A Decade of Change. *Monthly Labor Review*, Vol. 118, No. 4, pp. 45-57.

Gottschalk, Peter, and Sheldon Danziger. 1998. "Family Income Mobility—How Much Is There and Has It Changed?" In James A. Auerbach and Richard S. Belous, eds., *The Inequality Paradox: Growth of Income Disparity.* Washington, D.C.: National Policy Association.

Gottschalk, Peter, and Timothy M. Smeeding. 1997. "Empirical Evidence on Income Inequality in Industrialized Countries," Luxembourg Income Study Working Paper No. 154.

Hayghe, Howard V. 1993. Working Wives' Contributions to Family Incomes. *Monthly Labor Review*, Vol. 116, No. 8, pp. 39-43.

Hirsch, Barry T., and David A. Macpherson. 1997. *Union Membership and Earnings Data Book: Compilations from the Current Population Survey (1997 Edition).* Washington, D.C.: Bureau of National Affairs.

Immigration and Naturalization Service. 1999. *Statistical Yearbook of the Immigration and Naturalization Service 1998*. Washington, D.C.: U.S. Government Printing Office.

Johnson, David S., and Timothy Smeeding. 1998. "Measuring the Trends in Inequality of Individuals and Families: Income *and* Consumption." Unpublished manuscript.

Joint Economic Committee. 1992. *Families on a Treadmill: Work and Income in the 1980s*. Washington, D.C.: JEC.

Kominski, Robert, and Eric Newburger. 1999. "Access Denied: Changes in Computer Ownership and Use: 1984-97." Unpublished paper, Census Bureau (August).

Koopman, Siem Jan, Andrew C. Harvey, Jurgen A. Doornik, and Neil Shephard. 2000. *STAMP Manual*. London, U.K.: Timberlake Consultants Ltd.

Leete-Guy, Laura, and Juliet B. Schor. 1992. *The Great American Time Squeeze: Trends in Work and Leisure, 1969-89*. Washington, D.C.: Economic Policy Institute.

Mishel, Lawrence, and Jared Bernstein. 1994. "Is the Technology Black Box Empty? An Empirical Examination of the Impact of Technology on Wage Inequality and the Employment Structure." Presented to the Labor Economics Workshop, Harvard University. Unpublished.

Mishel, Lawrence, and Jared Bernstein. 1996. "Did Technology's Impact Accelerate in the 1980s?" Paper presented at the Industrial and Relations Research Association meetings, San Francisco, Calif., January.

Mishel, Lawrence, and Jared Bernstein. 1998. Technology and the Wage Structure: Has Technology's Impact Accelerated Since the 1970s? *Research in Labor Economics*. Vol. 17, pp. 305-355. Mishel, Lawrence, and Ruy Teixeira. 1991. *The Myth of the Coming Labor Shortage: Jobs, Skills, and Incomes of America's Workforce 2000*. Washington, D.C.: Economic Policy Institute.

Muñoz de Bustillo, Rafael and Rafael Bonete. 2000. *Introducción a la Unión Europea: un análisis desde la economía*. Madrid, Spain: Alianza Editorial.

Murphy, Kevin, and Finis Welch. 1989. "Recent Trends in Real Wages: Evidence from Household Data." Paper prepared for the Health Care Financing Administration of the U.S. Department of Health and Human Services. Chicago, Ill.: University of Chicago.

National Association of Colleges and Employers. Various years' September issues. *Salary Survey*. Bethlehem, PA: National Association of Colleges and Employers.

National Research Council. 1995. *Measuring Poverty: A New Approach*. Washington, D.C.: National Research Council.

Neumark, David, Daniel Polsky, and Daniel Hansen. 1997. "Has Job Stability Declined Yet? New Evidence for the 1990s." Working Paper No. 6330. Cambridge, Mass.: National Bureau of Economic Research.

Organization for Economic Cooperation and Development. 1995. *Economic Outlook.* Paris: OECD.

Organization for Economic Cooperation and Development. 1996. *Employment Outlook.* Paris: OECD.

Organization for Economic Cooperation and Development. 1997a. *Economic Outlook.* Paris: OECD.

Organization for Economic Cooperation and Development. 1997b. *Revenue Statistics 1965-1996.* Paris: OECD.

Organization for Economic Cooperation and Development. 1999a. *Economic Outlook.* Paris: OECD.

Organization for Economic Cooperation and Development. 1999b. *Employment Outlook.* Paris: OECD.

Organization for Economic Cooperation and Development. 2000a. *Main Economic Indicators.* Paris: OECD.

Organization for Economic Cooperation and Development. 2000b. Standardized Unemployment Rates, 06 April 2000. (http://www.oecdwash.org/PRESS/CONTENT/frstat.htm).

Organization for Economic Cooperation and Development, Statistics Directorate. 1998. *National Accounts, Main Aggregates, Volume 1, 1960-96.* Paris: OECD.

Oxley, Howard, Thai-Thanh Dang, and Pablo Antolin. 1999. "Poverty Dynamics in Six OECD Countries." Paper presented at the European Economic Association Annual Congress, September.

Pierce, Brooks. 1998. "Compensation Inequality." U.S. Department of Labor, Bureau of Labor Statistics, Washington, D.C. Manuscript.

Polivka, Anne E. 1998. "Using Earnings Data for the Current Population Survey After the Redesign." Working Paper No. 306. Washington, D.C.: U.S. Bureau of Labor Statistics.

Polivka, Anne E., and Stephen M. Miller. 1995. "The CPS After the Redesign: Refocusing the Economic Lens." Unpublished BLS paper (March).

Poterba, James M. 2000. "Stock Market Wealth and Consumption," Journal of Economic Perspectives, vol. 14, no. 2, Spring 2000, pp. 99-118.

Rose, Stephen J. 1995. *Declining Job Security and the Professionalization of Opportunity.* Research Report No. 95-04. Washington, D.C.: National Commission for Employment Policy.

Ruggles, Patricia. 1990. *Drawing the Line: Alternative Poverty Measures and Their Implications for Public Policy.* Washington, D.C.: Urban Institute.

Ryscavage, Paul, Gordon Green, Edward Welniak, and John Coder. 1992. *Studies in the Distribution of Income.* U.S. Department of Commerce, Bureau of the Census, Series P-60, No. 183. Washington, D.C.: U.S. Government Printing Office.

Schmitt, John, and Lawrence Mishel. 1996. "Did International Trade Lower Less-Skilled Wages During the 1980s? Standard Trade Theory and Evidence." Technical Paper. Washington, D.C.: Economic Policy Institute.

Scott, Robert E., Thea Lee, and John Schmitt. 1997. "Trading Away Good Jobs: An Examination of Employment and Wages in the U.S., 1979-94". Briefing Paper. Washington, D.C.: Economic Policy Institute.

Sekscenski, Edward S. 1980. "Women's Share of Moonlighting Nearly Doubles During 1969-79." *Monthly Labor Review*, Vol. 103, No. 5.

Shapiro, Isaac. 1987. *No Escape: The Minimum Wage and Poverty.* Washington, D.C.: Center on Budget and Policy Priorities.

Smeeding, Timothy M. 1997. "Financial Poverty in Developed Countries: The Evidence from LIS," Luxembourg Income Study Working Paper No. 155.

Stinson, John F., Jr. 1986. Moonlighting by Women Jumped to Record Highs. *Monthly Labor Review*, Vol. 109, No. 11.

Towers, Perrin and Company. Various years. Worldwide Total Remuneration.

U.S. Department of Commerce, Bureau of the Census. Current Population Reports. Various dates. *Marital Status and Living Arrangements.* P-20 Series. Washington D.C.: U.S. Government Printing Office.

U.S. Department of Commerce, Bureau of the Census. Current Population Reports. Various dates. P-60 Series. Washington, D.C.: U.S. Government Printing Office.

U.S. Department of Commerce, Bureau of the Census. Current Population Reports. 1990. *Trends in Income, by Selected Characteristics: 1947 to 1988.* P60 Series, No. 167. Washington, D.C.: U.S. Government Printing Office.

U.S. Department of Commerce, Bureau of the Census. Current Population Reports. 1991. *Trends in Relative Income: 1964 to 1989.* P60 Series, No. 177. Washington, D.C.: U.S. Government Printing Office.

U.S. Department of Commerce, Bureau of the Census. Current Population Reports. 1995. *Household and Family Characteristics.* P20 Series. Washington, D.C.: U.S. Government Printing Office.

U.S. Department of Commerce, Bureau of the Census. Current Population Reports. 1996. *A Brief Look at Postwar U.S. Income Inequality.* P60 Series, No.191. Washington, D.C.: U.S. Government Printing Office.

U.S. Department of Commerce, Bureau of the Census. Current Population Reports. 1997. *Money Income in the United States: 1996.* P60 Series, No.197. Washington, D.C.: U.S. Government Printing Office.

U.S. Department of Commerce, Bureau of the Census. 1973-99. *American Housing Survey for the United States*. Washington, D.C.: U.S. Government Printing Office.

U.S. Department of Commerce, National Telecommunications and Information Administration. 1999. *Falling Through the Net: Defining the Digital Divide*. Washington, D.C.: Government Printing Office.

U.S. Department of Education, National Center for Education Statistics. 1997a. *Projections of Education Statistics to 2008*. NCES 98-016. Washington, D.C.: U.S. Government Printing Office.

U.S. Department of Education, National Center for Education Statistics. 1997b. *The Condition of Education 1997*. NCES 97-388. Washington, D.C.: U.S. Government Printing Office.

U.S. Department of Education, National Center for Education Statistics. 1999. *Projections of Education Statistics to 2009*, NCES 1999-038, by Debra E. Gerald and William J. Hussar. Washington, D.C.: U.S. Government Printing Office.

U.S. Department of Labor. Bureau of Labor Statistics (BLS). 1988. *Labor Force Statistics Derived from the Current Population Survey, 1948-87*. Washington, D.C.: U.S. Government Printing Office.

U.S. Department of Labor, BLS. 1989. *Handbook of Labor Statistics*. Bulletin No. 2340. Washington, D.C.: U.S. Government Printing Office.

U.S. Department of Labor, BLS. 1995a. *International Comparisons of Hourly Compensation Costs for Production Workers in Manufacturing 1975-94, Supplementary Tables for BLS Report 893 June 1995*. Washington, D.C.: U.S. Government Printing Office.

U.S. Department of Labor, BLS. 1995b. *Contingent and Alternative Employment Arrangements*. Report 900, August 1995.

U.S. Department of Labor, BLS. 1997. *Contingent and Alternative Employment Arrangements, February 1997*. Report 97-422, December 1997.

U.S. Department of Labor, BLS. 1998. *International Comparisons of Manufacturing Productivity and Unit Labor Cost Trends, 1996*. Washington, D.C.: Bureau of Labor Statistics.

U.S. Department of Labor, BLS. 1999. *Contingent and Alternative Employment Arrangements, February 1999*. December 21, 1999.

U.S. Department of Labor, BLS. 2000a. *International Comparisons of Manufacturing Productivity and Unit Labor Cost Trends, April 2000a*. News Release: (http://stats.bls.gov/news.release/ prod4.toc.htm.)

U.S. Department of Labor. BLS. 2000b. *Comparative Civilian Labor Force Statistics, Ten Countries, 1959-1999*. April 17, 2000.

U.S. Department of Labor, BLS. Various years. *Employer Costs for Employee Compensation*. Washington, D.C.: U.S. Government Printing Office.

U.S. Department of Labor, BLS. Various years. *Employment and Earnings.* Washington, D.C.: Bureau of Labor Statistics.

U.S. Department of Labor, BLS. Various years. *Monthly Labor Review.* Washington, D.C.: Bureau of Labor Statistics.

U.S. Department of Labor, BLS. Various years. *Productivity and Costs.* Washington, D.C.: U.S. Government Printing Office.

U.S. Department of Labor, BLS, Foreign Labor Statistics. 2000 (http://stats.bls.gov/flshome.htm).

U.S. Department of Labor, BLS, Office of Productivity and Technology. 1998. *Comparative Real Gross Domestic Product Per Capita and Per Employed Person, Fourteen Countries, 1960-1996.* Washington, D.C.: Bureau of Labor Statistics.

U.S. Department of Labor, BLS, Office of Productivity and Technology. 1999. *Comparative Civilian Labor Force Statistics, Ten Countries, 1959-98.* Washington, D.C.: Bureau of Labor Statistics.

U.S. Department of Labor, BLS, Office of Productivity and Technology. 2000. *International Comparisons of Hourly Compensation Costs for Production Workers in Manufacturing, 1975-1998, Supplementary Tables.* Washington, D.C.: Bureau of Labor Statistics.

U.S. Department of the Treasury, Internal Revenue Service. 1998. *Publication 15, Circular E, Employer's Tax Guide.* Washington, D.C.: Internal Revenue Service.

U.S. Department of the Treasury, Office of Tax Analysis. 1998. *Average and Marginal Federal Income, Social Security, and Medicare Tax Rates for Four-Person Families at the Same Relative Positions in the Income Distribution, 1955-99.* Washington, D.C.: U.S. Department of the Treasury.

West, Sandra A. (Undated). "Measures of Central Tendency for Censored Earnings Data From the Current Population Survey." Unpublished Bureau of Labor Statistics report.

Wolff, Edward N. 1992. "Changing Inequality of Wealth." Paper presented at the American Economic Association Meetings, Boston, Mass., January.

Wolff, Edward N. 1993. "The Rich Get Increasingly Richer: Latest Data on Household Wealth During the 1980s." Briefing Paper. Washington, D.C.: Economic Policy Institute.

Wolff, Edward N. 1994. Trends in Household Wealth in the United States, 1962-1983 and 1983-1989. *Review of Income and Wealth,* Series 40, No. 2.

Wolff, Edward N. 1996. "Trends in Household Wealth During 1989-1992." Paper submitted to the Department of Labor. New York, N.Y.: New York University.

Index

About EPI

The Economic Policy Institute was founded in 1986 to widen the debate about policies to achieve healthy economic growth, prosperity, and opportunity.

Today, despite recent rapid growth in the U.S. economy, inequality in wealth, wages, and income remains historically high. Expanding global competition, changes in the nature of work, and rapid technological advances are altering economic reality. Yet many of our policies, attitudes, and institutions are based on assumptions that no longer reflect real world conditions.

With the support of leaders from labor, business, and the foundation world, the Institute has sponsored research and public discussion of a wide variety of topics: trade and fiscal policies; trends in wages, incomes, and prices; education; the causes of the productivity slowdown; labor market problems; rural and urban policies; inflation; state-level economic development strategies; comparative international economic performance; and studies of the overall health of the U.S. manufacturing sector and of specific key industries.

The Institute works with a growing network of innovative economists and other social science researchers in universities and research centers all over the country who are willing to go beyond the conventional wisdom in considering strategies for public policy.

Founding scholars of the Institute include Jeff Faux, EPI president; Lester Thurow, Sloan School of Management, MIT; Ray Marshall, former U.S. secretary of labor, professor at the LBJ School of Public Affairs, University of Texas; Barry Bluestone, University of Massachusetts-Boston; Robert Reich, former U.S. secretary of labor; and Robert Kuttner, author, editor of *The American Prospect,* and columnist for *Business Week* and the Washington Post Writers Group.

For additional information about the Institute, contact EPI at 1660 L Street NW, Suite 1200, Washington, DC 20036, (202) 775-8810, or visit www.epinet.org.

About the authors

LAWRENCE MISHEL is the vice president of the Economic Policy Institute and was the research director from 1987 to 1999. He is the co-author of the previous versions of *The State of Working America*. He holds a Ph.D. in economics from the University of Wisconsin, and his articles have appeared in a variety of academic and non-academic journals. His areas of research are labor economics, wage and income distribution, industrial relations, productivity growth, and the economics of education. He will soon be retiring as co-commissioner of the Takoma Park Babe Ruth Baseball League.

JARED BERNSTEIN joined EPI as a labor economist in 1992 and is currently the director of Living Standards Program. Between 1995 and 1996, he held the post of deputy chief economist at the U.S. Department of Labor, where, among other topics, he worked on the initiative to raise the minimum wage. He is co-author of four previous editions of *The State of Working America* and co-author of *How Much Is Enough? Basic Family Budgets for Working Families*. He specializes in the analysis of wage and income inequality, poverty, and low-wage labor markets, and his writings appear in popular and academic journals. Mr. Bernstein holds a Ph.D. in social welfare from Columbia University.

JOHN SCHMITT is a labor economist at the Economic Policy Institute. He has written for general and academic publications on wage inequality, the minimum wage, unemployment, and economic development, and he is a co-author of the last two editions of *The State of Working America*. Mr. Schmitt has an A.B. from the Woodrow Wilson School of Public and International Affairs at Princeton University and an M.Sc. and Ph.D. in economics from the London School of Economics.